The Chitlin' Circuit

THE
Chitlin' Circuit

And the Road to Rock 'n' Roll

Preston Lauterbach

W. W. NORTON & COMPANY

NEW YORK   LONDON

For information about permission to reproduce selections from this book,
write to Permissions, W. W. Norton & Company, Inc.,
500 Fifth Avenue, New York, NY 10110

For information about special discounts for bulk purchases, please contact
W. W. Norton Special Sales at specialsales@wwnorton.com or 800-233-4830

Manufacturing by RR Donnelley, Harrisonburg
Book design by Lovedog Studio
Production manager: Anna Oler

Library of Congress Cataloging-in-Publication Data

Lauterbach, Preston.
The chitlin' circuit : and the road to rock 'n' roll /
Preston Lauterbach. — 1st ed.
p. cm.
Includes bibliographical references and index.
ISBN 978-0-393-07652-3 (hardcover)
1. Jazz—History and criticism. 2. African American jazz musicians.
I. Title.
ML3508.L39 2011
781.64089'96073—dc22
2011007209

W. W. Norton & Company, Inc.
500 Fifth Avenue, New York, N.Y. 10110
www.wwnorton.com

W. W. Norton & Company Ltd.
Castle House, 75/76 Wells Street, London W1T 3QT

1 2 3 4 5 6 7 8 9 0

To my mom

Contents

List of Illustrations

The Chitlin' Circuit

Nondescript Places

The singlewide doesn't look inhabitable. It's stuffed half-way down the throat of a mangrove jungle. Two minivan carcasses, red and green, slump in the sandy driveway. But the address is right. A half-inch-thick sheet of particleboard stands in for the staircase. The ramp crunches under my weight. I smack the trailer 1, 2, 3, and a voice invites me in. Drab bed sheets cover the windows. A beam of sunshine breaking in through a floor-to-ceiling crack in the trailer's body provides the only light. Eighty-six-year-old Sax Kari, the fattest man of such advanced age I've ever seen, sits in a swivel office chair in the trailer's living room. He appears to be of tangled ancestry, sporting a crushed baseball cap and a short-sleeved, button-up shirt the color of rare steak. He's surrounded by an audio mixing board and four- and sixteen-track recording decks, which are set up along the living room's front and side walls. Four-inch and ten-inch reel-to-reel tape machines stand atop his keyboard and mixing board. A recent history of portable audio devices piles around him: transistor radios, most faceless, with their guts spilling out, and a circa-1987 silver shoulder-mount Venice Beach model tape deck. His red and white Fender Telecaster hangs from a ceiling hook in the corner behind him. He modified what

Mother Nature gave him to compensate for what Father Time took away—arthritis stiffened his once-supple guitar-plucking fingers, so he has grown his fingernails out and become more of a picker. His full name is the stuff of nursery rhymes: Isaac Saxton Kari Toombs.

Sax spent nearly eight decades in entertainment, beginning in the late 1920s, when he performed comedy on Butterbeans and Susie's vaudeville show, and was paid in candy. He learned to play keys, guitar, and reeds in school, which gave him the flexibility to adapt with musical fashion. He led a big band, then played gutter blues, rock 'n' roll, exotic soul, and disco. He recorded for several of the independent labels that served the black music market then, now coveted by collectors—Apollo, States, Great Lakes, Checker, Chess, Instant, Flick, and JOB. He worked as a bandleader, straight man, bag man, producer, concert promoter, record distributor, and shop owner, in musically fertile Chicago, Detroit, Memphis, New Orleans, and Miami.

In 1951, just after Sax's thirty-first birthday, the black *Memphis World* newspaper dubbed him "an old favorite." The next year "Daughter (That's Your Red Wagon)" by Swinging Sax Kari hit the top 10 of the rhythm and blues charts. "He astounded me," a fan from those days recalled. "I've seen him solo on saxophone, organ, and guitar—he was good on all of them, brother."[1] The next year in Detroit, Sax produced the first recordings of a curvy brownskin singer named Della Reese, long before angels touched her. He recorded novelty jams "Chocolate Fizz," "Hurry, Arthur Murray," and "Goldie the Green-Eyed Octopus," sometimes working under pseudonyms Ira Green or Dirty Red Morgan—as if the name Isaac Saxton Kari Toombs lacked color. Still in Detroit in the late 1950s, Sax produced the sublime "You're So Fine" by the Falcons, a doo-wop-rhythm-and-blues supergroup that included Mack Rice, who would go on to write "Mustang Sally," incendiary guitarist Robert Ward, soul hit-man-to-be Eddie Floyd, and young Wilson Pickett.

In New Orleans, Sax managed Esquerita, the flamboyant artist from whom Little Richard borrowed sartorial and musical style.

Sax Kari, right, promoting records at Memphis radio station WDIA, with disc jockey and entertainer Rufus Thomas, 1961. *Author's collection*

During the same period, he produced the Hollywood Jills, Polka Dot Slim, and Chris Kenner, of "Land of a Thousand Dances" fame. Then, in the 1970s Sax composed the score for a blaxploitation flick called *The Six Thousand Dollar Nigger* and recorded a Latin best-seller, "Besame Mucho." Sax wrote for Rock Candy Records, an early New York hip-hop label, in the early 1980s.

In 1982, back on the road with his band Four Sticks of Dynamite and the Fuse—with a tantalizing female dancer playing the fuse— Sax signed on for a week's residency at the One Stop Inn, a nightclub built on the sand beside a disused state highway in Seffner, Florida, a little east of Tampa. Local orange pickers packed the One Stop every night, and the club held him over for a second week. And a third. He liked the town, and the feelings seemed to be mutual, so he bought a little shack from the fellow who ran the One Stop. Sax refreshed another one of his old nicknames—Butterbeans and Susie, the husband and wife vaudeville team who gave Sax his start in show business, called the freckly little boy Candy Yams. After settling in Seffner, Candy Yams played organ and sang to piña colada–slurping tourists at waterfront resorts around Tampa–St. Petersburg.

Which is all perfectly interesting, but doesn't tell you why I was at his trailer door.

In the summer of 2003 I was working for *Living Blues* magazine, writing a feature about an artist named Bobby Rush. Bobby, a nonstop, glowingly charismatic man with his Jheri curl, rhinestone jumpsuits, and gluteusly gifted dance team, flipped my understanding of the blues. No longer was it the dark soundtrack of our national drama, but a still-vital music of spry wit. Bobby's audience, large and African-American, killed my assumption that blues appealed overwhelmingly to middle-aged white men. Bobby and a handful of other contemporary-minded black performers were at the center of a thriving subculture: the chitlin' circuit. (Bobby refers to himself in certain company as the "King of the Chitlin' Circuit.") *Their* blues shows, which typically feature upward of five acts and go on for hours, sell out rodeo arenas and civic centers, mostly in the Deep South. These scenes resemble a cross between a professional wrestling event and the pimp-of-the-year contest from *I'm Gonna Get You Sucka*. The musicians mingle with the crowd throughout the night, posing for Polaroids with their fans in front of airbrushed backdrops for ten dollars a pop. One of these tapestries, called "Wipe Me Down," shows a green, convertible Rolls with gold rims and upholstery, and a tinted windshield stuck in a downpour of hundred dollar bills, and if you look closely you see Ben Franklin, wearing diamond-studded shades, tugging on a plump joint. "Soul Heaven" depicts a last supper of fallen greats: Marvin Gaye, Johnnie Taylor, Bob Marley, and someone who resembles Frederick Douglass. The big concerts attract both young and nostalgic fans, and everyone has a very good time, dragging coolers and bottles in and feasting on smoked turkey legs, fried catfish, and pulled-pork-shoulder sandwiches. Industry personnel organize an annual Grammy-type celebration, called the Jackson Music Awards, held in Jackson, Mississippi. Dozens of radio stations—small, AM, but—still program their music. A grab bag of contemporary blues song titles includes "Lick It Before You Stick It," "You Ain't Cheatin' by the Rules," "I'll Drink Your Bathwater, Baby," "Everything I Like to Eat Starts with a 'P,' " "If I Can't Cut the Mustard (I Can Still Lick around the Jar)," "Your Dog's about to Kill My Cat," and "It Ain't Cheatin' until You Get Caught." Above all, the chitlin' circuit is fun, which isn't the first word most would use to describe the "authentic" blues scene. My fascination grew.

Bobby's cohorts proved every bit as intriguing as he. A former gospel singer named Marvin Sease wrote a song called "Candy Licker" in the late 1980s, and has enjoyed steady chitlin' circuit headliner status since. More than mere song, "Candy Licker" is a sometimes belligerent, ten-minute liberation of cunnilingus from black man taboo, sung from the perspective of Jody, a mythical lover conjured from the mists of Yoruban trickster lore. Jody does what other men do not deign discuss. Even more subversively, he cares about female satisfaction. Jody calls out the sorry-ass men who won't go down. A sharp ploy, considering the conventional wisdom, dating to the 1930s, that black women buy more blues records than black men do.

Sitting in the makeshift dressing room, really a boiler closet, at the Leflore County (Mississippi) Agri-Center in October 2004, I asked Sease how he devised his shrewd approach to such a controversial topic. "It came to me in a dream," he said.

This would make a hell of a book, I thought, and told a few people about the idea. One in particular, *Living Blues* co-founder Jim O'Neal, who would gently pose several door-opening questions during my ensuing years of research and writing, asked if I'd spoken to Sax Kari. I called Sax, and told him about the book I thought I was writing. He chuckled. "I worked for the man who *invented* the chitlin' circuit."[2]

✳   ✳   ✳

Back in the trailer in Seffner, Florida, in September 2005, Sax scoots in his office chair over to a Murphy bed in the corner of the living room–recording studio, and he grabs a chunk of promotional fliers, empty contract blanks, and pictures from a pile on his cot. "See if I can find a skeleton or two," he says, and plucks a fading snapshot of a light-skinned, heavily rouged African-American woman. Grinning, he whimpers, "This was my last real girlfriend," he bursts into fake tears, then shuts them off and straightens up. "Billy Eckstine beat me to her. She had a baby by Billy, but never had no children by me."

Sax cycles through a few more pictures and winds up his pitch to secure my representation as his manager, a natural development in the relationship between washed-up entertainer and naive enthusiast. "This business is the easiest in the world to make money in," he says. "I'm going to tell you something you don't know—you got no competition."

He searches for the right photo to use in his press kit, and shows me two portraits taken at an Olan Mills studio in the mid-1980s. In both, he wears a navy blue blazer and thick polyester tie and has fluffy sideburns and a pile of rust-colored hair. In one, he cuts his eyes suspiciously toward his right shoulder, chin square to the camera, eyebrows raised. In the other, he looks directly into the camera, a concerned pucker creasing his lips and brow, his "she was my last real girlfriend" pose. He smiles in neither. I ask if he'll sign one for me. He rocks back in his chair and says, "My signature is worth $10,000."

We dine that night at a fried-fish buffet, sitting under wicker ceiling fans at one of fifty or so tables of senior citizens and prolific eaters. Sax, having spent the previous quarter century out of the loop, asks after a few old friends.

"Sam Phillips?"

"He died," I tell him.

Sax Kari's concerned face and $10,000 inscription. *Author's collection*

"Sam's dead?"

The news hits Sax full. He scrunches the bushy eyebrows together, and his jaw drops. It sinks in for a moment before he shuts his mouth and resumes chewing. Every name on his list—Tyrone Davis, his old Indianapolis pal Jimmy Coe, Rufus Thomas—pushes him through the stages of grief in fast-forward: the pained facial expression, barely perceptible head shake, a moment of reconciliation, then acceptance, and return to the food. Brought up to speed, Sax recovers his characteristic good cheer as he plots our future. He has been writing songs for decades, so there's plenty of material. He owns a publishing company and manufactures his own CDs. We'll reconstruct the old chitlin' circuit, and he'll play Elks lodges from here to Texas. The public are idiots, he assures me, and will love to see this cartoon bear of an old man in his wheelchair playing the organ just as they had packed theaters to see a blind man, Ray Charles, perform.

"A blind man!" Sax shouts.

We finish supper, and I wheel him toward the exit. "You won't believe the amount of money we're going to make," he says. Before we reach the door, Sax asks me to pull his wheelchair up beside an empty table. I oblige. He picks up a ramekin of packaged sweeteners from the table and dumps them into his shirt pocket.*

The next morning, I arrive at the trailer, crunch up the ramp, knock, and push the door aside. Sax sits at his mixing board looking like a silent-film victim of either electrocution or exploding cigar—no ball cap this time, his springy white hair blown out at the back and sides, accentuating his resemblance to Jerry Stiller. He wears dark-gray slacks pulled well past his navel and wide black suspenders, but no shirt. He peers at me through thick, black plastic-rimmed, square-lens spectacles. Sax has been up all night writing songs and programming instrumental tracks and is anxious to share. He mashes a button that launches a synthetic rhythm track, and he sings a bluesy ballad he calls "What Is This Feeling?" Finishing the song, he leans back in his chair and howls a sweet "ooh-oohooh-wooh." Grinning, he tips his head toward me, nodding to the electronic beat. As the track's last bars fade out, he flips his hand dismissively: "You'll be surprised, the amount of money we'll make."

---

* A disclosure: I hasten to distance myself from the deplorable practice of check-book journalism, but nonetheless I provided my informants various compensatory items. During my three-day visit with Sax Kari, I purchased for him one cup of decaffeinated coffee with Sweet'N Low and half-and-half, two toasted bagels with egg and cheese; one $8.95 buffet admission; one order of sweet-and-sour pork, one order of egg foo young from a strip-mall Chinese take-out; and three apples and three oranges from a roadside fruit stand. Sax took it easy on me compared to Sir Lattimore Brown, who, in the span of just under two hours, set me back one order of beef with broccoli at a shopping-mall foodcourt, one gallon of 5W30 motor oil, one quart of automatic transmission fluid, one six-pack of Busch Light canned beer, and twenty dollars in cash.

I had studied the background of the chitlin' circuit as best I could in preparation for meeting Sax, but found nothing definitive on its origins. I did, however, notice a trend in many of the books that mention the circuit. Artists were *relegated* to the chitlin' circuit. Working it was a *grind*. Even its title is depressing, derived from what black people call a hog's small intestine, the cuisine of relegation. This chitlin' circuit seemed to be an unpleasant place, located in our nation's bowels, and better left unexplored. Sax's stories about the inventor and beginning of the circuit, however, revealed people of vision and an industry of intricate, far-reaching design that struck me as anything but shameful.

"I met Denver D. Ferguson out of Indianapolis, Indiana, in 1941. I had run away from home, and I got a gig working there for a funeral parlor. There was an affair at this big nightclub, dance hall, the Sunset Terrace. Taylor Seaths—he ran the Sunset Terrace for Denver— told me that Ferguson also had a booking agency. The lady who ran the [agency] office was Twyla Mayfield. Aside from all [Ferguson's] gabbing, she was really the one who handled all the booking. She introduced me to the old man.

"There were certain things [Ferguson] liked to do himself. He liked to make promoters, that was his thing. Ferguson made his promoters in the little small towns, shadow promoters. He collected phonebooks, and he located every black barbershop and beauty shop, every nightclub, bar or sooky joint in the South. Then he would send runners out to recruit them. He took those small-town people and made them dollar wise, and showed them how to promote his dances. Unless it was a moneymaking town, the white agencies didn't fool with it. He had his own printing press, where he could make his own placards [to advertise dances], and send them to the promoters. They would take up money at the door. Every band that came in had a road manager who worked for Ferguson, and sat there by the promoter at the door and counted the money.

"In the '40s, there were about twenty-two black promoters on

Denver Ferguson's list. The top man was Tom Wince, who was in Vicksburg, Mississippi. The next top man, Ralph Weinberg, was in Bluefield, West Virginia. Don Robey was in Houston. Howard Lewis in Dallas. Before you go out onto the road your whole tour was booked. Black promoters worked only with black acts, and Ferguson was the only black booking agent at that time. The promoters respected one another's territory. Tom Wince would do about twenty to twenty-five dates a year, Weinberg would do about twenty, and Lewis would do whatever he could get.

"This became—for the people that worked for him and the artists that was booked by him—the chitlin' circuit. Chitlins to black people were like caviar to Europeans. It's played out now, but it was a delicacy. The average chitlin' dinner was a dollar. You could go to one place and buy supper, drinks, and see an orchestra perform. It doesn't exist now as it did then. Back then you had big bands, anywhere from ten- to twenty-piece bands that had to squeeze themselves into a corner if there was no bandstand. There were no inside toilets at many of the places; you had to use privies. Now, when you got into a place that had running water inside, why you were fortunate. They sold ice water. They didn't have air conditioners; they had these big garage fans: two on the bandstand and one back at the door. These were wooden buildings on the outside of town; there were very few concrete buildings or places in town. It was seldom you'd find anyplace for blacks that would hold more than six hundred. The people'd be damn near on top of you. We'd get the brass and reeds on the back of the stage and get the drummer and rhythm section down front where you could see over their heads. You would play for two and a half hours straight, then take a thirty-minute break, then come back and play for the next hour and a half. Four-hour gigs.

"I was as good as Basie, Dorsey, any of 'em. Radio was just being born and they had all the big white bands on there. This is what blacks were listening to. If you couldn't get up to that standard, they didn't come to see you. You had to be dynamite. I had eighteen pieces.

My lowest salary a night would be $300 to $350 [for the band]. But the circuit was never about making big money—it was about making constant money.

"I was fortunate enough to have a bus. If you had an off day, you could fend for yourself. I would park my bus right in front of the biggest restaurant, and bullshit for a day or two. You go over to the radio station and say, 'Sax Kari and his orchestra will be in town for a couple of days,' and you could get a crowd together like that. A lot of times I'd get a gig on my own on the road, and old man Ferguson would call and say, 'I heard about you down in Vicksburg, well where's my part of the money?'

"In the South there was nothing but farming: tobacco fields, rice fields, sugar cane, cotton fields. [Black people] worked all week, and Saturday night was their night to howl, get drunk, and fornicate. They just wanted to know when the next dance was gonna be.

"I was like Ferguson's son. He taught me everything I know today, and kept me from getting screwed in so many ways. I worked in the office, out of the office, anything he wanted done, 'Sax, do it.' He was grooming me to take his place, but I never wanted an office job. I doubled as bandleader, road manager, whatever it took to make money out of the agency.

"Denver never kept any records. First thing he taught me was, 'Don't ever write anything down. Avoid big municipal auditoriums— that's where the IRS man is going to be there with you on the door counting your tickets. Go to the nondescript places.' "

* * *

Sax brought this project to a turning point, away from the story that I wanted to tell and toward one much more urgent. I traced the circuit from Sax's roadmap, and revelations appeared. The chitlin' circuit story that unfolded through old newspapers, interviews with aged jitterbugs, torn scrapbooks, and city directories crossed unexpected backroads: the numbers racket, hair straighteners, multiple murders, human catastrophe, commercial sex, bootlegging, international scandal, female impersonation, and a real female who could screw a light bulb into herself—and turn it on. I found that racketeering and bribery were indispensable factors in the growth of black music, and that nonmusical forces molded the chitlin' circuit, from the great migration to urban renewal. I was most surprised, though, to find how the circuit had musically evolved—how life and business on the circuit tinged its sounds, and how the sounds struck back and shaped the circuit's business and culture. There are other eras of chitlin' circuit history—from 1960s soul to Bobby Rush and Marvin Sease's circuit today—that deserve exploration. The different threads of chitlin' circuit action have their stories too—the comedy chitlin' circuit that spanned from Butterbeans and Susie to Red Foxx, Dolemite, and Richard Pryor, and the drama chitlin' circuit that August Wilson championed, where Tyler Perry got his start. This book, however, focuses on how the chitlin' circuit for live music developed during the 1930s and nurtured rock 'n' roll from the early 1940s to the mid-1950s.

These are the intertwined stories of booking agents, show promoters, and nightclub owners, the moguls who controlled wealth throughout the black music business. Until records eclipsed live shows as the top moneymakers, new sounds grew on the road and in nightclubs, through the dance business rather than in the recording studio. Though the moguls' names are not recognized among the important producers of American culture, their numbers rackets, dice parlors, dance halls, and bootleg liquor and prostitution rings financed the artistic development of breakthrough performers—Jimmie Lunceford, Louis Jordan, Joe Turner, Wynonie Harris, T-Bone Walker, Amos Milburn, Roy Brown, B.B. King, Ike Turner, Johnny Ace, Little Richard, and James Brown, among them. There are quite a few other musicians here who mattered in subtler ways, whose reputations haven't endured so well, such as Walter Barnes, Clarence "Gatemouth" Brown, Sax Kari, Bill Harvey, and Luke Gonder to mention a few. While more artists could have justifiably appeared, these emerged in my research as representative of and pivotal to their times. Some were monumental.

Their stories play out across a cityscape that no longer exists. While the ghetto's contours reverberate through the music in ways that often defy notation, rock 'n' roll simply couldn't have happened anyplace else. The streets of Indianapolis, Memphis, Houston, New Orleans, even Macon, Georgia, are as fundamentally crucial to this story as the people who walked them. As money and power flowed through the ghetto during the 1930s and '40s, creativity and musical innovation followed. But as black downtowns atrophied and disappeared thereafter, not only was their influence diminished, their mark faded from America's cultural history.

It begins not with an old song, but a lost world.

A Hundred Dollars Crooked

Long before black became beautiful, there was Bronzeville. In 1930 on the south side of Chicago, newspaper scribe James J. Gentry watched his neighborhood fill with Southern black émigrés. He noted the new residents' off-the-farm optimism and thirst for big-city glamour, and in the spirit of the moment, he gave the neighborhood its bright new moniker. Bronzevilles grew in Detroit, Milwaukee, Indianapolis, and elsewhere, functioning as black towns within white cities throughout the segregated North.

Indiana Avenue—*The* Avenue to locals—pulsed at the heart of Indianapolis's Bronzeville. The Avenue shot diagonally northwest from the city's center and bottomed out eight blocks later at Fall Creek. Avenue habitués understood local geography a little differently. "It runs from a pawnshop to a hospital," they'd say. True enough. Many nights along the strip began with the hocking of a watch chain at one of the brokers in the 200 block, and ended in the municipal clinic at the far end. In between lived the barbecue stands, cafés, soda fountains, barbershops and beauty parlors, tailors, cleaners, shoeshines, cabstands, billiard rooms, taverns, and nightclubs with fast and furious floor shows. A fellow named Denver Ferguson had a problem there in 1941. The Indiana State Alcoholic Beverage Commission revoked the permit to serve liquor at his nightclub, Sunset Terrace, the last Avenue stop before the hospital and the finest Negro dance hall between Chicago and New York.

Denver, "D.D." to associates (middle name, Darius), was built like a bulldog, short and compact at about five feet six inches. He was handsome, with reddish brown skin, wavy dark-brown hair flecked gray, and wide, light-hazel eyes. He had done well for himself during the previous two decades, beginning with an innovative numbers game he introduced to the Avenue in the early 1920s. When his liquor board problems began, Denver counted among his holdings a busy printing shop, a service uniform factory, and bits of real estate, including the Sunset Terrace and Sunset Cafe. His round-the-clock schedule gave him a rumpled, slouchy appearance—his suits were fashionably cut of fine fabric yet poorly cared for—but he seldom looked hurried. He liked the cream off the top of the morning's milk bottle and enjoyed fine, fat cuts of meat down to the gristle and bone. Denver motored through Bronzeville in a café au lait Buick Super. By then, he had cleansed his diction of any lingering Kentucky twang. He piled placards advertising the Sunset's next engagements around the house, and his kids laughed at the funny names: Fats Waller, Tiny Bradshaw, and Fatha Hines. Though quiet, Denver was not without a penchant for the grandiose. When he advertised opening night at the Sunset, he promised the Bronzeville citizenry, "You will enjoy this more than anything you ever attended in your life."

Denver, his brother, Sea Ferguson, and Harry "Goosie" Lee were the only black nightclub owners on the strip and, coincidentally, the only Avenue club owners to lose their booze licenses in 1941. Denver had grown accustomed to this sort of ankle biting during his twenty years outside the law. Every white politician up for office threatened Denver's livelihood with pledges to clean up the Avenue, hassling his gaming operations to play tough for white voters. That was, at least, until their first taste of the bribes. Though buying off the police and officials helped, Denver had gotten rich and then dodged punishment all those years thanks to his keen powers of anticipation—he sensed developing trends and trouble and acted decisively, correctly, on his hunches. And in early 1941, Denver thought the time was right for a venture beyond Bronzeville and the Avenue.

✳   ✳   ✳

Denver and Sea were born not in Bronzeville, but in Brownsville, down Kentucky way. Brownsville sits in lush, hilly Edmonson County on the Green River, atop a labyrinth of limestone caverns. Their parents, Mattie and Samuel, were born there just after the Civil War. In late-nineteenth-century Brownsville, most residents grew tobacco for cash and food for their households, and spawned their own workforces. Denver landed on the kitchen table on February 19, 1895, and Sea followed on December 22, 1899. Sam farmed, and schooled his brood in rural self-sufficiency—logging, stone and brick masonry, carpentry, and surveying. "Nothing could have been farther from the vocation that was born in me," Denver later wrote.[1] But Sam instilled values in his boys that would prove useful to the lives they chose. Sam, son of slaves, knew that property equaled power. He steadily acquired little pieces of Brownsville until he owned more of it than anyone else. Sam gave generously to municipal projects, providing land for a county reservoir, donating a downtown lot for a new church for his white neighbors, accruing favors and a begrudging respect from the community. Uncle Sam was okay, for colored.

As a boy Denver preferred to spend his time alone. A toy printing press Sam ordered from the Sears, Roebuck and Co. catalog captured Denver's fascination. At age nineteen, Denver acquired a linotype through Sam's machinations and printed a weekly broadside called the *Edmonson County Star*, Brownsville's first newspaper. Already a lad of innovation and accomplishment, Denver said good-bye to Brownsville to fight the Great War in 1917. "[It] was easily the happiest portion of my life," he would reflect, "because I could trust people en masse."[2] Following his return from the front, Denver joined the hundreds of thousands of African-Americans who left the South. He didn't go far. Indianapolis sits just over two hundred miles due north of Brownsville. He didn't go alone either. Indianapolis's black population swelled from 21,816 to 34,678 between 1910 and 1920 and continued to grow in the ensuing years, with most of these émigrés arriving from the Blue Grass State. They found a budding Negro district around Indiana Avenue in the city's northwest corridor, where colored saloons, confectioners, and brotherhood lodges bunched around the *Indianapolis Recorder*, the black newspaper.

Still, the city Denver came to in 1919 hardly fit the image of the free North. The rise of Indianapolis's black population coincided with a Ku Klux Klan revival. According to one estimate, Klan membership in Indiana swelled between 1920 and 1925 to include one-fourth of the state's male citizenry. The state's Grand Dragon, D. C. Stephenson, established his office in Indianapolis in 1923, a dirty trick on folks like Denver—city of black refuge becomes Kluxer Kapitol. In addition to their usual political strong-arming and intimidation tactics, the White Knights here dabbled in popular culture. KKK Records pressed titles such as "Daddy Swiped Our Last Clean Bed Sheet and Joined the Ku Klux Klan" and "The Bright Fiery Cross" (sung to the tune of "Old Rugged Cross"), both accompanied by the "100% Americans Orchestra." The blood-red label was stamped with the company's fiery cross logo, and the address printed in gold letters: "Best in Klan Music— The American, P.O. Box 871 Indianapolis, Indiana."

In 1920, Denver moved into a small home at 412 West North Street, abutting the Avenue's south end. He'd arrived with enough money to open the Ferguson Printing Company, and after some initial success running the business out of the house, he set up shop nearby at 322 Senate, overlooking Indiana Avenue, which would hold Denver's headquarters for the next twenty-five years.

From Denver's office, the Avenue streetcar line stretched horizon to horizon. The trolley clambered along the cobblestones, where the

A dapper, young Denver Ferguson, war veteran and cigar enthusiast, around the time of his settling in Indianapolis. *Courtesy of Carole Finnell*

last stubborn carriages frustrated motorists. Buildings on the Avenue's south end near Denver's shop were brick, some oxblood red, others sandy brown with black flecks, two and three stories tall. They extended from two storefronts to a half-block wide. They housed junkmen, fish and game shops, clothiers, and cobblers. Striped canvas and painted tin awnings reached from the façades over the sidewalk, shading the concrete in the absence of trees. After sunset, electric lights, five milky-glass globes on an iron post, a half-dozen per block, wiped away the darkness in soft yellow puffs. Avenue men dressed the same, in long-sleeved, collared, white shirts, suspenders, and dark trousers. A few sported vests; fewer wore suits. The greatest variety was seen atop their heads: newsboy caps, ivies, derbies, bowlers, straw boaters, and fedoras. Ladies' fashion functioned primarily to keep male imaginations active. Continuing up the street, broad brick buildings shrunk to double storefronts, with one- and two-story, tin-roofed wooden buildings interspersed among them. The architecture appeared increasingly modest farther up toward Fall Creek—raw plank shops and homes that would have blended in fine on an unpaved thoroughfare in the Old West.

The Avenue's first picture-show house, of corrugated iron, stood on bare ground. Each evening's show began with a fresh scattering of wood shavings to absorb the torrents of tobacco juice. The nearest thing to an orchestra in those days—a trio of piano, violin, and fiddle— sawed through the night at Vinegar Hall, where patrons dipped whiskey from a communal barrel. Another of the era's recreation spots, Bob Parker's Hole in the Wall, occupied the entire second story of a quadruple storefront. It was remembered only as "an institution of wide notoriety," a truly awesome distinction in this open town.

People lived above Avenue storefronts, where it stayed loud, and then spread throughout the rooming and shotgun houses along the cross streets. By 1920 most residential blocks adjacent to the Avenue were nearly 100 percent black. Sprawling family homes were divided to board the latest arrivals, and black families filled rooms where once a single white body had slept. Migrants adapted old Kentucky architecture to its new, high-density urban setting. They dug wells around back, and in one tenement installed a two-story privy that upstairs tenants had to reach by braving a wobbly, splintery footbridge. In winter, coal smoke from stoves and furnaces blackened the foggy, chill air, and ashy-gray snowmelt sloshed in the gutters. In summer, the fragrance of tomato plants punched through the humidity.

The Jews hung on around Indiana Avenue—Abraham Tavel and the Sachs Brothers ran their pawnshops, and the Schaeffer cleaners and Kappeler jewelers still did business—but the migrants had begun to transform the strip and were deep in the process of making it their own. Small-town Kentucky ways translated well to the Avenue. People lived intimately, publicly. Most homes lacked comfort, so folks spent their time visiting, out on the porch, walking the

street, or lounging in a café, many of which served "Kentucky oys-
ters," local code for hog intestines. Consequently, the track buzzed
night and day. Everybody living on top of and in front of each other
lent the weekly *Indianapolis Recorder* a penetrating vitality. It kept a
second-story office halfway between the pawnshops and the hospital,
where it saw and reported on everything. You might open it Saturday
afternoon and learn who your sweetheart was seeing on the side, go
find the cheaters in a café, cut their asses in front of everybody, and
end up in the next edition.

Though opening a print shop in this abruptly handmade city
hardly seems an entrée into the sporting life, it became just that.
Denver's first major clients at the print shop ran a street lottery in
New York known as the numbers game. He printed their ticket slips,
receipts, and tally cards. He may also have printed the dream books
that interpreted the numeric value of images appearing in gamblers'
fitful rest.

According to Herbert Asbury, informal chronicler of the American
degenerati—he called dream books "the real bestsellers of American
literature"—numbers games originated in London lottery shops in
the early eighteenth century. Sly clerks ran games on the side of these
legal raffles, catering to the farthing-ante set who couldn't afford the
price of a regular ticket. This shabby clientele sneeringly referred to
the clerks as "insurance solicitors," and bets as "policies." The names
stuck and the game spread to the States. Policy shops opened in New
York and New Orleans and grew unrestrained until the first anti-
gaming legislation passed in the early nineteenth century. As is reli-
ably the case with vice crackdowns, the game had become so popular
by the time anyone thought to outlaw it that it had no trouble moving
underground. Italians, Irish, and African-Americans ran the games
among themselves. Policy appealed to the poor in the States just as it
had to the meaner sort in London, and by the early twentieth century
it had become as universal as cholera in the ghetto.[3]

Policy developed a slightly different character in each community but had a few standard features. Bettors could wager as little as three cents. Black players preferred gambling on three-number sets known as gigs. Popular combinations developed their own titles, like 4-11-44, the "washerwoman's gig." Most games offered 200-to-1 odds on a gig despite the nearly 75,000 possible variations. This rather healthily favored the house. In some towns the spin of a policy wheel in the back room of a laundry, a tavern, or a grocer—someplace a crowd could gather without arousing too much suspicion—determined the winning gig. Other places used a set of digits from the published price of cotton or the Federal Reserve reports appearing in the evening news, something remote enough to be impossible to rig—or at least to appear that way. A so-called policy banker supplied the cash flow to back the game. He employed the numbers runners, who collected the bets and distributed winnings, and he reaped the inevitable profits from the games, which, despite the veneer of legitimacy, were fixed.

Denver moved up fast in the new world. By 1923, four years after arriving in Indianapolis, simmering with ambition and thorough in his comprehension of local matters, Denver scanned the Avenue storefronts of his neighboring black businesses—Archie Works's cigar shop, Lucius Wilson's shoeshine stand, James Dice's soft drink parlor, Arch Greathouse's billiard hall, and Monroe Buford's barber shop—and decided to play a little policy himself. As former Ferguson employee Jimmy Coe recalled, "Denver would rather make a hundred dollars crooked than a thousand dollars straight."

Very well, Mr. Coe, but in Indianapolis, crooked *was* straight. The side effects of racist policy and racist culture extended well beyond residential segregation and violent attitudes, black and white. Bright, ambitious black men like Denver could choose from only a strangling few professional options. Aside from busting his back and knuckles on the farm or in a factory, he could go straight and work as a pay-what-you-can physician, dentist, or attorney serving a poor population. This simply wouldn't do. So, as Coe explained, "Denver invented a numbers game . . . baseball tickets."[4]

Denver designed his daily lottery slips to resemble a baseball score-
card, with columns for runs, hits, and errors for every game scheduled
on a given day. Players filled their three-digit "gigs" into a team's runs,
hits, and errors column—just keeping track, officer. The outcome of real
baseball games, however, had no bearing on the winning numbers. The
daily report of the Indianapolis bank clearings and debits determined
the winners. The clearings and debits typically ran seven or eight digits
long, so players guessed which numbers would appear in the hundred-
thousandth, ten-thousandth, and thousandth spots. Players could bet
on as many three-digit possibilities as they could afford, logging their
predictions on a baseball ticket in a team's runs, hits, and errors box,
and paying their runner accordingly. A visual would be lovely, but while
memories of Denver's baseball ticket game are legion, most players wad-
ded their tickets in disgust and tossed them to the gutter.

It seems like an awful lot of trouble to go through just to gamble openly, but the baseball ticket design performed crucial, decep-
tive functions. Gambling devices were illegal, so the piece had to at
least appear to be *intended* for clean amusement—whatever sordid
deeds people performed with them were beyond the printer's culpa-
bility. Players placed their bets somewhat clandestinely, and no laws
prevented carrying pockets full of coin and baseball tickets. Players
enjoyed the novelty of it all, and the feeling of putting one past the
authorities. Far more important, Denver could control one or two
locally generated bank reports far more simply than he could rig the
outcomes or reported scores of baseball games. Bank reports came
out in the evening paper. Of course, wise policy bankers recognized
the importance of winning, and arranged for a daily hit or two on
lightly played gigs.[5]

The ebb and flow of Avenue life dictated the modes and rhythm
of the Ferguson policy racket. Numbers runners spread out to collect
tickets and bets and to distribute winnings, while hangouts like the
billiard halls and the ubiquitous barber and beauty shops housed policy stations for walk-up business and the latest results. Participation

among the poor citizenry was nearly universal. As Avenue habitué
Joe Hester recalled, "We all played the baseball tickets, man. That
was the only way we got over."[6] Street-level credibility meant everything. Bettors needed to know that their money would find the game
and that their windfall would find them. Runners needed to be visible. "They wouldn't solicit you, you had to contact them," Hester
said. And they weren't hard to find. They lolled on street corners and
smoked under the eaves along the Avenue. They stationed themselves
on apartment-building steps—the Avondale, the Marguerite, and
the Palma on Senate Avenue, the Lexington on Capitol Avenue, the
Roslyn on New York Street, toward Indiana Avenue's south end, and
the Lincoln Flats on West North Street a few blocks up—waiting for
the house girls to head home from the white folks' or for the waiters
and night janitors to make their way to the streetcar stop and toward
the professional buildings downtown. Ferguson's insurance solicitors ran thick along Blackford, Blake, Michigan, Minerva, North,
and Vermont streets southwest of Indiana Avenue, but lighter in the
blocks of Ransom Place, the neighborhood of choice among black
professionals on the northeast side. Denver bought an interest in a
taxicab company early in the racket, and drivers could easily be found
at the curb or flagged down cruising.[7] Bettors crowded policy stations
in the evening, waiting for the daily bank-clearings announcement,
then gutter-balled their losing tickets en masse—a daily ticker-tape
Avenue parade. The rare winner bought rounds of cloudy ale in the
back of Arch Greathouse's poolroom.

Commissions ranging between 10 and 15 percent of the bets collected kept the runners from taking off with a day's wagers. Even
when they did split, a single defection or even several in a day would
scarcely harm a game the size of Ferguson's. Though modest when
compared to the New York and Chicago rackets, the Ferguson game
employed two hundred in an area no larger than twenty city blocks.[8]

Denver orchestrated the racket from his shop, where he showed up
daily in his dungarees to wear the printer's heavy canvas smock. As

the only black printer on the Avenue, Denver did a steady honest trade running off promotional fliers (distributed at no additional cost by the firm's tireless pavement pounders), in addition to his own "novelties," as he called the baseball tickets. Goosie Lee, the leading black bookie at the time of Denver's arrival, could drive his gold Cadillac Roadster around like Jack Johnson and prance along the thoroughfare with a diamond-tipped cane—Denver kept his profile low and his fingers inky. As baseball tickets flowed into the streets from 322 Senate, Ferguson paid off the local cops at the back door, with rank determining an officer's take. A promotion in the force translated into a bump up the Ferguson weekly bribe scale: ten dollars for patrolmen, twenty for sergeants, thirty for lieutenants, and fifty bucks for a captain.[9]

Enthusiasm for the pastime ran high on the Avenue, as locals tracked the results of Cuban, Mexican, and Panamanian winter baseball with a zeal that matched their daily devotion to the major and Negro leagues from spring to early fall. Ferguson's baseball tickets either tapped into an already prevalent trait in Indianapolis gambling culture or began a local fascination with novelty games that persists to the present.*

The fever spread so that by 1925 Denver had attracted competition and needed help. A pair of Russian Jews, Joe and Isaac Mitchell, opened an Avenue dive in 1923, calling it a café. Prohibition, you understand. Joe managed this at 408 Indiana, a few hundred feet from Denver's print-shop headquarters. Isaac, known as Tuffy from

---

* Federal authorities prosecuted baseball ticket rackets into the 1970s, while another gambling institution that goes back to the early twentieth century, the pea shake house, still operates with legal immunity throughout black Indianapolis. Pea shake games anticipated today's Powerball lotteries. Dried peapods, each marked with a single digit, fill a scooped-out, dried gourd. Gamblers try to predict the series of three or four digits that appear after a shake of the gourd and a roll of the peas. No dummies, the Indiana State Lottery introduced a Powerball game in 1992 and within two weeks the Hoosier State led the nation in Powerball ticket sales. To this day, however, some Indianapolis gamblers prefer to place their bets in the intimacy of a backroom at the neighborhood dry cleaner rather than with the anonymity of a convenience store.

his days as a boxer, supervised the gaming suite above the café and masterminded the brothers' numbers racket. Theirs was an intimate rivalry. Their respective headquarters were so close you could stand outside Denver's print shop and smell the Mitchell hole's astringent gin. They acknowledged each other on the street, but Denver privately cursed these Yids, and the Mitchells muttered about that arrogant *schvartza*.

At this point, though, Denver concerned himself less with his swarthy opponents and more with a surplus-cash dilemma. The stuff piled up faster than he could bribe everyone off and safely spend it—beyond his fancy cars and fine food, Denver never flaunted; he smoked cheap, drank moderately, and lived decently. Denver sent for his brother, Sea, a freshly minted Lincoln University graduate. Denver was a better big-picture strategist than front man, so affable Sea became the Ferguson operation's public face. He was short like Denver—though not so plump—light-skinned, trim-mustached, and memorably attired. Although Denver reached Indianapolis first, Sea eventually overshadowed his older brother. Sax Kari came to the Avenue in 1939, and he considered Denver his mentor, but he acknowledged that around Bronzeville in its heyday, "Sea was the big man."[10] Unlike his aloof brother, Sea cultivated a reputation for generosity and good cheer among the Avenue citizenry. As Denver's daughter Carole Ferguson Finnell recalled, "If we wanted a dime to buy candy, we'd never bother daddy, we'd go to Uncle Sea." When he died in 1974, Sea was buried wearing his favorite gumball-red blazer. "He was flashy," Finnell recalled. "I thought that just suited him so well."[11]

The struggle between the two sets of brothers, Kentuckians and Russians, would shape underworld politics in Indianapolis for years to come.

Sea opened a real estate brokerage, and he and Denver became community developers. The Fergusons extended loans and credit for their constituents to rent or buy property and launch legitimate concerns. They gave generously to charitable causes, functioning as a de facto community foundation.[12] Today we might look cynically upon a reputed gambler who puts uniforms on little leaguers, or chalk in schoolteachers' hands, but in those days no one else offered the Avenue much charity. The Fergusons signaled their commitment to the Avenue and were applauded as *race men*, whose wealth, power, and openhandedness lifted all Negroes. The term *race man* applied to legitimate black business people and men like Denver and Sea alike, as a guiding ethical principle that outweighed the legality of one's activity.[13]

Not long after Sea got to town, a curious structure sprouted from the Avenue near Denver's print shop. The flatiron shot four stories up from a triangular base where diagonal Indiana Avenue and vertical North West Street cross like opening scissors, and spread a half-block up the Avenue. It was the picture of modernity, with its grand marquee and golden-hued brick. Two-story-tall red letters atop the building announced the Walker Theatre, named for the nation's first black female millionaire. The letters were visible from numerous vantage points citywide and sent a long shadow across the Avenue.

Born Sarah Breedlove in Delta, Louisiana, in 1867, Madam C. J. Walker developed her Wonderful Hair Grower and patented hot combs through experimentation on her own uncooperative scalp, parched and patchy from her childhood years picking cotton in the dry dust under Louisiana's scorching sun. Having worked her way up from the depths of the Southern plantation belt, through Western towns and industrial Northern cities, Walker saw that black people resided at the outskirts of American geography just as surely as they lived at the margin of its society. Not only did she invent products exclusively intended for black use, she created a system for finding black consumers in the out-of-the-way places they lived, in rural backwaters and urban ghettoes. She groomed agents and dispersed them territorially so that she could sell product even where no beauty shops existed. She built Walker beauty schools in bigger towns, where she might train hundreds of agents and beauticians. Her graduates sold Walker products and practiced Walker salon techniques, benefiting themselves, Madam, and the race as a whole, so the pitch went, as it liberated black women from white people's kitchens and set them up as independent business people. Madam mastered the system after settling down in Indianapolis in 1910, where she built a fine house and an adjacent cosmetics factory barely a block off the Avenue, at 640 North West Street. Walker agents sent all monies and orders to Indianapolis, from where Madam produced and shipped all the hot combs and straightener.

Walker's business grew steadily even after her death in 1919. The product line stretched until Madam's original Indianapolis factory couldn't meet demands for moisture-resistant Satin Tress, jet-black Liquid Hair Coloring, Glossine pomade, and Tetter Salve. So the company, under the leadership of Madam's daughter A'Lelia and Indianapolis attorney Freeman Ransom, established new headquarters at the heart of the Avenue. Success had never entirely satisfied Madam. A race woman to her core, she made statements on her people's behalf—they could be industrious, inventive, respectable, and tasteful without surrendering themselves. The new headquarters was such a proclamation, if delivered more in the day's exaggerated formality than Madam's decorum.

The Madam C. J. Walker Building opened the day after Christmas 1927. Its four stories housed the expanded cosmetics factory and company offices, with a telephone center to field orders, a beauty parlor, and Walker Academy, plus a modern drug store, coffee shop, and plenty of office space to rent to Indianapolis's black attorneys, dentists, and physicians. An ornate African-motif theater filled most of the ground floor. Designed to showcase opera and ballet, its décor melded ancient Egyptian and West African imagery, celebrating

black ancestry at its most regal and robust. The low arts were practiced high on the fourth floor in the Grand Casino Ballroom, where
the décor honored Denver and Sea's profession. The orchestra performed on a giant roulette wheel, flanked by a set of seven-foot-tall
dice. Giant cards, racing forms, and policy wheels adorned the walls.
Wonder where a fella can find a baseball ticket?

Chapter 2 ✳ ✳ ✳ ✳ ✳ ✳ ✳

The Midget Maestro

In Chicago, home of the original Bronzeville, journalist-musician Walter Barnes deduced that entertainment, at its core, is an act of victimless deception. His weekly *Chicago Defender* columns often discussed elite orchestra leaders, including Walter Barnes. His musical arrangements invariably concluded with him blowing the climactic note, issued with horn poised to the heavens. He wore white tails on stage, and his orchestra donned black tuxedos. He waved the baton some and also played alto, baritone, and tenor saxophones and clarinet. Barnes looked sharp off stage too, sporting a collection of striped and polka-dotted bow ties and flashing his gold incisor. A *Defender* colleague observed, "Walter Barnes, that midget maestro, seems undaunted by the prevalent depression. He drives a big car with double-breasted tires, and has several smaller ones to bring up the rear. . . . Fems drag out boy friends to hear Waltah. Boy friends look at Waltah, growl, and bare their teeth."[1]

Barnes was born on July 8, 1905, in Vicksburg, Mississippi, one of fifteen children. He grew up and got music in Mississippi, then landed in Chicago in 1924. After studying with Benny Goodman's mentor, classical clarinetist Franz Schoepp, Barnes joined the band of a verified former New Orleans pimp and all-time bullshit *artiste* named Jelly Roll Morton. Barnes never conceded that he'd learned much music from Jelly, though he clearly took tips on self-promotion and self-preservation from the old master. A good bandleader put his name first. He exuded hype and crafted a catlike knack for landing upright. By 1927, Barnes was leading his own band for white crowds at two of hustler Paddy Harmon's north-side dance palaces, the Dreamland and the Arcadia, and had begun to assemble his notable wardrobe and fleet of automobiles. The dapper young maestro's career percolated: Barnes and his Royal Creolians, now a fourteen-piece orchestra, cut a few numbers for Brunswick Records in late 1928. When Paddy Harmon unveiled his crowning achievement, Chicago Stadium, on March 28, 1929, Barnes's band was part of the festivities. He enjoyed being photographed in his clothes and cars, and sharing the shots with scores of family members who'd followed him north. His nieces and nephews always liked to see him coming, jingling the change in his pockets.

Barnes ingratiated himself to Al Capone and led the house band at Capone's Cotton Club, near Chicago in Cicero. He joked to friends that he insisted Capone pay him by check rather than counterfeit. Capone was truthfully a regular guy, though, Barnes said. Capone called Barnes "Brother," the maestro's family nickname, and flexed his ballyhooed reputation to Barnes's advantage once, with historic consequences. The midget maestro went to a radio station to see about arranging a live broadcast from the Cotton Club. The station manager dismissed Barnes summarily: "We don't air colored." Back at the club, Capone asked, "What'd they tell you, Brother?" Barnes explained, and Capone went with him to follow up. "But we don't air colored," the station manager repeated.

"You do now," Capone said.

In late 1930, Barnes led the first black Chicagoland big band to broadcast live, over WHFC.[2] His media footprint expanded, as he began contributing a rundown of the local big-band scene to the *Chicago Defender* as well.

Walter Barnes,
Chicago, 1927, in
his early twenties,
already leading
the Arcadia
Ballroom orchestra.
*Courtesy of Toya
Johnson*

The black swing world—there was a Caucasoid one too, led by the fortuitously christened Paul Whiteman—evolved like Barnes's career: nurtured in mobster clubs, then it took to the road. In 1929 and 1930, Barnes and Duke Ellington were ensconced in their respective Cotton Clubs, in Cicero and Harlem. Change arrived by late 1930. The Depression strung dollars out thinly and forced the bands to go get them. This world was divided by race, earnings brackets, and geography, though some performers moved across the lines. Artists like Ellington worked the thin-upper-crust, big-city theaters: New York, Detroit, Chicago, Los Angeles. The Ellington brain trust synched up with the NBC radio chain, which guaranteed broadcasts across the country, which in turn guaranteed ticket sales wherever he played, a system of an elegance befitting the Duke. He rarely performed for black audiences, though. Management's priorities were strictly finan-

Walter Barnes and the Royal Creolians, the latter donned in satin overalls at Chicago's Cotton Club in 1931. They were the first black Chicago band to be broadcast on radio, thanks to Al Capone. *Courtesy of Toya Johnson*

cial, and nowhere could black dollars outbuy white ones. Despite this, Duke was no turncoat in black America's eyes. He hadn't hamboned or blackfaced his way into the white sanctum; he earned white respect with his impeccable manner and pure, obvious genius—on his own terms. This was the program. The zeitgeist swirled from Duke's baton. Every black band's book included his numbers. He affected the way people dressed, and what they named their dance halls throughout black America. Few other black artists made it as far as Duke. Louis Armstrong was there, and an exuberant fellow who looked like Duke and clowned like Satch, Cab Calloway, was breaking through in early 1931. Their place in the music business was a rarefied one. White patronage was clearly the key both to sustenance and to great fame in the orchestra business.

Though Capone was still capable of throwing his weight around, his strength was clearly on the wane. In and out of the city, Capone's routine cycled from court to jail. Brother Barnes, till then a strictly local, exclusively for-white bandleader accustomed to extended residencies, needed to get creative. While Capone went to trial to face federal contempt-of-court charges in February 1931, Walter Barnes and his Royal Creolians left Chicago on tour. Capone was convicted on February 28, and four months later he would plead guilty to charges of tax evasion and Prohibition violations, which ended his highly visible underworld career.

Barnes returned home from his first tour, a few weeks' jaunt through the Virginias and Ohio, with a broadened perspective. "Times have changed—and how," he wrote in the *Defender*. "Bands, I mean big bands, are now taking to the road rather than hold one stand indefinitely. There's more money on the road and in barnstorming, even in one-night jumps. . . . Big name bands who are now barnstorming or will soon be are . . . Duke Ellington, on a theatrical tour, Noble Sissle, Eubie Blake . . . and any number of bands who could get stands if they wanted them. But the road calls with more appreciative audiences and bigger do-ra-mi."[3]

He also found good news waiting for him. Perhaps a parting gesture from Capone, the white-run Chicago talent agency Music Corporation of America (MCA), which had booked jazz combos throughout Capone's speakeasies before assuming a more prominent status in the jazz business, signed Barnes to an exclusive management deal. He spent May in a couple of Iowa clubs, then June entertaining at a spa in Minnesota. Waltah had rebounded nicely. He swung out on the road periodically in the summer and fall. He played in Illinois, Indiana, Nebraska, Minnesota, and the Dakotas. He pumped his image in the *Defender*. "Many of the white nightclubs, which have never before used Colored musicians or entertainers in their clubs, are beginning to use our artists for variety," he wrote in December 1931. "Tiny Parham went to work this week at Al Quadbach's famous Granada cafe, which formerly had such artists as Guy Lombardo and Paul Whiteman. Walter Barnes and his internationally famous Royal Creolians opened at the beautiful as well as unique Club Congo. These are only two examples of orchestras having important engagements."[4]

Success intoxicated him. It warped his journalistic perspective. "Talkies are passé," he wrote one week, then "[the] depression seems to have passed," another.[5] But Barnes's dizzying ride ended too soon. MCA delivered the boot in early 1932, for reasons unreported. The maestro paused.

Without heavy agency backing, or his white underworldly consorts, ofay dances were over. He still had the *Defender* on his side, though, and with its readership, his reach could extend across black America. A plan formed. "Walter Barnes would like to communicate with all promoters and clubs who are interested in first class dance attractions," he wrote in February 1932.[6]

Responses were not far ahead.

* * *

When Denver and Sea Ferguson were little boys in Brownsville, Kentucky, their father devised a highly personal expression of the motto "Bury Me Face Down So the World Can Kiss My Ass." Sam Ferguson owned more of the town than any dozen white residents combined, but they still called him *Uncle* Sam. Among his numerous property acquisitions over the years was a grassy hilltop at Brownsville's north side. The highest point in town, Sam christened it the Ferguson Cemetery and commissioned a pair of ten-foot-high granite obelisks for himself and his wife, Mattie. Though white Brownsville insisted on looking down on the Fergusons in life, it'd have to look up to them for eternity.

When Sam's sons left Brownsville, they carried this attitude with them to Indianapolis. Denver and Sea controlled one of the few high-performing Depression-era businesses. As their street lottery spread, they bought properties throughout Indianapolis just as their father had in Brownsville. At the time when Walter Barnes and the Royal Creolians first hit the road, the Fergusons made their first grandiose gesture, taking over a white social club headquarters, the Odd Fellows Hall, in 1931. Three stories high, built of brick, the Odd Fellows Hall stood with the decorous dignity of a Moroccan king, its eight-foot-tall arched windows capped with Arabian filigree, and its cast-iron cornice jutting up like a crown. Though the building was located at the corner of Senate and Vermont, diagonal Indiana Avenue shot right past it, and therefore it was considered *of the Avenue*. The brothers rechristened it the Ferguson Building and divvied it up. Sea installed his real estate brokerage in a ground-floor suite. With a daily flood of liquid assets pouring in from the baseball ticket game, the Fergusons founded or acquired multiple legitimate businesses along the Avenue, extended credit to other black entrepreneurs, set relatives up in a variety of businesses, and initiated brick-and-mortar improvements to black Indianapolis's rickety infrastructure. Already awake with music, laughter, and fights, the Avenue got dressed up as the Fergusons transformed black Indianapolis into Bronzeville.

Sea opened the Cotton Club in 1931, a round-the-clock joy spot that covered most of the lower level of Odd Fellows Hall. The Cotton Club kitchen churned out chili and chop suey, the latter an alleged hangover cure, while an orchestral rotation of Race Horse Williams and his Red Hot Revue, Chick Carter and his Rhythm Band, and Red Washington and his Cavaliers played through the night. William Benbow, a black entertainment veteran who washed up in town after black vaudeville wrecked, emceed at Sea's place. With its courteous and immaculately uniformed staff, professional entertainment, and tasty cuisine, the Cotton Club set the standard for local nightspots. "There had been so many requests for a clean, decent, respectable place to spend leisure time, so Mr. Ferguson responded," an Avenue resident remarked. "He has endeavored to do all a real kindness, and at his own expense."[7]

With their cash-heavy prosperity, and well-earned reputation in the local leisure industry, the Ferguson brothers were a perfect fit in

Denver Ferguson
enjoys a victory cigar
outside the Ferguson
Building (left), where
he opened the Trianon
Ballroom on the third
floor and his brother
Sea ran the Cotton
Club on the two floors
below. Senate Avenue,
Indianapolis, 1931.
*Courtesy of Carole
Finnell*

the emerging black dance business. Denver converted the top floor
of Odd Fellows into the Trianon Ballroom, answered a *Chicago
Defender* columnist's summons to promoters and clubs interested in
first-class dance attractions, and showcased Walter Barnes and the
Royal Creolians at his new dance hall on March 29, 1932. Coming
via highway from the Windy City, Barnes's caravan— the maestro's
Cadillac followed by a Packard with a trailer—grumbled down the
Avenue, passing the hospital and the shanties and Kentucky oyster
cafés on the north end, before entering the modern blocks, hanging
a right on Vermont and parking outside the Ferguson Building. Up
in the Trianon, which was functional but nothing showy, the band
members found a long room with high ceilings, a wood floor scuffed
from the Odd Fellows' polkas, and a view that ranged from the pawnshops back up to the hospital. The Trianon was the proper launch site

for Barnes's strategic shift to a black audience. From Indianapolis, Barnes played Cincinnati, then headed South, where his fame was strongest and the competition weakest, opportunity beckoned and danger waited.

As a native, Barnes knew the South, and thanks to his presence in the *Defender*, the black South knew him as something of a celebrity. To Southern readers, the *Defender* was a forbidden pleasure, an ally from the outside world, and a trusted source for style points, and with his debonair photograph and well-chosen name-dropping in the paper every week, Barnes was wrapped up in this romantic package. Barnes would leverage his *Defender* connection shrewdly. It gave him both valuable perspective on the entertainment business at that moment down South—he saw demand as great in most cities as it was yonder—and the tools to exploit the circumstances. Once dominated by traveling variety companies, the situation had lately been reset.

The Depression eviscerated black vaudeville. Its biggest centralized organization, the Theatre Owners Booking Association (TOBA), went toes up in late 1930.[8] TOBA theater owners sold out to talky companies. Traveling troupes without a circuit of franchise theaters to ply atomized on the road, scattering performers throughout the countryside. They cabled back to Barnes at the *Defender*, and he relayed their circumstances to his audience: "Iris Perrin among those stranded with the Shufflin' Sam company writes that she is taking her meals and will take her mail at the Gem Sweet shop, Knoxville, Tenn. . . . Willie Cracker, comedian, says he is not a dancer, but is able to make them laugh, may be found this week at 1001 Desiard Street Monroe, La. . . . James Jordan who admits that he is the 'world's greatest comedian' says he will give any show a try who sends him a ticket at Box 474 Moorhead, Miss. . . . Little Skinnie Robinson, ivory tickler, is ready to hit the road again, replies should be sent to 212 S. Fourth Street Memphis."

Stranded . . . will give any show a try . . . ready to hit the road again. Stuck, stopped, static, with a strong hint of desperation.

Despite this, showbiz news from Dixie was not all doom and gloom. As Barnes contemplated his post-MCA maneuvers, he received cables from Southern territory bands. These colorfully named orchestras worked according to the lean scale the Depression imposed. Many held a hotel ballroom residency and broadcast from there over low-watt radio stations, then toured as far as their reputations and broadcasts carried. Around these acts grew the rudimentary infrastructure of the Southern black dance business: dusty dance halls, hustling dance promoters, and hucksterish advance men, who went around drumming up gigs and publicity. In the absence of full itineraries, they barnstormed, packing into a Ford AA bus or Model A Woody, tying their instruments down to the roof, to catch gigs as they could.

They traveled leaner than vaudeville troupes did, usually eight to ten pieces at a time so they could afford to charge fewer dimes for a show. Their size and flexibility allowed them to move on fast from a dead town. They played informal venues, anything from the colored high school to agricultural outbuildings, thus the *barn*storming label. They sent Barnes their locations and provided as much of a plan for the future as they had scripted: "Lee Trammell and his Spotlight Entertainers are barnstorming Arkansas. Skeet Reeves is traveling in advance. The unit will route for northern states in March and may be reached this week at Stuttgart, Arkansas." Though he began as Chicago orchestra columnist and self-publicist, Barnes rapidly became central dirt dispatcher for traveling black jazz bands. Barnes's readers learned the whereabouts (and names) of Dittybo Hill and his Eleven Clouds of Joy, Herman Curtis and his Chocolate Vagabonds, Walter Waddell and his Eleven Black Diamonds, Jack Ellis and his Eleven Hawaiians, Belton's Society Syncopators, Smiling Billy Steward and his Celery City Serenaders, and A. Lee Simpkins's Augusta Nighthawks.

Though Barnes didn't mind helping, he sensed possibilities for himself in the territory-band movement. If they could pull audiences down South, why couldn't he outperform them? So, he placated local bands and managers, publishing their information in exchange for road intelligence: dance-hall locations, promoter contacts, colored-friendly lodgings and eateries. He plugged his band into the territory-band network and fused these previously separate entities into a more cohesive whole. He performed along the *Defender*'s underground circulation route, and learned how darktown functioned. In print, he ego-stroked the local fat cats and granted favors to those in the business who might help him. "All organized bands headed toward Memphis, Tenn., get in touch with Prof. Maurice Hulbert, manager of the Barn Night Club, an unusually unique club for our people."[9] He planted psychological seeds in the audience—Jelly Roll had blabbed himself up as the creator of jazz, and whether everyone bought it or not, at least he inserted himself into the conversation. While designing his Southern strategy, Barnes had written, "Among some of the name bands now on the road are Walter Barnes and his Royal Creolians. . . . Earl Hines, who is traveling eastward, and Duke Ellington, who is headed for the western coast."[10] In making himself the brightest star of the South, he extolled the exploits of Walter Barnes and his *internationally famous* Royal Creolians, "taking Tennessee," turning dancers away from the packed Barn nightclub on renowned Beale Street in Memphis, "going over big in the Sunny South," making "the sensation of the season" in Bloomington, Illinois, or en route to a return engagement at Cincinnati's Paradise Ballroom. He pumped his erudition and status at every opportunity. He received a Belgian book about American jazz, "written entirely in French. After reading this interesting book I have come to the conclusion that Europeans are far advanced in the American style of jazz music. Among the famous leaders whose pictures appear or about whom something is written are Walter Barnes Jr., Duke Ellington, Louis Armstrong, Jimmie Noone, Fletcher Henderson, and many other of our well-known musicians."[11]

Truthfully, Barnes and Ellington traveled different paths. While Barnes did it himself—he had incorporated the Walter Barnes Co. Music Corp. in the spring of 1932—Duke Ellington's career belonged to the most powerful forces in the entertainment business, the big money bloc of talent management firms—including Barnes's former rep, MCA—the musicians' union, and the mob, known as "the syndicate." Out of necessity, Barnes worked a lower stratum of the black swing world. While he performed at the Barn on Beale Street in Memphis, Ellington delighted the London Palladium and sipped gimlets with the Prince of Wales. Though the midget maestro would have traded places with the Duke of E in an instant, his dual occupation nevertheless placed him in a unique spot to both shape and write a new chapter of American music history.

Chapter 3 ✳ ✳ ✳ ✳ ✳ ✳ ✳

The Stroll

It was late summer of 1932. Walter Barnes, behind the steering wheel of his Cadillac, headed home from Ohio. Six of his musicians dozed in the car, beside and behind him. Contracts called for them to perform until late anyway, and the maestro always got revved and played overtime when the place was packed and the people kept dancing. To make it up to his band, he drove and they snoozed.

As a black independent band on the road, the group faced financial disadvantages. "Well-known popular bands have been receiving guarantees from $350 up, and get one-third or one-half up front," Barnes wrote, observing pertinently, "These bands are managed by white agents."[1] Bands that lacked organizational muscle, such as the Royal Creolians, were typically asked to work for the *first money in the door*, leaving them broke and hungry in the event of a poor turnout. But Barnes's crew earned well enough to keep the caravan rolling through Bristol, Knoxville, Atlanta, Vicksburg, and Memphis.

Outside Dayton, he snapped awake with the car upside down in midair. Before he could scream, it ground to a stop on its flat top. Everyone but the Caddy escaped serious harm.

Despite the risks on the new frontier, plenty of other important developments followed Barnes and company down South in the early to mid-1930s. A cousin of "the syndicate" saw the same potential in the South that Barnes had begun to exploit. The Seeburg juke-box company, with mob backing, installed coin-op phonographs in every colored café in any excuse for a town, providing a valuable new outlet for artist promotion, and an overnight pop-culture phenom-enon.[2] The earliest black orchestra to take advantage of the suddenly ubiquitous Seeburg and its marketing potential belonged to Jimmie Lunceford.

Lunceford, born in Fulton, Mississippi, in 1902 and educated at Nashville's Fisk University, developed his first big band while teach-ing music, English, and Spanish and coaching football and track at Manassas High School in Memphis, Tennessee, in 1927. Until that time, formal musical training was unheard of in Memphis's black pub-lic schools. Without a budget or directive other than his own motives, Lunceford initiated music education in black Memphis schools, a pro-gram that flourished over time and produced dozens of professional musicians. The first group to emerge was Lunceford's own Chicka-saw Syncopators, whom he molded from among his students and a few Fisk University classmates, then took on the road in 1930. After a successful run at upstate New York resorts, Lunceford teamed up with manager Harold Oxley in the summer of 1933. According to Lunceford biographer Eddy Determeyer, Oxley booked Lunceford "from the largest ballroom in Los Angeles to the most ramshackle barn in South Carolina."[3]

Hip to the zeitgeist, Lunceford and Oxley retagged the band the Harlem Express. The athletic Lunceford stood around six feet tall, weighed two hundred pounds, and was dark and handsome to boot. A nondrinker, he dressed immaculately, and his band glinted as sharply as a military review line. He could play a number of instruments, but his true gifts were for organization and leadership. He fined his men for wearing the wrong socks and conducted his orchestra on stage with a long baton. The group blended acrobatics and physical disci-pline, learned under Coach Lunceford, with musical acumen to create one of the most thrilling spectacles in the business: mesmerizing choreography, spit-polish appearance, unsurpassed musicianship, and boundless swing. "They'd start to rock," Count Basie recalled, "and they'd just rock all night long." Oxley linked Lunceford with Duke Ellington's manager, Irving Mills, for bookings and got Lunceford on the syndicate career track. By late 1933, Lunceford's band challenged Cab Calloway's and Duke Ellington's for supremacy, then in early 1934 it pushed Cab's to the curb as the new house attraction at Harlem's Cotton Club, like Cab had succeeded Duke in 1931.[4]

Though Lunceford would prove every bit an equal to Duke, Cab, or Count Basie as a recording artist and a draw, his unwillingness to play by the syndicate rules proved problematic.[5] Lunceford balked at the membership policies of the musicians' union: The 802 required all orchestra players to maintain union status locally wherever they worked, and imposed lengthy probation periods before activating new memberships. Nonunion orchestras needn't have applied for prestige gigs. A hornblower had to wait six months to get legal and play in a given location, or the union would fine and ostracize the leader. The arrangement encouraged lengthy single-club indentures, protecting the boss's interests over the band's. What could a union band do if a club fired them, without touring as a fallback? Lunceford and Oxley had been around enough to know that the 802 enforced its dominance in the cities but found the sticks not to be worth the trouble. They couldn't come after nonunion bands on the road anyway, so it left Lunceford a choice: big Harlem or little Harlems. He bought his contract out from Irving Mills's syndicate booking agency in December 1934, and he and Oxley entered full partnership as the orchestra's co-owners. Self-demoted from the syndicate, Lunceford turned to the Southern circuit. Lunceford followed Walter Barnes's writing—he congratulated the maestro after the announcement of Barnes's short-lived MCA contract back in 1931. He may have seen promise for himself in Barnes's running story in the midst of his syndicate troubles in 1934.

Lunceford was dark-skinned, from Mississippi, through Nashville and Memphis—a whole different world from that of Duke and the Hi-De-Ho Man, both high-yellow Yankees. The Lunceford band had Harlem credibility, thanks to the glorious Cotton Club run, and country panache, thanks to the Memphis boys in the band—Memphis was nothing but a big country town, everybody was from Arkansas and Mississippi. The band's sound, though as precise as its peers', was hot and lazy—Southern—characterized by a dragged-out backbeat. Bass player Moses Allen ad-libbed this preacher bit that made the people fall out, laughing. He cued the trumpet solo: "Oh, Gabriel, I want you to go down this mornin', I want you to place one foot on the land and the other foot on the sea; I want you to blow that silver trumpet calm and easy. . . . Oh, I imagine I can see him bust the bell of that trumpet wide open." The Harlem Express went over big. From the time Barnes first toured the South, the biggest name on regular tour down there was Earl Hines. When Lunceford arrived in early 1935, he eclipsed them both. Willie Smith, Lunceford sax man since the band stormed out of Memphis, said, "We'd go on the road for 364 days and play New York one night."[6]

The promotional activities of the Lunceford-Oxley organization rivaled its musicians' fire and creativity. Born in Jackson, Tennessee, in 1909, Dave Clark formed a swinging combo called the Hoodoo Men that played around town during the early 1930s. "I didn't believe that the only thing a black person could do was teach school, preach, be a doctor, or go to a mail order law school," he said. "I saw all this money floating around out there and didn't any of it come from those professions." Clark's personality suited a behind-the-scenes role rather than one on stage. His uniform consisted of a wide-brimmed hat, black horn-rims, slept-in-the-car stubble, and a cigarette. He spoke in a high voice, his enunciation muffled from a cleft palate, and used the word *baby* like punctuation. He coined little witticisms, referring to himself as "a member of the world's largest dues-paying

Dave Clark, left, member in good standing of the world's largest
dues-paying organization, pictured here with Ernie K-Doe, singer of
"Mother-In-Law," New Orleans, 1962. *Author's collection*

organization—the black race." He ran around for a Jackson dance
promoter, tacking up posters advertising the next show. He saw the
Seeburgs go into places the Hoodoo Men played—"every pool room,
in every dance hall, every joint that sold whiskey in it, everywhere
that they could stick a jukebox in, they stuck a jukebox in there,"
Clark said. "I came up with a idea that every town Lunceford was
playing, I could go in front of the band and get [his] record on the
jukebox," he said.[7]

It sounded to Oxley like an idea whose time had come. Clark
moved a few paces ahead of the endless Lunceford tour to hang placards, book print ads, and place Lunceford records on café jukeboxes
before the Harlem Express pulled in for its show. He rode the Greyhound bus and "got everything that went with black." As radio stations opened, Clark added them to his checklist. "First thing they'd

say is, 'Nigger, what do you want?'" One radio station manager released a hound on Dave, but "he must have thought I was another dog, cause he come to bite and just whined and played."[8]

✳   ✳   ✳

Meanwhile, Barnes played his one strength. "Just now one of the biggest box-office attractions is the Walter Barnes Royal Creolians, touring the South," a *Chicago Defender* colleague wrote in the spring of 1935, "and believe it or not the outfit refused to stay put in any one place no matter how good the engagement looks."[9] Though he may not have welcomed Lunceford's company, Barnes was doing fine. In the winter of 1933, he had established winter headquarters in Jacksonville, Florida, from where he would conduct his now annual late-fall-to-spring Southern tours. He replaced the ripped-up Cadillac with a gold Nash, and had his pretty wife do the driving while he reclined across the backseat. In July 1932, Barnes had wed Dorothy Parrott, herself a *Defender* correspondent and secretary of the Walter Barnes Buddy Club. The vows snagged her a promotion to road manager of the Walter Barnes Co. Music Corp. Their configuration in the car resulted from some serious strategic thought. Dorothy was fair-skinned, and if you sped past the Barnes's gold Nash on the highway, the car would've caught your eye first, then you would have noticed its occupants' contrasting skin tones. This would have sparked trouble. Dorothy and Walter considered seating Dorothy in the back, with darker-skinned Walt driving, to play the chauffeur trick on passersby, or hiding her, but then determined that creating the appearance of a lone "white" person driving the flashy car with Illinois tags was the least provocative option. A less ostentatious vehicle might have spared them this dilemma, but the Nash, parked outside the dance hall, elicited "oooh's." It was part of the package.

While Dave Clark fed the Seeburgs, Walter Barnes brightened his aura. Folks in Chicago scoffed at Barnes's Duke Ellington posturing, but he knew that black revelers below the Mason-Dixon line were suffering Harlem fever delusions. The more he toured the South, the more Cotton Clubs he played, and the more Little Harlems and Little Lenoxes the band stayed in, the more he noticed that the big men in little towns—bootleggers, racketeers, and undertakers, the impresarios of the Southern night—shared his pretension, and he played on this through his *Defender* presence. In Barnes's words, dirt-road hustlers became *financiers* or *capitalists*, and their burlap-curtain, sawdust-floor joints were *ballrooms*. And with his fair bride, white tails, and the gold Nash, Barnes became their Ellington. Big-city folks might have disparaged Barnes's tour route as the *chitlin' circuit*, but you'd sure never hear such terminology from him.[10]

The maestro remained committed to modernity. After swing supplanted Dixieland as the jazz lingua franca, the Royal Creolians became the Kings of Swing. Barnes and the Royal Creolians' 1928 and '29 recordings are swirling, Dixieland-flavored, with a dash of screechy flapper vocals, as in "Birmingham Bertha," and a little scatting. The band also covered popular blues, Leroy Carr's plaintive "How Long, How Long Blues" and the tawdry Thomas Dorsey–Hudson "Tampa Red" Whittaker duet "It's Tight Like That." Latter-day critics have found little to admire, but let's face it: Barnes's music was never intended for contemplation—it was supposed to be fun. The band configuration, too, adapted to swing—the banjo player became an upright bass, and a guitarist joined the group. As his affluence grew, Barnes added a pair of trombones, a trumpet, and another saxophone, bringing the total to fifteen pieces. The Barnes caravan grossed thousands of dollars—at eighteen dollars a show for five to seven nights a week, the musicians earned well above the union-mandated sixty dollars a week, and Barnes had no trouble recruiting. A Basie orchestra veteran who recalled earning around six bucks a night with the Count said that several of his colleagues quit to go South with maestro Barnes.

In the fall of 1936, the band embarked on its most ambitious Southern one-nighter tour yet. Barnes had patched and webbed his network

Walter Barnes, clad in white tails, and the tuxedoed Royal Creolians, 1933. *Courtesy of Toya Johnson*

of territory-band promoters and dance halls across the entire South. No dot on the map was too large or small: Ardmore, Muskogee, Oklahoma City, Taft, and Tulsa, Oklahoma; Houston, Longview, and Tyler, Texas; El Dorado, Hot Springs, and Little Rock, Arkansas; Monroe, New Orleans, Shreveport, and Tallulah, Louisiana; Greenville, Hattiesburg, Jackson, McComb, Vicksburg, and Yazoo City, Mississippi; Dothan and Gadsden, Alabama; Athens, Atlanta, Augusta, Columbus, Cordele, Macon, Savannah, and Waycross, Georgia; Jacksonville, Pensacola, St. Augustine, St. Petersburg, Sarasota, Tampa, and West Palm Beach, Florida.

Three months in, three months out, fifty-five cents admission every night.

"Read The *Defender* weekly for news of your hometown," Barnes instructed his audience. "I'll be there soon."[11]

Whatever pains Barnes and the Kings of Swing endured out there would remain private. It was all very well for black editors and activists to decry lynching and Southern black conditions from their offices in New York and Chicago, but Barnes made his living on the ground in the South and could not afford to stir up controversy, since vengeance could easily locate the gold Nash and the white bus full of black men. Barnes was no activist anyway. He preferred to change the reality of black Southerners in a fantastic, if fleeting way in print and on stage. As Barnes worked from town to town down South, he noticed a pattern. Any place with a sizable black population grew a darktown, and each of these black districts centered on a main thoroughfare, a world unto itself. The maestro, in his hep vernacular, called it "the stroll." He dashed off dispatches from every stroll he hit on the 1936–37 tour, leaving behind a neon and mud portrait of black Main Street in the South—the unfolding filaments of the chitlin' circuit.

The maestro left readers few hints about his crew's nonmusical activities. They found a Baptist church some Sundays, and according to Barnes family lore, they tested alcohol's effects on a pet monkey. As news of Lunceford's Southern success spread, Barnes crossed paths increasingly with syndicate-represented black acts—Andy Kirk and His Clouds of Joy, Erskine Hawkins, Chick Webb, and Lucky Millinder. Barnes and the Kings of Swing still worked many nights for the *first money in the door*, the standard contract language on the chitlin' circuit.

The tour kicked off in Tulsa, Oklahoma, the week before Thanksgiving, where Barnes found "Black Wall Street" bustling. "Greenwood is the name of the colored district of Tulsa, and one can get anything here from a shoe shine up." Barnes highlighted the stroll's musicians, dance promoters, dance halls, and its dentists, barbers, pharmacies, cafés, cab companies, and lodgings, always stressing the up-to-date. "I stopped with my entire orchestra at the modern and exclusive Small Hotel" in Tulsa, "one of the best equipped in the country, having newest electrical fixtures, telephone in each room,

Walter Barnes and his Kings of Swing in a self-produced promotional flier. Gone are the banjo and satin overalls. *Courtesy of Toya Johnson*

bath in every room, and modernistic furniture." The Kings of Swing played the Crystal Palace Ballroom, "the last word in beauty," and hung around the Goodie Goodie Club, Cotton Club, and Del Rio. "There's plenty niteries here."[12]

The stroll was more than a big-city phenomenon. In Muskogee, Oklahoma, where Second Street was the stroll, Barnes found two black nightclubs, the New Deal and Oasis Tavern, a dance promoter, and "Hubert's Restaurant, where all the show folks meet." Must have been hell, getting a table.

In late November, Barnes wrote, "This week in Houston was just like a regular jam session, what with my good pal Duke Ellington and his orchestra here at the same time. Plenty of handshaking and back-slapping."[13] Duke, it should be said, was down to play the university in Austin and an ofay club in Dallas. It was classic maestro, milking a polite greeting for maximum self-aggrandizement. He knew whose ego to caress as well, and dropped an unfamiliar name. "Don Robey, a clean cut young fellow, and industrious businessman, along with his partner Morris Merritt, presented Walter Barnes' orchestra at the Harlem Grill, to a crowd of 3,000."[14] Barnes's bluster would prove accurate over the next four decades, as the "industrious businessman" Don Robey became the most formidable black man in the black music business up to the dawn of disco. He started out, like the rest of Barnes's road contacts, a territory-band promoter, though his vision would extend well beyond the territories. Robey and Merritt were developing a new circuit enterprise as territory promoters. They booked Barnes in Houston, then Merritt toured Barnes through east Texas on into Louisiana. Of course Barnes did what he could to put those places on the black entertainment map as well—what benefited Robey might benefit the maestro.

"We are now driving down Desiard Street, the stroll in Monroe," the maestro wrote in December 1936. "The Red Goose Barber Shop is the place where all the boys have their grooming done. . . . Lovely Brown's Beauty Shop is where all the ladies get their fancy waves for the dances. . . . The Grog Cafe is the dining place of the profesh, and what good, Southern, home-cooked meals they serve here. . . . The Frog Pond ballroom located at 1003 Desiard Street is the most beautiful and spacious dance palace here."[15] Not coincidentally, the Frog Pond showcased the conductor and his Kings of Swing.

Beyond Robey and Merritt's territory, Barnes and company hit Mississippi in a freezing rain at the end of 1936, with shows in a different town every night. First to Greenville, they made the short trot down to Yazoo City to play the Afro Auditorium, then on to "Vicksburg, birthplace and stamping ground of yours truly," Barnes wrote. "The old home town turned out en masse to welcome the maestro." Members of the Cavalier Club sponsored the Barnes dance at the black-run Continental Ballroom there, corner of Washington at Jackson Street. After MCA cut Barnes loose, and he began to focus on touring the South, the savvy maestro had set his Uncle Alan up as head of the Dance Promoters of Vicksburg, and he enjoyed a stronghold in south Mississippi since. In Jackson, he stayed at a whorehouse run by the girlfriend of a blues pianist and fellow road band leader named Little Brother Montgomery. From there, Barnes commuted to gigs in New Orleans, across the gulf, and up the Mississippi pine belt through Hattiesburg. This time, Barnes found himself on the heels of a Windy City rival, pianist Earl "Fatha" Hines. Hines had played Vicksburg the previous weekend. "He went over big, but they say the admission was a little high, Earl."[16]

Though the cornerstone of Earl Hines's legacy—the Hot Five recordings with Louis Armstrong—was in place, he was scuffling just like our maestro of lesser repute. Still, Hines had plenty in his favor. He fronted the house orchestra at Chicago's Grand Terrace, and like Barnes and very few other black orchestras, Hines spread his band's renown well beyond the Windy City through mass media, a regular radio broadcast that carried from the South Side to the Deep South. His Southern tours were arranged by one of the first men to recognize the down-home black audience's economic potential, Professor Sherman Cook. The Professor ran with the Louis Armstrong retinue on its tours in the early 1930s and founded a Chicago-based booking agency, specializing in chorus-line revues, theatrical packages, and jazz orchestras.

On to Jackson, Mississippi, where the Barnes band played the Crystal Palace on Farish Street, the capital city's stroll, then the new Harlem Club, eighty miles south in little McComb.

The group's "June in January" promised to thaw their numb, weary hands. "I am unpacking my palm beaches and linens, preparatory to spending a winter in good old Florida, where the temperature is 98 degrees the year round," Barnes bragged in December 1936. In Jacksonville, "the telephone lines started buzzing, taxis started running, the tailors, the restaurants, and in fact, the whole stroll turned out on W. Ashley Street in this city's young Harlem when Walter Barnes and his orchestra returned," he humbly began. Barnes had installed the band's winter quarters in Jacksonville for the previous few years, ensuring a strong turnout of the gracious gentleman's many Floridian friends. Fun-makers came from Palatka, Fernandina, St. Augustine, Gainesville, Daytona, and Tallahassee, by the maestro's account, to join Jacksonville's cream at the Flajax club for the big dance. "This was the first time in the club's life that a band the caliber of ours furnished the tunes." Green and maroon streamers flowed through the auditorium. The women in long evening gowns swayed in the arms of tuxedoed gents. The band swung into "How Long Blues" at ten o'clock the evening of January 4, 1937, and beat out the last chorus of "Barnes Stomp" at three the next morning.

After the dance, the leading colored citizenry of Jacksonville, "where joy reigns supreme," feted Walter, Dorothy, and the boys. Doctors, attorneys, president of a nearby black college, and the standard assortment of morticians and dentists toasted the midget maestro. The party made its way down West Ashley to the Lenape, the largest sepia bar around, for champagne on the house, and then to the Green Front café for breakfast and a complimentary picnic basket for the trip. Barnes sat behind the bus driver on the way out of town, drowsily jotting notes, nibbling at a piece of cornbread. "All in all, Jacksonville is a very fly town," he admitted.[17] They played around the state for the next month, down to Sarasota, Miami, and West Palm Beach, up to Tampa and St. Petersburg, and finally back nearly to where they started in Jacksonville.

They zigzagged back and forth across the Gulf of Mexico, up the Florida panhandle to Dothan, Alabama, back down to Pensacola and over to Pascagoula, Mississippi, where the maestro observed, "Some very beautiful lassies in this town. Mixed with Spanish, French, Mexican, ofay, and what have you." Then over to the birthplace of jazz— "Rampart Street is the stroll," Barnes declared from New Orleans in March 1937. The band arrived at the Astoria, a hotel, restaurant, and gambling hall, and, Barnes wrote, "What a welcome the gang and I received, as we brought back one of the prodigal sons, Punch Miller, who had been away from home more than ten years." The maestro, working the baton, looked the crowd over from the bandstand at the Astoria's Tick Tock Tavern, an eyebrow raised. He smirked at those fine "Creole babies with big, flashing eyes." He spied baseballer Satchel Paige, "swinging high," and then turned back to the orchestra, who sat behind lecterns, four on the floor, four on the stage, with drums and strings standing at the rear. Before the show, Dorothy draped the black felt banner with "Walter Barnes and his Kings of Swing" lettered in gold felt over the far left podium. The stage was swathed in purple and gold pleated curtains. Black bunting with gold fringe dangling down and a sharp, gold *fleur-de-lis* embossed on each dip was spread across the top of the curtains. "The band went over so big, that they said there is not a place large enough to hold the crowd if we were to return."[18]

With home four months behind them, the band was run ragged. If the most modern accommodations notably offered cold *and* hot water, and those were found only in the wealthiest black enclaves, then you have to wonder how comfortably the group lived the rest of the time, which was by far *most* of the time on tour. In smaller towns they stayed in private homes, and spot-scrubbed their suits in the sink. They scooped through vats of Apex pomade trying to stay slick. Barnes spared readers the unpleasant details of touring life, preferring, from either braggadocio or optimism, to stress the pluses, like Florida's 98-degree temperatures in the dead of winter. Even a vibrant city like New Orleans, which had a variety of black amenities, put pressure on the band by offering equal parts temptation and trouble for young musicians. Drug trafficking, the sex trade, and undertaking thrived on South Rampart during the Depression's tough times.

In the first week of April 1937 Barnes's bus pulled onto "Sweet Auburn," as the Atlanta stroll was known, where fans had lined up for blocks to glimpse the band. "Atlanta is reputedly the most progressive Southern city where the race is concerned," Barnes observed.

"The atmosphere here is almost Windy Cityish." Alfred Angel ran the show on Sweet Auburn and presented the maestro on the rooftop Club Royale. After the performance, Barnes enjoyed a sneak preview of the lavish Top Hat Club, with its hardwood dance floor, neatly varnished and buffed to spread the warm glow of crystal-drenched chandeliers. "This will surpass all clubs in the state for swank," the maestro predicted.[19] On the next stop, Walter and Dorothy meandered through Charleston, South Carolina, but found "no stroll in this town." Still, they marveled at the Geechies and played for the Harlem Ace social club at Dart's Casino. They trudged back through Alabama, Mississippi, and Louisiana—"So all you dance fans, get your best togs out, because we will be swinging when we come."[20]

The morning of May 7, 1937, dawned on Barnes in his old boss Al Capone's favorite Southern haunt, Hot Springs, Arkansas. As attractions went, the restorative powers of the town's namesake steam baths finished a close second behind the town's casinos and whorehouses. True to form, though, Barnes kept his column clean—whatever happened in Hot Springs stayed in Hot Springs, except that the boys "played a very successful dance at the Casino Ballroom, which was promoted by Haskin T. Clark. All the elite of Hot Springs turned out en masse to greet the maestro and his orchestra for their last appearance in Hot Springs for the season."

After the show on May 9 at Little Rock's Dreamland Ballroom, the gold Nash, the white bus, and one cirrhotic monkey pushed home to Chicago.

"The boys were all in smiles," the maestro wrote. "After a very successful tour, they were all glad to be back."[21]

Chapter 4 ✶ ✶ ✶ ✶ ✶ ✶ ✶

Sunset

One of the corner lots Denver Ferguson acquired in Indianapolis during the Depression sat on a wide curve where the buses and streetcars stopped, toward the squalid north end of Indiana Avenue, near the hospital. Shanties littered both sides of the Avenue here, blocks from the street's core near Denver and Sea's Trianon Ballroom–Cotton Club complex. The end of Prohibition had flipped Avenue joints from hush-hush to wide open. Proprietors hung signs and decorated. Joe and Tuffy Mitchell, the Fergusons' rivals, fancified their dump with Italian travertine-tiled interior walls, arched windows, a polychrome ceiling stenciled with hazy clouds, and a stucco façade, in Joe's words, "for the benefit of colored friends whose generous patronage . . . has been the foundation of [our] financial success."[1]

Back in 1933 Denver had heard that the federal government planned to build a housing project over the shanties, and surmised that this land held far greater value than its appearances indicated. His tipster proved accurate—in 1934 the government acquired twenty-two acres directly across from Denver's corner parcel. Though we don't think of housing projects as progress, the February 5, 1938, *Recorder* hailed the opening of Lockefield Gardens: "The beautiful Lockefield

Gardens out Indiana–Avenue-way is really a sight to behold . . . the beauty of the architecture[,] the wide rambling walks[,] the new-born lawns wet with the morning dew[,] the placid atmosphere." Lockefield included 738 units, built of regionally quarried limestone, inlaid with big, bright, steel-framed windows.

Denver relished his racketeering tactics: the elaborate trade in favors, the hidden political machinations that any gambling syndicate requires to evade difficulty with the law, the chess-match thinking to keep allies in the fold, and the militaristic organization of underlings. His disposition suited the necessarily detached charisma of leadership. And he loved the money, the new car each year, and lamb shanks every night. He cultivated a certain mystique, keeping an aristocratic distance from the sinful public who filled his pockets. He assembled a staff that made it difficult for even his family to see him during work, which usually ran into the dark hours of morning. Haughtiness, shyness, and a natural inclination to live within his intellect—to create and solve problems—certainly shaped Denver's public image. As brooding and introspective as brother Sea was outgoing and gregarious, however, Denver reluctantly stepped forward as a public figure in bustling Bronzeville when he opened the Sunset Terrace.

As Lockefield Gardens' first tenants unpacked, Denver unveiled "The Night Club Where the Smart Set Goes" across the street on icy February 7, 1938. "You will enjoy this more than anything you ever attended in your life," Denver promised. "This is the crowning event." Sunset Terrace was by far the largest and grandest cabaret the Avenue demimonde had seen—a modern, brick façade, stretching nearly a half block. With the exception of Sea's Cotton Club, you could stand in the doorway of any other Avenue joint and hit the back wall with a roll of dice. Unlike the other clubs, which were built in the 1890s as stores or fellowship halls, Denver designed the Sunset specifically to its purposes.

Under the striped canvas awning at 873 Indiana Avenue, you could enter through the double-door and head left, down to the Sunset Cafe, a barroom with billiard tables, or right, to the ballroom and bandstand, where a stage was built three feet above the dance floor, ringed with copper railing. Sunset's signature feature, a balcony overlooking the dance floor and stage, wrapped around half of the building, tied in the same copper ribbon that ringed the stage. Tiny Bradshaw and his Famous 14 Demons of Syncopation stormed the stage that first night. Chorus girls swayed umbrellas as a rainbow of lights meandered every direction along the ceiling and walls at morphine speed. Behind this spectacular front, Denver built a labyrinth of card and dice parlors. In advertising the Sunset, he promised "The Best of Wines, Beer and Liquers," and "a place of gracious dignity to you and yours."[2] But a certain grim sensation wafted through the Sunset. "Every time I was there I wished for a bulletproof vest," Avenue pianist Errol Grandy recalled. "I didn't have one, but I wished for one." A former baseball ticket player and Sunset regular named Joe Hester concurred. "Everybody carried a gun in there," Hester said. "I had my little .32," he added, a revolver that fit just as neatly in the palm of the hand as into the inside pocket of a man's coat. Denver provided a security force, as Hester recalled. "Brawny motherfuckers, grab you by the shoulders and deposit you on the street, say, 'Get *out!*' "[3]

Denver admired Chicago's Grand Terrace, once known as Sunset Cafe, and regularly brought in its house band, led by Walter Barnes' old Southern road rival Earl Hines. The Hines big band played lush, brassy swing behind the leader's rhythmic, up-tempo piano. Though Denver presented Ellington and Ella Fitzgerald soon after opening, Sunset regulars preferred Hines. "Duke Ellington came to the Sunset one Sunday night," Grandy recalled. "He was on stage, and I heard fighting in the darkness. They threw whiskey bottles and beer bottles toward the bandstand and messed up his suit, and he said he'd never come back there, never."[4] Hines's blend of the glamorous and gutbucket endeared him to Indy's Bronzeville. His band men stood and pumped their horns in the air like pistols, and shouted him on through his strident solos as they would in a Southern hole-in-the-wall—"*Swing it, Fatha Hines!*"

✶   ✶   ✶

The Bronzeville renaissance was in full swing. After some of that Ferguson action, the Avenue's big players outdid one another with the most lavishly appointed nightclubs. Denver and Sea's flamboyant colleague Goosie Lee—a black Indianapolis 500 bookie—dumped "bales of mazuma"[5] into the swank Oriental Cafe, according to the *Recorder*. Lee practiced the same amoral philanthropy the Fergusons did. He collected black dollars in underworld trade and gave back to the community at large, carving economic independence out for himself and employing black locals. When Lee died in 1943, he was eulogized as a "very charitable soul . . . strictly a Race man . . . constantly working to get better jobs for his people."[6] An estimated two thousand Bronzevillians crowded outside 507–511 Indiana Avenue on March 22, 1938, halting street traffic to get a look at the Oriental, a "beautiful nitery with its large expansive doors of bronze, large slanting French windows, snug fitting Venetian blinds, [and] colored stucco." Lightning flashed across a pink sky and cold rain pelted their hats, but the crowd stood firm. The rain slick asphalt refracted the café's "multi-colored 75-foot neon sign, truly a dazzling picture beneath a berserk sky."

Inside, "a bevy of lovely damsels scurried busily with trays of chilled wines . . . until the wee hours of morn—A trio of mixologists bore up well under the strain of 'a dash of bitters here and a jigger of absinthe there,' to the tune of a melodious two-step played by Frank Reynolds and his 'Cats' during the evening," the *Recorder* reported. "Gorgeously gowned ladies with handsome escorts sat at decorated tables and imbibed gleefully. . . . It was a howling success. . . . Bronzeville nightlifers were on parade, if you weren't there you missed the treat of a lifetime."[7]

Denver and Sea's rivals, the Mitchell brothers, expanded their tavern across four storefronts a block below the Oriental, its growth unimpeded by its reputation. While scraps broke out in all the Avenue's crowded, drunken joints, the Mitchellyne attracted an exceptionally boisterous element. Its clientele, while not as polished as the smart set Denver and Sea appealed to, still had flash. Not long before the Sunset opened, the Mitchellyne was the site of a melodramatic scene that would be retold with disbelieving laughter. Upon entering the Mitchellyne on February 20, 1937, Annabel White, twenty-one and rather country, had spied her common-law spouse, Raymond Clark, twenty-eight and of suave comportment, entertaining a damsel. Annabel marched to the Seeburg and dropped in a nickel. As Billie Holiday wailed "My Last Affair," Annabel glided over to Raymond and stabbed him to death.[8]

Vinegar Hall, the tangy old barrelhouse where people drank and danced during Denver's early days in town, receded into yellow, bloodshot memory. The Avenue sparkled from the Cotton Club in the upper 300 block, to the Mitchellyne a few doors up at 406–410, to the Limehouse Club at 415, The Smokehouse at 438, Rainbow Tavern at 451, the Oriental at 507–511, Simplex Club at 525, New York Cafe at 526, Denny's Dreamland at 541, the Blue Eagle at 648, and the Sunset Terrace at 873 Indiana. Vinegar Hall's former manager Charlie Coleman remarked that the Avenue had transformed "from cobblestones to asphalt."[9] And though the Avenue still ran "from a pawnshop to a hospital" in local terms, its action bounced from the Cotton Club to Sunset Terrace.

Weeks after the Sunset and Oriental opened, the *Recorder* sponsored Indianapolis's first election for the mayor of Bronzeville. Black newspapers across the country hosted mayor-of-Bronzeville races (first in Chicago, 1934) to bestow honorary titles on their most popular citizens, poll-tax free. The leading colored men of Indianapolis— attorneys, doctors, and church elders—leafleted the Avenue and stumped on its corners to no avail. Sea Ferguson carried the day,

Denver Ferguson's Sunset Terrace, 873 Indiana Avenue, Indianapolis. The swankiest nitery to hit the Avenue, yet still too rough for
Duke Ellington. *O. James Fox Collection, Indiana Historical Society*

notching twenty thousand votes, double the runner-up's total. To
white Indianapolis, insofar as they'd heard of him, Sea was known as
a gambler and bootlegger. To Bronzeville, however, being of the play-
boy element was a plus. Sea had money, connections to elite black
culture, and—judging by the "real" mayor's presence at his inaugural
ball—downtown's attention.

Twenty-five hundred filled Tomlinson Hall the night of April 15,
1938. Sea, trim and dapper with his neat mustache and gray wool
three-piece suit, climbed the dais, grinning and wrapped in a purple
satin sash emblazoned with his new title in bronze. His wife, Ver-
noca, wrapped in Asian silk, clutched his arm. He thanked "our real
mayor," Walter Boetcher—who attended along with many of Indianapolis's elected officials and neighborhood bosses—then began his

Walter Barnes
advertising placard,
hand-edited, from his
final tour. *Courtesy of
Toya Johnson*

acceptance speech, a chitlin' circuit manifesto delivered in Constitutional tones: "We the brown people should favor with our purchases
the business establishments where [we] may also find employment. . . .
Our greatest problem today is our economic situation. . . . Our inability to find jobs and our exclusion from money labor unions makes it
imperative that we nurse and develop our own enterprises."[10]

Giddy Bronzevillians toasted the first family and celebrated the
public coronation of an underworld kingpin well past sunrise.

Some of that Avenue effervescence eventually bubbled over to
Chicago's Bronzeville, and summoned the dean of nightlife letters.
"Yours truly," Walter Barnes wrote in the fall of 1939, "stopped over
in Indianapolis and found this town to really be jumping." Impressed
with the strip's transformation since his gig at the Ferguson Build-

ing in 1932, Barnes and company made the stroll. "Grooving around, our first stop was the Cotton club, which features two orchestras. Fred Wisdom's six-piece swing unit does the jamming downstairs. . . . Upstairs the jitterbugs are jittered by Bill Christen and his Hot Six.

"At the Joe Mitchell's Inn, we found two more hot bands swinging out: Lionel Reison downstairs, while Bryant's Eight Syncopators hold the spot upstairs.

"The Oriental cafe features George Robinson and his six-piece orchestra. The P and P club offers a swing pianist and a lovely girl vocalist rendering the latest popular numbers." In the maestro's discerning eye, however, "Sunset Terrace is the most elaborate of them all."[11] There was no time for Barnes to go into detail, as another of his annual fall-through-spring tours took him below the Mason-Dixon line.

✳   ✳   ✳

Venues less elaborate than the Sunset were still the norm down South. One such place, the Rhythm Club, sat near the corner of St. Catherine and Pine streets in the black precinct of Natchez, Mississippi, known as the Triangle. The club, a former hardware store and Pentecostal church, was 150 feet by 60 feet and made of lumber and corrugated tin. A dozen or so buddies known as the Moneywasters Social Club hoisted a Jax Beer sign above the building's front door in 1938. They drank and threw dice and dances there.

In the spring of 1940, the Moneywasters booked Tiny Bradshaw, who had played the grand opening of Denver Ferguson's Sunset Terrace, to perform at the Rhythm Club. The Moneywasters deemed the affair a "Baby Doll Dance," after the femme fashion of the moment. They decided on a Tuesday night, April 23, in hopes that the local black high school's commencement celebration would carry over. Advance tickets sold briskly at the neighborhood's barbershops and the Moneywasters' speakeasy at St. Catherine and Pine.

Bradshaw planned to gig his way across the Gulf from Florida to

Natchez, when he received a telegram. Frank Schiffman, manager of Harlem's Apollo Theater, pitched Bradshaw a one-week stint. Bradshaw cabled his regrets to the Moneywasters and put them in a dilemma. The solution had presented itself weekly in the *Chicago Defender* for most of the previous decade. The Moneywasters had read Walter Barnes's indiscriminate entreaties to "any and all dance promoters." They called the *Defender* and eventually got in touch with Dorothy Barnes. She typically traveled with her husband's coterie but had broken off early toward Chicago to prepare for the band's homecoming—the group was due back on April 24 after completing another six-month Southern tour. Dorothy wired Walter. *One more dance . . . Natchez.*

Barnes carried all new musicians in the band for the tour of 1939–40. Even trumpeter Punch Miller, who had ridden shotgun on most of the maestro's previous runs down South, stayed in Chicago. Barnes added a footloose young cornetist in Miller's place, twenty-one-year-old Paul Stott from Indianapolis. Stott and some other boys had left home to join the Hagenback-Wallace Circus. The circus went broke in North Carolina, where Stott, with only the clothes on his back, hitched up with the maestro in November 1939.

In preparation for the big night, the Moneywasters wove dried Spanish moss through the Rhythm Club's rafters and cascaded it down the building's support beams. Baby dolls and their escorts would enter the Rhythm Club and escape to a magical place, as if the white-tuxedoed maestro and his boys in their black bow ties were serenading them, backlit by the moon, on the edge of Pearl Bayou. The moss was spritzed with a little kerosene to protect the dancers from a less romantic feature of the bayou night: mosquitoes. The Moneywasters also liked to protect their investments from unpaid spectators—they boarded the club's windows and barricaded every door save for the front entrance on St. Catherine Street. World-weary musicians called this the "toilet" setup—one way in, one way out. Alan Barnes, Walter's brother and the band's advance promoter, pulled the group's big bus to the curb across the street from the Rhythm Club on the afternoon of April 23, and the musicians straggled inside to set up on the big bandstand. Drummer Oscar Brown nailed the components of his drum kit down to keep them from wandering off. He secured the high hat and tossed his hammer aside.

At 11:30 that night, Barnes called "Clarinet Lullaby." Money-waster Walter Audrey, working the bar, heard scuffling near the lone door as the tune began, but thought nothing amiss; he had wondered what took the obligatory fight so long to break out. The orchestra swung through the number until the drummer broke rhythm and tailed off. Barnes, incensed, glared at his band and saw their eyes widen. They lowered the horns from their lips as Barnes turned around and watched fire dance up the wall around the door.

Barnes had played a thousand woodsheds and seen plenty of flames, spilling from kicked-over potbelly stoves or flashing from a tossed match. Fire was a constant worry to people who lived in tinderboxes with open heat, and they learned to react quickly and coolly, to snuff it or step out. He'd seen jitterbugs douse flames with their setups without missing the beat. But this fire raced through the kerosene-laced Spanish moss, following a hundred fuses in all directions. The club's walls, sheets of tin nailed either side of the wooden building frame, shielded the fire from water and radiated heat like an oven.

Barnes didn't move. "You can all get out if you keep calm," he called.

Perhaps he underestimated the blaze's severity. Or perhaps he recognized that he and the band were last in line to reach the door and had no choice. In any case, he had learned to play through chaos at Capone's Cotton Club—music soothed the savage beast. His breath quickened. He faced his band and directed them to start "Marie," a lilting Irving Berlin tune.

Drummer Oscar Brown wasn't going along. He stood from behind his kit, picked his hammer up, walked toward a boarded window behind the stage and smashed his way out. The other musicians played as flames scampered across the ceiling, tickling up the volume of the crowd's scream. "I was standing by the door," recalled Julius Hawkins, "and it just spread over everything."

Dancers ran shrieking toward the only exit. They pushed, trampled, dove, struggled through the door, and sealed it shut, while exhaust fans fed the flames. The Rhythm Club cooked. A woman tore off her clothing and hid in a refrigerator. A brawny man elbow-punched through a boarded window and hurled his date through the shards out onto St. Catherine Street. Reverend Edward Doherty, a Triangle resident and assistant pastor of the Catholic church across the street, awoke to cries but rolled over and tried to go back to sleep. "Negro women having a good time in the club frequently screamed like that," he would say.

Barnes exhorted his troupe through the thickening smoke, "Play, play!"

Eye-witness Frank Christmas would say, "The only calm person in the building was Mr. Barnes. . . . I think that [he] knew the danger he was in, but believed that if he could prevent the crowd from piling up around the door . . . he could fix it so most of the people could get out. But that crowd was beyond human control."[12]

A doctor's report read, "As reckless fear and mounting excitement kept pace with the racing flames, and when it became clear that there was little escape through the door, chairs and other objects were used to smash the few windows in means of escape. In desperation bare hands and fists broke out panes under the fierce drive of consuming heat and strangling smoke."[13]

The band kept playing.

With the final breath of his life, trumpeter Paul Stott blasted a note, just as the inferno gulped the remaining oxygen, collapsing the tin roof and walls, and crushing every still-heaving lung. The building's support beams snapped, and the flaming ceiling slumped over the stage, like a fiery curtain descending on Walter Barnes and his Kings of Swing.[14]

Two hundred and nine souls left this world through the Rhythm Club, hearing Stott's note blend into Gabriel's on the other side. The flames never touched most of them. They succumbed to smoke inhalation, fell under trampling feet, and were smothered. Firefighters and police smashed into the smoldering remains of the Rhythm Club and found young bodies "stacked like cord wood" against the walls where death captured them—young ladies clad in bobby socks, pedal pushers, baby doll dresses, pastel skirts, and pink scarves; men in boleros, red bow ties, and white bucks. Plus, the band—Stott, James Coles, John Henderson, Clarence Porter, John Reed, Calvin Roberts, Harry Walker, and Jesse Washington—and the vocalist, a beautiful, still-baby-fat nineteen-year-old named Juanita Avery. Alan Barnes had been guarding the band bus and helplessly took in the nightmare—the sights and sounds and smells—from the curb across the street. As the police and coroner's office counted the bodies, Alan identified the man in the white tails. Someone had already plucked the maestro's gold watch and about five hundred dollars, the night's gate, from the body.[15] Walter Barnes was thirty-four.

Over the next few days, Alan drove his brother's empty bus home to Chicago, while the band members' caskets traveled in every direction by train.

The people crowded in and outside Chicago's Pilgrim Baptist Church for Walter Barnes's funeral on April 30. Reverend Junius Austin compared Barnes's band to the heroic musicians who went down with the *Titanic*, still playing. Dorothy Barnes, shaken but resolute, said, "I have always known Walter to be unselfish and courageous. . . . It was because of his unselfishness and bravery that he lost his life."[16] The *Defender* reported that fifteen thousand had attended the funeral.

As Dorothy spoke, twenty-three-year-old John Gray circulated leaflets that blamed the fire on Jim Crow. Police arrested the young activist and threw him in jail. He sat there for a week until the Inter-

The dapper
maestro Walter
Barnes, as he
would want you
to remember him.
*Courtesy of Toya
Johnson*

national Labor Defense raised his fifty-dollar bail and argued successfully for the dismissal of charges.[17]

Of the outpouring of Barnes tributes in the black press, it was his old *Chicago Defender* colleagues who knew his legacy best. Barnes was "one of the first top notch band leaders to exploit the Deep South. Coming from a section of the country [Vicksburg, Mississippi] where few of the big name bands of the northern cities appeared, he struck upon the idea of making an annual tour of the South. Jacksonville, Fla. was his winter headquarters, and working out from there he covered every city and town of any size in the South. He soon became the idol of this section."[18]

Tiny Bradshaw, the bandleader originally booked for April 23, 1940, at the Natchez Rhythm Club, sat in the dressing room of the

Apollo, where news of the fire found him. "I'm still dazed over the tragedy," he told a reporter. "Going through the South I noticed more than 500 such fire-traps that they call dancehalls. I honestly think that some law should be passed abolishing these buildings." The reporter added, "Many name bands which are booked to go on tour have cancelled engagements calling for jobs in the South."[19] Syndicate talent agent Joe Glaser issued a press release, saying, in part, "Of course, it's shameful that colored people are not permitted to use more modern dancehalls in many parts of the South, but in the future, if they are unable to secure them, they will get none of our attractions."[20]

After the funeral, Dorothy sat in her apartment on Forty-fifth Street in Chicago and wrote to Paul Stott's father in Indianapolis. She wished to return Paul's only possession, the trumpet he blew as the Rhythm Club exploded. She requested a macabre detail in exchange. "Please tell me how Paul looked," she wrote. "Some of the boys were in such a condition that they could not be viewed. My husband, Walter Barnes, was fixed rather nice, but did not look like himself."[21]

Tribute songs "Mississippi Fire Blues" and "Natchez Mississippi Blues" by Lewis Bronzeville Five, "The Death of Walter Barnes" by Leonard "Baby Doo" Caston, and "The Natchez Fire" by Gene Gilmore came out within weeks. Richard Wright, born near Natchez, in Roxie, Mississippi, in 1908, reenacted the fire in his 1958 novel *The Long Dream*. In the 1950s and '60s, blues greats Howlin' Wolf and John Lee Hooker waxed their own accounts of the event. The fire has endured as the greatest catastrophe theme in the blues. Elmo Williams and Hezekiah Early, who were small children in Natchez the night the Rhythm Club went down, recorded a version of "The Natchez Burning" in 1997. Dorothy Barnes was around for all of it. She moved to Los Angeles with family in 1959. She never remarried, and seldom spoke of her late husband or the events of April 23, 1940, in Natchez, Mississippi. She died in 1999.[22]

Rock and Stomp Opus

Paul Stott came home to Indianapolis May 2, 1940, on a train, wrapped in a white cotton burial shroud and tucked in a longleaf pine casket. Stott's father, three brothers, and grandmother were among thousands of mourners who committed his remains to the earth on the sunny afternoon of May 4, below the branches of a sapling oak in Floral Park Cemetery.

As Stott went beneath the ground, Denver Ferguson stood at the pinnacle of his local power. *Indianapolis Recorder* reporter Wesley O. Jackson noted, "Clubs have popped up like mushrooms," and after an Avenue numbers inquest came up empty, "D.D. Ferguson beat the best that local politicians could offer and by recent stories that are circulated, he stands to play a good hand with the cards dealt."[1]

Gone were the days of country-come-to-town fashion, starched collars, and gingham frocks on Indiana Avenue. Zoot suits bloomed along the treeless street, draped over lean brown frames, shading every corner, and flapping in the breeze from pawnshop awnings. As one observer described in the spring of 1940, "From the entrance to the curb in front of every beer joint is cluttered up with every type of lounge lizard, rug cutters, scratch cats, and . . . such clothing . . . trousers too long to be short and too short for long . . . coats, my, my

... looks like a bass fiddle with legs. The more one's face resembles a hatchet, the wider the hat."[2]

The galley doors at Sea Ferguson's Cotton Club swung open to the metallic grin of Champion Jack Dupree, boxer, blues piano banger, and now bouncer at the Naptown nitery, clad in his black chalk-striped suit and white tie. Inside, patrons grabbed a seat and a bite in the ground-floor café while live music pumped in from the Sunset Terrace over a loudspeaker. Others dropped an extra two dimes in Champion Jack's glove and headed up to the third floor to behold the menagerie. Slick White "The Colored Caruso," Dorothy Jackson "Rope and Accrabat Dancer," Whistling Bruce "A Real Novelty," Ophelia Hoy "Like Aged Whiskey Always Good," and Sonny George "The One Arm Dancing Sensation" entertained in the former Trianon Ballroom, which became the Blue Room after Denver moved out to open Sunset Terrace.

J. St. Clair Gibson, devout sinner behind his nom de plume, "The Saint," drank of the Avenue's spirits and glorified its sporting life in his *Recorder* column "Bronzeville in Indianapolis." He would describe the Avenue as "the midway where hep chicks and overhepped wags try to beat out a spiel from early morn to midnight dusk. . . . Where tender dumplings play 'shoo-shoo baby' all day long . . . then you'll find the old ladies brigade making a hefty pull for the young blades with an offering of wine, mazuma, and togs."[3]

The perpetual scowl across the face of Opal Tandy, *Recorder* reporter and former Indianapolis police detective, balanced Gibson's boozy grin in the paper's pages. "Indiana Avenue, which St. Clair Gibson calls Bronzeville, reminds me of a large sewer pipe running through to mar the otherwise beautiful and artistic structure of a modern and attractive home." He continued, "The Main Stem of the Negro section snakes its way along, never complaining about the blood that floods its aged sidewalks and never having a sympathetic answer for the mothers who question it about the havoc and grief it has caused their home."[4]

Avenue beat cops, bribed to their badges, interfered little if at all with the many brawls. Though violence struck most Bronzeville residents as random and pointless, one bloodletting set off a chain reaction that certainly redirected Denver Ferguson's career, and quite possibly changed the trajectory of American music history.

On July 6, 1940, twenty-five-year-old Robert Chambers entered the arched doorway into the Mitchellyne, and sauntered up the narrow staircase past the pearly wall tiles and above the cloudy chrome ceiling into the joint's second-floor gambling room. Though the Mitchells appointed the ground-floor club lavishly, the casino upstairs remained dim, sparse, and windowless, where yellow smoke clung like algae and the gamblers' shouts drowned out the band downstairs. Chambers and a buddy angled their way to the craps tables, where Chambers drank a bottle of beer as his friend rolled. And won. But an argument erupted as the friend accused the house banker of shorting his winnings. In a blurry motion, Chambers either opened and raised a switchblade or did not, according to conflicting eyewitness reports. Mitchellyne bouncer Justus McReynolds moved toward the scuffle, drew his revolver, and gut-shot Chambers.

Gamblers scurried out of the Mitchellyne, and while McReynolds searched for Joe and Tuffy Mitchell, Chambers bled and gasped on the floor. Joe and Justus dragged Chambers, still heaving, downstairs, out a side door to the alley, and dumped him. Chambers died there on the pavement.[5]

Police seized pea shake materials, a baseball-ticket printer, and craps tables from the Mitchellyne. They arrested Justus McReynolds and charged him with murder. They arrested Joe Mitchell and charged him with vagrancy. Meanwhile, detectives interrogated their briber Tuffy Mitchell and his secretary Henry Vance, both of whom had been in the Mitchellyne's ground-floor cabaret and missed all the fun. Tuffy claimed that Justus McReynolds rented the second-floor space for purposes he was neither aware of nor a partner in. Within a couple hours, Joe Mitchell posted a $1,000 bond and went home.[6]

Respectable Indianapolis seldom noticed Avenue murders. The killing of Robert Chambers, though, shook the city. The *Recorder*, surveying the general mayhem on the Avenue, opined, "Never in the long and varied history of Indiana avenue has there been such contempt for human life and safety. . . . Since there are undoubtedly more joints, taverns, and smokers in colored sections than in any previous period, the matter of sufficient policing becomes of paramount importance, for persons gambling and drinking under the same roof invariably are encouraged to violence."[7] Significantly, the *Recorder* excoriated Joe Mitchell, a regular advertiser in the paper, weeks after the killing, saying, "Nothing has ever come up in this town, even in under world life, as vicious and dangerous an example of ingratitude to this city . . . than Joe Mitchell's record."[8] Mayor Reginald Sullivan, a sixty-four-year-old Episcopalian Democrat, promised a stronger police presence in Bronzeville, including an influx of new (unbought) officers to the area. "Not for many years have the police entered these places [i.e., Avenue joints] in the frequency and authority in evidence since [Chambers's killing]."[9]

Previous Avenue blockades, always a convenient, temporary fulfillment of a standard political campaign promise to clean up the city, had never discriminated—what hurt Denver hurt Tuffy, and everyone from lounge lizard up to financier who drew his wages from the street. Vice raids of years past had targeted Denver's baseball-ticket distributors and Tuffy's game tables equally, more or less. But the Chambers murder backlash was different. The Alcoholic Beverage Commission got involved, revoking liquor licenses, but only from the Avenue's three black-owned nightclubs: Harry "Goosie" Lee's Oriental Cafe, Sea Ferguson's Cotton Club, and Denver Ferguson's Sunset Terrace. *Recorder* reporter Opal Tandy predicted, "The big shots will straighten things out, then there will be more murders, the wheels of fortune will turn again, and the bright lights will glimmer on the Gay White way."[10] Denver and Sea knew that the Avenue's appearance might be restored, but the liquor board's intervention signaled a

disturbing and likely irreversible development—Jim Crow's arrival to
the Indianapolis underworld.

*   *   *

Champion Jack Dupree, with a break from the Cotton
Club door, rode the Big Four train to Chicago in January 1941, where
he recorded several sides for Okeh Records, including his addict
anthem "Junker Blues," its lyrics peppered with Avenue low-life lingo.
Fats Domino would mimic the melody eight years later in his recording "The Fat Man," considered by some the first rock 'n' roll song.

Back on the Avenue after his session, Champion Jack joined the
chorus circled outside the shuttered Cotton Club. "Suppose you take
all the white people in Indianapolis and put them together . . . and
give them six or seven blocks," he spat, "when any great number of
people only have one street and just about five or six decent places
to go, there's bound to be some sort of trouble. . . . Now why in the
world should people kick against such men as Sea Ferguson and Denver and Goosie Lee?"

It was not only the fortunes of those enviable men at stake, the
Champ said, but the future of black America. "Wouldn't it make you
feel nice to be able to see our girls coming home from work with their
hair waved out and their nails manicured, sitting up on the streetcar
looking cheerful where they had been working in a department store
or a big firm instead of coming out of the white folks kitchens where
they have been crawling around on their knees all day long, scrubbing
and washing and ironing. . . . [I]t's up to us to do something about it
instead of tearing down the little bit we have accomplished."[11]

A longbeard in a charcoal coat chimed in—"Are all Negroes on
the spot who operate places of business which take in $100,000 a
year? . . . It all seems to me to be a determined effort to stop these few
Negroes from climbing too high financially. Now, other groups are
trying to put us out, because somebody has realized the money in it.
Look at the baseball ticket racket. Who controls it now?"[12]

And so, we're back in Bronzeville, 1941, with Denver Ferguson and his problem. The lid eventually lifted from Bronzeville's black-owned niteries, though Sea would close the Cotton Club in less than two years and open a bowling alley. Denver continued his participation in the baseball-ticket racket, competing against Tuffy Mitchell for years to come. The Sunset Terrace would return to supremacy, but Denver, astute economic forecaster, sensed this as the right time to expand beyond Bronzeville.

*   *   *

Denver's young children heard the floorboards give late each night as their father walked down the hallway to bed. They could smell his scent of burnt cigar. Other than the occasional ride in his latest Buick, this was about all Denver's children got out of him. He woke up after they had left for school, and breakfast was the only meal he would take at home.

The simmering ambition of Denver's youth boiled to hypertensive frustration. Now forty-six, Denver kept close quarters with advisors Taylor Seaths and Twyla Mayfield, meeting each day in the office above noisy Ferguson Printing Company. Seaths, fifteen years Denver's junior, managed Sunset Terrace and served as vice president or first secretary in Denver's other entities. Mayfield outlasted all of Denver's wives, keeping him focused on business instead. Denver's daughter Carole remembers Mayfield standing in Denver's office door, blocking the Ferguson children from their dad. They heard him back there, talking on the phone, but Mayfield held a finger to her lips and shook her head. Even when the kids pushed past Mayfield, their old man rebuffed them all the same. "I ain't got time," he'd scowl.

Indeed he didn't. With fierce competition gnashing at the local racketeering business, and white authorities' sudden interest in black nightclubs, the Indiana Avenue capitalist assembled his most ambitious and far-flung venture yet.

On December 10, 1941, as the nation armed for war, Indiana Sec-

retary of State James Tucker's office approved articles of incorporation filed by the Ferguson Brothers Agency, Inc. The agency's listed
purpose was "to engage in the business of booking agent, promoter,
sponsor and artists' representative for bands, orchestras, shows,
revues, sporting, theatrical and athletic acts, concerts, games, contests, dances, shows and all other kinds of amusement enterprises."[13]
Ferguson Bros. established its offices at 328 North Senate, adjacent to
Denver's print shop. Its inaugural board of directors consisted of Taylor Seaths, Twyla Mayfield, Denver's top policy officer Cy Graham,
and *Indianapolis Recorder* columnist J. St. Clair Gibson.

Denver's breakthrough finagle was a tie-up with Chicago's
Bluebird Records. By now all the syndicate agencies had mutually
exploitative record-company affiliations—bookers needed records
to promote their bands, and record companies needed personal
appearance tours to promote records. Bluebird recorded hard blues,
which didn't fly with the white audience the syndicate courted, and
so popular blues artists who sold a lot of records still couldn't snag
big agency contracts. Enter Denver Ferguson. As the owner of a
nightclub the syndicate bands played, he understood the syndicate–
record company synergy. He proposed a similar scheme, pushing
Bluebird's nationally known blues artists through Deep South blues
country.

Denver had made some calls back in the spring of 1941 on behalf of
Bluebird's Lil Green, a Texas-born singer. Things clicked. Lil Green's
band featured a cost-effective but hard-hitting trio of Big Bill Broonzy
on guitar, Ransom Knowling on bass, and Simeon Henry on piano.
They were tough, especially up front. Big Bill plucked spiffy, Django-
flavor lead runs. Lil sang praises of assisted orgasm, "Romance in the
Dark," unassisted orgasm, "Rockin' Myself," and reefer, "Knockin'
Myself Out." The crowd went wild and the tour made money.[14] Six
months later, just before the official opening of Ferguson Brothers
Agency, Denver booked a highly successful run for up-and-coming
bandleader Jay McShann—*orkdom's newest band sensation com-*

Denver Ferguson
strikes a pose
befitting the
granddaddy of rock
'n' roll. *Courtesy of
Carole Finnell*

*bines Ellington reeds, Basie bounce, and gets gutbucket when vocal-
ist Walter Brown uncorks "Confessin' the Blues."*

From there, Denver easily recruited orchestras to represent.
Tiny Bradshaw and Claude Trenier and the Bama State Collegians
had played the Sunset. They were low-priority syndicate bands that
believed themselves worthy of greater attention. The Carolina Cotton Pickers, King Kolax, Snookum Russell, Milton Larkin, Clarence
Love, Gene Pope, and the International Sweethearts of Rhythm were
territory bands of renown that Denver promised wider geographic
exposure. Doctor Clayton and the combo of Roosevelt Sykes and St.
Louis Jimmy were nationally known recording artists who'd found
hard blues acts unwelcome within the syndicate's respectable circles.
The roster grew as "Boogie Woogie Piano and Accordion Queen"

Christine Chatman spun off from Snook Russell's group, and the "Hey Lawdy Mama," better known as Big Maybelle, broke out from Gene Pope's Genial Gentlemen.

William Little, known to hinterland jazz fans as King Kolax, was a seasoned entertainer and experienced bandleader with an ear for budding genius. Tenor sax player Gene Ammons, drummer Earl Palmer, who would contribute rock 'n' roll's distinctive backbeat rhythm, and a lanky North Carolinian named John Coltrane all played in the Kolax big band during its time with Ferguson Bros. Kolax whipped himself to a froth on stage, soloing fiercely till sweat poured down his face, and exhorting his sixteen-piece to the same. Multi-instrumental virtuoso Yusef Lateef remembered going to see them during World War II. "I walked in and Gene Ammons was standing on top of the piano, playing," he said, "so impressive."[15]

"I really liked this band," Coltrane recalled. "which was truly my 'school.' "[16]

Recognizing, perhaps, that talented musicians and spirited stage play were not everyone's tipple, Kolax brought along a full revue, featuring a drag-queen kick line. Shortly after joining Ferguson Bros., Kolax hired Dave Clark, Jimmie Lunceford's former advance man and an innovator in chitlin' circuit promotion.

Earl Palmer, he who made the backbeat, offered an intriguing explanation for Ferguson client Snookum Russell's chitlin' circuitness. Unlike the elegant Ellington, the foxy Billy Eckstine, or the professorial Lunceford, Russell "was the ugliest little sonofabitch you ever seen," Palmer said. "Looked just like a fish. . . . terrific piano player, great arranger, and a hell of a good singer, too. But he was ugly."[17] Nonetheless, plenty of talented youngsters played in the Snookum Russell band too, including trombonist J. J. Johnson, trumpeter Fats Navarro, and bassist Ray Brown. Annie Laurie, a big-league beauty and Paul Gayten's duet partner on a few New Orleans rhythm and blues hits in the late 1940s, got her start beside Snookum on the chitlin' circuit.

The Carolina Cotton Pickers began as a fundraising gimmick for the Jenkins Orphanage in Charleston, South Carolina. The fifteen-piece ensemble wore baby blue, double-breasted tux jackets and black bowties and trousers, while bandleader Leroy Hardison dressed like a matador in bolero jacket and billowing slacks. With so many young men of troubled upbringing in the group, perhaps it is not so surprising that their greatest difficulty came from within. Hardison, the man in charge of payroll, developed an aggravating habit of abandoning the Cotton Pickers mid-tour, leaving them penniless and orphaned once more.

The all-girl International Sweethearts of Rhythm began, similarly to their stablemates the Carolina Cotton Pickers, in the late 1930s as a moneymaker for the all-black Piney Woods Country Life School near Jackson, Mississippi. Piney Woods founder Laurence Jones assembled the group and bestowed the "international" tag to empha-size the Chinese sax player, Hawaiian trumpeter, and Mexican clari-netist in addition to the fourteen African-American girls in the group. Rae Lee Jones, whom the school assigned to chaperone the girls on their travels, had convinced the ladies to throw off their amateur status mid-tour in early 1941, astutely pointing out that they could top their Piney Woods–mandated eight-dollar-per-week salary. They absconded to Arlington, Virginia, under the guidance of real estate developer Al Dade, who assumed their management. Piney Woods principal Laurence Jones did not take the news well. He reported the band bus stolen and several of the band's underage members miss-ing. The Sweethearts ditched the bus in Montgomery, Alabama, and made it to Memphis, where a roadblock netted the fugitives. Four of the girls returned to Piney Woods, and the decidedly square Laurence Jones threatened to withhold diplomas from the rest. They seemed to prefer Dade's tutelage, who reportedly introduced them to the won-ders of makeup. He lodged the refugees at his property, redubbed "Sweetheart House," and they called him daddy. Clearly in need of a positive role model, the Sweethearts joined forces with Denver Fergu-son as one of the first major acts at Ferguson Brothers Agency. Tiny

Davis, a three-hundred-pound, proud lesbian vocalist, joined the group just prior to "one of the greatest one night tours ever staged by any attraction," as did Toby Butler, the group's first white member.[18] The Sweethearts had as many nicknames as members of a male orchestra, counting "Rabbit" Wong, "Vi" Burnside, and "Trump" Gipson among their membership, and claimed to have musical chops on par with any bunch of no-good men. Still, the ladies understood femininity's value to the blues crowd. As vocalist Anna Mae Winburn sang, "I ain't good looking and I don't have waist-long hair, but my mama gave me something that can take me anywhere."

Though the Sweethearts aren't well remembered, they impressed one Southern boy. Ike Turner said, "I forget what their name was—a girl band—it was like 20 of them! But they could play, and they were doing big stuff like Count Basie and Tommy Dorsey, Jimmy Dorsey, they were doing that kind of stuff. Yeah, they could play, it's a black college down there in Piney Wood, Mississippi, and we used to go to hear them play man, and they was b-a-d man."[19]

Tiny (Myron) Bradshaw, a graduate of Wilberforce University in Ohio, had been featured opening night at Denver Ferguson's Sunset Terrace four years before Ferguson Bros. launched, and then slimly escaped memorial in all those Natchez burning songs that commemorated Walter Barnes. Of lean build and mocha skin tone, Bradshaw sang lead, could pass for a poor man's Cab Calloway, and tried to, much to the dismay of critics who wrote off his music as derivative. He had at least one thing working for him, though: a conscience. Tiny rejected a *yah-suh* role in the Walt Disney motion picture *Song of the South*, which showcased the toothily grinning Negro folktale teller Uncle Remus. The Disneyfied depiction of bronze folk "set back my people by many years," the plaid-suited bandleader told the press. Critics be damned, Tiny's modern, dignified exuberance won the admiration of his peers. Louis Jordan, master of the sort of gleeful showmanship Tiny trafficked, said of Bradshaw, "He was my favorite entertainer that never got big."[20] A team of ten jitterbuggers swarmed the stage the moment the curtain lifted. Tiny ran on full speed as the male dancers tossed their partners in the air. Flailing his arms, he shouted—"Zah-zah-zah zoo-zoo-zoo zay!" He darted from brass to reeds across the bandstand, yelling like a pep-squad captain unhinged, "Let's go! Let's go!"

"Whatever these black orchestras lacked in precision and technical perfection," wrote Preston Love, a territory-band leader who went on to lead the Motown house orchestra, "they more than compensated in originality, creativity, spontaneity, and raw provocativeness."[21]

Ferguson Bros. booked rocking blues acts as well as middle-shelf swing bands.[22] Roosevelt "The Honeydripper" Sykes, a cigar-chomping, red-complexioned fire hydrant of a man, teamed with St. Louis Jimmy Oden, described by rhythm and blues historian Arnold Shaw as "a big-toothed man, with heavy-lidded eyes and pronounced cheekbones. Even early in life he had a receding hairline that made him look as if he wore a skullcap."[23] Sykes, from Helena, Arkansas, specialized in two-fisted barrelhouse blues piano that bubbled forth from deep Dixie lumber and turpentine camps. He sang in high bursts, as if shouting over a sawmill. Oden, a vocalist, composed the blues classic "Going Down Slow" and recorded it in 1941, just before the duo joined Ferguson Bros. and teamed with a fifteen-piece orchestra under Sykes's foremanship. Having to play to contract specifications—a pair of two-hour sets—quickly taught them the value of the old standards. "I was specializing in the blues, my records was hot out, and they booked me on account of my records," Sykes said. "But I played some of everything once I got out there. . . . I learned to play 'Stardust,' anything." Sykes recalled the headaches of big-band accounting as another challenge he hadn't met in the saw-mill juke joint. "Them fellows, you know you got to be a mama and a daddy. They come up, say, 'Hey man, put me in the book for five,' 'Hey man, I'm in a tight spot, I wants ten, man,' . . . You got watch 'em, keep 'em from getting drunk. . . . I had a lot of that."[24]

Doctor Clayton, a Bluebird recording star, wore his hat a size small, a shrunken suit, and lensless white glasses, looking as though he'd been kicked off a minstrel show in 1919. He played the vengeful cuckold, promising to murder his baby if she continued her unfaithful and dishonest practices. It sounded mean enough on a record, but his stage appearance, the goofy garb and his loopy fist-wagging, cast an air of idleness over his threats. Clayton's gig in Houston in August 1942 ended in a hail of debris after he took the stage at a packed house too trashed to sing. "Clayton staggered on the stage, with his hair standing on his head and suit wrinkled as if he had been sleeping in it for a week," the *Houston Informer* reported. "Then when instead of singing, he began to holler and clown, the patrons couldn't stand any more. Bottles, paper cups, and everything else were hurled at him. Words of indignation were shouted to such an extent that the massive City Auditorium became a turmoil of confusion. Policemen were forced to rush him off the stage to prevent his being seriously injured."[25] His orchestra stepped from the stage onto their bus without the drunken Doc, and left.

For the problem of making names for a bunch of no-names, Denver turned to board member J. St. Clair Gibson. Known on the Avenue as "The Saint," Gibson cranked the Ferguson publicity machine from his office at the *Indianapolis Recorder*. He concocted stories about Ferguson clients and placed them on the Associated Negro Press wire, a news service for the country's black papers. An illustrated serial of Richard Wright's *Native Son* circulated via the wire, just as Ferguson's dispatches initially appeared there. The Ferguson briefs always ran in the *Indianapolis Recorder*, but when they appeared in the *Chicago Defender* or *Pittsburgh Courier*, they reached all of black America. This was the case with the King Kolax creation myth: "They were holding a jam session at the Savoy Ballroom one night in the month of May 1940 . . . and all the cats had their axes sharp for some deep cutting. . . . As the session started and the cats started swinging . . . a young fellow came up from out of nowhere and asked to sit in. . . . This young fellow with his horn under his arm hit the stage in two jumps and told the pianist to take 'Honeysuckle Rose' in E flat. . . . This kid raised his horn toward the ceiling and started blowing and for 10 choruses he kept them jumping, hitting the high notes with a different riff for every chorus. When this kid had finished, one of the old timers said, 'There is your new King of the Trumpet' and this new king was King Kolax."[26]

Gibson urged dance promoters to contact him about "the best bands in the country," and after introducing readers to the same, he dashed off news briefs to convey the life of a chitlin' circuit star—"Christine Chatman Gets Hot Trumpet Player by Airplane" and "Snookum Russell Has Police Escort." It was the Walter Barnes publicity program, magnified.

Delicious hyperbole showed up in the Ferguson Bros. correspondence too. "Dear Sir," Denver Ferguson wrote to J. Neal Montgomery, owner of the Sunset Casino in Atlanta, Georgia,

> We wish to advise you we will have available for you Monday, August 23, KING KOLAX AND HIS NBC – SAVOY BALLROOM ORCHESTRA, undoubtedly the greatest swing orchestra in existence.
>
> If you like Kirk, Basie, or Lunceford, you will love and admire KOLAX. In our twenty-three years existence, we have never heard any orchestra that blows so much music and works as hard as this one does. Every man really loves to work. Every man is a STAR and KOLAX, himself, is undoubtedly the "King of the Trumpet."
>
> Louis Armstrong, Harry James, Erskine Hawkins, Roy Eldredge, nor Cootie Williams surpasses him as a trumpet man, and honestly and truly he has the greatest swing band in the world today, and should receive a guarantee of twice what we ask.
>
> Terms, however, can be arranged at $350.00 guarantee with privilege of 50% of gross receipts. And, as we are closing his

itinerary in your territory now, will you be courteous enough to advise us immediately by WESTERN UNION TELEGRAPH or Air Mail Special Delivery letter, whether or not you can use KOLAX on the above date?

Thanking you for a prompt reply and for past cooperation, we are

Yours very truly,
FERGUSON BROS. AGENCY, Inc.[27]

Of Twyla Mayfield's role in the new business, Sax Kari recalled, "Aside from [Ferguson's] gabbing, she was really the one who handled all the booking." [28] As Denver's children had learned, all Ferguson Bros. business went through Mayfield. Denver focused on the big picture, while Mayfield oversaw day-to-day operations.

Denver, knowing well how the syndicate controlled black bands in the big Northern cities, built his circuit in the territory Walter Barnes had pioneered for black bands in 1932 and virtually closed with his death in 1940. Unlike the syndicate, Denver put the black audience first, a simple variation at the core of his innovation. Denver knew the black South intimately—as Madam Walker of Indiana Avenue did before him. Denver understood the ways black neighborhoods functioned, and he knew that because of racial segregation, all-black enclaves existed in every excuse for a town. Whether he had read Barnes writings or not, Denver was in touch with the *stroll* concept and its prevalence across the map. He brought his own street-financial expertise to the enterprise. The money principles of the numbers game applied: the Negro individual lacked financial resources, but the stroll possessed collective wealth in nickel and dime increments. Add those nickels and dimes, multiply by numerous bands playing different joints simultaneously with a percentage of proceeds from each flowing back to Ferguson, repeat nightly, and you come to see, as Denver correctly surmised, that there was serious cash down there.

Denver had seen the black population growing on Indiana Avenue and started a street lottery. He built his successful nightclub on a tip about the new Avenue housing projects. The launch of Ferguson Bros. proved his impeccable timing—or superb luck—once again as the war solved overnight the problem of underemployment in the black South.

While building his talent roster, and exaggerating its greatness throughout the black press, Denver laced together a vast network, mostly down South—like Madam Walker and the *Chicago Defender*—of agents embedded in black communities. Denver called them *shadow promoters*. They were the natural extension of his philosophy and design to work around and beyond the established entertainment syndicate. Denver would dispatch runners to explain the system to the local agent, who would go to the black barber and beauty shop, restaurant and bar, building momentum for a show. Denver approached his relationship with these far-off promoters just as he had his numbers runners on the Avenue. If a promoter failed to pay Denver or his act according to the terms of their deal, then Denver would drop them from the circuit. No need for violent repercussion. He could always make another promoter. He wanted his freelancers, either in the street or on the circuit, to recognize the long-term value of their arrangement. He wanted them to see that they would make thousands more dollars with him over time than the few hundred they'd make off with by disappearing with the proceeds of a single dance. If they were incapable of this, let them go, Denver said. This was the closest thing to loyalty that he could breed.

Additionally, Denver plugged into established territory-band promoters who had thrown shows together since the barnstorming days, like Ralph Weinberg, former boxing promoter in Bluefield, West Virginia. Weinberg stretched Denver's circuit by the length of the Virginias' coal belt plus tobacco road in the Carolinas. Denver's bands ran across the white sands of the Sunshine State too, via Bill Rivers, who controlled south Florida from his Rockland Palace nightclub on Miami Beach, plus Cracker Johnson over in West Palm, and Charlie Edd, who supervised north Florida from his Jacksonville club, the Two Spot, to the Gulf of Mexico at Pensacola. J. Neal Montgomery, jazz pianist turned promoter, was Ferguson's man on Sweet Auburn, Atlanta's stroll, and Robert Henry, a Beale Street fixture, became the Ferguson man on black Broadway in Memphis. Denver made another set of key contacts among the more enterprising black nightclub owners. Like Denver, their vision extended beyond their respective localities. Howard Lewis ran the Rose Room in Dallas and plenty of action in west Texas. Lewis's competition with Houston club boss Don Robey, whose contacts included the finest gambling parlors from dusty towns down to the state's palm-shaded Gulf coast, sowed fertile ground throughout the Lone Star state, across the Gulf to New Orleans. A barber-turned-club-owner named Frank Painia booked acts at his New Orleans hub, the Dew Drop, and along spokes into the bayou toward Bogalusa and across the Gulf to Mobile. Tom Wince, a light-skinned Mason who ran the Blue Room in Vicksburg, Mississippi, booked shows for the little dice and assignation houses tumbled across the vast Mississippi Delta. Clint Brantley's connections extended from his Macon operation, the Cotton Club, into roadhouses hidden among the Georgia pines.

A successful promoter promoted himself first. The best present-day example of a classic promoter is Don King, who has managed to make himself as much of a story over the years as he has the boxing matches he organizes, ostensibly, to make his living. Fighters come and go, but there is always Don King. Same was true for Wince and Robey—and Ferguson himself—whose charisma and outsized exploits ushered them into the national discourse despite their distance from the real Harlem or the original Bronzeville. Like Denver, these fellows helped finance their local papers' entertainment pages, to ensure constant publicity for their taverns and galas. An elegant synergy unfolded as promoters booked Ferguson acts. The Saint's news items about King Kolax, Christine Chatman, and the rest, crackling over the Associated Negro Press wire, suited the promoters' need to create buzz and sell tickets, and so flowed through the *Houston Informer, Louisiana Weekly*, and others just ahead of the various touring schedules. This worked to the promoters', artists', and agency's favor, helping everyone get paid. These bulletins also mentioned "the country's leading sepia theatrical agency," and as it behooved the men behind the entertainment news to inflate Ferguson's status, briefs that had nothing to do with next week's show appeared—"Brown Skin Models Get Contract with Ferguson Brothers" and "Ferguson Announces $1,000 Weekly Contract for Snook Russell." It reinforced the local promoters' big-man status around Vicksburg or Macon to transact with such a prestigious organization. Readers had no idea that the agency generated this "news" or, for the most part, rigged its placement. As the circuit hit its full stride, Denver's old printing press whirred day and night, reeling off a few baseball tickets still, but mostly churning out advertising materials—press kits, handbills, and window placards—and tickets to be couriered to future tour stops. Within months of its inception, Ferguson Bros., having mastered Walter Barnes–style hyperbole and turned it loose on the black South, had established a trusted, time-honored brand, all from shop-spun hocus-pocus.

These promoters also plugged touring bands into home-style accommodations, since working the circuit required playing places too small to support black hotels. "We couldn't stay in the white hotels," bandleader Andy Kirk recalled. "I'm glad now we couldn't. We'd have missed out on a whole country full of folks who put us up in their homes, cooked dinners and breakfasts for us, told us how to get along in Alabama and Mississippi, helped us out in trouble, and became our friends for life."[29]

Where venues lacked, Denver improvised. As Sax Kari recalled, Ferguson taught his homegrown promoters to press a tobacco barn, warehouse, or fraternal lodge into duty in the absence of a regular dance hall. "There were no inside toilets at many of the places, you had to use privies," Sax said. "When you got into a place that had running water inside, why you were fortunate." Denver's contracts specified that a promoter provide a public address system but made no mention of modern plumbing.

Denver negotiated for his talent to ensure that the act, and agent, got paid before anyone else regardless of attendance. Denver and the promoter settled on a guaranteed fee. Denver extracted a deposit from that figure, paid before the show to "guarantee" the appearance—like the $350 he attempted to extract from J. Neal Montgomery—refundable only if the artist failed to show. If the gig proceeded smoothly, Denver kept the deposit and the artist kept the remainder of the guarantee, which the artist collected from the promoter at intermission. The promoter kept an amount equal to the artist guarantee, and if profits exceeded payouts, the artist and promoter split the surplus, according to the term of their deal referred to in contractual lingo as the "privilege," often, but not always, 50 percent. A chunk of this also went back to the boss. A Ferguson-employed road manager (who might also be the bandleader, as in the Carolina Cotton Pickers' unfortunate case) accompanied the agency's acts to count heads in the dance hall and then wire the cash into Denver's pockets—just like an Avenue numbers runner.[30]

Though the chitlin' circuit touring model—one-night stands, revolving through promoters' respective hubs and spokes—was built to sustain itself, Ferguson's big bands operated with little room for error. Bus fuel and maintenance, the band's food, clothes, and instruments, and salaries for a crew of twenty, not to mention makeup and high-heel repair for the queens, required steady cash. A single cancellation—and there were always cancellations—stranded bands. And many a *good* day left them threadbare. Earl Palmer recalled that groups were "always traveling, working one night stands. Barely getting by, but [sounding] good. The raggedy bands, we called them, big raggedy road bands."[31] Invariably, they wired back to headquarters for help. Of course, Denver, still administering his baseball-ticket game, not only made plenty of money but also needed to invest it quickly. So every sucker who crumbled a losing baseball ticket into the Avenue gutter did his part to help the future inventor of the backbeat and the messengers of bop survive another day in the music business.

Chapter 6 ✶ ✶ ✶ ✶ ✶ ✶ ✶

The Loser Goes to the Hospital, the Winner Goes to Jail

If indeed Denver Ferguson used his phonebook collection to locate a promoter in Houston, Don Robey was easy to find. The name of Robey's joint—Harlem Grill—was simple code for a black nightclub anywhere during the Ellington zeitgeist. Though Denver liked to *make* his promoters, Robey needed zero training.

Robey's grandfather Franklin, son of a South Carolina planter and a South Carolina slave, established his clan as one of colored Houston's more respected. Franklin practiced medicine and settled in a big house in the Third Ward, where generations of Robeys would enter the world. Don Deadric Robey was born there on November 1, 1903. He would come to believe his biracial background had endowed in him leadership characteristics from both cultures. "I'm a white man and a black man," he was fond of remarking. "I'll outsmart you *and* kick your ass."[1]

The city of Houston, during Robey's youth, exuded country spirit. When torrential rain flooded the streets waist-high, Robey's Third Ward neighbors put on their swim trunks. On warm days, kids played hooky and headed to a bend in Buffalo Bayou known as the Dump to swim in the snaky water and make out on the bank. The Robeys stayed dry, preferring to mix with local Creoles who claimed ancestry of Louisiana's free Afro-French. Despite his family's polite social status, Robey quit school and took lessons in street math as a numbers runner. White bosses controlled the Houston game (local adaptations were called the Big Four and the Hi-Lo lotteries) so Robey could never ascend to the heights Denver reached in Indianapolis. Perhaps this underworld kinship—numbers runner and numbers boss—explains the compatibility between Robey and the Fergusons. Robey was light-skinned, and with his wide-set, squinty dark eyes and slicked-back feathers he resembled a bird of prey. Like Denver, he preferred thinking to talking, and neither would be remembered as having much of a sense of humor. Unlike Denver, Robey never did mind being noticed. As an associate of later years recalled, "I remember seeing him driving down the street in a Buick that was yellow . . . [wearing] a green hat with a red band on it."[2]

Robey realized that his grandfather's respectability could carry the family only so far. They still paid the poll tax, and Houston still hit its Negroes hard. During the early to mid-1930s, Robey's early days in the Houston nightlife, a white vice cop named Eddie Bussard terrorized black dives. In one 1936 incident, Bussard raided a Fifth Ward joint and smashed his pistol butt into one patron's skull, which caused the gun to go off and kill a bystander. Authorities quickly ruled the shooting accidental, and Bussard's marauding continued. Days later, a white streetcar operator shot a seventeen-year-old black kid on the trolley, explaining that the boy planned to rob the car. The boy didn't survive to tell another side—case closed.

Houston's Negroes hit each other hard too. The sprawling black wards provided some shelter against violent whites, but hardly offered escape from hostility. Their layout led to a different way of living than on Indianapolis's compact Indiana Avenue. You could disappear into one of these worlds within the city, where people converted their homes into beer joints and card rooms. These dotted the Third, Fourth, and Fifth wards. With fried fish in the kitchen, whiskey buried out back, and the sparse furniture pushed to the walls, they were the kind of place where fellows like Jelly Roll Pearson ran dice games and shot whoever disputed his victories. Some of the more legitimate if not always lawful joints, the Cotton Club on Lyons Avenue, the Dew Drop Inn on Dowling, and the Hollywood Tea Room on Ennis, operated a bit more formally, throwing thirty-five-cent dances with a local orchestra. As far as big-time black entertainment was concerned, Houston stood somewhere on the outskirts of the hinterland.

Don Robey opened his first backroom amusement parlor, the Sweet Dreams Cafe, in 1933 at 2630½ Odin Avenue in the ethnically mixed Fifth Ward. Jews and Italians had made their homes and livings nearby, and Odin had become a hub of black business, with the offices of one of the local black newspapers, the *Texas Freeman*, near more modest operations like Lee's Lightning Shoe Repair and Robey's little gaming suite. Robey expanded quickly, opening the Lenox Club at 407½ Milam Street in 1934. Hereabouts, he changed the name of the Sweet Dreams to the Manhattan Club and commenced raising Houston's showbiz profile. Determined to bring in the best bands he could from outside Houston, Robey presented Frank Tanner and His Melody Makers on February 10, 1935: "First Time South . . . Kansas City's Greatest Band," the ad went. Meanwhile, the white-run Metropolitan Theater denied entry to black patrons who wanted to pay to see black acts such as Ethel Waters and the Mills Brothers perform. Whether irked by Jim Crow or enlightened by the sight of those black dollars, Robey resolved to give his people what they wanted.

Robey and Morris Merritt, both gamblers (*capitalists* if you prefer), had pooled their piles from a night at the craps table back in 1934 to stage a battle of local bands. The money multiplied by the end of the night, and the budding tycoons purchased the Harlem, at the corner of Heiner and West Dallas in downtown Houston, for a reported six hundred dollars. Robey paid out of pocket to upgrade the Harlem to first class, and he and Merritt unveiled it on March 1, 1936. Calling the joint "Houston's and the entire south's finest, most colorful and modern amusement spot," the *Houston Informer* noted its black and red deco interior and high-fidelity sound equipment. Robey, described as "promoter of various enterprises," was identified as the Harlem's proprietor, and Merritt as its manager.[3] A neon banner throbbed out front, and Champagne Type 2 Beer chilled inside. Robey and Merritt assembled a floor show featuring the "World's Greatest Feminine Tap Dancer Baby Briscoe, former celebrity of Broadway." They showcased locals like Giles Mitchell and the Birmingham Blue Blowers. The Creole Kings and Ace High social club functions, where men donned tuxedos and ladies wore silk and satin, were held at the Harlem, along with Houston's Bronze mayor ball. The jitterbug element congregated there as well. Reefer was openly smoked along West Dallas, and local vipers—as jazz-age stoners were known—made the Harlem Grill their pit. Patrolmen always knew where to catch Snake Henry selling sticks.

Not long after the Harlem unveiling, the *Houston Informer* sent a reporter to survey the West Dallas Avenue strip after midnight. A prostitute hey babied him over the brittle clap and baritone din drifting from Johnson's Domino Parlor. The hickory smoke from Snow's Barbecue teared up his eyes. He passed Wing Chong Grocery as another, more descriptive whore announced her evening menu and market prices. He passed Madam Jones, Spiritualist Divine, who promised, "I take away evil conditions and make you master of destiny." The *stroll* became the *stagger* as he reached the Harlem Grill.

Boy, oh boy, the action started. Every conceivable avenue of pleasure was rampant at this center of activity, a drunken man being dragged home by a good Samaritan, a couple of painted lilies standing in the corner smoking and indulging in that favorite West Dallas pastime—profanity. I paused to hear the deluge of obscene language coming from everywhere. A boy, apparently twelve years of age, walked up and asked for a cigarette. I gave him one on his nerve. He took two out of the package. A nickel Victrola started playing "Baby Won't You Please Come Home?" Couples dancing, couples drinking, some talking in tones that I could not understand.

A woman walked up and asked me to put a nickel in the Victrola. In obedience to her command, I placed a nickel in the slot and she requested that I play "Baby Don't You Stay All Night." The earthworm wiggling that started with the music was below my dignity, so I moved on down the avenue of "good times."

He pushed through threadbare gamblers and "women of the street plying their age-old profession," to the steps of a church, "used as an auction place by members of that profession. . . . An ambulance screaming its emergency warning roared past. . . . I moved on to the crowd gathered around the ambulance. As I arrived, the victim of a Texas jack was being hurriedly placed in the ambulance. The fresh odor of blood stirred my reporting instinct. I investigated and, to my surprise, he was cut because of the difference between seven and eight on the dice. . . . The loser goes to the hospital, the winner goes to jail. What a street!"[4]

Robey's aspiration to bring Houston the finest in black entertainment coincided with Walter Barnes's effort to deliver the same, and the maestro hit the Harlem Grill over Thanksgiving weekend, 1936. Even the optimistic Barnes remarked on the decrepit state of West Dallas Avenue. "The sidewalks are badly in need of repairing," he wrote, though was more complimentary of Robey, calling him clean-cut and industrious. Already, Robey's circuitry sparked. Robey and a partner, either Merritt or Julius White, had scouted the region for venues to stage dances in other towns and for co-promoters who could handle advertising and pre-show collections locally. Work and play were inseparable. They gambled their way across the Gulf Coast and occasionally got popped. In February 1937, Robey and Julius White were captured in a raid at Margaret's Place on Twenty-ninth Street in Galveston. The dapper pair stood nonchalant while other gamblers dove out of Margaret's back windows.[5] Traveling constantly to refresh relationships and fatten the Rolodex, Robey's modus operandi for the rest of his career, they developed contacts and located dance halls to pitch shows throughout east Texas and most of Louisiana. Barnes's band rode the Robey circuit first.

The week after Barnes's 1936 Houston show, Robey brought in Don Albert—"a master showman" who "has perfected a sensational musical unit that will captivate with its toe tapping syncopation." Albert was a New Orleans Creole, *née* Albert Dominique, who had established a territory band working out of San Antonio, Texas. Don Albert and the Ten Pals wore matching suits with vests (gray Scotch plaid in Houston), and bounced between Corpus Christi, Dallas, Oklahoma City, and Little Rock, and then occasionally to towns in Mississippi, southern Illinois, and West Virginia. Albert had taken to billing them "America's Greatest Swing Band." Earlier that year, a bulletin was issued in the *Pittsburgh Courier*: "NOTICE! Don Albert, director and manager of the famed Dixie orchestra which bears his name is requested to get in touch with Joe Glaser . . . immediately."[6]

Glaser, Louis Armstrong's manager, and one of the best-connected syndicate talent brokers, offered to manage "America's Greatest Swing Band," but Albert refused. After Albert and the rest of the world witnessed what Glaser did for Louis Armstrong, Albert would say that this had been a mistake. Though he would forever be kicking his 1936 self for lacking foresight, his decision to maintain independence helped steer him into a significant, if underappreciated role in black music, as Don Robey's man in San Antone.

In early 1938, a young orchestra led by trumpeter Milton Larkin played the Harlem. Once more, the *Informer* captured the scene. "Girls in dresses above their knees, anklets, high heel shoes. Boys with drapes starting six inches above their ankles and ending in a bunch of accordion pleats six inches below their necks! [E]veryone drunk and smoking, a girl swinging out alone, popping her fingers and imitating a crooked streak of lightning . . . everybody singing. Everybody is jazz mad, the orchestra is screaming like a bunch of freight trains, the crowd is stomping like a herd of cattle stampeding—boy what a time! The popping of beer bottles is keeping time with the music. Lights blue and green flickering on a lake of whiskey, a sea of wine, and an ocean of beer. . . . The trumpet sounds a long note, it is farewell for the day."[7] Impressed, one of the Robey ringleaders asked the young bandleader, " 'Well Milt, would you like to play a gambling club?'

"I said, 'I don't know, where is it?' He said, 'You'd get a hundred.' "[8] Fair enough, Milt supposed.

The Robey ring was set. Julius White split his time between civil rights agitation, managing the Harlem and another venue, the Downtown Grill, and promoting Houston dances. Robey was the organization's contact person and financier. From Frank Tanner and his Melody Makers in 1935 and Walter Barnes and his Kings of Swing in '36, Robey brought in successively bigger-name bands, Andy Kirk, Earl Hines, and Jimmie Lunceford before the end of 1936. He ingratiated himself to the top agents for black talent, Moe Gale, Joe Glaser, and Harold Oxley, and smeared his local competitors, establishing himself as the go-to syndicate promoter in Houston.[9] By 1940, all the premium acts played Houston—Duke, Cab, Ella Fitzgerald, Lionel Hampton, you name it. Robey conducted constant diplomatic excursions throughout his territory: Austin, Bay City, Beaumont, Corpus Christi, Fort Worth, Galveston, Longview, Lufkin, Marshall, Mexia, Orange, Port Arthur, Rosenberg, San Antonio, and Tyler, Texas; Franklin, Lake Charles, Minden, Monroe, New Iberia, New Orleans, Opelousas, and Shreveport, Louisiana.[10] Merritt worked as the legman, leading orchestras through the outfit's Texas-Louisiana dice trail, collecting at the door, and funneling funds back to Robey. People like San Antonio bandleader Don Albert operated on the fringe, promoting Robey attractions in his home base and scouting for tal-

ent. Milton Larkin's orchestra of future stars was the first band the
consortium repped. Tenor sax honkers Illinois Jacquet and Arnett
Cobb, pianist Wild Bill Davis, and guitarist Aaron "T-Bone" Walker
all traveled this dusty trail. Eddie Vinson, who would go on to prominence as a rhythm and blues bandleader, started off on saxophone
with Larkin. He bad-lucked himself into a nickname out there, trust-
ing Lucky Lou hair dressing's promise to make hair *really* straight."
Vinson burnt his straight off, and as he vowed to shave it off and
leave it that way, he became known, first to the chitlin' circuit, then
the ages, as "Cleanhead."[11]

Don Robey had much to offer Denver Ferguson in 1941: Houston
venues of all sizes, a sizzling band, and the ring of Gulf dance halls.
Denver realized he didn't have to *make* Robey as a promoter, so
much as enlist him. In fact, Denver owed his early success to Robey.
Houston had arrived as a spot for big-time entertainment, but action
on the lower circuit had slowed considerably since Walter Barnes's
death. In the late spring of 1941, a year after the Natchez Rhythm
Club disaster, Denver ventured to resuscitate the chitlin' circuit. The
first tour Denver booked down there, Lil Green's quartet, turned a
tidy profit under Morris Merritt's guidance across Robey's route.

When Merritt got home, Robey reminded him, and everyone else
who happened along the stroll, who was in charge. The partners had
bickered behind closed doors over use of the Harlem Grill—Robey
wanted to convert it to his band-booking office, while Merritt wished
to keep the club. Rumors of a power struggle fluttered around. Rather
than settle things privately, Robey saw Merritt making rounds on the
busted-up West Dallas Avenue sidewalk in the afternoon sunshine,
chased him down, and punched him behind the ear. Words flew one
way. Bystanders popped eyes and grumbled. The Don huffed off.
Remember the man's motto: I'll outsmart you *and* kick your ass. Having made his point and regained composure, Robey later explained to
a reporter, "I didn't think Merritt was treating me right, especially
when I realized all I had done for him. Why, just several days before

that, I paid Merritt $1,020 by cutting him in on the Lil Green tour, so when he came out of the door past me, I was so mad the only thing I could think of was hitting him."[12]

Denver showed the squabbling Houston partners his all-out appreciation for the Lil Green tour by booking the Milton Larkin orchestra at his Sunset Terrace and deploying his hype machine—"Milton Larkin, the dapper maestro and his terrific band from the wide open plains of Texas are provin' that they are the greatest band of musicians that hit the road during the year. The folks in this city agree with the critics in Harlem when they say this is the greatest discovery since Count Basie came out of Kansas City."[13]

✳   ✳   ✳

Almost as quickly as Denver Ferguson revived the chitlin' circuit, wartime allocations threatened to deflate the entire black joy trade. Uncle Sam's paratroopers needed fabric more than the stroll's zoot suiters did, and tailors flattened pleats and tightened drapes accordingly. The amusement industry's situation eerily resembled the death of vaudeville a decade before—road-hopping big bands and their big buses guzzled far too much gasoline to work in these days of allotment. In June 1942, the Office of Defense Transportation announced a bus ban in line with fuel rationing, though it designated five buses for the all-important defense function of orchestral travel, and issued one to Ferguson Brothers Agency, which assigned it to Claude Trenier and his Bama State Collegians. Wrote *Informer* reporter Ted Williams, "The ruling . . . might mean the swan song for Negro bands on the road. This faces them with the greatest crisis in the history of the entertainment world. For the one-nighter dance circuit is the life of sepia bands."

Adaptation to this great crisis had already begun, however, as Williams noted: "Louis Jordan has developed the best little band in the country."[14] When Jordan, the former big-band alto saxophonist, went solo, he couldn't afford to maintain a full orchestra, so he organized

a compact combo he called the Tympany Five. In November 1941, a
month before both the attack on Pearl Harbor and the birth of Ferguson Bros., Jordan and the Tympany Five recorded "Knock Me a
Kiss" and "(I'm Gonna Move to the) Outskirts of Town." This new
band format, its new sounds, and ballsy originality would revolution-
ize American music.

Jordan, born on July 8, 1908, hailed from Brinkley, Arkansas,
where his father fronted a brass band, and Louis first saw his reflection in the shiny brass of an alto saxophone perched in a pawnshop
window. Both Jordan men lit out with the Rabbit Foot Minstrels, a
barnstorming entertainment troupe that planted its tent at the edge of
town and announced its presence with a Main Street parade. Later,
Louis Jordan got modern with "Tuna Boy" Williams's band in the
anything-goes Arkansas resort town of Hot Springs in the late 1920s.
He enjoyed a stint in the Chick Webb Orchestra, from 1936 to 1938,
much of his tenure overlapping Ella Fitzgerald's in the Savoy Ballroom house band. He went solo thereafter, and formed the Tympany
Four, playing the Elks Rendezvous in Harlem. Later adding another
to make the Tympany Five, he rehearsed his group tight, and landed a
record deal with Decca, the place to be.[15]

A chronic hernia forced Jordan into a truss. No one in the audience, seeing him bounce, kick, and stalk like a preacher in possession,
would know. He emulated black artists of yore, working Mantan
Moreland's pop-eyes and Bert Williams's incongruous dignity into
his own elaborate stage persona. He had a round, happy face and a
countenance that beamed like a lantern. Blessed with a peach-brandy
singing voice, Jordan delivered lyrics fast-paced, but in charge.

Jordan would captivate a generation, just as Duke Ellington had,
although with a drastically different approach. Ellington enchanted
black America with his magical baton, inducing a dreamlike sense of
escape. Jordan adopted a more pragmatic, though no less effective
style. He sang for the people who splashed through Houston's flooded
streets in their swim trunks. Though he'd spent a decade playing in big-

city swing bands before going solo, he was billed as "That Man Who Sings the Blues," a wink to everyone else who'd come up with a privy out back. His minstrel-show moves evoked home, but his dazzling word play and lavender suit let everyone know it was okay to grow into something else. With Jordan's new direction, the Harlem fantasy would no longer be the primary creative force behind black popular music. Instead, he embraced the funny, confusing, violent reality of farm folk in the city. And as Ellington had stood as the most influential figure in black popular music since the late 1920s, Jordan would be the key role model to virtually every black pop performer for the next fifteen years. Diverse stylists, Charles Brown, Fats Domino, B.B. King, and James Brown, for starters, all acknowledged their debt to him.

At the time the United States entered World War II, though, Louis Jordan was one of a million cabaret acts moored in places like Rapid City and Wichita. He had cut some good records and developed much of his relaxed, rambunctious style, but his career hadn't progressed as he and his management had hoped. The surprising sales of his "Knock Me a Kiss" and "I'm Gonna Move to the Outskirts of Town"—a claimed 300,000 by early 1942—tantalized Jordan with the possibility of bigger crowds and fatter paydays, a move from playing to hundreds of fans for hundreds of dollars, to playing to thousands for thousands. Significantly, Jordan had tried since 1938 to reach the big time as a solo act through recording. It was the chitlin' circuit, not the record industry, that vaulted him to stardom. He and his young manager, Berle Adams, the new kid at syndicate talent agency General Amusement Corporation, in a move both desperate and inspired, scheduled a Southern tour, Jordan's first as a solo act. They set Jordan's guarantee at a King Kolax–like $350 per night to minimize a promoter's risk on the unproven act, still a fat payout for a five piece. Jordan and Adams's strategy involved making a big splash down South, proving that Jordan could be a profitable attraction, and thus worth a slot in the major Northern theaters. For the Southern strategy to work, Jordan would need to accumulate impressive ticket sales, which called for gigs in large nightclubs and auditoriums. Both contingencies required a muscular promoter.

Don Robey had just the combination of cash, constitution, and contacts Jordan and Adams's scenario called for. Robey bought a sequence of Louis Jordan dates, scheduling Jordan in big halls throughout the Texas-Louisiana trail where he and partner Morris Merritt had gambled and pitched dances for the past few years. Robey reasoned that folks would object to paying a full big-band auditorium ticket price for a lounge combo. He needed a cheap orchestra to pad the program stats. Who would you call? Denver Ferguson set Robey up with Claude Trenier and his Bama State Collegians, thereby getting his cut of one of the most important tours in chitlin' circuit history. A carefully worded preview stressed, "The complete show consists of twenty people"—Jordan's five and Trenier's fifteen. A less cautious bulletin cried, "Dance fans throughout Texas and Louisiana will have the first opportunity to thrill to the music of Louis Jordan and his orchestra. . . . This is his first appearance in the South and he is expected to be the biggest attraction of the season. . . . The versatility of this group is unsurpassed. They swing, they sing, and they clown. Louie is not only a topflight saxophonist and also became popular as a singer, dancer, leader, and composer. . . . And this is just another 'Don Robey Attraction' which means the best Houston can get in the entertainment field."[16] Robey played Jordan first at the Harvest Club in Beaumont on June 19, 1942, then at Galveston's City Auditorium on June 23, then introduced *Louie* Jordan "That Man Who Sings the Blues!" to the Houston City Auditorium on June 25. A pile-up of broken beer bottles forced the auditorium manager to close the dance floor that night.

Three nights after Houston, Jordan played to a riotous mob one thousand strong at the Rhythm Club in New Orleans. *Louisiana Weekly* reported, "Several persons who went to the dance emphatically called the affair a wild, drunken orgy." The fists flew in all directions, faster than attendee Johnny McGee could count. "It looked just like a wild west movie," he said. "You know, the 'Honky Tonk' kind." At nearly one o'clock in the morning, a twenty-year-old barber named Sanders Harris staggered out of the club onto Jackson Avenue, bleeding through his gray plaid suit. A cabbie rushed Harris to Charity Hospital, where he died from stab wounds to his chest and stomach. New Orleans's finest arrived at the Rhythm Club at half past one and found only the bartender. The club owners, the Mancuso brothers, longtime entrepreneurs of the New Orleans night, declared that all in attendance enjoyed "a lovely time." The three police on duty in the hall had seen nothing at all amiss.[17]

Jordan's manager placed a hear-ye tour report in *Billboard*, tallying the small band's big paydays in Little Rock, St. Louis, Beaumont, and Galveston. Hopeful for Northern attention, the item rang with unintentional prescience. Jordan's "unusually good biz . . . may lead to other tours for five and six piece outfits."[18] The *Billboard* plant achieved its desired effect: Jordan got a call from the big leagues, Chicago's Regal Theater. The boss agreed to give Jordan a shot. At the low-ball guarantee of $350, there was little risk and far greater financial upside than a big band could mathematically offer—there were only so many seats to sell, and the less a band cost, the more money a promoter kept. Adams had learned to appeal directly to the thrifty, sour-stomached sensibility of the theater booker. Jordan packed the Regal on September 25, three months to the day after his Houston debut. Adams disseminated news of this and Jordan's Dixie triumphs, and talent buyers lined up.

It had taken Jordan but four years and a chitlin' circuit push to achieve overnight fame. Don Robey, who had been content to bring the stars to Houston, began to realize he could make his own.

✳   ✳   ✳

World War II hurt the record business—jukebox factories converted to martial production shortly after Pearl Harbor, while shellac rationing halted record manufacturing in 1943—but stimulated Don

Robey and Denver Ferguson's corner of the trade. The cool-down on
bus use did nothing to subdue demand for live music in black America,
particularly as war jobs stuffed millions of empty pockets with cash.
As reported in the *Indianapolis Recorder* on May 15, 1943, "Christine Chatman and her 'Boogie Woogie' Seven who recently played an
engagement at Jerome Stacker's Royal Tennessee club [in Clarksville]
were such a sensation the manager held the aggregation over for two
nights. More than 1,700 soldiers stationed at one of the largest camps
in America . . . jammed the spacious club and have crowned Christine
the 'Darling of Boogie Woogie and Blues.' "

Ticket prices shot from the 50- to 75-cent range in 1942 to the 75-
to 99-cent range the next year, with some acts costing a Count Basie–
like $1.25, as a Tiny Bradshaw show at the Sunset Terrace did in June
1943: "The 'Killer diller' music man Tiny Bradshaw [was] recently
crowned king of the jitterbugs. . . . He leads a hectic life jumping
from one rug-cutting emporium to another meeting and greeting the
subjects of his empire of jitterbugs. King Tiny comes direct from Chicago where he's been busy breaking records nightly. . . . Advance tickets are 99 cents. Dancers from out of town are advised to make their
reservations early, thereby being assured of a table when they arrive
in the city for this mammoth swing attraction. $1.25 at the door."

The anticipated "great crisis" that the bus ban portended never
materialized. Denver could afford to buy his bands cars with this sort
of money flying around.

More after-dark entrepreneurs wanted to catch some of that
cash—black nightclubs opened all over the sunbelt. The phones at 328
Senate Avenue rang like London sirens. Six bookers handled incoming calls to Ferguson Brothers Agency. Founded on sawdust social
halls in the South, the circuit grew to unforeseeable places. Just over
a year after launching the agency, Denver tunneled toward the Pacific,
opening a Ferguson Brothers West Coast branch in Los Angeles to
follow the black migration toward Southern California naval yards.
Money poured in, and the Ferguson roster cycled through the Deep

South, Midwest, and California, and a few spots in the Northeast. Don Robey's old gambling haunts proved consistently profitable.

The Saint warned dance fans in Greenwood, Mississippi; Anniston, Alabama; and Atlanta and Columbus, Georgia: "Prepare for a BLACKOUT! Draw the Curtains! Douse the lights! Here comes the Blitzkrieg of Swing—Snookum Russell and his 'All Reet' orchestra."[19]

Barney Johnson and his Brownskin Models plied Robey's territory in late January and early February 1943 with a menagerie of burlesque, comedic, and musical talent unmatched below the third floor of Sea Ferguson's Cotton Club: Funny Bone Ferebee, Aarzanya "Queen of the Jungle Dancers," Leroy Watts and Chocolate Jones, and the Lee Twins, a dance team. The International Sweethearts of Rhythm swung through Robey's domain in March. Christine Chatman followed in June, Milton Larkin came back home in July (*sans* his outstanding supporting cast from the old Harlem Grill days), the Sweethearts returned in October, and King Kolax came in November, followed closely by the Carolina Cotton Pickers in December. Everyone spent at least a dozen nights retracing Robey and Merritt's dice parade through Louisiana and the Lone Star State. Lil Green tore through again, this time with Tiny Bradshaw's band.

While admission prices soared, Denver scrambled to develop new talent, or if not talent, new bands. He proved himself a better executive than evaluator. He heard about a couple of young guys on Indiana Avenue, one a guitar player, the other a pianist. He arranged to attend a rehearsal, which the duo conducted late every night at the piano player's place of straight employment, Willis Mortuary, around the corner from Ferguson Bros. headquarters. Denver sat in the chapel's front row, hat on lap, and listened. The guitarist, a dark boy, perched on a stool on one side of the room, Denver's left, while the pianist, lighter than Denver, with long, straight hair, played the funerary organ on Denver's right. A closed casket gleamed between the young musicians. Denver feared that the guitarist, while obviously talented, was too young to travel and front a band. The organist, though, came off as polished and self-assured. He called the tunes and played well. After the jam, Denver told the organ player to come up to Ferguson Bros. the next day, and within months the organist, a beaming lad named Sax Kari, was touring the chitlin' circuit. The guitar player, a local kid named Wes Montgomery, went back to jamming along with Charlie Christian records in his bedroom, though he would be lauded as one of the two or three most important modern jazz guitarists. The casket was a display model, the funeral home's finest.

Ferguson Bros. broke Sax into the practiced routine beginning with a booking at the Sunset, and a flood of inflated news of his success: "Fresh from a sensational run at the Sunset Terrace Club . . . Sax Kari and His Swing Caravan were acclaimed by Oklahoma City night-lifers as tops in the entertainment field."[20] Just as Sax hit the road, a young singer from Jackson, Tennessee, came into her own. "May Belle, new Ferguson Bros. singing find knocked the house out. . . . This buxom bit of rhythm is sure to go places as she is in the class with America's leading feminine vocalists." Sure enough, the *Chicago Defender* reported on July 31, 1943, from Buffalo, New York: "Maye Belle, 'The Hey Lawdy Mama,' really came on in this city last night when she set the Memorial Auditorium on fire with the blues in everybody's key. . . . Maye delighted the fans with her original style of swinging and singing the blues. And, when she fell in the groove on her favorite number, 'Hey Lawdy Mama,' the house started jumping until the wee hours of morning." Maye Belle would become better known as Big Maybelle. One of the toughest female vocalists of early rock 'n' roll, she recorded a number called "Whole Lotta Shakin' Goin' On" two years before a Bible college dropout named Jerry Lee Lewis got hold of it.

The Carolina Cotton Pickers commanded the highest fees, played the most dates, and earned Denver more cash than any other big, raggedy road band. The band added a great blues belter, former Walter Barnes orchestra vocalist Dwight "Gatemouth" Moore, to its already energetic show, and ventured above the Mason-Dixon line for a rare Philadelphia gig in 1943. A *Billboard* reviewer gushed:

> For the past dozen years the Original Carolina Cotton Pickers . . . have been confining their powerhouse tooting to the race dances below the Mason-Dixon line. Sometimes venturing into the Chicago territory, this is the first time the Cotton Pickers have hit an Eastern port. Expert in blaring for race gigs at the tobacco warehouses and armories down South, [the] band is strictly in a race groove.
>
> Playing with abandon and packing terrific power in their ensemble, the Cotton Pickers know none of the fine polish and finesse acquired by such contemporaries as Count Basie, Lionel Hampton, Jimmie Lunceford, et others. Their music is basically solid swing in its raw stage. Boys have no truck with the hit parade tunes or standards. [Their] books are loaded with original rock and stomp opuses with frequent dips into the large fund of race blues. Instrumentation takes in four trumpets, three trombones, five saxes, and four rhythm.[21]

The Cotton Pickers raised a few more eyebrows on the road, including the bushy pair belonging to Joe Glaser.

Glaser epitomized the syndicate that dominated black music on the road from the 1930s until the 1970s. Born in Chicago on December 17, 1896, young Glaser made himself a roaring-twenties renaissance man. Chicago police arrested him for hosting racially integrated dances at his jazz club the Sunset Cafe, and in March 1928 a judge closed Glaser's Plantation Cafe for a year to stem chronic Prohibition violations.[22]

Glaser is remembered as tough and uncompromising, though not without generosity. His dealings with black musicians are viewed, in retrospect at least, with suspicion. But he knew how to show them love. In the mid-1920s Glaser posted a sign advertising the two-week residency of an up-and-coming horn player outside the Sunset Cafe: "Louis Armstrong, World's Greatest Trumpeter." The gesture stuck with Armstrong, who reached out to Glaser during his search for a personal manager in 1935. The two hadn't seen each other in a decade, but they formed a partnership that lasted the rest of their lives and made them both rich.

Glaser traveled steadily, scouting new talent. He studied audience reaction to an act, and saw the Carolina Cotton Pickers drive the people wild. Glaser was about eight years into his partnership with Armstrong when he called on Denver Ferguson in mid-June 1943. He had added other black entertainers to his roster, including the troubled genius he came to Indianapolis to discuss, Billie Holiday. Ferguson and Glaser were about the same age. They shared a worldview, plenty of acquaintances, and tastes. Denver admired Glaser. He had named his Sunset Terrace after Glaser's renowned Chicago joint. Denver was apprehensive of Glaser as well. Whatever he and Glaser had in common, he felt that Glaser was more akin to his Avenue rival Tuffy Mitchell, another affable, cold-blooded, albeit shorter, Jew. But while Denver felt powerless against Tuffy, unable to retaliate without putting his life and freedom at risk, he felt equal to Glaser, advantaged in some ways, in the unsupervised world of the chitlin' circuit.

Glaser pitched syndicate-circuit unity: a Carolina Cotton Pickers–Billie Holiday double bill. He promised to make the Carolina Cotton Pickers stars, featuring them in big-city theaters and cabarets. In return, Glaser asked Denver to book the Cotton Pickers–Holiday bill and other syndicate talent on one-nighters through the chitlin' circuit en route through the entertainment capitals of the East, Midwest, and West Coast. Denver initially declined Glaser's proposition, purportedly telling the syndicate boss, "You can keep New York, I have the entire South."[23] By the spring of 1944, however, the *Chicago Defender* had announced a Glaser-Ferguson tie-up, noting that Glaser had booked the Carolina Cotton Pickers into Detroit's Paradise

Theatre.[24] The William Morris Agency subcontracted with Denver too, for the purpose of booking their acts through the chitlin' circuit.

As the war effort marched on and black dollars multiplied, new nightclubs fortified the chitlin' circuit. In Chicago, a group of high-profile investors, including Joe Louis, opened the Rhumboogie Club, and Denver Ferguson fronted a cadre that purchased Joe Glaser's old Sunset Cafe–Grand Terrace Club.[25] In Memphis, nightclubs returned to famed Beale Street. In Houston, local street pugilist and "nationally known figure in the amusement world" Don Robey caught the fever.

The Bronze Peacock

A hard winter rain pelted Houston as Don Robey entertained the first patrons inside his lavish new nightclub. The Bronze Peacock—a vanity tag if there ever was one—opened on February 18, 1946, and the celebration carried well into the next morning.

Robey had banished Morris Merritt, but otherwise the ring was unbroken. Don Albert, Robey's man in San Antone, emceed opening night around an assault-on-the-senses floor show: "Champion Jitterbug Couple" Mack and Ace, "Famed Tap Dancer" "Snake Hip" Galloway, "Renowned 'Shake' Dancer" Princero Thyllisioth, and the I. H. Smalley orchestra. Robey claimed to have poured $50,000 into the Bronze Peacock, eight thousand square feet of bar, dance floor, and bandstand. "That was a beautiful, nicely appointed club," drummer Earl Palmer said. "Not a run-down joint with gingham tablecloths." It served international cuisine, fine champagne, and wine, and in its hidden square footage, it housed a room each for cards, dice, and the wheel. It was the Don's own little duchy at the far reaches of the Fifth Ward, built among vacant lots four miles east of downtown Houston. "At night you could look out the Peacock and see lights from another part of town," Palmer said. "In between was an expanse of darkness."[1] Robey minted his own money, plastic chips stamped in bronze with the club's feathery logo, called "Peacock pennies" by the clientele, good for the victuals, rum, and tables, once the $1.50 admission was paid.

The Bronze Peacock's opening gala finally wound down well past 2:30 in the morning. Bronze Houstonians dressed in their finest—the Atomic Super Deluxe One-Button Roll was the rage among men—staggered out into muddy ankle-deep water. Despite its sludgy beginning, the Bronze Peacock was a triumph. "Now another era has hit the bayou," *Informer* reporter Jay Don Davis wrote.[2]

Another era hit the bayou, indeed.

✳   ✳   ✳

Pan wide: During the war's last year, markets for glass bricks, neon tubing, and plastic palm trees had picked up all over New Orleans and Miami, as well as into less notorious sanctums of black entertainment in Macon, Georgia, San Antonio, Texas, and smaller towns yet, as nightclub construction boomed.

Problem: Immediately after the war, black prosperity, impetus behind the nightclub boom, busted as defense jobs evaporated. This time it *was* like the Depression had done vaudeville. Folks' leisure cash vanished, equaling bad news for big bands. Unlike the Depression, when old vaudeville theaters simply sold out to talky houses, nightclub owners had just made major investments and started their businesses, and there was no next big thing to fold into. They *were* the next big thing. They needed to make this work.

Just in time, Louis Jordan and the Tympany Five's overwhelming success had begun to transform black pop music. Since his breakthrough chitlin' circuit tour in the summer of 1942, Jordan made a series of hit records, among them "Caldonia," "G.I. Jive," and "Is You Is or Is You Ain't My Baby?"—which remarkably reached the no. 1 spot on the country and western chart, meaning white people bought it. His personal appearance fee had skyrocketed from $350 to between $1750 and $2000 per night. His blend of down-home diction and uptown tempo had yielded six no. 1 records on the race charts, and none of his dozen 1946 releases peaked below no. 3. It was the year of "Salt Pork, West Virginia," "Choo Choo Ch'Boogie," and "Ain't Nobody Here but Us Chickens." Jordan and the Tympany Five recorded some of the earliest music videos—with the band garbed up as dandy cowboys, singing to a stable of livestock for "Don't Worry 'bout That Mule"—that were distributed throughout the country's movie theaters. Jordan's hot streak was unlike anything the black music world had seen, and his style quite unlike anything black music had heard.

Jordan's influence on the chitlin' circuit was best summarized by Dwight "Gatemouth" Moore, a chitlin' circuit warrior from its earliest days as a vocalist with the Walter Barnes orchestra and then with the Carolina Cotton Pickers. "He was playing . . . with five pieces," Moore recalled. "That ruined the big bands . . . he could play just as good and just as loud with five as 17. And it was cheaper." Among the big bands Jordan put out of commission was one Moore and Sax Kari led that last toured in 1947.

In addition to altering the typical band configuration, Jordan's popularity made the vocalist the main draw after an era dominated by bandleaders and featured instrumental soloists. As Moore explained, "With the bands in the '30s, the band singer was like the porter. The singer had to set up the bandstand," he said. "The singer, he wasn't the attraction in those days. But it done changed. But I'm talking about, when I was a vocalist, we set up the bandstand. We loaded the bus."[3]

Louis Jordan never loaded any bus.

Instrumentally, Jordan threw a little grit over the smooth swing horn sound, paving the way for the staccato, honking and screaming style of saxophonists in the next era.

Crucially, the dance business and not the record business stirred the new cocktail. Booking agents, not record companies, controlled artists day to day, deciding how many musicians they could afford to

carry, where they went, and how long they stayed. Acts built on the
Tympany Five model simply required less cash flow to tour than did
big bands—fewer members meant fewer uniforms to buy and clean,
fewer instruments to buy and maintain, fewer vehicles to fuel and
rooms to rent, which translated neatly into lower performance fees,
with the savings passed down the line to cash-strapped partiers. After
decades of big-band music, audiences were ripe for novelty. Naturally,
promoters and club owners pushed these cheaper acts out of financial necessity. These sweeping artistic and economic trends catalyzed
black pop's modification from swing to rock 'n' roll. Small bands like
Joe Liggins and the Honeydrippers, Johnny Moore and the Three
Blazers, and Jack McVea's combo, single acts like Ivory Joe Hunter,
and several more we shall presently meet, stormed onto the national
black music scene with electric guitars and wailing saxophones. The
few surviving chitlin' circuit big bands adapted to the new style.
Lucky Millinder continually cycled young vocalists and soloists into
his big band, and Buddy Johnson, leader of an eighteen-piece orchestra, sold himself as "King of the One-Nighters" and "Inventor of the
Walkin' Rhythm."

Of course, the chitlin' circuit business model evolved too. After
Louis Jordan's rise pushed the vocalist into the limelight, the band
became an afterthought. Early rock star-attractions Joe Turner,
Wynonie Harris, T-Bone Walker, Cecil Gant, and Ivory Joe Hunter
traveled without bands. Hell, *anyone* could be the band, as long
as the star, whose voice you heard on the jukebox and face you'd
seen on the posters, was there on stage. Dives could afford to book
cheaply traveling single attractions. Consequently, the top names—
not just fringe players like King Kolax, Christine Chatman, and
Snookum Russell—appeared in rural joints and small-town nightclubs on the chitlin' circuit. As the popularity of small bands grew,
they pushed into bigger venues. As *Billboard* noted in the summer
of 1946, "Switch from big band policy to cocktail type combos . . .
throughout the country was predicted by Midwest bookers, per-

sonal managers, and theater execs this week. . . . Records and radio are giving smaller units plenty of box office appeal. . . . Biggest name in the small org field is Louis Jordan. Jordan's Tympany Five . . . got its start in 1942 when [Jordan's manager] Berle Adams . . . got them some ballroom dates. . . . With the air and records building them in the public eye and bookers plugging them to theater ops, the trios, quartets, quintets, and slightly larger units seem to be headed toward the nation's spotlight."

At the heart of the reasons for the switch, in *Billboard*'s view, was that "the nut [i.e., guarantee] for a small unit is much lower than for a 20-piece band."[4]

The new rules spawned new players in the business, beginning with talent agencies. Ben Bart learned the circuit as a booker for the Gale Agency, routing Hot Lips Page, Erskine Hawkins, Buddy Johnson, and Lucky Millinder on Southern one-night tours during World War II. From this position, he forecast the big band's demise and then quit Gale in June 1945, founding Universal Attractions to develop the rockin' small-band- and single-star-attraction market on the chitlin' circuit. Universal Attractions flourished for decades to come, representing the biggest stars of black pop, and of the black band agencies that ran the field in the 1940s, only Universal Attractions and Joe Glaser's Associated Booking Corporation still operate today.

While the music and the business overhauled, the language evolved. The term *rock*, deployed in a musical rather than sexual context—it was black slang for coitus going back to at least the 1920s—gained popularity right around the time Louis Jordan and his small band blew up in the summer of 1942, and some permutation of it in noun, verb, or adjective form could be found sprinkled throughout the black music vocabulary thereafter. *Houston Informer* reporter Ted Williams wrote in his paper's August 5, 1942, edition, "On Friday night of the past week, I happened to be on hand when [Doctor Clayton] sang a couple of songs at the Eldorado and take it from me he had the house *rockin'* in rhythm." Williams turned it loose again a month later in his coverage of the Houston wartime electricity ration "dim-out," assuring readers that despite the stroll's lackluster appearance, "all one needed to do was enter any of the old rendezvous and . . . he would find the place rocking."[5] According to a white-penned *Billboard* review of a Carolina Cotton Pickers show, published August 18, 1943, the group's "rock and stomp" music was, to parse a little, "strictly in a race groove." Usage of the lingo spread, while black nightclubs multiplied and Louis Jordan's stardom boomed, even though the black economy had busted after the war. One of the most beloved black artists of the day, Nat "King" Cole, toured the South with his small band in late 1945. The King Cole Trio's newspaper ads appeared in New Orleans and Houston, and their window placards were tacked to every lightpost in between, emblazoned with a coat of arms and the words "Royal Rockin' Rhythm." Dolores Calvin, reporting on a Louis Jordan concert, wrote in the *Chicago Defender* on January 19, 1946, "The Royal Theater [in Baltimore] was rocking and the boys moved in to do a week there [for] an audience of scream-ing kids and applauding adults." Scoop Jones wrote in the June 22, 1946, edition of the black *Louisiana Weekly* that Dave Bartholomew's band at the Graystone in New Orleans "made the house 'rock.' " On May 31, 1946, Club Rock-It (later redubbed Club Rocket), which would showcase the new Joe Liggins and the Honeydrippers and Jack McVea's Louis Jordan–style quintet, plus Dave Bartholomew's band, opened at the corner of Jackson Avenue and Derbigny Street in New Orleans, former site of the Rhythm Club that Jordan rocked in the summer of 1942.

Though the white trade press would dub the new sounds rhythm and blues, black music had begun to rock. The new sound spread quickly along a specific geography, and occurred hyperactively in Houston, New Orleans, and in between, where all the right people mixed with just the proper friction. Though no single rock innova-tor, birthplace, or inaugural record should be irrefutably claimed, the music followed a few key performers, and Don Robey's Bronze Pea-

cock immediately became a major hub for rock 'n' roll's early businesspeople and artists.

✳   ✳   ✳

Joe Turner honed his vocal power while singing and sling-
ing suds in a Kansas City bar during Prohibition. Breaking over the
din, the toasts, and fights, Turner's voice became, in Nick Tosches'
term, "oceanic." John Hammond, the best white friend black music
ever had, pitched a party like no other, the Spirituals to Swing concert, on December 23, 1938, at New York City's Carnegie Hall. There
Joe reunited with Pete Johnson, the Kansas City pianist who had provided much lightning to his thunder since the Vine Street speakeasy
days. Joe sang that night as he did in the barroom, without a microphone. His song predicted Arthur Crudup's 1946 "That's Alright
Mama," a tune we wouldn't be talking about if not for the rendition
Elvis Presley recorded in Memphis in 1954, the greaser's debut on
commercial wax. The title refrain goes back, at least, to Little Brother
Montgomery. Do you remember him? Walter Barnes used to crash at
the whorehouse Little Brother's girlfriend madamed off Farish Street
in Jackson when touring south Mississippi in the chitlin' circuit's
earliest days. Little Brother recorded "Something Keeps A-Worryin'
Me" in October 1936 (less than two months before the midget maestro reappeared on the Jackson stroll), which includes what became,
nearly verbatim, the opening stanza of Crudup's, and later Presley's
version of, "That's Alright Mama." And even before Crudup adapted
the theme, Louis Jordan recorded "It's a Low-Down Dirty Shame"
in July 1942, which includes the same stanza. The obvious question
becomes, did the "That's all right . . ." theme originate with Little
Brother Montgomery? I don't doubt that it came from such a gifted,
prolific writer, but I can't prove it either. That answer was embedded
in long-decayed slats of Vicksburg cathouses and turpentine camp
commissaries from Natchez to Hattiesburg.

"That's alright, baby, that's alright for you," Joe belted across

Carnegie Hall. He would work variations of the melody and delivery of the song he performed at Spirituals to Swing into his own epochal 1954 recording you may have heard of, "Shake, Rattle and Roll." Joe clapped the fast beat, hooted, and bulged his big eyes in disbelief as Pete's fingers flew across the keys. "Roll 'em boy," Joe sang, "let 'em jump for joy."

Fifteen years before rock 'n' roll appeared as a pop-music marketing term, Joe Turner, an illiterate bootleg barkeep, laid the music down in Carnegie Hall. The audience seemed unprepared. He called, "Yes, yes," to them but got no response. "Well alright then?" he bellowed. Nothing. Clearly, Joe and his audience this night had hung out in different speakeasies. They politely applauded as he sang "we gone" and Pete banged the last note.

Later, Joe joined up with a man who knew where to find crowds that could "yes, yes" and "alright then" at the appropriate time. Denver Ferguson booked Turner into Don Robey's Bronze Peacock on the club's first weekend, February 22, 1946. Joe stood on the brand new Peacock stage, a high-buffed hardwood slab that shined like a bowling lane, and hollered "My Gal's a Jockey," his current version of the motif that would become "Shake, Rattle and Roll."

In three weeks, Robey introduced another rocker to Houston. Wynonie Harris was born in Omaha, Nebraska, in 1913, purportedly the product of high-plains teenage miscegenation. His mother was a fifteen-year-old black girl, his father, a young Native American named Blue Jay. Wynonie started on the Omaha stroll, where he made as much of an impression with his dancing as he would with his singing.[6] Wynonie inherited or developed a weakness for firewater, a hot temper, and a devilish mischievousness, all of which fed his art and inflated his aura. His first records as a featured vocalist were cut during a brief tenure with Lucky Millinder's orchestra, where he brought appropriate urgency to the musical question "Who Threw the Whiskey in the Well?" Fans heard the mischief and the raspy effects of many late nights in Wynonie's vocals.

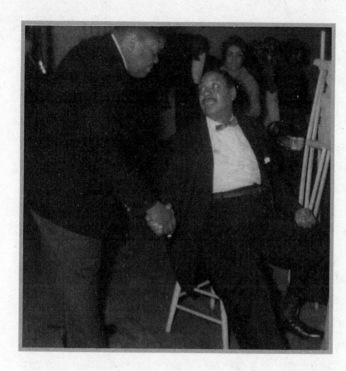

New Orleans disc jockey Popcorn Wylie pays tribute to Joe Turner (seated) in 1963. *Photo-Sax Kari/ Author's collection*

Wynonie was long-limbed, lean, light-skinned, and straight oily-haired with pale blue eyes. His trademark smirk tinged all he did. Fans could hear it in his records, see it on the placards announcing his next appearance, and finally behold it up on stage. It's clearly present in an article he, or an empathetic publicist, wrote for the October 1954 *Tan* magazine that Nick Tosches later excerpted in *Unsung Heroes of Rock 'n' Roll.* Wrote Wynonie, "The crooners star on the Great White Way and get swamped with Coca-Cola drinking bobby-soxers and other 'jail bait.' I star in Georgia, Texas, Alabama, Tennessee, and Missouri and get those who have money to buy stronger stuff and my records to play while they drink it. . . . I like to sing to women with meat on their bones and that long green stuff in their pocketbooks. You find them mostly down South."[7]

On the rare occasions when Wynonie couldn't find anyone to pour strong drinks, he enjoyed cock-blocking his more fortunate colleagues. Bandleader and drummer Johnny Otis, who traveled with

Harris, recalled that the singer would sneak up on another musician and his girl for the night, and say, " 'Excuse me young lady, but this no good motherfucker is married to my sister, and I don't appreciate what's going on here.' "[8]

Singer Roy Brown recalled, "He'd walk into a bar and shout 'Here come the blues . . . the drinks are on me—get to the bar.'

"Now you talk about conceited," Brown continued, "I thought I was conceited, but this guy! He and Joe Turner would be on the same stage. He'd walk up to him and say, 'What you gonna sing fat boy?' Joe Turner couldn't read or write and Wynonie would say, 'Sign this autograph!' "[9]

Behind it all lay an inner tenderness, old Omaha friends hinted. But if it's true that insecurity drove Wynonie, it took him too far. He jilted managers as often as girlfriends. He scratched gigs when the mood told him. He faced indictment in Virginia, where he allegedly instructed his entourage to beat the valet of Larry Darnell, an artist scheduled to face off against Wynonie in a "Battle of the Blues." Wynonie's growing fame only made him more reluctant, brooding, and self-destructive.

Perhaps the speed at which Wynonie transformed from Omaha hoofer to national celebrity left him dizzy. Millinder hired Harris into his big band in the spring of 1944. "Who Threw the Whiskey in the Well?" came out in April 1945. He built his reputation as "Mr. Blues" on Millinder's parade of Southern one-nighters and, having made that name for himself, bolted the group for Los Angeles. There he recorded "Around the Clock," and by the spring of 1946 he had booking agents scuffling over his date book, eventually landing with Harold Oxley, who had helped build the chitlin' circuit as Jimmie Lunceford's booking agent. Wynonie canceled on one Houston club owner to play the Bronze Peacock instead, on March 11, 1946, drawing rebuke from a local scribe: "That way lies extinction in the entertainment world." But Wynonie proved exceptional to this old rule.

Next came T-Bone Walker, an electrifying performer from up the road in Conroe, Texas, north of Houston.

As a boy in Dallas's Oak Cliff neighborhood during the 1920s, Aaron Thibeaux Walker absorbed mercurial rhythm from Blind Lemon Jefferson, a family friend and popular blues guitarist. As the nickname suggests, Jefferson needed help getting around, and Walker guided him to the bustling street corners where a handicapped musician might pick up a little change. Born on May 28, 1910, Walker inherited his Cherokee grandmother's steep cheekbones and tawny skin. As a child, he flirted with the Spirit, nuzzled beneath an open window at a bouncy Pentecostal Sunday service. "My pulse would be racing when the hand-clapping got going real good," he said.[10] Walker's corrupted middle name became his moniker: T-Bone. He learned to tap dance, and lit out with traveling medicine shows and vaudeville troupes. Back in Dallas in the early 1930s he won a talent show at the Majestic Theater, and with it a week-long stint in Cab Calloway's group. T-Bone's showmanship impressed Calloway, and the bandleader let the teenager perform a banjo routine that T-Bone completed in the splits. No one wanted to follow that finale, especially after T-Bone had matured into a sharply attired leading man, and dropped the banjo for a solid-body Gibson electric guitar. In Los Angeles in the early 1940s he'd sling the guitar behind his head and slow-split smooth as melting ice. By early 1943, T-Bone was wowing them at heavyweight champ Joe Louis's Rhumboogie club— a *Billboard* reviewer noted the audience's "wild response." T-Bone separated women from their undergarments using only his guitar. Alternating between L.A.'s Central Avenue and the Rhumboogie, with record companies fighting over him, and syndicate boss Harold Oxley booking his dates, T-Bone was at his acrobatic best in the late spring of 1946 when he first played the Bronze Peacock.

While no one could upstage T-Bone, his opening act was worth showing up for.

Robey misbilled him as Amos *Melbrum*. Born on April 1, 1927, one of a dozen children to devoutly Baptist parents, Amos Milburn grew up fast. He quit school after seventh grade and eventually joined the navy underage. He served three years and saw the Pacific before coming home and forming a five-piece band. Amos soaked up the potent Houston scene—drinking with Joe Turner, jamming with Wynonie Harris, while tearing up San Antonio via Don Albert's Keyhole Club. He warmed the Peacock audience for T-Bone Walker on June 1, 1946, sitting at the piano on the verge of stardom. Swing fans had always been wild, but Amos Milburn was one of the first artists to capture their bottle-busting enthusiasm and throw it back at them.

Opportunity found Amos in Robey's web. A freelance talent scout named Lola Anne Cullum—she discovered the pride of Houston's Third Ward, Lightnin' Hopkins—saw Amos back at the Keyhole, and pitched Amos his deal with the devil. She cut demo tapes and sent them to Aladdin Records in Los Angeles. Amos and Lola Anne traveled to L.A. to record in mid-September 1946, and Aladdin rushed the resulting sides out to favorable press. "Milburn shouts the wordage to his bright keyboard grooving," wrote a *Billboard* reviewer.[11] Milburn and his gang of five played every Houston joint, the Peacock, the Boston Lion, and the Big Apple, but they harbored a special affection for a rustic camp outside the city replete with picnic grounds, sixteen cabins for rent, and a commissary that served deep-fried shrimp, steak, and chicken all night. Though formally known as Sid's Ranch, Milburn cooked up a theme song for the place called "Chicken Shack Boogie," a sure enough portrayal of a classic chitlin' circuit dive. Milburn lays down friendly, half-spoken verses, elaborating on the shack's out-of-the-way location and humble architecture, then leads his band through torrid instrumental breaks to illustrate the fun all would have. On stage, Milburn perched at the edge of the piano stool nearest the audience, turned his body toward the crowd, pumped that right leg, lashed his pompadour toward the keyboard, tore through his set, and ruined the audience for anyone less charismatic than T-Bone. As a jazz quartet leader who was to follow Amos at the Keyhole recalled, "He was supposed to open for us, but we couldn't go on."[12]

Beer flowed, almost freely, since the Houston Office of Price Administration capped prices at twenty-two cents for a Jax, Pearl, or Falstaff. Passengers on the Dowling–San Felipe trolley sang like drunken sailors from the Downtown Grill to the Eldorado Ballroom on Elgin in the Third Ward to the Boston Lion at Calhoun and Ennis. Cheap taverns rocked as hard as Don Robey's high-class club. The Big Apple club proudly advertised its electric guitarists. A fellow known as Iron Jaw, "the man who not only dances with a table clasped in his teeth, but who seats a woman at the table," entertained at the Whispering Pines. The Harbordale Drive-In employed your fundamental rock 'n' roll combo of sax, guitar, piano, and drums, and the same setup worked Mary's, a whorehouse whose employees listlessly smoked and sipped canned beer until tapped.

These rougher establishments had their stars as well. Cecil Gant, born in 1913 in Nashville, Tennessee, made a popular record in 1944, "I Wonder," a suspicious soldier's lament delivered in Fats Waller's half-spoken style. Gant could play the piano as softly as a rippling bordello curtain, but preferred the thunderstorm boogie-woogie that heavy-stacked men like Albert Ammons, Meade Lux Lewis, and Joe Turner's buddy Pete Johnson elevated to an art form among New York jazz circles. It was basically the same strain that longtime Ferguson Bros. client Roosevelt Sykes, who Denver billed as Fats Waller no. 2, spread across the chitlin' circuit during the war years. Unlike the founding fathers of stride piano, Gant brought another instrument, electric guitar, to the top of the mix. Like seemingly all the early rockers, Gant drank unquenchably. He sang through his palate in the tone of a mallard's quack. Perhaps Robey found Gant, a dark man with a drifting eye, a bit barrelhouse for his trendy establishment. So Denver Ferguson booked Gant down at the Green Pasture, well south of Houston on Chocolate Bayou, which seems a suitably named body of water for Gant's boggy sound.

Robey the promoter cycled hot small bands like Joe Liggins and the Honeydrippers, and Johnny Moore and the Three Blazers, through the Houston City Auditorium, and every musician in town gathered at the Bronze Peacock for the afterparty. Nineteen forty-seven began fittingly, with Louis Jordan's return. After a sold-out auditorium show New Year's night, Jordan starred at the Bronze Peacock afterparty. Even the dice stopped rolling when Robey climbed the stage and introduced Jordan to ear-splitting applause.

Robey took out a half-page in the *Houston Informer* the next week to say, "Louis Jordan and Don Robey wish to thank their dance patrons in New Orleans, Monroe, Shreveport, Dallas, Ft. Worth, San Antonio, Houston, Galveston, and Port Arthur for the splendid reception." Jordan, via Robey, pronounced, "The Bronze Peacock is about the finest entertainment place this side of Chicago and Don Robey about the finest person and dance promoter in the country." He promised to record an homage, "Boogie Woogie at the Bronze Peacock."

In the dark hours of morning, Robey locked the Peacock doors, sat back in his windowless office, and counted his money. He liked to stay up all night, sorting the denominations, wrapping paper bands snugly around the piles, and filling burlap sacks. After sunrise, he loaded a fresh clip into a .45 caliber pistol, snapped two shells into his 12-gauge shotgun, and with the guns, money, and an associate, drove downtown.

Out of the car, in daylight on the city street, Robey dumped the moneybags in a red wagon. His associate pocketed the .45. Robey, finger in the shotgun trigger loop, slung the weapon over his shoulder. Remember, this *is* Texas. He pulled the wagon behind him along the sidewalk and into the bank, with his associate covering his back. More than one startled bank guard fumbled for his own holster at the sight before he realized what was happening.

Louis Jordan, left, the pivotal entertainer in pop music's transition from big-band swing to small-band rock 'n' roll, his soon-to-be ex-wife Fleecie Moore, and Don Robey, the promoter who helped Jordan break national, at Robey's Bronze Peacock nightclub in Houston, January 1, 1947. *Getty Images-Michael Ochs Archives*

✳   ✳   ✳

Indianapolis, January 1947

Strains of "Open the Door, Richard" stumbled onto Indiana Avenue from every barroom and pool-hall jukebox. It was a hammed-up number, unabashedly imitative of some of Louis Jordan's comical cuts. Jack McVea, a professorial L.A. baritone sax player and Ferguson Brothers Agency client, recorded it and saw it become the biggest hit in chitlin' circuit land, itself widely imitated. On the icy Avenue, though, "Open the Door, Richard" clashed with a gloomy atmosphere.

Denver Ferguson,
looking prosperous
and battle-tested,
1947. *Courtesy of
Carole Finnell*

At fifty-one years old, a quarter century into Avenue affairs, Denver Ferguson still had a full head of wavy curls, but no more dark ones. He had grown quite plump and taken to wearing wide-brimmed hats to keep his silk shoulders dry. The Avenue baseball-ticket numbers game had flourished during the war years. The Sunset Terrace still held the high ground among Avenue nightclubs, and Ferguson Brothers Agency remained a vital band-booking firm. Denver weathered waves of challenge on the Avenue and in the music business. This time, a Negro patrolman named Jacque Durham started the fuss. Durham had served five years on the force, enjoying a promotion to detective early in his career. But in late 1946, he was busted down to car patrol duty on Indiana Avenue. He did not take the demotion well. He witnessed widespread corruption among his colleagues on the Avenue. He squawked to his superiors about the time-honored graft that kept the Avenue's vice trade up, which in turn financed nightclubs, bands, and everything else that lent the strip its glory. Durham's gripes were news to absolutely no one. After he went public with allegations that high-ranking white cops, the graft recipients, enjoyed city hall protection, however, the Indianapolis elect needed to prove its cleanliness to white voters.

Marion County prosecutor Judson Stark summoned the alleged bribers, including Denver, to city hall, where they mumbled, "I have never paid any bribes to any police officer of any rank and don't know who has." Indianapolis mayor Robert Tyndall directed his employees, the accused politicians and policemen, to report their income of the previous four years. Chief of police Jesse McMurtry ordered his men to knock out every gambling joint on the Avenue. Consequently, "the regular dice and poker games have taken a nose dive underground, completely out of sight. . . . Even the junk dealers—peddlers of dope—have taken to the bushes," the *Recorder* noted. Hip-pocket bootleggers plied their late-night and Sunday trade with unusual caution. Baseball tickets, though, proved more difficult to corral than cards and dice. The gambling gentry who orchestrated ticket games, however, faced a foe unforgiving as death and, unlike Indianapolis police, above bribery—the IRS. The federal revenuers seemed less concerned with legal issues than whether or not they had received their share of the proceeds, ill-gained or not.[13] Bribery as the Avenue had known it for decades was over, and a serious blow landed against the city's fertile underground. The end had begun, and if one disgruntled cop could bring down a civilization as resilient as the Avenue, the entire chitlin' circuit was vulnerable, even during its brightest days.

Chapter 8 ✳ ✳ ✳ ✳ ✳ ✳ ✳

The Gate Swings

The folks from Conroe, Texas, swarmed forty-two miles down to the Bronze Peacock to see native son T-Bone Walker in early 1947. T-Bone, wearing his smooth process and pearly white tails, had fans reaching for the smelling salts, the local press reported. "His blues singing and 'geetar' playing 'send my very soul' as one lady elegantly put it. To give Walker due credit, he puts on a real show, giving patrons a run for their money (and believe you me he surely receives plenty of money from the hipped up women who come to be transported 'out of this world' by his down to earth blues)."[1]

As his show reached its climax, T-Bone pushed his guitar above his head, still playing, extending his arms, building to the song's crescendo. As he inched the guitar down behind his head, he spread his feet and slid his slender legs farther apart, still playing, the room's ecstasy building. Now the guitar strings ran parallel to T-Bone's shoulder blades, he popped a last pyrotechnic note, and as he landed the splits, the floor around him was covered with cash and feminine undergarments. "The chicks didn't snatch their drawers off and throw them," bandleader Johnny Otis noted, a little disappointed maybe. "They brought extras in their purses. I know because I was watching like a hawk."[2]

Young Clarence Brown, just twenty-two, idolized T-Bone, whose effect on an audience bewildered and inspired him. "T-Bone Walker," he would say, "had the people just screaming and hollering, women falling out, knocking down the walls, tearing down chandeliers, and I said, 'God Almighty, what is this guy doing to these people?' "

It seemed to Clarence the right sort of life. So he followed T-Bone, asking for pointers and begging to sit in. "I was trying to figure out what could make one do that," he explained. T-Bone tolerated the young man and reluctantly shared an occasional tip while offering little on the art of inciting property destruction.

Clarence caught a break in San Antonio. He joined New Orleans drummer Bob Ogden's band at the Keyhole Club, working for chitlin' circuit broker Don Albert, Don Robey's man in San Antone. Robey visited the Keyhole during young Clarence's tenure, and Albert connected the two. Robey gave the young man a business card, embossed with the Bronze Peacock's sparkling, feathery logo and address, 2809 Erastus Street. "Next time you're in Houston, come by the place," Robey told him.

"That next time was pretty soon," Clarence recalled. "I hitch-hiked to Houston." Robey's business card was the only paper kicking around his pockets when he arrived. He had to depend on the pro-prietor's kindness for admission, and once in, he sat beside the band-stand. Thursday night, March 13, 1947, marked T-Bone Walker's ninth straight at the Peacock, and another mighty hometown throng awaited. T-Bone suffered with chronic ulcers thanks to youthful binge drinking and Texas homebrew, and the successive late nights had worn him down. Clarence saw T-Bone take the stage and heard the shrieks building behind him. But before the first note, T-Bone set his big Gibson down and hurried back to the dressing room. Robey had a sellout crowd, already seated, and no act. In a panic Robey grabbed Clarence: "Boy, go up there."

"I picked up his guitar," he said, "and for no reason on earth I started in E-natural, that's the only key I knew, and I invented a tune right on the spot."

My name is Gatemouth Brown and I just got in your town

The repeated first line of a blues gives the performer a moment to plan ahead, which can come in handy when making up a song on the spot in front of five hundred people as if your career depends on it.

My name is Gatemouth Brown and I just got in your town
If you don't like my style I will not hang around[3]

The women went for their purses, the men reached in their pockets, and the crowd responded to Clarence "Gatemouth" Brown's spontaneous composition with an impromptu storm of cash and coin. He riffed and Robey stared. "I was broke," Gatemouth recalled, "and I made $600 in 15 minutes."

T-Bone, however, was not amused. As Gatemouth finished his boogie, T-Bone, restored by the sounds of his Gibson and feminine screams, marched on stage and seized the guitar from Gatemouth. "Look," T-Bone barked, "as long as you live and breathe, don't you ever pick on my guitar again."

Gatemouth, stuffing his pockets, looked up. "I'm sorry, Mr. Bone. I don't know what made me do it."[4]

At least that's how Gatemouth told it. Other accounts differ from his on certain points, but they lack his flair.

Clarence "Gatemouth" Brown was born on April 18, 1924, on the Louisiana side of the Sabine River, and raised on the Texas side in Orange. He learned guitar, mandolin, banjo, and bass while tagging along and filling in with his father's string band. Playing swamp-side house parties for five years with his dad, Gatemouth amassed the courage to pick up Cajun music's lead instrument, the fiddle. He loved its human cries, but eventually recognized there was more money to be made on guitar. The singers he heard around Orange moved him. "I listened to these blues outta what they call juke joints," Gatemouth recalled. "I wasn't big enough to go in, so I would sit across the street and listen to these blues. And my mind would leave my body and travel for miles away, but it seemed to me it would be traveling to the disastrous part of this man's life. And I said music's got to be a little different than that."[5]

Gatemouth made a big enough splash from the Bronze Peacock stage to attract press coverage. A *Houston Informer* report days after Gatemouth's debut confirms the suddenness of his appearance that fateful night and the enthusiasm of the Peacock crowd, without including any of the more sensational details Gatemouth later provided. "Altho this man did not sing like T-Bone," entertainment editor Ted Williams wrote, "he has him skinned forty ways when it comes to guitar playing. Gatemouth drew almost as much applause from patrons as T-Bone."[6]

The crowd's response affected Robey the same way a celebrated event had moved W. C. Handy a half century or so earlier. At a 1903 performance in the hamlet of Cleveland, Mississippi, Handy and his trained orchestra left the stage and allowed a local trio to play a few numbers. The country boys strummed their beat-up instruments and patted their splay feet while Handy's educated men smirked in the wings, until "a rain of silver dollars began to fall around the outlandish, stomping feet," as Handy described the event in his 1941 autobiography. "The dancers went wild. Dollars, quarters, halves—the shower grew heavier and continued so long I strained my neck to get a better look. There before the boys lay more money than my nine musicians were being paid for the entire engagement. There I saw the beauty of primitive music."[7] That night, Handy claimed, a composer was born. On March 13, 1947, at the Bronze Peacock, a producer was born. Gatemouth said, "What happened was that Don Robey, with all this commotion, saw all these women giving me all this money and men as well, and he couldn't understand it. He had me under a contract the next morning."

Robey had graduated from numbers runner to backroom casino operator, wood-plank dance-hall owner, territory-band promoter, and the man who sprung Louis Jordan, finally becoming boss of the fashionable lifestyle center known as the Bronze Peacock. Though it seemed that the previous decade had set up Robey to make a star out of Clarence "Gatemouth" Brown, his first crack came off amateurish. The Houston scene buzzed with the news of T-Bone Walker's ouster at the hands of a young rival—Gatemouth was fifteen years T-Bone's junior—but the next time anyone saw Gatemouth, he was posed in a picture in the newspaper, dressed like a birthday party magician in black tails and cummerbund, white starched collar and bowtie, wearing a black top hat cocked to the northeast, tall enough to hide a full-grown rabbit. The price tag hung from a tuning peg of the Gibson L-500 Robey bought. Gatemouth grinned broadly, nervously, his feet spread as if straddled across a rumbling fault line.

The ad copy for Gatemouth's first night headlining at the Peacock didn't exactly dispel the notion of a rush job: "Clancece (Gate Mouth) Brown," it read.[8] By the time Robey learned to spell Brown's first name, it didn't matter anymore, for the talent began to show through the silly trappings. Gatemouth was all the talk. "There have been some nights that they have stayed until five in the morning still applauding for some more of that 'Gatemouth' Brown," the boss told the press. Robey planned to develop Gatemouth as Berle Adams had made Louis Jordan. He hit the road, working it like a barnstorming advance man, touting his find to other club owners and shopping him around for a record deal. According to the *Informer*, he'd gotten a few nibbles. "Nightspots in other cities are already calling for him as well as a couple of Record Companies, so if you want the treat of your life in entertainment take our advice and see Mr. Gatemouth Brown do his number before he leaves town."[9] Gatemouth spent late spring and early summer playing Houston, mostly at the Peacock, and building his set. Robey hooked Gatemouth up with L.A.'s Aladdin Records, where another Peacock alum, Amos Milburn, rocked. Gate's debut on wax was the tune he'd improvised as T-Bone's ulcers flared up, "Gatemouth Boogie."

* * *

Meanwhile Louis Jordan's torn-suit popularity, Joe Turner's shaking, rattling, rolling verses, Wynonie Harris's blood-shot style, Cecil Gant's hard-drinking boogie, Amos Milburn's atomic piano, and the pile of panties at T-Bone Walker's feet rock 'n' rolled across Don Robey's territory from Houston to the Keyhole in San Antonio, Bluchise's in Port Arthur, and beyond, inciting crowds and infecting the youth. At the other end of this fertile swamp lay the Crescent City, where, back in the spring of 1946, the local black paper reported, "forthcoming events are T-Bone Walker, Joe Turner, Cecil Gant, and trash singing-talking Wynonie Harris."[10] As it happened in Houston, musical mayhem followed these gentlemen to New Orleans.

Rip Roberts, Louis Messina, and the Mancuso brothers, the latter Don Robey's local hook-up, threw dances at Lincoln Theatre or Labor Union Hall. People celebrated, mourned, and politically orga-nized to street music; they partied every night and, during Carni-val, around the clock, in nightclubs as widely dispersed as the city's African-American population. The venerable Dew Drop Inn opened in 1939 and numerous other joints blinked on during the next eight years. The Hurricane, Shadowland, Club Desire, Robin Hood (with its Sherwood Forest mezzanine), Club Graystone, Rip's Playhouse, Club Rocket (*née* Rock-It, at the former Rhythm Club, where Louis Jordan started a riot in 1942), and the Foster Hotel's Rainbow Room regularly booked live entertainment from among the deep local talent pool and one-nighting chitlin' circuit acts. Proprietors decorated as lavishly as they could afford to, and competed to offer the best enter-tainment. They bid against each other, not only for the services of the top musicians, who all got around, but also for performers like exotic

New Orleans's legendary Dew Drop Inn, as it looked in 1961, with Danny White on stage doing "The Twitch." *Photo-Sax Kari/Author's collection*

dancer Baby Irene, who was said to induce men to throw their whole wallets on her good nights.[11]

Black New Orleanians were quite forward-thinking on the issue of drag queens in civic life. Some attained true public-figure status, while others gained a level of renown in entertainment circles that some musicians would have traded a horn for. One memorable Crescent City freak could have inspired a 1945 Louis Jordan hit. In "Caldonia" Jordan notes his woman's unusual height, curveless frame, and extraordinary shoe size, admitting he loves her nonetheless, but still wonders about the cause of her astonishingly stiff cranium. Or is it a cranium at all? Speaking of crania, Professor Longhair, in trio with professors Short Hair and No Hair, made music behind the All-Star Female Impersonators Show at the Caldonia Inn in early 1948. By which time Caldonia had aroused a Louisiana country boy named Irving Ale to become Patsy Valdalia (*sic*, Vidalia), a sobriquet borrowed from local john jargon. Ladies of the night were "onions," so Patsy was of the sweet variety.

Big names couldn't count on nostalgia to sell tickets in New Orleans. Erskine Hawkins and the Ink Spots, each hugely popular during the sweet swing era, flopped at the auditorium in early 1946. Scoop Jones, *Louisiana Weekly* reporter and local Johnny Appleseed of "rockin' " verbage, noted that postwar economic conditions, which saw war-era employment drop, worked against big bands.[12] That's assuming that big bands wanted to play the South, a point Ella Fitzgerald disputed. She claimed that black "name" bands, without naming any, turned their backs on the South and its race trouble, although, she said, "Every artist who has made any real money, particularly bandleaders, has made it on the Southern one-night circuit."[13] The economic and social situations that worked against Erskine Hawkins and other big-name big bands proved advantageous to Cecil Gant, Joe Turner, Wynonie Harris, and T-Bone Walker, who traveled solo, cheaply, and required a local pick-up band for gigs. In 1947 in New Orleans, the top ticket price to a Wynonie Harris show cost $1.00; for Duke Ellington, $3.10. New Orleans was perfectly suited for the new-style chitlin' circuit action. Places like the Rainbow Room and Dew Drop Inn could feed, lodge, and showcase a traveling single act at no additional cash outlay for the promoter, which translated into lower ticket prices for the consumer and steady exposure and flow for the artists. Thanks to its local jazz tradition, the city was full of talented bands. The early rockers' records were simple and well known, easy for New Orleans's many learned musicians to pick up in a pinch if they didn't already know the songs. Plus, early rock 'n' roll was wind-driven thanks to its swing roots, and New Orleans boasted an abundance of horn players. Finally, a number of cutting-edge small bands, the Gondoliers, Flashes of Rhythm (who'd broken in Gatemouth Brown in San Antonio before his Bronze Peacock debut), and Dave Bartholomew's combo had assembled there, and could strongly back up any incoming chitlin' circuit riders.

When the police punished black New Orleans, they hit the night-clubs. The black press condemned the local cops' "Hitler tactics."

Such language and tactics were in use when Roy Brown (no kin to Gatemouth) showed up in spring 1947 wearing his only suit and a pair of shoes he'd resoled with cardboard. Born in the Crescent City on September 10, 1925, Roy carried barely 140 pounds on his six-foot-tall frame. He was dark-skinned, and his hair stood up like a crown and settled into a widow's peak. His father, Yancy, was some-place in the city, but the man had run off during Roy's toddlerhood. Roy had cycled back to his birthplace after being on the move most of his twenty-one years.

As a boy in a Cajun prairie town called Eunice, Louisiana, on the other side of Baton Rouge, Roy had organized a quartet and wrote a song called "Satan's Chariots Rolling By." With the power of the Lord and six or eight ounces of blackberry wine behind them, Roy and his boys sang it in church and had the sisters clapping, tapping their feet, and shouting. Roy's pride swelled at the sight of his mother, True Love Brown, coming to him after the performance. But she didn't return his wide grin, just yanked him outside and marched him home without a word. At the house, True Love told Roy to snap a limb off the peach tree near the front step and disrobe.

"I'm gonna teach you to jazz up spirituals," she said, and whipped him.[14]

The tight family of two relocated farther down Louisiana. Roy went to work in the boggy sugarcane and rice fields, battling relent-less heat and mosquitoes among the cypress knees between Morgan City and New Iberia. Remembering the peach switch, he dared not sing, but he listened to the other workers and digested their words, rhythms, and melodies.

Pneumonia took True Love from Roy there when he was only fourteen. After she died, Roy quit school and headed to Los Angeles. He developed muscular biceps and forearms and a powerful grip in the cane fields, and a scrappy reputation in small-town street brawls.

Roy became a professional welterweight boxer in L.A., but couldn't stand the sight of blood. Way behind on the rent in a Central Avenue flophouse, he went against his late mother's wishes and began to sing. Roy fared better on stage than in the squared circle, winning cash-prize amateur nights around L.A. doing Frank Sinatra and Bing Crosby numbers.

He then drifted to Galveston, Texas, and fell in with Mary Russell, an enterprising lady who, according to Roy, ran brothels, sold dope, paid off the police and mayor, and, of course, employed all the good musicians around at her Club Grenada.[15] Roy organized a six-piece unit and dubbed them the Mellodeers. In addition to filling requests for the latest hits and golden standards at Club Grenada, the Mellodeers fielded patrons' orders for reefer, and ran to the stash spot during intermission. Mary Russell greased the Mellodeers' way on to the air via KGBC radio, where they would promote that night's show at the Grenada. Roy had composed a ditty about Mary Russell's for his broadcasts, a crazy little thing. True Love Brown's son had no trouble conjuring colorful characters: Deacon Jones, Sioux City Sue, and Fanny Brown appeared in the lyrics. Roy sung it fast and loud, quite unlike the Bing Crosby stuff, and over the airwaves it infected the good people of Galveston. They didn't want to miss out on what the song's title promised, that over at Mary Russell's there'd be "Good Rockin' Tonight."

In the midst of all the fun, Roy had to depart suddenly, fearing that his affair with the wife of a Club Grenada backer would be exposed. He slipped onto a bus without a word to Mary Russell or the Mellodeers.

Roy returned to New Orleans on Sunday, April 6, 1947. Short on finances again, he scribbled the lyrics to his Galveston whorehouse jingle on a brown-paper grocery sack in hopes that he could peddle it to his role model, who happened to be in town. "When I was in high school, I used to attend the auditorium dances when Wynonie Harris was singing with Lucky Millinder," Roy said. "I'd always say if ever I was going to be a blues singer, I'd like to be like that guy. He was flamboyant, a good-looking guy, very brash. He was good and he knew it. He just took charge, I liked the style."

Roy walked a couple miles from the Greyhound bus station to find the music, not toward South Rampart Street, the stroll of Walter Barnes's day, or Bourbon Street in the sharply segregated Vieux Carré. Roy headed toward LaSalle Street, where Wynonie Harris and Cecil Gant were scheduled to appear. He crossed the cradle of Orleanian opulence at St. Charles Avenue. Grand antebellum architecture had been wasted, tucked in swamps where no one could see it, so the gaudily wealthy brought the palatial extravagance of the plantation manse here to the city, to St. Charles, where it could attract more regular admiration. Live oaks arced overhead, and calcified bivalve shells crumbled underfoot like busted chalk. In his cardboard shoes, Roy hoofed eight blocks above the mansion district to the new black playground. New Orleans's darktown buzzed furtively after a shake-down the previous week, when police arrested six hundred night-clubbers. Most were dragged to headquarters and released without booking, which fueled speculation among Negro business leaders that the police sought only to disrupt commerce.[16]

On the corner of LaSalle and Seventh sat a camelback, two stories at the sidewalk, growing to three levels past the entry, of gray stone and pink siding, with glass cube windows to spoil the view in from the street: Foster's Hotel and Rainbow Room.

Roy wanted to get just a few dollars for "Good Rockin' Tonight." Nary an intellectual-property attorney in sight, Roy shuffled rather timidly up to his idol at the Rainbow Room bar. Wynonie, luminous in a white suit and horizontally striped brown and beige Bohemian tie, curled his lip and raised his eyebrows at the dustily attired boy.

"What is it?" Wynonie asked.

"I've got a song," Roy said.

"Oh, not another one of these songs," Wynonie flailed.

"Yes, I want you to hear it."

"Don't bother me, son." Wynonie slithered off, sneering over his shoulder.

Hurt, Roy folded up his grocery sack and headed past a block and a half of rooming houses to the Dew Drop.

A diligent and fastidious Creole of color named Frank Painia had opened a little barbershop on LaSalle Street at Sixth Avenue before the war, across from where the sprawling Magnolia housing projects were going up. As the project residents moved in, Painia expanded. He bought a pair of two-story buildings, which became a restaurant, hotel, and nightclub, collectively known as the Dew Drop Inn. Even after the nightclub became black-nationally renowned, Painia continued to park his long Cadillac outside his old barbershop every morning, go in, and cut hair all day.[17]

The Dew Drop, as Roy Brown saw it, exuded Tunisian glamour, with its arched doorway and blue and white tiled façade. He pushed in and heard the piano rapid-fire.

Cecil Gant was dressed in starched khakis to remind fans of his wartime fame as Private Cecil Gant, and sported a black tie with his first name spelled down it in white block letters. He played piano and rolled his eyes around like Fats Waller when he sang. "He didn't have a sensational voice," Roy recalled, "but he had something in that voice, something catchy . . . he made you feel what he was trying to convey to you. He was terrific, he was beautiful, he was responsible for my career."

Gant finished his set, stepped off the stage, and lit a smoke. Roy stopped Gant's trip to the bar, and delivered the same spiel he'd inconvenienced Wynonie Harris with. Gant listened, then asked to hear the song. Gant liked "Good Rockin' Tonight," not just the words, but the voice as well. It was 2:30 in the morning, but Gant called to wake up Jules Braun, president of DeLuxe Records, in New Jersey.

Roy sang "Good Rockin' Tonight" into the cigarette-stinking Dew Drop payphone. Braun said nothing. Roy stood there, paralyzed, thinking he'd put Braun back to sleep. But Braun cleared his throat and asked Roy to sing it again. Roy did it. Braun asked Roy to return the phone to Gant, and Braun told Gant, "Give him fifty dollars and don't let him out of your sight."

A month made a damn difference: On May 12, 1947, Roy Brown hit the stage at the Black Diamond, a club at the corner of North Galvez and Conti streets in New Orleans's Tremé section. At Jules Braun's urging, Roy had composed three songs in addition to "Good Rockin' Tonight." He came up with "Lollypop Mama," "Long about Midnight," and "Miss Fanny Brown." The band that Roy sang with at the Black Diamond, Bob Ogden's Flashes of Rhythm, was the same group that had backed Clarence "Gatemouth" Brown the night Don Robey first saw Gatemouth in San Antonio.

Presently, Roy and Ogden's band—piano, trumpet, tenor, bass, and drums—crammed into a studio stashed at the back of a record store at North Rampart and Dumaine, at the Vieux Carré's hemline. The studio belonged to Cosimo Matassa, an Italian grocer not much older than Roy. Seated in a closet-size control room, Matassa brushed the shavings away as the stylus bore a groove into a rotating cellulose disc, literally, as the audiophile says, "cutting" a record. Roy bent sideways and sang into the piano's mic. "I merely sung the song," he would explain, generously crediting the Flashes of Rhythm. "They did a very good job, they did the arrangements. . . . It was a good rockin' thing, you know, and man, I just started singing . . . and I felt right at ease." "Good Rockin' Tonight" had been played live on radio, sung through the telephone lines between the Dew Drop and Jersey, and performed before connoisseurs of the bawdy in Galveston and Tremé. Now it had a shot at immortality.

*   *   *

Pounding piano, chanting lyrics, rhythmic hand clapping, and frenetic sax drove Roy Brown's songs. The music was blues-based, but thanks to Joe Turner and Louis Jordan, so-called blues verses had broken from the traditional AAB structure, and "blues" songs took on a hook-heavy narrative quality. Roy's lyrics departed from the pretentious black vernacular of the late 1930s and early 1940s, of flotsam "ballrooms" and racketeering "capitalists." Roy hollered it as he'd seen it in joints like the Black Diamond. The music abandoned T-Bone Walker's restraint and Louis Jordan's measured cool. Roy torched the blues with spiritual fire, just as the blackberry wine drenched his preteen gospel-singing. He sang, at plaster-cracking volume, about the pleasures of drink, receiving fellatio, watching females brick-fight, rocking the joint, and tearing its roof off. These were scenes from the stroll. Only Amos Milburn's "Chicken Shack Boogie" neared Roy Brown's frankness in depicting black street life. A Deep South guitarist said it best: "As a singer, he had balls," B.B. King recalled. "He belted out tunes like 'Rockin' at Midnight' and 'Boogie at Midnight' that everyone wanted to hear. . . . Listening now, these records sound like early rock 'n' roll—but then again, so does Louis Jordan."[18]

It can be safely said that "Good Rockin' Tonight" popularized "rockin' " to new extents, and since we know how big rockin' became, the song seems important now. Of course "Good Rockin' Tonight" wasn't the first song to extol rockin' (even that seems to go back to Duke Ellington, with his 1931 recording "Rockin' in Rhythm"), though it might be the first, and certainly was the biggest to use its new frame of reference, no longer exclusively a stunt word for intercourse, but as a more musical, good-time catchall. It also looks important in hindsight because "Good Rockin' Tonight" was the second Elvis Presley single Sun Records released in 1954 (after the Little Brother Montgomery–Joe Turner–Louis Jordan–Big Boy Crudup—and who else?—amalgamation "That's Alright Mama"). In its time, before Presley and before "rock 'n' roll," Roy Brown and "Good Rockin' Tonight" carried more than linguistic consequences. Roy Brown would spread the sound and aesthetics of rock 'n' roll well beyond its Gulf Coast bastion, farther than Joe Turner or Wynonie Harris had ever ventured. But first he would have to cement his local reputation.

✳   ✳   ✳

South Rampart Street ran north and slightly east, parallel with the Mississippi River as it turns up to form the eastern swoop of New Orleans's distinctive crescent shape. *Back of town*, as black downtown was known, stretched nearly ten blocks of South Rampart, from Howard Avenue on its south end up to Common Street, just shy of Canal Street and the Vieux Carré. Late-nineteenth-century two-story brick Italianate commercial buildings lined the strip. Many had their brick plastered over and had been painted in confectionery pastels, but looked plenty dusty by Roy's time. Louis Armstrong had pulled a coal wagon up and down South Rampart's blocks, past the Chinese restaurant-laundry-opium den, saloons, and theaters where Kid Ory and King Oliver once blew. Buddy Bolden's ghost swirled around South Rampart's gabled parapets and rushed through its cast-iron vents. The Astoria, a hotel, restaurant, saloon, gambling hall, and home of the Tick Tock Tavern, where Walter Barnes and his Kings of Swing performed in the spring of 1937, sat at the high end, at 225 South Rampart. Club Downbeat sat at the low end, at 712.

Of all South Rampart's old tricks, only opium was still widely enjoyed in the summer of 1947. Customers waited quietly, if not quite patiently, between the old storefronts and cafés for the man to walk by. They signaled him like a bidder in the heat of auction. Down the alley, a wordless swap occurred. Often, these transactions led to disputes over the amount of product or cash that had changed hands. One thickly humid evening, twenty-one-year-old dealer Wesley Hewitt sat on a stool at a tavern, at the corner of Rampart and Gravier. As Hewitt lifted a glass of Jax to his lips, one of his junking buddies, thinking Hewitt stiffed him on a recent transaction, pumped three .32 bullets into Hewitt's heart.[19]

A few blocks away at Club Downbeat, Roy Brown stood beside the jukebox listening to himself sing. He and a boy from Baton Rouge named Clarence Samuels, who had landed in town with the Carolina Cotton Pickers and stayed after the group disintegrated there, had been performing as the Blues Twins at the Downbeat. The joint's manager wisely jacked up the admission and Roy's salary as "Good Rockin' Tonight" blasted back-to-back-to-back from the Downbeat jukebox and gushed out of seemingly every open jalopy window on the stroll. With just a drummer and pianist Walter Daniels, one of Bob Ogden's Flashes of Rhythm, the Blues Twins tore the Downbeat up. "This spot rocks from the early P.M. until long after daybreak," *Louisiana Weekly* reported on August 9, 1947. The twins were still making the sun rise a month later. "The other night Roy Brown sang 'Good Rockin' Tonight' which has just been released and is madly being played the town over on jukeboxes. When Roy rendered this number, he brought the house down and despite efforts to quell the shouts for encores was forced to sing the number twice."[20]

Of the heady days at the Downbeat, Roy recalled, "I was getting ten dollars, my own room, I was a big shot—all the girls I need and my blackberry wine."

'Tween the Tip In Inn
and the Church of God

Beginning in the midsummer of 1947, the chitlin' circuit hit its full, hectic stride, with important events and new artists breaking all over the map, all at once. The circuit had fundamentally altered the black music landscape. At the decade's beginning, a talented black musician would have to leave the South to try to make it in New York or Chicago, and pray to get picked up by a name orchestra. Now, Southern cities and towns that had been inconsequential were growing into lively hubs, with nightclub work, recording opportunities, and strong connections to national talent agencies.

Macon, Georgia, might seem like a strange place to search for the country's next big star, but not so to Lucius Venable "Lucky" Millinder. He witnessed the rise of the South as a syndicate-bossed bandleader and had something to do with it. He scouted new talent for his orchestra, discovering and showcasing rising stars like the smirking blues singer Wynonie Harris and sanctified Sister Rosetta Tharpe. He kept the band stocked with the freshest musicians. Saxophonist Bull Moose Jackson and pianist Bill Doggett were featured in Lucky's band before their successful solo careers. Lucky's emphasis on the modern kept his big band in business after others went belly-up.

"Millinder couldn't read music," booking agent Irving Siders recalled, "but he had the greatest ear. He could find songs, and he made the band swing like it had never swung before. He found good arrangers, good musicians, and whipped the band into shape."[1] Millinder made a striking impression on folks, as Siders recalled. "Short, very suave, and handsome," and most important, "he could con you."

He also stood up for his people. Back in 1940 *Down Beat* magazine predicted that Negro orchestras were on their way out, which provoked a passionate response from Lucky in an *Amsterdam News* editorial. "Can *Down Beat* tell us what hit swing song past or hit swing arrangement the white bands have featured that colored bandsmen or arrangers haven't had something to do with?" he wrote. "I get sick and tired of hearing would-be white critics on colored music telling us how bad colored music is, and yet praising white bands to the skies for playing the Negro's creations."[2]

Millinder possessed business acumen to complement his ear, charm, and testicular fortitude. When *Billboard* reported orchestra earnings in 1948, it placed Millinder in the A category of earners in excess of $200,000, along with Louis Armstrong, Count Basie, Cab Calloway, Nat Cole, and Duke Ellington.

Lucky hailed from Anniston, Alabama, so he knew talent could come from any little old place. When he got to Macon, he'd lately recorded a tribute to one-nighter towns, "Chittlin' Switch." The placards tacked to telephone poles and mounted in barbershop windows around Macon got the town buzzing. They showed Lucky—dubbed the "Dynamaestro"—grinning like a salesman, announcing, "Lucky Millinder's National Talent Discovery Quest—See Stars of Tomorrow—Local Singers & Instrumentalists, Talented Entertainers Seeking Fame and Fortune." The program would broadcast over radio station WBML.

Macon owed its prominence in the black music world to Reese Dupree and the world's largest copper-domed structure. At considerable expense, in 1930 the city constructed the grand, columned Macon City Auditorium at the corner of First and Cherry, with a dome that shined like a new penny, and thanks to this, Dupree had a decent venue in which to showcase the top bands. Dupree, a Macon native, worked as the syndicate's black man down South in the 1930s, leading Fatha Hines, Jimmie Lunceford, Chick Webb, Ella Fitzgerald, and Count Basie through Macon, which enjoyed more consistent, high-level black entertainment than a town its size deserved. Macon's jitterbug element danced and brawled to the same bands, in person, that fans in New Orleans, Houston, and Memphis did. Throughout the flush World War II years, Dupree partnered with "Fat Jack" Howard to co-promote shows at the auditorium. Walter Barnes had mentioned Fat Jack—"owner of Macon's only complete newsstand, and *Chicago Defender* booster"—back in 1937, near the circuit's beginning.[3]

Lucky Millinder brought his national talent search to Macon, at what folks called the million-dollar auditorium, on July 2, 1947. The locals appearing that night included the Three Tones singing trio, the Heavenly Gospel Singers, singer-entertainer Melvin Welch, and a fourteen-year-old performer whose surname was misspelled in the *Macon Telegraph* preview, Richard *Pennman*. In time he would drop the troublesome last name, and the world would know him simply as Little Richard.[4]

Richard Penniman, born in Macon on December 5, 1932, was the third of a dozen children, and "the most trouble of any of 'em," his mother, Leva Mae, recalled.[5]

The Pennimans moved every few years but stayed in Macon's Pleasant Hill neighborhood, the modern-day servants' quarters downhill from the white palaces on College Street. At the time Lucky Millinder brought his star search to town, the Pennimans lived on Woodliff Street between the Tip In Inn and the Church of God. A perfect spot:

Little Richard would be influenced as profoundly by Macon's theatrical holiness as its dark-end-of-the-street hustlers. Bud Penniman, Richard's dad, sold bootleg whiskey to the Tip In (he buried the jugs in his neighbor's collard greens patch to conceal them from the police) and the family gospel group sang at the Church of God.

Richard looked like the fused halves of incompletely formed twins—one eye bigger than the other, one leg and one arm each longer than their opposites. He walked bowlegged. His childhood mischief crossed the border into maliciousness. He once defecated in a box and gave it to a neighborhood lady called Miz Ola for a birthday gift. The crippled woman was so incensed that she jumped off her porch to go after Richard without her walking stick. "I laughed like a cuckoo!" he recalled. Richard's mother didn't understand his behavior, except as a manifestation of Satan.[6]

Rather than fish and fight with neighborhood boys, Richard preferred to hang around with little girls. "See I *felt* like a girl," he would explain. When he and his cousins played house, he always wanted to be the momma. The kids griped that he'd played the momma yesterday. He'd sneak into his mother's room and dab rosewater on his face. His flamboyance bloomed from there—Richard liked to put on his sister's pedal pushers and run bowlegged through the housing project until the boys chased him out.[7]

As Richard strolled along Woodliff Street, he heard the ladies' chorus as they hung their wash out. One sang the first line of a spiritual, and the others picked up the harmony. The sounds of Ma Sweetie, the holiest roller down in Pleasant Hill, "praying, *crying* to God" resonated for blocks. He rode around with Ma Sweetie in his Uncle Willard's Model T to the camp meetings in Logtown, Forsyth, and Cordele, little country towns near Macon.[8] Richard heard local gospel singers—the groups with their matching satin shirts, jagged pocket kerchiefs, and sweet harmonies—the Carnation Echoes, Heavenly Singers, Flying Clouds, and a big woman named the Georgia Peach spread the Word. The Penniman kids liked to clown at the

Pentecostal church down the street. They washed their dirty feet in the holy water and danced and pretended to speak in tongues.

That experience and Richard's encounters with a street prophet named Doctor Nobilio, combined with his own natural mischief, encouraged him to masquerade as a faith healer, making fat women fall out at his touch. Doctor Nobilio walked Pleasant Hill streets at a mystical pace, wearing a turban and a gold-lined red cape. He carried a gnarled black walking stick and a Devil's Child, a mummified creature with claws and horns. Richard hollered, strengthening his already impossibly loud voice, to draw crowds around Doctor Nobilio. The people jotted questions for Nobilio onto slips of paper that he'd burn without reading before giving his answer. The smoke whispered to Nobilio of his strange little assistant's splendid future.[9]

Richard found more inspiration at the Macon City Auditorium, where he sold buckets of bottled Coke on ice and enjoyed the big bands and entertainers. His favorite was Sister Rosetta Tharpe. She traveled with Lucky Millinder during World War II. Mindful of Tharpe's dual citizenship in Jerusalem and Sodom, Lucky dubbed her "Harlem's Holy Roller Rhythmaid." With Lucky, Sister Tharpe had reached a vastly wider audience than she could have accessed in the gospel world alone. On her own since 1946, she reigned as the most popular spiritual attraction on the road. Like her secular circuit counterparts, she had a Cadillac-driving entourage. She played auditorium dates, often with her evangelist mother, Madame Bell, and Marie Knight, "The California Nightingale." While the rocker circuit played little shack ballrooms, the holy-roller circuit played one-room country churches. And while many of the rockers on the rise played piano, gospel entertainers, Tharpe included, chose the guitar, an easier instrument to carry along on street sermons.

Sister Tharpe played Macon, Memphis, New Orleans, Houston, and spots between, as frequently as Louis Jordan, Wynonie Harris, and T-Bone Walker did during the formative years of rock 'n' roll. In fact, they frequently ended up in the same places. Sister Tharpe and Louis Jordan would jam late night at Houston's Bronze Peacock in 1950. Men like Don Robey and Macon promoter Clint Brantley saw no controversy in making money off both sacred and profane musics, and promoted concerts by hard gospel singing groups like the Swan Silvertones, Dixie Hummingbirds, and Blind Boys of Alabama with a fervor equal to that with which they promoted doo-woppers like the Ravens, Clovers, and Orioles, who sang of the Lord's fruit of temptation.

No one on either side was quite like Sister Rosetta, though. Born in Cotton Plant, Arkansas, on March 20, 1915, she began traveling with her evangelist mother. She made gospel records backed with popular-style accompaniment, including that of Lucky Millinder's orchestra, in the late 1930s. She wore long, shimmering gowns on stage and kept her curls short. Most male gospel singers preferred a soft, harplike guitar accompaniment, but Sister Tharpe banged on her guitar. She played a resonator early in her career, but by 1947 she played a big, solid-body Gibson like T-Bone Walker's, plucking the notes as cleanly and forcefully as T-Bone as well. Her voice escaped her short, plump frame with Devil-crushing urgency, and in this cool era of black music, she rocked as hard as anyone.

No record of Little Richard's performance at Lucky Millinder's National Talent Discovery Quest exists. Nevertheless, promoter Clint Brantley remembered Richard's next public appearance for the rest of his life. Brantley was due to present a big show on October 27, 1947. He recalled, "I had Rosetta Tharpe . . . at the City Auditorium. Little Richard wasn't nothin' but a little boy. . . . He came to me before the show started and said, 'Mr. Clint, Sister Rosetta said I could open the program.' I said, 'Boy . . . you can't open no program.' When the curtain lifted, reckon who was there?" Brantley said. "Little Richard, singing like hell! I said, 'Well, shit, this boy *can* sing.' "[10]

The fans cheered, Sister Tharpe pressed a few bills into his hand, and Richard was hooked.

✳   ✳   ✳

While Richard came out publicly as an entertainer, he sneak-
ily explored that side that had always been with him. His first sexual
experience was with a gay railroad worker known in Pleasant Hill
as Madame Oop. Richard's parents didn't know he hung around
Madame Oop and another gay man who went by the name of Sis
Henry. "They would not have approved," Richard said. Madame
Oop and Sis Henry swished along Broadway, past the Cotton Club,
pushing through crowds of soldiers and chirping in their high voices.
Between the out members of Macon's gay black community and the
white perverts stalking around in cars looking for little black boys
like Richard, his homosexuality found plenty of encouragement.[11]

✳   ✳   ✳

July 12, 1947, a week and a half after little Richard Penniman's debut, was a day of departures. Four months after Gatemouth
Brown's sudden emergence at the Bronze Peacock, Don Robey sent
him out on the circuit. Robey had seen the Louis Jordan operation
up close, and felt he could duplicate its success. He needed someone
to follow Gatemouth around and count all his money, and so Robey
recruited his old legman. Since the Harlem Grill closed, Morris Merritt hadn't managed anything bigger than Lena Mae's Chicken Shack,
a little restaurant he and his wife owned. Robey's call found Merritt
half past ready to shed his apron and hit the road.

Gatemouth landed at the Dew Drop Inn, and Robey ensured that
the papers kept his star in the headlines. "Talk of New Orleans this
week is a slender little fellow with varied formal attire and a voice
that shouts the blues." The July 12 *Louisiana Weekly* called Gatemouth "a new find and a sensation that has been rockin' Texas."

New Orleans's hottest bandleader passed Gatemouth going the
other way, en route to filling Gatemouth's void at the Bronze Pea-

cock, beginning July 19. "Don Robey was the one that brought me there," Dave Bartholomew said. "He came to New Orleans and saw me play at the Robin Hood."[12] Robey, scouting venues in preparation for Gatemouth's first tour, discovered the phenomenal young Bartholomew just as the bandleader's rhumba-infused New Orleans sound matured. At the Peacock, Bartholomew met Lew Chudd, a white, thirty-five-year-old owner of a Los Angeles record company that specialized in Latin novelties. Bartholomew, with his distinctive twist on the new sound, and repertoire of original material, impressed Chudd. And their encounter, in the words of one writer, "would have major consequences for the course of American popular music."[13] Chudd told Bartholomew, as the latter recalled, "One day I'm gonna make you a big man." Bartholomew replied, "Uh-huh, I heard this story before."[14] In two years Bartholomew would produce the debut recording of New Orleans pianist Fats Domino for Chudd's Imperial Records.

Just as Gatemouth's long road run and Bartholomew's seismic career began, a man beloved and admired across the circuit met an abrupt end. Jimmie Lunceford collapsed while signing autographs in a record shop before a gig in Seaside, Oregon. He was taken to the hospital and pronounced dead at age forty-five. Rumors of poisoning emanated from his band, who saw Lunceford clash with a Seaside café owner who had refused the black men service at lunchtime, shortly before the bandleader's appointment at the record shop. The medical examiner certified heart attack as the cause of Lunceford's death.

"Duke is great, Basie is remarkable, but Lunceford tops them both,"[15] Glenn Miller had remarked when those three bands stood at the peak of their fame in the early 1940s. The Lunceford legacy, though, encompasses more than his recordings, sold-out performances, and the admiration of his peers. He had been a chitlin' circuit trailblazer, his big-name orchestra being the first of its level to perform almost exclusively for black audiences. Though he certainly inspired many up-and-coming musicians along that way, Lunceford left a greater mark in Memphis, where he had raised his first orchestra, the Chickasaw Syncopators. He returned to perform in Memphis at least annually, usually several times a year, and always played, gratis, at local black high schools the day of his show, and used the Manassas High band as his opening act for the evening's paying gig. Whatever explanations exist for Memphis producing so many more black musicians between the 1930s and 1960s than other Southern cities with sizable black populations did—indeed, for a multimillion-dollar music industry developing in the city, largely around home-grown, African-American musicians—they begin with Lunceford's introduction of music education to Memphis's black public schools.

Isaac Hayes, Booker T. Jones, bandleader-producer Willie Mitchell, members of the vaunted Hi Rhythm Section and the Bar-Kays—who would form the backbone of the city's music industry during its heyday from the early 1960s to the mid-1970s—and those who found recognition elsewhere—Richard "Pistol" Allen of Motown Records' house band the Funk Brothers, Phineas Newborn Jr., in critic Nat Hentoff's words, "one of the three greatest jazz pianists of all time," Hank Crawford, leader of Ray Charles's orchestra in the early 1960s, George Coleman, Booker Little, Frank Strozier, and Charles Lloyd, who gained respect in the jazz world, plus dozens of skilled sidemen—all sharpened their chops in Memphis public school bands. Though he made Harlem his home after hitting it big, Jimmie Lunceford chose to be laid to rest in Memphis's Elmwood Cemetery.

Chapter 10 ✳ ✳ ✳ ✳ ✳ ✳ ✳

Roy Brown's Good Rockin' Revival

Wynonie Harris hit the studio to copy the hottest song around New Orleans. This time, Wynonie showed greater interest in "Good Rockin' Tonight," the Roy Brown composition he'd shot down without a glance at the Rainbow Room eight months earlier.

Wynonie's "Good Rockin' Tonight" became a bigger hit than Roy's original on *Billboard*'s Best-Selling Retail Race Records and Most-Played Juke Box Race Records indexes, placing high, staying long on both, and feeding fire to the rockin' phenomenon in black music. Wynonie's cover would finish 1948 as the third most-played "race" record according to *Billboard*. Since Louis Jordan's leap to fame—and black pop's resulting shift from big-band jazz to small-band blues—the chitlin' circuit's status in black entertainment had graduated. In the early part of the decade, Walter Barnes and then Denver Ferguson's groups had traded on the absence of alternatives for music fans in the Deep South. None were important contemporary artists. But by 1948, the circuit's top acts—Wynonie Harris, Joe Turner, Amos Milburn, and Charles Brown, while Jordan reigned supreme—were some of the top artists in black music as a whole, with national reputations.

The Good Rockin' originator plugged away throughout 1948. Roy Brown's autobiographical "Mighty Mighty Man" drew a strong national review for its "rocking blues shout sandwiched between some wooly jazz licks."[1] In June, both Wynonie Harris's and Brown's version of "Good Rockin' Tonight" were among the top-15 race records sold. Roy continued tearing up New Orleans, while jumping at chances beyond his home turf. He held down a residency at Club Ebony in Montgomery, Alabama, and took a bow at the Cotton Club in Philadelphia. In the week before Christmas his "Long about Midnight" reached no. 1 on *Billboard*'s black record chart. The most important executive, arguably, in the black music business noticed Roy's moves.

Since founding his Universal Attractions talent agency in 1945, Ben Bart had ingeniously merged the upper-circuit theaters and auditoriums with the lower-circuit nightclubs and juke joints. He cycled single attractions, either a small band or a star act that toured without a band, through smaller venues individually, then brought them together on big package shows, with up to ten acts appearing in one night, to play the large venues. Bart leaned heavily on regional bosses like Tom Wince in Vicksburg, Mississippi, and Clint Brantley in Macon, Georgia, a pair of Denver Ferguson's key promoters during the chitlin' circuit's infancy. Wince ran the Blue Room in Vicksburg and booked bands through a dozen more small-town joints, including Jones Nite Spot in Indianola, Red Ruby Edwards' in Leland, Casa Blanca in Greenville, and the Harlem Nightengale in McComb, Mississippi, as well as Preston's in Bogalusa and the Green Lantern in Tallulah, Louisiana.[2] Even small-town and little-city promoters like Wince and Brantley ran complex operations. They employed bands and the complementary components of a club show, emcees, exotic and interpretive dancers, and comedy-sketch teams. They sent these entertainers out on tour, simply plugging in a name attraction like Eddie "Cleanhead" Vinson, Percy Mayfield, or Wynonie Harris, bought from an agent like Bart, at the top of the bill.

A gamble on Roy Brown as a live attraction in late 1948 would be the same as the one Don Robey took on Louis Jordan back in the summer of 1942—both were promising artists, each with a fresh sound and record sales strong enough to suggest they could draw a crowd. Thanks to his hit records and respectable-enough box office statistics, in late 1948 the chitlin' circuit got behind Roy and pushed.

Ben Bart booked a tour that would spread chitlin' circuit rock 'n' roll coast to coast, from the ballrooms Walter Barnes had played, up to big-capacity theaters in New York, Chicago, and Los Angeles. Bart sold blocks of Brown dates to the chitlin' circuit's most powerful promoters—Howard Lewis in Dallas, B. B. Beamon in Atlanta, Ralph Weinberg, and Don Robey—and booked Roy "Around the World," as the upper-echelon Northern black theaters, Harlem's Apollo, Baltimore's Royal, Washington's Howard, the Paradise in Detroit, and the Regal in Chicago, were collectively known. The chitlin' circuit and Around the World were each a grind in their own ways. The chitlin' circuit's pounding succession of one-nighters kept bands on the road, sleep-deprived and sardine-fed, for hundreds of miles a day through poor weather and past cops who took exception to a Cadillac limo or flexi-bus full of slick black dudes. Around the World engagements lasted a week, which eliminated the road grind, but traded it for a relentless schedule of several shows per day.

Roy had assembled a band in New Orleans—drummer Ernie Roth, pianist Edward "Lil' Tatum" Sentino, trumpeter Teddy Riley, alto saxophonist Johnny Fontenette, and tenor man Leroy "Batman" Rankins. They came to be known as the Mighty Mighty Men after the sexually proud "Good Rockin' Tonight" lyric that had grown into its own song, one of many anthemic Roy Brown titles. The group had performed together for over a year, building confidence and chemistry. In December 1948, Roy "Good Rockin' " Brown and the Mighty Mighty Men hit the road. In Memphis, the group played the Palace Theatre, an old vaudeville house on illustrious Beale Street. "Roy Brown Puts Blues Singing on a New Kick," a *Memphis World* headline read. "[Brown] sings the blues with a spiritual shouting rhythm."[3] The Palace was a warm-up for the biggest performance of Brown's life—on February 4, 1949, when Roy and his Mighty Mighty Men hit Harlem's Apollo Theater.

The Apollo's notoriously critical audience and 'round-the-clock show schedule made it an unusually challenging place to play, but Roy and the Mighty Men proved up to it. Back in New Orleans, they jumped all day and night during Carnival at the San Jacinto Club for sodden crowds and body-painted Zulu Indians. The Apollo seemed subdued by comparison. Roy and the band stormed the stage at full speed, launching into song. Batman Rankins swooped down from the rafters. He "flew around with that tenor sax," Roy recalled. "He walked the tables, he walked the bars." The band wore matching, vibrant suit jackets and shoes, coordinated with their popular songs— red for "Good Rockin' " and blue for "Mighty Mighty Man"—and choreographed dance steps to each tune. No one outworked the leader. Roy sweated through four suits an hour.

Once they hit the chitlin' circuit, there was no stopping Roy "Good Rockin' " Brown and the Mighty Mighty Men. Roy recalled a Nashville auditorium date, where his standard contract called for a $400 guarantee and 50 percent privilege over $800. He took $2500 back to the colored rooming house that night. As the cash piled up, Roy bought a Cadillac limousine for the band, a Ford van for their instruments and uniforms, a station wagon for wives and girlfriends, and a Fleetwood for himself. His payroll hit $565 a night, and he often cleared twice that. Roy's aftershow meal consisted of two whole fried chickens, two orders of fries, and three bottles of Jax beer. The first time his wife dined with Roy after the show, she reminded him that she didn't eat much, and doubted the need for each of them to have their own chicken. "You order what you want," Roy told her, "that's for me."[4]

DeLuxe Records, the firm that had brought the world "Good Rockin' Tonight," released another wrinkle on the theme, "Rockin' at Midnight," in the early spring of 1949. *Billboard* raved, "Brown swings with a strong vocal with [band] rocking hard in the back."[5] Another release, "Young Man's Rhythm," contained, in the term of one rock historian, an "astonishing" line: "Good Rockin', that's my name, they're gonna put my rock in the hall of fame."[6]

Roy's agents at Universal followed the Walter Barnes–Ferguson Bros. publicity model, flooding black papers with press releases. As dance promoters and club owners typically financed the black entertainment pages, and scribes knew who buttered their bread, the publicity blasts ran everywhere that held a financial stake in a forthcoming stop of the Good Rockin' revival. Denver Ferguson saw that Brown releases appeared in the *Indianapolis Recorder*, Don Robey placed them in the *Houston Informer*, and Roy's New Orleans manager, Rip Roberts, supervised the legend's local inflation. Readers all over the country followed Roy's crusade. "There's no depression in the music business as far as Roy Brown is concerned," the news from Cincinnati read on June 1. "Roy is racking up a spectacular record . . . with not a single vacant date on his booking calendar. The demand for Brown and his engaging musical unit reached a new high during the month of May. The great little band, with the blues shouting leader, was engaged every one of the month's 31 days!"[7]

July found Roy in Ralph Weinberg's territory. The white, Bluefield, West Virginia–based promoter, a heavy smoker with a doughy physique and chronically sleep-deprived appearance, Weinberg had monopolized the black dance business from his home base down to Georgia, and nearly to the Mississippi River. Weinberg, Howard Lewis in Dallas, and Don Robey in Houston made a booking agent's job easy by buying dates in bulk. Then they either subcontracted the dates to other promoters for a marked-up guarantee or followed the act on tour to work the door and count the money. Booking agents enjoyed the consistency of dealing with a single promoter for weeks at a time, and the agents and heavy promoters developed a collegial faith in one another that the business lacked in its earlier days. Steady promoters provided other advantages as well, as the news from July 10 in Charlotte, North Carolina, illustrated:

> Blues-singing, bandleading Roy Brown came within an ace of landing in the local clink last Thursday as a case of mistaken identity caused the local gendarmes to pick him up for the real culprit they were seeking who answered to the same name.
>
> Brown had arrived in town to play a one-night dance engagement and had just stepped from his Cadillac when an officer of the law "apprehended" him. . . . The whole affair was adjusted in the nick of time as Promoter Ralph Weinberg met the party practically at the courthouse steps and identified Brown as the leader of the band playing for him at the armory.[8]

After Fayetteville and Greensboro, North Carolina, Roy was deemed "turnstile magic."

Roy Brown's hard-rockin' tour overlapped notable news in the black music business. *Billboard* renamed its African-American music bestseller list from "Race Records" to "Rhythm and Blues Records" in the summer of 1949. The chart change belatedly confirmed what industry players already knew—the sound Louis Jordan pioneered and popularized in the early part of the decade had all but pushed jazz out of the black pop picture. The typical Harlem Hit Parade chart during 1942–43 included light pop fare such as the Ink Spots, big-swing-band tunes from Duke Ellington and Earl Hines, plus torch songs from Billie Holiday and Ella Fitzgerald. By 1944, Louis Jordan dominated the list, typically with numerous titles appearing throughout the top 15, while the other leading black small band, the King Cole Trio, and bluesy chitlin' circuit big bands led by Cootie Williams and Buddy Johnson nudged their way into the parade. After the war, Louis Jordan rode highest as more cool small bands, Roy Milton and His Solid Senders, and Joe Liggins and His Honeydrippers joined the party. By the fall of 1948, rockers had almost fully taken over the Race Records chart with Bull Moose Jackson, Charles Brown, Ivory Joe Hunter, Memphis Slim, and Wynonie Harris crowding Jordan out of the top spots. The last race charts in early 1949 read like the results of a revolution. Even the mighty Jordan had been toppled. Amos Milburn, Roy Brown, and Wynonie Harris pushed Jordan, Ella, and Billy Eckstine to the end of the list, and relegated Ellington and the swing generation to nostalgia.

The recognition *Billboard* gave chitlin' circuit music at the time was monumental; however, the semantics of "rhythm and blues" have muddied black music's rock 'n' roll legacy since. Influential gatekeepers have tended to treat "rhythm and blues" as a genre-defining term rather than what it was, a marketing phrase, shorthand for black popular music in whatever form happened to be selling. The standardized definitions of rock 'n' roll, courtesy of institutions such as the Rock and Roll Hall of Fame and *Rolling Stone* magazine, emphasize a fusion of black rhythm and blues and white country-western sounds, as if the two styles brought distinct elements to a new mixture. While that certainly applies to Bill Haley and Elvis Presley, some of the first rock 'n' roll stars as such, it implies a shared primacy that simply didn't exist at the true dawn of rock 'n' roll. While black music was clearly rockin' by 1949, country and western fans delighted to the sounds of yodels, waltzes, accordions, fiddles, and steel guitars—great stuff, but not the stuff of rock 'n' roll.

Back to 1949, when the papers hailed Roy Brown's rescue of the black music business following his August 10 Atlanta show. "Blues-shouting, rhythm dispensing Roy Brown and his band have put a stop to the dropping graph of attendance and revenue on the one-night dance circuit. . . . Thanks to Brown, it is felt that the low-point has been reached and things will begin looking up now that the fans have been brought back to the box office."[9] Roy wasn't the chitlin' circuit's sole savior. The other acts on the new Rhythm and Blues chart, Memphis Slim, Buddy Johnson, and Bull Moose Jackson (picture Eddie Murphy with a huge gap-tooth grin, gold-rimmed specs,

and baritone sax), filled clubs and theaters too. None other than Roy
caused as much hysteria, though, as the foot-stomping Houston pianist Amos Milburn, whom circuit fans, to paraphrase one of his hits,
liked better than chicken fried in bacon grease. Amos's rockin' chitlin' circuit anthem "Chicken Shack Boogie," which harkened back to
Houston's rowdy dives, and his sweet ballad "Bewildered" charted in
two of the top 3 spots on *Billboard*'s bestseller list in early 1949.

Shaw Artists, a Chicago-based black talent agency, repped Amos.
Its founder, Billy Shaw, had booked Southern one-nighters for Count
Basie, Billy Eckstine, Earl Hines, and the Nicholas Brothers tap duo
for the William Morris Agency during World War II. Shaw split
off specifically to work black acts as the small-band vogue spread,
and would eventually boast a powerful clientele that included Ray
Charles. In 1949, Shaw had Milburn touring as heavily as Roy Brown
did, and the two would run up against each other in Memphis later
that year.

By the middle of the year, *Billboard* ranked Roy Brown (no.
2) and Amos Milburn (no. 3) as two of the top 3 best-selling race
recording artists, behind Paul "Hucklebuck" Williams, another new
act, and comfortably ahead of Louis Jordan (no. 12), Wynonie Harris (no. 14), and T-Bone Walker (no. 31). Rock 'n' roll was energizing
the black music business from the Apollo to its Southern barrelhouse
roots.

The Good Rockin' tour reached Ferriday, Louisiana, on September
14, 1949, when Brown and the Mighty Mighty Men invaded Haney's
Big House. After returning home from World War I, Will Haney had
trudged Ferriday's streets selling insurance to black consumers. A nice
but no-nonsense guy, he stood a shade under six feet tall and weighed
around two hundred pounds. After successful years as a salesman,
he opened a barbecue stand in the 500 block of Fourth Street. Haney
added a barroom in the late 1930s. His years going door-to-door had
put him in touch with every black household in town, which made
him just the sort of community connector Denver Ferguson liked to

have promoting his dances. Though it's not known whether the two worked together, Haney began hosting live entertainment just as Ferguson was building the chitlin' circuit in the war years. It's unlikely the two didn't cross paths as the barbecue shack–barroom grew into the Big House.

Structurally, Haney's was no Sunset Terrace or Bronze Peacock. Outside, weeds sprouted around the cinder block building where the men emptied their bladders in the dark. Pale dirt spread around the lot and hung in the still air as the cars pulled up on Saturday night. As everyplace else around Ferriday slept, the Big House hummed with nuclear energy. The low lamps and neon Jax and Regal signs inside glowed through the windows. The music crackled from the house PA, and the rhythmic bouncing on the dance floor shook the walls. Standing across Fourth Street you could see the place vibrate. Neighborhood boys combed the dirt around Haney's on their way to church on Sunday morning, searching for cash misplaced from midnight craps games in the dust, and gold teeth dislodged in late-night brawls.

Liquor bottles, every brand, stood tall behind the bar. The kitchen fried anything and stayed open all night. Around the bar from the kitchen, the Big House opened up to dozens of tables and chairs, seating about two hundred, and the stage. Slot machines lined the walls, and a brass-knuckled bouncer patrolled the floor. A pair of aces named Bootsy and Poor Boy staffed the gambling shack around back, and seldom lost at poker.[10]

Local baron Lee Calhoun was all the authority Haney needed to appease in order to operate the Big House. Calhoun was Ferriday's feudal lord. He owned the land under Haney's club and much of the rest of Concordia Parish. Calhoun protected his tenant from Ferriday's Klannish white populace and redneck cops. A couple of Calhoun's teen-aged nephews liked to roam Ferriday after dark. By the time Roy Brown hit town, Jimmy Lee Swaggart and Jerry Lee Lewis regularly stopped to peek through Haney's windows. The proprietor, who understood the precariousness of his position in the world, warned the boys Uncle Lee would kill him if he found out they hung around the place. Of Haney's, Jerry Lee would say, "It was giving birth to a new music that people needed to hear. Rock & roll—that's what it was."[11]

Not only did black musicians rock Ferriday, it rocked back. Eddie "Cleanhead" Vinson, playing Haney's a few weeks after Roy, found the windows of his DeSoto broken. He "heaved a deep sigh of relief" upon learning the vandalism "was not the work of a band of Klansmen but rather that of two groups of teen-agers in a stone battle." One wonders about Jerry Lee and Jimmy Lee's alibis. Cleanhead chuckled about the dust-up, remarking, "You can't blame a guy for being nervous in these parts, can you?"[12]

By organizing a band and taking it on the road, Roy chose artistry over money. He could have easily worked as a single act, demanding the same guarantee and earning the same percentages, while performing with local pickup bands at his shows. The system had evolved to suit this arrangement. Instead, he carried the travel expenses and salaries of six men. The results were seen at Roy's shows and heard on his records. "Patrons . . . were treated to an all out battle between the two sax aces [Leroy "Batman" Rankins and Johnny Fontenette] of the Roy Brown band, which had . . . the crowd in a frenzy." They tried their new songs out live, and by the time they recorded them, they knew which hollers, moans, sax squeals, and trumpet bursts hit the audience's pleasure center. Just a week after their date in Ferriday, Roy Brown and the Mighty Mighty Men stopped in Dallas to record "Boogie at Midnight." It captures the group's explosive form fans heard on the epic 1949 tour. As he had with "Good Rockin' Tonight," Roy sang it as he saw it on the chitlin' circuit in "Boogie at Midnight," in *Billboard*'s description, "a frantic, shouting, hand-clapping, job that sounds like cash in hand."[13] The song rocks harder than Roy's previous records, and would become his biggest hit to date, peaking at no. 3 on the *Billboard* R&B chart. You can hear rock's New

Orleans brass roots, the sanctified hand-clapping and choir-chanting Roy brought to the sound, and Roy and Batman pushing each other higher up the rafters. No more compelling document exists of rock 'n' roll as it was made on the chitlin' circuit.

Roy came back through New Orleans in October to play two shows for promoter Don Albert, Don Robey's old San Antonio side-kick dating to Walter Barnes's days, and former proprietor of the Keyhole Club, where Amos Milburn and Gatemouth Brown were discovered. The press called Roy "the man who has the nation singing 'Good Rockin' Tonight.' " Roy rocked old chitlin' circuit strongholds Monroe and Shreveport, Louisiana, for Don Robey, Vicksburg's Blue Room and Hattiesburg's Harlem Club in Mississippi, from down in St. Petersburg and Tampa, Florida, to Knoxville and Clarksville, Tennessee, Richmond, Virginia, and Logan, West Virginia, under Ralph Weinberg's aegis, and also stormed north to the Showboat in Philadelphia for six standing-room-only nights. "The Brown band has been the heaviest coiner of folding money at the box office among all aggregations playing the one night circuit."[14]

Brown's Cadillac caravan dipped back South to Tupelo, birthplace of Elvis Presley. It hit Wynonie Harris's hometown Omaha, Nebraska, then Oklahoma. Tulsa promoter Irving Fields answered the demand in his town with a doubleheader, two shows in one night at the Big Ten club. The tour stretched southwesterly, into more new territory. In the desert thirty miles outside Tucson, Arizona, members of the Choctaw nation ceremonially inducted Roy Brown into their tribe. The Choctaw bestowed Roy an Indian name that translated as "Big Blow."[15] Big Blow vacationed briefly in Havana, returned to New Orleans for a day, then hit the road again on Christmas Eve.

*   *   *

In 1984, a reporter for the *Macon Telegraph and News* interviewed Melvin "Percy" Welch, who had led an interesting if not richly rewarding career as a chitlin' circuit bandleader. The reporter asked

Welch's assessment of Michael Jackson, who then stood on top of the pop world, having just collected eight Grammys for the *Thriller* album. A comparison occurred to Welch. "Every so often there comes an artist . . . with something different to offer, and he'll catch a wave and ride the tide for a while," Welch said. "Like Roy Brown when I was just a kid—he was the number one black artist. . . . I used to go to the auditorium and serve Coca Cola just to get in and hear Roy Brown."[16]

You can listen back through the ages and say that Mississippi guitarist Robert Johnson, who died in 1938, and German composer Wolfgang Amadeus Mozart, who died in 1791, are among the most important musicians in rock 'n' roll history, or that an obscure side cut by the Mississippi Jook Band in 1936 bears the marks of rock 'n' roll, and so has a supportable claim as the genre's earliest record. The problem with this perspective is that neither these artists nor their music resonated as "rock" in their times, and rock 'n' roll is every bit as much a popular phenomenon as it is a sound. Roy Brown was both. Roy and his agent, Ben Bart, deserve credit for elevating rockin' music to new heights in pop culture and spreading it farther across the map—if only in black America, where Roy could be remembered as on par with the most phenomenal black pop act of the century, while never reaching the mainstream. Roy Brown shook black popular music. He brought tough, lewd lyrics—the essence of chitlin' circuit song and a staple of rock 'n' roll ever since—from down in the barrelhouse to the top of the *Billboard* charts and from coast to coast across the country in 1949, two years before Cleveland disc jockey Alan Freed initiated popular use of the phrase *rock 'n' roll*, four years prior to Bill Haley's "Rock around the Clock," and five years before Elvis Presley covered Roy's composition "Good Rockin' Tonight."

Female Trouble

One pale winter afternoon, right about the time Batman Rankins swooped from the Apollo rafters, Denver Ferguson sat smoking a cigar, reading a magazine in his office. The booking agency headquarters had been pretty quiet lately.

Denver flipped through *Ebony* and noticed two portraits, especially the one of a young woman with a fine-boned profile and porcelain skin. He read the attached copy with mounting interest:

WANTED: TWO HUSBANDS

You'll be probably very surprised to receive a letter from two German girls. The explanation is very simple. We were just reading your article, "Eligible Men," in the EBONY of November. Perhaps it sounds strange to you that we like to meet Negroes. We met through our work so many different Americans and found out that Negroes have much more heart, more sense of human beings. We had many talks about the problems of your race and got the opinion that color means nothing. Only the personality counts.

You perhaps can understand that there are many doubts for us in having a future in Germany, even in Europe. It is so very hard for a girl to make a living here. So many people are jobless. We are young and hoping for a better future. Our desire is to get married, to build a family, to raise children and be a good housewife and companion, living a happy life.

Both of us were engaged during the wartime to German officers who got killed in Russia. Often we had chances to get married, but we never could find what we wanted. German men changed a lot. They are much different now than they were before.

Perhaps EBONY can help us to find the right husbands. We are 27 years old.[1]

This intrigued Denver.

While he had accumulated numerous professional achievements, his four marriages collapsed. His success had victimized him. As the chitlin' circuit took off in the late 1940s, pulling circuit artists up to the top, white-bossed talent firms, business at Ferguson Brothers Agency declined. Once an influential conductor of chitlin' circuit activity, he was now just another stop on the endless string of one-night stands. Locally, his Sunset Terrace remained the jewel of a still-bustling Indiana Avenue nightlife. Denver's young adjutant Taylor Seaths kept the Sunset hip, booking Roy Brown, Amos Milburn, Bull Moose Jackson, Hucklebuck Williams, Wynonie Harris, the Ravens, and Dizzy Gillespie in the first half of 1949. Seaths introduced a weekly bus excursion to draw patrons to the Sunset from other communities, as far as Champaign, Illinois, and Terre Haute, Indiana. Denver enjoyed a steady income, as his printing press churned out numbers slips and show posters. He owned several pieces of property, including a two-story modern home on West Maple Road. He had fought and finagled his way to a comfortable position, built himself a solid brick monument to the African-American dream, and energized commerce on Indiana Avenue. Indy's Bronzeville boasted a modern hotel, two black record shops, a dinner theater, plus the time-honored taverns, poolrooms, nightclubs, and other small businesses. In recent years, Denver had helped his former employee, comedian Toots Hoy, to open the Red Snapper Supper Club, and backed his cousin "Rags" Ferguson, from back home in Brownsville, Kentucky, in a new hotel that bore their surname. Denver could see from his office window the difference he made on the Avenue over thirty years.

He could hardly rest on his laurels, however, as the battle raged between white authority and black underworld. Indianapolis mayor Al Feeney took office in 1948, promising to tighten the grip on illegal activity, and unlike past candidates, he meant it. This represented a major deterioration in legit downtown-underworld noir relations from the high point ten years earlier, when Indianapolis's elected mayor Walter Boetcher attended the celebration following Sea Ferguson's election as the honorary mayor of Bronzeville, signaling tacit approval of Bronzeville's ways. The police, once Denver and Sea's allies in black economic development—so long as they took their bribes and stayed out of the way—suddenly became bad for business. They kept the heat on Avenue gambling operations. They conducted raids every weekend, bringing hundreds of Avenue nightlifers to jail on petty vice charges. Bronzeville's revenue stream ran sluggish. Residents were forced to apply for police permission to throw a party, or risk being arrested on bootlegging charges. The police harassed every pastime, from the policy rackets to a men's room dice game. Gamblers felt they were still cheating by the rules, and when assaulted, they defended their ground. The police raided a small after-hours club in early 1949, charging upstairs with clubs drawn. The seventeen crapshooters inside heard the approaching squad and wielded their beer and booze bottles. The two lines clashed, and the cudgels prevailed among a storm of broken glass. The cops seized about fifteen dollars, eleven cases of beer, three decks of cards, and a set of brass knuckles.

A beleaguered Denver may have finally been ready to settle down.

Decades of cheap cigars and marbled meat weakened his heart, and diminished his redoubtable energy. And it is entirely possible that he recognized, in the German woman so openly seeking black romance, his last grand gesture to the white world. Denver gathered his still-considerable hyperbolic talents and typed, "I have since my childhood dreamed of being married to such a beauty. Now I have found her."[2]

The cops-versus-citizens race clash escalated. Before dawn on May 2, 1949, a few weeks after Denver sent his letter to *Ebony*, a pair of Indianapolis policemen stopped their cruiser next to a parked car in which two men and two women sat chatting and crunching fried shrimp. The men in the car were prominent black citizens, physician and former city councilman Lucian Meriwether, and Harvard law school graduate and juvenile court referee Mercer Mance. Their dates were light-skinned sisters from one of Bronzeville's prominent families, the Stuarts, Emilie, a schoolteacher, and Catheleen, a social worker. The cops wanted to know what these white women were doing in a car with a couple of niggers.

Though a little ruffled at the cops' ham-handed intervention, the couples shared puzzled glances and chuckled a little. The Stuart girls explained that, despite appearances, they were Negroes. One of the policemen, disbelieving and none too appreciative of fancy colored sass, grabbed Emilie out of the front passenger seat, tearing her coat. When Mance protested from the driver's seat, the other cop accused the former Marion County attorney of public drunkenness and slapped on the handcuffs. The cops carried Mance and Emilie Stuart to the station and charged Emilie with disorderly conduct, vagrancy, and resisting arrest. The duo posed for mugshots and waited the rest of the night in jail. A judge dismissed all charges.

"The Stuart girls pose a difficult problem to the Indianapolis police department," wrote former IPD detective Opal Tandy in the *Recorder*. "They are not white and yet cannot be seen with Negro men. What does [Indianapolis police] chief Rouls intend to do with them? Will he instruct the police to issue a certain type badge of identification to be worn by the Stuarts for the benefit of all white policemen?"[3]

A few days later, an envelope reached Denver. The porcelain profile from *Ebony* had launched four thousand letters, but she responded only to Denver's. Her name was Lilo Rentsch, and she was a secretary in Wiesbaden-Biebrich, not far from Frankfurt, West Germany. "I am ripe for love," Lilo wrote Denver. "I wish only to live for you."[4]

Meanwhile, Indianapolis police harassed Denver's closest associates. "The ticket shops, gambling houses, race horse bookies, and houses of prostitution are tight now," Tandy wrote in the August 13 *Recorder.* They shut down Toots Hoy's Red Snapper Club as a public nuisance, and raided the Ferguson Hotel, where the cops claimed that Denver's cousin Rags was running a whorehouse. This was no big deal in and of itself, so the cops justified the raid by alleging that Rags catered to interracial couples. "I cannot say that this is a devious plan formulated to throttle the potential power of the negro," Tandy added, "but I can certainly say it looks that way. . . . There seems to be a deliberate attempt to keep these places closed until every Negro businessman is forced to close up. Strangely, a few of the white places remain open [on the Avenue], but the police just can't seem to catch or see what they are doing."

Yet another raid targeted Cy Graham, Denver's top numbers man, who operated a busy policy station next door to Sunset Terrace. Police seized hundreds of baseball tickets, cash, and a craps table. Denver's old newspaper ally J. St. Clair Gibson—"The Saint" who had spun magnificent tales as Ferguson Bros. publicity man—urged bronze folk to "stop compromising and begin [fighting] for the things that are right even if it means death. Too many Negroes are always saying—'Well what's the use, just let it drop.' As long as we maintain this attitude, we'll forever be kicked around. When the time comes that our most reputable places and persons are being kicked around, we say it's high time for action."[5]

Tandy interviewed Mayor Feeney about the lockdown. "Does anybody have the go sign, mayor, anybody at all?" Tandy asked. "If they think they have," Feeney gamely responded, "we'll raid them now, this very minute. We'll have the police push them around, and I mean hard, too. I'd better not hear of the police allowing anybody in town to run anything illegal."[6]

As Mayor Feeney squeezed Bronzeville, Denver's letters to Lilo increased in frequency and ardor. He promised an undying love and unending wealth. He was older than she, forty-four (fifty-four in truth, exactly twice her age), but, he persuaded her, this only made him a better mate—he was emotionally mature and financially set.

After hitting Denver's neighbors, his friends, and his relatives, Indianapolis authorities finally attacked the big man. At high noon on Monday, November 14, two squads of Indianapolis policemen and U.S. Treasury suits busted into Sunset Terrace and the Ferguson Brothers Agency building. They ousted Denver's employees and seized his printing press from Ferguson Manufacturing and the grand piano and two TVs from Sunset Terrace. They logged estimated values of the fixtures inside each facility for a planned auction of Denver's assets before padlocking the doors and slapping lien proclamations on the buildings. Taylor Seaths later reached the boss at home and told him what happened. The revenuers had monitored Denver for two and a half years, ever since Jacque Durham—the demoted policeman who had squealed to the papers about his colleagues accepting bribes to enable the black vice trade—exposed Avenue graft.

Denver's phone rang again. This time, a reporter at the white *Indianapolis Star* wanted his reaction. Denver, with Germany and sweet Lilo on his mind, called the property seizure a "Gestapo tactic."

The reporter cited common knowledge that Denver printed numbers tickets on the confiscated press. Denver hotly denied this. He'd been out of the racket for ten years. Common knowledge needed revision.

The U.S. Treasury action stemmed from an $82,410.11 tax debt. Denver described the local collector as "ambitious" and the levy as "arbitrary." Denver had paid $4,000 of the "arbitrary" $12,500 tab the IRS had sent him back on July 1, 1947. Penalties accrued as Denver failed to make further payments, the reporter pointed out.

"If I couldn't pay it at first," Denver responded, "it was preposterous for them to think I *could* at the higher figures which came afterward." Denver bade the reporter good day.[7]

In a clandestine act of Avenue wizardry, Denver made it all disappear the next afternoon. At a meeting at the Federal Building downtown, he presented the "ambitious" chief deputy internal revenue collector Wilbur Plummer with $10,000 in cash to cover his personal liability. Plummer apparently had more than 10,000 reasons to leave Denver be. "While Plummer adhered to federal policy in not revealing details of the quick settlement, he admitted that he had received calls from a number of prominent persons in the business world," the *Recorder* reported.[8]

Lionel Hampton made his scheduled appointment at Sunset Terrace, on Thursday, November 17, 1949, a little more than seventy-two hours after the government had padlocked the joint.

Denver wrote to Lilo, and promised to pay her passage and finance a luxurious life ever after.

✳　　✳　　✳

Houston

We last saw Don Robey armed like an outlaw, hauling bags of money *into* the bank. This scene repeated dozens of times in the years since the Bronze Peacock opened. Repetition bored Robey, however—we should be so unfortunate—and 1949 found him after new kicks. While Denver's fuses fizzled, Robey's fired.

Gatemouth Brown moved steadily across Robey's chitlin' circuit territory, zigzagging through Texas's black nightclubs, and border-hopping to Louisiana rarely with a day off.* "A fine station wagon, newly bought and lettered with all his latest hits, sure hits yokels in the eye when he arrives in their town," the *Houston Informer* noted.[9] But Robey had hoped to impress more than the yokels by now. Two years after sending Gatemouth on the road, Robey had realized Gatemouth wasn't Louis Jordan. Robey felt that Houston star Amos Milburn's success came at a cost to Gatemouth. Both artists recorded for Aladdin Records, but there the comparison ended. Amos's tunes sold fabulously, and the company focused its promotional efforts on him, while releasing only two Gatemouth couplings during their two-year contract. Robey knew he couldn't get Gatemouth out of the territory and into the national scene without more records and broader marketing. And Robey knew he wouldn't be able to do it alone.

Not long before Gatemouth materialized at the Bronze Peacock back in early 1947, a dreaded event had brought Robey unexpected, pleasant results. Six months after the Peacock opened, the IRS scheduled a visit. Perhaps an agent had witnessed Robey's dramatic bank deposits. Robey's business manager panicked. She called a coolheaded, smart friend, Evelyn Johnson. "I have a problem," the busi-

---

* The typical Gatemouth trek, as published in the *Houston Informer* on January 21, 1950: Club Flamingo in Wharton, Texas, Wingo Bar in Columbus, Texas, Club Raven in Beaumont, Texas, West Side Auditorium in Port Arthur, Texas, Catholic Hall in Orange, Texas, Club 90 in Ames, Texas, Oriental Gardens in Victoria, Texas, Morris Social Club in Bay City, Texas, City Auditorium in Galveston, Texas, Black Cat Country Club in Lufkin, Texas, Dallas Park in Shreveport, Louisiana, Dovie Miller Auditorium in Austin, Texas, White Eagle Club in Opelousas, Louisiana, Karimu Hall in Tyler, Texas, the fair grounds in Rosenberg, Texas, Carolls Auditorium in Monroe, Louisiana, Hollywood Club in New Iberia, Louisiana, Webster (High School) Auditorium in Minden, Louisiana, Dreamland Inn in Longview, Texas, North Inn Park in Brenham, Texas, Skylark Terrace in Corpus Christi, Texas, San Antonio Auditorium, Greystone Grill in Alexandria, Louisiana, Powell's Hall in Lake Charles, Louisiana, Clover Club in Mexia, Texas, Rainbow Terrace in Ft. Worth, Rose Room in Dallas, Club Raven in Beaumont (again), and the Houston City Auditorium, all one-night engagements between January 20 and February 22.

ness manager told Evelyn. "I need to get these books straight so we can beat this tax audit." So Evelyn took her first trip to the Bronze Peacock. In her patent leather heels, she stood nearly a head taller than Robey. Evelyn's confident air, azure eyes, and sculpted physique made Robey's heart palpitate. He found Evelyn's book-cooking as appealing as her looks—she aced the revenuers—and he wanted to keep her around. Evelyn happened to have been between jobs after overabsorption of radiation ended her career as an X-ray nurse. Robey hired her as secretary of the Bronze Peacock nightclub, but she quickly assumed leadership of day-to-day operations. She was at the Bronze Peacock during its finest hours—T-Bone Walker's panty parties and Gatemouth Brown's debut.[10] And as Robey and Johnson realized that Aladdin had abandoned their prodigy, an idea for all Robey's free time and extra money dawned on them.

"Don Robey was a very enterprising person," Johnson recalled. "He welcomed any challenge. His whole attitude was that we didn't need Aladdin to put out records on Gatemouth Brown.

"I said 'well how do you make a record?'

"He said 'Hell, I don't know, that's for you to find out.' "[11]

Robey helped more than Evelyn let on. He came up with the company's name: Peacock Records. He developed a strategy for growing the Peacock brand, based on the old model that he and Morris Merritt had used to promote dances in the 1930s. He would establish partnerships in other places, with people who could get records on jukeboxes and sell dance tickets. He and Johnson founded Buffalo Booking Agency, with Evelyn as its licensed agent, for the express purpose of booking Gatemouth Brown.[12]

She also learned on the fly, thanks to Robey's carte blanche, the particulars of the record business, eventually mastering licensing and copyright intricacies, plus the brass tacks of production and manufacturing. They jumped into the retail end of the trade, swapping out Robey's liquor store on the Houston stroll of Lyons Avenue and installing a record shop. There, the first Peacock Records issues of Gatemouth Brown's "Didn't Reach My Goal" backed with the remarkable "Atomic Energy" were sold. Johnson conducted the early administrative duties for Buffalo and Peacock while wedged in an office in the back that doubled as Peacock Records warehousing and distribution center. Robey hoped it would be a self-feeding beast, this Buffalo-Peacock: personal appearances would create a demand for records, with proceeds benefiting Peacock, and popular records would sell dance tickets, fattening the Buffalo. The key factor would be Robey's ability to forge and expand alliances beyond his Texas-Louisiana territory.

Chapter 12 ✶ ✶ ✶ ✶ ✶ ✶ ✶

All Part of the Game

By the early World War II years, while black nightclubs began to flourish virtually everywhere else in the country, Beale Street, Memphis's vaunted stroll, had run dry. Storied clubs like Pee Wee's, the Brick, the Monarch, and the Hole in the Ground—the sorts of places that inspired the music and colored the lyrics in W. C. Handy's revolutionary trilogy, "Memphis Blues," "St. Louis Blues," "Beale Street Blues"—vanished after a prolonged political assault on the street. Beale's vice trade scattered, so roadhouses up Highway 51 from the city rocked, and nightclub action moved across the Mississippi into West Memphis, Arkansas. War-era Memphis, with its vaudeville-style talent shows and numerous local big bands, jug bands, and park-bench guitar pickers, seemed a bit nostalgic next to Houston and New Orleans, and compared to those cities, modern black music emerged slowly in the Bluff City.

Beale Street rose eastbound from the cobblestone Mississippi River landing, where the cotton steamers waited. It climbed steeply onto a bluff, and then let down easy, past the Orpheum Theatre at Main Street, the intersection of white downtown and black downtown, into the shopping district over Second Street, past the modest brick cafés and pawn shops whose signage cluttered the view, by A. Schwab's two-story dry goods store, the cast-iron storefront at Epstein's Loan Office, and the glorious, three-story Gallina's Exchange, with its brick arches and torchlike cornices.[1] Gayoso Bayou, a paved-over subterranean waterway, snaked under Beale, and stuck the chill to your skin in winter the same as it did the heat in summer. The street-car sparked along past all-night chitlin' joints and chop suey restaurants. Rooming houses clustered around Beale for blocks on either side, and on the numbered cross streets, where thousands of black renters stayed.

The city dedicated Handy Park in 1931 at Beale and Third to show the composer its appreciation. Evangelists prophesied fire, and jug bands sputtered, creaked, and moaned in Handy Park, a dirt patch with benches that stretched to Hernando Street and the foot of a one-block theater district called the Rialto. Hallowed ground: roots of modern black music sprung from the now-abandoned taverns on this block where Handy heard the plaintive folk melodies and peculiar notes of cotton pickers and low-down rounders that he modified to his formal band scores and popularized as the blues. Roots of modern black activism sprawled from the block too, where a journalist named Ida B. Wells began her crusade against lynching. Through Handy, Beale Street's ancient dirges were in the books of Duke Ellington, Benny Goodman, and Louis Armstrong, and Ella Fitzgerald's band. From there, Beale Street inspired motion pictures and pop songs. It appeared in the literary works of William Faulkner and Richard Wright.

The Rialto sidewalk filled up by nightfall, people milling, loping, stopping, talking. Dusty farm clothes rubbed razor-sharp gabardines. Brogan scuffed Stacy Adams. The juiced snored away down alleys. You could consult hoodoo priests and priestesses or drop a dime to peek in the carnival tent. Hip Beale Streeters had dubbed this block with respect to the Italian entrepreneurs who had built the street's theaters in the early twentieth century, which added character and architectural splendor to the street. The three-story Palace showed movies, played orchestras, and hosted amateur contests where The Lord High Executioner dismissed contestants with a blank fired from a pearl-handled revolver. The Daisy—where Handy and Bessie Smith stepped from their limousine to a red carpet on opening night of *St. Louis Blues* in 1929—was North Africa meets boardwalk, its hexagonal ticket booth tucked in a recessed dome ringed with twinkling lights. The boxy, modern New Daisy shaded the sidewalk with its grand marquee directly across the street from the old Daisy. Music filled the Rialto air. Local dance orchestras—Howard Yancy's, Ike Peron's, Conny Connell's, and Ben French's, the latter Jelly Roll Morton remembered as being Beale's top piano player as of 1909—kept second-story studios around the Palace, either side of the street. They threw their windows open, and their sounds, Yancy's banjo-plucking ragtime and Connell's sweet Ellingtonian swing, mingled with the jukebox tunes and the scent of fried pork skin blaring from the One Minute Dairy and Lunch below. But still, no nightclubs—Memphis's powerful political boss E. H. Crump had closed down the sinful stations of gambling and prostitution after an embarrassing exposé of his machine's coziness with vice had appeared in *Collier's* in 1935.

Despite Beale's fame as the birthplace of the blues, lengthwise there wasn't much to it—two or three crowded blocks.

While the chitlin' circuit activated music business across black America, making places like Houston and Macon viable for the first time, Beale Street would be its great revival job. In late 1941, just as Denver Ferguson officially entered the band-booking business, a man named Robert Henry rented a second-floor room above a liquor store between the Peron and Yancy studios in the heart of the Rialto, and opened a dance promotion office, across the street from the saloon where Handy had scribbled the notes to what had become "Memphis Blues."

Born in Tupelo, Mississippi, in 1889, Robert Henry migrated to Memphis in 1909. Henry stood no taller than a pool cue. He was light-skinned and fleshy, with a broad nose, pointy little eyes, and round shoulders. He wore his hair and mustache scraggly and his shirttail out. He constantly leaned, a bent elbow on a bar top or a shoulder pressed against a pillar. He mixed evenly with Beale Street's diverse clientele—his unpretentious appearance comforted rural folk, and his elegant wit impressed the rest. Henry fell in love with the city's bands as soon as he arrived, and organized a series of dances featuring them at different locations. Robert Henry's Moonlight Ball became a widely anticipated event. "That's when they was doin' the Cootie Crawl . . . the Slow Drag and all them different dances," he'd say. "At twelve o'clock we'd put the lights out in the dance hall. The people, they got a lot of kick out of being in the dark. Understand? Pretty girls, pretty clothes."[2]

By the late 1920s Henry had begun hosting his Moonlight Ball in a hall behind his South Memphis home, next door to historically black LeMoyne College. He called this backhouse club the Pink Rose. The time period, residential location, and arrangement, even the suggestive name, all fit the speakeasy profile, but in his disarming way Henry insisted that the Pink Rose served "nothin' but coke colas." The joint's name was its most colorful feature. No tables or chairs inside, just a bandstand and dancing room only.

Through World War II, Henry established himself as the Rialto's big-time band buyer and local band seller. He brought Count Basie, Cab Calloway, Duke Ellington, and Fats Waller to the Palace, and presented Jimmie Lunceford's homecomings up the block at Beale Avenue Auditorium. Perhaps taking his inspiration from political machinist "Boss" Crump, Henry appointed himself representative for the local colored American Federation of Musicians. His Beale footprint had expanded by 1944, with a record shop across the street from his office, and a billiard lounge a few doors from there. For a roadhouse booking, he could assemble an orchestra from spare parts in Handy Park and the saloons, usually in under an hour. He studied the street, resting against the poolroom doorway, gathering intelligence on newly arrived musicians, and holding a finger to its economic winds. He noted black soldiers spending cash in greater quantities than he had seen from common folk, and thought the time right to carefully bring back nightclubs.

Henry threw a dance on January 12, 1945, in the Hotel Men's Improvement Club, located at the gateway to the Rialto at Beale and Hernando streets. He showcased local orchestras first, not wanting to invest much in case the political boss's bullies dismantled him. In late February 1945, Henry felt safe enough to spend money on an out-of-town act, and Ferguson Brothers' classically hyperbolic publicity adorned Beale's shop windows: "Dance Dance Dance to the Music of King Kolax and the 'Hottest Dance Orchestra in the World.' "

Meanwhile, a husband and wife tandem carefully opened another new nightspot on the fabled boulevard. Born in Memphis on November 6, 1906, Andrew "Sunbeam" Mitchell had grown up on Beale Street. If he wasn't born a hustler, he became one early in life. His father, a drayman, taught Sunbeam to lead a horse-drawn vegetable cart throughout the densely packed district. The closest thing to an education Sunbeam got took place behind the cart, where he learned to calculate his inventory and prices of various goods, the basics in mental arithmetic that would lay the foundation for his career. The street never closed so Sunbeam enjoyed very little time off. On slow nights, Sunbeam hitched his cart beside the Savoy Club, where he could hear the stylings of stiff-moving whorehouse pianist Money Clark, and a dance caller named Cat Eye, who led couples through the Black Bottom and Shimmy She Wobble in comical rhymes. "I never was a dancer," Sunbeam said. "I was an observer. I was trying to make some money some way."[3]

Sunbeam worked in a Detroit factory during World War II. Having made some money, he returned home in 1944 and fell in with a young woman named Ernestine McKinney. Fourteen years younger than Sunbeam, she would become his business partner, then his bride. They leased two stories above the Pantaze Drug Store on the corner of Beale and Hernando opposite the Hotel Men's Improvement Club.

Previously, the space had housed a ponderously named joint, the Royal Gardens (no royalty, no gardens). "That was a little high powered place," Beale musician Piano Red recalled. "Fellows throat cutting and throw them out the window, three stories down onto Beale and Hernando."[4] Ernestine and Sunbeam opened a rooming house on the third floor, letting rooms at $3.50–$5.50 a week. Ernestine kept all the records, paid the bills, and charted monthly expenses, often listing Sunbeam as one of the heaviest. Just a few months into the hospitality business, with Sunbeam losing interest, she found herself staggering under mounting responsibilities. She wrote to a friend on January 15, 1945, "Sunbeam, he want to do nothing but sleep, eat, go to the show, come in at 1–2, any time he feel like, and I don't have no body to help me. West Memphis have closed down and Bully Freddie and Kid Henry stay in the street all the time."[5]

The latter issue inspired Ernestine's solution to the former. Much of Memphis's black nightlife had spread across the Mississippi River to West Memphis, Arkansas, during the previous decade, and West Memphis's closure certainly created new opportunity on the river's Tennessee side. Or perhaps they simply saw what Bob Henry was doing across the street, and followed suit. Either way, Ernestine and Sunbeam built a modest bandstand, and installed a bar and grill downstairs from the rooming house. Drug store customers entered the Pantaze at street level, from the front of the building on the Beale side, while a skinny catwalk led up from Hernando Street to the floors above, where Ernestine and Sunbeam opened the Domino Lounge and Mitchell Hotel on May 4, 1945. Slyly, Ernestine kept her man close to home, and though the fates of Bully Freddie and Kid Henry remain a mystery, Sunbeam Mitchell would become the catalyst to black Memphis music's renaissance.

Sunbeam's experience on the vegetable cart taught him the value of a constant street presence. A casual, heavyset fellow with a high hairline, Sunbeam was oddly mannered. His hands shook. He stammered in a high, nasal voice. He dressed like a barkeep, in white shirts, sleeves rolled up, dark trousers, and black necktie. His jowls hung and his belly protruded. Sunbeam would become a human-interest story in his later days. Reporters would depict him as an avuncular, charmingly grizzled patron of the blues. In these remembrances, Ernestine and Sunbeam's place had been like a Norman Rockwell soda fountain, only with blacks. Sunbeam and Ernestine were the pop and mom who kept a pot of chili on and their doors open for their adopted, nomadic children who might drop in broke or hungry at any time. They nurtured B.B. King, Bobby "Blue" Bland, Johnny Ace, Little Junior Parker, and Little Richard. "So many out of town musicians would come in," Sunbeam told a *Memphis Commercial Appeal* reporter in 1985. "They didn't have money, nothing to eat. They'd try to get things going. I'm the one that helped them along, gave them something to eat. That chili."[6]

There was significantly more to Sunbeam's operation, however, than a soft heart and hot chili.

"Sunbeam was a nice man," drummer Howard Grimes said, "but dangerous."[7]

Like Grimes, saxophonist Emerson Able worked for Sunbeam. As Able explained, Sunbeam flourished during this locked-down time on Beale thanks to high-level protection. "Sunbeam was Abe Plough's ace nigger. Didn't nobody fuck with Sunbeam, man."[8]

Abe Plough was born in Tupelo, Mississippi, in 1892, and the Ploughs moved to Memphis a couple of years later. Abe's only enduring educational experience came from a grammar-school teacher who imparted a method of paperless arithmetic. Beyond that, Plough typified the self-made man. At age sixteen, Plough quit school and borrowed $125 from his father, Moses. In a room above Moses's store, Abe concocted and bottled Plough's Antiseptic Healing Oil; Plough must have seen the ubiquitous Sunbeam working Beale Street from the time Plough opened the Pantaze Drug Store at Beale and Hernando in 1914. He learned black vanities and superstitions on the street, and amassed great wealth with his Black and White cosmetics, a line of skin bleaches and hair straighteners that Plough launched in 1917 at prices below those for Madam C. J. Walker's beauty products. Concoctions such as Plough's Mexican Heat Powder found prominent use in hoodoo spell recipes. He advertised heavily in black newspapers. In 1920, Plough moved into pharmaceuticals and developed St. Joseph's aspirin. He remained interested in grassroots black culture after his shift from black commerce into the business of mainstream beauty products like Coppertone suntan lotion. By the end of World War II, Plough ranked among the richest men in Memphis, strictly a limousine-to-work kind of man. Nevertheless, Plough was Jewish, and Memphis society limited Jewish country club membership and participation in Cotton Carnival, the city's annual celebration of planter aristocracy. Perhaps an outsider kinship formed between Plough and Sunbeam, hard-grinding hucksters up against an unforgiving social barrier. Plough was careful to keep his distance from Sunbeam on paper—the Mitchells paid Abe's brother Sam the rent—and while there's no doubt that Plough helped Sunbeam, no one can say how much Plough knew about Sunbeam's activities above the Pantaze.[9]

Sunbeam's racket began modestly enough. "He never stopped selling bootleg whiskey," Emerson Able recalled. "He could be talking to the chief of police and say, 'Excuse me, chief.' Then go get a half-pint and sell it to the guy next to the chief." Sunbeam was no moonshiner. He sold legally produced, bottled-in-bond liquor, making it more conveniently available than did liquor stores that closed certain hours of the day and days of the week. Sunbeam's service to patrons was comparable to what Abe Plough had provided two generations prior with his 140 proof Antiseptic, which was good, according to its label, "for cuts, bruises, wounds, sprains, rheumatism, neuralgia, headache, stiff joints and pains in the back." Recommended dosage: "as often as the severity of the case requires."

In very little time, Sunbeam discovered a substantially populated, legally inconvenienced constituency of liquor lovers below the state line in dry Mississippi, and he would develop an interstate vice distribution system that worked like an old-time medicine show, albeit with sex, gambling, bottled-in-bond booze, and entertainment by the rising stars of black music.

✳   ✳   ✳

Memphis caught up to the rest of the black music world by the middle of 1946. Bob Henry had sold white promoters the idea of showcasing the top black orchestras, and so Basie, Ellington, and Lunceford performed matinees at the white Orpheum Theatre, just a few blocks from the Rialto, before their nights at the Palace on Beale. White promoters Nate Evans and Chalmers Cullins, recognizing the city's large, underserved black population beyond Beale, built a theater on Park Avenue in Orange Mound, south of downtown. They recruited Kemmons Wilson as a partner. Wilson started out as a teenage dropout selling popcorn at the picture shows, then distributed pinball machines and jukeboxes before hitting it big as a builder. He went on to found the Holiday Inn motel chain in 1952. In 1946, Wilson and friends completed the W. C. Handy Theatre and hired Bob Henry to "showcase the finest in Negro entertainment."[10]

While Henry promoted high-profile acts on Beale and at the W. C. Handy, Sunbeam Mitchell's low-down juke joint simmered. "We never could get it to an A-class club," Sunbeam said. His clientele mostly "didn't have the money to go to better places."[11] He charged fifty cents admission. The place sat about two hundred, with nary a tablecloth, but plenty of good food. The grill churned out veal chops, bell peppers, mashed yams, and fried fish as well as that sought-after chili. Patrons drank Pabst and Sterling beers by the quart, in addition to Sunbeam's medicinal compound. With thirty-five rooms in the Mitchell Hotel, and no more than ten boarders at a given time, Ernestine let several of the rooms out on a short-term basis, as former regular Ford Nelson recalled. "I would access some of those 'by the hour' rooms, have me a little fun back up in there."[12]

Around this time, an eternally upbeat and highly talented tenor saxophonist named Bill Harvey organized Sunbeam's house band. Harvey mimicked Louis Jordan's bug-eyed stage antics, but his clowning exterior hid a genius for band leadership—how to whip a group into shape, to highlight its strengths and downplay weaknesses, and to show budding musicians the respect they needed to yield to his guidance. On Beale Street after the war, the man had no peer. As Ford Nelson recalled, "We would leave our respective jobs, try to get out as early as we can to hear him blow tenor saxophone."

Harvey's band shared residency at Sunbeam's with Tuff Green and the Rocketeers. Richard "Tuff" Green had studied music with Professor Jimmie Lunceford in the late 1920s at Manassas High in North Memphis. Tuff operated the city's first black recording service, out of his home in musically wealthy South Memphis. Tuff made his recordings and rehearsed the Rocketeers at 406 Simpson Avenue, exactly a block parallel to the little frame cottage on Lucy Avenue where Baptist preacher C. L. Franklin's family lived, including daughter Aretha, and less than a mile from Lunceford's tomb. Tuff Green and the Rocketeers' circuit began with city housing-project auditoriums, extended to dance halls in the Arkansas Delta and Greenville, Mississippi, and ended up most nights at Sunbeam's. Tuff played bass and, like Harvey and Lunceford, loaded his band with promising young musicians. Noted jazz pianist Mose Allison said, "I always tell people that the original rock-n-roll band was Tuff Green in Memphis. . . . I used to go to the Mitchell Hotel, man, they used to sneak me in in '47 and '48."[13] The Rocketeers included, among others, drummer Phineas Newborn Sr., saxophonist Ben Branch, and twenty-one-year-old tenor wizard Leonard Campbell, known as "Doughbelly."

Though Sunbeam didn't formally schedule or advertise live music at his place, everyone, including the big acts Bob Henry promoted, learned where to find the all-night jam session. Sunbeam's music contacts grew as his informal jam sessions and cheap lodging became the exclusive spot for traveling black performers and their entourages.

The musicians at Sunbeam's competed in head-cutting contests, play-offs between soloists. Beale Street lifer Rufus Thomas recalled, "After each would take a solo, then one would take a part of the sound and play maybe four bars, and then the other fellow would pick up four bars. Then the other one would play eight, and [his opponent] would play eight. So they battling back at each other . . . and these just were beautiful." Black stars playing Memphis often stopped to test their chops against locals at the Mitchell. "They'd put their horns under their arms and go to the jam sessions," Thomas said. Pianist Ford Nelson recalled, "When Nat Cole came through, I heard them say 'nobody at the Mitchell Hotel gonna cut his head.' Nat Cole, he took care of business." Describing other contenders, Emerson Able said, "Saxophone players were looking for the little fat man in the fez: Doughbelly," who counted Wardell Gray, hard bop stylist then with the Basie orchestra, among his victims. Of Doughbelly, Rufus Thomas said, admiringly, "Terrible. I mean, [he'd] blow somebody off the bandstand."[14] According to Ford Nelson, house bandleader Bill Harvey was a "force to be reckoned with." Tuff Green's second tenor man Ben Branch challenged Harvey, but "of course Bill would take care of him," Nelson said.

Piano challengers also had to deal with Bill "'Struction" Johnson, who earned his sobriquet from what unsuspecting newcomers met in competition with him. Beale Street's rollicking musical history pumped through Johnson's fingers. Handy-era orchestra leaders Howard Yancy and one-eyed Ike Peron—the fellows who kept second-floor rehearsal studios above the Rialto—groomed him to play tinkling melodic accompaniment like Duke Ellington, and forceful stride leads like Earl Hines. 'Struction rolled just as comfortably with small blues combos like Howlin' Wolf's, providing a jackhammer rhythm. His deeply laid-back, almost sleepy, demeanor and chuckling good humor belied his cutthroat competitiveness. Robert Lockwood Jr., Robert Johnson's protégé, a nimble-minded, inventive guitarist, said of 'Struction, "He's one of the best musicians I've ever known."[15]

While the big orchestras still rehearsed above Beale as they had in W. C. Handy's day, Sunbeam's place was becoming a laboratory for new sounds.[16] The first person to recognize this and act on it was a fancy fellow from Houston whose gold teeth were his only discernibly Negro characteristics. Don Robey dropped into the Mitchell in the summer of 1947, probably during the same trip that led him to Dave Bartholomew in New Orleans. Kindred spirits, Robey and Sunbeam took to one another immediately. This association opened musical trade between Memphis and Houston that would boost these cities to the top of the black music world over the next two decades. Asked to explain the Houston-Memphis connection, Robey's business partner Evelyn Johnson recalled, "It was primarily through promoting bands, with Andrew Mitchell, who was lovingly called 'Sunbeam.' It was a medium of exchange, because we had bands that came out of Houston, and he'd promote them over there and vice versa."[17] On August 30, 1947, Mitchell regulars Tuff Green and the Rocketeers became the first black Memphis orchestra to play Houston, gigging at the Downtown Grill for Robey's partner Julius White.

Though Sunbeam already had the cream of Memphis's white business community on his side, he added a little more protection to his home base in October 1948 when the Memphis Police Department swore in its first black officers. Blacks weren't permitted in the downtown police station unless in handcuffs, so the new black force needed a place to change into its uniforms and call roll. Their beat was segregated as well, limited to Beale Street after dark until midnight. Sunbeam opened his door to them, and Memphis's original colored cops began their first roll call next to the Seeburg, before spilling down the catwalk to Beale. One of the new officers, Jewel Jubirt, shared a few strategic insights with a newspaper reporter. "When the old people get out of line, we're going to run them home, but we're going to clean up these jitterbugs—they're going down to the station. We're going to stop all this 'playing the dozens,' " he added, explain-

Two of Beale Street's first black patrolmen, Jewel Jubirt and Roscoe McWilliams, calling roll at Sunbeam Mitchell's joint at Beale and Hernando, night of November 8, 1948. *Special Collections, University of Memphis Libraries*

ing with a chuckle that the dozens is a game of traded barbs "about someone's female ancestors" that typically foreshadow a knife fight. "We're going to stop prostitution on Gayoso [the street parallel to Beale]," Jubirt concluded, saying nothing about the oldest profession on Beale. Along the sidewalk, the street appeared tame by comparison to its younger self. The scent of buttered popcorn clung to the air around Fourth and Beale, at the edge of the Rialto, competing with the peanut roaster and boiled hard crabs at the One Minute Café— "get a few drinks and start wearing out and peanuts and crabs taste good," a Beale Streeter remarked. A long-timer noted, seemingly with a wink, "People look at Beale and say 'What is there to it?' " but "Old Beale's still here just like it always was. They just don't know where to look."[18]

Sunbeam behaved as if he had been deputized by his arrangement with the police. Never shy with his six-shooter, Sunbeam would make

The second Mitchell Hotel, located above the drugstore at the corner
of Main Street and Calhoun Avenue in downtown Memphis, as it
looked when Sunbeam and Ernestine Mitchell assumed its operation
in 1949. Remembered as a skinning joint during its heyday, it's
now a popular hangout and tourist attraction called Ernestine and
Hazel's. *Special Collections, University of Memphis Libraries*

news for thwarting would-be robbers, and earn an off-the-record
reputation for settling violent disputes with violence.[19]

As 1948 bled into '49, Ernestine and Sunbeam spread the Old
Beale magic, opening a second Mitchell Hotel and grill. Like the first,
it occupied the second floor of one of Abe Plough's drug stores. This
one stood at the corner of South Main Street and Calhoun Avenue,
across from the main train and bus terminal. The place earned immediate notoriety as a skinning joint. The prostitutes working the rooms
there were more inclined to knock johns unconscious and pick their
pockets than actually screw anyone. Green hornblowers and rubes

after harvest were the favorite clientele. Many a band left Memphis after a good night in worse shape than it had arrived in. Sunbeam loaned bandleaders gambling money, for they were virtually all inveterate players, then took them for it at his tables while his Main Street sirens, or the ones upstairs on Beale, fleeced the boys in the band.

By now, area band activity all ran through Sunbeam, as the Mitchell Hotel became an informal musicians' employment agency, a regional chitlin' circuit hub. Like New Orleans's Dew Drop, Dallas's Empire Room, and Indianapolis's Sunset Terrace, bandleaders organizing tours of the region would check in at Sunbeam's cantina to find musicians to hire. Rain or shine, night or day, someone could be found. In March 1949, tenor saxophonist Charles "Jazz" Ferguson, bandleader for guitarist Jimmy Liggins's rockin' eight-piece, stopped into the Mitchell to fill a hole for a couple weekends in Mississippi. Jazz picked Emerson Able Jr., a sixteen-year-old alto saxophonist, from the ever-changing Mitchell house band lineup, along with a couple other youngsters.

Their first show went off at a skating rink in Hinds County, near Jackson, Mississippi. Since Jackson was strictly policed, bootleggers and gamblers set up outside the city limits, north, toward the skating rink, and east, across the Pearl River on what they called the Gold Coast. Also known as "'cross the river," the Gold Coast gained well-deserved notoriety for its hotly competitive nightclub scene. A 1946 shootout between rival club owners took out one of the businessmen and the county constable. A month prior to Liggins's skating-rink dance, Gold Coast club operator Sam Baker shot and killed "Brother" Reed following a game of that risky insult contest known as the dozens.[20]

As the Liggins band played, on April Fool's Friday in 1949, Jazz Ferguson noticed a local in the crowd approach his wife for a dance. He was pleased to see her reject the man, a barber-in-training named Jerry Brasfield. The barber refused to back down, however, and Jazz shouted at him from the bandstand to back off. The barber, according to a press report, "became vulgar and abusive." Jazz leapt into the crowd. The barber flashed his razor, slashing Jazz across the arm, back, and neck.[21] "The people were hollering, 'Band, start playing, start playing,' " Able, the schoolboy saxophonist recalled. "Everybody thought music was gonna soothe the savage beast, and get them to stop fighting, and start dancing."

Instead, the guns came out, sounding to Able like they were firing from all directions. The men on stage didn't know which way to run, so they froze. The star of the show, Jimmy Liggins, stood spotlighted at center stage in the middle of the shootout. The melee paused as Liggins's head jerked, his cheek splashed against the rink wall, and his body dropped. Able glanced down at his shirt collar and saw a fragment of Liggins's jawbone stuck there. Then the stampede was on. More jitterbugs were trampled than shot or cut. Liggins narrowly survived, requiring numerous blood transfusions, reconstructive surgery, several weeks of convalescence at Jackson Baptist Hospital, and then a benefit dance at the skating rink to pay his medical bills and put enough money in his pocket to get the hell out of Mississippi.

Sunbeam sent a henchman named Bilbo Brown to collect the Memphis boys and take them on to their next gig with the Ligginsless Liggins band in Biloxi. Brown got Able and company to the gig, then took off with the money, leaving the boys in a Gulfport rooming house. The house lady confiscated their horns and carried the boys to the Western Union office, where they called their parents to wire them enough to pay their board and catch a bus home.

"I didn't tell my daddy about what happened to Mr. Liggins," Able said, "and he finally read about it in the *Pittsburgh Courier*."

Nevertheless, young Emerson convinced his father to let him play another weekend gig. Besides, this was with a group of his classmates, not some hard-running professionals. "We were the Rhythm Bombers," Able said, a big band made up primarily of Manassas High graduates. Their leader, Mr. W. T. McDaniel, liked to season them with extracurricular gigs, which also supplemented his meager teaching wage. The Bombers played for Sunbeam, but not at Beale and Hernando. "During that time, Sunbeam had gambling tables all up and down [Highway] 51," Able said. "He would take hoes up there that was hanging around his hotel selling pussy. Ernestine minded the hoes. This was part of the game. You had hoes there, and in the backroom guys were shooting dice through the horn at a big craps table. The white sheriff [of Tipton County] came through to get his collection on a bad night, and Sunbeam told him he didn't have no fuckin' money, 'cause wasn't nobody at the club. They got in a big argument, and we had to get to playing to curb the disturbance."

Able hoped it wasn't another night like the one last weekend at the rink.

"Then we heard 'crack-crack!' And the people said 'Lord, have mercy, Sunbeam done shot the sheriff!'

"Once again, I became a track star. No bullets hit me because I'm a little bitty dude. I ran the wrong way on 51—started going north instead of south. I couldn't tell my daddy nothing about this, or he'd stop me from playing."

The sheriff survived and no charges were ever pressed. "I don't know whether Sunbeam paid him off or whether Sunbeam said he was gonna tell the people the sheriff was taking money from him," Able said. "They were dealing in corn whiskey, and it was an illegal gambling joint, so everybody had to keep their mouths shut."

A Little Like Going to Heaven

Sunbeam and Bob Henry weren't the only powerful forces in black Memphis music. A struggling pop and country western radio station—WDIA, 73 on your dial—had introduced an all-black format in October 1948, and within a year the station featured a lineup of all-black on-air talent. Though select black ensembles had broadcast as far back as the 1920s—recall Al Capone's assistance in integrating the Windy City airwaves—and stations played black records during certain programs, WDIA was the first station entirely committed to programming for the black audience. The station's impact on Memphis music was profound and immediate. The *Memphis World* opined at the end of 1949 that a "galaxy" of talent had come to WDIA the previous year.

One star in this new galaxy was a skinny guitarist and singer from deep blues country named Riley King. Born in Itta Bena, Mississippi, on September 16, 1925, Riley grew up on spirituals and took up guitar as the sanctified instrument of choice. He sang in gospel quartets around Indianola, Mississippi, and drove a tractor before fleeing for the city. He arrived in Memphis in 1947 and stayed for a while with his cousin Booker White, a hard-core blues guitarist who'd made

records in the 1930s. In the city, Riley was drawn to one spot in particular—"going to Beale Street, in the mind of . . . Riley B. King, was
a little like going to heaven," he would say.[1] He ran to W. C. Handy
Park and listened to the musicians there for hours but kept his own
guitar tucked beneath his arm. Beale guitarists "seemed to have four
hands," he said. "I felt like I had all thumbs."

He wandered around, ogling the painted ladies and dice games:
Heaven.

After a brief return to Mississippi, Riley moved to Memphis again
in late 1948, determined to stay and make a living in music. Someone
in Handy Park told him to go see ol' Bob Henry in his office above
the liquor store on the Rialto.*

"In the beginning," Henry recalled, "I got Nat to give [King] a
job."[2] Henry was speaking of Nat D. Williams, a dark little man with
thick glasses and nubby fingers who taught at Booker T. Washington
High School, wrote the *Memphis World* column "Down on Beale,"
was the first black disc jockey WDIA hired, and emceed amateur
shows at the Palace Theatre, where Henry had booked acts for the
previous two decades. Henry had grasped radio's power as immediately as he recognized Riley King's *something*. After acing an audition
for WDIA owner Bert Ferguson with an impromptu jingle for a station sponsor, cure-all serum Pepticon, the charming and humble Riley
B. King broadcast daily, playing records and performing. He'd picked

---

* This differs from B.B.'s account in *Blues All around Me*, but comes from a much
earlier source, a March 29, 1952, story by Jim Roberts in the *Memphis Tri-State
Defender*, "From Itta Bena to Fame: B.B. King." The article touches on specific,
personal details of King's upbringing, early places of worship, his education, and
work history. King's job as a disc jockey began when "acting on a tip, Riley searched
out the veteran Memphis showman, Robert Henry. He found the friend of struggling artists on a wet and dreary afternoon, and soaking wet with drenched guitar,
Riley sought his help. Shortly thereafter, Riley King . . . was producing a popular
radio show of his own." Subsequent events explain the omission of Robert Henry
from future repetitions of the B.B. King story. As it's told now, B.B showed up to
WDIA, four and a half miles from his Beale Street hangout, in the pouring rain.

up the tag "Blues Singing Black Boy" in Handy Park, and abbreviated it for his deejay handle. The station billed him as Bee Bee King.

Henry specialized in auditorium and theater bookings, something Bee wasn't up to. Enter Bob's buddy Sunbeam Mitchell. Sunbeam booked the budding radio star into juke joints as far out as the WDIA signal traveled, and Bee Bee advertised his next appearance from the electric pulpit. He played little joints out Highway 51 toward Dyersburg, Tennessee, back down Mississippi's Highway 61, and over the river in Arkansas.

On a cold night in December 1949 in Twist, Arkansas, a fight broke out in a drafty juke joint heated by an oil drum half full of burning kerosene. Grappling, the brawlers tumbled down and toppled the drum on their way to the floor, spilling fire everywhere. It could have been like April 23, 1940, in Natchez all over, but everyone escaped. Until Bee Bee realized he'd left his instrument inside. Too poor to let it burn, he dashed back in. The fire roared over the shouts of "don't." It was like Hell in there, flames lashing at him as he ran, chunks of ceiling dropping all around, but he grabbed the guitar neck and turned back. He rolled out of the shack, smoldering. He heard that the two men had thrown blows, nearly killing each other and everyone else in the joint, over a waitress named Lucille, and he named his guitar after her, so the story goes.[3]

Bob Henry understood radio's transformative effect on the black music business. Ellington, Basie, and Lunceford spent years drilling their bands, juggling lineups, experimenting with arrangements, developing repertories, and building reputations. Now one song could do it. Any fool could comprehend Bee Bee's talent, feel his charisma, and see the audience sway the way he swayed. He only needed the song.

Henry fed Bee Bee records to play on his show, and pushed those of whomever he had booked next at the W. C. Handy. After Bee Bee returned from his nightly foray into Sunbeam's cotton town junket— "mainly raunchy roadhouses," he recalled—he headed up to the Mitchell Hotel to check Bill Harvey. "That was a thrill and an education," King would say.[4] By the time Bee Bee started calling his guitar Lucille, Bill Harvey had moved into the Mitchell Hotel at Beale and Hernando, literally an artist-in-residence, and begun to groom several gifted young musicians. These were products of Jimmie Lunceford's legacy of music education in Memphis's black public schools, including, though not exclusively fixed to, saxophonists Irvin Reason and Fred Ford and trumpeter Nathaniel Woodard. The club seldom shut its doors, and so Sunbeam employed numerous house musicians to rotate throughout the days into nights. The head-cutting never stopped. Phineas Newborn Jr., then a teenage prodigy, dominated the piano. "Phineas cut me," fellow tinkler Ford Nelson admitted, "the only one that ever got to him was a fellow named Oscar Dennard."[5]

Though Sunbeam, with his shaky hands and stammer, was memorably unmusical, he exerted artistic influence in his club, and that influence, however unwittingly, helped define his city's distinctive style for years to come. He felt that bebop, which the musicians loved experimenting with, would alienate his fifty-cent clientele, but he understood musicians' creative needs. "Sunbeam was very practical," said Ford Nelson, by this time a rotation pianist at the Mitchell. "He knew the audience preferred blues, but that the musicians preferred jazz, so he gave us some leeway." The Sunbeam style was masculine, yet refined, the blues stirred up with tight, polished jazz. This cocktail, whether called rhythm and blues, rock 'n' roll, or soul—heard on record labels from L.A., Houston, and Chicago—would be a vital force in American popular music for three decades to come. Like the musical education Jimmie Lunceford introduced to black Memphis schools, Sunbeam laid a cornerstone of what came to be known as the Memphis sound. You can hear its bluesy beginnings in B.B. King's early 1950s hits, "You Know I Love You," which was recorded in Tuff Green's South Memphis living room, and "Woke Up This Mornin'," cut in Houston but with Bill Harvey's band from the Mitchell. It's in Rosco Gordon's "No More Doggin'," the rockin' orchestral expression of a drunken leer, honed at Sunbeam's, and Little Junior Parker's

"Next Time You See Me" and "Driving Wheel," another Mitchell alum who recorded for Don Robey's record conglomerate in the late 1950s.

As recording grew into a multimillion-dollar local industry, and the Memphis sound became a trademarked advertising slogan in the mid-1960s, the basic musical formula remained no more complicated than what Sunbeam understood back in 1949. The people want to hear blues, and the musicians want to play jazz. Many of the musicians that the local music industry was built around had come up working for Sunbeam under that philosophy. Strains of what began at Sunbeam's—those punchy, blue horns—can be heard through the glorious Stax Records catalog in the early to mid-1960s. A former member of Tuff Green and the Rocketeers named Willie Mitchell (no kin to Sunbeam) produced a decade-long string of hits at Memphis's Hi Records, beginning with his own bluesy party instrumentals, and with such diversely styled vocalists as the unflappable Ann Peebles, brimstone-fiery O.V. Wright, and hypersexual Al Green. And do we hear echoes of Jimmie Lunceford in Hi's nonchalant backbeat?

Some folks will say Sunbeam's formula, a little blues for the people, a little jazz to keep the musicians alert, characterized much of the day's black popular music, and they'll be right to a certain degree. Still, it's uncanny that so many musicians who enjoyed extraordinarily long runs in a fickle business can trace their origins to a barroom above a drug store at the corner of Beale and Hernando in Memphis. Musicians who hung around the Mitchell's outstanding house players, talented locals sitting in, and visiting stars, in an environment that was both highly competitive and carefully nurturing, soaked up a quantity and quality of lessons that were simply not available anywhere else.

Sunbeam's influence spread to Houston through his house-band leader Bill Harvey. Working for Don Robey in the recording studio, Harvey shared his tricks with Grady Gaines, who led Little Richard's Upsetters in the mid-1950s, and Harvey groomed Joe Scott, who started as trumpeter in Harvey's band then became the producer-arranger for Bobby "Blue" Bland, Robey's most consistent earner from 1955 to 1973, and himself a Mitchell soldier.

*   *   *

By the time Robey started Peacock Records in late 1949, the prime New Orleans talents—Roy Brown, Dave Bartholomew, and by extension Fats Domino—were making someone else rich. He knew that Memphis in 1949 offered the same opportunity, and thanks to the Sunbeam Mitchell talent pipeline, Robey wouldn't miss the rush this time. In December 1950, Bill Harvey signed with Robey's Peacock Records and Buffalo Booking Agency. Harvey hopped on the endless Gatemouth Brown tour at the Del Morocco club, a few doors down from Sunbeam's, and would be a regular on the road and in Robey's recording studio for much of the next decade. One of Harvey's first assignments on record was to back pianist Marie Adams on the prophetically titled "I'm Gonna Play the Honky Tonks."

Chapter 14 ✳ ✳ ✳ ✳ ✳ ✳ ✳

Crossover

Denver Ferguson sidestepped the IRS in 1949, but the Feds picked up his trail again in 1950. Late that year, U.S. Senator Estes Kefauver, a Tennessee Democrat, spearheaded an investigation of Indianapolis's gambling as part of his far-reaching crackdown on organized crime and political machinery. The Kefauver probe found that Indianapolis lottery operations grossed a combined ten million dollars annually. Federal tax agents followed one of the racket's revenue streams to Indiana Avenue. They interrogated Avenue numbers runners and backroom policy house operators and planned to uproot the city's resilient bribe system from the street level to game bosses up to police and politicians. The January 13, 1951, *Indianapolis Recorder* reported, "Along the 'main stem' the 'grape vine' has been buzzing for several weeks [that] . . . the two big number house operators [presumably Tuffy Mitchell and the Fergusons] of the Westside, or several persons in both organizations, may be put on the spot."

Indianapolis rewired its power structure to complement the Feds' efforts. The next week a Marion County (Indianapolis) delegate introduced a bill in the state legislature to ban the printing or possession of numbers slips, the street lottery's unit of play, including the cleverly elusive baseball tickets that Denver had designed. The general assembly also considered granting the state attorney general unprecedented supervisory authority over county prosecutors and sheriffs, a preemptive strike against racketeers moving operations out of Indianapolis to give officials in a new county a taste of the bribes, then smuggling tickets back into the city. The same measure could have merely shifted the bribery to a higher place—the state attorney general's office—but Indianapolis's current tough-talking mayor, Philip Bayt, took another unprecedented step against the Avenue racket. He stationed police outside known ticket stations 'round the clock, including the oft-raided one nearest Sunset Terrace. Restrictions on the game heavily limited the kind of cash flow it needed to pay bribes.

Ultimately, Kefauver strangled Indiana Avenue's financial resources. Ferguson Brothers Agency could not survive on King Kolax's and Snookum Russell's receipts alone, and without capital from another source, Denver shut his agency down.

Denver, softened by the promise of new romance, decided not to fight on. He closed Ferguson Printing and Ferguson Bros., sold the building they occupied, and put out the word that he'd left the business. Denver's new plans required him to cooperate with the federal government, even share his personal financial data with them, which is what immigration officials demanded before they would authorize his German pen pal Lilo Rentsch's entry to the United States. He obliged and swore in affidavits, agreed to property appraisals, and provided his tax returns, which only reconfirms that love will make a man do crazy things.

The revenuers focused on Tuffy Mitchell (Denver's white long-time rival) and Denver's brother instead. Wilbur O. Plummer, the same collector Denver outfoxed in 1949, slapped a $173,967.67 lien on Sea Ferguson's property on December 13, 1951. Special Agent A. Robert Nelson, a forensic tax auditor, calling Sea "one of the big boys on the Avenue," said that Sea failed to report income earned from his bowling alley, liquor stores, and filling stations between 1942

and 1949. "[Sea] also did not report everything on the lottery during those years," Nelson added. The white *Indianapolis Star* referred
to Sea as "Indiana Avenue kingpin" and noted the former Mayor
of Bronzeville's impressive record of arrests on gambling and liquor
violations.[1]

Sea strolled into the tax collector's office, wrote out a check for
$128,882.48—the amount he and the government settled on, a record
in Marion County—then turned and walked out without a word.
From then on he concentrated on his bowling alley and real estate
practice, and encountered no further legal challenges.[2]

Denver, too, felt free and clear. The Avenue roughed him up pretty
well at times, but here he stood—thirty years after introducing his
novel numbers game to black Indianapolis, nearly twenty years after
building the glamorous Sunset Terrace, and a decade and a half past
developing the chitlin' circuit—retired and awaiting the arrival of his
bride. He had enabled hundreds of friends and relatives to make their
living in the black world. He fought valiantly against white encroach-
ment, he evolved to stay on top, and now he was ready to live out his
golden years with the porcelain profile from *Ebony* settled on the pillow beside him each night.

✳   ✳   ✳

Senator Kefauver hadn't limited the scope of his inves-
tigations to the Indianapolis vice trade—he attacked political racketeering as well, and hence he had the paradoxical effect of toning
down the Indianapolis scene while blowing Memphis wide open.
There, longtime machine boss E. H. Crump had restricted nightlife on Beale Street, with exceptions for operators with powerful
protection.

The lifting of the Crump lid in 1950 changed Memphis much as
the repeal of Prohibition had everyplace in 1933—joints that had
operated quietly under the lid improved their looks, and new places
opened up. A renovated Currie's Club Tropicana opened on Thomas

Street in North Memphis, Del Morocco plugged in to the Beale scene between the Hotel Men's Improvement Club and Sunbeam Mitchell's hotel on Hernando Street. A skating rink called the Hippodrome on Beale's east end began hosting live rock 'n' roll and remote radio broadcasts as well, as 1951 started fast in Memphis. On March 2, our pals Gatemouth Brown and Sax Kari performed at the W. C. Handy for Bob Henry. WDIA announced a new program, Bee Bee's Jeebies, hosted by Bee Bee King, airing weekday afternoons between one and two o'clock. The shows at the W. C. Handy and Hippodrome cost between sixty cents and a dollar, and you could buy locally brewed Goldcrest 51 Beer there in ten-cent "splits."

Just as Sax and Gatemouth left town, a group of teenagers motored up Highway 61 from the Mississippi Delta, their instruments and PA equipment tied on top of their car. Nineteen-year-old Ike Turner drove.

Ike came up in Clarksdale, Mississippi, where poor men made music with broom wires and broken bottlenecks, and Ike brought this spirit to the new sound. He and his band buddies mended slack piano wire with steel belt from radial tires, and patched worn-out horn pads with bits of chamois and cork from soda bottle caps. They called themselves the Top Hatters, but a schism divided the members who preferred big-band swing from those who saw greater promise in the modern style. The modernists, not hurting for confidence, declared themselves Kings of Rhythm. Their core lineup included bandleader Ike Turner on piano, Jackie Brenston on baritone sax and vocals, Raymond Hill on tenor sax, Willie Sims's drums, and Willie Kizart's guitar. Bee Bee King, playing Clarksdale on Sunbeam's cotton-town juke-house circuit, had seen the Kings of Rhythm perform and recommended they visit Sam Phillips at Memphis Recording Service.[3]

Sam C. Phillips, a twenty-eight-year-old red-headed Alabamian, loved black music. The prospect of recording it lured Sam from steady employment at a radio station into the rhythm and blues record business. He rented a shop at 706 Union Avenue amidst used-car dealerships, a few blocks east from downtown Memphis. He acoustic-tiled the walls and ceiling, and bought a few microphones and a recording deck. Sam subcontracted for Chess Records in Chicago and Modern Records in Los Angeles, independent producers for the black record market.

As the band of Mississippi boys drove up Highway 61, they hit a bump that sent their equipment flying from atop the station wagon. They diagnosed a fractured cone in the guitar amplifier.

In deference to black music's rawness, Sam was developing a minimalist record-producing philosophy. He wanted the artists he recorded to be comfortable, to be themselves. So when Ike and his band showed up with a busted amp, they improvised a solution, placing a crumpled newspaper in place of the damaged speaker cone to help carry the guitar's sound.

Though the band recorded several numbers that day, a boozily cruising tune called "Rocket 88" stood out thanks to Ike's boogie-inflected piano, Raymond Hill's sax—straining through its chamois-patched holes—and that fuzzy-crackling guitar. Its most original aspect, according to singer Jackie Brenston, was its lyric, which the group had composed on Highway 61 between stops to tie down their shit.

Sam played the "Rocket 88" demo for Dewey Phillips (no relation), a white Memphis disc jockey who straddled barriers of race and ordinary reality. He proclaimed his cultural allegiance more loudly than Sam, however, by shopping at the Beale tailor the black sports favored, and speaking in a rapid-fire hipster dialect. Dewey dug the song. Sam too heard a hit, and with no other recourse to get rich from it, he became Brenston's manager.[4] With his interest vested in Brenston and not the Kings of Rhythm unit, Sam sent the master recording up to Chess Records in Chicago as "Rocket 88" by Jackie Brenston and his Delta Cats, and set about transforming his client into a star.

The song stirred up a sensation in Memphis. Dewey used "Rocket 88" as the theme song for his late night "Red, Hot, and Blue" program on radio station WHBQ. Oldsmobile dealerships—a powerful Olds Super 88, with its fat fenders and V8 engine had inspired the tune—located a few blocks on either side of Sam Phillips's Memphis Recording Service on Union Avenue, set public address speakers out, and blared "Rocket 88." Raymond Hill's shrieking sax echoed up and down Union, and Willie Kizart's guitar blended with the V8s' rumble in traffic. The song made front-page news in the white *Commercial Appeal* on March 28, 1951. "You may not have heard this musical explosion yet," wrote Lydel Sims, "but . . . I'm afraid you are utterly doomed to." By the time Sims's article hit front porches, Memphis's Plastic Products—an extraordinary operation where apron-clad women baked records like hot biscuits on equipment invented by owner Robert "Buster" Williams—had pressed thousands of Brenston's "Rocket 88" and distributed them to mom-and-pop record shops throughout the South. "Sam is convinced," Sims reported, "the Rocket will move out of the race field into general popularity."

In the years since, critics have debated whether "Rocket 88" was the first rock 'n' roll record, though plenty of sonic evidence, courtesy of Roy Brown and Amos Milburn among others, nixes that possibility. By Jackie Brenston's own reasoning, "Rocket 88" was the second generation of black rock. The Kings of Rhythm cribbed the music from "Cadillac Boogie" by Jimmy Liggins, he whose cheek rested in pieces in a Mississippi skating rink. Brenston would tell *Living Blues*, many years later, "If you listen to the two, you'll find out they're both basically the same. The words are just changed."[5] Nevertheless, "Rocket 88" was probably the first black rocker to cross over since Louis Jordan successfully marketed to white people, or "general popularity" in Sam Phillips's nice euphemism. A white deejay broke the song, a white company embraced its advertising power, and the white paper picked the story up, a rare combination of events. A couple days after the front-page story ran, an ad appeared in the white *Commercial Appeal*. It told readers to go to Orange Mound, the black neighborhood, next weekend to a theater named after black

Memphis icon W. C. Handy and drop sixty cents to see a black band. The ad carried a promise from Jackie Brenston: "WE ARE GONNA TEAR THE HOUSE DOWN!" The group played the weekend of April 7–8 at the W. C. Handy. An ad in the black *Memphis World* listed a Saturday 11:30 p.m. showtime, while the *Commercial Appeal* ad said, "Show for White . . . Sunday 11:30pm."

While they may not have torn racial barriers down, the music, as Sam Phillips hoped, reached a new audience for black rock 'n' roll in Memphis. The *Commercial Appeal* published results of its disc jockey write-in popularity poll the second day of the run, April 8, 1951, with Dewey Phillips finishing second. The most surprising result, however, according to the paper's radio editor: "Who could have known that card after card would stare us in the face with nothing on it but 'Please play "Rocket 88" . . .'." The request perplexed the editor. He wondered, "What in tucket is 'Rocket 88'?"

While Brenston, Turner, and crew played the W. C. Handy, one of the theater's owners, Chalmers Cullins, performed in a black-face comedy about purloined poultry in the city auditorium. Then there was ol' Bob Henry, whom Cullins and Wilson had brought in to run the show at the W. C. Handy years before. Add the men of destiny Ike Turner and Sam Phillips to the mix and you've got quite a cast. All lent their muscle to Memphis's first hit record. "Rocket 88" soared to the top of the *Billboard* Rhythm and Blues charts in July 1951. Sam Phillips's star search, however, would have to continue. "Everything went smooth for a while," Brenston explained. "But I guess everybody got the big head, including me. . . . I was a greenhorn. I had a hit record and no sense." Brenston never matched his initial success. Sam, with his sights set on "general popularity," recorded Jackie singing a country song "Tuckered Out" as a follow-up to "Rocket 88."

"It was lousy," Brenston would reflect.[6]

Sam Phillips learned a few lessons of his own.

Meanwhile, the growing power of radio on the chitlin' circuit vaulted another Mississippian in Memphis to stardom, though in a roundabout fashion.

✳   ✳   ✳

Lowell Fulson had a paralyzing case of stage fright. The big red Oklahoman seldom played theaters, and here he was at Memphis's W. C. Handy. Though His "Every Day I Have the Blues" was one of the biggest rhythm and blues grooves going, he froze there in the wings all the same. His band vamped the introduction to his opening number one more time. Bob Henry had seen this before. He waddled over to Lowell, leaned on the big man's shoulder like they'd been tight for years, and suggested in his disarming way, "You just walk out there like you going to the bathroom or somewhere. Like you don't particularly care about coming on stage." Lowell took a few steps and peeked through the curtain. "All them people sitting out there looking," he thought. Lowell feared he might get run off. Lowell looked back at Bob Henry, who gave his head a half shake, and drawled, "Get on out there."[7]

Lowell's warm-up act and pianist that night was a handicapped twenty-one-year-old known by his impairment, Blind Ray Charles. Ray made thirty-five dollars a week and lived the chitlin' circuit cycle, performing daily, chain smoking and shooting dice on the bus between stops, and flopping in a furnished room. After beginning as a section player, he now led Fulson's band for a couple of sets, and was featured in another. His vocal style had matured from the medium cool he borrowed from Nat Cole earlier in his career, to his own poly-textured sound. Fulson and Charles presented contrasting styles. Lowell, affable, overweight, and gold-tooth grinning, played loose, country blues. He couldn't read music. Ray, trim, clean-cut, and detached, could hear every note the band played clearly as if isolated from the rest of the song. Keeping track of the composition as a whole, he identified and corrected mistakes during the group's rehearsals, and tightened the Fulson band into a precise unit. Trade papers and black entertainment pages began to notice.

So Lowell's apprehension that night may have stemmed from the perfectly rational fear of following Ray Charles.[8]

Lowell had twenty-six-year-old local deejay Bee Bee King to thank for the intimidating crowd. King played Lowell's records in heavy rotation on his daily program, as he always did to help publicize his manager Bob Henry's promotions. King and Henry hoped to parlay the airplay into more than good ticket sales. "You the onliest one to fill this place," King told Fulson after the show. "I pat myself on the back cause I laid on your records." Lowell thanked Bee Bee. "But tell you what you can do," Bee Bee continued, "you can let me do that 'Three O'Clock in the Morning.' "

Fulson had recorded the song five years earlier and guessed it had outlived its usefulness to him. He had never heard Bee Bee sing anyway and figured why the hell not, the kid helped him make a little money. "Why sure," Lowell said. "You can do the song."[9]

Bee Bee wasted no time. Independent rhythm and blues record companies had scouts working around Memphis and could swiftly arrange ad-hoc recording sessions in makeshift locations, like Sam Phillips's Memphis Recording Service, WDIA's cramped studio, Tuff Green's living room (where they hung blankets on the walls and windows to muffle the outside world), and the colored YMCA at the corner of Vance Avenue and Lauderdale Street toward downtown.

In late 1951, King (listed as "King, Bee B." in the city directory) and his wife, Martha, rented a cozy room a couple blocks south of Beale Street at 376 South Lauderdale among once grand homes that had been subdivided tenement-style. Bee Bee was a local celebrity, on the radio and playing guitar in clubs, but you could see his shirts hung out to dry like everybody else's. The Big Y building at Vance and Lauderdale, where Bee Bee and his pickup band would record "Three O'Clock Blues," sat barely a block from the Kings' flat.

Bill Harvey, under contract to Peacock Records, couldn't participate. Otherwise, the Memphis sound's past, present, and future were well represented at the session. Tuff Green, a former student of Jimmie Lunceford and leader of one of the many after-hours bands at Sunbeam Mitchell's, played bass.

Alto saxophonist Hank Crawford also learned to play at Manassas High. Crawford would join Ray Charles's band as a one-night replacement in Memphis in 1958 and sign on full-time. He became Charles's bandleader until leaving in 1963 to start a solo career. Despite possessing virtuosic ability, Crawford remained rooted in the down-home Memphis sound. "I found out as a young musician growing up in Memphis," he told the *Los Angeles Times*, "that if you weren't reaching people, and having them tap their foot, then there was nothing happening."[10]

The dashing Willie Mitchell played trumpet. His early growth as a musician owed both to the Lunceford legacy and the Mitchell Hotel scene. As a bandleader in the early 1960s, Willie Mitchell would record several successful instrumentals and work steadily in nearby clubs. He would achieve musical immortality in coming decades as producer-auteur at Hi Records in South Memphis. Working in an old movie theater-turned-studio in a tough neighborhood a horn's blast from Lunceford's grave, Mitchell would help create Al Green in the 1970s, as well as the soul-stirring songs of Syl Johnson, Ann Peebles, Otis Clay, and O.V. Wright.

Ben Branch, a former member of Tuff's band, the house bandleader at Currie's Club Tropicana in North Memphis, played tenor sax. His band would include musicians both great and unknown; singer Isaac Hayes, bassist Donald "Duck" Dunn, and drummer Howard Grimes, who would define the Memphis sound at its pinnacle of popularity in the 1960s and early 1970s. Branch would lead the Southern Christian Leadership Conference's Operation Breadbasket Choir and Orchestra, which performed in conjunction with Dr. Martin Luther King Jr.'s civil rights rallies. On the evening of

April 4, 1968, Branch stood in the parking lot of the Lorraine Motel, just a mile from the Y, looking up at Dr. King on the motel balcony, as King asked Branch to play "Precious Lord, Take My Hand" "real pretty." They were among King's last words before an assassin's bullet ended his life.

Though barely twenty, pianist Ike Turner had already led a band on a hit, "Rocket 88." He was as tireless a talent scout and producer as he was a performer, and Memphis cats B.B. King and Bobby "Blue" Bland—who, like Ike, are now Rock and Roll Hall of Famers—would credit him with sparking their recording careers. In fact, Ike had connected B.B. to RPM Records out of Los Angeles, which supervised the session and released "Three O'Clock Blues." Ike's own stardom would reach its peak in duo with Tina Turner. Their version of "Proud Mary" would win a Grammy award for the best song of 1971. But she would quit him and allege spousal abuse, and the depictions of that abuse in Tina's autobiography and subsequent drug arrests overshadow Ike's contributions to popular culture.

That day at the Y, "Three O'Clock Blues" belonged to B.B. King. The accompaniment is spare and atmospheric. The horns melt into a low moan. Ike punctuates B.B.'s guitar phrases. B.B.'s urgent vocals and slashing guitar carry the song. This song would soon change his life.

The Memphis sound rocked the black music world. "Three O'Clock Blues" was an instant smash hit—soaring past Ray Charles's "Kissa Me Baby"—landing atop the charts for best-selling rhythm and blues singles and earning the most jukebox plays in the R&B category by mid-February. Its only competition came from B.B.'s buddy Rosco Gordon, another regular at Sunbeam's, whose "Booted" was recorded at Sam Phillips's and released on Chicago's Chess Records.

Bob Henry's New York connections, from his big-band-booking days, benefited B.B. early on. Talent agencies contacted their man in Memphis when "Three O'Clock Blues" broke. "They called me and asked who he was," Henry said, "so that's when I made arrangements for B.B. to go out on the road."[11] Henry signed B.B. up with Ben Bart's Universal Attractions, the agency that propelled Roy Brown's blockbuster 1949 tour. Henry then took B.B. to Paul's tailor shop on Beale and outfitted him in two suits, one merlot and one lavender, with black and red shoes, a shirt, socks, and tie to match.

Shootin' and Cuttin' and Shit

Richard Penniman had left his home in Macon, Georgia, with a snake-oil showman named Doc Hudson in 1949. Doc Hudson toured like the old barnstormers. He hit small towns that lacked black restaurants or accommodations, so the entertainers slept out under a tent in a field. On the Doc's medicine show, Richard whooped the only secular number he knew then, Louis Jordan's "Caldonia." In Fitzgerald, Georgia, a lady named Ethyl Wynnes, who owned a club called the Winsetta Patio, took pity on Richard, lured him away from Doc Hudson, brought him under her roof, and fed him chitterlings and pigs' feet. When her club's vocalist got sick, she plugged Richard into the band. They hired him on, and Richard became a lead singer in the chitlin' circuit's darkest furrows with the B. Brown Orchestra. Richard's sister recalled "the most exciting thing . . . that ever happened to the family. B. Brown's band came to town and taped to the station wagon was this placard with the name Little Richard all over it. That was the first time he was called Little Richard."[1] The family's joy was short-lived. Richard split the B. Brown group to join the Sugarfoot Sam from Alabam minstrel show. "That was the first time I performed in a dress," he recalled.[2] They changed his name from Little Richard to Princess Lavonne. He couldn't navigate in high heels, so the band carried him to the microphone before the curtain opened and plopped him down on the stage. Princess Lavonne joined a popular tradition of black transvestite entertainers. From Billie McAllister packing chic Chicago cabarets, to Patsy Valdalia strutting her hairy legs through New Orleans's rough joints, there were as many impersonators as blues singers in black clubs.

Though the Princess Lavonne persona died off, Richard Penniman absorbed a part of her. He quit Sugarfoot Sam, and landed in Atlanta, seventy-five miles or so up the road from Macon. There he met Billy Wright, a cookie-cutter rhythm and blues singer who curled his hair up high. Wright influenced Richard's style, from his mulberry shoes to his makeup: Pancake 31. Wright also helped Richard record for the first time. On October 16, 1951, eighteen-year-old Little Richard Penniman, still yet to play piano professionally, cut four tunes for RCA, one a Penniman composition, "Every Hour." Teenage Little Richard sang like an evening-gown blues chanteuse.

Down in Macon, Richard's father, Bud, had expanded his moonshine operation, managing the neighborhood juke joint, the Tip In Inn. The Tip In was a one-room café that dealt in fried food and cold beer. Though Bud and his effeminate son had tied tails, Bud supported Richard's career choice and played "Every Hour" as often as possible on the Tip In jukebox.

Back home in late 1951, hanging around the Macon Greyhound bus station trying to get laid, Richard met Esquerita, a pompadoured boy from South Carolina who shared Richard's sexual inclination. Esquerita, born Eskew Reeder Jr., wasn't much older than fifteen when he and Richard met. Esquerita worked then in a promotional capacity with a charlatan named Sister Rosa who sold "blessed" bread. Richard invited Esquerita home, where Esquerita showed Richard a trick or two on the piano, playing "One Mint Julep" high on the treble, with a rolling bass. Esquerita had long, spidery fingers. "He was," Richard recalled, "one of the greatest pianists and that's including

Esquerita, Little Richard's inspiration, with a fan in New
Orleans, 1963. *Photo-Sax Kari/Author's collection*

Jerry Lee Lewis, Stevie Wonder, or anybody I've ever heard. I learned
a whole lot about phrasing from him."[3]

RCA called back, and Little Richard recorded another batch of
four songs on January 12, 1952, still just as a vocalist despite Esquerita's piano lesson. The euphoria lasted all of a month.

At 11:30 p.m. on February 14, 1952, Macon police found Bud Penniman's body sprawled across the floor near the Tip In Inn entrance,
victim of multiple gunshot wounds to the chest. Bud had warned a
fellow named Frank Tanner about tossing firecrackers into the Tip
In's wood stove on this cold night. When Tanner disobeyed, Bud went
for his gun, but Tanner shot first. The club sat a block or so from the
Penniman home at 1540 Fifth, and Bud's family heard the news fast,
may have even heard the fatal blast and ignored it—another night on
Pleasant Hill.

With all those children and without Bud, the Penniman family became punch-line poor. According to Richard, they pulled wood off their house to burn on cold days. Twenty years old now, Richard took a job at the Greyhound station, washing dishes in the café where he'd met Esquerita. Can you see it? Little Richard in a hairnet and smudged apron, scraping half-eaten chicken fried steaks and gravy mashed potatoes into the garbage, those fiery fingers dishwater-wrinkled. He wouldn't stand there long. Richard's longtime cohort Percy Welch said that the trauma of Bud's death "led [Richard] to come into rock-n-roll."[4] Whether his motives were financial, existential, or both, Richard knew exactly who to see for passage into that world. On his break, Richard would slide down Fifth Street from the 'Hound station to harass Clint Brantley, Macon's black entertainment kingpin at the Two Spot.[5]

Born in Sandersville, Georgia, in 1902, Clint moved to Macon in 1922 and opened a barbershop. He began his music career behind the drums. He organized a band and learned how to work behind the scenes. "We'd play little dances at the school and so forth," he recalled. He built contacts throughout his Georgia musical travels, his band playing joints that were little more than four walls and a roof, "just so [you] weren't playing in the woods," he said, for people who liked to drink, dance, and gamble. "Yeah, fight like hell, too."[6]

Clint was tall and stout with long arms and heavy hands. He spoke profanely and directly. Unlike Don Robey, man of fashion and standing, Brantley wouldn't have drawn attention on a crowded Macon street. In late March 1942, twenty years after settling in Macon, Brantley opened a nightclub. The Two Spot sat at the corner of Fifth and Walnut, a two-story lumber building looking down on smaller, similarly rustic shops. The plain row of them looked like farm buildings of various sizes—a barn, smokehouse, cellar, and coop—placed side by side and plastered with enticements to drink Nehi. Fifth Street, a hub of transportation, heavy industry, and black entrepreneurship, ran southwest from the lazy Ocmulgee River under a railroad trestle. The tracks swung around, parallel to Fifth, right

Fifth Street, the stroll in Macon, Georgia, ca. 1940. Clint Brantley's Two Spot occupied the two-story building at the right and the structure with the double-arched entries. An unknown Maconite named Richard Penniman begged for work here during the early 1950s, and a group of raggedy young men led by James Brown auditioned for Clint Brantley here in 1955. *Middle Georgia Archives, Washington Memorial Library, Macon, Georgia*

past Obie Brooks's fruit stand, City Fish Market, a peanut stand, and the Two Spot. Train traffic and nearby paper and lumber mills kept the pungent block vibrating. The Two Spot's proximity to the colored U.S. Army dispensary, the Terminal Station—where numerous railroads converged, and city and interstate buses picked up and dropped off—and the city jail ensured it a boisterous clientele. "Shootin' and cuttin' and shit," Clint recalled. "I run under many a table."

Though rumors circulated of Clint's participation in the local numbers racket—known here as "the bug," players "caught the bug"—he maintained that his earnings had escalated solely through his increasingly ambitious musical endeavors. He began throwing big parties at harvest time, one of which put him over. "I had a Farmer's Ball," Clint said. "I made between five and six thousand dollars. That was the first big piece of money I made." Brantley then took over the Cotton Club on Broadway—one street up from Fifth—Macon's red-light strip, where the soldiers from Camp Wheeler crowded the street, and everyone played their numbers at a cabstand outside the Douglass, a colored theater that had been a stop on the black vaudeville circuit before motion pictures learned to talk. Brantley publicized the Cotton Club as "Middle Georgia's Finest Nightclub" and advertised the "Chitterlings for Sale" at the humbly furnished, 150-seat room. Clint's Sultans were the Cotton Club house band, featuring Luke "Fats" Gonder, a straight-up blues pianist sometimes billed as Count *Basic*.

Being both a barber and a small-club owner, Brantley was just the type of fellow Denver Ferguson sought in the chitlin' circuit's early days. Brantley kept busy during the war years, cutting hair by day on Fifth Street and showcasing territory bands at night at the Two Spot—'Fess Chambliss from Atlanta, and Johnny Walker and his Augusta Night Hawks—and Ferguson's chitlin' circuit bands at the Cotton Club. Boogie Woogie piano and accordion queen Christine Chatman, then the rock and stomp Carolina Cotton Pickers played Brantley's 12:01 dances in March 1944. A Macon tradition, these were scheduled weekly at a minute past midnight Sunday in observance of the Sabbath blue law.

In the weeks preceding Lucky Millinder's 1947 talent show and Little Richard's debut, early rockers Joe Turner and Wynonie Harris, and Ferguson band the Snookum Russell Orchestra played Clint's Cotton Club. After Lucky's talent search and Richard's memorable opening for Sister Rosetta, Brantley began billing his Cotton Club as "a swell place for teens and twenties," and urging, "if you can sing, play, or dance, then be on hand Wednesday nights"—a timely move considering the new sounds rising. Luke Gonder emceed Clint's teen talent nights at the Cotton Club, and learned to spot a good prospect. Gonder would drop by the Penniman home and work with Richard on the family's piano.

When Richard came to Clint in 1952, Clint knew Richard's ability and appreciated the value of having new records out. Little Richard's second batch of records generated some buzz, getting his name in the trade papers and, more important, the black news.* Richard wanted to get the hell out of Macon and do something for his widowed mother, ten siblings, and the new one on the way. As far as Clint's connections went—in most of Georgia and a little into Tennessee—the records didn't have to be hits to draw crowds so long as Little Richard could be billed as a "recording artist." Brantley had expanded his operation while promoting Denver Ferguson's acts, and he'd become a territorial promoter for Universal Attractions, booking the agency's single acts into his route of sawdust ballrooms. To support this action, he had groomed a band, led by young Maconite Percy Welch, who had tried out for Lucky Millinder the same night as Richard back in 1947. The package also included emcee, pianist, and Richard's first piano teacher, Luke Gonder.

✳   ✳   ✳

Memphis

John Alexander Jr. was a minister's boy, born in Memphis on June 9, 1929. He grew up, one of ten children, in the family home at 899 Fisher Alley in South Memphis.[7] He and his buddies patrolled the neighborhood. They picked fights mostly, and John distinguished himself in a more graceful pursuit—he was a beautiful roller skater. Kids followed him up hilly Williams Street to watch him pirouette down, and they crowded Sylvester Thomas's living room on Porter Street to listen to John play the piano.[8]

John and his pals gravitated to Beale Street and hung around outside Sunbeam Mitchell's. Once John came of age he stayed in Sunbeam's, where he knew he could fall into gigs simply by being on hand. Club operators in the little towns outside Memphis called Sunbeam at the last minute, and bought whatever band he could scrape

---

* A blurb that appeared on page 10 of the August 9, 1952, *Memphis World* dubbed Little Richard RCA's "new disc find."

together from the barroom. B.B. King recalled playing with all different musicians and combinations. Alexander, Ford Nelson, Rosco Gordon, or Phineas Newborn Jr. might have played piano behind B.B. on a given night, just depending on availability. Bobby Bland tagged along to sing a few. Some nights, John Alexander found himself in Joe Hill Louis's band.[9] Louis went over big in the sticks. He squalled harmonica, and beat his electric guitar through a well-seasoned amp while kicking the bass drum. He called himself the one-man band but packed a few accompanists on live gigs.

Sunbeam plugged these acts into joints across a widening empire. His connections now ran from Memphis's leading businessman to the depths of the Negro underworld. Despite his dizzying responsibilities around Memphis, Sunbeam sought new territory for his bootlegging operation and found a thirsty market due south of his home city. Mississippi would not repeal Prohibition until 1966, more than thirty years after ratification of the Twenty-first Amendment. Ingeniously, and much as the classic gangsters of the Prohibition era had done, Sunbeam built a circuit of black nightclubs in the Magnolia State. He provided libation and song and persuaded people to join the business much as Denver Ferguson had done to begin the chitlin' circuit.

Milton Barnes of Hattiesburg in southeastern Mississippi recalled, "At the time it behooved me to go into the club business, I knew nothing about clubs. The man I got [the idea] from, he was out of Memphis, colored guy and his wife. . . . I told him, 'I don't know nothin' about the club business, what do I do?' " Sunbeam explained the modern-day medicine show concept. "He made me a proposition," Barnes said. "He made his money on whiskey, cause we's dry. . . . You see, when you get that big crowd for a concert, you gonna sell lots of whiskey. I had B.B. King on a Sunday night, place was packed. I had sold out of tables, chairs, so we stacked Coca Cola crates. [We] made money."[10] Barnes earned his from the door. Barnes built the Hi-Hat club in Hattiesburg around 1950, and in no time he was running joints, down to the Mississippi Gulf Coast, on similar principles. The presence of Sunbeam's wife, Ernestine, suggests that more than whiskey could be obtained at the Hi-Hat.

To advertise a dance, Barnes would ride whoever was scheduled to play through Palmer's Crossing, as a section of black Hattiesburg was known, on a flatbed equipped with a loudspeaker, like a rustic Mardi Gras float, blaring the attraction's latest recording as they waved to the people. Barnes's territory became such a stronghold in the 1950s that B.B. King would call Hattiesburg his second home. Following his great success in the after-dark trade, Barnes bought the Hattiesburg Black Sox semipro baseball squad, and sent them barnstorming the same juke joint towns that B.B. played.

Sunbeam forged another long-standing allegiance not fifty miles south of Memphis in the Mississippi Delta, where he and Tunica County kingpin Harold "Hardface" Clanton partnered in a dice and entertainment venture.[11] Segregation and Prohibition: The laws and customs implemented to keep men like Sunbeam, Milt Barnes, and Hardface in line instead made them wealthy playboys.

The sharecropper system dominated Tunica society, yet Hardface proved exceptional to its rules. Born in 1916, Hardface fought in World War II and gained respect from the rich cotton family white men of his native land. They looked out for Hardface after that. Like ambitious black entrepreneurs everywhere after the war, he set up a nightspot. Clanton distributed liquor there—corn and sealed, it was all bootleg in Mississippi—with Sunbeam as his supplier. Hardface didn't need to bribe anyone since Tunica officials, and those aspiring to power, knew that an affront to Hardface offended the county's richest men. Hardface clearly valued proper appearances and permitted the sheriff a roundup every month or so. Regulars took turns checking into the Tunica jail for the benefit of all. A half hour later, they'd be back at the craps table.

Like Sunbeam, Hardface dressed plain. He hid his lone extravagance—a fleet of antique roadsters he restored—on a fenced-off piece of rural land, and cruised the cars late at night on deserted

Delta roads. Also like Sunbeam, Hardface practiced paperless accounting—their mathematical acumen made both formidable gamblers. Hardface played Skin, a strain of poker that rewards the best card counter, who, in the Tri-State Delta region, seems to have been Hardface. He and Sunbeam traveled to gamblers' conventions, riding in one of Hardface's classic cars, the two of them dressed uncharacteristically raffish. They planted marked, resealed decks in general stores, shipping or couriering the cards days ahead of their arrival to the convention. Once the games began, they'd remark that, nothing against the house of course, it was only gentlemanly to start with a fresh deck.

✳   ✳   ✳

Mitchell Hotel regulars B.B. King, Rosco Gordon, and Joe Hill Louis had all broadcast from Memphis's WDIA by 1952, and they began to pull other young Beale Streeters, namely, John Alexander Jr. and John's South Memphis pal Bobby Bland, into the radio station's studio to perform and tout their next gigs. Once B.B. hit with "Three O'Clock Blues," WDIA program director David Mattis launched Duke Records to capture the staggering Beale Street sound.

Of this bunch, the shy pianist John Alexander Jr. seemed the least hungry for stardom. B.B., Rosco, or Bobby Bland handled the vocal chores at their shows, and John seemed as happy behind the piano, out of the spotlight. John showed up at WDIA's studio in May 1952 to back Bobby Bland's first Duke Records session. Bland hadn't nailed down the lyrics, though, and Mattis scrapped him last minute. The pianist, getting tuned up and screwing around with Ruth Brown's hit "So Long," sounded pretty good. Mattis tweaked the lyrics on the spot, and recorded John Alexander Jr.'s impromptu debut single. John's name sounded too dull, and in a hell of an inspired fifteen minutes, John Alexander Jr. became Johnny Ace and "So Long" became "My Song." Mattis credited accompaniment to the Beale Streeters.[12] It's about what you'd expect from a mop-up group: choppy, out-of-

tune piano and sodden saxophone. Johnny Ace's vocals are monoto-
nous, but sincere and distinctive. "You could go down the block and
find ten boys who could sing better than Johnny, but he had that certain something," Evelyn Johnson recalled.[13]

Dave Mattis, the man who made "Johnny Ace," self-identified as
a bleeding heart. He saw real social value in WDIA's black broadcasting, and as a white Southerner who staked his career on his progressive racial views, he was clearly ahead of his time. He could not,
however, have been further out of his league than when he began to
run with the outlaws in the black record business.

Don Robey knew the talented crop Mattis made records of
through his association with Sunbeam Mitchell. Hearing of Mattis's Duke Records venture, and sensing Mattis's deficiencies, Robey
sent his white sales manager Irving Marcus to Memphis to broach
a partnership. Robey's muscle and Memphis talent seemed to Mattis a powerful combination. The merger appealed to Mattis's sense
of racial justice as well—a Southern musical conglomerate of black
entrepreneur and white bleeding heart would be momentous. Mattis
agreed to the partnership, the particulars of which remain unknown,
and in August 1952 Robey announced the merger of Mattis's Duke
Records and his Peacock Records.

Robey leveraged his contacts to market Johnny Ace double-time,
bringing exactly the strength to Duke Records that Mattis lacked. In
his tested chitlin' circuit method—the same approach that got Louis
Jordan noticed a decade ago—Robey stuck his neck out, booking
Johnny top-of-the-bill throughout his territory. Sunbeam Mitchell got
it rolling at the Hippodrome, the skating rink–ballroom he controlled
four blocks east on Beale from the Mitchell Hotel. There Johnny Ace
appeared for the first time as a headliner, on August 23, 1952, though
the avid skater may have already tested the track. His opening act
that night was Bobby Bland, the performer he'd trumped last minute
at his first recording session, billed here as "Bobby Blue." The Hippodrome was quite a graduation for Ace and Blue after being seasoned

at Hardface's clubs in the flat center of nowhere. The Hippodrome
had just begun hosting dances the previous year, and quickly became
a regular hotspot, the first Beale club to cater to teenagers. Skaters
spun and glided around the buffed-pinewood oval during shows,
while jitterbugs twirled and tossed their partners across the infield,
and fans crushed against the bandstand to get a closer look or shake a
hand. Louis Jordan and Lionel Hampton, among others, had graced
the stage, and every Sunday, a white disc jockey from West Memphis
hosted his eponymous Jack the Bellboy dance at the Hippodrome,
with music by Tuff Green, broadcast live over KWEM.

Black-formatted radio had quickly become the concert promoter's
most powerful tool, doing what newspaper ads and window placards never could. It had matured rapidly in Memphis since WDIA's
black format hit the airwaves less than four years earlier. Even without payola (and there was payola), Johnny Ace's "My Song" would
slide smoothly into black radio's web of financial interests and Memphis music's network of mutual back-scratching. No one would have
to explain the importance of playing the record to Jack the Bellboy,
friend of the Hippodrome. Dick "Cane" Cole at WLOK was a longtime Sunbeam foot soldier, and Dewey Phillips at WHBQ could be
relied on to spin a hot new local disc. David Mattis, as a partner in
Duke Records, stood to benefit financially from "My Song" sales and,
as WDIA program director, could play the thing every ten minutes.

This maximum exposure sold tickets for Sunbeam and records for
the Robey-Mattis partnership. Beyond Johnny Ace's homemarket, a
hot record spread in the same way a hot attraction did—concert promoters and radio programmers caught sparks from Memphis, news
of heavy airplay and a sellout crowd. Programmers and promoters
thought alike, wanting to provide fans what they wanted in order to
boost ratings and sell ads, or sell tickets. Johnny Ace—or whomever
the people loved, the name mattered not—could make them money.

From its Memphis launchpad, "My Song" took off. It hit no. 1 on
Billboard's Rhythm and Blues chart on September 27, 1952, just a

month after Sunbeam showcased Johnny at the Hippodrome. Forces beyond John Alexander Jr.'s grasp now officially controlled his life. He unwittingly stepped into an ethical vacuum—a new business where the financial opportunities emerged far ahead of regulatory constraints. Back in Denver Ferguson's day, an executive chose the business for the love of music and the outlet for money laundering. These were decent guiding principles as far as the health and liberty of the artist were concerned. Aside from a few purely figurative back-stabbings, no one got hurt back then.

In the coming months, Dave Mattis saw none of the cash a major hit should have generated, since Robey handled distribution and collection for their company. Mattis quit WDIA in November 1952, planning to become Robey's active partner in Duke Records' Houston operation. Mattis showed up at the old Bronze Peacock unannounced to share this plan with Robey, and, "that's when the .45 came out . . . ," Mattis said, and he didn't mean the emerging single-play record.[14] Mattis eventually accepted $10,000 for his share of the company and got out.

Fame came at Johnny Ace fast. If you've visited Graceland, you understand the excess poor Southern boys are capable of once their limits are lifted. He drank heavily, screwed around with the women, and developed a highly disturbing, but safely rigged, good-luck ritual. He liked to spin his revolver's empty cylinder, snap it into place, cock the hammer, jab the barrel against his temple, and press the trigger.

*   *   *

Right around the time Don Robey and his gun dissolved the Duke Records partnership, Little Richard commenced his first tour as a featured attraction, though he dumped Clint Brantley's group in favor of an ensemble of entertainers he encountered on the road. Richard met Raymond and Mildred Taylor, Barry Lee Gilmore, Billy Brooks, and Jimmy Swann at the New Era Club in Nashville in late 1952 and formed the Tempo Toppers. Brantley's band returned to Macon as the Tempo Toppers played their way to New Orleans's Dew

Drop Inn, where they performed with female impersonator extraordinaire Patsy Valdalia. "He didn't even shave off his mustache!" Richard recalled. "He looked like a woman who had been hit with a board and didn't get well."[15] Princess Lavonne could be so catty. Little Richard played piano in the Tempo Toppers, his first professional turn at the instrument. They rambled to Houston from the Dew Drop, where they caught on at Club Matinee on Dowling Street.

The *Houston Informer* reported on the group's debut there on February 14, 1953—a year to the night from the murder of Richard's father. "The crowd was small, but I think it safe to say that they made a hit with those of their new fans who were around at the close of the show. The entire aggregation is working every minute during their performance." They performed Roy Brown and B.B. King hits, and each Tempo Topper did at least double-duty: Gilmore shook maracas and danced with large pieces of furniture clenched between his teeth. Richard admired this and tried it himself, but stuck to piano and vocals. Jimmy Swann played guitar and banjo, Billy Brooks drummed, and Raymond Taylor rigged a trumpet and trombone on racks he could grab while seated at the organ. They sang quartet numbers and choreographed dance steps. Richard was the youngest and most noticeable Tempo Topper, with his powdery beige face, neatly plucked eyebrows, and a head of curls like black ocean froth.

The Tempo Toppers attracted Don Robey's attention immediately. Robey's Duke Records was hot, thanks to Johnny Ace, and Robey's Peacock Records would soon catch up. Just as the Tempo Toppers hit Houston, a song Robey had mothballed a couple years earlier and then released as an afterthought began to make noise in the business—Big Mama Thornton's "Hound Dog," the no. 1 record in R&B land in the spring of 1953. Robey, with confidence and resources to spare, signed the Tempo Toppers to Peacock Records and the Buffalo Booking Agency.

The group's reputation got around fast, and folks packed Club Matinee to guzzle Bull Dog Extra Stout Malt Liquor and catch the new act. The *Informer* reported on March 7, 1953, "The Tempo Toppers again brought down the rafters at the Matinee. . . . Little Richard sang HAVE MERCY MERCY BABY until he was nearly exhausted."

But the group couldn't transfer that energy from Club Matinee to the recording studio. It is, after all, difficult to capture the sound of a man dancing with a table in his mouth. As Richard remembered it, Robey had a rather subduing effect on the Toppers. "Don Robey was a disciplinary person, almost like a dictator," he said. "He wore great big diamonds on his hand and he was always chewing this big cigar, cussin' at me round the end of it. . . . He was so possessive."[16] The Tempo Toppers' records sound conservative—you might even use the critic's smug dismissal *derivative*—by the day's standard.

Though Richard was never too proud to borrow, he recognized the same low career ceiling for an instrument-juggling, furniture-biting cover band as he had seen over Princess Lavonne. He continued to seek himself out, to develop his artistry, but not without the tentativeness of a person in transition, reluctant to go all-in on one version of himself. He played piano and sang solo in the Matinee's Anchor Room. Bandleader Johnny Otis, a Robey employee, saw him there. "I remember it as being just beautiful, bizarre, and exotic, and when he got through he remarked, 'This is Little Richard, King of the Blues,' and then he added, 'And the queen, too!' "[17]

✳   ✳   ✳

By now, the black pop record business generated substantial amounts of money, and unlike during World War II, when an artist could make a living on the circuit based on his reputation, making records had become an indispensable component of an artist's success. The companies that recorded chitlin' circuit music had booking agency tie-ups—it's no overstatement to call these relationships intimate—and when a promising new artist recorded, the record people referred the artist to an agent. King Records teamed up with

Universal Attractions, whose respective principals Syd Nathan and Ben Bart were brothers-in-law. Chicago's Chess Records sent people across town to Shaw Artists, Specialty Records referred theirs to Ben Waller, both in Los Angeles, and Peacock Records sent artists to Buffalo Booking Agency, whose respective principals Don Robey and Evelyn Johnson worked, and often slept, under the same roof.

The record and talent companies saw their work as intertwined, with personal appearances potentially increasing record sales, and impressive record sales leading to high demand for personal appearances and, thus, higher guarantees for the artist and commissions for the agent. This entwinement blurred the lines between a booking agent and record company's respective responsibilities. As head of Universal Attractions, the leading chitlin' circuit booking agency of the early 1950s, Ben Bart cultivated personal relationships with influential disc jockeys. Bart recognized that jocks directly impacted his own income. He learned their preferences and weaknesses, for boys or girls or dope, and negotiated favors from a position of strength. Both agencies and record companies kept expense accounts on artists, and so "loans," Cadillacs, and clothes all counted against future record sales and appearance fees. The company-store analogy comes to mind. Still, the tie-ups were not hard and fast, and plenty of savvy artists worked their own deals, and booking and recording companies poached talent all the time. As we know, ladies and gentlemen played hard out there. And as our Memphis friend Bob Henry would learn, it's best to keep an eye on Don Robey.

In the spring of 1953, Robey, flush with Big Mama Thornton and Johnny Ace fever, visited Henry in Memphis with an offer to buy thirty B.B. King dates to play throughout Texas, Oklahoma, and Louisiana. Henry's twenty-seven-year-old protégé had followed his 1951 breakthrough hit "Three O'Clock Blues" with what King deemed "respectable" sellers. B.B. quit his job at WDIA in 1952 to perform full-time, still recording for L.A.-based RPM Records and touring via Universal Attractions.

King and Robey had known one another through Sunbeam Mitchell for a couple years, and to King it must have seemed that all career paths led back to the Bronze Peacock. King had seen Johnny Ace's "My Song" surpass one of his own on the *Billboard* charts thanks to Robey's might. B.B. had recorded in Houston with Mitchell alums and Robey employees, the Bill Harvey band, and B.B. played some of his earliest road dates after "Three O'Clock Blues" with Milton Larkin and the X-Rays. Larkin and Robey went way back—Larkin conducted Robey's first house orchestra at the Harlem Grill back in the late 1930s, and his was the first band Robey booked out into the territory, well before Gatemouth Brown came along. Virtually every young musician with whom B.B. jammed at the Mitchell and played Mid-South roadhouses had signed with Robey. Robey clearly wanted to bring King under the Duke, Peacock, and Buffalo banners—he had already tried, unsuccessfully, to liberate King from RPM Records.

If you'd placed Henry and Robey side by side, and asked an ambitious black musician to choose his manager on appearances alone, it wouldn't have been a contest. Henry, plump and slouchy, looked his sixty-four years. His wiry gray hair poked out from under his blown-out cap, and the chalky Beale Street dust clung to his brogans. Robey, with his dark hair slicked down, appeared younger than his fifty-one years, peering alertly from behind black horn rims. His suits fairly shimmered, and a prosperity-minded fellow would not have missed his diamond tiepin and gold ring.

Henry took the money and sent B.B. off. Robey hooked B.B. up with a familiar band: Bill Harvey's from the Mitchell Hotel. They had jammed after hours at Mitchell's place, and Harvey regularly worked as King's bandleader in Mississippi joints like the Hi-Hat in Hattiesburg or Hardface's in Tunica.

Robey's longtime legman Morris Merritt traveled with the coterie. Merritt, with a suavely intimidating presence very much like his partner's, offered B.B. the persuasive combination of cash and cars to leave Bob Henry for the Buffalo Booking Agency, and Don Robey

The Memphis-Houston connection (left to right): Johnny Ace, unknown, B.B. King, unknown, Bill Harvey, and Willie Mae Thornton, 1953. The men all began their careers at Sunbeam Mitchell's in Memphis, and either recorded for Don Robey's Duke-Peacock Records, toured for Robey's Buffalo Booking Agency, or both. *Getty Images-Hulton Archive, Frank Driggs Collection*

thus acquired a new interest in the Memphis sound. Merritt bought B.B. a Cadillac to cruise the circuit in and a couple station wagons for the Harvey band to ride along.[18]

Henry hadn't invested anything in B.B. since purchasing those garish tuxedoes from Paul the tailor for King's first big tour. "Bein' hard-headed," Henry said, "I owned his contract, but I just tore it up and told him I could bill without him. Forget him. I went a long ways to try to help him. When he got to the place he could make some money, he broke his contract. So I got out of the business."[19] Not without a little vengeance. When B.B. came to the Beale Avenue Auditorium in August 1953, Henry had King's Cadillac impounded, and his pay for the night garnished through a writ of attachment. The auto belonged to Morris Merritt, not King, so a judge freed the

Caddy. The show's promoter, Andrew "Sunbeam" Mitchell, sensitive to the nature of Beale hustler politics, refused to pay King until the contractual matter found resolution. B.B. consequently scrubbed Robert Henry from all future renditions of the B.B. King story.*

Feeling burned, Henry quit fooling with music altogether. King left him without management clients, and at his age he had lost patience with the younger crowd at the shows he promoted. "I got out of the dance business," he said, because "I got $700 or $800 invested in the band and look up and some guy got two or three wine bottles and throw 'em across the house."[20] Henry remained a fixture of Beale Street's Rialto, selling records at his shop or shooting stick a couple doors down at his pool hall.

Back in Houston, Don Robey had converted the Bronze Peacock from a nightclub to the headquarters of Duke-Peacock Records and Buffalo Booking Agency. The companies' respective rosters brimmed with talent, primarily from Sunbeam Mitchell's sphere of influence—B.B. King, Bill Harvey, Little Junior Parker, Earl Forest, 'Struction Johnson, and Johnny Ace all toured the Buffalo circuit, and, except King, all recorded for Duke or Peacock. The new headquarters subsequently became a dysfunctional family home where the stern father was driven to distraction by his gay son and alcoholic, lesbian daughter. As Robey strained over piles of paperwork, he could hear Little Richard and Big Mama Thornton bickering down the hall, and progressively nearer, until the pair busted through his office door, Big Mama chasing Little Richard with a butcher knife, threatening to kill the faggot. Robey had to disarm Big Mama and scold the two for behaving like children in his place of business.[21]

---

* "From Rags to Riches—Story of B.B. King," *Houston Informer*, May 29, 1954, 9, says, "One day while sitting in Memphis' W.C. Handy Park B.B. was told by some friends to visit Professor Nat D. Williams, dean of Negro disc jockeys, who hired him to sing on a 15 minute show." An earlier article had specified Robert Henry as the man B.B.'s friends told him to see.

Evelyn Johnson, Robey's partner on the booking side, yearned for children of her own, but the turmoil at Peacock headquarters pretty well exhausted her maternal resources. Some of her clients required remedial reading education, many struggled with substance abuse, and all wanted for better grooming and etiquette. They all fought with each other and with Robey, mostly over money with the old man. Richard would later allege that Robey had beaten and severely injured him. In any case, their personalities clashed, and as the Tempo Toppers records clunked, Little Richard left Houston alone in October 1953. Robey banished Little Richard, with regards, to Sunbeam Mitchell's in Memphis.

Richard assembled the nucleus of his new band, the Upsetters, from among Sunbeam jam-session contestants, guitarist Thomas Hartwell and tenor saxophonist Danny Carmichael. They returned to Macon, where they recruited drummer Chuck Connors and saxophonist Lee Diamond. Clint Brantley, Richard's first manager, outfitted the band with uniforms and a station wagon and once again sent his trusty lieutenant, Luke Gonder—Richard's old piano teacher—with them down the road.

Still under contract to Robey's Buffalo Booking Agency, Richard and the Upsetters toured Robey's Texas, Oklahoma, and Louisiana circuit, multiplied by Brantley's territory through Georgia. They traveled as part of a package, a vicious one-two punch really, with yet another erstwhile house band at Sunbeam Mitchell's Memphis club, Little Junior Parker and 'Struction Johnson's Blue Flames. The *Houston Informer* reported on February 20, 1954, "Hotter than a fire cracker, Little Richard and his high-powered Upsetters . . . upset 'Sooners' with their atomic brand of entertainment at Oklahoma City's Dance Palace last week." The show's unnamed promoter remarked, "I've seen dances, but never have I seen showmen work any harder, nor a crowd react more favorably. Richard is in a class with Louis Jordan and B.B. King." Almost.

Chapter 16 ✶ ✶ ✶ ✶ ✶ ✶ ✶

The Hardest-Working Man in Show Business

An eyewitness to Johnny Ace's departure from this world swore she'd seen his hair stand on end in the moment between when his pistol fired and his body slumped to the floor.

On December 25, 1954, Johnny had just left the bandstand for an anteroom backstage at the Houston City Auditorium at about 11:00 p.m. He was due back out after an intermission, just long enough for a few swigs. He sat on a dresser table, and his Houston woman, twenty-two-year-old Olivia Gibbs, sat in his lap. A pint of vodka passed between Johnny, Olivia, Willie Mae "Big Mama" Thornton, and a couple others. Empties littered the dressing room floor: Christmas night cheer.

Johnny, compulsively fooling with his silver, snub-nosed .22-revolver, put the barrel against Olivia's head and pulled the trigger. Snap. It was the rigged good-luck ritual he'd repeated throughout the two and a half years since "My Song" pulled him from Sunbeam Mitchell's juke joint to the top of the black music world. It had been good to him so far.

After Johnny's big stage debut at the Memphis Hippodrome on August 23, 1952, he caught on fast, performing for a week at a Kansas City nightclub, before a week's run at Club Alabam on Los Angeles's Central Avenue in November. "My Song" began as a grassroots phenomenon, hitting on Washington, D.C., neighborhood jukeboxes then spreading. It eventually spent nine weeks as the no. 1 R&B record, despite numerous cover versions tearing at its sales.

Johnny refined his sound after "My Song," polishing a formula that distinguished a Johnny Ace number from anything else on the radio or the juke. He favored lyrics with the emotional depth and verse complexity of a teenage love note intercepted in a high school hallway. The musical accompaniments were music-box fragile and gentle, extremely so compared to B.B. King's playful, lusty swing and Rosco Gordon's red-eyed piano stabbings. In less than a year, Johnny scored two more hits. "Cross My Heart" made no. 3 on the *Billboard* R&B chart in January 1953, and "The Clock" made the chart on July 4, 1953, and stayed no. 1 for five weeks. Naturally, his drawing power increased. Evelyn Johnson, Robey's partner and head of Buffalo Booking Agency, packaged Johnny with Big Mama Thornton on tour. On October 24, 1953, they announced that they'd soon play the Apollo.

Though Big Mama never repeated the success of "Hound Dog," Johnny Ace stayed hot. "Saving My Love for You," released in December 1953, peaked at no. 2. Ace's bookings remained constant, and he could afford to haul an orchestra around as chitlin' circuit business boomed. *Billboard* reported on April 24, 1954, "Where the r&b agencies appear to have an edge on their competition in other fields is the manner in which they are constantly opening up new clubs in which to place their acts. Bookers in all of the key offices are constantly seeking new locations where r&b artists can be used. They often spend time on the road seeing café owners who have rarely used more than a pianist to convince them to try a show with a singer and [a band]." So the trade rag caught on to the Denver Ferguson model a dozen years after its origination. The territory for R&B personal appearances had expanded since Denver's day—the Ace-Thornton revue played New England in April 1954.

In five years since founding Buffalo Booking and Peacock Records, Don Robey and Evelyn Johnson's chitlin' circuit conglomerate had blossomed into the most elegantly functioning racket anywhere in the industry. Robey is a controversial figure in black music history, his reputation dogged by real and rumored violent episodes. The man had vision, however; he foresaw opportunities and, with his gun and his wits, pursued them. He made artists. He made promoters and nightclubs. From the time of Walter Barnes's 1936–37 tour and survey of the Southern black music business in its infancy, Robey alone stood tall in 1954. His partner, Evelyn Johnson, had proved every bit as formidable as he, without the sidearm. As boss of Buffalo Booking, she developed a system that carried weaker groups through the circuit on strong acts' coattails, bolstering record sales along the way. She explained, "As a booking agent, I had five groups. I staggered them out and put the best one out first, a mediocre one second, a [strong] one out third—these are single engagements on the same circuit, the chitlin' circuit. [Promoters would] buy the first one because they definitely want them, they buy the second one because they want the third one, they buy the fourth because they are waiting for the fifth. I kept them going. We got a rotation going where [we'd book the acts] where deejays are playing their records, and one hand scratches the other."[1]

Johnny Ace thusly pulled Little Richard, both with the Tempo Toppers in 1953 and with the Upsetters in 1954, along on Richard's way to brighter days.

Johnny's two-year chart hot streak cooled, however, throughout 1954. "Please Forgive Me," released in April, reached no. 6 in June, his lowest peak chart position. Then his October 1954 release "Never Let Me Go"—a quintessential slice of his sound, a vocal ballad with velvety purple accompaniment—reached only the jukebox plays chart, peaking at no. 9.

Don Robey announced a new Ace record, "Pledging My Love," in the December 25, 1954, *Billboard*. A little after eleven o'clock that night in the Houston City Auditorium dressing room, Johnny pointed his revolver at a young lady who'd come to the show with his girlfriend. He pulled the trigger and the hammer snapped. Everybody shrieked. He swung the snub barrel to his girlfriend's head. He pulled the trigger and the hammer snapped. He cackled and they yelled for him to stop. He said there was nothing to get excited about—the gun wouldn't shoot: see. He looked down the barrel, pushed it to his right temple, and pulled the trigger. With a quick pop, a bullet fired into Johnny's brain. The brain still had enough voltage to send a shock wave through Johnny, and Big Mama Thornton thought she saw his hair straighten. He went limp, drooped to the floor, and crashed among the empty pints and halves. His blood ran like spilled ink. That room cleared fire drill–style, and someone got Evelyn Johnson, who was taking tickets and counting money at the auditorium ticket window. She rushed back there and saw the penny hole in his temple and the smirk on his face.[2]

Rumor had it that Don Robey orchestrated the accident. Johnny Ace's sales had tanked, and perhaps Robey noticed the effect of death as a career move for Hank Williams, whose passing in 1953 sent "I'll Never Get Out of This World Alive" to the top of the country chart. How else could Robey get one last smash out of slipping Johnny Ace? Robey knew Ace's propensity for gunplay, how Ace liked to snap empty rounds at himself and friends, though rumor never accounted for how Robey knew to slip the bullet in the proper chamber so that Ace would shoot himself instead of his girlfriend. Robey didn't exactly go out of his way to squash the rumor. According to his son, the Don would smirk when the incident came up, and say that what hurt him the most about Christmas night 1954 were the three thousand refunds. The rumor has shaded Robey's reputation ever since, but it fit the persona he'd cultivated up to that point, beginning with the public sucker punch of his partner Morris Merritt in 1941. If no one had thought Robey capable of a ploy on the level of the Johnny

Ace hit, the rumor never would have gained traction. Still, a bullet to the temple is a vastly more grave matter than a fist to the ear.

A heavy drinker who carelessly toyed with his firearm, Johnny was certainly up to the task of accidentally blowing a hole in his skull. He played with the gun loaded and unloaded, and by 11:00 on a party night, he could have easily either forgotten a bullet he'd earlier breeched or sloppily dropped the rounds out of the revolver, leaving one shot chambered.

Whatever explanation suits you, there's no denying that Robey profited handsomely from Ace's death. He flew into action, hiring Memphis photographer Ernest Withers to document Johnny's funeral, ensuring a steady stream of pictures and copy for the Associated Negro Press wire. All the major black papers covered the story, and Withers's photos of Robey and Evelyn Johnson deplaning like dignitaries in Memphis—she in black mourning veil—and the throng at the funeral conveyed exactly Robey's intended impression of Ace's star magnitude.

Robey pushed for the largest possible Memphis venue to host Johnny's last rites. A who's who of Memphis music served as pall-bearers, honorary and true—Little Junior Parker, Phineas Newborn Jr., Fred Ford, Rosco Gordon, and B.B. King, among others. Before the funeral, they toasted Johnny at Sunbeam's, where they'd all begun as nobodies just three years earlier. They filed down the catwalk to Hernando Street and walked the block or so to Clayborn A.M.E. Temple in the cold, bright afternoon of January 2, 1955. You had to push through the crowd outside, as big a group as had ever paid to see Johnny alive. His band parked the Woody they'd logged so many circuit miles in on the corner of Linden and Hernando, beside the towering limestone-brick church.

An estimated five thousand mourners (probably Robey's guess, circulated through the press via an Ernest Withers news release—which Robey financed—and repeated into fact throughout black papers) overflowed Clayborn Temple, and sat or stood through a parade of sermons and solos. Afterward, the cortege, including Johnny's band-mobile, accompanied the body to New Park Cemetery, where John M. Alexander Jr., age twenty-five at death, rests.

No artist more poignantly signifies the rise of the record than Johnny Ace. He was worth more dead, a ghost voice on black vinyl, than in the flesh as a touring artist. The same would not, could not, have been true for Walter Barnes or the Carolina Cotton Pickers. Even Louis Jordan maintained his fame and made his living—and his manager's—in personal appearances. Dead Johnny on record accomplished a feat that live Johnny on stage couldn't have pulled off—events breaking from the death of Johnny Ace would change the chitlin' circuit as we've come to know it.

While the Ace story received immediate, maximum exposure across black America, white consumers too were taken with the tragic tale. They bought his records and heard the fragile, doomed voice. The January 15, 1955, *Billboard* noted, "The recent death of Ace gave added impetus to what would probably have been heavy first week sales in any case. It is spiraling upwards at dazzling speed." Most important, the review continued, "['Pledging My Love'] is almost as popular with pop customers, as with r&b." Johnny Ace was crossing over.

None of this caught Robey flat-footed. The same day *Billboard* recognized Ace's mainstream buzz, Robey agreed to share half of publishing revenue from "Pledging My Love" with Wemar Music if Wemar could convince a well-known white pop singer to record the song, thereby gaining Robey backdoor entrance into an other-wise forbidden market. Pre-Motown, pre-Stax, good luck making money in pop as a black-run company. Robey did it. Sure enough, Wemar arranged for Teresa Brewer to cover "Pledging" and her ver-sion charted. In March, Johnny's version reached no. 17 on the *pop* chart (while holding the top R&B spot), and Brewer's version hit no. 30.

Not only did seemingly every other firm in the record business produce Ace tribute songs or covers, but an insanely devoted fourteen-
year-old fan in West Palm Beach, Florida, died by Russian roulette
in a misguided imitation of his hero. "Pledging My Love" became
a pop sensation, as the Four Lads and even Louis Armstrong covered the tune. Johnny's original spent ten weeks atop the R&B chart,
eventually winning the triple-crown as the year's top seller and leader
in both jukebox and radio plays. Robey rushed a greatest-hits LP to
press. Another single, "Anymore/How Can You Be So Mean?" came
out in July and reached the R&B top 10.

Toward the end of 1955, *Billboard* signaled a major turning point
in American music history. The recording industry recognized that
the chitlin' circuit sound had become the driving creative force, not
just of black pop, but for the business as a whole. What's more, they
recognized our boy Johnny's significance. In a November 12, 1955,
article, "The Year R&B Took Over Pop Field," *Billboard* noted,
"Ironically, spin-wise, the pace setter is the late Johnny Ace whose
Duke recordings continue to sell after his accident."

In the decades following Ace's end, "Pledging My Love" became
something of a standard and its ill-fated singer a legend. Diana Ross
and Marvin Gaye sang a duet version; Elvis Presley, who had risen to
fame from Memphis during Johnny's heyday, recorded it just months
before his own death in 1977; and Emmylou Harris cut it country-
style. Aretha Franklin, who was born a mile from where Johnny grew
up, covered several of his tunes. Paul Simon wrote a tribute, "The
Late Great Johnny Ace." The boy made his mark.

The Woody that Johnny and his band navigated the chitlin' circuit in—the one that led his funeral procession—landed behind the
stable on Robey's horse farm. Robey's son, born a decade after Ace
died, saw it there looking like an old gangster sled—weeds sneaking
through the floorboards, "My Song" and "Cross My Heart" lettered
faintly in white across its body—and wondered how such an odd relic
ended up in his backyard.

Dave Mattis, the Memphis radio executive who unwittingly launched Johnny Ace, remarked after seeing Johnny's body in state that the boy had been much happier as a cheap piano player.

The people who grew up idolizing plain John Alexander Jr. in South Memphis prefer to remember him roller-skating down Williams Street, graceful and carefree.

*   *   *

As Johnny Ace sunk below the Memphis soil, Little Richard returned home to Macon a new man. He'd fought with Don Robey and steeped in the Memphis sound at Sunbeam Mitchell's, while Macon's chitlin' circuit status had grown from port to hub. Hank Ballard and the Midnighters, the originators of "The Twist," would stay close by for most of 1955–56, and boogie man John Lee Hooker and crew relocated to Macon during the spring of 1955. "Our booking agent was old Clint Brantley," Hooker said, ". . . he booked us all over Georgia, Alabama, some parts of Mississippi once in a while, everywhere he could book us."[3] Macon had as many black nightclubs showing live music as Memphis did. Club 15 boasted the best hardwood dance floor in town. That and the Manhattan Club sat outside Macon on Highway 129 northeast toward Gray, Georgia. Brantley owned a couple such venues and controlled action at the rest. His entourage had grown with his holdings. "The niggers I had with me were big and strapping sons of bitches." The cops? "I never did have no trouble with them. They always respected me." Once Brantley began promoting big concerts at the auditorium, he learned the value of police protection, and hired at least a dozen plainclothesmen to work his shows. "I have seen it up there when the floor was so bloody you couldn't walk on it."[4]

No other chitlin' circuit promoter had as profound an effect on the development of superstars from small-town, bloody-floor origins. Clint Brantley groomed not one but two of the most innovative, celebrated artists in American popular music. Denver Ferguson had a gift for mass marketing and one for big-picture thinking. Don Robey had a knack for making money. Neither seems to have known what the audience would like before the audience liked it. Clint Brantley, however, astutely judged talent and facilitated its growth like a minor league baseball farm system gets its prospects ready for the majors.

Downtown, Brantley booked acts at the Elks, the VFW, and the million-dollar Macon City Auditorium, all in the heart of the little city. Black music was no longer confined to Broadway (technically Fourth Street) and Fifth, the city's World War II–era strolls. Brantley brought in as many one-nighters as he booked out. Jimmy Liggins and his reconstructed jaw were favorites for holiday dances, playing the Valentine and Halloween balls at the Manhattan in 1955, and Billy Wright, who inspired Little Richard's hair and makeup, played the same spot. Though Richard had spurned Brantley to join the Tempo Toppers back in 1953, the big man welcomed the unpredictable one back and committed his considerable resources to preparing Little Richard for the galaxy beyond Macon.

Upon his homecoming, Little Richard and his Upsetters "upset the VFW Friday night, February 4."[5] Brantley, understanding that the world for chitlin' circuit entertainers was expanding, booked Richard to play a white club, Ann's Tic Toc on Broadway. He performed at Club 15's weekly 12:01 dance throughout February and March. Then Brantley tested him. On March 21, Little Richard played his first headlining gig at the city auditorium. Not only was this his biggest local show to date, but also Brantley pitted him in a "Battle of the Blues" against a tested pro, the original rockin' pianist Amos Milburn. The battle turned out to be more than seasoning for Richard. As Phil Walden, significantly, a white teenager back then, told Peter Guralnick, Little Richard blew Amos Milburn away. "Amos Milburn and the Chickenshackers were headlining a two-billed show, and the opening act was Little Richard. Strictly a local act. And I can remember Amos Milburn kind of disappointed

Preparing to cross over: Little Richard and band entertain at Ann's
Tic Toc Lounge, a white club on Broadway in Macon, Georgia, 1954.
*Middle Georgia Archives, Washington Memorial Library, Macon,
Georgia*

me, [he was] just a fat guy sitting at a piano. But Little Richard just
destroyed me."[6]

Brantley continued rotating Richard through different venues,
putting him in front of new crowds, playing Richard at the Elks Club
Easter dance. The next week, Brantley ramped up the challenge—
"Little Richard and His Upsetters to clash with Roy Brown and His
Mighty Men," the news read. "This will be one of the greatest Jitterbug jamborees in the history of Macon when Rocking Roy and Rocking Richard meet Friday night." Brantley promised, "Little Richard
will have surprises for you."[7] By now Richard was flourishing—with
the drag act and the cabaret act behind him, he had begun to look like
the "quasar of rock-n-roll." Richard wore a silvery cape and his hair
high. And while no one would say it was easy to be gay, the people at

home forgave his eccentricities and allowed him to be himself. That's just Richard, little boy used to run around in his sister's pedal pushers. Unlike his time with Don Robey, Richard felt comfortable. He played on stage with exotic dancers Princess Dee and Tokita Lopez, and female impersonator Mose "Vicki" Jackson. Old friends. He honed original material to suit his swelling persona and outrageous show. "One song which would really tear the house down was 'Tutti Frutti,' " he said. "The lyrics were kind of vulgar . . . it would crack the crowd up."[8]

After an intensive six months in Macon, Brantley plugged Richard into the network he'd activated as a Ferguson promoter during the chitlin' circuit's infancy. Richard's extravagant reputation preceded him into the Peach State's juke houses. He was more confident, playing more piano and wailing like a man aflame. Little Richard and his band played no fancy places, but they worked every night. By now the band's lineup mixed New Orleans, Houston, and Memphis players and came with a built-in emcee and bandleader, Brantley's longtime aide de camp and Richard's first piano instructor, Luke Gonder. Gonder's job had as much to do with holding volatile Richard's hand and ensuring the cash flow back to Brantley as it did introducing the group and playing a little piano. As Brantley's ears and eyes on the circuit, Gonder would not only supervise Little Richard but also make a monumental discovery.

When Little Richard and the Upsetters arrived in Toccoa to play Bill's Rendezvous in early August 1955, they were the biggest thing in small-town Georgia. "Even so," James Brown recalled, "the Rendezvous was our turf and we were determined to cut him if we could."[9]

By *we*, James meant the Flames.

Born on May 3, 1933, in Barnwell, South Carolina, James Brown came up in an Augusta, Georgia, brothel his aunt managed. Like Little Richard and many other budding entertainers of the day, James found inspiration in a Louis Jordan film short, "Caldonia." In 1949,

not long after seeing "Caldonia," James was arrested for armed rob-
bery, convicted, and shipped to the Georgia juvenile detention center
at Toccoa. There he met Bobby Byrd, a good kid from outside. Byrd
played on a baseball team of town boys who competed against Brown
and other juvey inmates. Byrd also sang in a gospel group that performed at talent shows at the lock-up, and he heard James sing at
these programs, impressively. When James got out, Byrd brought him
into the Gospel Starlighters.

They shifted from gospel and patterned themselves after vocal
groups like Billy Ward's Dominoes, the Five Royales, and the Midnighters. They landed their first regular gig at Bill's Rendezvous
Club in Toccoa, a café with a piano and dance floor. They covered
hits, but as they couldn't afford instruments, the group stomped
the rhythm and whistled or hummed instrumental sequences. They
picked up gigs in Lithonia, Hartwell, Cleveland, Cornelia, Kings-
ville, and Athens—some of the same towns Little Richard had seen
on Ma Sweetie's revival tour and Clint Brantley's circuit—and across
the line in Greenville, South Carolina. The boys took turns on the
Rendezvous piano and, in James's words, "learned to make a whole
lot of noise with very few resources."[10] He would say that he built his
superhuman performance stamina in these jukes, alternately stomping, singing, and playing piano for as long as the people wanted to
drink, dance, and gamble. The group named themselves the Flames,
and burnt as hot as anyone possibly could around Toccoa. They
saved their jingling gig money and bought some real instruments, and
James Brown emerged as their leader.

The Flames lingered around the Rendezvous that night to study
the band from Macon. Little Richard took no notice. Once the
Upsetters got started, James recognized his advantage over Richard.
Though he sang feverishly and looked wild—decked out in a shimmering cape, made up like an opera singer, with his high, curly pompadour—he couldn't dance. At the Upsetters' intermission, local fans

urged James and the Flames to take the stage. They rushed on and bounded into their act. Richard initially feigned disinterest, but as the place throbbed, he lost control.

"Get 'em off!" he cried to the club manager. "*Get them off!*"

Richard accepted defeat as honorably as could be expected. "You're the onliest man I've seen who has everything," he reportedly told James, before theatrically stalking off.[11] Luke Gonder hung around. He thought he'd seen every wishful singer in the state, but he hadn't witnessed anything quite like James and the Flames. Gonder told James to go to Macon and see Clint Brantley. Brantley recalled, "Luke came back that night and said, 'Some little niggers got down and sure could sing. They call themselves the Flames. I gave them your address and how they could get you, and they said they'd be down here.' "

Clint Brantley sat in his old joint the Two Spot nursing a hangover one Saturday morning in late August 1955. The place smelled like mildew and dry beer, and the heat and the whiskey-head kept Clint pretty still. The trains steadily rumbled past the Two Spot and their sudden, ear-splitting whistles jangled him.

"Four or five little niggers walked through the door," Clint said. "And you could tell they were country." They introduced themselves and said they wanted a manager. Hung-over Clint was in no mood. "And I said, 'Well I don't want to.' " They turned to head on back out, but Brantley stopped them. Feeling a little contrite, he asked them to sing a good spiritual before leaving. He thought it might lift him.

"And goddamn—man—them sons of bitches, they sang 'Looking for My Mother.' Goddamn, they looked for her, too." The Flames split up around the Two Spot, singing and peering under tables and around the bar, looking for their mother, already adept at the sort of theatrics that would make the James Brown show unlike any other showbiz attraction in the coming years. Clint told them he might be able to help after all and encouraged them to stick around Macon. The Flames moved into Dean's Hotel, just a few doors down from the Two Spot, toward the Ocmulgee River.

*   *   *

Further down the road, Little Richard met Lloyd Price, a fellow client of Don Robey and Evelyn Johnson's Buffalo Booking Agency. Richard envied Lloyd's car, a black and gold Cadillac—as shiny as the one at the funeral home, and you didn't have to die to ride. Price liked Richard's style and recommended he send an audition tape to Specialty Records. Though a fellow named Art Rupe owned Specialty, the company's ears belonged to Bumps Blackwell, a classical musician from Seattle who had nurtured Ray Charles and Quincy Jones. Bumps was looking for someone to compete with Ray when an audition tape arrived at Specialty's Los Angeles office, "wrapped in a piece of paper looking as though someone had eaten off it," he recalled. The enclosed songs had the gospel-inflected blues Ray Charles rang the cash register with and a little something all their own. "The voice was unmistakably star material," Blackwell said.[12]

Bumps found Richard, he of the star-quality voice, in Macon and sent for him to come to New Orleans. They met on September 13, 1955, after Little Richard's last 12:01 dance at Club 15.

Bumps summoned a band to J&M Studios at Rampart and Dumaine, where Roy Brown made "Good Rockin' Tonight" back in 1947. Earl Palmer, inventor of rock 'n' roll's backbeat, joined on drums. Palmer's career spanned from the Ferguson circuit, through Don Robey's Bronze Peacock, to recording with Fats Domino. The presence of guitarist Edgar Blanchard, who'd recorded some of the earliest rock 'n' roll with Roy Brown, and Fats's sax man Lee Allen rounded out a formidable lineup.

Bumps, seeing Little Richard, expected him to perform wildly, but instead the singer seemed subdued. The session stuck in the same mundane place as Richard's earlier recordings. Hours in, they'd completed a few numbers, but nothing worthy of the expense. Bumps called lunch break to sort things out, and everyone headed to the Dew Drop. In these hallowed walls—where an indigent Roy Brown had sung "Good Rockin' Tonight" to a record executive over the phone and a cross-dressed freak like Patsy Valdalia had become a starlet—something came over Richard. Seeing the crowd and the unmanned piano on stage, he couldn't resist. He took the stage and broke out that vulgar song from his show. It opened with machine-gun piano pounding and Richard belting, "Awop-bop-a-loo-mop-a-good-god-dam, Tutti Frutti, good booty, If it don't fit, don't force it, you can grease it, make it easy."

Bumps hollered, "That's what I want from you Richard. That's a hit!"

Now funky and gay were definitely the wrong kind of black. Bumps knew it, and Richard knew it too. He hadn't come to New Orleans to cut "Tutti Frutti." The lyrics needed tidying, but it had the fire.[13]

A couple days before Little Richard's epochal recording session, Clint Brantley had announced his latest discovery in the Macon paper.

> The Flames of Washington D.C.
> A New Sensation in Music and Band
> Appearing at the Elks Club Saturday Nite,
> September 17, 1955
> 8:00 P.M. until ?
> Adm. $1.00[14]

The Flames assumed Little Richard's 12:01 gigs and played club Les Amis, while Clint Brantley juggled his many duties. On October 7, Brantley promoted "The Big Rock and Roll Show" at the auditorium, with the surprising headliner Clarence "Gatemouth" Brown. Gatemouth was still recording and touring for Don Robey's Duke-Peacock-Buffalo conglomerate, and his latest records were instru-

mentals, not exactly the leading pop trend. The fellow who appeared
third on the bill (after Buddy Johnson) had a better handle on that—
Chuck Berry, singer of the rising hit "Maybellene." The song had
been out barely six weeks and was destined to carry Berry over to a
predominantly white audience, making him the briefest tenured of
chitlin' circuit artists during rock 'n' roll's rise. After this, "Maybellene" would reach no. 5 on *Billboard*'s pop chart, Chuck would enjoy
a marathon run of popularity interrupted only by the occasional
arrest, and Gatemouth could tell his grandkids about the night Chuck
Berry opened for him.

Little Richard's abrupt departure for the West Coast after the
"Tutti Frutti" session left Brantley with a problem, namely, unfulfilled
bookings. So for a few weeks during the fall of 1955 around Georgia,
you could have seen James Brown as Little Richard, and Bobby Byrd
as James Brown with the Flames. Brantley plugged James right into
Richard's gigs, touring with Richard's Upsetters, traveling in a station wagon adorned with Richard's name and song titles. James took
it in stride, teasing about Richard's magical ability to perform in two
places at the same time. Emcee Luke Gonder worked the joke into his
nightly introduction of the band on stage. After rattling through the
lineup, he reached the star of the show.

"Ladies and gentlemen, *the hardest-working man in show business* today—Little Richard."[15]

So the man who taught Little Richard's first tricks on the piano
also coined one of the most distinctive brand names in entertainment
history. You can hear Gonder himself deliver the intro, updated with
James Brown's name on the *Live at the Apollo* album.

James sang "Tutti Frutti," and so for that matter did Pat Boone
and Elvis Presley, giving a gay-sex anthem probably the widest listen-
ership, if among an oblivious audience, that such a tune has ever had,
from Georgia moonshine dens to *American Bandstand*. James gradually shed Richard's identity, mixing his own knockout closing num-

Alvin Luke "Fats" Gonder, aka Count Basic, was one of rock 'n' roll's great unheralded role players. He taught Little Richard beginning piano chops, helped discover James Brown and the Famous Flames, and named Brown "the hardest-working man in show business." *Middle Georgia Archives, Washington Memorial Library, Macon, Georgia*

ber "Please, Please, Please" into his Little Richard set, and breaking it to the folks on his way out that they'd been duped. To the best of anyone's recollection, no one asked for a refund.

Brantley arranged for the Flames to record a demo of their own material, and at radio station WIBB, the group recorded a rough cut of "Please, Please, Please" as an audition for record companies. The station's R&B deejay Hamp Swain played the cut on the air repeatedly, which certainly helped pack Club 15 late on Sunday nights.

Rock 'n' roll was but one factor of the Macon community's vitality at this time, for the city nurtured an active spiritual life as well. On October 23, 1955, a young minister from Montgomery, Alabama, named Dr. Martin Luther King Jr. preached at Macon's Tremont

Temple. "Dr. King is a young man, just 25 years old, who is acclaimed one of the most powerful preachers of our time," the local paper said.[16] And so you could have heard Dr. King at noon, just a half mile from Clint Brantley's Two Spot, and danced to James Brown at a minute past midnight.

Brantley seasoned the Flames as he had Richard, installing them as the band for Club 15's 12:01 weekly dances, then mixing them in at the Elks and VFW. James became himself again, and reunited with his group. Having successfully packed nightspots throughout Macon, the band earned an upgrade. Leading up to their November 5, 1955, Macon Elks show, they were billed for the first time as the *Famous* Flames. The Famous Flames progressed fast, and Brantley deemed them ready for the big stage under the world's largest copper dome, and announced, for November 11, 1955, "The Big Battle Is on Armistice Night: Macon's Own to Challenge the Nation's Best."[17] In this case Ruth Brown represented the nation's best, and it was no exaggeration. A poll of rhythm and blues deejays, published in *Billboard* that week, rated Ruth Brown the second favorite artist after Fats Domino. *Cash Box* contributors chose her as the favorite female R&B artist for the second year running.

To represent Macon's own, Brantley chose his Flames, of course, with a notable change. Brantley ran a photo of James Brown in the ad for the Armistice Night battle, verifying what everyone who listened to Hamp Swain's show already knew, that James stood out in front of the Famous Flames. James dressed in a white suit with black shirt and gray tie, posed like a gospel singer, leaning a little to his left with his left arm bent up and fingers extended, the mic stand elevated in his right hand so the microphone tilted above his head, his famous process hair just attaining its lusciousness.

A month later, Little Richard returned home. "Tutti Frutti" had reached the *Billboard* R&B top 10, and there was perhaps no hotter spot anywhere than the:

Big Christmas Rock 'N Roll Dance Featuring . . .
The Sensational Flames—Plus—The Upsetters
At The New Elk's Club Monday December 26
From 11 until 2 A.M. Adm. $1.00[18]

While Richard's record was climbing the charts, Brantley sent copies of the Famous Flames' "Please, Please, Please" dub to every R&B record company in late 1955. He and James visited a few companies in person, and called at Duke-Peacock Records in the Bronze Peacock building on Houston's outskirts. Evelyn Johnson and Don Robey gave the dub a listen. "My attitude was like, oh so repetitious," Evelyn recalled many years later. Chuckling, she said, "They received a contribution from here to further their journey." Then she paused and added, dead seriously, "Mistakes were made because of poor judgment."[19] Don Robey had officially blown it with both of Clint Brantley's star pupils.

Ralph Bass of King Records in Cincinnati—whose roster included Roy "Good Rockin' " Brown among others—recognized the Flames' talent and arranged a phone conversation with Brantley. Their link was Universal Attractions, the booking agency for whom Clint Brantley had served as regional promoter several years prior. Universal's president Ben Bart and King Records' president Syd Nathan were brothers-in-law. Bass was anxious to meet James and the Flames. Brantley invited Bass to Macon, but he emphasized caution. Bass recalled, "He said to me—this is like a James Bond story—'Now at eight o' clock you park your car right in front of this barbershop, which is right across the street from the railroad station. When the lights go on and the blinds go up and down, after they go down, you come on in.' "

The location Bass described was Brantley's Fifth Street barbershop, right next to the Two Spot, across from the tracks. Bass did as Brantley instructed, pulling his car beside the tracks on a rainy winter night. Brantley watched and signaled Bass as he'd explained. Bass

An early James
Brown publicity
shot that manager
Clint Brantley
commissioned for
use on placards
and newspaper
ads throughout
Georgia, 1956.
*Middle Georgia
Archives,
Washington
Memorial Library,
Macon, Georgia*

went inside, and the two men stood among the tonsorial spin chairs discussing the future of the Famous Flames. Bass hadn't been the first to try to sign the Flames, Brantley informed him, and produced a contract from Chess Records. Bass countered with two hundred cash dollars. "Clint, this is for you," Bass said.

There wasn't much more to say. Brantley took the cash and promised that the Flames would sign with King Records. Bass wanted to make sure the group he signed was the same he'd heard on the tape, so later that night Brantley brought him to the Flames' performance at a club on the Ocmulgee called Sawyer's Lake. As a cold rain poured outside, James Brown crawled on his back across the stage singing "Please, Please, Please." Bass said, "It was fantastic."[20]

James Brown and the Famous Flames drove to King Records' Cincinnati studio in a station wagon with Little Richard's band name, the Upsetters, still painted on the panel. "Please, Please, Please" came out on March 3, 1956, less than six months after James and the Flames had landed in Macon. And, of course, the group signed with Universal Attractions to book their dates. On Thursday, March 8, 1956, they battled Hank Ballard and the Midnighters at the Magnolia Ballroom in Atlanta, and "walked off winners." The Midnighters challenged the Flames to a rematch in the Macon Auditorium on March 23, which kicked off the Flames' first cross-country tour.

Things looked bright for the young parolee from Toccoa. Booking agent Dick Alen recalled, "I booked one of [the] first dates for James Brown and The Famous Flames. Everybody in the station wagon, pulling a trailer with a Hammond B-3 organ on it, would be $400 a night, and everyone [was] very happy."[21]

✳   ✳   ✳

Just as Johnny Ace had once pulled Little Richard along the chitlin' circuit on his coattails, Richard followed Johnny's breakthrough to the white record-buying market. Once "Tutti Frutti" hit, a long string of bookings materialized, and he needed a band and road support. Richard sent a 1956 canary yellow Fleetwood Cadillac and an envelope full of cash to Percy Welch back in Macon to arrange everything. They had been on the Lucky Millinder amateur program together as teenage boys back in 1947, and toured together briefly before Richard joined the Tempo Toppers in 1953. Now Percy became Richard's road manager and spent the next couple of strenuous years driving and flagging down hot meals.[22]

Richard could be generous, petty, loyal, and fickle. Bobby Byrd of the Famous Flames asked Richard for a little help on the road, while the Flames were still in the $400-a-night category and Little Richard was pulling in thousands. Richard grabbed a wad of bills from an attaché case he kept in the trunk of his car and gave them to Bobby as if they were paper napkins. B.B. King hit up Richard for $500 out there and offered to sign an IOU. "Darling, there ain't nothing for you to sign," Richard said. "If you see me out there hungry and you got some bread, give me a piece."

Percy ran all day for Richard. "He'd call and say, 'Go get me a pot of coffee,' and he'd already have a pot," Percy said. " 'Well, get me a fresh pot.' Sometimes, he'd have three or four pots of coffee and wouldn't be drinking none of it. . . .

"He'd [order steak], take one cut outta that meat and then he would get on the phone and get to talking. And that steak would get ice cold. He'd never touch it again," Percy said. "I [almost worked] myself into a nervous breakdown. I was the road manager. I was the chauffeur. I was the valet. I was the go-fer. He called me so many times a day it was pathetic."

On the day of a show, Richard dressed for the stage and walked the low-down black parts of town, pulling eyeballs like Doctor Nobilio did back on Macon's dusty streets. Richard liked to pick up the raggediest little urchin he could get his hands on, hug him, and autograph a twenty-dollar bill for the child. "Go tell your momma Little Richard gave that to you."

Percy said, "That night, everybody on that street would be at the show . . . there wouldn't be standing room."

At dances, Percy watched the door and counted the group's money, which meant chasing unscrupulous promoters down and standing between armed robbers and the coveted cashbox. The situation went from inconvenient to maddening as the group played a white club in Bell, Texas, in early 1956. While the crossover success of "Tutti Frutti" opened new opportunities to this band of chitlin' circuit veterans, they found the same old bullshit on the other side.

"Now all during the show, Little Richard was knocking them out, I mean left and right," Percy said. "They were screaming and hollering the whole time we were playing. So after the show, we were waiting to get paid. Little Richard was in his dressing room changing his clothes. About this time, it looked like all the Texas Rangers bust in the door. Now, I was getting paid, one of the big sheriffs said, 'That's him right there who was up on stage doing all that vulgar dancing.' They grabbed me and handcuffed me to the rail that went around the bar. . . . So this little district attorney, that was about four feet tall, he went into the dressing room to whip Little Richard . . . there was this big commotion and all of a sudden the door flew open like an explosion and this D.A. came out sliding across the dance floor and his head hit the concrete wall and knocked him out."

The lawmen locked several band members up, to the tune of a $7,000 bond, $5,000 on Little Richard alone. Percy had about $12,000 in the famous attaché case, but he sensed a scam. He contacted a black attorney in town who told him to sit tight until the next morning when he could straighten the situation out more economically. Richard saw things differently. Give them the $7,000, he said, "I don't care. I want to get out of here right now." But Percy waited it out, and sprung Richard and the boys for $500 apiece with the local lawyer's help the next morning.

Percy's responsibilities left little time for relaxation. Unconsciousness offered no safety from his boss's antics. About the only time Percy could try to rest was when he handed Little Richard the keys, "but I couldn't sleep . . . cause he was a reckless driver."[23]

If life with Little Richard wasn't trying enough, the group regularly found themselves in the bizarre position of carrying the attaché case full of money and having nowhere to spend it. They worked seven nights a week, made thousands a night, slept in their Cadillacs, and lived on sardines and saltines. Late one night in Virginia, with Percy, half-starved and totally exhausted, at the wheel, the other band members lounging around, and Richard asleep in the backseat, the caravan drove past a brightly lit diner. They could see truckers in there eating, and the diner door painted all white and stamped with the word *only* in harsh black letters.

Percy pulled into the town square and cruised around it slowly. He shifted, punched the gas pedal, and peeled his tires. Sure enough, as Percy's car exited the square, blue lights popped into his rearview mirror. The sheriff stopped Percy, told him to get out, and asked him where he was headed in such a hurry. Percy said, "I'm looking for you."

"What did you want with me?" the sheriff asked.

"I'd just like to get one decent, hot meal in my stomach this week," Percy replied. "If you could take us up to that truck stop, and get them people to let us sit down and eat, I'll give you a hundred dollar bill."

"Follow me," said the officer.

The band ate well in that white café, and after they finished, Little Richard autographed a hundred-dollar bill for the policeman, same as he would sign a ghetto kid's twenty. And the crooked road rolled on.

✳   ✳   ✳

Indianapolis: 1952–57

The five years from Johnny Ace's debut to Little Richard's pop breakthrough had been transformative—artists of the black music underground became the most popular acts in the country. Though Denver Ferguson stayed out of the game, he fought the sorts of obstacles in his personal life that his former industry encountered. The short version: crossover was no panacea, and crossing back was damn tough.

On a bright, cold March day in 1952, he had waited in New York to see his beloved glide down the gangway from the transatlantic ship. But his angel never landed. A woman who must have weighed two hundred pounds insisted through a Bavarian accent thick enough to fill pastry that she was Lilo—the porcelain profile, Denver's pen pal of three years. Denver lost his breath. His chest tightened. He had to sit down. The sight must have shocked Lilo as terribly as she distressed Denver. In his letters, he was in his mid-forties but virile, the product of good farm genes. The gasping and snowy hair made him look twenty years older than the man he had described to her.

Denver had funded Lilo's passage from Germany, and he promised to do the same for her return, but she refused. She was his responsibility. To transport her unwed across state lines back to Indianapolis could constitute a violation of the Mann Act, the legislation that criminalized interstate transportation of women for immoral purposes. He had to marry her. On March 14, 1952, Denver D. Ferguson and Lilo Rentsch became man and wife. A few days later, the Marion County Criminal Court found Denver's longtime rival Tuffy Mitchell guilty on seven gaming charges.[24] Of the two, Mitchell would have a far easier time with his sentence.

Denver began preparing for his divorce shortly after his wedding. Fearing that Lilo would loot him in their settlement, he had property to stash. He hoped instead that she would become destitute after the divorce and thus be forced to return to Germany, an outcome Denver longed for more desperately than he had ever wanted her company. He signed his land holdings over to his brother Sea and hid his furniture.

The divorce proceedings publicized Denver's private suffering during his time with Lilo. *Ebony*, the national black magazine that brought the ill-fated couple together, wisely kept its distance. *Ebony*'s looser sister publication, *Jet*, however, noted that the legal proceedings brought "lurid charges and counter-charges" to light. Denver claimed that the marriage was never consummated. "On one occasion, he said, his wife tried to rape him which made him suffer a heart attack." Lilo countered, however, that Denver's impotence and "peculiar bedroom mannerisms" prevented their commencement of a sex life. Without divulging specifics, she charged that Denver tried to engage her in abnormal sex acts, from which she fled before locking herself in another room. After discovering that Denver slept with a hatchet under his pillow, she never entered the master bedroom again. Except once, to be photographed for the *Jet* article, stooped over the bed, lifting a pillow part way up from the mattress with her left hand and pointing her right index finger at a hatchet that lay there.[25]

Lilo admitted one lie—instead of a picture of herself, she had sent *Ebony* a picture of a friend, but had done so to protect herself from a feared backlash from her employer, the U.S. Air Force, and not to mislead her thousands of suitors. Denver and Lilo's divorce became final on February 24, 1953.

Jet stuck with the story and reported in its November 12, 1953, edition, "Denver Ferguson, wealthy Indianapolis club owner who proposed to German-born Lilo Rentsch and married her after seeing her picture in Ebony Magazine in 1949, was divorced from his foreign wife and ordered by the Indianapolis Circuit Court to pay her $25,000 alimony and $5,000 attorney fees." Denver unsuccessfully sought an annulment on grounds of her false advertising in *Ebony* and dishonesty in their correspondence. The affair amounted to an international scandal, as it was reported in Lilo's homeland, then picked up in a Spanish publication.

Denver's difficulties mounted in early 1954 as his legal battle with Lilo continued, when a special prosecutor identified several prostitution "pick up spots," including Sunset Terrace, his nearly twenty-year-old nightclub in downtown Indianapolis. The already dramatic fallout with Lilo took a surreal turn. Denver, having stashed real estate with his brother and claimed poverty, refused to pay a cent of the $30,000 awarded Lilo in alimony and legal fees almost a year earlier, but the tactic backfired spectacularly. Lilo's attorney led deputy sheriffs and a court-appointed receiver into Sunset Terrace and took control, ejecting Denver's employees and seizing the cashbox. Lilo's attorney explained that Denver's sudden cash-flow problems forced Lilo to protect his only remaining asset. Three years earlier, as Denver haggled with U.S. Immigration to bring Lilo from Germany, he had claimed a net worth of around $300,000. Now, Denver entered involuntary bankruptcy, and his beloved Sunset Terrace belonged to the person he despised above all others.

He dared not return to the Sunset and, with his income cut off, spent most of his time at home. At eight o'clock on the bright morning of Monday, May 25, 1954, a most unwelcome group of visitors— Lilo's lawyer and the sheriff's deputies again—called on Denver there. This time they parked a moving van out front. Lilo had provided an inventory of furniture and appliances inside, and armed with a court order, they seized Denver's few remaining possessions. A crowd gathered on the sidewalk as the deputies marched rugs, tables, chairs, beds, and lamps into the moving van.

Lilo's attorney wondered about the whereabouts of the new gas range and big refrigerator Lilo told them to confiscate. As Denver's stuff passed by, the attorney loudly remarked, "Well we won't get much out of a sale of this stuff, but we're going to keep trying to collect our money." He hinted not so subtly that his next plan would force the sale of Denver's house.[26]

With the weight of catastrophe on his head, Denver suffered a devastating stroke.

For nearly thirty years Denver Ferguson publicly clashed with white gamblers and politicians. His victories were celebrated throughout Bronzeville, and his setbacks stung many. His battles now were private, the most basic problems of getting himself fed, bathed, and dressed after the crippling stroke. He treated himself with a variety of liniments and tonics, though, and recovered some movement. His daughter Carole came to cook breakfast in the mornings, and Sea visited some. He spent most of his time in bed, where the acres of headstones visible in the cemetery outside his window unsettled him.

An appellant judge forgave Denver's indebtedness to Lilo in 1955, ruling, in part, that "alimony allowances would reach astronomical figures in a great many cases were they to be based upon the self-appraisal and representations of an ardent suitor during courtship."[27] Consequently, Denver's home furnishings were returned to him. As he recovered his belongings, his old inventive spirit stirred. He filed a patent for a letter-sorting device in 1956.

Denver dragged himself to his desk on the morning of December 20, 1956. He heard a knock at the door and, expecting Carole or Sea, invited the visitor in. Two federal marshals entered. They saw Denver, face half-sunken, at his desk, little patent medicine bottles lined up before him, and a stack of dog-eared pamphlets and a copy of "Dollar Maker Tips," a guide to operating a home business, within reach. They arrested him for making false statements on Sunset Terrace's admission tax returns from late 1951 and early 1952. Denver had dishonestly listed his assistant Taylor Seaths as Sunset's owner and filed, according to the government's allegation, twenty-seven false income reports.

They looped their arms under Denver's and hoisted him up from the desk. He asked if they would let him drink a glass of milk before the trip. They agreed, and stood there with him in the kitchen, between the refrigerator and range he had hidden from the sheriff's deputies who had seized his stuff for Lilo a few years back. The marshals, knowing Denver's condition, brought an ambulance along, but Denver said he preferred to ride downtown in the marshal's car. Denver whispered hoarsely about his weak heart and made the marshals take their time down the front steps.

One of the marshals waved the ambulance away and drove Denver to the federal courthouse, just about a mile from Sunset Terrace, blocks from the former Ferguson Brothers Agency headquarters and the print shop where he had reeled off thousands of numbers tickets. Unlike the backroom resolution of Denver's 1949 tax trouble, there would be no funny business this time. He was going before a judge.

U.S. Commissioner Edwin Haerle detailed the charges and penalties (a maximum of ten years' imprisonment and $5,000 fine for each) and set a hearing date three weeks out. Denver feigned confusion, as if the marshals had apprehended the wrong person entirely and dropped him into someone else's nightmare. Haerle warned Denver against leaving town, to which Denver scowled and pointed down to his stroke-numb leg. "I can't go nowhere," he said. Haerle asked how much bond Denver could bear. "None, I haven't got a cent," he responded.

Haerle said that Denver had been around. "You should know all about judicial proceedings." A zero bond was out of the question. Haerle set it at $5,000, which Denver posted and then went on back home.[28]

The IRS granted Denver numerous extensions due to his health. The arrest sapped his remaining strength, and he spent virtually all of his time contemplating the Crown Hill Cemetery.

J. St. Clair Gibson, better known as the Saint, Denver's old friend, longtime newspaper columnist, and public relations man for Ferguson Bros., published the first in a series of tributes to Denver in the May 4, 1957, *Indianapolis Recorder*. Denver "has fought a courageous fight . . . always taking a boot in the buttocks from people he helped." The Saint reminded readers of the many jobs Ferguson created, and he mistily recalled the dirty, delightful old days at Sunset Terrace, "rated at that time as one of the finest danceries in the nation . . . the music played on and on and on."

Sea stopped in to Denver's for a visit on May 11, 1957. The second installment of the Saint's tribute had just been published, listing people who owed Denver money. This would please him. The Saint called Denver "the man who made more Negroes wealthy than any other person in Naptown. . . . He employed hundreds of musicians and entertainers and booked them all over the country. His agency was considered among the top four in the nation . . . with a phone bill running better than a thousand dollars a month plus station wagons, automobiles and buses." He reminisced on all the old acts: Lil Green, Jay McShann, Snookum Russell, Big Maybelle, Doc Clayton, Tiny Bradshaw, King Kolax, Christine Chatman, and the International Sweethearts of Rhythm.

But Denver never saw it. Inside, Sea found him lying next to his bed, where Denver died trying to stand up.

After a viewing on the Avenue, Denver's body was taken to his birthplace, Brownsville, Kentucky, then carried up the highest hill in town to Ferguson Cemetery, and laid to rest beside his father and mother.

Renewal

This ought to be where the Royal Creolians, International Sweethearts of Rhythm, Chickenshackers, Mighty Mighty Men, Tempo Toppers, and Famous Flames face off in an apocalyptic Battle of the Blues, but I'm afraid closing the chitlin' circuit is not so simple. Such a slippery organization does not just topple. Headlining performers died or went cold, big-time promoters quit, posh nightclubs shut down, and the circuit as a whole outlived all such strife. From Walter Barnes winking at dancers as he flourished his baton on the Afro Auditorium stage in Yazoo City, Mississippi, to Marvin "Candy Licker" Sease flaring his tongue at the Agri-Center crowd in Greenwood, Mississippi, seventy-five years later, no underground American music scene has survived nearly as long or accomplished as much as the chitlin' circuit.

This first twenty years on the circuit, from Barnes, Fatha Hines, Tiny Bradshaw, and Lucky Millinder to B.B. King, Little Richard, and James Brown was only the beginning. And rock 'n' roll, though a key aspect of this story, had been no more of a deliberate destination for the chitlin' circuit than it was the circuit's end point. But the chitlin' circuit is in sharper focus now than it was back then. We can view its evolution through a wide angle, clearly seeing important events and monumental changes that may not have been recognized as such in their chaotic times. We can see how a cultural fad for Louis Jordan's small band and harsh post–World War II economic conditions forced black promoters to turn from big, expensive swing bands to small, cheap, loud combos, thus revolutionizing black music. We can see how darktown's lively atmosphere inspired violent, sexual, hedonistic lyrics—Roy Brown's "Good Rockin' Tonight" and "Boogie at Midnight"—and how it all unwittingly, incrementally shaped rock 'n' roll.

We can also now recognize how the circuit was transformed as black rock 'n' roll went mainstream in the mid-1950s. The tour business, which had been the leading moneymaker in black music during the circuit's first twenty years, was demoted.

Back in the 1930s, ill-fated bandleader Walter Barnes made no money, for himself or anyone else, from his few recording opportunities, but he earned his entire salary in the dance hall. The same rule applied to Denver Ferguson's artists: his top drawing act during the World War II years, the Carolina Cotton Pickers, never made record one, much less their first dime from anything other than a dance. Louis Jordan couldn't reach stardom through records and cabaret residencies during the same period, and hit the chitlin' circuit in the summer of 1942 to build his audience and fatten his pockets. T-Bone Walker, Joe Turner, Wynonie Harris, and Cecil Gant made outstanding records after the war, but still made their livings on the circuit. Consequently, the money and power in the for-black music business were with agents, promoters, and club owners, people like Denver Ferguson, Don Robey, and then Ben Bart and Billy Shaw, who decided which artists and styles would be appealing to the public and profitable to themselves. The recording industry's black niche grew all the while, but the chitlin' circuit still saw records as a promotional tool.

Records nudged ahead gradually, beginning with the introduction of *Billboard*'s Rhythm and Blues chart in 1949, which separated chitlin' circuit music from other black styles, notably jazz. It conferred status too, establishing the music's value in the marketplace. Cross-over for the black record business came with increased radio exposure and continued respect from the industry at large in the coming years, punctuated by the death and ascent of Johnny Ace on Christmas night 1954. By 1956, *Billboard* had desegregated its charts, and Little Richard, Fats Domino, Clyde McPhatter, and Ray Charles regularly appeared on the Best Selling Records list and on the Honor Roll of Hits, mixing with Elvis Presley, Carl Perkins, Perry Como, and the unforgettable Kay Starr, whose "Rock and Roll Waltz" outsold 'em all that year. In January 1957, *Billboard* marveled at the sudden diversity of the once homogeneous mainstream record market. "The most numerous invasion force . . . came right out of rhythm and blues. As the adulterated product known as rock and roll caught on, the dee-jays led the kids in the appreciation of the true, original article. This led to the pop success of such performers as Little Richard."[1] With radio behind black music, as the *Billboard* reporter noted, and the pop record market desegregated, there was a new way to make it big, open for the first time to chitlin' circuit artists. This caused a simple, seismic shift—following Little Richard's breakthrough, chitlin' circuit performers could think seriously about making a living, perhaps a fortune, in the recording studio.

The tour business had shaped the sounds of World War II–era black music as it went small band and rocked, and the music, in turn, shaped the tour business. From this point forward, however, the record business replaced the tour business in this equation.

The original circuit's geography experienced even more drastic upheaval than its business model. While the circuit's creative and economic energies shifted from the nightclub to the recording studio, the circuit as we've come to know it on its road to rock 'n' roll was eliminated by degrees as urban renewal programs eviscerated once vital black neighborhoods nationwide. There would be no return to the old circuit, and reminders of black Main Street's importance to American culture were erased from sight. The decade from the late

1950s to the late 1960s was a transformative period. By the end of
it, the circuit would offer new opportunities, but it would no longer
look like its old self.

Just as Sax Kari pointed me down the road to rock 'n' roll, Howard Grimes's story, and what happened in his hometown, illumi-
nate the next phase. Howard was born in Memphis, Tennessee, in
1941. He learned to play drums, and thanks to his talent and some
favorable breaks, he laid the rhythm behind a decade and a half of
Memphis hitmakers, from Rufus and Carla Thomas to Al Green.
Like Sax, Howard is an underappreciated figure. Even among Memphis soul aficionados, his reputation rates behind that of Al Jackson
Jr., the house drummer at Stax Records. Also like Sax Kari, Howard's lack of celebrity in no way reflects the value of his story or his
importance to history. For the drummer sees all, and behind his kit
Howard witnessed the rise of soul music. Hearing him speak, you get
the sense he was born wound-down to supply the laid-back rhythm
that would become a crucial component of Hi Records' hit formula
and the Memphis sound. His voice affects you like his drumming on
one of those masterful recordings, maybe the one that put Al Green
over, "Tired of Being Alone"—his speech is clear, deliberate, and sustained. There are no hiccups, pauses, or "you know's," and no rush.
It slows your pulse and heightens the suspense. His physical stature
fits the nickname he was given during the heyday—Bulldog—though
he was a skinny thing then, and he still embodies the calm tenacity
that goes with it.

Grimes, another descendant of Jimmie Lunceford's musical lin-
eage, played in the Manassas High School band in the mid-1950s.
Emerson Able, who once picked a fragment of Jimmy Liggins's shattered mandible from his shirt collar, was Manassas band director at
the time. Able consciously carried forth the Lunceford legacy—he
drilled his band to perfection. Able also worked for Sunbeam Mitchell and knew the realities of the band business for black musicians.

Able recognized Howard's talent—a blessing of perfect rhythm—and sensitivity. He took special interest in Howard's musical apprenticeship. Able bragged about his pupil among other local bandleaders, and Grimes soon found a job with entertainer Rufus Thomas. The outfit's salty veterans kidded Howard about being so green. "His lean is so clean you could stir cabbage with it," one of them said as they rode up Highway 51, nearly causing Rufus to crash the station wagon.[2]

From playing cafés in Memphis's black enclaves, teenage Howard graduated to one of Sunbeam Mitchell's road bands. The venerable bootlegger still sent several of these units out to play rural roadhouses every weekend, keeping a princely one-third of each group's earnings even though 10 percent was the industry standard. Howard joined a guitarist, pianist, and horn player, emcee Willie Britt, known as the "King of Comedy," and the ensemble's star attraction, an exotic dancer called Ms. Shake Right. Their first assignment carried them from Memphis to Houston, Texas, in 1958, Howard's farthest venture from home yet. "That's where I learned my lesson about Three-Card Monte," Howard said.[3]

In Houston, Howard and the three other guys in the band headed to Caldwell Tailors on the Fifth Ward stroll, Lyons Avenue. (Ms. Shake Right customized her apparel, and "Comedy" Britt dressed to set himself off from the group.) They stepped out from Caldwell's like a con man's answered prayer, greenhorns grinning in new gold blazers and black trousers. As Howard recalled, "Here was this dude on the corner, shuffling these cards. Being young, I thought my eye was quick. He let me win a couple times, then he clipped me for my money."

On top of cracking jokes, Comedy Britt served as the road band's accountant and supervisor, carrying a small attaché case and a pair of shoulder-holstered .38 revolvers. After Howard told Comedy about his misfortune, they headed back to the tailor shop and went into the lounge next door, where they found the Monte dealer nursing a high-ball at the bar. "This was the first time I ever saw how serious this business is," Howard said.

Comedy snapped those two pistols out on the dealer. Laugh, motherfucker, laugh. "The cat gave Comedy my money," Howard said, "and I still can't gamble, can't play no cards, or shoot pool."

That night, the boys in gold played behind Ms. Shake Right.

"I'm going to tell you the most fascinating thing about that woman," Howard said. "She'd be out there dancing, splitting and wiggling her hips. This lady, when she laid down on the floor to do her thing, she'd take a lightbulb, put it in a certain place, and it'd jump on and off! I'm thinking, 'This woman got something hot down there.'

"I had to grow up to find out what that secret was. For years, as I grew up and moved from Sunbeam's band to Bowlegs' band, she was singing from the Flamingo Room to Club Handy [as Sunbeam's Beale Street club was known after the late 1950s]. I seen her one day, and I asked her about that act, 'Ms. Shake Right'—that's what we knew her by—'I played behind you all those places, and I'm curious about that lightbulb.' She started laughing. 'Oh Howard, I had a magnet in the center of my suit, right where it was cut at the vagina, and when I screwed that bulb in, it would flick on and off when it hit the magnet.'"

Before graduating from high school, Howard Grimes and his per-fect time were well liked among Memphis bandleaders, if not always justly compensated. Anyone seeking a reliable backbeat had nothing to worry about once Howard grabbed the rhythm. His steadiness on the drums seemed to him about the only certainty in this business. The older bandleaders Howard drummed for played tricks when it came time to pay at the end of the night. Ben Branch liked to wad a five around a ball of ones, and Bowlegs Miller would fold Howard's money into a tight square, toss it up in the air to him, and be headed out the door by the time it hit Howard's hand. Nonetheless, How-

House band at the Plantation Inn, West Memphis, Arkansas, ca. 1961, that included saxophonist Floyd Newman (standing in the center), drummer Howard Grimes (kneeling on the left), and Isaac Hayes (kneeling on right). *Courtesy of Howard Grimes*

ard spent the late 1950s and early 1960s in these bands, primarily Branch's outfit, the Largos. They were the human jukebox at Currie's Club Tropicana in North Memphis, covering Hank Ballard and the Midnighters, the Five Royales, Ray Charles, and Brook Benton, and keeping the dance floor sweaty. When these acts came to Memphis, they called the Largos for backup.

In Memphis during the late 1950s, a couple of hopeful record companies assembled studios in abandoned movie houses near where Tuff Green once ran the city's earliest black recording service. Creativity blossomed in these new studios much as it had in old nightclubs. The doors remained unlocked and the atmosphere was as free-flowing and relaxed as at a Bronze Peacock afterparty or anytime at the

Mitchell Hotel. Musicians dropped in to jam and joke, pass the jug, and blow through the latest hits. Maybe somebody brought some lyrics. Howard was well on his way to becoming a chitlin' circuit drummer like dozens of pace-setters before him who bounced through traveling orchestras or worked in the source bands regional promoters employed to back touring singers. Instead, as the Southern black music business began to emphasize records over dances, he became a choice studio drummer whose beats would crackle out of transistors, hi-fis, and conversion van eight-tracks, later to be sampled in top-10 pop hits and heard in TV shows and motion pictures. In 1960, Howard Grimes's old boss Rufus Thomas called him with a thrilling offer to record. In the studio, the group talked through most of the song's accompaniment, but they were stuck on the rhythm. They hit on a pattern based on one of the songs Howard played with the Largos at Currie's, "Ooh-Poo Pah-Doo" by New Orleans drummer Jessie Hill. It clicked on Rufus's song, an up-tempo duet sung with his daughter Carla called " 'Cause I Love You." The song reached no. 5 on *Billboard*'s R&B charts and crossed over to no. 10 on the pop list, ringing the cash box a half-million times, jump-starting the company soon to be known as Stax Records.

While the black record business took off, the original chitlin' circuit infrastructure crumbled. Racial integration, a new moral streak in city government, and a far-reaching federal program together reshaped the African-American cityscape. Urban renewal spun out of the federal Housing Act of 1949, which provided cities with federal funding for the purchase of slums. The idea was to replace blight with vibrancy, but urban renewal in practice often replaced functioning minority neighborhoods, initially with high-rise public housing and then, after the 1956 Federal-Aid Highway Act, with interstate highways. African-American novelist James Baldwin called it *Negro removal*. Renewal merged with more aggressive policing of black downtown. Think about Indianapolis: When Denver Ferguson introduced the numbers game in the mid-1920s, cops were satisfied to take their bribes and look the other way. A quarter-century later, police on the same beat hassled every Negro social function from craps games and private parties to double dates. Similar circumstances would unfold on Memphis's Beale Street, where covenants of bribery and protection that had kept the street culturally vibrant and free from white control since the nineteenth century dissolved.

The basic argument against urban renewal, according to its most visible early critic, Jane Jacobs, is that it destroyed communities and the *innovative economies* therein by isolating residential properties from commercial districts. Anyone who's read this far will appreciate the italicized phrase's implications. Dense, African-American precincts—"the stroll" in Walter Barnes's hip 1930s jive—fostered such innovative economies as Madam C. J. Walker's cosmetics system, the numbers game, and the black nightclub business, the latter two respectively feeding and housing the creative economy of black music up to rock 'n' roll. Denver Ferguson built the chitlin' circuit around the urban design of the stroll, through community hubs, barbers, and bars where literally everyone socialized, where blanket advertising through placards and handbills could reach a complete audience, and a few, always nearby retail outlets, whether barber and beauty shops, drug stores, or saloons, could serve the demand for tickets, and everyone could walk or catch the trolley to the show-place. Naturally, the removal of such an elegant system hurt the chitlin' circuit business model.

Beale Street had become more than a local stroll by 1959, when Memphis authorities first broached renewing it. Beale Street was a national icon. Its mystique wafted through American culture, high and low, black and white, thanks to its fame as the birthplace of the blues.

It began by word-of-Negro-mouth. It reached a Florence, Alabama, youth named W. C. Handy in the late nineteenth century, who heard "life was a song from dawn to dawn" there and felt "a yearning for Beale Street and the . . . universe it typified."[4] He satisfied the yearning, arriving on Beale in 1906 with a job heading Memphis's Colored Knights of Pythias band. A formally trained bandleader in the Sousa bag, Handy found the street teeming with gamblers, brawlers, cotton-bale haulers, brass bands, flesh for hire, and hoo-doo conjurers. In Beale's lavish taverns he heard syncopated piano and barflies dropping improvised verses. Women danced up against the wall as if flat on their backs. Taken with the universe Beale typi-fied, Handy composed and published tunes based on the sights and sounds that struck him there, most notably, "Memphis Blues," "St. Louis Blues," and "Beale Street Blues," between 1912 and 1917. The mystique went mainstream in 1919, when Gilda Gray sang "Beale Street Blues"—an eight-to-the-bar boogie woogie in the style of the house pianist at Beale's Monarch tavern, with lyrics glorifying chit-lin' cafés, pickpockets, and ladies of the night—in *Schubert's Gaieties* on Broadway.

In the late 1920s, Beale's feral sounds spread along all routes of the Great Migration on records by Memphis Minnie, Jim Jackson, Cannon's Jug Stompers, Frank Stokes, and Furry Lewis. The mys-tique crossed over into peckerwood and literary elite circles in 1931, when the country's most popular hillbilly singer, Jimmie Rodgers, teamed up with its greatest jazz soloist, Louis Armstrong, to record "Blue Yodel No. 9"—set down in Memphis on the corner of Beale and Main. William Faulkner bit a "St. Louis Blues" lyric for the short-story title "That Evenin' Sun," published in 1931, and flashed furtive glances down Beale in *Sanctuary*, also out that year. In 1934, Beale orator George W. Lee's book *Beale Street: Where the Blues Began* introduced Handy, Nine-Tongue the gambler, and brawler River George to middle America as a Book of the Month Club selection.

All the while, Handy's Beale Street songs permutated: They influ-enced George Gershwin's "Rhapsody in Blue" and were in the books of every big band from Duke Ellington, Ella Fitzgerald, and Louis Armstrong to Guy Lombardo, Glenn Miller, and Benny Goodman. The blues took on a life of its own, echoing from Deep South dives to

Carnegie Hall. Its status upgraded from craze to American art form and popular music bedrock.

Handy's 1941 autobiography further entrenched himself as *Father of the Blues* and cemented Beale in the public mind as where it all began. Richard Wright riffed on Handy imagery in 1945's *Black Boy*: "I found Beale Street . . . the street that I had been told was filled with danger: pickpockets, prostitutes, cutthroats, and black confidence men." The street surprised Wright, for "it was on reputedly disreputable Beale Street . . . that I discovered that all human beings were not mean and driving."[5]

Two years after Wright's book came out, B.B. King hit Beale and picked up the tag the *Blues Singing* Black Boy. He would say, "I found Beale Street to be a city unto itself. It was exciting seeing so many people crowded on the streets. So much activity, so much life, so many sounds. . . . Beale Street did look like heaven to me. . . . Even if I never saw [Handy] in person, I could feel his esteem. His stature gave the blues pride and his presence made Memphis, at least in my mind, the capital of the blues."[6]

White Memphians crossed Beale on their Main Street errands, catching scents of cornbread, fish frying, and pork shoulder sweetly barbecuing, though most dared not explore further. Handy would remark, "White people of Memphis have never understood just what Beale Street really meant and means to my people."[7] Still, outside ofays revered the strip. Comedian Danny Thomas visited in 1955, and shocked to see that the world famous *street* was officially called Beale *Avenue*, he recorded "Bring Back Our Beale Street" and led a successful campaign to have its colloquial name restored, just in time for Nat "King" Cole to star as Handy in the film *Beale Street Blues*.

The 1959 tourist attraction plan made a certain amount of sense, considering Beale's pull on the outside world. Suspicion greeted the news on the street, though. Matthew Thornton was a longtime Beale fixture, head of the local Colored Knights of Pythias brotherhood who had brought Handy to Memphis in 1906, and in 1938, as the

"Mayor of Bronzeville" craze swept black America, Thornton was elected "Mayor of Beale Street." He never relinquished the title and continued to function as an emissary between Beale and the outside world. As such, he had mastered the subtle art of Southern black diplomacy. Throughout Thornton's time frame, white Memphis was content to look away from Beale as long as its votes and graft were properly delivered. The street's distinctiveness, the fame Memphis's city fathers were poised to exploit, derived from black independence thus secured. It was a fragile but time-honored balance. When asked about the tourist attraction plan, Thornton remarked, carefully, cryptically, "The white folks of Memphis want a better Beale Street just like the colored folks do."[8] Their suddenly *wanting* Beale after nearly a century of laissez-faire was a dark omen.

The Memphis Housing Authority, urban renewal's local agent provocateur, sized Beale up in 1961. MHA director Walter Simmons said, "We looked around and saw where some improvements can be made. We have no desire to destroy the things that made Beale Street famous nationally. Later, maybe, we can do something about urban renewal around Beale, after we go into it thoroughly."[9]

Renewal wasn't the only force of change lurking around Beale. The street's packed sidewalks had owed to the fact that black people couldn't shop, dine, cabaret, or go to the movies in white downtown. A series of 1962 sit-ins at the Main Street Woolworth lunch counter won black Memphians the right to spend their almighty dollars across a wider swath of downtown Memphis, and these opportunities pulled irreplaceable funds from Beale. The street that had once symbolized protection and independence from whites began to look like a vestige of racism. This scenario affected strolls everywhere—integration into mainstream society disintegrated black downtown. Robert Henry, Beale's dance promoter and B.B. King's former manager, would remark, "What we need is some urban re-OLD-al," but his nostalgia was apparently not shared by the civil rights generation.[10]

Beale Street still produced talent, though not in the most obvious places. A lab tech named Roosevelt Jamison ran a blood bank in a squat, flat brick building next door to where W. C. Handy had published Memphis's early blues hits. Roosevelt moonlighted in gospel music. Between extractions, he wrote songs and rehearsed a spiritual quartet in a storage room. One of the singers was Overton Vertis Wright, who went by "O.V." Born in the country outside Memphis in 1939, O.V. hung around the blood bank more than the other guys, writing lyrics with Roosevelt and honing his voice. In 1963, Roosevelt composed a nice lyric, though not of strictly holy sentiment, called "That's How Strong My Love Is." Roosevelt wrote it with Sam Cooke in mind, but O.V. heard it and told Roosevelt it suited O.V. Wright better than Sam Cooke. After a few run-throughs accompanied by refrigerator hum in the blood storage room, Roosevelt believed him. Now Roosevelt understood the business enough to know the real money flowed not to he who sings but he who holds the copyright. He didn't know, though, how to transcribe a melody, a necessity for legally registering an original composition. Roosevelt heard that a fellow who lived up in Sunbeam Mitchell's old hotel could help.

Bill Harvey had come home to die. Harvey led the first Mitchell Hotel orchestra and the first Peacock Records house band, then traveled and recorded with Memphis stars B.B. King, Johnny Ace, and Bobby "Blue" Bland. Years of gin, sleep deprivation, and grinding bus rides, though, had nearly worn him away. Suffering with diabetic lesions on one of his legs, he retired to his room. Now he earned a few stray dollars by writing charts and lead sheets for bands. Roosevelt stood in Harvey's sparse flat and hummed the melody to "That's How Strong My Love Is" while Harvey transcribed the tune into notes. In late 1963, Roosevelt had the lyrics and melody copyrighted, recorded a demo of O.V. Wright singing it, and began searching for a record company to release the song.

Roosevelt found a partner at Goldwax Records, and by late summer in 1964, O.V. Wright's "That's How Strong My Love Is" got hot. *Billboard* reported it as the no. 1 R&B song in the Miami market on

August 1, 1964, and then named it a Regional Breakout Single on September 19, 1964. Influential deejay John R at Nashville's powerful WLAC reported it a "smash" in the October 10 edition of *Billboard*. The attention brought O.V. Wright more misery than bliss. Before starting his solo career with Roosevelt, O.V. had recorded several tracks for Don Robey's Peacock Records as a member of the Sunset Travelers gospel group. While O.V. figured that his contractual obligation covered only his work with the Sunset Travelers, Robey saw it differently. He sued O.V. for breach and won damages rumored to have been in six figures. O.V. didn't have that kind of cash. He had to work it off Robey's books instead.

*   *   *

Despite Memphis Housing Authority's reassuring public tone, longtime Beale Streeters understood the likelihood that they'd have to move to survive. "They were getting ready to tear things down on Beale Street," Sunbeam Mitchell recalled. "Urban renewal was coming through there and we knew it was going to come up." Sunbeam moved his base from Beale and Hernando to Georgia Avenue in South Memphis, where he would open Club Paradise, with his old protector Abe Plough's help, in March 1965. Sunbeam did his best to import the Beale Street magic. He outfitted Paradise with a gambling room and hosted a weekly "Sissy Night" for transvestites. The new club had a house band and floor show, featuring the spangled-bikini–clad Mitchellettes. Club Paradise, however, was a cavernous, three-thousand-seat showplace, well suited to major touring acts, but without the intimacy of the old Mitchell Hotel. This was the aspect of urban renewal most destructive and antiseptic to the chitlin' circuit: decentralization. While the Mitchell Hotel had stood at the heart of Negro America's Main Street, Club Paradise was isolated in South Memphis. "Down here in this ghetto," Sunbeam said.[11] The trolley lines had fed Beale from black neighborhoods on the north

and south sides of town, and the street appealed universally throughout the rural black population for hundreds of miles. Georgia Avenue
had neither advantage. Though Sunbeam saw the move to a large
hall as a plus, he hated what was happening on Beale, and resented
the force-out. Nonetheless, Club Paradise would become one of the
circuit's gold medallions during the soul era, if only for big shows
and not incubation. Off the strip, Sunbeam moved from chitlin' circuit power broker and talent maker to elder statesman—still in the
game, but without his once mighty influence over the circuit's dollars and sounds. Sunbeam's status drop reflected a broader circuit
trend. Disc jockeys had usurped the old-school promoters. Now that
they controlled the strongest media outlet, they were pushing artists
on radio as Denver Ferguson, Don Robey, and Sunbeam had in the
black entertainment press. Never again would a promoter function as
crucially to artist development in black music. That power was now
vested in producers.

Willie Mitchell (no relation to Sunbeam)—a lean, light-skinned
man with gleaming eyes and an aristocratic air—had played in
numerous Memphis bands, including Tuff Green's. He studied Bill
Harvey, and served a lengthy apprenticeship with music teacher Onzie
Horne. Willie Mitchell's own band leadership experience dated back
to 1948, at least, when a group under his guidance played a black
society dance in Indianola, Mississippi.[12] He played trumpet on B.B.
King's breakout hit "Three O'Clock Blues" in 1951, then led a nightclub dance band that played, mostly for whites, at Memphis's Manhattan Club and the Plantation Inn across the river in West Memphis,
Arkansas. His band leadership skills translated smoothly to record
production, beginning at Memphis's Home of the Blues label, where
he worked with Roy "Good Rockin' " Brown among others in 1960.
Willie, through the ascent of the record business and his pursuit of
the new possibilities there, would become a force in black music, a
figure of financial power and profound artistic influence. Had Wil-

lie been born twenty years sooner he could have and probably would have become a top bandleader on the black side, but never a shaper of mainstream pop music taste.

By the mid-1960s, Willie Mitchell had become boss producer at Hi Records' Royal Recording Studio in South Memphis, near Stax Records and Club Paradise. The studio was built inside a low neighborhood movie house with a sandy brick façade, circa 1920, wedged deep into a ghetto maze among pink and aquamarine Queen Annes and brick courtyard apartments. The Royal's lone architectural purpose was to barrier the outside world, no light, no sound. It had only one door, which opened to a small lobby furnished with wicker thrones, decorated with plastic flora and cigarette-yellow shag carpet. A corridor, lined with cheap trellis, led to the studio, with fiberglass insulation rolled across the ceiling and Willie's wood-paneled control room in the middle. He would own Hi Records and Royal Studio eventually. He took control of the sound immediately.

Willie began cultivating a rhythm section—the three young Hodges brothers, guitarist Teenie, bassist Leroy, and organist Charles—as intensively as his mentor Onzie Horne had schooled him in the art of arranging. He put them up in his home and refined their chemistry. They cut demos at Royal and backed Willie on gigs. The brothers seemed good to go, but the band hadn't found a reliable pace-setter. That is until guitarist Teenie Hodges saw Howard Grimes playing at the Thunderbird Lounge in the fall of 1966. Howard's command of the rhythm impressed the group and their mentor. Willie, who kept everyone loose with his gift for similes and a vocabulary to make a sailor blush, halfway embarrassed and honored Howard with a new nickname. While sitting around listening to a session playback, Willie got fired up for the new drummer. "Here he come," Willie said. "Listen to that foot [on the kick drum], like a nigger walking mad through the house—knocking over furniture—he don't want to be fucked with. *Get out the way!* When he clamps down on the beat, he's locked in like a bulldog."

The Hi Rhythm Section: Memphis bandleader and producer Willie Mitchell groomed four young musicians, here with singer Otis Clay, into one of the tightest, most versatile and distinctive bands of the soul era (left to right): drummer Howard Grimes, keyboardist Charles Hodges, bassist Leroy Hodges, Clay, and guitarist Mabon "Teenie" Hodges, at Willie Mitchell's Royal Recording Studio in Memphis, 1971. *Courtesy of Howard Grimes*

Howard became "Bulldog," and the Hi Rhythm Section was complete.

At Royal, Willie controlled the sound and whatever might affect it. Bulldog smoked weed for the first time before a session, but, leery of the herb's powers, limited himself to two tokes. Everyone indulged openly around the studio, so casually that Howard wouldn't have guessed that anyone noticed. When it hit him, "Everything came to life," he said. "I could hear what we were going to play so clearly. I was locked in. We nailed that first song in one take." Before the next day's recording session, a joint circulated as the band warmed up. Willie called over the intercom from the control room, "Don't give the Bulldog more than two hits."

Hi Rhythm's apprenticeship with Willie Mitchell had overlapped years of mounting anger in black Memphis. Memphis Housing Authority bulldozers hit Beale Street on June 19, 1965—Sunbeam got out just in time—and began leveling 625 targeted structures (141 buildings had been marked for preservation) to make way for a "Gaslight district" tourist area patterned on Bourbon Street in New Orleans. Beale's run as a community hub ended. The plan called for the demolition and replacement of housing in the Beale district, improvements to business infrastructure, and the construction of tourist services and a new headquarters for the local utility company. The federal department of Housing and Urban Development awarded MHA a $10.9 million grant to finance the project, funneling the first half-million in July 1965. In 1966, Beale property owners were given the option of following an MHA-scripted rehabilitation plan or selling. City building inspectors deemed virtually the whole strip "substandard," forcing owners into repairs that few could afford. Beale merchants fought these demands steadfastly but without victories, and dug in for a futile "last ditch" stand in court in March 1967. One longtime property owner noted the discrepancy between MHA's destructive actions and preservationist rhetoric. "You're forgetting one thing. If you tear down all these buildings you will no longer have Beale Street and you will defeat your purpose."[13] A hand-painted sign in a shop window mixed a dose of the day's grim pragmatism and sweet nostalgia from the W. C. Handy lyric that put Beale on the map a half-century before: "When you gotta go, you gotta go, but I'd rather be here than any place I know."

As black Memphis music died and resurrected concurrently, one outsider, long involved with Beale Street, accurately judged the shift and jumped on the right trend. "Houston mafia's coming," Willie Mitchell told his group one day at Royal. Bulldog expected a mob, but "Houston mafia" turned out to be one guy, white-looking at that. Howard saw the gold flash when Houston mafia spoke, though, and knew this was no Caucasian. Later that afternoon, a white limousine stopped on Lauderdale Street outside Royal Studio. A dark little man in light blue disembarked the limo under the blank sky. Howard appreciated the man's dramatic entrance, if less so than his choice of footwear—house shoes. Howard liked O.V. Wright off the bat.

By this time, Willie Mitchell had produced an O.V. Wright album and some Bobby "Blue" Bland songs for Don Robey—the only old-school chitlin' circuit promoter to cleanly transition into a power position in the new era—and the new Memphis-Houston connection was about to yield its biggest hit yet. The first song O.V. recorded with Willie's new Hi Rhythm Section was called "Eight Men, Four Women." The mood and melody drew from the Animals' version of "House of the Rising Sun," and "Eight Men" is no less of a lament. Its title characters are the jury that convicts O.V. of loving the wrong woman. The record went gold.

Meanwhile, Beale Street's coffin was in the ground, about to have dirt kicked over it. On February 1, 1968, two African-American Memphis sanitation workers were killed by a malfunctioning garbage truck. Fed up with the low wages and nonexistent benefits they received to work in such dangerous, dirty conditions, Memphis sanitation workers went on strike. Clayborn A.M.E. Temple, where Johnny Ace's funeral had taken place in early 1955, became the workers' rallying point. In a few weeks, uncollected trash piled on many of the city's streets, and picketing garbagemen filed daily along Beale and Main.

Nearly two months in, Martin Luther King Jr. came to lead a peaceful march on the sanitation workers' behalf. By now the workers were experienced demonstrators, having solemnly endured mace from the police and verbal backlash on the streets. The garbagemen's plight, however, attracted a younger, angrier protest element to the streets. The two factions gathered on the morning of March 28, 1968, to walk down Beale Street behind King. As the throng moved, shop windows shattered, and when the omnipresent police intervened, a riot erupted. Televisions and mannequins and suits spilled out on the sidewalk, tear gas filled the air, rioters threw stones, bottles, and

Looters smash
the front
window at
Paul's tailor
shop on Beale
Street, where
B.B. King had
bought his first
show tux in
1951. *Special
Collections,
University
of Memphis
Libraries*

punches at the police, who clubbed anyone within swinging range.
King drew heat for leaving the scene.

After the riot fizzled, National Guardsmen and police patrolled
Beale and stood sentry at every intersection. That night, gunshots
crashed into the concrete all around the guardsmen down below Sunbeam Mitchell's old joint at Beale and Hernando. The area had been
secured, with armored vehicles and soldiers blocking every inroad and
alley—the only direction the shots could have come from was up.

Memphis never went up in full torch like Watts and Detroit.
Instead, a liquor store burnt here, a grocery there. You could still see
fire everywhere. The Hi crew had obtained police permission to break
a citywide curfew in order to go to work, so Bulldog's Oldsmobile
98—painted gold, with a tangerine Plexiglas roof—had the streets to
itself. Usually, there was so much noise and clamor, cars and trucks

Riot cops on the Rialto: Memphis police patrol Beale Street on March 28, 1968, marching east past Sunbeam Mitchell's club. *Special Collections, University of Memphis Libraries*

and crowds, Bulldog could hardly hear his own car stereo. Now he drove through empty streets. While pieces of the city burned around them, the men at Hi worked and honed their craft, and created art of enduring, transcendent beauty. A noble sense of restraint, an improbable calm, washes over the music made in those desperate days. By no means were the artists at Hi detached from what happened all around them. The damage reached next door to the studio, when a Molotov cocktail crashed through an apartment window. Many of the people who smashed and burned and were shot and clubbed and gassed were the same age as the fellows at Hi, same race, grew up in the same circumstances. The Hi band kept cool and stayed organized. They were masterful and composed in the middle of chaos and fire.

On April 4, 1968, in Memphis, an assassin ended Martin Luther King's life with a shot fired from a flophouse bathroom window to the balcony of the Lorraine Motel. The interpersonal aftereffects of the King assassination fractured Stax Records, the company that had set up shop a mile from Hi Records and improbably grown into a hit-record factory. Stax had built its formula on interracial collaboration to this point, mixing groups like Booker T. & the M.G.'s and accompanists the Memphis Horns. This, the assassination compromised. While paranoia and distrust suddenly haunted the once harmonious Stax studio, the assassination had the opposite effect a mile down the road at Hi Records. You can't hear the anger or the fire from the street outside on Willie Mitchell's "Soul Serenade," which was recorded in the South Memphis ghetto during the tense times of early 1968. That may be the ultimate testimony to their art. As Hi Rhythm gelled in the spring of '68, Royal Studio took off. Willie Mitchell recorded a string of hit instrumentals—"Prayer Meetin'," "30-60-90," and "My Babe"—under his name, while attracting new artists to the Hi label and producing hits for other imprints as a freelancer. Mitchell worked at the studio until four most mornings, and was back a few hours later, by ten, refreshed and immaculately dressed.

Months after the King assassination, Memphis Housing Authority officials still uttered their oft-repeated company line: "An effort is being made to retain as much of the famous Beale Street flavor as possible." It was a thin euphemism for leaving a few of the street's storied buildings upright while bulldozing thousands of residential units in the area and most of the businesses on the eight key blocks of Beale and four blocks on either side of it. The Beale Street Urban Renewal project had become a $15 million deal still without positive results. A promised high-rise residential development to upgrade substandard housing around the street would never materialize. As for the new concept of Beale as a tourist attraction, a high-rise Holiday Inn, and tourist plaza and bank complex—ambitious projects that were used to justify renewal in the first place—either never happened or appeared drastically scaled-down. And it wasn't just Memphis. The same results played out across every stroll in America—Indiana Avenue in Indianapolis, West Dallas Street in Houston, little Desiard Street in

Monroe, Louisiana, and on and on. The streets Walter Barnes cruised
in 1936–37, which he found brimming with black barbershops, dentists, tailors, cafés, hotels, theaters, dance halls, and nightclubs, today
are interstate freeway ramps, parking lots, weeds, or, in Beale's case,
souvenir shops, biker bars, and the Hard Rock Cafe, as a private
developer made good on MHA's Beale Street tourist attraction plan,
reopening the street in 1983 after a decade of emptiness.

Of course, there was another side to these changes for the chitlin'
circuit. When Willie Mitchell and Hi Rhythm went on tour in late
1968, they encountered plenty of the time-honored road traditions,
such as the groupies who robbed them at automatic pistol-point—we
love you, Detroit! Instead of flopping at boarding houses or whorehouses along their way, though, the band stayed in Best Westerns,
waking up late to doze by the pool. They played a few craps-table
nightclubs, but also a TV dance party and a gig at Disneyland. An
instrumental group, they worked with a variety of vocalists on the
circuit. In Midland, Texas, they were scheduled to play with one who
had a hit record called "Back Up Train." The guy showed up looking
like a bum, dressed in an old army jacket with a hand-sewn fur collar. Willie and the band knew his song, and halfway disbelieving that
this vagrant was Al Green, they started "Back Up Train." As they
remember it, every other activity ceased when he opened his mouth.

If Al had been born in 1926 instead of 1946, his best-case scenario
would have been something like Roy Brown's career—hot and then forgotten. Willie Mitchell would make Al Green, not on the road as Clint
Brantley had made Little Richard and James Brown fifteen years earlier, but at Royal Studio. On his 1969 debut album, Green flashed his
talent, not to mention that of his backup band and producer, for rendering pop standards in his own image. An undaunted nobody, he con-
quered the Beatles' "I Wanna Hold Your Hand." By the measurement
of heavy radio play or record sales, though, no one seemed to notice.
Then Hi released *Al Green Gets Next to You* in 1971, which planted
his flag on top of the pop world, with five hits, including deconstructed

The Beale Street district, after urban renewal. The Rialto stands at right, the light-colored building with the arch is the Daisy Theatre, and Beale Street Baptist Church, the imposing, dual-towered white structure, stands at left. *Special Collections, University of Memphis Libraries*

versions of Junior Parker's "Driving Wheel" and the Doors' "Light My Fire" plus his break-out hit "Tired of Being Alone."

Though Willie Mitchell used drummer Al Jackson on certain Green sessions—moving Bulldog Grimes to the conga for "Call Me," "I'm Still In Love with You," "Here I Am (Come and Take Me)," and "Let's Stay Together"—this local group with direct circuit ties back to Jimmie Lunceford, Don Robey, and Sunbeam Mitchell would generate millions of pop record sales, laying the soundtrack for countless conceptions.

✳   ✳   ✳

Word reached Howard "Bulldog" Grimes backstage at Club Paradise that he had visitors in the crowd. The emcee led him out to

Howard "Bulldog" Grimes, riding high Memphis style in the 1970s. *Courtesy of Howard Grimes*

the ballroom to see who'd sent the message. There at a long table, with his wife and friends, sat Emerson Able, Howard's high school band director and mentor. Howard had Able to thank for many of the good things this life brought him. With all the recording and touring, however, Howard hadn't seen Able in years. He felt like an ingrate, ashamed he hadn't kept up. In his tough-loving style, though, Able let him know that nothing had changed since their days in the band room at Manassas High. "I got my ear on you, and if you fuck up, I'm gonna know it."[14]

Not long after that night, Bulldog and the members of Hi Rhythm assembled at Royal Studio to record Al Green. Willie called over the intercom, "Count us off, Mr. Dog." That crunchy tapping you hear at the beginning of "Love and Happiness" is guitarist Teenie Hodges

kicking a Coca-Cola crate. Bulldog clamped down on that beat as if
Mr. Able, Sunbeam, Comedy Britt, and Willie all had their ears on
him. The band slid into the groove behind him and stayed. Willie
danced from the control room into the studio, and proceeded to get
down.

✳   ✳   ✳

Though the chitlin' circuit's transformation from its rockin'
nights to the vinyl era was complete, its old spirit sauntered ahead.

The circuit stayed grounded in its dirty roots. As the real money in
the business came from record sales, powerful disc jockeys controlled
airplay and ruled the 1970s, getting payola in goods and services—
ego-stroke record deals for jocks, jock conventions featuring an orgy
room and Mt. Cocaine. The rise of the bagman and the pusher-pimp-
parasite-"manager" followed. More blood oozed.

Still, the hot acts plied it, ladies' men like Latimore, Tyrone Davis,
and Johnnie Taylor and glitzy groups like the Chi-Lites and the
Impressions, as did perennial blues stalwarts B.B. King and Bobby
"Blue" Bland. The Apollo programmed black pop, Motown style,
while the circuit played to the Southern sensibility. As soul faded from
the popular music scene, artists outlived their mainstream popularity
but felt love just the same on the circuit. Audiences were older and
nostalgic. Audiences obsessed on middle-age drama—infidelity and
prowess loomed lyrically large.

The circuit became an underground haven for music that evolved
the wrong kind of black for the mainstream: bluesy and erotic. Race
segregated it in the old days; tastes would segregate it from now
on. Z. Z. Hill said as much in his 1982 classic-to-be "Down Home
Blues," if not in so many words. The theater-revue scene had wilted,
and circuit action transferred to fringe nightclubs exclusively, a basket of pork rinds on every table and a guy selling half pints from a
briefcase—Remy, Crown, Canadian Club, Dark Eyes, and 7. Little
Milton, an artist with 1950s Memphis roots, sang about it in "Annie

Mae's Cafe," an echo of Amos Milburn's "Chicken Shack Boogie." In the 1980s, the circuit sound went synthetic—computer beats and electronic horns. The ladies Millie Jackson and Denise LaSalle shed their pop ambitions and turned lyrical tricks. A new puppeteer, Otis Redding's brother Rodgers Redding, emerged as the circuit's dominant booking agent. In 1987, a gospel singer pushing forty named Marvin Sease announced the dawn of a fantastically filthy new era with the epic "Candy Licker." Bobby Rush assembled a one-of-a-kind dance crew.

Rodgers Redding revived the package tour in the 1990s, selling down-home tradition that's still hot in the twenty-first century. A placard—popsicle-colored cardboard, low-ink typesetting, black-and-white headshots—hanging in a darktown barbershop window tells you where to hear sixty years of black music history somewhere tonight: Bobby Bland rasping through "Stormy Monday," Denise LaSalle advising "Lick It before You Stick It," Bobby Rush serenading an ass that's visible from the nosebleed seats, and Mel Waiters singing his hit "Hole in the Wall," echoing "Annie Mae's Cafe," echoing "Chicken Shack Boogie."

Afterword

Though the white pop music world opened itself to black artists like Little Richard and James Brown, it remained closed to their mentor **Clint Brantley** and other black professionals like him. So, as the Macon, Georgia, stroll withered, Brantley's fortunes sunk. He ran a tavern on Broadway called the Key Club until the mid-1970s, then spent a couple years simply hanging around the decrepit strip telling lies, as the old folks say. In 1978, James Brown learned that his benefactor was in failing health, and took Brantley into his care in Augusta, Georgia. Brantley died there in 1980.

Clarence "Gatemouth" Brown reflected on his early years in a 1993 *Living Blues* interview. "Most of the people, and most of the buildings that I used to see, they've all disappeared like an old mining town in Colorado or Nevada. I think that's pretty sad to see the history go away forever." Rather than fade away with them, Gatemouth evolved, shedding the corny top hat and tails Don Robey had decked him out in for a beat-up cowboy hat and blue jeans. After leaving Peacock Records and Don Robey in 1967, Gatemouth embraced his eclectic musical heritage. He recorded in a variety of styles and on numerous instruments, and with roots music practitioners as varied as Roy Clark and Professor Longhair. He won a Grammy in 1982 and performed regularly for the rest of his life. He died on September 10, 2005, not far from where he grew up on the Texas-Louisiana border.

After breaking on to the scene with "Good Rockin' Tonight" in 1947, cementing his status as one of the top draws in black entertainment during his epic 1949 tour, and enjoying top-draw status on the chitlin' circuit past the mid-1950s, the original "Mighty, Mighty Man" of rock 'n' roll plunged from atop the black music world. **Roy Brown** was convicted of wire fraud in 1961 after using B.B. King's name to con a promoter into sending him a couple hundred dollars. He then used his own name to peddle encyclopedias door to door, before gaining access to his songwriting royalties and retiring to Los Angeles. He enjoyed a hero's return to New Orleans at the 1981 Jazz and Heritage Festival, saw his daughter graduate from college a few weeks later, then suffered a fatal heart attack on May 25, 1981. Despite his accomplishments, he has yet to be enshrined in the Rock and Roll Hall of Fame.

Denver Ferguson's brother and sometime business partner **Sea Ferguson** died on March 10, 1974, in Indianapolis. His reputation as "Indiana Avenue kingpin" had slipped away, and Sea was lauded as a businessman, civic leader, and active member of the Urban League and NAACP.

Louis Jordan died on February 4, 1975, not long after telling writer Arnold Shaw that "as a black artist, I'd like to say one thing. . . . Rock-n-roll was not a marriage of rhythm and blues [to] country and western. That's white publicity. Rock-n-roll was just a white imitation, a white adaptation of Negro rhythm and blues." Back in December 1949, he had called for desegregated seating at his Southern shows, unsuccessfully it turned out. By the time the white audience for black rock 'n' roll forced the integration issue, Jordan's unprecedented run of hit records had stopped. For reasons neither Jordan nor his manager ever spoke about clearly, Jordan had listed his wife, the aptly named Fleecie Moore, as the songwriter on the hits he composed. She retained these rights and reaped the rewards even after their divorce.

Sax Kari died on October 1, 2009, a few months shy of his ninetieth birthday, in Tampa, Florida. He had spent his last years in a nursing home, plotting his escape and conquest of the music world.

The great bootlegger, gambler, promoter, and nightclub boss **Andrew "Sunbeam" Mitchell** died at home in Memphis on August 22, 1989, at the age of eighty-three. He had run Club Paradise in South Memphis from 1962 until he retired in 1985. Musicians who marveled at his toughness couldn't deny his generosity. Emerson Able offered this fitting epitaph: "He never fucked a musician over. They got what they asked for from him." The building that housed the Mitchell Hotel at the corner of Beale and Hernando streets in Memphis survived urban renewal, and the second Mitchell Hotel at South Main Street and G. E. Patterson Avenue lives on as Ernestine and Hazel's, a favorite downtown bar and grill. The second-floor rooms where Ernestine Mitchell's sirens skinned countless patrons are open for late-night drinkers, though their occupants have since alighted elsewhere. Ernestine died on March 30, 1999. Sunbeam and Ernestine are buried in Memphis's New Park Cemetery, where Johnny Ace rests.

Denver Ferguson's old Indiana Avenue rival **Tuffy Mitchell** proved the old adage "if you live in pool halls, you just may die in one," collapsing of a heart attack on September 30, 1970, during a billiards match in Indianapolis. He retired with forty arrests and nine convictions on his record, mostly on gaming and tax-evasion charges. He was free on bond at the time of his death.

Robert Henry was among the final, stubborn Beale Street tenants to let go, finally killing the lights in his poolroom for the last time in 1974, years after urban renewal had reduced his once proud street to dust and rubble. He died in Memphis on February 14, 1978.

Emerson Able and his pupil **Howard Grimes** both live in Memphis. Able retired from Memphis City Schools, and Grimes still works live gigs with the Hi Rhythm Section and, nearing the age of seventy, is again becoming the most sought-after studio drummer in the city.

Lilo Rentsch died in Indianapolis in 2001, having seemingly settled into a quiet life after her rather clamorous landing.

After building Duke-Peacock Records into an independent black music empire over nearly a quarter century, **Don Robey** sold it to ABC Records for $100,000 and a leased Cadillac in 1973. He died of a heart attack in Houston on June 16, 1975. His business partners Morris Merritt and Evelyn Johnson outlasted him. Merritt made it to March 1982; Johnson, to November 2005.

Acknowledgments

My correspondences and friendships with family members of some of the characters who appear in *The Chitlin' Circuit and the Road to Rock 'n' Roll* enriched both the story and my life. Very special thanks to Don Robey Jr. in Houston. St. Clair Alexander shared memories of his brother John "Johnny Ace" Alexander in Memphis. Dorothy Parrott Barnes's niece Joyce Taylor, of Los Angeles, introduced me to Walter Barnes's niece Toya Johnson of Chicago. Both ladies shared family stories that appear here, and Ms. Johnson provided photographs of Mr. Barnes. Last but foremost, words cannot express my gratitude to Denver Ferguson's daughter Carole Ferguson Finnell of Indianapolis and her family.

I was equally fortunate to encounter numerous able-minded archivists and librarians while researching the story. Not only did they provide access to important documents, but also they shared enthusiasm for and knowledge of their places and specialties that added important intangibles to this project. Thanks to the staffs at the Auburn Avenue Research Library in Atlanta and the Houston Metropolitan Research facility in Houston; Wilma Gibbs and Susan Sutton at the Indiana Historical Society in Indianapolis; Portia Maultsby, Brenda

Strauss-Nelson, and Ronda Sewald at the Archives of African American Music and Culture at Indiana University in Bloomington; Lynn Abbott at Tulane University's William Ransom Hogan Archive of New Orleans Jazz; Muriel Jackson at the Middle Georgia Archives at the Washington Memorial Library in Macon; my old buddy Greg Johnson in the Blues Archive at Ole Miss (University of Mississippi); Ed Frank in Special Collections at the University of Memphis Library; and G. Wayne Dowdy of the Memphis Public Library, whose encouragement and insight were especially inspiring.

Other point people provided indispensable information and contacts on this story's many fronts. Thanks to Roosevelt Jamison in Memphis; Christina Ayon, Dave Brewer, Paul Mullins of Indiana University–Purdue University Indianapolis, and retired Indianapolis police officer Richard Crenshaw in Indianapolis; Roger Wood in Houston; R. J. Smith, an L.A. guy who knows where to go in Macon, Georgia; Van Siggers of Tunica, Mississippi; and Allan Hammons of the B.B. King Museum in Indianola, Mississippi.

Dan Kochakian, John Broven, Mike Haralambos, Galen Gart, Billy Vera, and Charles "Dr. Rock" White have been writing about black music for longer than I've been breathing, and all were kind enough to answer questions and share their research or track down information, as did my valued friend and erstwhile co-conspirator Red Kelly. Mike Lydon graciously permitted me to listen to interviews he conducted while working on his excellent Ray Charles biography. *Juke Blues* editor Cilla Huggins and *Oxford American* editorial assistant Meghan Plummer came through with important data at the last minute.

Megan Pugh provided a writer's closest allies: high-grade caffeine and insightful proofreading. Scott Barretta has been both a great and a terrible influence, and I've enjoyed both immensely. Historians Ted Ownby and Ed Ayers provided writing advice and research guidance on earlier versions of this project that retained usefulness throughout its evolution.

I'm indebted to Jim O'Neal for making connections for me to get this project going, for sharing his own research and vast knowledge, and for all the thought-provoking e-mail and conversations. He's not one to beat his own drum, so I'll do it for him. Jim, through his work with *Living Blues* magazine and as a record producer and independent scholar, has committed his life to the history of the blues and its cousins, and has made incalculably important contributions to the historical record of black music.

I'm blessed to be working with agent Paul Bresnick and editor Tom Mayer, both of whom live in defiance of the *what's wrong with publishing today* clichés. Mayer's assistant Denise Scarfi helped out, and Mary Babcock provided expert copyediting.

My friends Emerson Able Jr., Howard Grimes, and the late Isaac "Sax Kari" Toombs made this book possible and changed my life, and I don't think I can thank them enough for all they've done.

Finally, my wife, Elise, and our daughter, Maggie Grace, enlivened motel rooms in nondescript places, and kept me laughing.

Preston Lauterbach
Memphis, Tennessee

Notes

Introduction **Nondescript Places**

1. Interview of Charles Thomas by author, September 30, 2005.
2. Interview of Sax Kari by author, September 28, 2005.

Chapter 1 **A Hundred Dollars Crooked**

1. "As I See Myself" written by Denver Ferguson, July 9, 1950, printed in his funeral program, which is on file at the Indiana Historical Society, Indianapolis.
2. Ibid.
3. Herbert Asbury, *Sucker's Progress: An Informal History of Gambling in America from the Colonies to Canfield* (New York: Dodd, Mead, 1938), 88–106. The "bestsellers" comment appears on page 94.
4. Robert L. Campbell, Dan Kochakian, and Armin Buttner, "The Jimmy Coe Discography," at hubcap.clemson.edu/~campber/coe.html, part of the fabulous Red Saunders Research Foundation, online at http://hubcap.clemson.edu/~campber/rsrf.html.
5. "Many People Are 'Skinned' in New Racket," *Indianapolis Recorder*, January 28, 1933, 1, 8.
6. Joe Hester quotes come from interview by author, August 30, 2007.

7. "Indianapolis Shocked by Divorce Scandal," *Chicago Defender* (National Edition), July 4, 1931, 1.

8. A 1941 study concluded that the South Side (black) Chicago racket employed 5,000. The pre–World War II Harlem game seems, by my reading of contemporary press accounts, to have been as vast and complex as the Pentagon and with just as many power struggles.

9. Interview of Carole Ferguson Finnell by author, November 15, 2008. The best breakdown of the game and its orchestration was published years later as authorities dismantled the racket. "Expose of Numbers Racket Rouses City," *Indianapolis Recorder*, July 30, 1949, 1, 3.

10. Interview of Sax Kari by author, May 3, 2007.

11. Interview of Carole Ferguson Finnell by author, November 15, 2008.

12. See Irma Watkins-Owens, *Blood Relations: Caribbean Immigrants and the Harlem Community, 1900–1930* (Bloomington: Indiana University Press, 1996) for a nice study of Harlem numbers boss philanthropy. Denver and Sea Ferguson were each noted from time to time in the *Indianapolis Recorder* as generous givers.

13. Sea Ferguson would be recognized for his charitable doings after reportedly awarding college scholarships to business-minded students from black Indianapolis. See J. St. Clair Gibson, "Bronzeville in Indianapolis," *Indianapolis Recorder*, June 8, 1940, 13.

Chapter 2 **The Midget Maestro**

1. [Salem Tutt], "Going Backstage with the Scribe," *Chicago Defender* (City Edition), February 7, 1931, 8.

2. William Howland Kenney, *Chicago Jazz: A Cultural History, 1904–1930* (New York: Oxford University Press, 1993), 157. Also, interview of Barnes's niece Toya Johnson by author, January 6, 2010.

3. "Orchestral Doings by Walter Barnes Jr.," *Chicago Defender* (City Edition), March 25, 1931, 9.

4. "Hittin' High Notes with Walter Barnes Jr.," *Chicago Defender* (National Edition), December 19, 1931, 5.

5. Ibid., December 5, 1931, 5, and December 19, 1931, 5.

6. Ibid., February 13, 1932, 5.

7. "Is the Avenue Doomed?" *Indianapolis Recorder*, January 4, 1941, 11.

8. Black vaudeville theaters had opened in great numbers around the turn of the century. Not necessarily black-owned, but always in service of black

patrons, the venues grew most abundantly in the dank conditions of the South—according to one historian's count, Mississippi's black theaters outnumbered New York City's. Black vaudeville pioneer Sherman H. Dudley managed the Mid-City Theatre in Washington, D.C., in 1919 and announced it in the papers as "the only theatre on Seventh Avenue catering to colored people that doesn't discriminate."

Dudley and his cohort formed the Theatre Owners Booking Association (TOBA) in early 1921. It's been misreported that TOBA began in 1909. A scholar at California State University, Northridge, published an annotated bibliography of TOBA news items in the black press, online at http://www.csun .edu/~htang/toba.html. See "New Organization," *Chicago Defender*, January 29, 1921, 4–5, for the news of TOBA's founding.

Shareholder theaters of decidedly ethnic ownership—Italians, Jews, and blacks, men with street commerce in their blood—comprised TOBA. Each held the same voting power and stock in the conglomerate. TOBA mended ragtag black vaudeville shows together under the centralized management of its president, Milton Starr, owner of the Bijou Theatre in Nashville, and booker Sam Reevin of Chattanooga, and ran them through a cycle of city theaters. Soon after its creation, the TOBA circuit, modeled on white vaudeville organizations such as the Keith and Orpheum chains, encompassed Winston-Salem (North Carolina), Greenville and Charleston (South Carolina), Nashville, Memphis, Shreveport, New Orleans, Dallas, Atlanta, Macon, Savannah, Pensacola, Jacksonville, Louisville, Cincinnati, Chicago, Detroit, Cleveland, St. Louis, Indianapolis, and Pittsburgh, plus Dudley's seven theaters in Washington, D.C. TOBA's circuit ventured as far west as Kansas City, Missouri. Some were indeed desirable spots, built in the intricately carved and gold-leafed aesthetic of the Gilded Age. Others, though, drew unfavorable comparisons to livery stables from TOBA performers, who said their organization's initials stood for *Tough on Black Asses.*

A basic TOBA troupe carried about all the variety a single stage could handle, not to mention all the personalities one sleeping car could hold: tapdancer Jack Wiggins, singing, dancing, joking duo Dick and Dick, spousalabusive comedy team Butterbeans and Susie, song-belter Stovepipe Johnson, ventriloquists, stage actors, opera prima donnas, and, finally, headlining blues singers like Ma Rainey, Bessie Smith, Sara Martin, and their respective orchestras all worked the farthest-reaching black entertainment network to date. They lugged trunks full of scenery drops, costumes, and props from town to town—Rainey ordered custom-made backgrounds emblazoned with the logo of her record company, Paramount. On stage she levitated from a giant phonograph, taking her place in the spotlight like a gold-toothed Venus.

Though Sam Reevin booked itineraries in Chattanooga and Milton Starr balanced the books in Nashville, a troupe's leading act, a woman more often than not, would handle the money on the road, and some better than others: Thomas A. Dorsey described Rainey's management skills as "lovely" simply because "she paid the help." She collected the night's receipts from the theater manager—a split of paid admission, lightened 5 percent by TOBA's cut—and distributed the earnings among the company.

TOBA held on for nearly a decade despite competition, infighting, stale shows, and performers who publicly griped about the poor pay. It was finally done in by the Great Depression. Dudley, one of the most important figures in the black vaudeville business, sold his theaters to a white-owned chain of talkie houses in 1930, then retired to a horse farm in Maryland. Most owners of black theaters followed his lead and sold out to motion picture companies. Dudley pondered TOBA's demise in January 1931: "Was it mismanagement of the organization or was it the shows? Salaries were small, but the actors worked all the time and could be working now if [management] had only made a study of the show business. This they did not do, so the audiences got tired of seeing the same thing week in and week out. . . . Now as to the managers: they never encouraged the producers of these shows for the TOBA to put out shows of the better kind by classifying them and paying a decent salary. . . . All they cared for was to count the receipts and live for today without looking into the future."

Though TOBA is seen as the chitlin' circuit's music business progenitor, it specialized in a different form of entertainment, and there would be little to no carryover from TOBA's entertainers, executives, and venues, to the chitlin' circuit's. Really, TOBA belongs as much at the beginning of the drama of chitlin' circuit's history as it does here.

9. "Hittin' High Notes with Walter Barnes Jr.," *Chicago Defender* (National Edition), August 6, 1932, 5.

10. Ibid., March 19, 1932, 5.

11. Ibid., August 6, 1932, 5.

Chapter 3 **The Stroll**

1. "Hittin' High Notes with Walter Barnes Jr.," *Chicago Defender* (City Edition), September 3, 1932, 6.

2. Gus Russo, *Supermob: How Sidney Korshak and His Criminal Associates Became America's Hidden Power Brokers* (New York: Bloomsbury, 2006), xii.

3. Eddy Determeyer, *Rhythm Is Our Business: Jimmie Lunceford and the Harlem Express* (Ann Arbor: University of Michigan Press, 2006), 63.

4. "Lunceford Crowds Duke and Cab for Popularity in East Now," *Chicago Defender* (National Edition), October 28, 1933, 5. Also, "Lunceford's Band Replaces Cab for Cotton Club Stay," *Chicago Defender* (National Edition), January 13, 1934, 5; and "Big Shots of the Stage to See New Cotton Club Show," *Chicago Defender* (National Edition), March 31, 1934, 9.

5. Determeyer, *Rhythm Is Our Business*, 74–75.

6. Ibid., 75.

7. Dave Clark, in interview with Portia Maultsby, April 9, 1983, transcript on file at the Archives of African American Music and Culture at Indiana University, Bloomington.

8. *Dave Clark thru '72*, Stax Records, SLE-0373.

9. Rob Roy, "Orchestras Find 'Pot of Gold' in Travels," *Chicago Defender* (National Edition), April 27, 1935, 11.

10. The term *chitlin' circuit* was strictly a word-of-mouth phenomenon, with precedents in Southern black culture. The hog intestine was a staple of Southern black cuisine dating to plantation hog slaughters during slavery, and remained popular during the decades of pervasive black poverty after emancipation. W. C. Handy mentioned chitlin' cafés in his 1917 composition "Beale Street Blues." On August 14, 1926, the National Edition of the *Chicago Defender* announced the "latest terpsichorean novelties among the elite of Asheville, NC," including the "Chitterling Strut," and the related plight of Wallace Walker, dance-hall proprietor: "Walker had been arrested charged with operating a dance hall without license, but he was released when it was found out that the cost of 'chitterling strutting' was only 15 cents a head at Walker's place." Shortly after Walker's near misfortune, a comic strip shot across the Associated Negro Press wire. It was set in just the sort of Southern, black anytown that Barnes circuited through and called "Chittlin' Switch." True to the chitlin' circuit's underground status, the phrase didn't appear in the black press until a December 23, 1972 *Chicago Defender* article about Ike and Tina Turner.

11. Walter Barnes " 'Tulsa Has Plenty Niteries' Says Dapper Walter Barnes," *Chicago Defender* (National Edition), December 4, 1936, 20.

12. Ibid.

13. Walter Barnes, "The Broadcast," *Chicago Defender* (National Edition), November 28, 1936, 21.

14. Ibid., December 12, 1936, 20.

15. Walter Barnes, "Felix Jenkins, Oil King in Monroe, LA., Banquets Walter Barnes and Band," *Chicago Defender* (National Edition), December 18, 1936, 20.

16. Walter Barnes, "If You Hate to Put Your Feet in Mississippi Mud, Don't Come This Way . . . ," *Chicago Defender* (National Edition), December 26, 1936, 20.

17. Walter Barnes, " 'Jacksonville, What a Flytown; Plenty Big Shots,' Writes Walter," *Chicago Defender* (National Edition), January 16, 1937, 24.

18. Walter Barnes, "Walter Barnes' Band Tremendous Hit at Big Dance down in Ol' New Orleans," *Chicago Defender* (National Edition), March 13, 1937, 24.

19. Walter Barnes, "The Broadcast," *Chicago Defender* (National Edition), April 17, 1937, 21.

20. Ibid., April 23, 1937, 21.

21. Ibid., May 8, 1937, 21.

Chapter 4 **Sunset**

1. "Joe Mitchell to Open New $3,000 Cafe," *Indianapolis Recorder*, August 5, 1933, 10.

2. From advertisements in the *Indianapolis Recorder*, February 5, 1938.

3. Interview of Joe Hester by author, August 30, 2007.

4. Errol Grandy, in interview by Gary Barrow and Will Wheeler, January 12, 1985, for the Indiana University Oral History Research Center, transcript on file at the Center for the Study of History and Memory, Indiana University, Bloomington.

5. "Gala Opening of New Oriental Cafe," *Indianapolis Recorder*, March 25, 1938, 14.

6. J. St. Clair Gibson, "The Avenoo," *Indianapolis Recorder*, December 18, 1943, 4.

7. "Gala Opening of New Oriental Cafe."

8. [Photo caption], *Indianapolis Recorder*, February 20, 1937, 1.

9. [J. St. Clair Gibson], "A History of Famous Indiana Avenue," *Indianapolis Recorder*, March 8, 1947, 10.

10. "Ferguson Outlines Concept of Bronzeville Mayor Job in Speech to His New Council," *Indianapolis Recorder*, April 23, 1938, 3.

11. Walter Barnes, "In the Groove with Walter Barnes," *Chicago Defender* (National Edition), September 16, 1939, 20.

12. Paige Van Vorst, "Walter Barnes & His Band of Heroes," *Mississippi Rag*, November 1998, 37–38.

13. "Orchestra Tried Heroically to Avert Stampede in 'Furnace,' " *Indianapolis Recorder*, April 27, 1940, 1.

14. "Local Boy Blows Last Note as 198 Die in Natchez Fire," *Indianapolis Recorder*, April 27, 1940, 1.

15. "Barnes' Body Is Looted," *Chicago Defender*, May 2, 1940.

16. " 'He Died a Hero,' Says Mrs. Barnes in Tears," *Chicago Defender* (National Edition), May 4, 1940, 8.

17. "Blames Jim-Crow for Natchez Fire; Jailed, Released," *Chicago Defender* (National Edition), May 11, 1940, 7.

18. " 'He Died A Hero,' Says Mrs. Barnes in Tears."

19. "Bradshaw's Ork Barely Escaped Barnes' Fate," *Chicago Defender* (National Edition), May 4, 1940, 20.

20. Van Vorst, "Walter Barnes & His Band of Heroes," 38.

21. Letter from Dorothy Barnes to Ernest Stott.

22. I'm indebted to Barnes's nieces Joyce Taylor of Los Angeles and Toya Johnson of Chicago, for sharing memories and family lore. Johnson provided primary and secondary source material and photographs as well.

Chapter 5 **Rock and Stomp Opus**

1. Wesley O. Jackson, "Naptown after Dark," *Indianapolis Recorder*, January 13, 1940, 10.

2. Clarence Brown, "In the Groove," *Indianapolis Recorder*, April 27, 1940, 11.

3. J. St. Clair Gibson, "The Avenoo," *Indianapolis Recorder*, November 9, 1946, 12.

4. Opal Tandy, "Bronzeville in Indianapolis," *Indianapolis Recorder*, November 3, 1940, 10.

5. The murder garnered front-page coverage in the black *Recorder*, with multiple stories in the July 13, 1940, edition offering varied tidbits of information about the crime and its immediate fallout. See "Jail Joe Mitchell, 2 Others in Murder Case 'Backfire,' " "Chambers Passes Mitchell's Last Time En Route to Cemetery," and "Tavern Owner, Equipment Seized in Avenue 'Visit.' " Additionally, the *Recorder* issued an open letter to Indianapolis authorities. Everything about the coverage was unusual, considering the frequency of violence on the Avenue and the matter-of-fact treatment killings received in the *Recorder*.

6. "Tavern Owner, Equipment Seized in Avenue 'Visit,'" *Indianapolis Recorder*, July 13, 1940, 1–2.

7. "Open Letter," *Indianapolis Recorder*, July 13, 1940, 1–2.

8. "Joe Mitchell and His Tavern on Indiana Avenue," *Indianapolis Recorder*, July 27, 1940, 8.

9. "Jail Joe Mitchell, 2 Others in Murder Case 'Backfire,'" *Indianapolis Recorder*, July 13, 1940, 2.

10. Opal Tandy, "Is the Avenue Doomed?" *Indianapolis Recorder*, January 4, 1941, 11.

11. J. St. Clair Gibson, "Bronzeville in Indianapolis," *Indianapolis Recorder*, January 11, 1941, 11.

12. "Is the Avenue Doomed?" *Indianapolis Recorder*, February 1, 1941, 13.

13. Quoted from the Articles of Incorporation for Ferguson Brothers Agency, Inc., on file at the Indiana State Archives, Indianapolis.

14. In an interesting look at Houston internecine dance promoter warfare, Don Robey let slip that he paid his co-promoter for this tour $1,020. Van Pell Evans, "Two Tiffs Occur on Promotional Front; Counter Charges Fly," *Houston Informer*, June 21, 1941, 13.

15. Lewis Porter, *John Coltrane: His Life and Music* (Ann Arbor: University of Michigan Press, 1999), 56.

16. Ibid., 57.

17. Tony Scherman, ed., *The Rock Musician: 15 Years of Interviews, The Best of Musician Magazine* (New York: St. Martin's Griffin, 1994), 225.

18. D. Antoinette Handy, *The International Sweethearts of Rhythm* (Lanham, MD: Scarecrow Press, 1998); Sherrie Tucker, *Swing Shift: All Girl Bands of the 1940s* (Durham, NC: Duke University Press, 2001).

19. Cilla Huggins, "Ike Turner: In the Beginning," *Juke Blues* 37 (Spring 1997): 11.

20. John Chilton, *Let the Good Times Roll: The Story of Louis Jordan and His Music* (Ann Arbor: University of Michigan Press, 1997), 217.

21. Preston Love, *A Thousand Honey Creeks Later: My Life in Music from Basie to Motown* (Middletown, CT: Wesleyan University Press, 1997), 236.

22. Eddie Boyd, a former Bluebird Records recording artist, told an interviewer, "It was a woman here [Chicago] called Prossie Blue at that time, and Ferguson Brothers from Indianapolis. And then it was the other cat in New Orleans called Quinchette or something like that. Those three people was the ones who were booking these blues artists all over America then." "Living Blues Interview: Eddie Boyd, Part Two," *Living Blues* 36 (January/February 1978): 18. My search for information about Prossie Blue and Quinchette continues.

23. Arnold Shaw, *Honkers and Shouters: The Golden Years of Rhythm and Blues* (New York: Macmillan, 1978), 37.

24. Margaret McKee and Fred Chisenhall, *Beale Black & Blue: Life and Music*

on Black America's Main Street (Baton Rouge: Louisiana State University Press, 1981), 177–78.

25. Ted Williams, "Doctor Clayton Pulls Drunk-Dance Flops," *Houston Informer*, August 29, 1942, 13.

26. "King of Trumpet Men Comes to Sunset July 31," *Indianapolis Recorder*, July 31, 1943, 4.

27. Letter from Denver Ferguson to J. Neal Montgomery, August 6, 1943, from the J. Neal Montgomery Collection at the Auburn Avenue Research Library, Atlanta.

28. Interview of Sax Kari by author, September 30, 2005.

29. Andy Kirk, as told to Amy Lee, *Twenty Years on Wheels* (Ann Arbor: University of Michigan Press, 1989), 89.

30. It's difficult to calculate the sum of money Denver's circuit generated, or to trace where it ended up. We can see only some scheduled concert dates that appeared in the *Indianapolis Recorder*, and, in terms of cash, know what Denver asked from Atlanta promoter J. Neal Montgomery, whose correspondence has survived. In 1943, Denver asked a guarantee of $400 or $500 for the Carolina Cotton Pickers, $300–$350 for Snookum Russell, $250–$275 for the International Sweethearts of Rhythm, and $175–$200 for Christine Chatman. For comparison, Louis Armstrong received a $1,000 guarantee for an October 4, 1944, appearance at the Atlanta City Auditorium, while Louis Jordan's guarantee ran to $1,500 in some cases. Based on averages of the Ferguson Brothers' bands figures, and assuming that the groups played only the gigs on the published schedules, the Ferguson Bros. office received just over $100,000 in deposits on those acts. Since Ferguson Bros. represented about eight more attractions, it's safe to guess that the business brought in at least $200,000 annually during World War II. This doesn't include the guarantees paid to the bands. The Carolina Cotton Pickers, by the scant figures we have, blew the rest of Ferguson's acts away, with $66,552 in guarantees. That works out to $3,697 per man, twice the average salary in nonagricultural industries during the early 1940s. Sax Kari remembered earning a minimum of $300–$350 while running his sixteen-piece big band, and paying out $12–$15 per day to the bandmen, which compares favorably with the International Sweethearts $8 weekly salary earned while playing for the charity of the Piney Woods School.

31. Tony Scherman, *Backbeat: Earl Palmer's Story* (New York: Da Capo Press, 2000), 82.

Chapter 6 The Loser Goes to the Hospital, the Winner Goes to Jail

1. Per his son Don Robey Jr., in interview with author, August 10, 2009.

2. James Salem, *The Late Great Johnny Ace and the Transition from R&B to Rock 'n' Roll* (Champaign: University of Illinois Press, 2001), 54.

3. "Harlem Grill Opens Spacious New Quarters," *Houston Informer*, February 29, 1936, 4.

4. V. E. Porter, "Houston after Midnight," *Houston Informer*, February 2, 1938, 3.

5. "Twenty Seven Held in Gambling Raid," *Houston Informer*, February 6, 1937, 6.

6. Christopher Wilkinson, *Jazz on the Road: Don Albert's Musical Life* (Berkeley: University of California Press, 2001), 130. Item appeared in the *Pittsburgh Courier*, February 8, 1936, section 2, page 7.

7. V. E. Porter, "School Children Dance and Liquor Flows Freely," *Houston Informer*, March 9, 1938, 3.

8. Milton Larkin Oral History, January 5, 1988, Milton Larkin Collection, Houston Metropolitan Research Center, Houston Public Library.

9. Robey admitted that he wrote letters to Gale and Glaser that slammed a local filling-station owner, last name of Cawthon, who promoted dances on the side. See Van Pell Evans, "Two Tiffs Occur on Promotional Front; Counter Charges Fly," *Houston Informer*, June 21, 1941, 13.

10. "Robey's Enterprises Are Dixieland's Strongest," *Chicago Defender* (National Edition), November 11, 1950, 20. Also, "Nite Life in Texas," *Chicago Defender* (National Edition), January 22, 1938, 19.

11. Larkin Oral History.

12. Evans, "Two Tiffs Occur on Promotional Front," 13.

13. "Band Routes," *Indianapolis Recorder*, May 31, 1941, 4.

14. Ted Williams, "Serenading the News," *Houston Informer*, June 20, 1942, 13.

15. John Chilton, *Let the Good Times Roll: The Story of Louis Jordan and His Music* (Ann Arbor: University of Michigan Press, 1994).

16. "First Appearance in South, Expected to Be Big Attraction," *Houston Informer*, June 20, 1942, 13.

17. "1 Slain in Rhythm Club," *Louisiana Weekly*, July 4, 1942, 1, 3.

18. "Jordan's Five-Piecer Does Swell Biz on One-Nighters," *Billboard*, July 11, 1942, 23.

19. "Russell's Orch. at Sunset Friday," *Indianapolis Recorder*, January 23, 1943, 5.

20. "Kari Combo Tops at Lyon's Grill," *Indianapolis Recorder*, October 30, 1943, 5.

21. Maurie Orodenker, "On the Stand," *Billboard*, September 18, 1943, 16.

22. "Plantation Cabaret Is Dark Again," *Chicago Defender* (National Edition), March 4, 1928, 4.

23. Per Sax Kari's recollection.

24. "Joe Glaser Makes Deal with Bookie," *Chicago Defender* (National Edition), March 11, 1944, 8.

25. "Hear Grand Terrace to Reopen Soon," *Chicago Defender* (National Edition), February 26, 1944, 8.

Chapter 7 **The Bronze Peacock**

1. Tony Scherman, *Backbeat: Earl Palmer's Story* (New York: Da Capo Press, 2000), 78.

2. Jay Don, "Violets and Ivy," *Houston Informer*, February 16, 1946, 14.

3. Peter Lee and David Nelson, "From Shoutin' the Blues to Preachin' the Word: Bishop Arnold Dwight 'Gatemouth' Moore," *Living Blues* 86 (May/June 1989): 11, 13.

4. "The Boys Who Sell 'Em See Combos Hogging Theaters," *Billboard*, August 10, 1946, 39.

5. Ted Williams, "Serenading the News," *Houston Informer*, September 5, 1942, 8.

6. Tony Collins, *Rock Mr. Blues: The Life & Music of Wynonie Harris* (Milford, NH: Big Nickel Publications, 1995).

7. Nick Tosches, *Unsung Heroes of Rock 'n' Roll: The Birth of Rock in the Wild Years before Elvis* (New York: Da Capo Press, 1999), 49.

8. Johnny Otis, *Upside Your Head! Rhythm and Blues on Central Avenue* (Middletown, CT: Wesleyan University Press, 1993), 89.

9. John Broven, "Roy Brown, Part I: Good Rockin' Tonight," *Blues Unlimited* 123 (March 1977): 6.

10. Helen and Stanley Dance, "Electrifying Texas Blues: Aaron 'T-Bone' Walker," in Pete Welding and Toby Byron, eds., *Bluesland: Portrait of Twelve Major American Blues Masters* (New York: Dutton, 1991), 103.

11. "Record Reviews," *Billboard*, November 9, 1946, 9.

12. Billy "Slam" Stewart, quoted in Christopher Wilkinson, *Jazz on the Road: Don Albert's Musical Life* (Berkeley: University of California Press, 2001), 221.

13. "Accusations Rock Politics of City; Gamblers Won't Talk," *Indianapolis Recorder*, January 11, 1947, 1, 2.

Chapter 8 **The Gate Swings**

1. "Ye Nite Lifer, by Sid," *Houston Informer*, March 15, 1947, 12.
2. Johnny Otis, *Upside Your Head! Rhythm and Blues on Central Avenue* (Middletown, CT: Wesleyan University Press, 1993), 87.
3. Quoted from Gatemouth's reminiscence: "I started a boogie in E-natural—never will forget it—created it on the spot—'My name is Gatemouth Brown, I just got in your town, if you don't like my style I will not hang around'—we called it 'Gatemouth Boogie.' " From "Feature-Gatemouth Brown," *Juke Blues* 60 (Early 2006): 26.
4. Clarence "Gatemouth" Brown, in interview with John Standifer, July 25, 1984, on file in the African American Music Collection at the University of Michigan, online at http://www.umich.edu/~afroammu/standifer/brown_clarence.html, accessed May 15, 2009.
5. Brett J. Bonner and David Nelson, "Gatemouth Brown: Music That's Right for the World," *Living Blues* 107 (February 1993): 11.
6. "Ye Nite Lifer, by Sid."
7. W. C. Handy, *Father of the Blues: An Autobiography* (1941; New York: Da Capo Press, 1991), 77.
8. In the *Houston Informer*, March 29, 1947, about three weeks after Gatemouth's debut.
9. "A Star Is Born in Houston Nightspot," *Houston Informer*, April 26, 1947, 13.
10. Scoop Jones, "Pot Pourri," *Louisiana Weekly*, March 16, 1946, 9.
11. Ibid.
12. Scoop Jones, "Pot Pourri," *Louisiana Weekly*, May 18, 1946, 10.
13. " 'Artists Must Join Liberals in Dixie to Make Southern Circuit Pay,' —Ella," *Louisiana Weekly*, October 5, 1946, 12.
14. Material on Roy Brown and quotes from Roy Brown in this chapter are from John Broven, "Roy Brown, Part I: Good Rockin' Tonight," *Blues Unlimited* 123 (March 1977): 6–11, with Broven's gracious permission.
15. Mary Russell makes a few appearances in Gary Cartwright's *Galveston: A History of the Island* (Fort Worth: Texas Christian University Press, 1998), 226, 248.
16. "600 Nabbed in Night Club Dragnet, Raids Peril Negro Business," *Louisiana Weekly*, April 5, 1947, 1.

17. Jason Berry, Jonathan Foose, and Tad Jones, *Up from the Cradle of Jazz* (New York: Da Capo Press, 1992), 54–64.

18. B.B. King with David Ritz, *Blues All around Me: The Autobiography of B.B. King* (New York: Avon Books, 1996), 124.

19. "City Is Being Overrun with Dope," *Louisiana Weekly*, August 23, 1947, 1.

20. "Blues Twins Get Big Ovation at Club Downbeat," *Louisiana Weekly*, September 20, 1947, 14.

Chapter 9 'Tween the Tip In Inn and the Church of God

1. Siders quotes from interview with Michael Lydon, Spring 1995, for the latter's Ray Charles biography, housed in the Michael Lydon Collection at the Archives of African American Music and Culture at Indiana University, Bloomington.

2. Lucky Millinder with Dan Burley, "Millinder Answers Down Beat," *Houston Informer*, January 4, 1941, 9.

3. Walter Barnes, "The Broadcast," *Chicago Defender* (National Edition), April 17, 1937, 21.

4. See the two *Macon Telegraph* stories announcing the program, June 29, 1947, 31, and July 2, 1947, 14.

5. Charles White, *The Life and Times of Little Richard: The Quasar of Rock* (New York: Harmony Books, 1984), 4.

6. Per Richard's description in ibid., 6–9.

7. Ibid., 9.

8. Ibid., 14.

9. Ibid., 21.

10. Clint Brantley, in interview with Milton Dimmons, 1978, on file at the Middle Georgia Archives, Washington Memorial Library, Macon, Georgia.

11. White, *Life and Times of Little Richard*, 10.

12. Interview of Dave Bartholomew by author, July 8, 2009.

13. Rick Coleman, *Blue Monday: Fats Domino and the Lost Dawn of Rock 'n' Roll* (New York: Da Capo, 2006), 39.

14. Dave Bartholomew, in interview with Portia Maultsby, May 14, 1985, on file at the Archives of African American Music and Culture at Indiana University, Bloomington.

15. Eddy Determeyer, *Rhythm Is Our Business: Jimmie Lunceford and the Harlem Express* (Ann Arbor: University of Michigan Press, 2006), 121.

Chapter 10 **Roy Brown's Good Rockin' Revival**

1. "Record Reviews," *Billboard*, February 7, 1948, 126.

2. Thanks to Jim O'Neal for bringing to my attention Wince's club circuit as published in the *Jackson Advocate*, February 5, 1949.

3. "Roy Brown Puts Blues Singing on a New Kick," *Memphis World*, January 28, 1949, 3.

4. Quotes from Roy Brown in this chapter are from John Broven, "Roy Brown, Part I: Good Rockin' Tonight," *Blues Unlimited* 123 (March 1977): 6–11, with Broven's gracious permission.

5. "Record Reviews," *Billboard*, March 5, 1949, 113.

6. Description and lyric quoted from Morgan Wright at http://www.hoyhoy .com/artists/roybrown.htm, accessed February 25, 2010.

7. "Roy Brown Has Full Date Book," *Houston Informer*, June 4, 1949, 12.

8. "Roy Brown Victim of Mistaken Identity Almost Lands in Jail," *Louisiana Weekly*, July 30, 1949, 13.

9. "Roy Brown New 'Golden Boy' on One-Night Circuit," *Louisiana Weekly*, August 13, 1949, 12.

10. Stanley Nelson, "Haney's Big House . . . ," *Concordia Sentinel*, November 26, 2007, at http://www.concordiasentinel.com/news.php?id=1047, accessed July 10, 2009.

11. Peter Guralnick, "Perfect Imperfection: The Life and Art of Jerry Lee Lewis," *Oxford American*, no. 63 (December 2008), 23.

12. "'Rock Battle' Gives Eddie Vinson KKK Scare in Ferriday," *Louisiana Weekly*, October 22, 1949, 11.

13. "Record Reviews," *Billboard*, November 5, 1949, 91.

14. "Roy Brown to Play First Northern Date in 3 Years," *Louisiana Weekly*, October 15, 1949, 10.

15. "Roy Brown Is 'Inducted' into Choctaw Tribe," *Louisiana Weekly*, December 10, 1949, 13.

16. Robert Nathan Dorrell, "No More Back Doors for Percy Welch," *Macon (Ga.) Telegraph and News*, March 12, 1984, 2B.

Chapter 11 **Female Trouble**

1. Quoted from the decision in *Ferguson vs. Ferguson*, Court of Appeals of Indiana, filed April 18, 1955, at www.versuslaw.com, accessed December 15, 2009.

2. Ibid.

3. Opal Tandy, "The Avenoo," *Indianapolis Recorder*, May 7, 1949, 12.

4. *Ferguson vs. Ferguson.*

5. J. St. Clair Gibson, "The Avenoo," *Indianapolis Recorder*, August 20, 1949, 12.

6. Opal Tandy, "The Avenoo," *Indianapolis Recorder*, August 27, 1949, 12.

7. "Tax Debt of $82,410 Is Charged," *Indianapolis Star*, November 15, 1949, 1.

8. "Sunset, 'Still Operatin' at Same Old Spot,'" *Indianapolis Recorder*, November 16, 1949, 7.

9. "Ye Nite Lifer, by Sid," *Houston Informer*, January 21, 1950, 14.

10. Evelyn Johnson, in interview with Portia Maultsby, May 12, 1985, on file at the Archives of African American Music and Culture at Indiana University, Bloomington.

11. Johnson quoted in James Salem, *The Late Great Johnny Ace and the Transition from R&B to Rock 'n' Roll* (Champaign: University of Illinois Press, 2001), 55.

12. There was one conduit between the Ferguson Brothers Agency and Buffalo Booking: Sax Kari. He said that he had shared Ferguson's contacts with Evelyn Johnson.

Chapter 12 **All Part of the Game**

1. For much of the building history in this section, I'm indebted to Richard Raichelson's work in *Beale Street Talks: A Walking Tour down the Home of the Blues* (Memphis: Arcadia Records, 1999). Raicheslon brings sanity to a dizzying history of who operated what, where, and when on Beale Street, while offering keen insights into the street's architecture and social texture.

2. Robert Henry, in interview with Margaret McKee and Fred Chisenhall, October 15, 1973, on file in the Memphis Room at the Benjamin Hooks Central Library, Memphis.

3. "Yes, Sunbeam Is Still Down at the Paradise," *Memphis Commercial Appeal*, March 15, 1985, 3.

4. Margaret McKee and Fred Chisenhall, *Beale Black and Blue: Life and Music on Black America's Main Street* (Baton Rouge: Louisiana State University Press, 1981), 137.

5. Ernestine McKinney to Mrs. Pittman, January 15, 1945, Beale Street Collection, Memphis Public Library.

6. "Yes, Sunbeam Is Still Down at the Paradise."

7. All quotes of Howard Grimes from interview by author, May 3, 2009.

8. All quotes of Emerson Able from interview by author, November 8, 2009.

9. The Mitchells' business records in the Beale Street Collection at the Memphis Public Library show records of rent payment for the Beale and Hernando property, and insurance payments for other properties to Sam Plough. The lease agreement, dated August 15, 1944, on file in the Club Paradise Collection in the archives of the Stax Museum of American Soul Music, is between Sunbeam and the United Corp., signed by United president L. Hayden, United Corp. The Ploughs' level of awareness of the Mitchells' activities is unknown, and it's entirely possible that the Ploughs saw the Mitchells as solely legitimate entrepreneurs.

10. "New Theatre in Orange Mound to Be Named for Famed William C. Handy," *Memphis World*, February 8, 1946, 1.

11. "Yes, Sunbeam Is Still Down at the Paradise."

12. All quotes of Ford Nelson from interview by author, July 8, 2009.

13. "Mose Allison: Still Looking for That Bo Hog Grind," *Blues Access* 33 (Spring 1998): 33.

14. From an extraordinary interview Rufus Thomas gave author Robert Palmer and Memphis music scholar David Less on October 28–29, 1976. A transcript is in Special Collections at the University of Memphis Library. Quote is on page 10.

15. Jas Obrecht, *Rollin' and Tumblin': The Postwar Blues Guitarists* (San Francisco: Miller Freeman, 2000), 175.

16. Sunbeam Mitchell's club at Beale and Hernando was known variously as the Domino, Mitchell's Hotel, and later, most famously, Club Handy. I've chosen to refer to it informally, so as to avoid calling it the wrong name for a given time (Sunbeam said he changed the name to Club Handy as a tribute to the composer who died in 1958, but the city directory notes no such change until the early 1960s), as well as any confusion with the W. C. Handy Theatre, a different venue that rates prominently in the present discussion.

17. Evelyn Johnson, in interview with Portia Maultsby, May 12, 1985, on file at the Archives of African American Music and Culture at Indiana University, Bloomington.

18. Robert Johnson, "A Historic Saturday Night on Beale Street—Negro Policemen," *Memphis Press-Scimitar*, November 11, 1948, 2.

19. "Cafe Owner, A. Mitchell, Is Attacked," *Memphis World*, December 19, 1950, 1. "Four men attacked Andrew Mitchell, owner of Mitchell Cafe at 195 Hernando recently in his living quarters above the cafe. A single bullet, pass-

ing through the abdomen of one man slammed into the arm of another." The suspects allegedly tried to rob Sunbeam at razor-point, a poor choice of armament in this case.

20. Thanks again to Jim O'Neal for the tip. "Widely Known East Jackson Operator Victim in Fatal Shooting," *Jackson Advocate*, March 5, 1949, 3.

21. "Jimmie Liggins Wounded . . . ," *Jackson Advocate*, April 9, 1949, 1.

Chapter 13 **A Little Like Going to Heaven**

1. Jas Obrecht, *Rollin' and Tumblin': The Postwar Blues Guitarists* (San Francisco: Miller Freeman, 2000), 98.

2. Robert Henry, in interview with Margaret McKee and Fred Chisenhall, October 15, 1973, on file in the Memphis Room at the Benjamin Hooks Central Library, Memphis.

3. B.B. King with David Ritz, *Blues All around Me: The Autobiography of B.B. King* (New York: Avon Books, 1996), 129–31.

4. Ibid., 139.

5. All quotes of Ford Nelson from interview by author, July 8, 2009.

Chapter 14 **Crossover**

1. George Lemanson, "$173,967.67 Lien Filed on Gambler," *Indianapolis Star*, December 14, 1951, 1.

2. "Sea Ferguson Makes Record Tax Settlement," *Indianapolis Recorder*, December 22, 1951, 1.

3. From the white *Memphis Commercial Appeal*, March 28, 1951: "B.B. King of Memphis, one of the race artists Sam [Phillips] has been recording, passed the word along to Ike Turner, a Negro bandleader of Clarksdale, Miss., that the market was open. Ike brought his band up for an audition."

4. "Playing Chess! Hwd. AFM Nix Brings Modern Counterclaim," *Billboard*, August 11, 1951, 16, identified Sam as Brenston's "personal manager." The local press coverage focused on Brenston and Phillips, not bandleader Ike Turner, particularly a front-page story in the white *Memphis Commercial Appeal*, which indicates behind-the-scenes string-pulling that a bunch of black teenagers from Clarksdale would not have merited ordinarily.

5. Jim O'Neal, "Jackie Brenston," *Living Blues* 45/46 (Spring 1980): 18.

6. Ibid., 19.

7. "Lowell Fulson," interview by Mary Katherine Aldin and Mark Humphrey, *Living Blues* 115 (June 1994): 22.

8. Michael Lydon, *Ray Charles, Man and Music* (New York: Riverhead Books, 1998), 71–81. Lydon's book is so excellent and thorough that I recommend it unreservedly and leave it to tell about Ray Charles's rise to fame from the chitlin' circuit.

9. This is Fulson's version of the story. B.B. King's more clipped account is in B.B. King with David Ritz, *Blues All around Me: The Autobiography of B.B. King* (New York: Avon Books, 1996), 124–25.

10. Jon Thurber, "Hank Crawford Dies at 74 . . . ," *Los Angeles Times*, February 5, 2009, at http://articles.latimes.com/2009/feb/05/local/me-hank-crawford 5/2, accessed January 12, 2010.

11. Robert Henry, in interview with Margaret McKee and Fred Chisenhall, October 15, 1973, on file in the Memphis Room at the Benjamin Hooks Central Library, Memphis.

Chapter 15 **Shootin' and Cuttin' and Shit**

1. Charles White, *The Life and Times of Little Richard: The Quasar of Rock* (New York: Harmony Books, 1984), 23.

2. Ibid., 24.

3. Ibid., 30.

4. Melvin "Percy" Welch interview, undated, on file at the Middle Georgia Archives, Washington Memorial Library, Macon, Georgia.

5. Jane Oppy, "Star Dust," *Macon News*, May 17, 1977, 12A.

6. All Brantley quotes come from his interview with Milton Dimmons, 1978, on file at the Middle Georgia Archives, Washington Memorial Library, Macon, Georgia.

7. Now Ferry Court.

8. I'm grateful to Dorothy Jean Griffin for sharing her memories of growing up in South Memphis.

9. Johnny's obituary in the *Tri-State Defender*, January 8, 1955, 2, says so, and Ford Nelson, a pianist who frequented the Mitchell Hotel and was disc jockey at WDIA during this period, recalled the same in our 2009 interview. Nelson said Louis, perhaps typically of the one-man show personality, was reluctant to share the limelight with his accompanists.

10. Interview of Milton Barnes by author, October 14, 2003. Though he did not mention Sunbeam by name—the interview took place before I knew who

Sunbeam was, and I only listened to the playback years later, after Barnes's death—there can be no doubt about the identity of the "colored man and his wife" with connections to bootleg whiskey and B.B. King, searching Mississippi for outlets for both.

11. I'm indebted to both Van Siggers of Tunica for sharing insight into his Uncle Hardface's career, as well as the entertaining and informative Mississippi Blues Trail marker in downtown Tunica, www.msbluestrail.org.

12. Galen Gart and Roy C. Ames, *Duke/Peacock Records: An Illustrated History with Discography* (Milford, NH: Big Nickel Publications, 1989), 28–29.

13. Evelyn Johnson, in interview with Portia Maulsby, May 12, 1985, on file at the Archives of African American Music at Indiana University, Bloomington.

14. Gart and Ames, *Duke/Peacock Records*, 35.

15. White, *Life and Times of Little Richard*, 36

16. Ibid., 38.

17. Ibid., 36.

18. "B.B. King, Famed Blues Artist, on Socko Tour," *Chicago Defender* (National Edition), May 9, 1953, 19.

19. Robert Henry, in interview with Margaret McKee and Fred Chisenhall, October 15, 1973, on file in the Memphis Room at the Benjamin Hooks Central Library, Memphis.

20. Ibid.

21. Gart and Ames, *Duke/Peacock Records*, 63–64.

Chapter 16 The Hardest-Working Man in Show Business

1. Evelyn Johnson, in interview with Portia Maultsby, May 12, 1985, on file at the Archives of African American Music and Culture at Indiana University, Bloomington.

2. James M. Salem, *The Late Great Johnny Ace and the Transition from R&B to Rock 'n' Roll* (Chicago: University of Illinois Press, 1999), 132–34. Salem's book is an indispensable source of information about the murky people and mysterious events surrounding John M. Alexander Jr.

3. Robert Shaar Murray, *Boogie Man: The Adventures of John Lee Hooker in the American Twentieth Century* (New York: Macmillan, 2002), 157.

4. Clint Brantley, in interview with Milton Dimmons, 1978, on file at the Middle Georgia Archives, Washington Memorial Library, Macon, Georgia.

5. "Little Richard and His Upsetters" advertisement, *Macon Telegraph and News*, January 30, 1955, 11.

6. Peter Guralnick, *Sweet Soul Music: Rhythm and Blues and the Southern Dream of Freedom* (New York: Harper and Row, 1986), 138.

7. "A Jitterbug Jamboree" advertisement, *Macon Telegraph*, May 1, 1955, 14.

8. Charles White, *The Life and Times of Little Richard: The Quasar of Rock* (New York: Harmony Books, 1984), 55.

9. James Brown with Bruce Tucker, *James Brown: The Godfather of Soul* (New York: Da Capo Press, 2002), 68.

10. Ibid., 56.

11. In Brown's telling, ibid., 68.

12. White, *Life and Times of Little Richard*, 46.

13. I'm indebted to Charles White's wonderful Little Richard biography for that scene, and you should read the whole book to truly appreciate everything that is Little Richard and all Little Richard has said he's done. Ibid., 49.

14. "The Flames of Washington D.C." advertisement, *Macon Telegraph*, September 11, 1955, 14.

15. White, *Life and Times of Little Richard*, 56.

16. "Dr. M.L. King Jr. Tremont Temple Guest Minister," *Macon Telegraph*, October 23, 1955, 16.

17. "The Big Battle Is on Armistice Night" advertisement, *Macon Telegraph*, November 6, 1955, 15.

18. "Big Christmas . . ." advertisement, *Macon Telegraph*, December 25, 1955, 16.

19. Evelyn Johnson, in interview with Portia Maultsby, May 12, 1985, on file at the Archives of African American Music and Culture at Indiana University, Bloomington.

20. This terrific anecdote and quotes of Ralph Bass come from John Hartley Fox, *King of the Queen City: The Story of King Records* (Chicago: University of Illinois Press, 2009), 90.

21. Dick Alen, in interview with Michael Lydon, May 30, 1995, transcript on file in the Michael Lydon Collection, Archives of African American Music and Culture at Indiana University, Bloomington.

22. Welch anecdotes and quotes come from the Melvin "Percy" Welch interview, undated, on file at the Middle Georgia Archives, Washington Memorial Library, Macon, Georgia.

23. Jeffrey Day, "Big 3 from Macon Left Lasting Influence on Rock 'n' Roll," *Macon Telegraph and News*, February 1, 1987, 1D, 2D, 11D.

24. "Await Prison Order for Tuffy Mitchell," *Indianapolis Recorder*, May 29, 1954, 12.

25. "Ind. Cafe Owner Seeks Divorce," *Jet*, March 19, 1953, 18–19.

26. "Seize Household Furnishings in $30,000 Search," *Indianapolis Recorder*, May 29, 1954, 1, 2.

27. Quoted from the decision in *Ferguson vs. Ferguson*, Court of Appeals of Indiana, filed April 18, 1955, at www.versuslaw.com, accessed December 15, 2009.

28. Carolyn Pickering, "Former Avenue Kingpin Nabbed on Tax Charge," *Indianapolis Star*, December 21, 1956, 22.

Coda **Renewal**

1. Bill Simon, "Who Juices the Spotlight? Jock Showcasing of New Talent Keeps Wax Fresh," *Billboard*, January 26, 1957, 58.

2. Interview of Mickey Gregory by author, December 11, 2008.

3. Howard Grimes quotes come from an interview by author, May 3, 2009.

4. W. C. Handy, *Father of the Blues: An Autobiography* (1941; New York: Da Capo Press, 1991), 16.

5. Richard Wright, *Black Boy* (St. Louis, MO: Turtleback Books, 2003), 208.

6. B.B. King with David Ritz, *Blues All around Me: The Autobiography of B.B. King* (New York: Avon Books, 1996), 98–99.

7. From the *Memphis Press-Scimitar*, November 16, 1955, quoted on the frontispiece of Margaret McKee and Fred Chisenhall's *Beale Black and Blue: Life and Music on Black America's Main Street* (Baton Rouge: Louisiana State University Press, 1981).

8. " 'Gold' on Beale Goes Unmined," *Memphis Press-Scimitar*, April 22, 1959, A-7.

9. Phil Moss, "Lt. Lee Is Glad to See Progress on Beale St.," *Memphis Press-Scimitar*, April 11, 1961, B-1.

10. Robert Henry, in interview with Margaret McKee and Fred Chisenhall, October 15, 1973, on file in the Memphis Room at the Benjamin Hooks Central Library, Memphis.

11. Walter Dawson, "From Beale Street to Club Paradise," *Memphis Commercial Appeal*, July 27, 1975, 3.

12. "Clarksdale Omegas Stage Big Dance," *Jackson Advocate*, December 25, 1948, 10.

13. Alvin Lansky, quoted in "Owners Protest Beale St. Plan," *Memphis Press-Scimitar*, February 17, 1967, 17.

14. According to Grimes's reminiscence in interview by author, May 3, 2009.

Index

Page numbers in *italics* refer to illustrations.

DEMOCRATIC
BY DESIGN

DEMOCRATIC
BY DESIGN

HOW CARSHARING, CO-OPS, AND COMMUNITY
LAND TRUSTS ARE REINVENTING AMERICA

GABRIEL
METCALF

St. Martin's Press

New York

www.stmartins.com

Library of Congress Cataloging-in-Publication Data

Metcalf, Gabriel, author.
    Democratic by design : how carsharing, co-ops, and community land trusts are
reinventing America / Gabriel Metcalf.
        pages   cm
    Includes bibliographical references and index.
    ISBN 978-1-137-27967-5 (hardback)
    1. Social entrepreneurship—United States. 2. Cooperative societies—
United States. 3. Social change—United States. 4. Equality—United States.
5. Democracy—United States. I. Title.
    HD60.5.U5M48   2015
    334.0973—dc23

                                                                    2015018296

ISBN 978-1-137-27967-5 (hardcover)
ISBN 978-1-4668-7928-7 (e-book)

Our books may be purchased in bulk for promotional, educational, or business
use. Please contact your local bookseller or the Macmillan Corporate and
Premium Sales Department at (800) 221-7945, extension 5442, or by e-mail at
MacmillanSpecialMarkets@macmillan.com.

First edition: November 2015

10   9   8   7   6   5   4   3   2   1

For Elizabeth and Kate

CONTENTS

ONE

INTRODUCTION

THINGS AREN'T RIGHT IN AMERICA TODAY—THE
emergence of a more unequal class structure; the corruption of our
democracy by unlimited campaign spending; our inability to do
anything about climate change; the wasteful sprawling of suburbia across the landscape; and the general sclerosis of our political
system, which seems to preclude solution-seeking.

But this is not a book about what's wrong. This is a book
about what to do about it—specifically, about an approach to social change that involves building alternative institutions.

The idea is to create living examples of a better society. These
projects can then be seen, studied, improved on, and copied.
People can join them or support them. If the alternative institutions are good enough at what they are trying to do, they will
expand and multiply. Eventually, some of them will actually begin to out-compete the mainstream institutions that they stand
alongside.

Participation in alternative institutions has been one of the
most widespread forms of progressive activism, yet it remains
undertheorized and poorly understood. Through this book, I
hope to change that. My goal is to provide a more substantial
intellectual underpinning for the institution-building strategy of
social change—to examine the historical precedents, explore how

alternative institutions work, and suggest some principles that will be useful for activists.

Many of the existing alternative institutions in the United States trace their roots to two waves of activity—the first in the 1920s and 1930s, which centered on consumer cooperatives, including food co-ops, rural electricity co-ops, and credit unions, and the second in the 1960s and 1970s, which included free schools, alternative media, community health clinics, and communes. A more recent wave of activity includes developing local currencies, community land trusts, and carsharing cooperatives.

A THEORY OF PIECEMEAL CHANGE

The central idea of the alternative institution strategy is that we should focus on creating elements of a better society today, one institution at a time. This approach means that we do not have to convince people to agree with a comprehensive critique of society's ills or have the same view of what a better society would look like. We simply have to find people who agree with us about better ways to achieve specific ends.

This is an important distinction. It is simply not possible to convince a majority of people to adopt a progressive analysis wholesale. It wouldn't be possible even if all progressives suddenly agreed with one another. There are just too many topics, and it is hopeless to try to win over a majority of people with a long list of platforms, proposals, and critiques.

The strategy of alternative institutions proceeds in an entirely different, and more achievable, manner. It suggests that we can work one project at a time, with as many people as we can get to join us on each project. We can work with people to create new institutions even if they have different motivations than we do. Alternative institutions are a strategy of minimum consensus. We only need to build agreement about what we want to create next. And this is hard enough. It takes years of work and strong organizing skills to build support for changing even one institution in a community. It takes wisdom and foresight to know which institutions are ripe for changing, which ones to take on first, and which ones to leave for later.

Underlying this approach to social change is skepticism about the usefulness of the concept of "social systems." Of course, many of us try to understand social problems in a systematic way—to perceive the underlying or structural causes of the problems we would like to solve. But there is not just one system; there are many. The military-industrial complex. The intertwined structures of race and class. Corporate agribusiness. Suburbia. Patriarchy . . . This list could go on and on, huge topics with oceans of ink written about them, each in need of change.

These big systems are not likely to be subject to sweeping transformation of a revolutionary or reformist variety. When the Left ascends, as historically it has done from time to time, it's not in a position to summarily remake any of these systems. It's only when we can address the individual parts of our social order that we can realistically hope to change them.

That's the basic theory of alternative institutions: society is composed of smaller institutions or organizations that are subject to change. Activists work to create new institutions, one at a time—each one building on the last, each new institution opening up possibilities for further changes.

THIS BOOK IS GROUNDED in a very personal experience. For six years, I worked to establish a carsharing cooperative with two of my best friends. We had worked on other projects together and talked about the potential of alternative institutions for a long time. We agreed that the existing alternative institutions, at least as far as we had experienced them, were not living up to their potential—in particular, because of their inability to involve people who were not already politically active. We set out with the explicit goal of building something that could become mainstream—that could successfully involve regular Americans of any political stripe.

It was a lot harder than it looked. In some ways, we met with incredible success: we helped bring carsharing to North America! In other ways, we fell far short of what we wanted to accomplish. We faced difficult choices about how much to compromise our ideals in order to allow the project to grow. And we learned a lot about the practical realities of building an alternative institution in the real world.

When it was time for me to step away from the carsharing project, I decided to write this book. It's my chance to share some of what I learned, as one activist trying to effect social change in a nontraditional way—in the hope that my experiences might be useful to others who can, with luck, carry the work farther than we did.

In addition to my experience with City CarShare, I have worked for more than twenty years in the field of city planning. While this is not a book about urbanism, my own interests in transportation, housing, economic development, regional planning, sustainability, and the other disciplines of urban policy will come through.

I develop the ideas in this book through stories about social movements and alternative institutions. Through exploring the divergent histories of many different kinds of these efforts, I try to discover the possibilities and the limitations of alternative institutions as a social change strategy and to develop a set of ideas that can inform future practice.

I use my own experiences with carsharing as the opening story in chapter 2. While acknowledging that I am far from an objective observer of this project, I hope that by beginning with this first-person story, I make the broader themes in this book tangible and relevant.

The next three chapters explore distinct types of alternative institutions. Chapter 3 discusses the institutions of democratic decision-making by reinterpreting the origins of the American Revolution. Chapter 4 examines economic institutions, and chapter 5 looks at place-based institutions. Through the lens of these different domains, we come to understand a broad set of circumstances in which alternative institutions can be effective.

Chapter 6 discusses the tricky concept of "selling out" and the dilemmas faced by organizations as they grow and become more mainstream.

Chapter 7 serves as a synthesis chapter, looking at three stories of progressive movements that managed to include alternative institutions as part of a broader set of strategies.

Finally, in conclusion, chapter 8 attempts to develop a "sociology" of historical change by drawing on the ideas presented earlier in the book.

My own values will be clear throughout. I am in favor of a society that is more democratic, more egalitarian, and more ecologically balanced. But my intent is not to lay out a detailed vision for a better society or even a critique of the current arrangements. This is a book about the means, not the ends. It speaks to one of the timeless questions faced by anyone who aspires to a better world: How do you change society? This book doesn't have all the answers, but it has some of them. My hope is that it will inspire a new generation of activists and theorists to carry these ideas in new directions and perhaps open up some new possibilities for American idealists, at a time when new possibilities are much needed.

TWO

THE STORY OF
CITY CARSHARE

IN 1997, MY FRIENDS AND I BEGAN TO ORGANIZE A carsharing cooperative in San Francisco as a way to test our theories about alternative institutions. We first learned about carsharing from an article published in 1994 in *RAIN Magazine*.[1] Two brothers in Berlin had started an organization called Stattauto Berlin, which literally translates to "instead of cars." The general idea is this: A co-op owns a fleet of cars and keeps them all over the city. Members of the co-op can use a car when they want. They pay based on how much they drive. It's that simple.[2]

In the case of Stattauto, which started in 1988, members made reservations by phone; an employee of the organization took calls and kept track of reservations. Keys were kept in a lockbox at each parking location, and members had the combination. People wrote down in log books how far they drove. There was an hourly fee and a mileage fee—the idea being that the hourly rate roughly covered the capital cost of the car and the mileage rate roughly covered the gas and the wear and tear. Membership in the organization included insurance.

City CarShare operated largely the same way, except that we automated the process of reserving a car, both because we came along a decade later and got to take advantage of new technology and because we thought the high-tech approach would be more appealing to our San Francisco audience.

One way of thinking about the economics of carsharing is that it converts most of the fixed costs of car ownership into variable costs. Under private ownership, the insurance, the purchase price of the car, and, depending on where you live, the parking are all fixed costs, regardless of how much you drive. In a sense, having already committed to those costs, most car owners think the only "real" cost of driving is the gas, so there is no economic incentive to minimize car use. In contrast, when you pay each time you use a car based on how long you use it and how far you go, there is a pricing incentive to be mindful of how much you drive.

The core work of organizing an alternative institution, just like other kinds of political organizing, is talking to a lot of people to find supporters who will help make it happen. We talked to hundreds and hundreds of people, from neighborhood leaders to bicycle groups, from developers to technology firms, from elected officials to more experienced activists. And from these conversations we found supporters, members, funders, volunteers, and— the core of the organization—board members.

We had a wonderful board. It organized itself into committees to deal with operations and technology, fund-raising, marketing, and—once we had staff and money—human resources and finance. Later, we organized committees for each sub-area of the region where we wanted to operate. This leadership model allowed us to distribute the workload and involve large numbers of people while still preserving the overall direction of the project.

People got involved for a wide variety of reasons. Some were committed environmental activists. Some cared about local economic development. Some were motivated by the negative impact of cars on cities. There was little ideological or political unity among us. In fact, we made sure to recruit board members who were connected to both the right and the left of the political establishment. We were confident that our institution would do its job if it succeeded in getting large numbers of people to abandon private car ownership (or at least to reduce the number of cars they owned) and switch to carsharing.

Ultimately we organized City CarShare as a traditional nonprofit, rather than a co-op. This allowed us to go after some important funding sources. And more important, we believed that the nonprofit form provided the greatest likelihood for the organization to stay true to its mission over time.[3]

We had some unexpected early success with fund-raising, and one of us (not me) quit her job to be the full-time director. We leased one car to try out the technology in it. We first signed up five friends, and then fifty, to test the system. We leased five cars, then another five. Once we were up above a hundred "testers," we launched. The story hit the newspapers, and members poured in faster than we could sign them up. The amount of time from our first efforts at serious organizing to our launch was about three years.

Each location where we kept cars was called a "pod." We lined up mostly free parking, relying on support from the city government, transit agencies, and businesses. Over time, as the project got bigger, we reached the limits of the free-parking strategy and had to rent spaces, but the contributed space from supporters was crucial to getting started.

Our outreach strategy at first was simply to contact the people we had been signing up for the previous three years and tell them they finally had their chance to join. Only gradually did we start to do "real marketing."

We immediately felt the stress of rapid expansion, especially never having enough money. We needed more staff to do the work than we could afford to pay, and we needed to put more cars into service than we could afford to lease. Demand was not a problem. The ability to service the demand was the problem.

The technology didn't work nearly as well as we had hoped. Eventually we got it right, but only after many false starts and spending way too much money. It was an area that none of the organizers knew well—a crucial mistake, in retrospect. Our dream had been to give away our software and hardware for free—to create open-source carsharing technology—but the set of software engineers we finally brought on board to fix all the problems refused to work in open source. We were still able to serve our members and grow the organization, but we did not succeed in starting open-source carsharing technology.

For a long time, we were also not sufficiently staffed to handle the demands on customer service. Staff members took turns being on call for emergencies, carrying around a pager and a laptop. As the organization grew, we did in fact get more efficient, and we were able to add staff, while still serving an ever-growing number of members per staff person. This was simply a function of the fact that our operation required us to be at a minimum size in order to work right, and we had to grow into stability. We got through it by having staff members work seventy-plus hours a week; having board members who served as de facto unpaid staff, putting in huge amounts of time themselves; and having a committed set of early users who were patient with us.

We learned quickly how to identify the right places to expand. Not surprisingly, the key is density: you need enough people within walking distance of the pod to support it. In areas that are too spread out, it's not convenient for people to walk to the car, and the cars don't get driven enough to cover their costs.

Meanwhile, there were major operational priorities tied to bringing down costs: getting a better deal on insurance, getting a better deal on the cars, improving the technology so that we could grow without adding too many staff members. Each of these projects is a story in itself, but we eventually managed to make them all happen. We had an incredible staff that was able to solve enough of the key problems to make the project work.

FUNDING STRATEGIES

Throughout the early phases of the project, there was tension between the desire to make the service as attractive as possible—and thereby out-compete the private automobile—and the limits of our funding. The goal of attracting people away from private ownership would suggest having fewer members per car (so people could always get a car when they wanted one, at a location close to them) and having prices that were as low as possible. But the imperative of breaking even financially would push in the other direction, toward more members per car and higher prices. This situation is, essentially, a version of the same dilemma all businesses face—or it may perhaps just be a fact of working in a world with finite resources. Nevertheless, each of us weighed these trade-offs differently. This question—of how high a service "quality" to provide—probably caused more disagreement during board meetings than any other issue.

Our fund-raising strategy evolved as well. In the beginning, we were very intimidated by the prospect of having to raise significant amounts of money, as most people are. But we soon understood that there could be no organizing without raising money, and we decided to treat it as a skill that could be learned like any other. There were essentially three funding sources for a project like City CarShare: (1) charitable donations, (2) contracts with public agencies, and (3) loans.

The funding strategy for City CarShare was an expression of the political culture within which we worked. The European carsharing projects were funded with giant government grants, and in some countries they were even run by government agencies as public programs. Our nonprofit, community-based approach, which required us to piece together funding from many different sources, reflects the United States' smaller public sector—or, looked at another way, our thriving culture of social entrepreneurship.[4]

One of the more successful funding approaches that City CarShare decided to try was financing by our members. We charged a refundable member deposit, which we would repay, without interest, when a member quit the service. It served as both a security deposit, reducing the likelihood that members would skip out on their bills, as well as an interest-free form of debt that could finance organizational expansion. Many alternative institutions have the potential to tap into this kind of grassroots financing, although it is a serious obligation that can only be taken on if there is truly a viable business model for the organization.

Some of the more innovative alternative institutional projects tackle the issue of funding directly—cooperatives pooling their resources to fund other cooperatives, either by making direct investments and providing management help, much like venture capitalists do, or by investing savings in cooperative banks, which then make the loans.

BECOMING THE NEW NORMAL

As our membership grew, our outreach strategy changed. We continued to emphasize face-to-face meetings with community groups whenever we opened a pod in a new neighborhood. But in recruiting potential members, we shifted our emphasis from the environmental and social benefits of carsharing to the personal benefits.[5] We did focus groups and surveys to see how our members learned about the program, what prompted them to join, what they liked and didn't like, and how best to explain the concept of carsharing to the uninitiated. And we were able to hire staff with more marketing experience, raising the level of sophistication.

Our goal was to get big—meaning to attract as many people as possible to carsharing. The project did eventually become financially self-sustaining, with hundreds of cars and tens of thousands of members. But for us, the ultimate social change metric was the car ownership rate in the city. We wanted to have more members of the carsharing organization in our service territory than people who owned cars—in other words, to out-compete the private automobile.

Organizational metrics are fundamental to a serious alternative institution strategy. They are the way organizers hold themselves accountable to do what they say they are going to do and, more fundamentally, the way organizers operationalize their broad social change goals into smaller pieces that can be achieved incrementally. We needed traditional business accounting metrics to manage the expenses and revenues as well as management metrics such as members per car, utilization rates, and net revenue per car. Eventually these evolved into "efficiency metrics" like days for each pod to break even, members per staff person, and the ratio of fixed costs to total costs. We pored over all of these at board meetings.

But given the premise that our goal was to get as many people as possible to use carsharing, we relied heavily on a set of growth metrics: new members per month, the attrition rate, and the cost to acquire each new member. There were two ways of looking at how big we needed to be: first, large enough to break even; second, large enough to affect the city.

WHAT DOES IT TAKE for an alternative institution to grow so big that it becomes the new "normal"?

First of all, it can't require broad political agreement to join. Anyone who is willing to participate should be welcomed. If the organizers have chosen their institution well, it will be a positive thing in itself for the institution to grow and thrive, and they can trust that its success will be socially transformative without a political litmus test.

In practice, we relied heavily on some community organizing techniques to connect with people.[6] Environmental organizations provided the base of our membership, because they were willing to communicate with their members and tell them about what we were doing. Neighborhood organizations found the parking spots for us because they saw carsharing as a way to help with on-street parking shortages. Business organizations connected us to firms that joined as business members, which was crucial for generating use of the cars during off-peak weekday hours. And developers ended up putting pods of cars in new buildings as an amenity for residents.[7]

We had a lot of explicit discussion about how the organization should evolve over time. It was clear to everyone that the structure that worked so well initially would not necessarily serve the organization once it was up and running. We knew we had to recruit more experienced board members and a staff leadership capable of running a large organization.

As new leadership took over, there were some funny moments. We had written the employee handbook to say that May Day, the traditional holiday for the workers' movement, was the only mandatory holiday—but it turns out there are federally mandated holidays with which the new managers had to make the organization comply. One of our original descriptions of the service, "methadone for car addicts," was also quietly dropped. The new leaders cared a lot about City CarShare, but they did not see themselves as part of a larger movement of alternative institutions; if anything, they saw themselves as part of the alternative transportation movement. I think this says a lot about the difficulty of linking up different alternative institutional projects across subject areas. But we stood by our decision to embrace the whole spectrum of motivations.

CHOOSING AN ALTERNATIVE INSTITUTION

Perhaps the most important question facing activists interested in creating alternative institutions is which ones to build, or, more ambitiously, which ones to work on and in what order. So—why carsharing?

Transportation touches all of us, and it was increasingly clear that the available options were not serving us well. Cars are quite destructive to our social and natural systems, and we need desperately to reform the way they are used. Global warming, the extractive industries that are required to manufacture cars, oil wars—most people are familiar with the downsides of automobile overuse.

Electric vehicles would not be enough: EVs take up just as much space in cities, and the ecological impact of making the cars is just as big as the impact of driving them.[8]

Highway builders, sprawl home builders, military contractors, and oil companies collectively dominate the politics of the United States. The patterns of U.S. settlement have been shaped by the automobile. Our federal government places a very high priority on subsidizing sprawl through highway construction and military adventures to secure the supply of oil. There are plenty of advanced industrial nations where these patterns are not nearly so prevalent. But we felt that in the United States, a project that questioned car ownership would inherently be significant.

And we believed that carsharing could reach beyond radicals to engage regular people because it answered a clear need that people already felt. Cars are expensive. Studies showed that around 15 percent of household budgets in the United States were being devoted to transportation costs.[9] Our models suggested that for people who drove less than a certain amount each year, carsharing could save them money. We imagined carsharing could work in densely populated cities that had good public transit—cities like San Francisco, New York, Boston, Seattle, and Chicago.

Finally, we thought that carsharing was a strategy that could be a bridge to a different transportation and land use system in the United States. If, rather than owning their own cars, people in cities were to use cars only when they needed them, the total number of cars that are kept in a city would be a fraction of the current number. That would mean all of the space devoted to storing cars would become surplus, available for other purposes. The areas that had been parking lots or parking garages would become apartments or workplaces or city parks. Buildings could be closer together without all the parking in between them, making it easier to walk. Cities would become more pedestrian-oriented instead of car-oriented.

The alternative institutional strategy depends on having the end in mind at the beginning: What would the world look like if the alternative succeeded in becoming the normal way of doing things? We were trying to create something that did not then exist in the United States, as well as making a transitional step toward a world in which cars played a smaller role in the overall transportation system.

The carsharing movement, as of this writing, is still evolving quickly, with new models and hybrids being invented, from peer-to-peer carsharing to dynamic ride sharing.[10] As driverless vehicles move toward becoming a reality, and as we witness a wave of business-led innovation in transportation services, carsharing has come to seem like just the small beginning of a broader change in urban mobility. In some senses, the early carsharing movement "proved the market." At the outset, we reasoned (obviously incorrectly) that for-profit carsharing was not going to be economically viable or it would have already existed. Instead, for-profit carsharing became dominant, and eventually we saw rental car companies and car manufacturers begin to get into the carsharing business and to explore new, related business models. Meanwhile, carsharing became part of a broader movement of collaborative consumption, which facilitates sharing all kinds of resources.[11] The need and the opportunity are different now as a result of all of these changes.

No one today would think of starting a carsharing organization as an alternative institution, for the simple reason that they already exist and are almost everywhere a for-profit business venture. But the kinds of questions we asked ourselves in starting City CarShare are still relevant for activists who are thinking about where to start. How do we know where to focus our energies? Which alternative institutions are the most important to work on first? Let me suggest, as a starting place, the following questions as a way to help figure out which alternative institutions we should put our energy into:

1. Do the organizers have the resources to succeed? Is the project practical, given the number of people involved, the skills of the organizers, and the funding they can access? Will the project be able to survive long enough to have an effect?

2. Does the project address problems people are already aware of? Or does it require a more fundamental "consciousness raising" before people will be interested in being part of it? How much of a stretch will it be to get people interested?

3. How many people will be touched by the project? Does it have the potential to reach into the "mainstream" and engage large numbers of people? Will it need a minimum number of participants before reaching stable size, and if so, is there a realistic plan for getting to that critical mass?

4. Does it have the potential to grow, spread, or replicate? Can it link up with other alternative institutions and form part of a network? Does it suggest fulfillment on a larger scale that can inspire others to build on it or add to it?

5. Are there preexisting institutions that can be transformed or added to so that they take on new roles—or must the alternative institution be created from scratch? If there is the potential to transform an existing institution, how hard will it be to make the changes? Is that institution open to new people? Is that institution tired, out of energy, and in a sense waiting for energetic people to take it over? Or is it strong and closely protected?

6. Will the alternative institution provide the people involved in it with a different way of relating to each other? Will it give the participants experiences that will be personally transformative? Will it provide opportunities for self-development or consciousness raising?

7. Is the alternative institution strategically located in relation to important institutions in our society? Will it trigger or suggest other changes in other institutions?

If it succeeds, would it open up new possibilities for organizing that could build upon it?

8. Does the alternative institution help us paint a picture of how things should work? Does it "prefigure," even if in a small way, a better society? Does it embody principles that, if fully extended, imply something about the nature of a society structured according to democratic or ecological values? Will the institution's success help people to believe that a better world is possible or imagine what a better world might look like?

Each location and each historical moment will call for its own unique set of potential alternative institutions. In some cases, institutions already exist in a nascent fashion that approximate the structure of a good society; in other cases, the institutions will have to be created from scratch. What will be a revolutionary new idea in one moment will be a boring repetition in another.

CONCLUSION

By our own criteria, our carsharing venture was only partially successful: we barely scratched the surface of replacing private car ownership with something else. But carsharing did turn out to be wildly popular, spreading around the country and the world. We were able to make something that normal, apolitical people could relate to. We learned a lot about taking an idea with radical implications and making it have a broad appeal.

After more than a decade of operations, it was time for City CarShare to come to an end as an independent nonprofit. It was clear that carsharing of that type was going to be replaced by a new wave of transportation services—one-way carsharing (which allows people to leave the car wherever they want rather than returning it to the home pod), dynamic ride sharing (which takes people where they want to go like a taxi), and perhaps eventually driverless cars, which would whisk people around and finally put an end to widespread personal car ownership. None of this is what we predicted at the outset. But we had a part in launching the great wave of transportation change that took place at the start of the twenty-first century.

I hope this story will be joined by many other stories of new alternative institutions. I hope other people will develop the theory better than I have done. I hope other people will build alternative institutions that are truly socially transformative, that join together to make a new world.

THREE

ALTERNATIVE
INSTITUTIONS
AND AMERICAN
DEMOCRACY

LET'S BEGIN WITH A FAMILIAR STORY: THE FOUND-
ing of the United States, via the American Revolution. In the
history of activism, few people have accomplished more: the revo-
lutionaries won, they created a new country and a new political
system to go along with it. But the story most of us learned in
school—how the battles of the Revolution were fought—is the
least important part.

In fact, the actual fighting came at the end of a very long
process—a process of political evolution as painstaking and important as the war itself. In this way, the American Revolution
provides a perfect case study of alternative institutions as a social
change strategy and a jumping-off place for exploring some more
recent attempts to use alternative institutions to reconstruct our
political system, renewing the ideals of democracy for the modern age.

POLITICAL SYSTEMS IN CONFLICT

American democracy didn't start with the Revolution. It grew quietly under British control and gathered strength gradually as a set
of institutions and practices were created beneath the notice of the
most powerful empire on the planet. Across the diversity of the

colonies, which ranged from early corporate enterprises organized for the purpose of trade to idealistic religious communes, what emerged over time was a de facto system of self-government camouflaged by formal subservience to the British crown.[1]

Town meetings provided an experience of democracy that still serves as the American ideal of self-governance. In these small religious communities, all eligible members—which eventually grew to include an estimated four out of five male residents— were invited, even expected, to show up and participate in the decisions of the community. To be sure, town meeting democracy was far from perfect. Women, nonwhites, and even white males without property were excluded. But the town meetings nevertheless provided a form of democracy that involved real discussion and debate, asking much more of participants than occasional voting for candidates. Over time, the authority of the town meetings grew, and they took on responsibility for levying taxes, settling disputes, building roads, and organizing militias. Since these towns and cities had very limited contact with the central regime, whether in Boston or in London, town meetings came to be viewed as the source of legitimate government.[2]

Most of the colonies had governors appointed by the king (all but Rhode Island and Connecticut). But they also had legislatures, elected by the colonists (at least, those who were eligible to vote). Over time, these elected legislatures asserted the right to carry out the larger functions of government—raising taxes, issuing currency, making decisions about "foreign policy" with other countries, and creating the laws that the courts would administer.

When state legislatures convened, town meetings elected delegates to attend, so that power really emerged from the bottom up.

It was the conflict between these two sources of political power—the governors and the legislatures—that would be central in the lead-up to the Revolution. The Stamp Act of 1765 was inflammatory not only because of the economic burden it imposed, but also because it asserted the right of the crown, rather than the colonial legislatures, to levy taxes.

In response to this struggle for power and authority, the town meetings and colonial legislatures across the colonies formed ever-denser networks of relationships with one another. The Boston Town Meeting created the first of the Committees of Correspondence in 1764, to "correspond" with other towns and rally opposition against the Currency Act. These committees then spread throughout Massachusetts, and eventually almost all the colonies, serving as a way for leaders across the colonies to be in dialogue with one another.

By 1774, the towns were sending formal delegates to meet together. At these conventions, Americans learned how to organize government on a larger scale that was still grounded in, and accountable to, the local democratic structures of the town meeting and other local legislative bodies. In September of 1774, Committees of Correspondence across the colonies organized the first Continental Congress in Philadelphia. The delegates debated various proposals for structuring permanent decision-making bodies to serve the colonies, began the boycott of commerce with England, and wrote a statement of Rights and Grievances.

Local government entities remained intact, but they were now networked with each other directly rather than through the political apparatus emanating from the king. They continued to act as though they had the right to govern. As crown-appointed governors tried to stop them from meeting, in some cases refusing to call the state legislatures into session, the Committees of Correspondence convened legislatures without any permission from the crown. By the time of the Second Continental Congress, war with England had already begun.

The American Revolution illustrates some of the key components of alternative institutions as a strategy. First, it succeeded at least partially because before war began, the people living in the colonies had created alternative institutions of self-government that made the British government superfluous.

Hannah Arendt, in her book *On Revolution*, contrasts the American experience of empowering an already-existing set of democratic institutions with the case of the French Revolution, which was not built on any such foundation:

> The great and fateful misfortune of the French Revolution was that none of the constituent assemblies could command enough authority to lay down the law of the land; the reproach rightly leveled against them was always the same: they lacked the power to constitute by definition; they themselves were unconstitutional. . . .
>
> Conversely, the great good fortune of the American Revolution was that the people of the colonies, prior to their conflict with England, were organized in self-governing bodies, that the

revolution—to speak the language of the eighteenth century—
did not throw them into a state of nature.[3]

After all of this education in self-government and all of this work
creating the new political system, independence was actually a
small step. There was no gap in time between overthrowing the
old order and establishing the new one. Each of the thirteen colonies began writing constitutions immediately, while the War of
Independence was still going on.[4]

Second, experience with self-government provided the colonists with the opportunity to learn how to solve their own problems and nurtured a sense of agency—the belief that they had the
ability to create or change the structures of collective life themselves. The decades of experimentation with self-government informed both the revolutionary strategies and the institutions that
were built after the war ended. This illustrates one of the great
virtues of alternative institutions—that by providing participants
with a different lived experience, they can begin to resocialize people into new ways of behaving.

Third, the leadership consciously reflected on the question
of institutional design. What were the best ways to give ongoing
expression to the spirit of the new democracy? How should fundamental disagreements be handled? What were the best ways to
structure the process of making decisions together?

What makes the writings of the Federalists and the anti-
Federalists so compelling today is that they were drafted by people
who had dedicated their lives to thinking about the institutional

design of democracy—people who had turned their inherited town meeting structures into a revolutionary government and overthrown a powerful empire. They had meditated as deeply as anyone in history on the fundamental questions of how to make social change and how to best embody the ideal of democracy. The constitutional law scholar Bruce Ackerman suggests that we should

> learn to see the Founders as they saw themselves: as successful revolutionaries who had managed, time and time again, to lead their fellow citizens in public-spirited collective action, even at great personal cost. So far as the Founders were concerned, these revolutionary acts of mobilized citizenship gave their public life a special quality—far removed from the pushing-and-shoving of normal life.[5]

The Founders tried to come up with a structure that would enable future generations to continue to develop and deepen the democratic tradition. We live with the results of this imperfect but visionary attempt every day.

Fourth, just as the Founders used competing centers of governmental power as a way to create change, institutional conflict remains ubiquitous and is very much a part of "normal" politics in the United States today. The realm of government is contested by different agencies, acting according to different logics of authority, on different scales, sometimes cooperating, sometimes competing. The country has fifty states, three thousand counties, around twenty thousand municipal governments, and more than thirty thousand special-purpose districts. Each has its own legitimate claim to express the "will of the people." The specific powers and limitations on powers that adhere to each unit of government are themselves the object of endless contestation: many of the great political dramas of American democracy consist of battles between different units of government, and movements for social change frequently use jurisdictional conflict as part of their strategy.

Sometimes we create new public entities to carry out new public purposes—for example, forming a transit agency in a city that doesn't have one or forming a public authority that can manage sea level rise in an urbanized coastal region. In other cases, we rely on one unit of government entering into conflict with other public agencies—for example, states challenging the federal preemption of gas mileage standards in automobiles in order to require greater efficiency. And sometimes we try to transform the inner workings of public entities within the same formal shell, a process sometimes called "conversion"—for example, when an energy utility gets repurposed to transition a community away from reliance on fossil fuels.[6]

Finally, not all of the institutions were changed. While many parts of the political system were replaced with something new during the American Revolution, other major institutions—the family, the system of landownership, the structure of business organizations, and most importantly, slavery—were left more or less unchanged. This is always the case with institutional change: There are many institutions in a society, each one created out of different historical circumstances. Changing one institution does not automatically change the others; in fact, the existing institutions form the context that will mold and shape the new ones, just as much as the reverse.

In one of my favorite books on American politics, *The Search for American Political Development*, Karen Orren and Stephen Skowronek call this phenomenon "intercurrence," meaning the simultaneous operation of different political systems. In the 1830s, slavery was entrenched at the same time that democracy was expanding for white male citizens. They write:

> [T]he institutions of a polity are not created or recreated all at once, in accordance with a single ordering principle; they are created instead at different times, in the light of different experiences, and often from quite contrary purposes.[7]

The dream of changing everything at once is only a dream—or more often, in the real world, a nightmare. There can be no single revolution that sweeps away all the oppressive institutions and replaces them with better ones. The work of creating a good society is never done.

We are not accustomed to thinking of institution building as an intentional strategy. We default to attributing change to "social forces" and "underlying causes" of historical change, rather than crediting the conscious, intentional acts that have gone into the creation of new social systems. But our own history should teach us otherwise: the institutions that make up our society are human creations, and social movements over the years have repeatedly tried to invent new institutions that would solve the problems they confronted.

TOWARD A NEW DEMOCRACY

In many ways, the ideal of the town meeting, with both its decentralism and its robust participation, has been our dominant image of the good society for hundreds of years. The decentralist tradition is often identified with Thomas Jefferson, whose legacy has been appropriated by both progressives and conservatives throughout American history. Jefferson believed that the township or ward should be the basic unit of American democracy:

> Divide the counties into wards of such size as that every citizen can attend, when called on, and act in person. Ascribe to them the government of their wards in all things relating to themselves exclusively. A justice chosen by themselves, in each a constable, a military company, a patrol, a school, the care of their own poor, their own portion of the public roads, the choice of one or more jurors to serve in some court, and the delivery within their own wards of their own votes for all elective officers of higher sphere, will relieve the county administration of nearly all its business, will have it better done, and by making every citizen an acting member of the government, and in the offices nearest and most interesting to him, will attach him by his strongest feelings to the independence of his country and its republican Constitution.[8]

The United States is more politically decentralized than any European country except Switzerland. But the Constitution says that power resides with the states, not with wards or cities, as Jefferson suggested. The debate over decentralism has existed as long as the country has, and it's not clear which side has the upper hand. Probably for most people, the Civil War, fought to overturn the defense of slavery in the guise of "states' rights," defined centralism as the more progressive approach. Following the Civil War, the struggle for racial equality continued to rely on federal power to protect minority rights against entrenched local opposition. Similarly, the Nixon era environmental laws relied on federal power to override state and local governments. One could make a long list of the environmental problems caused by *defensive localism,* which pushes environmental impacts to "somewhere else."[9] This has been among the chief causes of urban sprawl in America, along with many other problems.

On the other hand, progressives have also worked to decentralize power on certain issues, as when more recent environmental actions on climate change have been taken at the state and city level. In theory, a more decentralized system of government would allow communities to tailor their actions to the distinct ecological conditions of their locations.

There are strong arguments on both sides of the decentralism debate. However, I think it's worth separating out the ideal of participation in the democratic process as a worthy goal, regardless of the broader argument over scale. We use terms like "participatory democracy" (from the Students for a Democratic Society

Port Huron Statement in 1962) and "deliberative democracy" (the phrase favored by political theorists) to refer to the idea that all of us will actually discuss issues, work out problems, and make decisions together.[10]

Those of us who believe in deliberation have several different reasons: we think the process may result in better decisions—more informed, more aware of the distinct interests of different people, more fully thought through; and we believe the process of deliberating is potentially transformative for the people who do it—and that it nurtures qualities of empathy and understanding, that in some sense it raises consciousness.

Is there a way to retain the opportunity for greater participation in public life that seems to go along with decentralization, even while acknowledging that many decisions will be made on a larger geographic scale? If so, we need a new set of political institutions that can revitalize the process of political involvement and make it more widespread.[11]

We should acknowledge at the outset a hard truth about participatory democracy: community participation is ubiquitous in America, but it's not very good. The field of land use planning, where I have worked for two decades, relies intensively on community meetings and workshops to make decisions, but many kinds of public agencies also have their boards, commissions, and oversight bodies. While none of it approximates the total control of government by neighborhood assemblies that decentralist radicals might prefer, we would be wise to consider the lived experiences of participatory democracy that exist today before reflexively calling for more of it. Some problems to take note of:

- The conversations tend to be awful. People who talk the loudest, or are the least afraid of conflict, dominate. It's extremely rare that someone changes his or her mind as a result of anything said in a meeting. Instead of people figuring things out together, too often we see people showing up to repeat slogans, or at least reiterate previously held positions.

- Discussion is often lacking critical information and is thus ineffective at solving the problems it takes on. When problem resolution requires technical knowledge, the knowledge is often not available, either because the participants are distrustful of technical expertise or perhaps because the deliberative format privileges those with the loudest voices. So the discussions devolve into an exchange of opinion. A related problem: when actions proposed by one group of people will have a negative impact on other people, the affected groups are often not brought together to resolve the conflict. This exacerbates the problems of defensive localism and of communities being blind to the impacts of their actions on other communities.

- And perhaps the most fatal flaw is the phenomenon of self-selection. People tend to spend time with those who are "like" them culturally, which is increasingly showing up in people's choices about where they live, sorting towns and cities into culturally compatible residential locations.[12] So neighborhood-based convenings already tend to include people who are in some sense similar to each other. Beyond this fact, we know that people who choose to spend time at community meetings are wealthier, better educated, and less likely to have children than those who do not. Add to that the intense aversion to conflict that many people feel, and voluntary participation is likely to fragment along ideological lines, and people will prefer to participate in groups with others who share their beliefs rather than have dialogue with the full range of viewpoints. The version of participatory democracy that actually exists is not usually a fair representation of "the people," but rather just a representation of the very small number of people who show up.

We need institutional designs that can overcome all of these problems by making the conversations better, making full use of relevant technical information, and overcoming the fatal problem of self-selection to make the results more inclusive.

One of the most ambitious attempts to overcome these problems is the experimentation with "deliberative polling" developed by political theorist James Fishkin, with a large group of collaborators.[13] The basic idea is this: first, randomly select a group of people, as is done through opinion polls or juries, to make it more likely that the group of people will actually be a fair representation of society; and second, provide people with a lot of information, access to experts, and a chance to deliberate.

In Fishkin's experiments, facilitators work with experts from both sides of a debate to develop briefing materials that are balanced. They then bring the randomly selected group together to ask questions of panels of experts representing competing viewpoints. Facilitators try to create a safe environment for people to talk and debate.

The results are a projection of what an informed public opinion would be if people had access to information and had a chance to deliberate. In Fishkin's approach, it's essential to use the correct methods: use scientific sampling to ensure that the group is attitudinally and demographically representative and large enough (at least several hundred people) to ensure statistical validity; conduct in-depth polls both before and after the deliberation to see how attitudes change as a result; ensure that both sides of the debate agree on briefing materials in advance; and have the participants express their views anonymously to minimize social pressure to conform to the majority viewpoint.

An example was a deliberative poll of Texas utility customers in 1996 (later expanded to other utilities over the next several years). Fishkin, then teaching in Austin, was hired by the utilities to run deliberative polls as a way of complying with a state mandate to assess customer preferences. Several hundred randomly selected utility customers were brought together for "town hall" meetings to talk about choices they faced in utility policy, rates, and the mix of energy sources. A team of utility executives, regulators, and interest groups developed the poll questions and the briefing materials. The results, surprising to some, indicated that customers would be more willing to pay higher rates in order to support greater use of renewables, efficiency programs, and subsidies for low-income households. These policy goals were, more or less, enacted by a 1999 Texas utility reform law.[14] In this case study, regular Americans, rather than academics or policy professionals, were able to grapple with ethical trade-offs and complex policy decisions and come to a nuanced policy decision—evidence that deliberative democracy can work, under the right conditions.

The question of whether deliberative processes should be binding or just advisory is an important one. On one hand, it seems likely that more people will be motivated to participate if the results of a deliberation are actually binding.[15] On the other hand, it is not fair to empower a process that only involves a small number of people—even less so if they are self-selected rather than representative of the diversity within a polity.

Of course, deliberative processes within voluntary organizations should be encouraged as a place to practice the arts of democracy. When a voluntary association has a reasonable claim to represent the diversity of viewpoints in a polity, as is sometimes the case with broad-based civic groups, the results of its deliberations should be given even more weight.[16] But ultimately, these are advisory processes, and they do not include enough people to have a legitimate claim to actually exercise power. "The people" include conservatives as well as progressives—all the vast diverse viewpoints that exist within our society. Self-selected groups simply do not have a valid claim to be empowered to make decisions for the entire polity. In the example of the Texas utilities, which sponsored and implemented the results of a deliberative process, the ultimate decision was left up to the people with formal power, who were asked to use their own judgment about the results of the deliberation. That's probably a reasonable expectation for most cases.[17]

Vancouver, British Columbia, provides another approach to the question of how "binding" deliberations of citizen juries should be. The province has been experimenting with randomly selecting jurors, who deliberate for most of a year and then put policy proposals forward to voters for ratification.[18] But in general the deliberative poll is probably best thought of as an accompaniment to representative democracy—a way of providing a snapshot of informed public opinion to elected officials, who can choose to interpret and act on it in various ways—rather than a way of making the final decisions.

The great drawback of the deliberative poll as a democratic procedure is the mirror of its great strength: that only people who are invited to participate are allowed to participate. By ensuring fairness of representation, as in a jury, the deliberative poll means that most people don't get to experience the benefits of deliberation. It may be a way of arriving at the "best" answer to a complicated policy question, but it is not a way of nurturing the qualities of citizenship, raising consciousness, or making the abstraction of "democracy" into a meaningful experience for all citizens.[19] So it cannot be the whole answer. Democracy is a big concept, and it is in need of continual experimentation and revitalization by a lot of different people. There is certainly a need to support a greater proliferation of other deliberative forums.[20]

Deliberative polling falls squarely within the strategy of alternative institutions. Instead of just writing more political theory about the meaning of democracy, Fishkin actually went out and created a new institutional form of it—bringing real people together in a new way to talk about real decisions that our polity faces. These experiments demonstrate the possibilities of new democratic forms that go way beyond the inherited models of participatory democracy like the town meeting. The experiments are there for all of us to learn about, improve on, and expand upon. If they are successful, they can grow and become a more important part of our political system.

The ideal of participatory democracy is deeply embedded in American culture. It is, in some sense, the founding story of the country. But the early democratic structures like the New England town meeting cannot remain the only models, and the experiences of participation in public life today are not very widespread or very satisfying to the participants. We need a new round of innovation and experimentation to revitalize our democratic tradition. The approach of alternative institutions suggests that, rather than try to reform the "government" as a whole in a systematic way, we create new experiences of democratic decision-making from the ground up. If these new, admittedly small, experiments are successful, they can grow over time to involve more people. Ultimately they can provide a template for a renewed and meaningful experience of democracy.

FOUR

TRANSFORMING THE ECONOMY

PROGRESSIVE HISTORY IS FILLED WITH BLUE-
prints for new economic systems—some insightful and some
impossible.[1] But my approach here is different. Instead of a master plan for a whole new economy, I offer a view into the component parts, the wide-ranging landscape of socially responsible
businesses, co-ops, mission-driven investment funds, and other
emerging alternative institutions that are part of American economic life. I argue that the economy already contains a great deal
of institutional diversity, including many elements that show great
promise for further expansion and development. I look at specific
institutions, evaluate their potential, limitations, and impacts, and
then see what they add up to.

The chapter has three parts. First, I examine socially responsible businesses and worker co-ops—the most widespread types of
economic institutions that are trying to make money while doing
the right thing. Assessing the potential of this strategy, I argue that
the pressures of competition usually set some hard limits on the
ability of these types of firms to succeed.

Second, I assess efforts to expand the space for socially responsible businesses by creating socially constrained pools of investment capital and aggregating consumer demand. These strategies

work within the bounds of the market but provide a way for businesses to avoid the "race to the bottom."

Finally, I turn to nonmarket economic institutions that are especially important for managing natural resources.

All of these institutions, along with many others, have a role to play in efforts to build an economy that works for everyone.

HIGH-ROAD BUSINESSES AND WORKER CO-OPS

The most straightforward approach to transforming the economy is to create firms that can be financially successful while also being socially responsible. A good starting place for our exploration of the economy is the simple idea of paying good wages without polluting the environment—what sometimes gets called the "high road" business strategy.

A well-known example is Interface, a carpet manufacturer. In 1973 in Georgia, then the center of the American textile industry, Ray Anderson started Interface to bring the idea of carpet tiles from Europe to the United States. As Anderson tells the story in his book, *Business Lessons from a Radical Industrialist*, he built the business with an eye toward all the normal things that lead to profitability and managed to build a successful, growing company for twenty years. Then he had an epiphany while reading a book by Paul Hawken, one of the gurus of the sustainable business world:

Hawken's words haunted me as I thought about our factories, the smokestacks, the discharge pipes, the receiving docks stacked with raw materials made from oil, and the truckloads of scrap heading for the landfill, where they'd sit for something like the next twenty thousand years. . . . I stood indicted as a plunderer, a destroyer of the earth, a thief, stealing my own grandchildren's future. And I thought, *My God, someday what I do here will be illegal. Someday they'll send people like me to jail.*[2]

So beginning in the early 1990s, Anderson committed his company to change, to become the first sustainable carpet company in the world, to become a "restorative" company that gives back more to the earth than it takes. The company set out to eliminate all waste, all use of petroleum, and all toxic chemicals from its products. It set out to use 100 percent renewable energy. It invented new production techniques, new materials, and new machines to recycle carpets. It built solar arrays. It changed the practices of its suppliers and their customers. It developed new products.

Eventually, Interface began to convert customers from owning carpets to leasing them—the same transition from ownership to access that carsharing provides. By selling floor-covering services instead of selling carpets, Interface moved to a business model that allowed it to take responsibility for carpets at the end of their use and created an economic incentive to facilitate recycling.

Interface is of course not the only company like this. Many, many businesses are selling products or services that enhance the world—solar panels, windmills, organic farms, infill housing development, and countless other examples. And that's before we get to new business models and more esoteric realms of business innovation.[3]

Manufacturing businesses can often save money by reducing waste from their production processes. This is a big part of what Interface did, and many firms have found ways to redesign their manufacturing systems to reduce pollution or convert "waste" into a source material for some other business process. The consulting firm of William McDonough (an architect) and Michael Braungart (a chemist) described their redesign of the materials that went into a fabric by saying "Let's put the filters in our heads and not at the end of the pipes."[4]

Taking this a step further, some businesses actually manage to reduce how many things people need, by facilitating access instead of ownership. Carsharing, home exchange, tool sharing, and many of the various forms of "collaborative consumption" make it easy to share things between people who don't already know each other, thereby reducing the cost (and environmental impact) of producing quite so much stuff.[5] Appliances, carpets, and furnishings can be leased rather than owned, which enables manufacturers to take care of life cycle disposal and re-use, in theory both reducing manufacturing impacts and eliminating waste from landfills.

Reviewing the many experiments in socially responsible business should give us cause for optimism. There is a lot to be gained by unleashing the creativity of inventors and entrepreneurs to redesign our economy one firm at a time. The question we face, and will return to, is what it will take to make every business socially responsible.

Worker ownership is an entirely different tradition of socially responsible business, with just as much potential. From the earliest days of American industrialization, the notion of worker ownership has held an intuitive, and deeply felt, appeal: instead of fighting with an owner who treats us badly, let's be our own bosses and run this company ourselves. Over and over, the co-op has emerged as a strategy within the labor movement, either as an alternative to forming unions or as an accompaniment to forming them, a way for workers to take the power into their own hands.

As far back as the 1760s, tailors who went on strike to demand better pay formed cooperative tailor shops to support themselves during the strike. This pattern was repeated countless times. Eventually, as the working-class movement grew in sophistication, people began to plan to organize co-ops in advance of strikes and then as a way to never need to strike again. Worker-owned cooperatives were an important strategy of the National Trades' Union (1830s), the Protective Union movement (1840s and 1850s), the National Labor Union (1860s), the Grange (1870s and 1880s), the Knights of Labor (1870s and 1880s), the Farmers Alliance (1880s and 1890s), and the Seattle General Strike (1919), which is explored as a case study in chapter 7. The idea was that if the working class withdrew its labor from the capitalist system and instead put it into a system of cooperatives, the entire economy would be transformed.[6]

We can imagine what a network of worker cooperatives might look like at scale in modern times, because such a network already exists in Spain, with the Mondragon cooperatives. Founded in 1956 in the Basque region of Spain, Mondragon has grown into a network of more than one hundred worker-owned industrial and retail cooperatives, with more than thirty thousand worker-owners and another forty thousand nonowner employees. Mondragon sets aside money for workers' pensions and for reinvesting in the businesses. Profits and workers' savings are kept in a Workers Bank (Caja Laboral Popular), which has the mission of making investments to start new cooperatives. Education and training cooperatives run from preschool up through university. It's something like this that most people have in mind when they talk about building up a network of workers' co-ops, in which a worker-owned store would be selling products made in worker-owned factories, while keeping its money in worker-owned banks: a parallel economy.[7]

True workers' co-ops, in which workers actually participate in making management decisions and/or electing the governing body of the business, are relatively rare in the United States today. As of this writing, there are around 350 of them, with a total of at least five thousand employees and $500 million in annual revenues, including printers, manufacturers, food co-ops, restaurants, grocery stores, and other kinds of businesses spread all over the country.[8]

But worker ownership is much more common than true democratic cooperatives. The most common form of worker ownership is the Employee Stock Ownership Plan (or ESOP). Examples of ESOPs include Publix Super Markets; W. L. Gore, the makers of Gore-Tex apparel; CH2M Hill, an engineering and construction firm; and the New Belgium Brewery.

ESOPs were enabled by the federal Employee Retirement Income Security Act (ERISA) of 1974, and there are currently about twelve thousand of them employing a total of eleven million people.[9] But in the broadest sense, almost half of the companies in the United States have some form of employee ownership, including stock options for employees, which is common in tech firms.[10]

Worker ownership has been embraced by both the Left and the Right as a way to build wealth among the working class and provide workers with a stake in the growing economy. It's a short step from the American belief in widespread property ownership to a belief in broad-based ownership of businesses.[11]

IF WE TAKE HIGH-ROAD FIRMS as our starting place, and we are interested in expanding the space for businesses that are both socially and environmentally responsible, the question we face is this: What would it take to make the high road the better option for everyone?

What we are up against is the fact that competition between firms creates enormous pressures to reduce costs, and this often means that businesses are forced to cut wages and disregard their impact on the natural environment. When governments put laws in place that protect workers and the environment, firms often seek to move their activities to other locations to avoid those laws. The dynamics of competitive pressure are powerful.

Imagine a technology company that makes consumer products in the United States, following U.S. environmental laws and paying U.S. wages, trying to compete with a company that has moved its production to China, where it faces fewer environmental restrictions and can pay much lower wages. As things now stand, the company that is trying to be "responsible" by paying high wages and following U.S. environmental standards will have to sell its products for a higher price. Higher prices will lead to fewer sales and less revenue. This company will be less able to attract investors and will have fewer profits to reinvest in developing the company. Ultimately, it is likely to disappear, losing its competitive race against the less responsible companies. Or, said differently, in order to remain in business, the firm would be forced to cut costs by offshoring production in search of cheaper wages and more lax environmental standards.

This dynamic, of competition forcing businesses to be bad actors—to push down wages, externalize environmental impacts, and move to the places that are willing to accept these kinds of behaviors—is what's commonly called the "race to the bottom." The pressures for this kind of negative competition are built into our current economic system. These pressures are manifested in the normal motivations of the key actors:

- *Firms* are trying to make money. Specifically, they are competing with other companies to gain customers; to sell things for as high a price as they can get; and to produce things for as low a price as possible. They are also competing to attract investment, by convincing those who control pools of capital that they have high potential to make more profit.

- *Investors* are trying to make money too, betting on companies that have the potential to earn the greatest returns and trying to minimize the likelihood of loaning money that will not be repaid. Intermediaries of various kinds pool money from multiple investors and invest it for them, competing for investment dollars based on their own ability to generate high returns.

- *Consumers,* meanwhile, are trying to spend as little as possible to buy the things they need or want.

- Finally, *communities* are competing with each other to attract investment. Cities want to attract jobs because they want to provide employment for their citizens. And they want businesses in order to generate taxes, either directly from taxes that businesses pay to the city or indirectly from taxes that residents pay, with the money they earn from the jobs. A strong tax base, of course, is what enables cities to pay for schools, parks, police, and all the other public services. Cities that fail to attract investment (meaning jobs) will have high levels of unemployment and poor-quality public services. Communities that succeed in attracting jobs (and higher tax revenues) are able to thrive, providing a high quality of life and economic opportunity for their residents.

Adding these simple but powerful incentives together creates the situation we have in much of our economy today: firms that take the high road lose out on investment and customers to the low-road firms, while communities that impose high standards lose out on jobs and investment to low-road communities.

None of this is an argument against international trade. But it does suggest that the reason for trade should be comparative advantage rather than externalizing costs. More broadly, it suggests that we need a framework for competition that does not pit communities against each other in a race to the bottom, in which they compete for investment based on which location will have the lowest environmental and labor standards. In a new economic system, there would be some "reform corporations" with ownership models that embed mission-driven purposes into their structures.[12] But other firms would simply be trying to make money, which is fine. The point is that the democratic process would be able to set the terms of competition. No more oil companies fighting to keep the United States from taking action on climate change. No more car companies fighting against fuel economy standards. No more gun manufacturers fighting to block gun control laws. Corporations would do their work, but on the terms set by the citizenry.[13]

It's difficult to intervene in the dynamics of business competition at the level of the firm because socially responsible firms operate within the same constraints as all other firms. They are subject to the same pressure to compete for customers and sales and to come up with money to make needed investments.[14] But it's also difficult to intervene at the level of policy and regulation because our democracy is not strong enough.

On one hand, we want to celebrate and encourage all kinds of high-road businesses, from worker co-ops to B-corporations to regular businesses that are motivated to do good. On the other hand, we need to ask ourselves if there is anything that can be done to create more room for firms to take care of workers and the environment while still remaining profitable.

CREATING GREATER SPACE FOR DOING THE RIGHT THING: MISSION-DRIVEN INVESTMENT AND PROGRESSIVE CONSUMER DEMAND

The more we can change the dynamics of investment that businesses have to attract, and the demand that businesses have to serve, the more room we create for firms of all kinds to be responsible. And the more we change these competitive dynamics, the more we allow communities to hold companies to high standards, rather than pitting communities against each other.

If we could do this, there would still be market mechanisms at work, and the economic system would still be highly competitive. But the terms of the competition would be different. Companies would still compete for customers, but would do so while paying a living wage and minimizing pollution. Investors would still look for the best investments, but only within the set of opportunities that are ethical.[15]

To intervene in the dynamics of economic competition, I would propose two strategies that seem the most immediately viable:

First, create *socially constrained pools of investment capital,* which would be available only to firms that take a high road in terms of treatment of workers and minimizing adverse environmental impacts.

And second, *aggregate progressive consumer demand* to expand the pool of customers who will buy from socially responsible firms.

What are the possibilities of gathering up socially constrained pools of capital as a way to enlarge the space for businesses to act ethically—or even, perhaps, to nudge ordinary businesses in a positive direction? Right now, the "motor" of our economic system is fueled by investors' need to earn returns on the money they put to work. That's not the problem, so long as investors are choosing among options that are not destructive of the planet or of society. What would change the terrain for firms that are trying to take the high road is redirecting the capital that enables economic activity into socially responsible channels. Investors would still be looking for good investment opportunities, still be placing money with the firms that seem to have the most potential for growth, but the candidates for investment would be businesses screened for the focus on economic activities that will actually benefit communities and the planet.

There are already some interesting institutions set up for this purpose—and there could be a lot more. Among them are credit unions—cooperatives that provide financial services to ninety million Americans as of 2010 (about a third of the U.S. population). In the annals of alternative institutions, the credit union movement is probably one of the most successful. It's the branch of the cooperative movement that has the biggest reach; credit unions control more than $900 billion in assets from members' savings.[16] There is a whole support system for starting new credit unions, and they are linked together into insurance pools and other cooperative arrangements. Credit unions probably function more or less like regular banks today. But there is enormous *potential* for them to be more than that, to provide a source of financing for rooted, socially responsible forms of business. A legacy from earlier waves of alternative institution building, they could play a bigger role in a new wave.

The network of community banks—for-profit banks that are locally owned and operated—also has the potential to support high-road businesses. Even after decades of consolidation in the banking industry, there were still almost seven thousand community banks in the United States as of 2012, and these are sources of financing that are at least somewhat tied to local communities.[17]

Community Development Financial Institutions (CDFIs) can be banks, credit unions, or other types of entities, but they are focused on serving low-income communities. There are, as of this writing, more than one thousand CDFIs in the United States.[18] CDFIs are another source of mission-driven investment.

Moving beyond banking, there are other, potentially even more significant, pools of capital that could become sources of investment for high-road businesses. Charitable foundations control $662 billion in assets as of this writing.[19] That amount supports $49 billion in charitable contributions (about 16 percent of all charitable donations in the country). But the underlying assets could be invested to serve a social purpose rather than just to earn interest.[20]

The largest pool of funds that is, in theory, constrained to progressive purposes is the socially responsible investment (SRI) funds. By the most expansive definition, $3.74 trillion in assets are managed by U.S. funds that use some sort of social or environmental filter on their investments.[21] SRI funds represent slightly more than 11 percent of total U.S. investment capital. However, the reality of socially responsible investing is more modest than the term "socially responsible" suggests. Essentially, fund managers use various screens to weed out bad actors but, otherwise, virtually any company at all can claim to be "socially responsible." Paul Hawken, in his definitive analysis of this industry, found that more than 90 percent of Fortune 500 companies qualify.[22]

The pension funds that labor unions manage are another potential source of socially constrained capital. With more than $7 trillion in assets, pensions could be structured so that workers could demand that they support causes that matter to the labor movement. For the most part, however, pension fund managers simply try to generate high returns for their members' retirement savings. This has largely meant that fund assets are invested like any other source of capital.

Unions, by relinquishing control to conventional fund managers, are participating in the very race to the bottom that is the undoing of organized labor in the United States. An important analysis by people trying to reform labor's pension strategy concluded that while "one might expect the operations of capital markets to change to better advance the welfare and interests of the workers . . . for a host of reasons that range from control to consciousness to organization, there is no such symbiotic relationship."[23]

In short, we are in a situation where there are institutions controlling vast sums of capital for productive investment that are at least partially mission-driven—so the *potential* exists to direct investment to firms that will act responsibly and thereby avoid the destructive race to the bottom. To convert this potential into a reality, we are going to need a massive social movement—focused on credit unions, community banks, socially responsible investment firms, and, above all, labor pension funds—that actually establishes investment criteria that would redirect this portion of our society's capital into constructive socially and environmentally responsible firms.[24]

WHAT ABOUT TRYING to get customers to switch their purchasing power to socially responsible firms and worker-owned businesses? If we could do that at a large scale, it would provide more room for firms to do the right thing, and if enough of the purchasing power were aggregated in this way, it could even force firms to become socially responsible in order to fulfill the requirements of this customer base. How viable is this strategy?

Cleveland's Evergreen Cooperative Initiative is an interesting case study of what harnessing purchasing power can do. Starting in 2006, a group of leaders convened by the Cleveland Foundation set out to invent a new way to create viable businesses that would be rooted in the city, which is grappling with the effects of deindustrialization and faced with persistently high rates of poverty. The idea behind Evergreen was that the businesses would employ residents of the city's poorest neighborhoods, and the work would provide those residents with opportunities for wealth creation.

Inspired by a visit to the Mondragon cooperatives in Spain, the largest network of cooperatives in the world, the Cleveland Foundation, along with a group of the city's largest hospitals and universities, set out to launch networks of businesses that would be structured as worker-owned cooperatives. The co-ops would partner with the hospitals and universities that are the major employers in the city. Those institutions would agree to use their purchasing power to support the start-up companies. Foundations would provide money for a revolving loan fund, known as the Evergreen Cooperative Development Fund, which would both lend the start-up capital for the businesses and offer technical support to help the businesses succeed.

After several years of planning, the first two businesses launched in 2009. As of this writing, the Evergreen Cooperative Laundry is one of the largest commercial laundries in Ohio, serving hospitals, nursing homes, restaurants, and hotels in a state-of-the-art green facility. Ohio Cooperative Solar weatherizes homes and is the owner-operator of solar power installations on the rooftops of the city's biggest health care and education buildings. A third business, Green City Growers, opened in 2011 to operate a massive greenhouse in inner-city Cleveland, where it grows produce for local businesses and residents.

These three businesses provide jobs with good wages, training, and health care benefits, as well as longer-term assets in the form of ownership shares. Evergreen is actively developing new business ventures, with the goal of creating five hundred new jobs. Evergreen has also started a community land trust, which will purchase and own the land on which its enterprises are located.

The key innovation embodied in what people now refer to as the "Cleveland model" is that by aggregating the demand of anchor institutions—the local universities and hospitals, in this case—community-owned businesses can secure the necessary support they need to be both profitable and socially responsible. The purchasing power of mission-driven organizations is a powerful economic engine that can be harnessed to drive a market for products and services that offer something other than the lowest price point.[25]

Alternative institutions all over the country could replicate Cleveland's strategy. Not just hospitals and universities, but also energy utilities, local governments, labor unions, consumer cooperatives, and churches—the entire set of mission-driven organizations—could direct their purchasing power to further their broader missions. School districts could require all food in school lunches to be healthy and organic. Large consumer co-ops could work to elevate wages and working conditions for their suppliers. For many of these organizations, the added costs of using their purchasing power to support socially responsible businesses would be manageable. The combined spending of these anchor institutions is huge and could stimulate economic activity well beyond that now undertaken by worker-owned firms and socially responsible businesses. With it, the space for a different kind of economy is much bigger.

BEYOND THE MARKET: THE INSTITUTIONS OF LONG-TERM STEWARDSHIP

Much good comes from competition between firms. Those that do a good job grow; those that don't contract. There is an incentive to work hard and to try new things. Our economy becomes more efficient over time through the simple mechanism of differential rates of growth and decline in firms. Relying on markets for resource allocation also has the great advantage of leaving many decisions up to individual choice.

But that's not the whole story. There are enormous failures of the market—misallocated resources, pervasive environmental impacts, the race to the bottom that pits communities against each other.[26] And when the market becomes dominant over the political system, as it has in the United States today, we lose our ability to act thoughtfully for the public good, as if the entire direction of our society is on autopilot and cannot be changed.

The realm of natural resources is probably the area where the market economy is failing us the most. The ability of the land to support healthy ecosystems, the ability of the sky and oceans to absorb pollution, the supply of clean water on which all life depends—these natural life-support systems are being destroyed by our economy.

Many natural resources have the characteristic of being part of *the commons*—resources that are available to large groups of people, or even to all human beings—rather than being privately owned. The concept of the commons is quite old, originating in precapitalist pastureland and forests that were available to everyone in a community. Today, the term refers to natural resources—the air, rivers, oceans, and land, and the natural processes that operate on the earth—as well as universally available social resources like the Internet, the spectrum of radio waves, or even the societal trust that underpins a democracy.

The commons are managed in many different ways. Elinor Ostrom won a Nobel Prize in Economics for her research into voluntary institutions that govern the use of "common pool resources" like fisheries. She documented, through a review of sociological and ethnographic research (along with her own fieldwork on pasture management in Africa and irrigation system management in Nepal), an enormous variety of institutional arrangements, which she referred to as the "polycentric" governance of the commons.[27]

The famous problem of the "tragedy of the commons" was developed in reference to the idea of fishermen taking too much and thereby destroying the viability of the fishery on which they depend.[28] It was generalized to refer to the broader phenomenon of a group of people acting rationally for their own self-interest but producing an outcome that is bad for everyone in the long run. But Ostrom found many examples in which groups of people were able to successfully manage common pool resources like fisheries, pastures, forests, and irrigation systems. She cautioned against overreliance on governments or traditional private property rights. Ostrom proposed a series of eight principles for managing common pool resources for long-term sustainability:

1. Define clear group boundaries.
2. Match rules governing the use of common goods to local needs and conditions.
3. Ensure that those affected by the rules can participate in modifying the rules.
4. Make sure the rule-making rights of community members are respected by outside authorities.
5. Develop a system, carried out by community members, for monitoring members' behavior.
6. Use graduated sanctions for rule violators.
7. Provide accessible, low-cost means for dispute resolution.
8. Build responsibility for governing the common resource in nested tiers from the lowest level up to the entire interconnected system.[29]

The good news is that the economy today is pluralistic, with a wide range of institutional diversity. In addition to traditional firms, it includes public enterprises, like water and transportation utilities; nonprofit organizations, which provide around 10 percent of employment in the United States;[30] and many different types of organizations for governing the commons. We should view some of these organizations the same way we view the New England town meeting: inheritances from the past that can inspire a new round of institutional invention. We need new and better non-market institutions for governing the commons that can expand the scope of long-term stewardship over environmental resources.

Peter Barnes, a businessman who created the company Working Assets, has proposed a new set of common property trusts to manage key natural resources. These trusts would be nonmarket, nongovernmental institutions—nonprofit organizations whose job is to manage a resource for long-term preservation and sustainability. Barnes defines the idea of the commons this way:

> The notion of the commons designates a set of assets that have two characteristics: they're all gifts, and they're all shared. A gift is something we receive, as opposed to something we earn. A shared gift is one we receive as members of a community, as opposed to individually. Examples of such gifts include air, water, ecosystems, languages, music, holidays, money, law, mathematics, parks, the Internet, and much more.[31]

His proposal is to create a cap and dividend program that he calls a "sky trust." It would give all people an ownership right in the capacity of the atmosphere to absorb carbon. The trust would manage this carbon sink resource by issuing permits to pollute. On one hand, it would ensure that the capacity of the atmosphere is not diminished over time by strictly limiting how much pollution can be emitted. At the same time, it would generate a citizens' dividend for all Americans. It's a proposal for a new institution that could implement a cap and trade program and manage it for the long term.[32]

Many people know about land trusts (one of the key alternative institutions discussed in the next chapter) as stewards of land in perpetuity. If a land trust allows land to be used, say for farming or housing, the trust still owns the land and sets the terms of use. An interesting example is the system of "state trust lands" established in many states to pay for education.[33] When Ohio became a state in 1803, Congress reserved land to generate revenues to pay for public education. This idea was expanded with larger land grants up through the admission of Alaska to the Union in 1959. Because the trustees are directed by law to manage the resources for the benefit of students in perpetuity, the land managers have to both generate economically productive activity on the land and ensure that they are being stewards of the land for future generations.[34]

But the concept of a trust has much broader applications as well. Trusts are a legal tool for separating ownership, management, and the beneficiary of an asset. The trustor provides the assets and determines the beneficiary; the trustee is responsible for managing the asset; and the beneficiary receives the proceeds. This concept applies to situations as diverse as pension funds, managed for the benefit of retirees; charitable trusts, managed for the benefit of defined charitable purposes; and endowments, managed for the benefit of a college or other institution. Trustees can make mistakes; they are only human. But the trustee mode of decision-making has the great benefit of calling on people to manage economic assets for the long-run. It's a type of economic governance that we can use more frequently.

One of the models for this "sky trust" is the Alaska Permanent Fund. This fund collects the royalties on oil extraction. Most of the royalties are used to fund the government (and implicitly to keep taxes low), but 25 percent of the royalties go into the Permanent Fund—in essence, a big mutual fund that is managed for the benefit of all Alaskans. Every citizen receives a check each year from this fund.

What Peter Barnes proposes is to apply the concept of the trust to essential natural resources, like the air or the ocean. The trust would essentially own the rights to pollute that resource and would auction those rights to pollute at a level that is sustainable for the long run. It would then use the money it collects to pay dividends to all members of society. It's a great example of institutional innovation related to the commons. As part of a growing network of natural resource trusts, it could help us figure out how to make the human economy compatible with the natural world.

CONCLUSION

Alternative institutions are one way to piece together a parallel economic system—an alternative sphere of the economy that would fit into a more ethical, socially optimal system that won't flee high standards—that is rooted, even while being dynamic. This parallel economy would involve the creation of firms that are maximizing their efforts at social responsibility, the expansion of pools of socially constrained capital, and the aggregation of purchasing power to support locally rooted economic activity. At the same time, it would involve the establishment of new, nonmarket institutions, especially for the management of our commons.

The various parts of this new economy have to grow together. Businesses need the capital and the customers, purchasers of goods and services need places to buy them from, and the investors need places to put their capital to work. All parts have to be sized in proportion to each other.

If we were to succeed, there would still be a large market economy, with prices and competition, and the many virtues that markets provide for resource allocation. Firms would still compete with each other, and those that do a better job would grow. But the market economy would have a lot more room for socially responsible businesses, worker co-ops, and other "high road" firms. Our democratic process would be more able to set the terms of the competition—to structure a level playing field for business activity that requires all businesses to pay decent wages and minimize the environmental impacts of their activities. And we would be able to set up these rules without the threat of disinvestment. Efforts to protect human and environmental welfare through regulations and the other mechanisms of normal lawmaking will be greatly aided by the existence of progressive businesses, worker-owned firms, and other economic institutions that are actually aligned with the vision of a sustainable, humane economy, rather than against it.

One of the reasons it's so hard for many people to feel hopeful about the direction of our society is because our democracy has been taken captive by our economic system. Maybe some of the ideas in this chapter can help us take it back.

FIVE

CARING FOR PLACE

PLACE-BASED STRATEGIES OCCUPY A DISTINCT niche within the world of alternative institutions, with a focus on the structure and organization of our physical communities. From the religious communities of the earliest European colonies to the communes of the nineteenth century to the experiments of modern city planning, place-based alternative institutions have been an important expression of many different social movements.

SHARED OWNERSHIP OF THE LAND

Burlington, Vermont, nestled along the shore of Lake Champlain, is not simply a picturesque New England college town. Its political independence is well known. In 1981 it elected Bernie Sanders as its first socialist mayor and later sent him to Washington to serve as the only socialist member of Congress. The Progressive Coalition, influenced by the strands of the German Green Party, elected aldermen in the 1980s and 1990s. In 1984, seeking an alternative to conventional affordable housing programs, one that would reflect the city's demographics and social values, activists formed the Burlington Community Land Trust, the first municipally funded community land trust (CLT) in the United States.

The goal was to provide permanently affordable housing and offer residents some of the benefits of homeownership.[1]

The basic idea of a CLT is to separate ownership of the land from ownership of the buildings. Individuals can own the buildings, but not the land underneath. The trust serves in perpetuity as the owner and steward of the land. CLTs redefine and reallocate the rights and responsibilities that come with the ownership of these structural improvements through a ninety-nine-year ground lease between the CLT and a building's owner. Included in the ground lease are restrictions on how much the price can go up when one building owner sells to another. This allows owners to get some benefits of price appreciation while still keeping the units affordable for the next person.

Under typical private landownership, even if an owner of a building does nothing, the value of the building often goes up. Perhaps the people in the community tax themselves to build transportation facilities or public parks; the neighboring property owners invest in their buildings; or simple population growth increases demand for land in the area. These value increases are, in a sense, "unearned" by individual owners.[2] Over time, as the land values increase and privately owned properties are sold and resold, the prices increase and the value created by the community is siphoned off to the landowners exclusively. In high-demand communities, the net result is expensive housing. In contrast, the price of housing built on a land trust does not have to increase along with the rest of the private real estate market. Residents may get some of the money they invest in their housing back (unlike renters) and benefit in other ways from the increased value, but the housing itself remains affordable.

In areas suffering from disinvestment or population flight, the CLT serves a slightly different purpose, stabilizing neighborhoods and ensuring that properties are kept up rather than abandoned. CLTs have also proven to be especially effective in preventing mortgage foreclosures during downturns in the real estate market. The structure of ownership, in which land is used to benefit the community rather than individual citizens, remains the same in both situations.[3]

The Burlington Community Land Trust is, as of this writing, the largest in the country, with more than two thousand apartments and five hundred owner-occupied homes, along with commercial space. In 2006, it merged with the Lake Champlain Housing Development Corporation, a nonprofit developer of affordable housing funded by many of the same sources, to become the Champlain Housing Trust (CHT). Today the CHT has a full continuum of housing alternatives, from supportive housing for formerly homeless people to traditional nonprofit rental housing to limited equity cooperatives, condominiums, and houses, as well as assistance to help people buy their own homes.

The concept behind the CLT can be traced back to Henry George (1839–1897), whose widely read book *Progress and Poverty* (1879) argued that the root cause of poverty is the ownership of the land by a landlord class that benefits from the labor and investment of others: "If one man can command the land upon which others must labour he can appropriate the produce of their labour as the price of his permission to labour."[4]

George argued that government could pay for all public needs by eliminating taxes on labor and profits, instead relying on the "single tax" on land. The idea was to tax back the "unearned increment" of rent and use it for the benefit of the community. George's ideas had a major influence on progressive thought in the United States and led to many experiments with cooperative living. It inspired a few cities—predominantly in Quaker-influenced Pennsylvania—to institute a tax on land itself rather than taxing buildings on the land.

Conservation land trusts, whose purpose is to preserve undeveloped land, were invented in 1891. Today conservation land trusts range from large national (or international) organizations like The Nature Conservancy and the Trust for Public Land, to smaller, local land trusts (of which there are about thirteen hundred, as of this writing). This type of trust owns the land and removes it from the speculative real estate market. Some conservation land trusts grow food or make other uses of the land—these are also called agricultural land trusts—but for the most part, conservation land trusts do not encourage development, as community land trusts do.[5]

The founding of New Communities, the first CLT, dates from 1969. The National Sharecroppers Fund, established to alleviate the plight of poor, mainly black tenant farmers, helped to send a delegation of eight activists to Israel in 1968 to study the kibbutz and the moshav, cooperative agricultural communities that had been developed on leased land. They brought back a proposal for how cooperative farming on community-owned land might address the land tenure problems of African Americans in the rural South. In 1969, New Communities was incorporated by a group of civil rights activists. They began looking for land and found fifty-seven hundred acres in southwest Georgia, where they established what was the largest African American–owned property in that area in 1970.[6]

Over the course of the next decade, a half-dozen CLTs were founded, all in rural areas. The first urban CLT was the Community Land Cooperative in Cincinnati, and others came online in the 1980s. The urban CLTs were (and are) predominantly focused on affordable housing, although their activities have increasingly included commercial development and urban agriculture as well. The movement has grown steadily since then. There is a whole network of classes, funders, and providers of technical assistance, including the National Community Land Trust Network.[7] CLTs have overcome the problem of isolation that plagues so many alternative institutions. By 1995, there were one hundred, and as of this writing, there are more than 240 CLTs in the United States.[8]

The limiting factor for the size of both CLTs and conservation land trusts is money. Land trusts have an advantage in being permanent and, if they allow revenue-generating uses of their land, self-funding. But the initial cost of acquiring the land is a huge barrier—especially if the goal is to provide affordable housing in an expensive city or to conserve areas in popular locations. Land trust advocates are increasingly trying to make the case that governments should invest their affordable housing money in CLTs as a key way to expand the reach of this strategy.[9]

Land trusts prefigure a system of landownership that would be broadly beneficial if it became more widespread. They provide an incentive for making productive use of the land—building things, growing things—but the benefits from those investments flow to those who make the investments and do the work, rather than to those who passively own the land. The mission of the trust, as the landowner, is to maintain the long-term utility of the land and the long-term affordability, quality, and security of what is built upon it. The land trust model avoids the pitfalls of purely private ownership while still encouraging entrepreneurship and investment.

Kevin Lynch, one of the great designers and theorists of urban planning, wrote a beautiful essay called "A Place Utopia" as the conclusion of his book *Good City Form*. In it, he imagines a different way for humanity to occupy the land. He writes:

> The land . . . is owned by those who use it. But this ownership simply means the right of present control and enjoyment and the responsibility of present maintenance. The impossible dream of eternal, absolute, transferable, individual possession has evaporated. People now accept that the life span of any human owner is brief, while place abides, and that the territories of many other creatures overlap their own. In the more permanent sense, the intensively urbanized central areas and major transport routes are

held by local or regional governments, while all the remaining space is in the hands of special regional trusts.[10]

These regional land trusts are, he says, almost religious bodies, whose job is to manage land for the long term, to facilitate use in the present while keeping options open for future generations. It's just one man's version of utopia. But it evokes how things might work if we restructured our system of ownership so that land is taken care of for the long term.

NEW TOWNS

Ebenezer Howard (1850–1928) might accurately be called the "father of city planning." A British stenographer and one-time homesteader in the United States, Howard eventually returned to London and launched a series of experiments to create new communities on farmland outside the city. These experiments, which came to be called "garden cities," were very much within the tradition of alternative institutions and had an enormous influence on urban planning in the United States.

Howard's book *Garden Cities of To-Morrow*, originally published in 1898, lays out a strategy for decongesting London by establishing new towns in the British countryside.[11] These towns would be linked by rail and would allow their inhabitants to enjoy the benefits of both the country and the city—economic opportunity and access to nature; low rents and high wages; community and freedom. Howard envisioned a carefully planned cluster of towns, so designed that each dweller in a town of comparatively small population is afforded, by a well-devised system of railways, waterways, and roads, the enjoyment of easy, rapid, and cheap communication with a large aggregate of the population, so that the advantages which a large city presents in the higher forms of corporate life may be within the reach of all, and yet each citizen of what is destined to be the most beautiful city in the world may dwell in a region of pure air and be within a very few minutes' walk of the country.[12]

The layout of the garden city he proposed came to represent many city planners' ideal arrangement: neighborhoods in which everyone can walk to the necessities of daily life; a town surrounded by a greenbelt, so that the town cannot spread endlessly outward; a lifestyle that combines the efficiency of higher densities with access to nature; a mix of land uses; and a central rail station that connects people to a greater metropolitan world.

From the perspective of alternative institutions, Howard's key contribution is his detailed plan for how to organize and fund a garden city. The land would be purchased at agricultural prices. The organizers would borrow money to buy the land and build the buildings. As people and industries rented the buildings, the rent would pay back the loan and then be used for other public purposes such as old-age pensions, health care, and public improvements.

Howard saw himself as an inventor. With the garden city concept, he put together a series of ideas that were already in circulation—the idea of recolonizing rural areas to provide opportunity for the inner-city poor; the idea of land being owned by the public rather than privately; and the idea of a model physical community that combined the best attributes of the country and the city. He proposed a system of socializing the rents and using them to fund the needs of the community as the model of an entirely new economic system, an alternative to both capitalism and socialism. Each town would be an experiment in self-government, with services provided by the municipality or by people themselves organizing to do what needed doing.

But Howard's importance goes beyond the "invention" of the garden city. He devoted the rest of his life to actually putting the ideas to work. The year after he published *Garden Cities of To-Morrow*, he founded the Garden Cities Association to promote the concept. (This organization still exists as the Town and Country Planning Association, the UK's leading progressive city planning advocacy organization.)[13] Within a few years, Howard had recruited more than one thousand members, including prominent industrialists, academics, and politicians. But he was not simply trying to raise awareness; he was trying to raise the money to actually buy the land and create the world's first garden city as a "limited dividend" corporation. In 1902, the Garden City Pioneer Company was formed with start-up capital to survey sites; that same year the land that would become Letchworth, a city thirty-five miles from London, was purchased.

The enterprise was never financially successful, and of course it took much longer to organize than anyone anticipated, but the city of Letchworth was built. By 1938, it had fifteen thousand inhabitants, but it took government subsidies after World War II to get it to its full capacity of thirty thousand people. The city is filled with trees, beautiful cottages, and a town center; it is surrounded by a greenbelt of open space. Some industry came, though never as much as was hoped.

In 1919, Howard did it again: he purchased part of an estate fifteen miles from London at an auction, assembled a board of his wealthy friends to actually come up with the money, and established the UK's second garden city, which came to be known as Welwyn. Because it was so much closer to London, Welwyn had even less success attracting industry and ended up being more of a residential suburb than a city unto itself.

Both of the garden cities exist to this day as examples of how Howard's ideals could be made real, if imperfectly so. While most city planners today would say that Letchworth and Welwyn were successful as physical planning experiments, the plan to use rents on property to pay for public goods failed. Each city ultimately faced bankruptcy, and the bylaws were changed to try to get investors some of their money back. Howard's legacy after his death in 1928 would be felt in two ways: the physical model of the city would be influential in city planning, while the economic model was pursued within the land trust movement.

In the UK, almost thirty new towns have been built since the Letchworth and Welwyn experiments as part of the national government's growth management strategy.[14] In the United States, planners eagerly read *Garden Cities of To-Morrow* and went to study Letchworth. The first U.S. town inspired by this model was Forest Hills Gardens, in the Queens borough of New York City. Founded in 1908 and gradually built out over the ensuing decades, Forest Hills Gardens was an influential early prototype of suburbia, if suburbia had turned out according to the visions of the idealistic planners. The central square is by the train station. Higher-density apartments cluster around the center, with single-family homes farther away. The roads discourage speeding traffic, while welcoming walking. And of course, there is a great deal of greenery. It's not hard to see how this bucolic setting, still linked to the metropolis by rail, could feel like the antidote to the problems of the nineteenth-century city.

Radburn, New Jersey, located about twenty miles from New York City and founded in 1929, was another influential attempt to translate the garden city concept to the United States. It is similarly bucolic and similarly oriented around a rail station. Founded as "a town for the motor age," Radburn's designers explicitly took on the design challenge of the automobile and created a system of separate pedestrian paths that do not cross major roads at grade. This was an attempt to implement the enormously influential idea of the "neighborhood unit"—a carefully planned physical environment including homes, schools, stores, and open space, all designed to be accessible without having to cross major roadways.[15] In the hands of less sensitive designers, these "superblocks" became a new planning orthodoxy in postwar suburbia—one of the many ironies of the trajectory of the garden city movement.[16]

Many other new towns followed in the United States, including Sunnyside Gardens in Queens and Greenbelt, Maryland (one of several new towns established as a result of the New Deal). Reston, Virginia, was perhaps the first postwar planned community. Reston, however, was undertaken entirely as a private-sector, profit-motivated development, as was Columbia, Maryland. Both of these new towns greatly watered down the density and walkability of the earlier models.

There is a sad and ironic line leading directly from Letchworth to Radburn to Irvine, California, a very traditional suburb in terms of both its physical form and its business model, albeit one that was thoughtfully planned. In the hands of private developers, the American interpretation of the garden city model led to the banality of large-scale suburban developments, where no one can really get around without a car. But the hope that new towns can provide new models of urbanization persists.

The New Urbanist movement that emerged in the 1990s to reform the way American suburbs are planned brought another wave of new towns. Places like Seaside, Florida, and Mashpee Commons, Massachusetts, demonstrated their principles of good place-making: front porches; town centers that people can walk to; mixes of income levels and housing types in the same neighborhoods; hiding the cars and garages out of sight; creating public spaces that are framed by buildings; designing streets to be as narrow as possible. These prototypes were followed by dozens, some would say hundreds, of other New Urbanist communities.[17]

As long as the population is growing, there will always be new settlements created. It's time we become more thoughtful about how to design and build them, rather than just replicating what we already have.[18] It is probably not an exaggeration to say that the ideal of a garden city—a form of settlement that combines elements of both country and city—has been the single most influential idea in city planning for the past century. The dream of a decentralized metropolis that links multiple town centers together into a larger whole, while providing the benefits of small town life, combining the virtues of traditional face-to-face community with the benefits of modernist cosmopolitanism, has continued to be an elusive but attractive dream.

Some creators of new towns hoped they would become stepping-stones to far-reaching changes in the economy and society. Most have had more modest ambitions, namely trying to attract buyers. But whatever the motivation, the way we arrange human settlement on the land matters. Whether we cluster development together to conserve open space, whether we design opportunities for walking and biking, whether we make it possible for people of different socioeconomic backgrounds to live together—all of these "fundamentals" of city design are, in fact, institutions that need reform as much as any other in our society.

COMMUNES

From the earliest days of the European expansion to North America, people have tried to create settlements that would embody their ideas of the right way to live. These communes went beyond the physical planning and landownership changes that have been part of the new town movement; the organizers of communes were trying to actually create a more complete cultural break—to demonstrate whole new ways of organizing social life. Communes can perhaps be thought of as a kind of "internal secession"—an attempt to create an entirely new society within the confines of a settlement.

The model for communes was probably the monasteries of Christian Europe, where the religious orders would retreat into self-contained communities, with only very prescribed and specific interactions with the outside world. But the Puritan settlements in New England provide the most paradigmatic example of communes for the American context. The Puritans were not just seeking to be left alone to practice their chosen way of life; they aspired to demonstrate the superiority of that way of life to the rest of humanity. This is the oft-cited "city on a hill" metaphor that U.S. presidents have evoked in countless speeches. The phrase comes from Jesus's Sermon on the Mount, and the Puritan John Winthrop used it in 1630 in a sermon delivered to future settlers of the Massachusetts Bay Colony while on board the ship *Arabella*:

> We shall find that the God of Israel is among us, when ten of us shall be able to resist a thousand of our enemies; when He shall make us a praise and glory that men shall say of succeeding plantations, "may the Lord make it like that of New England." For we must consider that we shall be as a city upon a hill. The eyes of all

people are upon us. So that if we shall deal falsely with our God in this work we have undertaken, and so cause Him to withdraw His present help from us, we shall be made a story and a by-word through the world.[19]

The Puritan colonies contained some of the core elements of the alternative institution model of change.

First, create an alternative that prefigures a better world. Having decided to abandon the Church of England, the great effort of the Puritans went into building up their own traditions and fulfilling their own ideals of how to live a holy life. The focus shifted from fighting against something to building up something.

Second, recruit and inspire. The Puritans hoped that their experiments in the American colonies would inspire others to emulate them. Change occurs either when people join the new institutions or when people copy them.

Third, compete with the mainstream institutions. Once the alternative exists, there can be competition between real things rather than just between ideas. One of the most important ways that societies are changed is through competition between institutions, in this case churches. Some grow and attract more members, some decline.

Since the Puritan settlements of the 1600s, there have been several major waves of "communalism" in America. The largest wave of communitarian settlements took place between 1820 and 1850, as part of the country's Western expansion. Reformers and idealists of all kinds saw the opportunity of new development as a chance to change the course of history. Said one French socialist about America in 1854:

> If the nucleus of the new society be implanted upon these soils, today a wilderness, and which tomorrow will be flooded with population, thousands of analogous organizations will rapidly arise without obstacle and as if by enchantment around the first specimens.[20]

Both native-born and foreign-born "communards" saw the United States as the ideal place to build new settlements and test out their ideas of how society should be organized.[21]

Many of the communal movements were, like the Puritans, religiously motivated. The Shakers, who traced their origin to England in the mid-1700s, emigrated to America in 1774. They are well known today for their furniture, their singing—and for not having sex. The group could only grow by conversion or adoption.

The Shakers formed separate, self-contained communities in New England and the Midwest and worked to live lives without sin. Over time, a distinct culture developed, and they came to be economically successful, ultimately expanding to twenty different communities and a peak membership of six thousand. While the specifics of their beliefs may not have attracted widespread emulation, and their vow of celibacy doomed them to eventual extinction, the existence of apparently thriving Shaker communities inspired other communal experiments in the nineteenth century.[22]

Robert Owen, an industrialist known in Britain as one of the founders of the cooperative movement, came to the United States to establish the first secular socialist community. Owen had experimented with idealistic but paternalistic models of company towns in Glasgow's New Lanark mills, which he owned. In 1825, Owen purchased the town of New Harmony, Indiana, from a failed religious commune. He was able to recruit eight to nine hundred workers to this demonstration project of communitarian socialism, but they were never given real control over the city. Even as Owen came to embrace socialism, his paternalism remained intact.

Owen was largely absent from the commune, traveling the country promoting new towns as a way to solve the problems of early industrialism. His experiment lasted only two years. Owen returned to London, where he became a leading figure in the labor movement and a proponent of what Marx and Engels would later call "utopian socialism."[23]

A far more successful version of secular communalism was the Fourierist movement (also called "Associationism"). Charles Fourier (1772–1837) was another utopian socialist and a contemporary of Robert Owen. He invented an entire cosmology, writing about religion and sex and psychology. But he also developed a detailed proposal for cooperative communities that would unite people of all classes. He called these communities "phalanxes."

Each phalanx would have 1,620 people, and Fourier drew up detailed architectural and landscape plans for them.

The movement inspired thirty phalanxes in the United States. They were not exact fulfillments of the architectural specifics contained in Fourier's writings, but nevertheless they were real attempts to create cooperative, socialist communities. For a time, Brook Farm, the most famous and influential intellectual community in America, joined the Fourierist movement. As the leading historian of the movement explains,

> Fourierists saw themselves as a third voice in the debate over the social meaning of America. Opposed to both the free-labor system of northern capitalists and the slave-labor system of the South, their communitarian movement sought to transform both into systems of *cooperative* labor—and to convince Americans that their mission was to make their nation the socialist Promised Land.[24]

In the 1890s, a series of socialist communities were founded in California, influenced by the writings of the utopian author Edward Bellamy, the growing power of the socialist movement, and the active labor movement in the Bay Area. The Kaweah Cooperative Commonwealth ran from 1885 to 1890 in the Sierra Foothills (in what is today Sequoia National Park), gathering together hundreds of people to try to carve out a communal way of life based on a timber economy. After spending a half decade building a road to support the lumber project, the federal government ended up voiding the group's land claims in order to create the national park. Former residents went on to start other socialist communities, most importantly, Llano del Rio in the Mojave Desert east of Los Angeles, which lasted from 1914 to 1918. It attracted nine hundred residents and made progress building up a self-sustaining economic base until it was felled by the lack of water and the failure of its irrigation plans. The residents then moved the colony to an abandoned lumber town in Louisiana, where it continued until the Great Depression.

Koinonia Farm was another interesting take on the commune. Founded in 1942 in Georgia, the purpose of the farm was to demonstrate that blacks and whites could live together harmoniously under Christian values. Koinonia created a mail-order nut business to support the enterprise. Members farmed, worshipped, and studied together amid the constant threat of violence from whites in the surrounding area. The community lasted until 1993, when members reorganized as a more traditional nonprofit organization focused on affordable housing; some of the original members went on to form Habitat for Humanity. Koinonia still exists as a historic site and community, albeit without the intense communal focus of the Civil Rights era.[25]

Most of these socialist communes were not long lasting, and in general, the religiously motivated communities have had more staying power. But they were nevertheless important attempts to build an alternative society, complete with newspapers, orchestras, schools, holidays, weekly dances, and democratic governance structures. Their founders believed that seeing socialism in practice was the best way to expand the movement.[26]

And of course, communes—or as they are more often called today, intentional communities—are still around.[27] A wave of communitarian experimentation accompanied the countercultural movements of the 1960s and 1970s. Some, like The Farm, founded in 1971 in Tennessee, or Twin Oaks, founded in 1967 in Virginia, are still going strong.[28]

The strategy of "internal secession," in which a group tries to create its own place to live where it can follow its own cultural norms and beliefs, is in fact an essential part of American liberalism—a way for people with incompatible value systems to get along without killing each other. Distinct subcultures can live next to each other, and so long as they agree to impose their values only on their own members, they can be given wide latitude to live as a distinct society within a society. It is so natural to Americans, so firmly rooted in the history of North American colonization, so normalized by the examples of Mormonism, the Amish, and Indian reservations, that we take it for granted.

Modern American democracy imposes somewhat porous boundaries around these distinct communities. In theory, there must be free exit: any individual must be allowed to leave the community at will. Nevertheless, the ability to live with like-minded people, ignoring or avoiding whatever is most distasteful about the broader culture, is surely one reason that people of so many different beliefs have been able share this country without, very often, settling their differences by violence.

Today, the strategy of creating new communes lives only at the margins of American society. For the most part, intentional communities are content to serve as places of refuge, where people can live in community in ways that are consistent with their values. They are not challenging the "mainstream" world. It may be that in the middle of the nineteenth century, communes had a more transformative potential. As Carl Guarneri, one of the leading scholars of American utopian history argues, the people who put so much energy into organizing them believed that American society was at a pivot point and that the form taken by new communities could have a decisive influence on the direction the country ultimately took:

> Just as nineteenth-century communitarians believed that small colonies planted on the frontier might well become the dominant social institutions of later generations, the developmental habit of thought gave special significance to the form taken by the industrial towns and commercial centers expanding on the eastern seaboard and along major transportation routes: a single factory town or urban slum might determine the course of a region's future or even the nation's. Lowell and New York City's notorious Five Points district might well be harbingers of an approaching feudal order. To the mid-nineteenth-century mind, "potentialities were among the most real of all things." Associationists sincerely believed their society to be at a critical turning point, when new competitive industrial and commercial forms had to be reshaped before they became permanently entrenched.[29]

Out of all the social ferment of the nineteenth century—the mixing together of abolition, "free-thinking," women's rights, and, later, the labor movement, populism, socialism, and progressivism, so much cultural and economic change along with such diverse social movements—it's hard to disentangle what worked and what didn't. Were the various communitarian experiments important for incubating new cultural forms? Or were they always marginal in their impact on American society?

Inevitably, those who try to found new settlements that include comprehensive changes to the way people live find that it's impossible—at least all at once. In the real world there is no way to start from scratch. The roads and the buildings may be new, and in the case of more secessionist communes, even some of the cultural norms may be new, but these experiments inevitably take place within a set of existing social institutions. Internal secession is never complete. For every social norm that they try to change (say, ungodliness or materialism) there will be dozens that go unnoticed (patriarchy or classism, for example). So it must always be.

Thinking about place-based strategies on a continuum from comprehensive to piecemeal, we can see that piecemeal is vastly more common—precisely because it's more achievable. Communes and religious communities, which strive to create both a new physical form and a new culture, have been the exception. New towns, whether developed by idealists, by profit-oriented developers, or by a mix of both, are more common. Going even smaller—to new building styles, new forms of ownership, new types of the public space—we find that experimentation is ubiquitous.

CONCLUSION: CITY PLANNING AS AN INSTITUTIONAL CHANGE STRATEGY

City planning may sound like an unexpected place to look for alternative institutions, but in fact, the piecemeal nature of urban development lends itself to experimentation, in much the same way that other alternative institutions experiment with pieces of our social fabric. Cities, in this sense, can be understood in the same way we understand other institutional realms, both as systems that fit together in a functional sense and as assemblages of distinct parts, which are separately subject to change.

There are circumstances in which new cities are planned and created from scratch, but this is not the norm. Most cities in the United States, large or small, were built in pieces over a long period of time. Buildings and open spaces are created one at a time, funded by different people, designed and built by others. Even systems of urban infrastructure evolve in a piecemeal, uncoordinated way over time—a new rail line put in one decade, an upgrade to the sewer system the next.

People in each generation contribute to the city, according to their own ideals. The City Beautiful Movement of the 1890s and 1900s tried to create "civic centers" of well-matched buildings, reminiscent of nineteenth-century Paris, to create a sense of grandeur and order, while at the same time, the early skyscrapers were going up as monuments to commerce. Landscape architects like Frederick Law Olmsted created naturalistic parks to bring nature into the city, while the next generation created "reform parks" with play structures intended to provide socialization and exercise to immigrants and inner-city children. One of the wonderful things about cities is that these contributions representing very different ideals from very different times remain. The existing city is not erased and we do not start with a blank slate. As new parts are added, we have a layering of history, made visible, still inhabited, still living.[30]

Each generation builds to solve the problems it faces and to express its beliefs about how to live the good life. Social movements of many different kinds end up defining an urban agenda that leaves its mark on the city. Environmentalists invent new forms of sustainable architecture, from passive solar homes to skyscrapers, that generate energy. Social justice activists create affordable housing. And local chambers of commerce lead efforts to build major works of infrastructure to promote the prosperity of their towns.[31] Each contributes to the layering of ideas that produces a real city.

In cities across the country, there are place-based organizations that function as engines of institutional innovation. These range from community development corporations (CDCs), which work to solve problems in low-income neighborhoods, to general-purpose civic groups like the Regional Plan Association of New York, the Metropolitan Planning Council of Chicago, and my own organization, SPUR, in the San Francisco Bay Area.[32] These place-based organizations often generate new projects and new institutions designed to solve the practical problems they confront.[33]

Movements in city planning, like other movements that use alternative institutions, place emphasis on practical experimentation—demonstration projects that can be replicated and become more common if people take them up. These urban elements are more physical than what we generally think of as "institutions," so in this sense movements within city planning are a distinct variant on the broader model of alternative institutions that we are exploring in this book. But I would argue that they belong here as part of the discussion. Abstract goals like "sustainability" or "community," as well as social problems like "automobile dependence," have to be understood as physical arrangements, not just as ideologies. The way we make our society more ecological is to make it possible for people to walk, bike, and take public transit—and this requires redesigning the physical arrangement of buildings, blocks, streets, and neighborhoods. The way we foster trust and an exchange of ideas is to encourage people to spend time together in public—and this is enacted through a welcoming public realm of sidewalks, plazas, and parks.[34] I think it's useful to think about cities as systems with component parts that can be replaced and reinvented, just like any other set of institutions.[35]

Cities today are in need of a set of new institutions. It's time to take the land trust model to scale. It's time to finally replace car ownership with shared mobility as the primary form of getting around. It's time to scale up new forms of infrastructure, like small-scale solar energy installations, and this may require new forms of ownership and financing. It's time for a new set of place-based economic development institutions, which can better connect people with economic opportunities. In place of more suburban sprawl, it's time for another round of new towns that will push the envelope on compactness and ecological sustainability and that come with transit connections to other places as part of the overall package because they are designed at a large enough scale to support real transit investment. In these and other ways, it's time to use the tradition of alternative institutions in city building to remake our cities and towns again.

SIX

SUCCESS, FAILURE, AND THE FEAR OF SELLING OUT

OUR GOAL AS BUILDERS OF ALTERNATIVE INSTI-
tutions is to create a model, a living example of how things would
work in a new society. But that's just the start. Once the model is
up and running, we want it to expand or be copied. We want it to
become the new mainstream.

But what if a project loses its focus—changes in some way
to gain popularity, and in the process becomes less visionary, less
different? In other words, what if a project "sells out" or becomes
"co-opted"? Is there a way to grow and gain adherents while still
staying true to a transformative vision?

This chapter explores this set of very difficult questions that
lie at the heart of a political strategy that relies on alternative institutions. It starts with the story of the early public housing movement in the United States, which gained surprising success, but on
terms that fatally undermined its agenda. From there, we'll try to
draw some broader lessons about the danger of co-optation, as well
as the inverse problem: self-marginalization.

HOUSING FOR ALL

The goal of the progressive housing advocates within the New Deal
coalition was to create public housing not just for poor people, but

for the broad working class. But in one of history's tragic ironies, the movement to create "housing for all" turned into a program of slum clearance later known as urban renewal.

Activists such as Catherine Bauer, author of the 1934 book *Modern Housing,* took inspiration from the European "social housing" movement. European governments were building publicly funded housing projects, often designed by famous architects, to house workers, thereby treating housing as a public good rather than a private commodity. Bauer wrote about what she saw on a tour of Europe: "The land, construction, finance, and management of low- and medium-cost dwellings were removed from the speculative market: housing became a public utility."[1] American reformers saw in these European projects a vision of housing that would be better than what the private market could produce. Public housing of this type would be defined by things such as soundproof walls, an orientation to the sunlight, cross-ventilation, proximity to community facilities, protected children's play spaces, modern appliances and kitchen design, onsite gardens, and sturdy construction. Bauer's book lists many such "irreducible minimums."

The United States' first permanent federal housing legislation was enacted by Herbert Hoover in 1932, in the midst of the Great Depression. The financial crisis was causing homeowners to default on mortgages, while at the same time, lenders had run out of capital to fund either home purchases or home construction. The act established a system of federally supervised banks for mortgage lenders as a way of expanding the supply of housing capital. The theory was that by injecting more capital into the housing market, that part of the economy could be restarted.

Hoover's Secretary of the Interior, Ray Lyman Wilber, warned that if the government did not shore up the ability of private capital to produce significant amounts of housing, "housing by public authority is inevitable."[2] But the housing market continued to decline, and by the time Roosevelt took office in 1933, many families were faced with the loss of their single biggest investment, and many lenders were faced with insolvency.

A sense of urgency enabled Roosevelt to enact legislation that established, for the first time in the United States, public ownership of housing. Title II of the 1933 National Industrial Recovery Act (the section that initiated the public works programs) included a program of "construction, reconstruction, alteration, or repair under public regulation of low-cost housing and slum-clearance projects."[3] An Emergency Housing Division was established within the Public Works Administration (PWA). Over the four years of its existence, it financed or directly built fifty-eight housing developments with a combined total of twenty-five thousand dwelling units.[4]

The Housing Division's initial strategy was to fund housing development through local nonprofit or "limited dividend" community groups. This approach, the forerunner of today's Community Development Corporation, was implemented during Lyndon Johnson's Great Society program and is probably the dominant way of delivering affordable housing in the United States today. But in 1933 there were not enough local community groups organized to be developers, and in February of 1934, Harold Ickes, Secretary of the Interior and manager of the PWA, suspended the limited-dividend housing program.

In its stead, social housing became something that the government provided directly. This moment marks the beginning of "public housing" in the United States. Ickes also began to focus the federal housing program more on "slum clearance," to the dismay of activists like Catherine Bauer and Lewis Mumford. These critics were not necessarily attached to the existing urban fabric; rather, they believed that slum clearance would be too expensive. In addition, some of them did not like the fact that the affordable housing was being constructed at relatively high densities; they had hoped that affordable housing for the masses would take the form of new towns at the suburban periphery.

During the four years of its existence, the Housing Division of the PWA worked very much in the spirit of the progressive housing reformers who believed public housing would appeal to Americans of all classes. This makes sense when we consider the popularity of Social Security. Government programs that benefit all Americans (such as Social Security) have remained popular since the New Deal. By contrast, programs like welfare, which only benefit a small segment of the population, have a narrow and weak political constituency and are thus vulnerable to budget cuts. Reserving government housing for the poor and leaving the middle class to fend for themselves effectively "targeted" the public subsidies to those who needed them most, but undermined support over time while also stigmatizing their recipients.[5]

As it turns out, the early PWA housing program was almost too successful in building housing that would have a universal appeal. In 1936, Massachusetts Senator David Walsh complained, "[T]he houses which have been constructed [by the PWA] in New York, Cleveland, and Boston and elsewhere are really in competition with private property."[6] The president of the National Association of Real Estate Boards testified to Congress that American values tied to homeownership would be subverted by public housing because it would prove such an attractive option that "the urge to buy one's home will be diminished."[7] That same year Congress passed the George-Healey Act, which retroactively set income ceilings for residents of PWA housing projects. This meant that only very poor people were allowed to live there, marking a major shift in the program.

Middle-class people, by contrast, were expected to buy their own homes with federal assistance. The Home Owners Loan Corporation and the Federal Housing Administration were the two main avenues to subsidize home ownership. They did this, principally, by guaranteeing some of the risk of mortgage lending so as to drive interest rates lower than they would be in a "free" market. (After World War II, the GI Bill and federal highway spending would further deepen the federal commitment to middle-class homeownership by subsidizing access to cheap land at the urban periphery.) These programs would come to be taken for granted, and most middle-class people would believe that their property ownership was solely the result of their own hard work. The public housing program for the poor stood as the only overt, visible example of housing-related welfare in action.[8]

This idea of a two-tiered federal housing program was further institutionalized by the 1937 Wagner Public Housing Act (also known as the United States Housing Act). It enabled the program to become permanent by turning the PWA's Emergency Housing Division into the U.S. Housing Authority (after advocates failed to achieve this goal the two previous years). However, this was accomplished on terms that were not at all what the progressive reformers had wanted. The provisions of the bill promoting housing through nonprofits and cooperatives were killed. All decisions about how (and whether) to build public housing were left to local governments. The law mandated that for every unit of housing built by the government, one unit of "unsafe or unsanitary" housing must be eliminated.[9]

Perhaps most important, the Wagner Act set cost ceilings for residential construction so low that new public housing could not possibly be attractive to middle-income people. Under the PWA, the average cost per dwelling unit had been $4,975, with units in some cities costing significantly more; the Wagner Act established a maximum of $4,000 per unit (although in some larger cities it was set at $5,000).[10] Much of the unappealing character of public housing in the United States has been wrongly attributed to the influences of modernism as a design philosophy. But the legal spending caps, instituted by conservative legislators during the New Deal, deserve at least part of the blame.

With the Wagner Act, public housing was defined as being only for poor people, and that has made it permanently unpopular in the United States. By the 1980s, only 3 percent of all units in the country were owned by nonprofits or public agencies, compared to 15 percent in Germany, 23 percent in France, 43 percent in the Netherlands, and 30 percent in the United Kingdom.[11]

The 1937 Wagner Housing Act first linked the creation of public housing to the demolition of slums. This linkage was completed when the 1949 Taft-Ellender-Wagner Housing Act established a Division of Slum Clearance and Urban Renewal within the Housing and Home Finance Agency.[12] After World War II, the act's goal of "decent housing for all" was increasingly interpreted as a mandate to clear away the older, dilapidated parts of town and replace them with new, modern housing. This movement came to be known as urban renewal. During the 1950s and 1960s, the older parts of inner cities, often populated by minorities, were literally torn down, generally to be replaced with sterile office towers, grim and dehumanizing public housing projects, and convention centers. In many cases, the original occupants had no hope of returning to their old neighborhoods.

The dual nature of urban renewal—as both a federal program for decent, affordable housing and for tearing down inner-city neighborhoods—was already present in the progressive housing movement of the 1920s and 1930s. Many of the housing reformers saw these goals as inherently intertwined. It was logical to them that, as good housing was constructed, bad housing would be removed. But as the housing activists worked to bring their ideas to a national scale—to win a national affordable housing bill—their compromises with other interests created a deeply flawed model.

The program of urban renewal depended on the government gaining control over the private real estate market to acquire land by eminent domain. The land thus acquired would then be assembled into the large parcels that enabled modernist "superblock" redevelopment. Urban planners were given this power as part of the broader New Deal belief in the need for government intervention in the economy—and the results were so disastrous that planners have never again been given real power over the private real estate market.

Could there have been a program for rebuilding the United States' impoverished urban neighborhoods that was decentralized, that worked within the fine-grained fabric of small parcels of land, that promoted piecemeal change instead of wholesale rebuilding according to the stylistic beliefs of young bureaucrats? The answer, of course, is yes. Could there have been a public housing movement that created housing for the broad working class, and not just the poor, defining housing as a right like Social Security? The answer again is yes.[13]

But what happened instead is a poignant example of how activists, even with the best of intentions, can be co-opted by other interests. To launch a public housing program that could work on a national scale, housing advocates needed Congress to approve the program and the funding. But in exchange for that support, the advocates agreed to a series of compromises that would doom public housing to marginality and destroy inner-city neighborhoods.

THE PROBLEM OF CO-OPTATION

There is a big, fuzzy literature on the problem of "co-optation"—another word for compromising too much. But too often the worry about co-optation results in a self-defeating commitment to stay marginalized—pure and uncompromised, but at such a small scale that not very many lives are changed. I'd like to delve into the theory of co-optation a bit and then propose some more useful ways of thinking about the meaning of success and failure for alternative institutions.

Some critics of alternative institutions argue that these alternatives provide a place of retreat from an oppressive society, or that they offer a living example of a better way—but that they are only useful to the degree that they are connected to a radical political movement. George Katsiaficas, in his history of the New Left, is generally positive about the role of alternative institutions in sustaining progressive possibilities long after the self-destruction of Students for a Democratic Society and the rest of the organized New Left movement. While these bakeries, food co-ops, alternative newspapers, and free clinics might be marginal in scale and impact, he says,

> Nonetheless, they provide a space for the self-development of the individuals who work within them, and they provide a living example that the imperatives of profit-making and top-down structures of power are not the only possibilities for institutional

organization. The communities and individuals who have created and work within these counter-institutions may serve as base areas and become a source for new leadership which could be decisive factors in the formation of future social movements.

However, "More often than not," he worries,

the isolation of the counter-institutions from each other and from a larger movement has the effect of depoliticizing them, leaving them open to the criticism that, at best, they provide an escape for a few from the problems of society and that, at worst, they have degenerated and become a part of the very system they oppose.[14]

What Katsiaficas means by becoming part of the system they oppose is, I believe, getting big—as in having lots of customers or members. This, I also believe, is a totally mistaken analysis. *If an alternative institution does something good, we should want it to get big.*

Writing at the end of the 1970s, activist David Moberg expresses the same concern about the relationship between alternative institutions and a broader political movement, saying, "As a result of the fragmentation of the left and the counterculture, there is no movement with which alternative institutions can associate to reinforce their political character."[15] Both Katsiaficas and Moberg—and many others on the Left—assume that the "real" action occurs somewhere else, outside of alternative institutions—in the labor movement, in protest movements, perhaps even in electoral politics. If you don't think that the work of alternative institutions is actually significant in itself, then you pay attention to the other things that members of alternative institutions are doing or, even worse, to the language that the alternative institutions use instead of what they are doing. (Does it sound radical, or are they "playing it safe" to gain more members?)

My argument is that if we take alternative institutions seriously as a social change strategy, we should pay attention to the actual functioning of the alternative institutions—not just to the language used by the leaders, and not just to the other things that the members may do. For all of those who worry about alternative institutions being co-opted, the burden is on the worriers to specify what exactly the institutions would do or be like if they were not co-opted—or, as the phrasing seems to go, if they were attached to a broader social movement. It's only by being clear about what the alternative institution should be doing, rather than what its leaders should be saying, that we are going to get anywhere.

A BETTER WAY TO ASSESS IMPACT

There is a better way to evaluate the transformative impact that alternative institutions are having on society. I suggest that we use a two-stage process for evaluating an alternative institution: first, an internal critique that tries to ascertain if the organization is meeting its own goals; and second, an external critique that asks if the goals are the right ones and if achieving them will actually move society in a positive direction.

Evaluating the purpose or goal of an organization is a complicated process. In some cases, the organizers may not do a good job of articulating their own goals. But the harder problem, which arises in the external critique, is grasping the latent or unintended consequences of organizational action.

For example, a typical worker co-op may believe that its goal is simply to provide its members with decent jobs. An internal critique might start with some factual comparisons of wage scales between the co-op and other businesses in the area. It might then move to a more qualitative description of the interpersonal dynamics at the co-op in order to draw a more comprehensive conclusion about what it's like to work there. The external critique might note, for example, that the industry the workers are employed in—the business of the co-op—happens to cause significant environmental damage, thus raising larger questions about the organization's contribution to social good.

Or a community supported agriculture (CSA) farm, in which a group of people in a community invest up front in the crops of a farmer in exchange for a share of the yield, may list its goals as follows: provide sustenance in a way that is not damaging to the land; shorten the "supply lines" that are required to feed city-dwellers, and thereby reduce carbon emissions; and create a financial mechanism that enables small farmers to remain in business. An internal critique would focus on the basic social change goals in a fairly straightforward way: Are the crops being grown organically or does the farmer cut corners to try to lower costs? Do the members indeed live near the farm and is the distribution method efficient, so that the carbon cost per calorie of food is less than under conventional agriculture? It would also look to the basic business metrics: Does the CSA have enough members, and is it generating enough revenue to keep the farmer in business? For the farmer, these are the most pressing questions. An external critique might look at how the CSA is bringing people into a relationship with a broader network of sustainable living resources. Or it might explore the degree to which the CSA is helping to nurture an ecological awareness among its members.

For both the worker cooperative and the CSA—as for virtually every alternative institution—the external critique provides another dimension by considering the success of the movement as a whole: Are we gaining ground? Is the alternative becoming mainstream? Is the share of jobs in the economy that are within cooperatives growing? Is the share of food that is produced locally growing?

If an alternative institution is doing good work, if it embodies a set of principles that we want to see extended, then growth should be the goal. We want the alternative institutions to displace the older institutions.[16] Activists should not settle for the mere fact that an alternative exists somewhere as the proverbial beacon of hope. We should be aiming to win, and we can't shy away from comparing participation in the alternative institutions against participation in the mainstream institutions.[17] Businesses call this market share. Transportation providers call this mode share. The old agricultural extension services, when promoting crop rotation or soil conservation techniques, called it the penetration rate. I think this comparison between the size of the alternative and the size of the nonalternative should be a major part of any external critique of an alternative institutional strategy.

To take this idea further, we should look at the consequences if a particular alternative institution does grow. Does a cooperative model create upward pressure on wages, as other firms are forced to pay more to attract workers out of the cooperative sector? Is the success of CSAs, farmers' markets, and other strategies for re-localizing agriculture allowing productive land at the metropolitan periphery to remain in agricultural use?

Finally, moving beyond the question of market share, we should also look at how alternative institutions are networked with other types of institutions. Are linkages being established between credit unions—or better yet, public employee pension funds—and cooperative businesses? Are alternative schools—or better yet, public schools—switching to food that is locally produced?

And at the broadest political level, are the alternative institutions having an effect on the sense of political possibilities? Does the existence of a strong cooperative sector help create a climate in which the minimum wage can be raised? Does the existence of a viable local agricultural sector help provide support for an agricultural protection rezoning law to curtail suburban sprawl?

Does the concept of co-optation have a useful role to play in any of this analysis? Maybe at times. Getting big is not the same thing as being co-opted. But it does happen that organizations change what they do in some fundamental way in order to grow (or more often, just in order to survive), and the results of this change cause the organization to have a different kind of effect on society than the leaders aimed for initially. It is in this precise sense of the word that I think we should use the concept of co-optation. But I think we need to have a more sophisticated set of analytic tools with which to judge success or failure in alternative institutions. The internal and external critiques described in this chapter are one set of tools we can use for making our evaluations.

CONCLUSION: TOWARD AN ACCEPTANCE OF IMPERMANENCE

Many now-well-established organizations started out as alternative institutions. Everyone who is interested can listen to public radio. Working-class people can get banking services and personal insurance in ways that would have been unimaginable to the Populists who dreamed of providing the "common man" with access to these services in the late 1800s.

How should we think about these things? I suggest we call them victories. There is such a thing as succeeding and becoming integrated into the functioning of society. When this happens, I recommend that people who want to be involved with a more "cutting-edge" project should move onto new terrain.

Most alternative institutions never get off the ground. After a lot or a little work, the organizers give up and move on to the next thing. Of the institutions that do actually open, most fail to engage very many people or get big enough to have a real effect, and they eventually close. Even alternative institutions that are dynamic and able to grow mostly get crushed or run out of money or gradually lose the interest of their participants and wither away. It is a very small number that have the chance to worry about getting co-opted or "selling out" because they became widely adopted—in other words, mainstream.

There are all sorts of reasons that an organization sells out. The constant search for money to keep operating drives activists to do things they wouldn't have dreamed of when they were starting out on their project. The pressures of competition with conventional firms force some institutions to copy the very entities they were created to challenge. And on a personal level, the burnout from long hours causes founders to look for ways to hand off a project to someone—anyone—who will take it. And if they do hand the institution off, they are unlikely to have developed a coherent leadership transition plan.

I believe that co-optation is sometimes just a fancy word for the tendency to care too much about the perpetuation of the organization. When we begin to worry too much about the organization, rather than the goals the organization is supposed to achieve, we are in danger of doing too many things just to survive: telling the grant-makers what they want to hear, giving the regulators what will keep them off our backs, doing whatever is necessary to avoid burnout.

The logic that guides the organization, at this point, is like the logic that drives any business under capitalism. In order to survive, the institution has to provide what people want. It's actually the opposite of having something that the organizers think the world needs and trying to get people to want it.

This is not a problem with clear lines separating right from wrong. Of course we have to worry about the organization surviving, and of course we have to make compromises for that to happen. When an alternative institution is co-opted, it's not all or nothing. Some piece of the original work is abandoned, or some element of its identity is changed, or some higher potential is not realized. We need to become a lot more sophisticated at perceiving both what is given up and what is retained as alternative institutions struggle to persist under conditions not of their own choosing.

It's hard to make social change, no matter the strategy. Perfection will not be possible. Organizers will face hard choices about what compromises to make in order to continue to do as much of the work as possible. We need to take ourselves seriously enough that we try to figure out how to have the greatest impact on the world. It can't be enough to say "At least we're doing something."

Even though good people pour their passion and hope into the work of creating an alternative institution, even though it takes so much time and energy, even though it's fragile and precious, we have to be resigned to impermanence. If dedication to the institution's perpetuation comes to overshadow dedication to the goal the institution is supposed to achieve, we have been co-opted.

Many alternative institutions will be crushed, go bankrupt, get torn apart by internal conflict, and die in other inglorious ways.

There is tragedy in this truth. In spite of our best efforts, much of our work will not last as long as it deserves to.

Our attempts to prefigure a better world will be imperfect imitations of that world. Through the process of social change, as we learn more and as we fight on a terrain that has been altered by past actions, alternative institutional politics will come to look different. The alternative institutions we make now, as our attempts to imagine what a free world would look like, will be transcended, replaced by something better, creating a different kind of impermanence.

SEVEN

PUTTING THE
PIECES TOGETHER

ALTERNATIVE INSTITUTIONS WORK BEST AS PART of a broader political movement. One of our key tasks as activists is to build more robust connections, both across issues and across strategies. Electing good people to office, running ballot initiative measures, organizing to use the power of existing government institutions to make policy change, and above all, working to bring about a large-scale change in values are all key parts of the process. Big, successful social movements—the kind that change societies and make history—all have one thing in common: they were able to deploy a wide variety of approaches all at the same time.[1]

This chapter tells three stories about important social movements that managed to put the pieces together: the Populists of the late nineteenth century, the Seattle General Strike of 1919, and the modern sustainable food movement. These social movements managed to integrate alternative institutions, political organizing, and cultural change as part of a broader "movement of movements."

THE FARMERS' ALLIANCE

The Populists of the 1880s and 1890s began largely as a rural self-help movement but evolved into a network of alternative institutions—and eventually a serious attempt to create a national political coalition of "producers against plutocrats." They ultimately achieved key parts of their agenda through the Progressive era reforms at the start of the twentieth century and through the New Deal, though they never managed to win national political power themselves.

The leading organization of the Populist movement was the National Farmers' Alliance and Industrial Union—commonly referred to as the Farmers' Alliance, or simply the Alliance. Centered in Texas, and later expanding throughout the Great Plains and the South, the Farmers' Alliance emerged in response to desperate conditions that farmers endured.

In the 1880s, the majority of the country was still rural and earned its living growing crops. Agricultural prices fell during the last third of the nineteenth century, probably as a result of overproduction. Farmers were dependent on railroads to get their goods to market and in most cases had only one railroad to choose from.[2]

In the South, sharecropping, a particularly harsh form of agrarian export economy, predominated. Under this system, also called the "crop-lien" system, farmers would rent land by promising a "share" of their crop instead of renting with cash. Farmers would generally need to buy supplies, housing, and everything else they needed from "furnishing merchants" by promising an additional share of crops as payment. These same furnishing merchants were often the ones who bought the crops at harvest time. Individual farmers lacked the information or the economic power to effectively participate in this market. If their crops were not worth enough to cover their debts, the sharecroppers would be forced to work the following year to pay off the debt. They were trapped in a system resembling European serfdom more than American slavery. Yet the South lacked both banks and the industrial jobs that could provide alternative sources of employment.

The Farmers' Alliance emerged in 1879, after several false starts, and spread across Texas as a network of farmers' self-help organizations, in which farmers began meeting to talk about how to change their situation. It grew out of earlier organizations like the Grange (founded in 1867) and the Greenback Party (founded in 1876), as a response to the immediate problems of individual farmers.

The Alliance decided to create a series of cooperatives—first in the form of "trade stores." All the farmers in a county would pool their business to improve their bargaining power with the furnishing merchants. The Alliance quickly added cooperative buying committees for supplies (with elected purchase agents representing the farmers), cooperative crop storage yards, and other forms of self-help.

However, the Alliance had a difficult time finding buyers for its crops or manufacturers willing to sell supplies directly to the farmers. Banks boycotted these ventures as a bad credit risk, as did wholesale purchasers of crops, who were ideologically unsympathetic. The Alliance was never able to borrow money at reasonable interest rates, which ultimately proved devastating to the cooperative strategy. The Alliance also tried, unsuccessfully, to create new institutions like cooperative manufacturing enterprises, cooperative banks, and an alternative currency system.

But even where these efforts failed, the struggle to build up and defend the cooperatives transformed the members of the Alliance themselves.

Each county Alliance had a designated lecturer, whose job was to travel around the county organizing and to represent the Alliance at larger conventions. The county-level "suballiances" were increasingly networked together through meetings, conventions, and newspapers—a process of organizing that calls to mind the Committees of Correspondence and the Constitutional Conventions that were so important in the making of the American Revolution. Lawrence Goodwyn, the leading historian of the Farmers' Alliance, describes the way the Alliance organizers were changed by their experiences, which in turn led many of them to push the Alliance to examine the more fundamental roots of agrarian poverty:

> Closest of all to the economic anguish at the bottom of Texas society, they became increasingly activist. Day after day, the local lecturers traveled through the poverty-stained backwaters of rural Texas and met with farmers in country churches or crossroads schoolhouses. The small stories of personal tragedy they heard at such meetings were repeated at the next gathering, where, in an atmosphere of genuine shared experience, they drew nods of understanding. The most astute organizers soon learned that farmers were more likely to link their own cause to another, larger one

whose spokesman knew and understood their grievances. The difficulty was the lecturers themselves were altered by these experiences. They were, in effect, seeing too much. Hierarchical human societies organize themselves in ways that render their victims less visible; for a variety of reasons, including pride, the poor cooperate in this process. But the very duties of an Alliance lecturer exposed him to the grim realities of agricultural poverty with a directness that drove home the manifest need to "do something." Repeated often enough, the experience had an inexorable political effect: slowly, one by one—and in many instances unknown as yet to each other—local lecturers came to form a nucleus of radicalism inside the movement.[3]

Alliance members developed an increasingly broad view of the working class in America as people with a common cause who needed to fight together. Parts of the Texas Alliance tried to support the 1886 railroad strike organized by the Knights of Labor (one of the early attempts to organize industrial workers into a national political movement) through a boycott of the railroads and by providing food to strikers. But the Knights of Labor were defeated, and ultimately there was no organized movement of industrial workers with whom the Alliance could form a coalition.[4]

The Alliance began to look for opportunities to merge with other farm organizations and expand across the South and Midwest—even dreaming of a great union of farmers to unite against the banks, railroads, and merchants. Organizers were sent to every state in the South to organize county Alliances, trade stores, and cooperative warehouses. Another nucleus emerged in Kansas. In 1890, the Alliance began a national organizing campaign.

At Alliance conventions, delegates voted to adopt increasingly far-reaching political platforms including laws that would compel corporations to pay employees according to contracts, forfeiture of unused railroad land grants back to the government (and then transfer to new homesteaders), full taxation of land held by railroads and cattle companies, and a national currency that was inflationary and "flexible" rather than tied to gold.[5] In 1888, the Alliance began to call for the government to issue credit through a nationalized banking system and government ownership of warehouses for agricultural goods—in essence a plan to mortgage crops to the government at low interest rates to replace the "monopolistic rents" that furnishing merchants were collecting through the crop-lien system. The Alliance added planks calling for the direct election of senators, reduction of tariffs on imported industrial goods, a progressive national income tax, and government regulation and/or nationalization of the railroads and telegraph.

Goodwyn suggests that the experience of the Farmers' Alliance teaches us that people's consciousness develops over time, so that large numbers of people may become ready to take steps they were not initially prepared for:

> The sequential process of democratic movement-building will
> be seen to involve four stages: (1) the creation of an autonomous
> institution where new interpretations can materialize that run

counter to those of prevailing authority—a development which for the sake of simplicity, we may describe as "the movement forming"; (2) the creation of a tactical means to attract masses of people—"the movement recruiting"; (3) the achievement of a heretofore culturally unsanctioned level of social analysis—"the movement educating"; and (4) the creation of an institutional means whereby the new ideas, shared now by the rank and file of the mass movement, can be expressed in an autonomous political way—"the movement politicized."[6]

As the Alliance continued to organize larger and larger cooperatives and to articulate increasingly radical political demands, its members began to organize for more direct political power, first through the Union Labor Party and eventually, in 1892, through the People's Party (commonly referred to as the Populist Party). Organizers began by recruiting people into a set of alternative economic institutions because they addressed immediate concerns. But as participants began to appreciate their potential power and became more sophisticated about the nature of the existing social system, they began to engage in larger-scale political action.

The formation of the People's Party marked the point where the story turned away from alternative institutions and entered the realm of electoral politics. The People's Party won four states in the 1892 presidential election and seats in Congress and in state-level offices in both the 1892 and 1894 elections. Then in 1896, the Democrats tried to co-opt the Populists. William Jennings Bryan received the dual endorsements of both the Democratic Party and the People's Party (after some key concessions to the Populists' agenda). He was defeated decisively by William McKinley, receiving very few urban votes across the country, thereby ushering in an era of Republican Party dominance at the national level that lasted until Franklin D. Roosevelt assembled the New Deal coalition almost forty years later. The Populists were perceived as being too radical, and they were not able to win electoral support from the urban workers.

Meanwhile, the industrial working class was divided by race, ethnicity, language, and religion. The American Federation of Labor, which represented the vast majority of unionized workers in the country, had an ambivalent relationship to electoral politics and was itself largely unable to deliver the votes of its members.[7] Goodwyn believes the tragedy of the Populists was that they reached their peak of organization and power almost forty years before the labor movement was able to succeed in organizing urban workers—in essence meaning that there were no equivalently organized urban radicals for the agrarian radicals to enter into coalition with:

By the time American industrial workers finally found a successful organizing tactic—the sit-down strike—in the 1930s, a sizable proportion of America's agricultural poor had been levered off the land and millions more had descended into numbing helplessness after generations of tenantry. Thus, when the labor movement was ready, or partly ready, the mass of farmers no longer were. That fact constitutes perhaps the single greatest irony punctuating the history of the American working class.[8]

This, coupled with the crucial fact that the Populists were never able to transcend their own racism enough to successfully bring black sharecroppers into the movement, doomed their attempt to construct a national political coalition capable of winning power and bringing about a second American Revolution.

The cooperatives the Farmers' Alliance created did not endure in anything like the form the originators had anticipated (although some of the mutual benefit associations evolved into insurance companies). The problem of access to credit was never really solved, or at least not until it was too late. The Federal Reserve Bank system was established in 1913 as a way to pool credit across the economy and (in theory) drive down the cost of borrowing money, and later the farm loan acts of the New Deal created pools of credit specifically for farmers. But by then, the process of concentrating ownership over agricultural land was far, far along. The widely distributed landownership that the 1862 Homestead Act had made possible eventually devolved into quite concentrated ownership. This process might not have been so rapid or thoroughgoing had the Populists been able achieve their core objectives.

Nonetheless, many of the ideas that marked the Populists as radicals in 1890 and 1896 would be enacted over the next quarter century. The federal government began to levy an income tax in 1913 (with the passage of the Sixteenth Amendment to the Constitution).[9] Senators became directly elected in 1913 (via the

Seventeenth Amendment).[10] Railroads were eventually subject to meaningful—if not necessarily well-targeted—government regulation, and for a time the federal government worked to break up monopolistic "trusts" in order to restore competition to some industries.[11]

American labor historian Elizabeth Sanders interprets this string of major national policy and legal changes to mean that the movement was clearly successful and that "most of the national legislative fruits of the Progressive Era had their unmistakable origins in the agrarian movements of the 1870s, 1880s, and 1890s."

> In view of these regional tendencies, it seems appropriate to recognize the major reform legislation of the Progressive Era—the tariff, banking, income tax, railroad, shipping, and commodity exchange regulation and the antitrust, farm credit, highway, and education measures—as an "agrarian" agenda, albeit one now broadly endorsed in the periphery.[12]

With the disappearance of the Populists as a distinct political party, their agenda was absorbed into the Democratic Party in the South and the Republican Party in the Midwest.[13] For the simple reason that the majority of the voters in the "agricultural periphery" had been won over to many of the Populists' ideas, politicians began to promote them.

The Farmers' Alliance illustrates some of the fundamental elements of the alternative institutional strategy.

First, new institutions were created to solve immediate problems that people faced in their daily lives. The day-to-day work of the movement did not consist only of "educating" people about how things worked; it involved the creation of institutions to help solve the practical problems people faced. Experience with these efforts led people to a greater understanding of the broader context for the problems they experienced. Being part of these new cooperative institutions created a sense of community and shared understanding.

Confidence in the political movement was based in large part on the movement's success in running practical operations. Organizers worked to recruit people into institutions that would make tangible improvements in their lives, rather than recruiting people on the basis of ideology. There was, eventually, consciousness raising, but it wasn't the first thing on the agenda.

Second, the network of people who were involved in cooperatives provided a direct avenue for political organizing. The leaders and political visionaries who pushed for a more sophisticated agenda did not simply stand on the proverbial soapbox or start newspapers that no one would read. These leaders had a willing audience in the base of people who trusted them, and they had a preexisting network of communication through which they could convey their thinking.

People filter the messages they hear, based on their faith in the messenger. No matter how passionate and articulate we are, no matter how insightful our ideas, people won't be listening to us unless the message is spread through preexisting networks of trust and affiliation. Alternative institutions provide a mechanism for political engagement that connects with specific groups rather than approaching them as an undifferentiated mass.

Third, the cooperatives that served small groups of farmers were increasingly networked with one another to enable larger economies of scale and to pool risk across more participants. Because the institutions were networked, rather than freestanding, they were able to innovate with new economic institutions that took the form of "cooperatives of cooperatives." Eventually, the networks grew so extensive that they began to constitute a parallel economic system operating according to a different set of principles from the dominant economic system.

The success of the Populist movement is a rare example of these three principles working in American history. Alternative institutions are typically too small and too isolated. But the goal of any serious alternative institution must be to get large enough, and develop enough new relationships with other institutions, to create a whole new ecosystem of organizations that can begin to make its own rules. The Farmers' Alliance did not last forever, and nothing does. But it still managed to change American society, as many of the experiments it launched were taken up by reformers in later generations.

THE SEATTLE GENERAL STRIKE

In 1919, a three-day citywide strike in Seattle saw sixty-five thousand workers—in solidarity with strikers at the shipyard—walk off

their jobs. The size of the strike made for unexpected challenges—
thirty thousand workingmen who normally ate their meals in restaurants had to be fed after the waitresses' union walked out too.
The Labor Council organized communal kitchens. The mayor
threatened to call in troops.

The Seattle General Strike is one of the very few general
strikes to have taken place in the United States. But the real story
is about two large citywide cooperative networks that served as
the institutional core of the movement. The Seattle Consumers'
Cooperative Association, formed in 1918, started with eight grocery store branches, which were then joined by cooperatives of
tailors, jewelry makers, and a coal yard in 1919. The Cooperative
Food Products Association began as a cooperative meat market
founded by the butcher's union in 1918 and then grew into a
big network of producers' cooperatives. Dozens of other cooperatives including bakeries, restaurants, cafés, reading rooms,
barbers, shoe repairers, and longshoremen were created around
these two institutional pillars. Leaders of the Seattle cooperative
movement soon began reaching out to form national networks of
cooperatives.

This specific set of Old Left politics that went into the strike
and the Seattle cooperative movement are not what's important
here. We can, from a century later, be very critical of the messy
contradictions of workers going into business for themselves while
at the same time espousing anticapitalist values. But I still think
it's an interesting story for the simple reason that it illustrates
the potency of adding alternative institutions to a broader set of

strategies—in this case the traditional union tactics of striking for higher wages.

Dana Frank, the leading historian of the Seattle cooperative movement, describes the implications of this innovation for the broader labor movement:

> Seattle's "cooperative movement," spanning roughly from late 1918 through 1921, marked the postwar decade's most creative definition of what the "labor movement" would be. Cooperatives stretched the unions' definition of work. By crossing over from production to consumption, they expanded the areas of working-class economic life with which the AFL movement would concern itself. They broadened the definition of solidarity, offering white workers the opportunity to form "one big union of consumers." Finally, the cooperatives created an opening for the politicization of women's unwaged work as part of the working-class movement.[14]

The cooperative movement was still limited by the same racism and exclusivity that characterized the broader labor movement, but in some important ways it managed to include women and to provide new solutions to their immediate problems of managing households and family finances. The movement's leaders articulated a vision of institution building as an alternative path to a socialist society:

> Their theories began with the concept of the "workers' purchasing power," which, if organized collectively, could enhance working

class power. According to their model, the workers would first form consumer distributive branches, which would then unite in a wholesale operation. From these, in turn, producer cooperatives would be formed to produce the products consumed in the consumer cooperatives. From consumption to production, in other words, the movement would build outward to a vast cooperative sector of the economy, which would gradually expand the realm of workers' ownership and, finally, supplant capitalist institutions. As Warbasse [president of the Cooperative League of the United States] argued, "Cooperation penetrates steadily into the business of the capitalistic world and crowds it out." Another advocate explained in the CFPA [Cooperative Food Products Association] newsletter: "[T]he thing that it supplants will almost imperceptibly fade away as the new is developed to take the place of the old." The theorists' model, in sum, was one of evolution, even of secession. "Violent revolution not needed," as one promised.[15]

The theory of cooperatives, as developed in Seattle, stems from the insight that the "purchasing power" of people's normal household expenditures can be used as a force for change. If large numbers of people can be convinced to redirect their spending into new channels, there is potentially enough wealth to build new types of economic institutions.

The cooperative movement grew even more quickly immediately after the strike as people became more politicized and as they witnessed the support that the cooperatives were able to provide to the strikers. Workers who were unable to win concessions from their employers through strikes realized that they could, in a sense, go into business for themselves. The butcher's union opened a slaughterhouse, the building trades formed a cooperative contracting enterprise, and the longshoremen's union started a cooperative stevedoring company.

The cooperative movement in Seattle, as in the rest of the United States, lacked the support of strong national working-class unions or progressive political parties such as those that existed in Europe. But the city labor unions provided the financial backing and the membership that made the cooperative movement possible. In this sense, the movement stands as an example of what can be achieved when political organizing and institution-building efforts work in concert. The labor movement could not have won significant demands, and certainly could not have pulled off a general strike, without the cooperatives. By the same token, the cooperatives could not have grown so large without the support and organizational backbone of the labor unions.

Neither the radical labor movement nor the cooperatives ultimately survived the postwar recession. In hindsight, both were fragile. Following World War I, as shipbuilding was ramped down and the general labor shortage in the country eased, the business organizations in Seattle went on a successful offensive. At the same time, the movement was discredited by the fact that many labor leaders had started "pro-labor" businesses for themselves that turned out to be simply regular businesses intended for private enrichment—creating a sense of disillusionment and confusion about politicized consumption choices.

We cannot, a century later, sort out how much the Seattle cooperative movement was doomed to fail due to its own limitations and how much can be blamed on poor execution of the strategy. But versions of this story reappear throughout the history of cooperatives in America: they foundered on their inability to outcompete regular businesses—or, seen another way, their inability to define a distinct and significantly better set of offerings.

The Seattle cooperative movement illustrates some important lessons for progressive movements today.

First, a social movement needs institutions where people can come together and build community. This is the role that labor unions played in Seattle. The cooperatives added another dimension to the community. "Solidarity" is not an abstract idea; it's something that is enacted by the institutions and practices of the social movement.

Second, the purchasing power of labor is potentially very powerful if it can be directed into progressive channels. Like the Evergreen Cooperatives discussed in chapter 4, the idea of aggregating "demand" and using it for progressive purposes is a strategy with great potential. The personal savings (and today, the pension funds) of labor union members could do a lot of good if they were channeled into spending and investments that are aligned with union agendas.

Third, alternative institutions gain strength by networking with each other. The Seattle cooperative movement developed an innovative new system. Its network included not just individual stand-alone cooperatives but also cooperatives that bought from one another. It established cooperative banks that lent to the worker-owned firms. The "thickness" of these networks is an essential attribute of a successful cooperative strategy. Leaders of alternative institutions need to be looking for ways to connect institutions with one another in order to start to piece together the beginnings of a broader new system.

THE SUSTAINABLE FOOD MOVEMENT

The sustainable food movement is a complex undertaking that emerged from a multifaceted attempt, over several decades, to change the way Americans grow, cook, and eat food. Lodged largely within for-profit businesses, its leaders did not, for the most part, see themselves as trying to change "the economy" per se. And yet, by setting out to change the food industry, they were engaging with one of the economy's largest and most important sectors. In many ways, this movement can be seen to be the most broadly successful of our three case studies in how to build community by networking alternative institutions.

Food has been the focus of intensive activism and innovation for at least a century in the United States. In the nineteenth century, the advent of canning and the advancement of refrigeration technology, combined with improvements to the railroads and other forms of transportation, broke the link between cities and their surrounding "hinterlands" as sources of food. Now food could come from anywhere, and the emergence of a truly mass market for food created new opportunities for the food industry.

The overall effect of these early changes was to increase the variety and freshness of the food that was available to most Americans. But industrialization also created problems: food that was not healthy to eat, growing methods that were not healthy for the land, and labor conditions that were not healthy for workers. The pioneers of the organic farming movement sounded the alarm as early as the 1920s. Rudolf Steiner published *Agriculture,* a book promoting biodynamic farming, in 1924, and in 1942, Rodale Press began publishing *Organic Gardening* magazine.[16]

Many of the key moments in the modern food movement are also key moments of broader cultural change: the victory gardens during World War II; the publication of Rachel Carson's *Silent Spring* in 1962; the founding of the union that would become the United Farm Workers, also in 1962. Changing the way we eat would eventually become one of the signal contributions of the lifestyle changes that spread from the counterculture in the 1960s.

Food scholar Warren Belasco coined the term "counter-cuisine" to convey the way food became a nexus for a whole set of political issues in the 1960s, from fast food and industrial agriculture to environmentally destructive farming and the exploitation of foreign workers: "Unlike sporadic anti-war protests, dietary righteousness could be lived 365 days a year, three times a day."[17]

The movement grew from the network of early health food stores and vegetarian restaurants to become a major force that ultimately would change the way Americans eat, at least for the middle and upper classes. In 1960, supermarkets had almost no fresh (much less organic) produce, and what they did have was often flavorless and wrapped in Styrofoam trays. Today, any corporate grocery store has an array of healthy food, from produce to cereal, coffee to dairy. The countercuisine became mainstream.[18]

In a sense, the success of the food movement is extraordinary because it required so many changes. Farmers have had to grow their crops differently; stores and distributors have had to start offering different food for sale; new recipes had to be discovered or invented; and ultimately millions of individuals have changed the way they eat. It's a perfect case study of a social movement that was able to bring together multiple strategies, from cultural change to alternative institutions. And, significantly, many of the key actors and institutions began by working within the structure of small businesses. Cookbooks, restaurants, grocery stores, farmers, and manufacturers all contributed to a profound and lasting transformation.

In 1961, Julia Child published *Mastering the Art of French Cooking*. It quickly became the best-selling cookbook in the United States and remained so until 1982, when Martha Stewart published *Entertaining*. Julia Child altered American cooking as she amassed a devoted following. Her enormously popular television show, *The French Chef*, premiered in 1962. Over the next several decades, other authors followed with cookbooks with a more countercultural flavor. Frances Moore Lappé's 1971 *Diet for a Small Planet* outlined the environmental consequences of the meat industry and advocated vegetarian cooking. The book sold several million copies and influenced many other writers and works, including *The Vegetarian Epicure,* by Anna Thomas

(1972); *Laurel's Kitchen,* by Laurel Robertson, Carol Flinders, and Bronwen Godfrey (1976); and *The Moosewood Cookbook,* by Mollie Katzen (1977). In addition to the cookbooks, quite a few best-selling authors have taken food as their subject, including Wendell Berry and, more recently, Michael Pollan.[19] Having so many writers with strong change agendas connect with so many Americans is one of the signal achievements of the sustainable food movement.

Celebrity chefs and iconic restaurants had enormous influence on the culture of food as well. Chez Panisse, opened by Alice Waters in Berkeley in 1971, and Greens Restaurant, opened in San Francisco in 1979 and supplied by the Green Gulch Farm in Marin County, made sustainable food glamorous, bridging the gap between the counterculture and the mainstream.

In order to eat differently, people needed access to healthy and sustainably produced food, and for this to happen, grocery stores needed to change. The early pioneers were often, though not always, co-ops. But in a story that is repeated over and over, from credit unions to carsharing organizations, the nonprofit experiments in food sourcing demonstrated the existence of a new potential market, which attracted interest and investment from the for-profit sector. Whole Foods Market, which began as a small natural foods store in Austin, Texas, in 1980, has, as of this writing, more than three hundred stores around the country. Stony-field Farm, a small dairy operation founded in 1983, grew into the world's largest organic yogurt producer (and eventually was bought by a multinational corporate owner). Veritable Vegetable, a produce distribution business that began in the early 1970s as part of the People's Food Movement in San Francisco, is now a women-owned company that links organic farmers and retailers throughout California and parts of the southwestern United States. The mainstreaming of organic food into the normal capitalist business structure is, in a sense, a victory, even if it's not what was envisioned by the activists who worked so hard to invent the first organic food co-ops.

Farmers and food manufacturers, finally, had to provide different food to stock in those stores. It is probably true the transformation of the food industry was demand-driven, meaning that as consumer tastes changed, the businesses that grew, processed, and sold food to those consumers provided what people wanted to buy. But this process worked in both directions, and credit needs to be given to the food producers for the revolution in farming. New methods for growing food had to be invented, refined, and disseminated. Again, the vast majority of these farmers were acting as small businesspeople.

There have also been some notable attempts to restructure the relationship between consumers and farmers. Farmers' markets, which grew in number fivefold between 1994 and 2014 and now operate in virtually every American city, attempt to connect consumers directly with farmers.[20] Community supported agriculture (CSA) is a business model that farmers use to organize groups of people to buy "shares" in their crops. The members thus share the risks and rewards of the harvest with the farmer, creating what is often a more reliable income stream for the farmer.[21]

Farm-to-school initiatives are another strategy that tries to connect smaller farmers with institutional buyers like school districts. With farmers' markets, CSAs, and farm-to-school efforts, the farmers themselves are still small businesspeople, but they have access to somewhat larger and more reliable markets.

Most of the key actors who fueled the rise of the sustainable food economy have operated as small businesses. The story of the transformation of the food business is really about a movement that tried to change a piece of the market without changing the basic structures of the economy. That said, this story fits within the broader outlines of an alternative institutional strategy for the simple reason that progress was made by providing people with new choices, not just by legislating new regulations. It's a great example of how piecemeal changes can bring about a far-reaching cultural change. I see the following as some of the key factors.

First, the sustainable food movement did not require agreement about end goals. Some people were motivated by moral reasons, believing that sustainable food is better for the earth, while others were motivated by personal health reasons. The movement did not founder on questions of which motivation was the right one.

Second, the movement spoke to people's self-interest in a way that appealed to a broad range of Americans. The sustainable food movement, perhaps uniquely among social movements, has a strong claim to be a path for direct, immediate personal benefit in the form of better eating. So we should acknowledge the power of self-interest in making the offerings of this movement appealing to people who are not necessarily politically engaged.

This observation may also suggest a limiting factor for this strategy: ultimately, the sustainable food movement will not be able to fully displace unsustainable food production simply by providing a better product, if for no other reason than that sustainable food is more labor-intensive and therefore more costly. Many consumers, especially people with less money, continue to choose cheaper, less healthy, less sustainable options. At some point, the only way to make our entire food system sustainable may be to win in the realm of politics by changing regulations on farming and food processing. Now that the model of healthy food has proven itself and created a constituency, this is an argument that will be easier to make; but with food, as with so many other issues, the alternative institutional model of change works best as part of a broader set of strategies that includes political and regulatory change.

Finally, the idea of working to transform an industry as the right "unit of analysis" is interesting. It suggests that working at the level of industries or sectors of the economy, where progress on one piece mutually reinforces other pieces, could be extremely productive. The leaders of the sustainable food movement were not trying to change the economic system; they were trying to change the food system, just as the founders of City CarShare were trying to change the transportation system. This sectoral approach is a very promising way for activists to connect their projects to big, broadly transformative agendas.[22]

We shouldn't overstate the accomplishments of the sustainable food movement. While most Americans eat better than they did half a century ago, only a small portion of farming uses organic practices, the price of the healthy food is often so high that only the relatively well off can afford it, and many farmworkers continue to endure harsh working conditions. Nevertheless, it's an important example of a social movement that managed to use many different strategies to bring about some significant changes.

CONCLUSION

Looking at these very different social movements, from different eras in American history, we can see some important common themes. Their proponents had ideas about how the culture needed to change, and they built new institutions that gave people the opportunity to live in a way that embodied their values. They managed to weld together multiple strategies as part of a broader movement.

As case studies, none of them is perfect. We need to learn as much from their failures as from their successes if we want to go beyond what has come before us. But they provide us with at least some suggestive ideas about how to build successful, broad-based movements for change.

Observers have noted the tendency of alternative institutions such as co-ops to lose their political zeal when they are disconnected from broader political movements. But the reverse problem is also true. People who have their consciousness raised but lack the ability to translate their raised consciousness into different ways of living tend to drift into cynicism and withdrawal. Alternative institutions provide a means for people to live differently, to give concrete expression to their politics. In addition, they provide people with more ways to make contributions to the movement.

Cultural change and institution building should be mutually reinforcing strategies. Cultural change inspires people to participate in alternative institutions—it's what makes them aware that they want something different. And institution building provides a way for them to translate their values into practice.

The Old Left had a network of schools, summer camps, cooperative apartments, labor unions—tying together multiple strategies and a deep commitment to cultural change. It had artists, writers, and musicians working to promote its ideals of solidarity, secularism, and optimism about the future to the rest of America. The New Left of the 1960s had its own cultural agenda—including sexual liberation, the quest for community, and racial integration.[23]

Today's Left also has a cultural change agenda. Many of the struggles of the past, like antiracism and feminism, remain unfinished. And many of the core values that would underpin a free society—egalitarianism, the desire to play an active role in the democratic process, consciousness of our relationship to the ecosystems that support life—are not yet widely enough held in our society. We need to make those ideas real by offering a new set of institutional arrangements to embody them.

The Left suffers from having such a lack of institutional options to provide people once their consciousness is raised. It offers neither an experience of community that can compete with the evangelical churches nor a hope for material well-being that can compete with conventional jobs. The vast majority of progressive organizations, from the Sierra Club to the Service Employees International Union, ask nothing more than payment of dues and offer little or nothing in the way of a different life—the professional staff do the best they can to spend the membership dues effectively to make social change. The Left would benefit from a more robust set of alternative organizations and practices into which people can be recruited and through which meaningful and satisfying experiences can be provided. A network of alternative institutions would be the location where people meet each other, learn the issues, and talk about bigger ideas. Just like churches and labor unions serve to organize people into groups capable of taking collective action, alternative institutions could also provide a way to mobilize people for political action on many fronts.

We need multiple connections between alternative institutions, political campaigns, educational strategies, and other approaches to social change. A strong movement would have an entire ecosystem of approaches and organizations fitting together. Alternative institutions have a big role to play within a broader progressive movement.

EIGHT

THE MYSTERY OF SOCIAL CHANGE

WHAT CAN WE NOW SAY ABOUT HOW SOCIAL change occurs, about how we move from activism—the realm of projects, campaigns, and movements—to an actual change of social structure? This book concludes by trying to see what all of the analysis of the previous chapters adds up to in terms of a theory of historical change.

We have looked at social movements over more than two centuries of American history and explored some of the ways their leaders have tried to build a society that would live up to their ideals. We have focused on some specific efforts to create new institutions and build a new society within the shell of the old one.

We've analyzed political, economic, and place-based institutions. We've discussed the dilemmas faced by activists as they balance the need to scale up their experiments enough to have an impact with the desire to retain their visionary ethos. And we've looked at movements that managed to weave together multiple approaches to social action, from consciousness raising to institution building.

Drawing on the history of social movements and borrowing heavily from the academic literature on the sociology of social change, I would propose seven principles to explain how change happens.

I. SOCIETY IS MADE OF
MANY INSTITUTIONS.

A society is made up of smaller parts, which we can call "organizations" or "institutions."

Some are economic entities, like businesses and banks. Some are public agencies, like armies and transit authorities, or bodies of democratic governance, like legislatures and city councils. Churches and political parties are institutions, as are schools and prisons. All of these institutions and many others together make up what we call society.

These institutions exist in relationship to one another, and the nature of the relationships is important. For example, similar institutions sometimes are grouped together because of the way they function. A group of businesses that produces a set of interrelated products can be called an "industry." A group of churches affiliate into the same religion. A set of public entities grouped together as departments comprises the state.

Certain institutions influence, or sometimes even control, other ones. A governmental agency may have regulatory control over the conduct of an industry, and in turn that industry may try to influence the actions of the governmental agency.

We can think about society as comprising the entire set of institutions that exist at a given moment. This allows us to envision how change happens: instead of trying to change an entire society, we can work on the component parts—the institutions.[1]

2. THE INSTITUTIONS WITHIN A SOCIETY
DON'T ALL FIT TOGETHER NEATLY.

Social institutions are often internally contradictory. We can see this most clearly in the case of organizations that are explicitly working to change society—like conservative and progressive political organizations with quite distinct visions of the world, fighting each other to win people's allegiance and to influence the actions of government. Political organizations fight over everything from the teaching of evolution to the level of taxation to the scope of collective action on environmental problems—trying to mobilize, or to constrain, a powerful set of institutions for various purposes. Should an energy utility prioritize renewable energy or the lowest prices? Should our taxes go to support religious schools? There is a constant, roiling debate within our society about how various institutions should operate.

In other cases, it's not a matter of clashing values, but of misalignment of institutions. Our schools train people for jobs that don't exist anymore, meaning that our education system and our employment structure are misaligned. Our land use planning rules produce low-density suburbia, which our transportation infrastructure cannot adequately serve, meaning that our land use planning system and our transportation system are misaligned. Our food system makes people obese, which leads to diseases that overwhelm our health care system, because our food system and health care systems are misaligned.

Sometimes one set of institutions promotes a value system or a set of personal possibilities that are contradicted by a different set of institutions. Think of the expansion of women's access to college education—which ran headlong against the older institution of the family and the idea that women should primarily exist within the domestic sphere. In some ways, the second wave of feminism emerged as a way to resolve this conflict.

Then there are actual power struggles between sets of institutions. For instance, state and federal governments constantly clash over which level has legal jurisdiction—to regulate pollution, to define school standards, to impose labor standards, to manage the social safety net. Social movements try to choose the jurisdiction where they think they have their best chance of success, just as corporations do. There is a constant jockeying for position among all the players.

It's a mistake to think of American society as monolithic or unified. It's filled with contradictions and disjunctures.[2] Those who want to change the world should find this hopeful: there is great scope for action and innovation. As we get better at "reading" the social currents, we will find some that are moving in our direction, and others that are not.

3. EVEN AS SOCIETY IS TRANSFORMED, NOT ALL INSTITUTIONS CHANGE AT ONCE.

The institutions that comprise a society were created at different times, evolving out of different circumstances, and they often operate according to different logics. Following the American Revolution, the change of political structure did not change the institution of slavery.

The Catholic Church still exists after more than two thousand years, having persisted through multiple social, economic, and political upheavals.

New England town meetings still function, alongside the state-centric structure embodied in the U.S. Constitution, the post–New Deal empowered federal government—and even newer international organizations like the United Nations and the World Trade Organization.

Bureaucracies emerge through gradual accretion and transformation. Certain parts of our government date from the founding of the country. But other institutions have been developed over the ensuing centuries. When a new party wins an election and takes formal power, there is always a great deal of continuity with the previous regime.

Society emerges through a layering of different institutions over time. Academics call this process "intercurrence." At any given point in history, the set of institutions dates from different origins. Changing one institution does not mean that others are changed. They evolve and take on new roles sometimes, as the context around them changes.[3]

Social change does not happen all at once. The idea of revolution—the idea that "everything" changes—is a fairy tale.

Perhaps we can take some comfort in accepting this fact: we won't be able to mess everything up too badly if our work turns out to have unintended consequences, as it usually does. This means, of course, that our work will never be done. We make our society piece by piece, one institution at a time.

4. INSTITUTIONS OPERATE ACCORDING TO DISTINCT LOGICS OR PRINCIPLES.

When we create new institutions, succeed in attracting people to participate in them, and link the institutions up together, we are accomplishing social change. But what kind of change? What does the new set of interlinked organizations add up to? What principles structure this new system? What ends does it tend toward?

Different types of institutions express different values.

- The New England town meetings express principles about how to organize a polity: through democratic election of leadership, confederating from smaller geographic scales up to larger ones. Structuring the democratic process through a network of town meetings generates a specific, decentralized type of political life.
- Carsharing organizations embody a value system about how cities should work: with primary reliance on walking, biking, and transit, while using the automobile only to carry heavy things or to leave the city. Structuring car use through shared mobility rather than private car ownership

generates a distinct type of transportation system, which
in turn has implications for the agenda of bringing about
a more humane type of city.

- Worker co-ops change the nexus of control and power
within a business. While they are still in competition with
other firms, an industry that consists of worker-owned
firms would almost by definition operate according to the
value of fair treatment of workers.

As we organize new institutions, we should ask ourselves: If this
institution were to someday become the mainstream institution,
were it to someday be part of the predominant structure of our
society, what would that society look like and how would things
work?

Means and ends are connected in an institution-building
strategy of social change. The forms of the organizations we create
embody a larger vision.

5. COMPETITION BETWEEN
INSTITUTIONS IS WIDESPREAD.

Of course competition between businesses is inherent in a market economy. What is less well understood is that competition is
also an important engine of social change. As new business strategies and structures emerge, they cause changes to ripple across
many other realms of life. The railways weren't just a new form
of competition for ships and horses (along with canals and roads).

The railway industry helped invent the vertically integrated, hierarchically organized corporation in the nineteenth century—a corporate form that would later spread to many other parts of the economy. And the railways, in turn, reshaped settlement patterns, immigration trends, and commodity flows in our economy.

Similarly, the automobile wasn't just a new form of competition for the railroads. The auto industry invented another form of corporate organization. The term "Fordism" came to signify the entire model of mid-twentieth-century capitalism, with its heavily unionized workforces, high wages for male factory workers, and a social compact between labor and business. The emergence of mass automobile ownership also enabled suburban development and radically transformed land use patterns once again. There are countless examples like this, in which competition between businesses broadly transformed our society.[4]

But competition between institutions extends beyond businesses. Religious movements also compete for believers. At least since the emergence of Protestantism, there has been pervasive competition in the Western world for allegiance, and as the Protestant religion split into ever-more competing doctrines, the options for religious worship proliferated. As each branch of faith struggled to win converts, some grew, some shrank. And so the domain of religion, along with its accompanying values, was changed over time.

Political parties compete for votes. And those that win get the right to shape many of the institutions in our society.

Cities compete for investment in the form of companies being willing to locate there, create jobs, and pay taxes. Cities also compete for residents. Some grow, and some shrink.

People who are engaged in institution building as a social change strategy have to be comfortable with the idea of competition. Alternative institutions are in competition with mainstream institutions—to attract members, customers, or investment, and sometimes to be empowered or viewed as the more legitimate institution to take on a set of responsibilities.

Competition is ubiquitous, and it is one of the engines of history. As institutions grow or shrink, evolve or die, based on their competition with other institutions, the overall structure of society is changed.

6. SOMETIMES INSTITUTIONS ARE REPURPOSED. OTHER TIMES, NEW ONES ARE CREATED.

Institutional change can happen in different ways.

In some cases, existing institutions take on new functions. This process is called "conversion."[5] We see this often with public institutions, which seldom simply go out of existence. Thus, the three branches of our national government play quite different roles today than they did at the country's founding. The president has become the head of a large bureaucracy, something that was not contemplated originally, while Congress has much less power, relatively, than it once did.

When new institutions are created, they can sometimes re-place the existing institutions through a process of *displacement*.[6] That's what happened when the town meetings of Colonial America began to make decisions instead of the crown-appointed bureaucracy: one set of political institutions displaced another.

Sometimes, however, competing institutions do not push out the older ones, but rather coexist in a process of *layering*.[7] That's what happens when a new organization is created, like a transit district, without pushing aside any of the existing organizations. Multiple institutions exist in layers at the same time, acting according to their own logics and purposes.

Finally, in addition to conversion, displacement, and layering, we can identify several other mechanisms of institutional change over time: *drift*, in which institutions fail to change even while external circumstances might require active adaptation; and *exhaustion*, when institutions fade away or break down through their own internal failings or contradictions.[8] Examples could include some of the early national labor unions, like the Knights of Labor, which grew weary of the fight; the communes that ran out of steam and lost members; or a long list of co-ops that failed to attract enough customers or energy to keep going.

When activists create new institutions, the process of change will tend to involve displacement and layering. When activists repurpose existing institutions, the process is one of conversion. These terms are helpful for describing what happens when people intentionally accomplish social change through the creation (or transformation) of institutions that embody their ideals.

7. THERE IS NO PRIMARY INSTITUTION, AT LEAST NOT PERMANENTLY.

Institutions act on other institutions, influence them, and sometimes even control them. But there is no single unified theory of institutional determination that can explain everything.

For one thing, the relationship between groups of institutions changes. We can, for example, think about the emergence of capitalism as a relative increase in the power of economic institutions over political institutions. However, this power was never absolute or fixed; the question of how much influence our democracy can have over our economic sphere remains one of the central areas of struggle in our society.[9]

What this means for activists is that we have to develop proposals for every part of society that is broken. We can't assume that if we just focus on a "primary" institution, the other things will automatically change. There is no shortcut around developing working models for each institution, each form of oppression or dysfunction, that needs to be changed. If we fix our energy system, that will not exempt us from also having to reconstruct our transportation system—or our way of managing the land, or our food system, or anything else.

Institutions do influence other institutions. So making progress with one set of problems can certainly open up new possibilities for solving other problems. But our work will never be done.

CONCLUSION

This book has proceeded from a simple premise: that alternative institutions can play a bigger role in progressive strategy to bring about a better America. If we want to create a more democratic, more equal, more ecologically balanced society, then alternative institutions have an important place as part of a broader progressive movement.

Using alternative institutions, we create real-life examples of the kind of society we want to see. Instead of just criticizing what's wrong with the current system, we create something new and better. We give people choices between real things rather than just between ideas.

If the new institutions work, if they are successful at providing a better alternative, then the goal is for them to grow and reach more people. Eventually, if they expand and form networks with one another, they begin to form a new, parallel social system.

"Reform or revolution," the old Left once debated. Alternative institutions provide other options: replacement and reinvention.

Widespread, progressive change will require more than just alternative institutions. It will call on all the disciplines we know of, from community organizing to electoral strategies, from cultural agitation to education. But these strategies will work better if alternative institutions are also a robust part of the movement. They provide an answer to the question of what people can do to translate their ideals into action, and they can provide practical support to the rest of the movement. In some cases, they can become the primary drivers of change themselves.

In my own experiences as an organizer who is deeply involved with urban policy, I have been especially drawn to some of the place-based institutions, such as community land trusts. I also see enormous untapped potential in the institutions that aggregate capital and socially responsible consumer spending to enable a shift in resource investment patterns within our economy.

There is so much potential for innovation and change on the part of activists. If we do the hard work of translating our vision and values into specific proposals and organizational models, there is room to create far-reaching change by creating new institutions, creating a better society one piece at a time.

THE IDEA OF ALTERNATIVE INSTITUTIONS

WHERE DOES THE IDEA OF ALTERNATIVE INSTI-
tutions come from? I owe a debt to many thinkers from various
intellectual and political traditions. What follows is a highly selec-
tive, unorthodox intellectual history of the concept, which will
give the reader a sense of some of my influences and provide avenues for further exploration.

UTOPIAN SOCIALISM

There is a series of passages in *The Communist Manifesto* in which
Marx criticizes the "utopian socialists" for not understanding that
the only way to improve society was through class struggle and for

believing that they could bring about communism before capitalism had run its course. The utopian socialists, according to Marx, were products of an earlier era before the conditions were ready to make real social change:

> [W]hen feudal society was being overthrown, these attempts necessarily failed, owing to the then undeveloped state of the proletariat, as well as to the absence of the economic conditions for its emancipation, conditions that had yet to be produced, and could be produced by the impending bourgeois epoch alone.

The utopian socialists clung to the idea that their political agenda would benefit *everyone,* not just workers, and that *everyone* was a potential recruit to the cause:

> [S]ocialists of this kind . . . consider themselves far superior to all class antagonisms. They want to improve the condition of every member of society, even that of the most favoured. Thence, they habitually appeal to society at large, without distinction of class.

Finally, the utopians worked by setting up "experimental realization of their social Utopias" rather than building working-class movements:

> Hence, they reject all political, and especially all revolutionary, action; they wish to attain their ends by peaceful means, and endeavour, by small experiments, necessarily doomed to failure,

and by the force of example, to pave the way for the new social Gospel.[1]

Stumbling across these accusations, it feels clear that those of us who work through alternative institutions must have an affinity with these activists who did their work before socialism was codified into Marxist dogma. We agree with them: a better society does not automatically emerge out of the right historical conditions, but rather out of the right organizing. The orientation to growing alternative institutions tends to mean that we think of our projects as benefiting "everyone" rather than particular constituencies. And we do try to make social change through experiments (hopefully not doomed to fail) that pave the way for the new social Gospel, just as Marx claimed.

But some of his arguments still resonate as valid criticisms of many alternative institutions: the tendency to create communities that are disengaged from the rest of society and the dependence on winning favor from those who control wealth in order to fund their experiments.

The first explicit thinking about alternative institutions emerged out of the ferment of the nineteenth-century socialist movement. As part of the early reaction against the emergence of industrial capitalism, a huge variety of reform efforts and countermovements emerged in Europe and America. There was never a movement that called itself "utopian socialist" (again, the term came from Marx), but the name stuck because there were commonalities among a set of people who were trying to create living examples of a society free from oppression. The utopian socialists articulated many different versions of a free society, urged people to form autonomous communities that enacted those ideas, and tried in various ways to create their own versions of utopia.

For some of the most useful histories, see Carl Guarneri, *The Utopian Alternative: Fourierism in Nineteenth-Century America* (Ithaca, NY: Cornell University Press, 1991); Edward Spann, *Brotherly Tomorrows: Movements for a Cooperative Society in America, 1820–1920* (New York: Columbia University Press, 1989); Dolores Hayden, *Seven American Utopias: The Architecture of Communitarian Socialism, 1790–1975* (Cambridge: MIT Press, 1976); and the collection of essays in Donald Pitzer, ed., *America's Communal Utopias* (Chapel Hill: University of North Carolina Press, 1997).

ANARCHISM

The theory of alternative institutions owes its greatest intellectual debt to the social anarchists.

In general terms, anarchist thinkers can be thought of in two broad groups: individualist anarchists and social anarchists. Both share a critique of the state (meaning government) as coercive. However, social anarchism, emerging out of the broader nineteenth-century socialist movement, criticized not just the state but capitalism, religion, and eventually all forms of hierarchy.

Going back to the early conflicts with Marx (the anarchists were kicked out of the International in 1872), the anarchists developed a set of ideas that support alternative institutions as a strategy. To begin with, most social anarchists believed that radical ends should be achieved by democratic methods rather than forced on people through a seizure of state power. More fundamentally, they argued that mere "political revolution"—taking over the operation of the state—would not be sufficient to bring about freedom. Instead, "social revolution"—a change in all the forms of social relationships—was necessary. "Henceforth there can be no successful political or national revolution that does not translate as social revolution, and no national revolution that does not turn into universal revolution," said Mikhail Bakunin.[2] From this perspective, the anarchists tried to envision what a free society would look like in much greater detail than the Marxists did, and they eventually called for a broad set of institutional changes. The focus shifted from winning state power to restructuring life more broadly.

Unlike the Marxist tradition, which believed that one society would automatically create its successor, anarchists argued that many different paths could emerge from a particular historical moment. They saw history as contingent on human agency rather than predetermined by macro-historical forces. This made it possible to imagine that the kinds of cultures and institutions created in one period could have an influence on the ultimate trajectory of society rather than being just temporary stops on the way to a predetermined end.

Already by the 1860s and 1870s, the anarchists were developing detailed blueprints for how things would work "after the revolution" and approaching the concept that the means used by activists should "prefigure" the ends. Bakunin had expressed broad support for the cooperative movement as a training ground to "accustom the workers to organizing, conducting and running their affairs for themselves," arguing that, when the revolution comes, "every country and every locality should boast lots of cooperative associations which, if they are well-organized, . . . will carry society from its current state through to a state of equality and justice without unduly great traumas."[3] Gradually, this type of thinking evolved into more detailed proposals for new social institutions.[4]

Anarchism in this era exhibited a flowering of debates about how to organize society, and many activists tried to nurture a political culture that could remain open to multiple visions without degenerating into factionalism. Even the great divide between those who envisioned a society organized as a confederation of workplaces (industry-based) and those who advocated a federation of communes (place-based) could be incorporated into the broad movement.[5]

The idea of prefiguring the desired "end state" of a free society through activists' methods of social change themselves, ideally by building up pieces of the vision in the here and now, remains at the core of the alternative institutional strategy. This was, for the anarchists, the highest form of "direct action."

Fast-forwarding several decades to the most important American anarchist movement, we see similar ideas in the Industrial Workers of the World (often referred to as the "Wobblies"). This movement of workers, which was formed in the United States in 1905 and peaked in the 1920s, drew on the anarchist idea of prefiguration. The preamble of the IWW Constitution stated, "By organizing industrially we are forming the structure of the new society within the shell of the old." It's not that organizing workers is exactly an alternative institutional strategy, but we see in the IWW as in so many anarchist movements the idea of the present-day actions and organizations becoming the basis for a new society.

The classic anthology of anarchist writings is Daniel Guerin, ed., *No Gods No Masters: An Anthology of Anarchism, Book One* (San Francisco: AK Press, 1982). For useful overviews, see Peter Marshall, *Demanding the Impossible: A History of Anarchism* (Oakland, CA: PM Press, 2010), and Cindy Milstein, *Anarchism and Its Aspirations* (Oakland, CA: AK Press, 2010). On the IWW, see Melvyn Dubofsky, *We Shall Be All: A History of the Industrial Workers of the World,* abridged edition (Chicago: University of Illinois Press, 2000).

Finally, the theorist who most directly tried to argue for alternative institutions as the embodiment of anarchist political practice was Murray Bookchin. Bookchin draws on an eco-anarchist theoretical tradition that includes Kropotkin and Mumford, but his most original writing concerns the nature of politics in a free society. In essence, he proposes that public life be organized as a series of face-to-face assemblies where people come to debate issues and formulate decisions. The basic unit of self-governance for Bookchin must be small enough for the face-to-face deliberative democracy to work. In larger cities, neighborhood assemblies confederate together, and cities join into regional confederations. Each assembly sends a delegate to the larger coordinating body.

Bookchin's most relevant book, *The Rise of Urbanization and the Decline of Citizenship* (San Francisco: Sierra Club Books, 1987), traces the historical precedents for this model in the Athenian polis, the city-states of Renaissance Italy, the French Revolution and Paris Commune, the Spanish Civil War, the Swiss cantons, and the New England town meeting.

Under the name "libertarian municipalism," he called for activists to organize neighborhood assemblies, under whatever form of official government exists. Bookchin had an ambivalent relationship to anarchism, and toward the end of his life he decided that the word "communalism" better represented his thinking. Nevertheless, he was certainly the intellectual heir to a long anarchist tradition of thinking about alternative institutions. Start with his classic collection of essays, *Post-Scarcity Anarchism* (San Francisco: Ramparts Press, 1971). His study of the English, American, and French Revolutions is *The Third Revolution: Popular Movements in the Revolutionary Era, Volume I* (London: Cassell, 1996).

THE OLD LEFT AND THE NEW LEFT

Was there an Old Left theory of alternative institutions? Not exactly. Certainly the model of social change proposed by the Old Left—organize workers to ultimately take state power, either through revolution or through winning democratic elections—had little to do with alternative institutions. It was not a piecemeal theory of change, nor was it an approach that tried to prefigure the ends through the methods of activism.

On the other hand, many branches of the labor movement did experiment with co-ops, seeing in them the pathway to create the seeds of a new society in which workers worked for themselves. Over and over, the early labor movement traveled the path from going on strike to trying to go into business for itself. Three useful histories of this tradition are: John Curl, *For All the People: Uncovering the Hidden History of Cooperation, Cooperative Movements, and Communalism in America,* 2nd ed. (Oakland, CA: PM Press, 2009); Steve Leikin, *The Practical Utopians: American Workers and the Cooperative Movement in the Gilded Age* (Detroit: Wayne State University Press, 2005); and Edward K. Spann, *Brotherly Tomorrows: Movements for a Cooperative Society in America, 1820–1920* (New York: Columbia University Press, 1989).

The New Left (during roughly the 1960s) talked a lot about alternative institutions. Using the language of "dual power" and "parallel institutions," the New Left imagined that the movement could pioneer new styles of human relationships and new models for democratic practice, which could become more widespread and help transform the broader society.

In reality, the New Left was so brief and so quickly consumed by fighting the war in Vietnam that it did not get very far with its work on alternative institutions. My own judgment is that it loomed larger in theory than in practice. Wini Brienes, in her history *Community and Organization in the New Left, 1962–1968* (New Brunswick, NJ: Rutgers University Press, 1989), says, "Counterinstitutions (institutions outside the established order organized along radical egalitarian principles as a means of building the new society within the shell of the old) were one of the most important new left efforts."[6] She points specifically to the Economic Research and Action Project (ERAP), staffed by Students for a Democratic Society activists in 1964 and 1965. This was an effort by the white New Left to go into inner-city ghettos and organize poor people to take greater power within their communities. The ERAP organizers did some very promising work, and if it had lasted longer, could have shown the way for SDS members to have an impact beyond their own middle-class communities and campuses. But ERAP did not build alternative institutions, at least of the type this book has been discussing.

The food co-ops, alternative newspapers, free clinics, and other institutions of 1960s progressivism were seen by some radicals at the time as a distraction from real politics—a quest for self-fulfillment rather than an attempt to change the world. Nevertheless, it's these expressions of the counterculture that managed to touch large numbers of Americans and ultimately change the culture—the music we listen to, the way we eat, the way we raise children, and much else. It's only if we expand our scope of inquiry to include the counterculture as a core part of the New Left that alternative institutions begin to have a major role.

In sum, the New Left opened the doors to a bigger role for alternative institutions in two ways: first, by theorizing about new models of participatory democracy and parallel institutions as a way to change society, breaking with the older models of the Old Left; and second, through the counterculture, which actually built alternative institutions in spite of the fact that so many New Left intellectuals dismissed the significance of the counterculture.

Useful sources for learning more about the Old and New Lefts include George Katsiaficas, *The Imagination of the New Left: A Global Analysis of 1968* (Boston: South End Press, 1987); Greg Calvert and Carol Neiman, *A Disrupted History: The New Left and the New Capitalism* (New York: Random House, 1971); Richard Flacks, *Making History: The American Left and the American Mind* (New York: Columbia University Press, 1988); and Seymour Martin Lipset and Gary Marks, *It Didn't Happen Here: Why Socialism Failed in the United States* (New York: W. W. Norton and Company, 2000).

A history of the New Left that is attentive to the counterculture is Maurice Isserman and Michael Kazin, *America Divided: The Civil War of the 1960s,* 2nd edition (New York: Oxford University Press, 2004). In a completely different vein, Warren J. Belasco's *Appetite for Change: How the Counterculture Took on the Food Industry,* 2nd updated edition (Ithaca, NY: Cornell University Press, 2007), treats the cultural dimension of the 1960s New Left as the part of the movement that had the biggest impact and tells the story of the organic food movement in a way that recognizes the role of alternative institutions.

VOLUNTARY ASSOCIATIONS

Another source of thinking about alternative institutions is entirely outside the tradition of the Left, and here I'm talking about Alexis de Tocqueville, author of the founding text of political science in the United States, *Democracy in America,* first published in 1835. This French liberal from an aristocratic family traveled through the United States in 1831, ostensibly to research penal reform, but in fact to learn everything he could about the country that had helped inspire the French Revolution.

One of his strongest impressions of the United States was the tendency to create voluntary organizations rather than relying on the state:

> Americans of all ages, all conditions, and all dispositions constantly form associations. They have not only commercial and manufacturing companies, in which all take part, but associations of a thousand other kinds, religious, moral, serious, futile, general or restricted, enormous or diminutive. The Americans make associations to give entertainments, to found seminaries, to build inns, to construct churches, to diffuse books, to send missionaries to the antipodes; in this manner they found hospitals, prisons, and schools. If it is proposed to inculcate some truth or to foster some feeling by the encouragement of a great example, they form a society. Wherever at the head of some new undertaking you see the government in France, or a man of rank in England, in the United States you will be sure to find an association.[7]

There is a whole literature on civic participation that builds on de Tocqueville, arguing that participation in civic life is inherently good, because it builds the "habits of the heart" (phrases from de Tocqueville are like Shakespeare to political scientists) that support caring about more than just oneself.[8] Robert Putnam, author of *Bowling Alone: The Collapse and Revival of American Community* (New York: Simon and Schuster, 2000), argues that "social capital" is built through voluntary associations:

> Externally, voluntary associations, from churches and professional societies to Elks clubs and reading groups, allow individuals to express their interests and demands on government and to protect themselves from abuses of power by their political leaders. Political information flows through social networks, and in these networks public life is discussed. . . .
>
> Internally, associations and less formal networks of civic engagement instill in their members habits of cooperation and public-spiritedness, as well as the practical skills necessary to partake in public life.[9]

Building alternative institutions outside of government is as American as the New England town meeting. It is, in this sense, one of the founding ideas of our country. Clearly, it is not the influence of the utopian socialists that has caused America to be such a fertile ground for alternative institutions; it's the fact that they are in harmony with a long tradition of a weak state and a strong sense of civic capacity to bring people together in a community and solve practical problems. De Tocqueville helps us see that.

De Tocqueville has been used by people across the political spectrum. There is a fascinating right-wing appropriation of his thinking that promotes voluntary civic organizations as an alternative to government. Private land developers, private methods of dispute resolution, and homeowners' associations are all held up as examples of civic voluntarism in this American, anti-statist tradition. So are some institutions that are beloved by the Left, like land trusts and housing cooperatives. See, for example, the collection of essays in David Beito, Peter Gordon, and Alexander Tabarook, eds., *The Voluntary City: Choice, Community, and Civil Society* (Ann Arbor: University of Michigan Press with the Independent Institute, 2002).[10]

The most sophisticated version of this approach, which draws heavily on Ebenezer Howard and Henry George, argues that "the realistic choice in the provision of civic goods is not market versus government, but whether the governance that provides the collective goods is imposed or voluntary."[11] The conservative idealization of voluntary associations draws from the insight that making collective decisions that are binding on all members of a community is inherently coercive on the people who disagree with the majority's decision; it therefore seeks to maximize the areas of voluntary association as a counterforce to true public decisions that are binding in this sense.

The dream of voluntary communities is a staple of both the Right and the Left. In its extreme form, it involves a highly troubling attempt to escape from the messiness and complexity of dealing with people different from oneself. Let this be a warning to anyone interested in the alternative institutional strategy: the goal is not to escape into a homogenous world inhabited only by people who agree with one another. The only alternative institutions worthy of the name must be open to new people and oriented to engaging the broader society. Progressive strategy has to rely on more than self-generated, nongovernmental institutions. Of course we need governments of many kinds, and the progressive agenda will continue to make demands on various bodies of government to do things.

That said, it is true that sometimes, many times, government is the problem: it builds freeways through cities, subsidizes suburban sprawl, launches oil wars . . . and we could each build our list. Sometimes we really are trying to innovate outside of government—because government has been captured by other interests or simply for the honest reason that we haven't convinced a majority of people to see things our way.

Perhaps left and right can agree that the strategy of voluntary associations, including alternative institutions, is one acceptable response to the tyranny of the majority. It says, in essence, "We will create models of how we want to live and we will invite you to join us and copy us. We will not force you, however." This gentleness and respectfulness of the "otherness" of other people is what I hope people of many different persuasions will find appealing.

THE SOCIOLOGY OF INSTITUTIONAL CHANGE

I would recommend to the interested reader a series of writers who have explored the processes of social and institutional change at a larger scale.

The sociologist Goran Ahrne developed an "organizational theory of society," which proposes that we understand social systems in terms of organizations: "[S]ocial processes and social change must first of all be comprehended in their organizational settings and as the effects of the interaction among organizations in various constellations. The relations between individuals and society can best be understood in terms of organizational affiliation—membership, ownership, citizenship, kinship and employment."[12] See his *Agency and Organization: Toward an Organizational Theory of Society* (London: Sage Publications, 1990) and *Social Organizations: Interaction Inside, Outside and Between Organizations* (London: Sage Publications, 1994).

The fundamental sociological framework I have used in this book is the idea that society comprises institutions and that those institutions do not necessarily fit together neatly. The institutions date from different times and operate according to different principles. This is what makes it possible to change society by changing individual institutions. Several thinkers have been particularly helpful in formulating this approach. Manuel De Landa's *A Thousand Years of Nonlinear History* (New York: Zone Books, 1997) builds on the work of historian Fernand Braudel to describe how markets as economic institutions, with many recognizable features, go back to Roman times. The various institutions and practices that make up the modern capitalist economy emerged over hundreds of years and evolved through many different forms of political organization, religion, and family structure. This is a story in which institutions coexist with many other institutions dating from different times and places. For the source material, see Fernand Braudel, *Civilization & Capitalism 15th–18th Century, Volume I: The Structures of Everyday Life—The Limits of the Possible* (New York: Harper & Row, 1981). *Volume II: The Wheels of Commerce* (New York: Harper & Row, 1983) gives us the haunting image of capitalism being preserved "in a bell jar" from ancient times until it was unleashed upon the world.

Saskia Sassen's *Territory, Authority, Rights: From Medieval to Global Assemblages* (Princeton: Princeton University Press, 2006) covers more or less the same time period, but with a focus on the evolution of state institutions. Her thesis is that "critical capabilities built up in a given period can jump the tracks and get lodged into new organizational logics that may diverge sharply from the preceding ones."[13] She explains how the social system that exists at any one time is the result of many different institutions from many different origins being pieced together and repurposed.

Karen Orren and Stephen Skowronek in *The Search for American Political Development* (Cambridge: Cambridge University Press, 2004) develop a similar theory, specifically focused on American history. They write, "Institutions are products of the past processes, are adapted to past circumstances, and are therefore never in full accord with the requirements of the present."[14] I also draw heavily on the analytic framework proposed by Wolfgang Streeck and Kathleen Thelen in their "Introduction: Institutional Change in Advanced Political Economies," in Streeck and Thelen, eds., *Beyond Continuity: Institutional Change in Advanced Political Economies* (Oxford: Oxford University Press, 2005).

The science fiction writer Kim Stanley Robinson comes to the same conclusion in *2312* (New York: Hachette Group, 2012): "[I]n residual-emergent models, any given economic system or historical moment is an unstable mix of past and future systems. Capitalism therefore was the combination or battleground of its residual element, feudalism, and its emergent element—what?"[15]

For another useful perspective on institutional change, see Douglass C. North, *Institutions, Institutional Change and Economic Performance* (Cambridge: Cambridge University Press, 1990).

On the sociology of social change, I have drawn heavily on Piotr Sztompka, *Society in Action: The Theory of Social Becoming* (Chicago: University of Chicago Press, 1991) and *The Sociology of Social Change* (Oxford: Blackwell, 1993), as well as Anthony Giddens, *Central Problems in Social Theory: Action, Structure, and Contradiction in Social Analysis* (Berkeley: University of California Press, 1979).

On social movement theory, I found especially useful: Charles Tilly, *Social Movements, 1768–2004* (Boulder, CO: Paradigm Publishers, 2004); Elisabeth Clemens, "Organizational Form as Frame: Collective Identity and Political Strategy in the American Labor Movement, 1880–1920," in *Comparative Perspectives on Social Movements: Political Opportunities, Mobilizing Structures, and Cultural Framings,* eds. Doug McAdam, John D. McCarthy, and Mayer N. Zald (Cambridge: Cambridge University Press, 1996), 205–226; and in the same collection, Kim Voss, "The Collapse of a Social Movement: The Interplay of Mobilizing Structures,

Framing, and Political Opportunities in the Knights of Labor,"
227–258.

THE THEORY AND PRACTICE OF
ALTERNATIVE INSTITUTIONS

The writings from participants in alternative institutions are hard
to find, often scattered in self-published pamphlets. Each institution has its own story to tell, and I hope other scholars will spend
the time with them that they deserve. Some stories told in the
first person that I have learned from include: Michael Fullerton,
ed., *What Happened to the Berkeley Co-op? A Collection of Opinions*
(Berkeley, CA: Center for Cooperatives, 1992); Ann Ferguson,
"The Che-Lumumba School: Creating a Revolutionary Family Community" *Quest*, 5, no. 3 (1981): 13–26; and Craig Cox,
Storefront Revolution: Food Co-ops and the Counterculture (New
Brunswick, NJ: Rutgers University Press, 1994).

For excellent case studies by outside observers, see John Case
and Rosemary Taylor, eds., *Co-ops, Communes & Collectives: Experiments in Social Change in the 1960s and 1970s* (New York:
Pantheon Books, 1979). The first half of this collection includes
accounts of free clinics, alternative schools, alternative media, food
co-ops, urban communes, and legal collectives. The political theorist Jane Mansbridge profiles an anonymous participatory work-
place in part III of her magnificent *Beyond Adversary Democracy*
(Chicago: University of Chicago Press, 1980), 139–230. See also

Pauline P. Bart, "Seizing the Means of Reproduction: An Illegal Feminist Abortion Collective—How and Why It Worked," in *Qualitative Sociology* 10 (Winter 1987): 339–357; Paul Avrich, *The Modern School Movement: Anarchism and Education in the United States* (San Francisco: AK Press, 2005); Greg Pahl, *Power from the People: How to Organize, Finance and Launch Local Energy Projects* (White River Junction, VT: Chelsea Green Publishing, 2012); Peter Medoff and Holly Sklar, *Streets of Hope: The Rise and Fall of an Urban Neighborhood* (Boston: South End Press, 1994); and Janice Fine, *Worker Centers: Organizing Communities at the Edge of the Dream* (Ithaca, NY: ILR Press, 2006).

There is not a lot of theory about alternative institutions, but there is some. The most important writer I have learned from is Gar Alperovitz, a professor of political economy at the University of Maryland. His project, the Democracy Collaborative, tries to provide practical support for alternative institutions, while his writings provide a theoretical underpinning. See especially his *What Then Must We Do: Straight Talk about the Next American Revolution* (White River Junction, VT: Chelsea Green Publishing, 2013) and *America Beyond Capitalism: Reclaiming Our Wealth, Our Liberty, and Our Democracy* (Hoboken, NJ: John Wiley & Sons, 2005), along with Thad Williamson, David Imbroscio, and Gar Alperovitz, *Making a Place for Community: Local Democracy in a Global Era* (New York: Routledge, 2002). Alperovitz profiles dozens and dozens of alternative institutions that are operating in America today and tries to tease out of them a theory of broad-scale societal change, a process he describes as "evolutionary reconstruction."

Michael Shuman's book *Local Dollars, Local Sense* (White River Junction, VT: Chelsea Green Publishing, 2012) profiles many alternative institutions with a focus on financing and capital. Shuman himself is an important activist and advisor to many alternative institutions around the country.

A great essay on the history and theory of alternative institutions is David Moberg's "Experimenting with the Future: Alternative Institutions and American Socialism," in *Co-ops, Communes & Collectives: Experiments in Social Change in the 1960s and 1970s,* eds. John Case and Rosemary Taylor (New York: Pantheon Books, 1979).

I'm sure there is much more that I have yet to discover—and much more that has yet to be written. But these sources should provide the interested reader with a good starting place to delve deeper.

ACKNOWLEDGMENTS

I WOULD LIKE TO ACKNOWLEDGE SOME OF THE people who helped shape the ideas in this book, as teachers, comrades, and friends.

First of all, I would like to acknowledge the board of directors and staff of City CarShare—the people who actually built the experiment into a major institution that could demonstrate the success of alternative institutions as a model. I would also like to acknowledge SPUR for incubating this project and letting me spend so much time on it in the early days.

I want to thank some of the teachers I had who opened up the world of political thought to me—Hassan Rahmanian, who taught me organizational design; Frank Adler, who taught me critical theory; Todd Quinlan, who taught me sociology; and Murray Bookchin, who taught me that alternative institutions can be at the center of political practice. And I especially want to thank Michael Bader, who helped me learn how to say what's true in a way that people can hear it.

In terms of producing the book itself, my agent, Lisa Adams, and my editor, Emily Carleton, were indispensable. Erica Lee and Liza Hagan worked as my wonderful research assistants on several key chapters.

I want to thank some of the people who took their time to read parts of the manuscript and send comments to me, dramatically improving the final product: Allison Arieff, John Davis, Neal Gorenflo, Ben Grant, Rick Jacobus, Sharon Metcalf, Michael Monte, Matt Moore, Doug Smith, Randy Smith, Michael Tietz, James Tracy, Jennifer Warburg, and Eli Zigas.

My parents and my sister, Elena, all have worked to make the world better in their own ways. I am grateful to have come from a family of idealists.

My sons, Jonah and Orion, were on my mind constantly as I worked on this book. They are what matters the most to me. I can't wait to find out what they will do with their own ideas and dreams.

And finally, I have dedicated this book to Elizabeth Sullivan and Kate White, my oldest comrades, and the ones who started City CarShare with me. Thank you.

NOTES

CHAPTER 2

1. Michael LaFond, "Cooperative Transport: Berlin's Stattauto (Instead of Cars)," *RAIN Magazine* 14, no. 4 (Summer 1994), http://www .rainmagazine.com/archive/1994/cooperative-transport01252014.
2. Robert Cervero, Aaron Golub, and Brendan Nee, "San Francisco City CarShare: Longer-Term Travel-Demand and Car Ownership Impacts" (Berkeley: University of California at Berkeley Institute of Urban and Regional Development, May 2006), https://citycarshare.org /wp-content/uploads/2012/09/Cervero-Report-May-06.pdf.
3. The legal form of an alternative institution is far from a technical decision. On one hand, it must "fit" with the funding and organizing model, while on the other, it sets up the structure that largely determines how the values and workings of the organization will evolve over time. It's perfectly legal to not form a legal entity at all and just act as an unincorporated association. Probably the vast majority of alternative institutions start out this way, and many can remain so indefinitely. However, unincorporated associations cannot receive "charitable" donations that count as tax deductions, and unincorporated associations cannot protect board and staff members from liability. We were dealing with cars, and it was only a matter of time before someone got hurt. We needed to protect board and staff members from being sued.

For a long time, we referred to our project as a "car co-op" because this seemed like such a commonsense way to describe the idea. Co-operatives, technically known as "mutual benefit corporations," are a very common corporate form for alternative institutions. But as we learned more about the legal meaning of a co-op, we realized it didn't fit our needs for two reasons, one practical and one political. First, co-ops are not eligible for donations. We would not be able to receive grants from foundations or tax-deductible donations from individuals, so co-ops had the same drawback as unincorporated associations. Second, for our social change agenda, the big problem with being a cooperative was that we did not want to create an institution whose primary purpose was to benefit members, but instead one whose purpose was to benefit the city. Our analysis was that, over time, the non-profit form would better maximize the chances of the organization staying focused on the goal of improving city life. For a thoughtful study on the various ways to use the nonprofit legal form, see Peter Frumkin, *On Being Nonprofit: A Conceptual and Policy Primer* (Cambridge, MA: Harvard University Press, 2002).

4. There is enormous potential for charitable foundations in the United States to play a greater role in supporting alternative institutions. On the possible roles that community foundations can play, see Marjorie Kelly and Violeta Duncan, "A New Anchor Mission for a New Century: Community Foundations Deploying All Resources to Build Community Wealth," The Democracy Collaborative (November 2014), http://democracycollaborative.org/sites/clone.com munity-wealth.org/files/downloads/ANewAnchorMission_FINAL3 .pdf.

5. The term "early adopters" comes from *diffusion theory*, the study of how new ideas, products, or practices spread through a society. Everett Rogers, the leading theorist of diffusion theory, classified people into five categories based on their response to innovations: (1) innovators, (2) early adopters, (3) early majority, (4) late majority, and (5) laggards. We talked about diffusion theory a great deal in the carsharing project; it is a body of research with broad relevance to

the alternative institutional strategy. See Everett Rogers, *Diffusion of Innovation,* 5th ed. (New York: Free Press, 2003).

6. Randy Shaw, *The Activist's Handbook: Winning Social Change in the 21st Century,* 2nd ed. (Berkeley: University of California Press, 2013).

7. See Sarah Durham, *Brand Raising: How Nonprofits Raise Visibility and Money through Smart Communications* (San Francisco: Jossey-Bass, 2010).

8. See Keith Crane, Liisa Ecola, Scott Hassell, and Shanthi Nataraj, "Energy Services Analysis: An Alternative Approach for Identifying Opportunities to Reduce Emissions of Greenhouse Gases," RAND Corporation (2012), http://www.rand.org/content/dam/rand/pubs/technical_reports/2012/RAND_TR1170.pdf, especially chapter 4, "Personal Transportation: Sharing, Rather Than Owning, Vehicles," 19–40.

9. See the "Housing + Transportation Affordability Index," Center for Neighborhood Technology: http://htaindex.cnt.org.

10. Susan A. Shaheen, Mark A. Mallery, and Karla J. Kingsley, "Personal Vehicle Sharing Services in North America," *Research in Transportation Business & Management* (2012), doi:10.1016/j.rtbm.2012.04.005.

11. See Rachel Botsman and Roo Rogers, *What's Mine Is Yours: The Rise of Collaborative Consumption* (New York: HarperCollins, 2010); Lisa Gansky, *The Mesh: Why the Future of Business Is Sharing* (New York: Portfolio Penguin, 2010); and Gansky, "Policies for Shareable Cities: A Sharing Economy Policy Primer for Urban Leaders," Shareable and the Sustainable Economies Law Center, www.theselc.org/policies-for-shareable-cities.

CHAPTER 3

1. This telling of the American Revolution relies most heavily on R. R. Palmer, *The Age of Democratic Revolutions: A Political History of Europe and America, 1760–1800: The Challenge* (Princeton, NJ: Princeton University Press, 1959); Bernard Bailyn, *The Ideological Origins of the American Revolution,* enlarged ed. (Cambridge, MA:

Belknap, 1992 [1967]); and Murray Bookchin, *The Third Revolution: Popular Movements in the Revolutionary Era, Volume 1* (New York: Cassell, 1996). Two other books, which are more critical of the Jeffersonian strand of American thought and provide more useful and more sympathetic interpretations of the Founders' attempts to institutionalize the Revolution after the War of Independence, are Gordon S. Wood, *The Radicalism of the American Revolution* (New York: Random House, 1991), and Bruce Ackerman, *We the People, Volume I: Foundations* (Cambridge, MA: Harvard University Press, 1993).

2. Frank M. Bryan, *Real Democracy: The New England Town Meeting and How It Works* (Chicago: University of Chicago Press, 2004).

3. Hannah Arendt, *On Revolution* (New York: Viking Press, 1965), 164.

4. Murray Bookchin argues that the preparation for the Revolution went back much farther to the cultural autonomy of life in the colonies and even to the radicalism of the English Revolution in the previous century: "The less inflammatory character of the American Revolution can be attributed to the fact that American colonists had already been revolutionizing their society from the inception of colonization some two centuries earlier." In Bookchin, *The Third Revolution*, 145.

5. Ackerman, *We the People, Volume I: Foundations*, 165.

6. See the more detailed discussion in chapter 8 on mechanisms of institutional change, which contrasts *conversion* of an existing institution with *displacement* of existing institutions by newer ones.

7. Karen Orren and Stephen Skowronek, *The Search for American Political Development* (Cambridge: Cambridge University Press, 2004), 112.

8. Thomas Jefferson to Samuel Kercheval, 1816. ME 15:37—Quotations from the *Writings of Thomas Jefferson*, http://etext.virginia.edu/jefferson/quotations/jeff1050.htm.

9. The term "defensive localism" comes from Margaret Weir, "What Future Social Policy? Urban Poverty and Defensive Localism," *Dissent* 41, no. 3 (July 1994): 337–342. See Gerald Frug, *City Making: Building Communities without Walls* (Princeton, NJ: Princeton University Press, 1999), for a good overview of the legal history, and Jon

C. Teaford, *The Unheralded Triumph: City Government in America, 1870–1900* (Baltimore: Johns Hopkins University Press, 1984), for the major history of the urban reform movement in the nineteenth century.

10. For a good overview, see Amy Gutmann and Dennis F. Thompson, *Why Deliberative Democracy?* (Princeton, NJ: Princeton University Press, 2004); Benjamin Barber, *Strong Democracy: Participatory Politics for a New Age, Twentieth Anniversary Edition* (Berkeley: University of California Press, 2003); and Archon Fung, *Empowered Participation: Reinventing Urban Democracy* (Princeton, NJ: Princeton University Press, 2004).

11. For a different approach to solving the problems of collective decision-making in the real world, see Josh Lerner, *Making Democracy Fun: How Game Design Can Empower Citizens and Transform Politics* (Cambridge, MA: MIT Press, 2014).

12. Bill Bishop, *The Big Sort: Why the Clustering of Like-Minded America Is Tearing Us Apart* (New York: Houghton Mifflin Company, 2008).

13. James S. Fishkin, *When the People Speak: Deliberative Democracy and Public Consultation* (Oxford: Oxford University Press, 2009).

14. R. L. Lehr, W. Guild, D. L. Thomas, and B. G. Swezey, "Listening to Customers: How Deliberative Polling Helped Build 1,000 MW of New Renewable Energy Projects in Texas" (National Renewable Energy Laboratory (NREL), Golden, CO, June 2003), accessed from the Department of Energy's Office of Scientific and Technical Information website at www.osti.gov/bridge.

15. This is a point made convincingly by Frank Bryan in his study of the New England town meetings as they exist today in Vermont in *Real Democracy*. It is also the point made by Robert Putnam in *Bowling Alone: The Collapse and Revival of American Community* (New York: Simon and Schuster, 2000).

16. Broad-based civic organizations are working at every level to convene people to solve public problems. These voluntary attempts to create a public sphere to deliberate on the issues of the day are an important part of the public sphere today. I should note in the interests of full

disclosure that I have worked for more than a decade at one of the most venerable of these civic organizations, SPUR, an urban policy organization in the San Francisco Bay Area. Other examples range from the local, such as the City Club of Portland, to the national chapters of the League of Women Voters. America Speaks is a national organization devoted to running real-world deliberations (what it calls the "21st Century Town Hall") of all kinds. It often gets very large numbers of people involved, using techniques of community organizing and marketing to try for inclusiveness, but it does not rely on random sampling and cannot claim to achieve fair representation. See www.americaspeaks.org.

17. For this reason, I disagree with political theorists like Nancy Fraser who call for a move from "weak publics" to "strong publics." Fraser contrasts "weak publics, whose deliberative practice consists exclusively in opinion formation and does not also encompass decision-making," with strong publics that can "translate such 'opinion' into authoritative decisions." She calls for a proliferation of self-managed institutions that would make decisions with internal "mini" public spheres of a sort. I would argue that this progressive dream only makes sense within the narrow confines of voluntary associations and that it would be highly undemocratic for these "counter-publics" to lay claim to broader decision-making authority over units of government. See Nancy Fraser, "Rethinking the Public Sphere: A Contribution to the Critique of Actually Existing Democracy," in *Habermas and the Public Sphere,* ed. Craig Calhoun (Cambridge, MA: MIT Press, 1991), 109–142.

18. See Amy Lang, "But Is It for Real? The British Columbia Citizens' Assembly as a Model of State-Sponsored Citizen Empowerment," *Politics and Society* 35, no. 1 (2007): 35–70. The final report from this project can also be accessed here: http://www.citizensassembly .bc.ca/resources/final_report.pdf. See also the citizen jury process being used by Oregon to evaluate ballot measures in John Gastil and Katie Knobloch, "Evaluation Report to the Oregon State Legislature on the 2010 Oregon Citizens' Initiative Review," Healthy Democracy

Oregon, http://healthydemocracyoregon.org/sites/default/files/Oreg on%20Legislative%20Report%20on%20CIR%20v.3-1.pdf.

19. Indeed, Fishkin himself discusses what he calls the great "trilemma" of democracy: that of the values of the equality of all people; the value of deliberation as a way to make decisions; and the value of wide-spread participation in democracy. It is possible to create a system that optimizes for two but not three of these goals at the same time: "the fundamental principles of democracy do not add up to such a single, coherent ideal to be appropriated, step by step. . . . Achieving political equality and participation leads to a thin, plebiscitary democracy in which deliberation is undermined. Achieving political equality and deliberation leaves out mass participation. Achieving deliberation and participation can be achieved for those unequally motivated and in-terested, but violates political equality." In Fishkin, *When the People Speak*, 191.

20. See the Jefferson Center's work on citizen juries at http://jefferson -center.org.

CHAPTER 4

1. For examples of economic blueprints, which I reject but still find in-teresting, see: Patrick Devine, *Democracy and Planning: The Political Economy of a Self-Governing Society* (Cambridge, MA: Polity Press, 1988); John Roemer, *Equal Shares: Making Market Socialism Work* (London: Verso, 1996); Michael Albert, *Parecon* (London: Verso, 2003); and David Schweickart, *After Capitalism,* 2nd ed. (Lanham, MD: Rowman & Littlefield Publishers, 2011).

2. Ray Anderson with Robin White, *Business Lessons from a Radical In-dustrialist* (New York: St. Martin's Press, 2009), 13–14.

3. See the excellent collection of articles in *The Oxford Handbook of Cor-porate Social Responsibility,* eds. Andrew Crane, Abagail McWilliams, Jeremy Moon, and Donald S. Siegel (Oxford: Oxford University Press, 2008).

4. William McDonough and Michael Braungart, *The Upcycle: Beyond Sustainability—Designing for Abundance* (New York: North Point Press, 2013), 72.

5. See Juliet Schor, "Debating the Sharing Economy," Great Transition Initiative, http://greattransition.org/publication/debating-the-sharing-economy; and Lisa Gansky, "Policies for Shareable Cities: A Sharing Economy Policy Primer for Urban Leaders," Shareable and the Sustainable Economies Law Center, www.theselc.org/policies-for-shareable-cities.

6. The best history of this movement is John Curl, *For All People: Uncovering the Hidden History of Cooperation, Cooperative Movements, and Communalism in America,* 2nd ed. (Oakland: PM Press, 2009).

7. To learn more about Mondragon, see George Cheney, *Values at Work: Employee Participation Meets Market Pressure at Mondragon* (Ithaca: Cornell University Press, 1999); Greg MacLeod, *From Mondragon to America: Experiments in Community Economic Development* (Sydney, Nova Scotia: University of Cape Breton Press, 1997); Roy Morrison, *We Build the Road as We Travel* (Philadelphia: New Society Publishers, 1991); and William Foote Whyte and Kathleen King Whyte, *Making Mondragon: The Growth and Dynamics of the Mondragon Cooperative Complex* (Ithaca, NY: Cornell University Press and ILR Press, 1988).

8. For a good overview, see the website of the U.S. Federation of Worker Cooperatives, http://www.usworker.coop/about/what-is-a-worker-coop.

9. From the home page of the National Center for Employee Ownership, http://www.esop.org/.

10. Edward J. Carberry, "Employee Ownership and Shared Capitalism: Assessing the Experience, Research, and Policy Implications" in *Employee Ownership and Shared Capitalism: New Directions for Research,* ed. Edward Carberry (Champaign, IL: Labor and Employee Relations Association, 2011), 1–26. See also the publication from the Democracy Collaborative at the University of Maryland, *Building Wealth: A New Asset-Based Approach to Solving Social and Economic Problems* (Washington, DC: The Aspen Institute, 2005).

11. See Joseph R. Blasi, Richard B. Freeman, and Douglas L. Kruse, *The Citizen's Share: Putting Ownership Back into Democracy* (New Haven, CT: Yale University Press, 2013).

12. For a great survey of attempts to focus on the design of ownership structures to embed responsibility into the inner makeup of economic institutions, see Marjorie Kelly, *Owning Our Future: The Emerging Ownership Revolution* (San Francisco: Berrett-Koehler Publishers, 2012).

13. I would argue that the essential purpose of a corporation is to gather capital and spread risk among multiple investors—a sound purpose. The original English corporate charters were granted only by the crown—for example, the East India Company, chartered in 1600, or the Hudson Bay Company, in 1670. But in the early United States, every state could issue its own corporate charters. These corporate charters were granted for specific purposes and for a defined period of time—for example, to build a turnpike and then to pay back the investment by collecting tolls. State legislatures could revoke the charters of corporations that did not act in accordance with their defined public purpose.

    Starting in the 1830s, as states competed to attract investment, they began to issue charters with ever fewer restrictions. Many states allowed incorporation for general purposes, rather than specified business activities. And, perhaps most significantly, U.S. law evolved to protect investors from liability. Corporations could exist in perpetuity, as long as they made money; but if they lost money or were found to have violated the law, their investors would be shielded from risk beyond the possibility of losing their investment.

    A series of Supreme Court cases enabled this change. In *Trustees of Dartmouth College v. Woodward* (1819), the court ruled that the issuance of a corporate charter is a contract, which cannot be violated, meaning that state legislatures could no longer change the purpose of a corporation—or revoke the charter of a corporation no longer operating in the public interest. *Santa Clara County v. Southern Pacific Railroad Company* (1886) was interpreted to mean that corporations are legally persons and are therefore subject to the "equal protections" of the Fourteenth Amendment to the Constitution (the amendment intended to protect freed slaves). Following *Santa Clara*, corporations gained many additional rights, as the doctrine of corporate personhood was applied in new ways by the Supreme Court, up to and including the right to donate money to influence elections as a form of "free speech." All of this has weakened the ability of the democratic process to define the terms under which economic competition will take place.

On the history of corporate laws, see Kent Greenfield, *The Failure of Corporate Law: Fundamental Flaws and Progressive Possibilities* (Chicago: University of Chicago Press, 2006); and the work of the Program on Corporations, Law and Democracy including Richard L. Grossman and Frank T. Adams, "Taking Care of Business: Citizenship and the Charter of Incorporation," in *Defying Corporations, Defining Democracy*, ed. Dean Ritz (New York: Apex Press, 2001), 59–71.

14. Critics from the Left have derided worker co-ops as "collective capitalism" for more than a century. One of the classic critiques of the cooperative movement from the Left is contained in Beatrice and Sidney Webb's *The Consumer's Co-operative Movement* (London: Longmans, Green, 1921). See also J. K. Gibson-Graham's rejoinder to the Webbs in his discussion of Mondragon in *Postcapitalist Politics* (Minneapolis: University of Minnesota Press, 2006), 101–126.

15. It's worth noting that some "safe harbors" already exist, prior to an alternative institutional strategy, where government can regulate businesses without driving them away. Monopolies, such as water and energy utilities, have specific business territories and do not face competition within them. If required by their regulators, utilities can meet extremely high standards of social and environmental performance (for example, to use renewable energy) and can pass on these higher costs to their rate-payers. Another type of temporary safe harbor could be innovative businesses in newly emerging sectors of the economy. Industries tend to move through a "product cycle"

or "profit cycle" in which they begin with higher-value, higher-cost offerings, which require innovation. In the early stages, the leading companies may be selling something no one else sells, and they may be able to earn extraordinary profits for a period of time because they do not face any real competition. Such companies will typically be drawn to urban areas where they can rely on dense clusters of talent to innovate and continue to invent new things. Over time, industries tend to spread into new locations as more competitors emerge, and price becomes more important for the expanding customer base. At these later stages, production typically moves out to lower-cost locations. But in earlier stages, these firms are often perfectly capable of withstanding high wages and careful environmental standards. See Ann Markusen, *Profit Cycles, Oligopoly, and Regional Development* (Boston: MIT Press, 1985).

16. See "A Brief History of Credit Unions," National Credit Union Administration, http://www.ncua.gov/about/history/Pages/CUHistory .aspx. For asset size, see the "2010 Year End Statistics for Federally Insured Credit Unions," National Credit Union Administration, http:// www.ncua.gov/Legal/Documents/Reports/CUStat2010.pdf, 12.

17. A good overview is the "FDIC Community Banking Study," FDIC (December 2012), http://www.fdic.gov/regulations/resources/cbi/re port/cbi-full.pdf.

18. The 2012 Annual Report from the U.S. Department of the Treasury on CDFIs contains key statistics on this set of institutions: http://cd fifund.gov/impact_we_make/research/FY%202012%20CDFI%20 Fund%20Year%20in%20Review.pdf.

19. "Key Facts on U.S. Foundations," Foundation Center, http://foun dationcenter.org/gainknowledge/research/keyfacts2013/pdfs/Key _Facts_on_US_Foundations.pdf.

20. See the post by Judith Rodin, president of the Rockefeller Foundation, on the potential of impact investing, "Innovations in Finance for Social Impact," Rockefeller Foundation (September 5, 2014), http:// www.rockefellerfoundation.org/blog/innovations-finance-social -impact.

21. "Report on Sustainable and Responsible Investing Trends in the United States, 2012," The Forum for Sustainable and Responsible Investment, http://www.ussif.org/files/Publications/12_Trends_Exec_Summary.pdf, 11.

22. Paul Hawken, "Socially Responsible Investing: How the SRI Industry Has Failed to Respond to People Who Want to Invest with Conscience and What Can Be Done about It," Natural Capital (October 2004), http://www.naturalcapital.org/docs/SRI%20Report%2010-04_word.pdf. See also Eric Becker and Patrick McVeigh, "Social Funds in the United States: Their History, Financial Performance, and Social Impacts," in *Working Capital: The Power of Labor's Pensions,* eds. Archon Fung, Tessa Hebb, and Joel Rogers (Ithaca, NY: Cornell University Press, 2001), 44–66.

23. Dean Baker and Archon Fung, "Collateral Damage: Do Pension Fund Investments Hurt Workers?" in *Working Capital,* eds. Fung, Hebb, and Rogers, 13–43. For a more theoretical and historical treatment, see Robin Blackburn, *Banking on Death, or, Investing in Life: The History and Future of Pensions* (London: Verso, 2002).

24. This section draws heavily on the work of Michael Shuman. See *Local Dollars, Local Sense* (White River Junction, VT: Chelsea Green, 2012). Many smaller experiments illustrate the potential of this strategy:

    • The National Cooperative Bank, with $1.6 billion in assets, provides investment for co-ops of all kinds to form or expand. And there are smaller, geographically focused funds that do the same thing, like the Cooperative Fund of New England and the Northcountry Cooperative Development Fund in Minneapolis. (See www.ncb.coop; www.cooperativefund.org; www.ncdf.coop.)

    • The La Montañita Fund makes microloans to food-related businesses within the "foodshed" of its cooperative grocery stores in New Mexico. (See lamontanita.coop/fund.)

    • Co-op Power is a member-owned cooperative that is actually a network of locally owned energy co-ops in New England. It provides technical support and funding to Local Organizing Councils, each of which owns and runs its own renewable energy projects. (See www.cooppower.coop.)

- Local currencies like Ithaca Hours in upstate New York and BerkShares in western Massachusetts try to keep money circulating within communities and make more visible the distinction between the localized and the globalized economy. (See www.ithacahours.org and www.berkshares.org.)
- The Union Labor Life Insurance Company, formed in the 1920s as a life insurance company for unions, has established a private equity fund devoted to saving union jobs and investing in unionized companies. The Builders Fixed Income Mutual Fund uses labor pensions to invest in union construction projects around the country. (Many other attempts to harness the power of labor pension funds are profiled in Michael Calabrese, "Building on Success: Labor-Friendly Investment Vehicles and the Power of Private Equity," in *Working Capital*, eds. Fung, Hebb, and Rogers, 93–127.) And Heartland Capital Strategies, set up by the United Steelworkers of America, is a network of investment funds that specializes in using workers' pension funds to create good jobs. (Thomas Croft, "Helping Workers' Capital Work Harder: A Report on Global Economically Targeted Investments" (Heartland Capital Strategies, 2009), www.heartlandnetwork.org/images/pdfs/heartland%20cwc%20global%20eti%20report%202009.pdf.)

25. For more on the "Cleveland Model," see Steve Dubb, Sarah McKinley, and Ted Howard, "The Anchor Dashboard: Aligning Institutional Practice to Meet Low-Income Community Needs," The Democracy Collaborative (August 2013), http://community-wealth.org/sites/clone.community-wealth.org/files/downloads/AnchorDashboard CompositeFinal.pdf; and by the same authors, "Achieving the Anchor Promise: Improving Outcomes for Low-Income Children, Families and Communities," The Democracy Collaborative (August 2013),

http://community-wealth.org/sites/clone.community-wealth.org
/files/downloads/Achieving%20the%20Anchor%20Promise_com
posite_FINAL.pdf. See also Tracey Ross, "Eds, Meds and the Feds:
How the Federal Government Can Foster the Role of Anchor Institutions in Community Revitalization," Center for American Progress
(October 2014), http://www.scribd.com/doc/240183541/Eds-Meds
-and-the-Feds-How-the-Federal-Government-Can-Foster-the-Role
-of-Anchor-Institutions-in-Community-Revitalization.

26. There is an enormous literature on situations in which markets do
    not work well, often grouped under the category "market failure."
    Markets tend not to work well when large externalities are present
    (so the nominal prices are incorrect); when there are monopolistic or
    oligopolistic sellers; when both parties in a transaction do not have
    adequate information; when the good being exchanged is a public
    good (or common good), meaning people cannot be excluded from
    it; and other reasons, all of which are explained in any standard eco-
    nomics textbook. But much of the debate hinges on the question of
    how common these failures are. See, for example, John Cassidy, *How
    Markets Fail: The Logic of Economic Calamities* (New York: Farrar,
    Straus and Giroux, 2009), and Harry W. Richardson and Peter Gor-
    don, "Market Planning Oxymoron or Common Sense?" *Journal of
    the American Planning Association,* 59, no. 3 (1993): 347–352, doi:
    10.1080/01944369308975885.

27. See Elinor Ostrom, *Governing the Commons: The Evolution of Institu-
    tions for Collective Action* (New York: Cambridge University Press,
    1990); and Elinor Ostrom, *Understanding Institutional Diversity*
    (Princeton, NJ: Princeton University Press, 2005).

28. Garrett Hardin, "The Tragedy of the Commons," *Science,* 162 (1968):
    1243–1248.

29. Ostrom, *Governing the Commons,* 90.

30. Katie L. Roeger, Amy S. Blackwood, and Sarah L. Pettijohn, *The
    Nonprofit Almanac 2012* (Washington, DC: Urban Institute Press,
    2012).

31. Peter Barnes, *Capitalism 3.0: A Guide to Reclaiming the Commons* (San Francisco: Berrett-Koehler Publishers, 2006), 5.

32. Peter Barnes, *Who Owns the Sky: Our Common Assets and the Future of Capitalism* (Washington, DC: Island Press, 2001).

33. See Jon A. Souder and Sally K. Fairfax, "In Lands We Trusted: State Trust Lands as an Alternative Theory of Public Ownership," in *Property and Values: Alternatives to Private and Public Ownership,* eds. Charles Geisler and Gail Daneker (Washington, DC: Island Press, 2000), 87–119.

34. State trust lands encompass 145 million acres as of this writing, compared to 47 million acres under ownership by nonprofit land trusts. See the 2010 National Land Trust Census at www.landtrustalliance.org/land-trusts/land-trust-census.

CHAPTER 5

1. Some context for the Burlington story can be found in James M. Libby Jr. and Darby Bradley, "Vermont Housing and Conservation Board: A Conspiracy of Good Will among Land Trusts and Housing Trusts," in *Property and Values: Alternatives to Private and Public Ownership,* eds. Charles Geisler and Gail Daneker (Washington, DC: Island Press, 2000), 259–281.

2. In economic theory, the concept here is one of economic rent, which was defined by early political economists like David Ricardo and Adam Smith as payments made to someone who controls access to a factor of production—land, licenses, patents, and so on. Economic rents function more like bribes to be able to undertake economic activity rather than payments for actual contributions to economic activity. Adam Smith wrote in *The Wealth of Nations,* "As soon as the land of any country has all become private property, the landlords, like all other men, love to reap where they never sowed, and demand a rent even for its natural produce. The wood of the forest, the grass of the field, and all the natural fruits of the earth, which, when land

was in common, cost the labourer only the trouble of gathering them, come, even to him, to have an additional price fixed upon them. He must then pay for the licence to gather them; and must give up to the landlord a portion of what his labour either collects or produces. This portion, or, what comes to the same thing, the price of this portion, constitutes the rent of land." In Smith, *Wealth of Nations* (New York: Prometheus Books, 1991 [1776]), 52–53.

3. For some of the theory behind land trusts, see David Abromowitz, "An Essay on Community Land Trusts: Toward Permanently Affordable Housing," in *Property and Values,* eds. Geisler and Daneker, 213–231; and Chuck Matthei, "U.S. Land Reform Movements: The Theory behind the Practice," *Social Policy* (Spring 1992): 36–45.

4. Henry George, *Progress and Poverty: An Inquiry into the Cause of Industrial Depressions and of Increase of Want with Increase of Wealth* (Cambridge: Cambridge University Press, 2009 [1879]).

5. Richard Brewer, *Conservancy: The Land Trust Movement in America* (Hanover, NH: Dartmouth College Press, 2003).

6. This history of the community land trust movement is drawn from John Davis, "Origins and Evolution of the Community Land Trust in the United States," in John Davis, ed., *The Community Land Trust Reader* (Boston: Lincoln Institute of Land Policy, 2010), 3–47.

7. See the National CLT Network, www.cltnetwork.org.

8. See also the Urban Land Conservancy in Denver, http://www.urban landc.org, and the Philadelphia Land Bank, http://www.phillyland bank.org. The Dudley Street Neighborhood Initiative (DSNI) in Boston is an interesting example. DSNI is located in inner-city Boston, on turf that straddles two neighborhoods (Roxbury and Dorchester) that had been suffering from chronic disinvestment and property abandonment. What began as a collaborative effort among churches, social service agencies, and local businesses evolved into a permanent organization in 1984, one that has had extraordinary success in fostering community rebirth.

Initially, DSNI focused on basic neighborhood cleanup—removing trash from abandoned lots, towing abandoned cars, and so on.

With an emphasis on eliminating empty lots, the organization developed an agenda of building new housing and commercial space. In 1989, it created a subsidiary community land trust called Dudley Neighbors (DNI), and in 1990 it won a grant of authority from the City of Boston to undertake eminent domain on the empty lots. Under the rallying cry, "Take a stand, own the land," DNI developed more than four hundred of the thirteen hundred originally identified abandoned parcels into homes, schools, businesses, and parks. The organization also runs community centers, greenhouses, youth educational programs, and job training programs.

On the Dudley Street Neighborhood Initiative, see Peter Medoff and Holly Sklar, *Streets of Hope: The Rise and Fall of an Urban Neighborhood* (Boston: South End Press, 1994). For broader context, see also Robert Halpern, *Rebuilding the Inner City: A History of Neighborhood Initiatives to Address Poverty in the United States* (New York: Columbia University Press, 1995).

9. In 1992, an amendment to the National Affordable Housing Act enabled CLTs to receive designation as Community Housing Development Organizations and thus receive federal funding for affordable housing. City governments can support new CLTs by providing start-up funding or even transferring surplus public property to land trusts. It remains an open question whether the traditional governance model, which includes both community and resident participation, will persist when and if CLTs are embraced by local governments. See John Davis and Rick Jacobus, *The City-CLT Partnership: Municipal Support for Community Land Trusts* (Boston: Lincoln Institute of Land Policy, 2008), www.lincolninst.edu /pubs/1395_The-City-CLT-Partnership.

10. Kevin Lynch, *Good City Form* (Boston: MIT Press, 1981), 294–295.

11. The book was originally published under a different title, *Tomorrow: A Peaceful Path to Reform,* in 1898, and republished in 1902 as *Garden Cities of To-Morrow.* This section draws heavily on four works about Howard: Peter Hall and Colin Ward, *Sociable Cities: The Legacy of Ebenezer Howard* (Chichester, West Sussex: John Wiley and Sons,

1998); Stephen V. Ward, "Ebenezer Howard: His Life and Times," in *From Garden City to Green City: The Legacy of Ebenezer Howard,* eds. Kermit Parsons and David Schuyler (Baltimore, MD: Johns Hopkins University Press, 2002), 14–37; Robert Fishman, *Urban Utopias in the Twentieth Century: Ebenezer Howard, Frank Lloyd Wright, Le Corbusier* (Boston: MIT Press, 1982); and "The City in the Garden" in Peter Hall, *Cities of Tomorrow: An Intellectual History of Urban Planning and Design in the Twentieth Century* (Oxford: Blackwell, 1988), 86–135. Howard's ideas came from an idiosyncratic mix of influences, including the "nationalist movement" inspired by Edward Bellamy and the social anarchism of Petr Kropotkin, whom Howard might have known in London. Howard moved to Nebraska to homestead in 1871, but after deciding that farming was not for him, he ended up in Chicago before returning to London in 1876.

12. Quoted in Hall and Ward, *Sociable Cities,* 23.

13. See Dennis Hardy's history of the TCPA, "Tomorrow and Tomorrow: The TCPA's First Hundred Years, and the Next," Town and Country Planning Association, www.tcpa.org.uk/data/files/18991999.pdf.

14. Hall and Ward's *Sociable Cities* contains an excellent history and interpretation of the garden city idea in British town planning, along with the authors' proposals for the future.

15. See Clarence Stein, *New Towns for America* (Boston: MIT Press, 1957).

16. See Kermit Parsons, "British and American Community Design: Clarence Stein's Manhattan Transfer, 1924–1974," in *From Garden City to Green City,* eds. Parsons and Schuyler, 131–158; and Eugenie L. Birch, "Five Generations of the Garden City: Tracing Howard's Legacy in Twentieth-Century Residential Planning" in *From Garden City to Green City,* eds. Parsons and Schuyler, 171–200.

17. Andres Duany, Elizabeth Plater-Zyberk, and Jeff Speck, *Suburban Nation: The Rise of Sprawl and the Decline of the American Dream* (New York: North Point Press, 2000); and Peter Calthorpe, *Urbanism in the Age of Climate Change* (Washington, DC: Island Press, 2011). A good history of New Urbanism as a social movement can be

found in Emily Tallen, *New Urbanism and American Planning: The Conflict of Cultures* (New York: Routledge, 2005).

18. As Peter Calthorpe, one of the movement's key designers, argues, "This is the crux of the problem: Planned communities must be judged in contrast to suburban sprawl, not idealized urban environments. For the U.S., new towns are relevant because, though unconsciously, we continue to build them. A housing subdivision, shopping mall, and industrial park with a freeway network is an unmade new town." From Calthorpe, "A Short History of Twentieth Century New Towns," in *Sustainable Communities: A New Design Synthesis for Cities, Suburbs, and Towns,* eds. Sim Van der Ryn and Peter Calthorpe (San Francisco: Sierra Club Books, 1986), 234.

19. John Winthrop, "A Model of Christian Charity," 1630, http://religiousfreedom.lib.virginia.edu/sacred/charity.html.

20. Quoted in Dolores Hayden, *Seven American Utopias: The Architecture of Communitarian Socialism, 1790–1975* (Boston: MIT Press, 1976), 9.

21. Dolores Hayden explains how communes of the eighteenth and nineteenth centuries were supposed to cause more widespread change—a distillation of the theory of alternative institutions in general: "If the model community plan represented an inventor's theory, the settlement itself represented a working prototype, a 'patent office model' which proved that the theory would work in practice. A pioneering spirit, coping and practical, sustained experimental communities in the short run. In the long run, as an extension of the 'invention' simile, the successful prototype was expected to inspire national demand." Quoted in Hayden, *Seven American Utopias,* 20.

22. See Priscilla J. Brewer, "The Shakers of Mother Ann Lee," in *America's Communal Utopias,* ed. Donald Pitzer (Chapel Hill: University of North Carolina Press, 1997), 37–56; and Hayden, *Seven American Utopias,* 64–103.

23. See Donald Pitzer, "The New Moral World of Robert Owen and New Harmony" in Pitzer, *America's Communal Utopias,* 88–134.

24. Carl Guarneri, *The Utopian Alternative: Fourierism in Nineteenth-Century America* (Ithaca: Cornell University Press, 1991), 7.

25. "Koinonia History," Koinonia Partners, http://www.koinoniapart ners.org/History/index.html.

26. Robert Hine, "California's Socialist Utopias" in Pitzer, *America's Communal Utopias,* 419–431. On Llano del Rio, see Hayden, *Seven American Utopias,* 288–317.

27. One estimate says that the number of rural communes peaked in 1970 at 3,500, with about one thousand of them still in existence in 1978. See David Moberg, "Experimenting with the Future: Alternative Institutions and American Socialism," in *Co-ops, Communes & Collectives: Experiments in Social Change in the 1960s and 1970s,* eds. John Case and Rosemary Taylor (New York: Pantheon Books, 1979), 285.

28. Albert Bates and Timothy Miller, "The Evolution of Hippie Communal Spirituality: The Farm and Other Hippies Who Didn't Give Up," in *America's Alternative Religions,* ed. Timothy Miller (Albany: State University Press of New York, 1995), 371–378.

29. Guarneri, *The Utopian Alternative,* 108.

30. The story of the layering of components of the city over the ages is told well by Spiro Kostoff in *The City Shaped: Urban Patterns and Meanings throughout History* (New York: Bulfinch Press, 1991). The best history of the successive generations of city building through the lens of the value systems of city planners is Peter Hall, *Cities of Tomorrow: An Intellectual History of Urban Planning and Design in the Twentieth Century* (Oxford: Blackwell, 1988). On the successive eras of American park design, see Galen Cranz, *The Politics of Park Design: A History of Urban Parks in America* (Boston: MIT Press, 1989).

31. Robert Fishman, the leading historian of American planning, identifies the real engine of change in the physical landscape of our country as "the urban conversation" between civic groups, newspapers, business interests, and social movements. In a country with a weak centralized government and a distrust of government regulation, this is how change happens: "Although the specifics of the planning problems differ, the basic themes of the urban conversation are always

the same: how to justify public action to a society that is deeply individualistic; how to support long-term investment strategies in a society built on short-term gains; how to justify the taxation of private profit for the common resources and the common good. This urban conversation—rather than any centralized government—has been the ultimate source of the authority that generated the outputting of investment in roads, bridges, waterworks, schools, libraries, and other public facilities." Quoted in Robert Fishman, "The American Planning Tradition: An Introduction and Interpretation," in *The American Planning Tradition: Culture and Policy,* ed. Robert Fishman (Washington, DC: Woodrow Wilson Center Press, 2000), 5.

32. CDCs grew out of the War on Poverty in the 1960s. One of the first was Brooklyn's Bedford-Stuyvesant Urban Development Corporation, formed in 1964. By the early 1970s, they were established in virtually every major city in the country. Started with early funding from the Ford Foundation, CDCs were soon funded by the federal government via the Office of Economic Opportunity (later renamed the Community Services Administration). As the tide of New Left progressivism in America receded, direct federal funding dried up, but legislation like the Community Reinvestment Act of 1977 and the 1986 Low-Income Housing Tax Credit ensured that banks and corporations would continue to invest heavily in CDCs.

The original idea behind CDCs was to help poor neighborhoods take care of themselves. They offered support for new businesses of all kinds, along with job training, affordable housing, and other direct services. Over the decades, the focus of most CDCs has narrowed to one service in particular: affordable housing. But the ethos of more broad-based community regeneration remains intact for some of them. For an overview of the history of CDCs, see Neal Pierce and Carol Steinbach, *Corrective Capitalism: The Rise of America's Community Development Corporations* (New York: Ford Foundation, 1987); and Mitchell Sviridoff, ed., *The Trials and Errors That Shaped the Modern Community Development Corporation* (New York: New School University, Community Development Research Center, 2004). For one of the best critics of the CDC model, see Randy Stoecker, who argues that the exclusive focus on housing provision is robbing the movement of its broader community empowerment potential in "The CDC Model of Urban Redevelopment: A Critique and an Alternative," *Journal of Urban Affairs* 19 (1997): 1–22. Joyce Mandell critiques Stoecker's critique in "CDCs and the Myth of the Organizing-Development Dialectic," *COMM-ORG: The On-Line Conference on Community Organizing*, 15 (2009), http://comm-org.wisc .edu/papers2009/mandell.htm.

33. The Center for Neighborhood Technology in Chicago created a carsharing organization and an energy utility. Forterra in Seattle (formerly the Cascade Land Conservancy) created a "transfer of development rights" mechanism in which urban developers purchase development rights from farmers at the urban fringe in order to preserve open space. T.R.U.S.T. in South Los Angeles created a land trust and a program to develop affordable cottages in the backyards of single-family homes. Place-based civic organizations have incubated and otherwise helped launch affordable housing developments, worker co-ops, community banks, energy co-ops, business improvement districts, and other nongovernmental institutions—in addition to being a major source of innovations within government itself.

34. To learn more about the reformist agenda within city planning, see: Christopher Alexander, Sara Ishikawa, and Murray Silverstein, *A Pattern Language* (Oxford: Oxford University Press, 1977); Ellen Dunham-Jones and June Williamson, *Retrofitting Suburbia: Urban Design Solutions for Retrofitting Suburbs* (Hoboken, NJ: John Wiley and Sons, 2009); Alex Steffen, ed., *Worldchanging: A User's Guide for the 21st Century* (New York: Abrams, 2006); Peter Newman and Jeffrey Kenworthy, *Sustainability and Cities: Overcoming Automobile Dependence* (Washington, DC: Island Press, 1999); and Peter Calthorpe and William Fulton, *The Regional City: Planning for the End of Sprawl* (Washington, DC: Island Press, 2001).

35. Planning philosophies are often directly tied to political philosophies. Broadacre City, Frank Lloyd Wright's utopian plan, expresses a belief

in Jeffersonian ideals of universal property ownership and economic independence and in that sense can be understood as a symbolic, physical interpretation of American liberalism. The Radiant City, Le Corbusier's ideal city proposal, expresses a belief in central planning by experts and control over the land and can be understood as an attempt to create a physical expression of early-twentieth-century socialist ideals. In the realm of cities, it's easy to see the specific forms but sometimes hard to perceive that they are the result of political values. For more on Frank Lloyd Wright and Le Corbusier, in addition to Ebenezer Howard, see Fishman, *Urban Utopias in the Twentieth Century.*

CHAPTER 6

1. Catherine Bauer, *Modern Housing* (Boston: Houghton Mifflin Company, 1934), xvi.
2. Quoted in Gail Radford, *Modern Housing for America: Policy Struggles in the New Deal Era* (Chicago: University of Chicago Press, 1996), 88.
3. Radford, *Modern Housing,* 89.
4. Radford, *Modern Housing,* 93, 100.
5. Linda Gordon tells this story better than anyone. See her anthology, *Women, the State, and Welfare* (Madison: University of Wisconsin Press, 1990).
6. Radford, *Modern Housing,* 108.
7. Radford, *Modern Housing,* 189.
8. The classic history of suburbia in relationship to federal policy is Kenneth T. Jackson, *Crabgrass Frontier: The Suburbanization of the United States* (New York: Oxford University Press, 1985). See especially chapter 11, "Federal Subsidy and the Suburban Dream: How Washington Changed the American Housing Market," and chapter 12, "The Cost of Good Intentions: The Ghettoization of Public Housing in the United States."
9. John H. Mollenkopf, *The Contested City* (Princeton, NJ: Princeton University Press, 1983), 69.

10. Radford, *Modern Housing*, 190.

11. Radford, *Modern Housing*, 200.

12. Mollenkopf, *The Contested City*, 77–81.

13. On the history of the modern affordable housing movement and the emergence of nonprofit developers as the critical institution, see David J. Erickson, *The Housing Policy Revolution: Networks and Neighborhoods* (Washington, DC: The Urban Institute Press, 2009).

14. George Katsiaficas, *The Imagination of the New Left: A Global Analysis of 1968* (Boston: South End Press, 1987), 194–197.

15. David Moberg, "Experimenting with the Future: Alternative Institutions and American Socialism," in *Co-ops, Communes & Collectives: Experiments in Social Change in the 1960s and 1970s*, eds. John Case and Rosemary Taylor (New York: Pantheon Books, 1979), 282.

16. Chapter 8 explores the mechanisms of institutional change in more detail, contrasting *displacement*, when a new institution replaces or pushes aside an existing institution; *conversion*, when an existing institution is repurposed; *layering*, when a new institution is added onto a set of preexisting institutions; *drift*, when an institution fails to change in spite of changed external circumstances that would require adaptation; and *exhaustion*, when an institution loses its relevance and eventually disappears.

17. There has been a lively debate about how to think about "experiments" for a long time. I stumbled upon a reference from 1933, when a group of young anarchists calling themselves the Vanguard Group criticized the idea of forming "colonies" where radicals would withdraw from mainstream society to demonstrate new possibilities for community: "There is too much superstitious awe about the word experiment. An experiment . . . cannot be indefinitely pursued without taking stock of all the previous failures without introducing a certain variant in each and every attempt. The history of such attempts, for nearly a century, to solve the social problem via colony building has clearly shown the futility of such a method. To keep repeating the same attempts without an intelligent appraisal of all the numerous failures in the past is not to uphold the right to experiment, but to

insist upon one's right to escape from the hard facts of social struggle into the world of wishful belief." Cited in Andrew Cornell, *Oppose and Propose: Lessons from Movement for New Society* (Oakland, CA: AK Press/Institute for Anarchist Studies, 2011), 57–58.

CHAPTER 7

1. There is a vast literature on social movement theory. One of my favorite sources is Charles Tilly, *Social Movements, 1768–2004* (Boulder, CO: Paradigm Publishers, 2004). See also Gerald F. Davis, Doug McAdam, W. Richard Scott, and Mayer N. Zald, *Social Movements and Organization Theory* (Cambridge: Cambridge University Press, 2005). For an insightful discussion of the reasons for the weakness of electoral strategies for the Left in the United States, see Seymour Martin Lipset and Gary Marks, *It Didn't Happen Here: Why Socialism Failed in the United States* (New York: W. W. Norton and Company, 2000). For a practical guide to the skills of organizing, see Randy Shaw, *The Activist's Handbook: Winning Social Change in the 21st Century*, 2nd ed. (Berkeley: University of California Press, 2013).

2. This story is based on Elizabeth Sanders, *Roots of Reform: Farmers, Workers, and the American State, 1877–1917* (Chicago: University of Chicago Press, 1999); and Lawrence Goodwyn, *The Populist Moment: A Short History of the Agrarian Revolt in America* (New York: Oxford University Press, 1978). The Populist Moment is a shortened version of Goodwyn's longer treatment from two years earlier, *Democratic Promise: The Populist Moment in America* (Oxford: Oxford University Press, 1976). Goodwyn has been criticized by other historians for not paying attention to many other strands of the Populist movement, which in fact consisted of a large number of quite divergent movements in different parts of the country over a number of years. I think it's best to read Goodwyn not as a historian of the entire Populist movement, but as a historian of a particular set of institutions and organizers that are important as precedents for the alternative institutional strategy. For a more complete treatment of the

Populist movement, I have relied most heavily on Robert C. McMath Jr., *American Populism: A Social History, 1877–1898* (New York: Hill and Wang, 1993).

3. Goodwyn, *The Populist Moment,* 47.

4. Kim Voss, "The Collapse of a Social Movement: The Interplay of Mobilizing Structures, Framing, and Political Opportunities in the Knights of Labor," in *Comparative Perspectives on Social Movements,* eds. Doug McAdam, John D. McCarthy, and Mayer N. Zald (Cambridge: Cambridge University Press, 1996), 227–258.

5. It is hard for most of us today to understand the debates over monetary policy that occupied so much Populist energy in the second half of the nineteenth century, but the issues were very real. After the Civil War, the federal government contracted the amount of money in circulation, making money scarcer and thus driving up its purchasing power and worth over time. Industrial and financial leaders argued that this policy was necessary for economic development: unless money retained its worth, people with money would not invest in risky industrial ventures. Farmers wanted an expanding supply of money. In part, this was because there was not enough currency in circulation (especially in the South). More importantly, in an inflationary environment, debts are repaid in money that is worth less than when it was borrowed, while in a deflationary environment, debts are repaid in money that is worth more than when it was borrowed.

6. Goodwyn, *The Populist Moment,* xvii.

7. Sanders, *Roots of Reform,* 71–100.

8. Goodwyn, *The Populist Moment,* 297.

9. The federal government actually started collecting an income tax in 1863 to finance the Civil War, but it was repealed in 1872. Under pressure from the People's Party, Congress passed the Income Tax Act of 1894 to levy an income tax on wealthy citizens, but the Supreme Court struck it down the same year on the grounds that any tax levied on individuals by the federal government had to be in proportion to the state's population (not in proportion to the wealth of the individuals being taxed). So it took the Sixteenth Amendment to enable

the federal income tax, followed by the Underwood Tariff Act (also passed in 1913), to finally begin charging the tax.

10. In the original U.S. Constitution, senators were chosen by the state legislature, drawing on the Revolutionary precedent of having states send delegates to the Constitutional Conventions. In practice, the states elected their senators according to widely diverging practices until 1866, when Congress began to regulate the election of senators, in response to deadlocks in some states that caused Senate seats to sit vacant. (There were deadlocks in twenty states between 1891 and 1905.) The campaign to have direct election of senators became a national cause, promoted by the Populists and others. Oregon and Nebraska began directly electing senators on their own, and by 1912, almost thirty states did so. The popular pressure, along with the thirty or so directly elected senators who believed in this system, allowed the passage of the Seventeenth Amendment in 1913. The 1914 Senate elections used direct election across the entire country.

11. The Populists' attack on the railroads is not necessarily the most coherent part of their agenda. There were numerous regulations on the railroads before, during, and after the Populist movement. This story is one of the central themes in the evolution of capitalism in the second half of the nineteenth century and is the subject of many of the classics of economic and business history. See Alfred D. Chandler Jr., *The Visible Hand: The Managerial Revolution in American Business* (Cambridge, MA: Belknap, 1977); and Robert Wiebe, *The Search for Order, 1877–1920* (New York: Harper Collins, 1977). Among the legal milestones were the Interstate Commerce Act of 1887, the Sherman Antitrust Act of 1890, the Elkins Act of 1903, and the Hepburn Act of 1906. *Santa Clara County v. Southern Pacific Railroad Company* (1886), the court case that granted corporations the legal status of "personhood," including the protections enumerated in the Bill of Rights, was a case involving railroads. It would not be a stretch to say that the modern corporation was invented by railroads. So it should be no surprise that the Populists' demands regarding railroads, which can essentially be viewed as wanting to pay less money to ship

agricultural goods to market, would become a small part of the larger story. Eventually, price controls were imposed on railroads—leading to underinvestment by the railroads in their physical infrastructure and a slowed response to the rise of the automobile.

12. Sanders, *Roots of Reform,* 159.

13. The "afterlife" of the Farmers' Alliance was not just in the form of Progressive era legislation. In 1902, a new farmers' organization was created, the Farmers Educational and Cooperative Union of America, or Farmers Union for short, out of the ashes of the Farmers' Alliance, to continue to organize cooperatives and the political demands of farmers. Sanders describes the union this way: "Chastened by the failure of the Alliance, the FU was more cautious and less radical than the old Alliance, more an organized interest group than a movement (and in this respect it had more in common with the AFL than had the Alliance). Nevertheless, its political agenda was probably the broadest and most 'progressive' of any grass-roots organization of this era." Quoted in Sanders, *Roots of Reform,* 151.

14. Dana Frank, *Purchasing Power: Consumer Organizing, Gender, and the Seattle Labor Movement, 1919–1929* (New York: Cambridge University Press, 1994), 41.

15. Frank, *Purchasing Power,* 43–44.

16. For a useful overview, see Harvey Levenstein, *Revolution at the Table* (Berkeley: University of California Press, 2003).

17. Warren Belasco, *Appetite for Change: How the Counterculture Took on the Food Industry,* 2nd updated ed. (Ithaca, NY: Cornell University Press, 2007), 28.

18. Looking at the officially labeled "organic" part of the movement, we can see that there has been huge progress, but there is still a very long way to go. By 2010, the sales of organic food had grown to more than $26 billion annually, with almost five million acres of land being farmed organically. But organic food sales are still only 4 percent of overall food and beverage sales, and less than 1 percent of cropland is under organic production. Statistics from the Organic Trade Association, www.ota.com/organic/mt/business.html.

19. See Wendell Berry, *The Unsettling of America* (San Francisco: Sierra Club Books, 1977) and *Bringing It to the Table* (Berkeley: Counterpoint Press, 2009); and Michael Pollan, *The Omnivore's Dilemma: A Natural History of Four Meals* (New York: Penguin Press, 2006).

20. USDA, "National Count of Farmers Market Directory Listing Graph: 1994–2014," http://www.ams.usda.gov/AMSv1.0/ams.fetch TemplateData.do?template=TemplateS&leftNav=WholesaleandFar mersMarkets&page=WFMFarmersMarketGrowth&description=Fa rmers+Market+Growth.

21. See Steven McFadden, "The History of Community Supported Agriculture, Part I," The New Farm, http://newfarm.rodaleinstitute.org /features/0104/csa-history/part1_print.shtml.

22. Dan Solomon, an architect and one of the founders of New Urbanism, contrasts the food movement favorably with his own attempts to change American culture: "Architects and urbanists frequently look with envy to the foodies for their huge cultural accomplishment. They have not only created a new American cuisine of amazing quality, but they have had an impact on the supermarket, where decent produce and tasty, nutritious products are much less of a rarity than they used to be. Even fast food has not been totally immune to the influence of the foodies." Quoted in *Global City Blues* (Washington, DC: Island Press, 2003), 15–16.

    The analogy between cities and food is clear: if we want to change city building to make communities more sustainable, we need to change the practice of a whole set of professions. There are the practitioners that design and plan cities, whether city planners and architects or engineers and transportation planners. There are contractors who actually build new buildings and the mortgage and finance industry, which plays such a large role in deciding what gets funded. And ultimately, just as with the sustainable food movement, we need to also change consumer tastes.

23. Michael Kazin argues that the American Left has traditionally had its greatest influence on the "culture" and way of thinking of Americans without actually winning political power. See Kazin's *American*

Dreamers: How the Left Changed a Nation (New York: Alfred A. Knopf, 2011).

CHAPTER 8

1. Throughout this book, I have been using the words "institution" and "organization" more or less interchangeably. I have built on many social theorists to develop this approach, but I owe a particular debt to the sociologist Goran Ahrne. He argues: "The implication of an organizational theory of society is that social processes and social change must first of all be comprehended in their organizational settings and as the effects of the interaction among organizations in various constellations. The relations between individuals and society can best be understood in terms of organizational affiliation—membership, ownership, citizenship, kinship and employment." In Goran Ahrne, *Agency and Organization: Toward an Organizational Theory of Society* (London: Sage Publications, 1990), 141. See also Goran Ahrne, *Social Organizations: Interaction Inside, Outside and Between Organizations* (London: Sage Publications, 1994). Another important influence on my sociological theorizing is to be found in the work of Piotr Sztompka. See his *Society in Action: The Theory of Social Becoming* (Chicago: University of Chicago Press, 1991) and *The Sociology of Social Change* (Oxford: Blackwell, 1993).

2. It should be clear that the ideas sketched in this section reject the Marxist lens on history entirely. While Marx believed that each "mode of production" bore within it internal contradictions that would lead to social transformation, he also described society in unified terms as flowing from the organization of the economy, and treated other parts of society as deterministically given by the economic structure. The view of historical change that I have sketched here also differs a great deal from the idea of social wholes that we have inherited from classical anthropology, which treated societies as if they were self-contained, coherent units in which the parts fit together. Instead, the view offered here is that (a) societies are always evolving; (b) societies

are always in contact with other societies; and (c) they are always internally divided. They comprise different groups of people trying to do different things, which are only sometimes mutually reinforcing. On the emergence of the concept of "culture" in anthropology, see George W. Stocking Jr., "Franz Boas and the Culture Concept in Historical Perspective," in his *Race, Culture, and Evolution: Essays in the History of Anthropology* (Chicago: University of Chicago Press, 1982), 195–233. For a version of history that emphasizes the connections between cultures, see J. R. McNeill and William McNeill, *The Human Web: A Bird's-Eye View of World History* (New York: W. W. Norton and Company, 2003).

3. See Manuel De Landa, *A Thousand Years of Nonlinear History* (New York: Zone Books, 1997), especially Part I, on the history of cities and the economy in Europe from AD 1000 to the present.

Karen Orren and Stephen Skowronek develop a similar theory based specifically on American political institutions: "Pluralism has traditionally referred to competition among interests structured by 'rules of the game' upon which all parties agree; it is, at base, a description of order amid conflict. Intercurrence, by contrast, refers to the simultaneous operation of different sets of rules, to a politics structured by irresolution in the different sets of rules, to a politics structured by irresolution in the basic principles of social organization and governmental control, and it describes the disorder inherent in a multiplicity of ordering rules." In *The Search for American Political Development* (Cambridge: Cambridge University Press, 2004), 118.

See also Saskia Sassen, *Territory, Authority, Rights: From Medieval to Global Assemblages* (Princeton, NJ: University of Princeton Press, 2006).

4. See Alfred D. Chandler Jr., *Strategy and Structure: Chapters in the History of the American Industrial Enterprise* (Cambridge, MA: MIT Press, 1962); and Alfred D. Chandler Jr., *Scale and Scope: The Dynamics of Industrial Capitalism* (Boston: Harvard University Press, 1990).

5. This terminology comes from Wolfgang Streeck and Kathleen Thelen's analysis of political institutions. They describe the mechanism of institutional *conversion* as follows: "Such redirection may come about as a result of new environmental challenges, to which policymakers respond by deploying existing institutional resources to new ends. Or it can come about through changes in power relations, such that actors who were not involved in the original design of an institution and whose participation in it may not have been reckoned with, take it over and turn it to new ends." Quoted in Wolfgang Streeck and Kathleen Thelen, "Introduction: Institutional Change in Advanced Political Economies," in *Beyond Continuity: Institutional Change in Advanced Political Economies,* eds. Streeck and Thelen (Oxford: Oxford University Press, 2005), 26. See also Kathleen Thelen, "How Institutions Evolve: Insights from Comparative Historical Analysis," in *Comparative Historical Analysis in the Social Sciences,* eds. James Mahoney and Dietrich Rueschmeyer (New York: Cambridge University Press, 2003), 208–240.

6. Streeck and Thelen describe *displacement* as follows: "Such change often occurs through the rediscovery or activation—and always the cultivation—of alternative institutional forms. As growing numbers of actors defect to a new system, previously deviant, aberrant, anachronistic, or 'foreign' practices gain salience at the expense of traditional institutional forms and behaviors." In Streeck and Thelen, "Introduction: Institutional Change in Advanced Political Economies," 20.

7. Streeck and Thelen describe the process of *layering* this way:

> What is most interesting about change through layering is that it can set in motion path-altering dynamics through a mechanism of what we might think of as differential growth. The classic example from the welfare state literature is the layering of a voluntary private pension system onto an existing public system. While the established public system may well be unassailable, faster growth of the new private system can effect profound

change, among other things by draining off political support for the public system. . . .

Since the new layers created in this way do not as such and directly undermine existing institutions, they typically do not provoke counter-mobilization by defenders of the status quo.

In Streeck and Thelen, "Introduction: Institutional Change in Advanced Political Economies," 23.

8. See Jacob Hacker, "Policy Drift: The Hidden Politics of U.S. Welfare State Retrenchment," in *Beyond Continuity,* eds. Streeck and Thelen, 40–82.

9. The classic study of the takeover of the political realm by the economic realm is Karl Polanyi, *The Great Transformation: The Political and Economic Origins of Our Time* (Boston: Beacon Press, 1944).

APPENDIX

1. Karl Marx, "Manifesto of the Communist Party," in *The Marx Engels Reader,* 2nd ed., ed. Robert C. Tucker (New York: W. W. Norton and Company, 1978), 497–498.

2. Mikhail Bakunin, "Program and Object of the Secret Revolutionary Organization of the International Brethren," in *No Gods No Masters: An Anthology of Anarchism, Book One,* ed. Daniel Guerin (San Francisco: AK Press, 1982), 156.

3. Mikhail Bakunin, "On Cooperation," in *No Gods No Masters,* ed. Guerin, 182.

4. For example, Cesar de Paepe presented a report to the "anti-authoritarian" International in 1874, following the split in the First International, describing a detailed program for providing public services in an anarchist society. It called for decentralizing power to local "communes"—local assemblies, which would confederate together. "The Commune becomes essentially the organ of political functions or what are described as such: law, justice, security, the guaranteeing of contracts, the protection of the incapable, civic society, but at the same

time it is the organ of all local public services." From "On the Organization of Public Services," in *No Gods No Masters,* ed. Guerin, 194.

5. Adhemar Schwitzguebel saw this diversity of approaches as an expression of openness in the process of making history, arguing that different strategic approaches to organizing would lead to different, but equally good, revolutionary outcomes:

> [I]t is inevitable that the Revolution will be subject to extreme variation. Doubtless we shall see every socialist theory, communism, collectivism and mutualism, being implemented to a more or less restricted or comprehensive extent, according to whatever great currents the Revolution is to follow. . . .
>
> In what respect will it halt the proletariat's revolutionary march, if Germans make a reality of the workers' State, while the Italians, Spaniards and French make a reality of the Federation of Communes? And indeed if, in France, certain communes hold on to individual ownership while collective ownership prevails elsewhere?

Adhemar Schwitzguebel's Reply to César de Paepe, "The Question of Public Services before the International," in *No Gods No Masters,* ed. Guerin, 200–201.

6. Wini Brienes, *Community and Organization in the New Left, 1962–1968: The Great Refusal* (New Brunswick, NJ: Rutgers University Press, 1989), 52.

7. Alexis de Tocqueville, *Democracy in America, Volume 2* (New York: Vintage Books, 1990), 106.

8. In addition to Putnam's work, see Sean Safford's critique and extension of Putnam's concept of social capital, *Why the Garden Club Couldn't Save Youngstown* (Cambridge, MA: Harvard University Press, 2009). See also Peter Frumkin's discussion of voluntary associations in "Civic and Political Engagement" in his *On Being Nonprofit* (Cambridge, MA: Harvard University Press, 2002), 29–63.

9. Robert Putnam, *Bowling Alone: The Collapse and Revival of American Community* (New York: Simon and Schuster, 2000), 338.

10. Key essays in this collection include: Stephen Davis, "Laissez-Faire Urban Planning," 18–46; Daniel Klein, "The Voluntary Provision of Public Goods? The Turnpike Companies of Early America," 76–101; Robert C. Arne, "Entrepreneurial City Planning: Chicago's Central Manufacturing District," 102–119; and Fred E. Foldvary, "Proprietary Communities and Community Associations," 258–288.

11. Foldvary, "Proprietary Communities," 286.

12. Ahrne, *Agency and Organization,* 141.

13. Sassen, *Territory, Authority, Rights,* 27.

14. Orren and Skowrenek, *The Search for American Political Development,* 108.

15. Kim Stanley Robinson, *2312* (New York: Hachette Group, 2012), 126.

SOURCES CITED

Abromowitz, David. "An Essay on Community Land Trusts: Toward Permanently Affordable Housing." In *Property and Values: Alternatives to Private and Public Ownership,* edited by Charles Geisler and Gail Daneker, 213–231. Washington, DC: Island Press, 2000.

Ackerman, Bruce. *We the People, Volume I: Foundations.* Cambridge, MA: Harvard University Press, 1993.

Ahrne, Goran. *Agency and Organization: Toward an Organizational Theory of Society.* London: Sage Publications, 1990.

Ahrne, Goran. *Social Organizations: Interaction Inside, Outside and Between Organizations.* London: Sage Publications, 1994.

Albert, Michael. *Parecon.* London: Verso, 2003.

Alexander, Christopher, Sara Ishikawa, and Murray Silverstein. *A Pattern Language.* Oxford: Oxford University Press, 1977.

Anderson, Ray, with Robin White. *Business Lessons from a Radical Industrialist.* New York: St. Martin's Press, 2009.

Arendt, Hannah. *On Revolution.* New York: Viking Press, 1965.

Arne, Robert C. "Entrepreneurial City Planning: Chicago's Central Manufacturing District." In *The Voluntary City: Choice, Community and Civil Society,* edited by David Beito, Peter Gordon, and Alexander Tabarrok, 102–119. Ann Arbor: University of Michigan Press, 2002.

Bailyn, Bernard. *The Ideological Origins of the American Revolution,* enlarged ed. Cambridge: Belknap, 1992 [1967].

Baker, Dean, and Archon Fung. "Collateral Damage: Do Pension Fund Investments Hurt Workers?" In *Working Capital: The Power of Labor's Pensions,* edited by Archon Fung, Tessa Hebb, and Joel Rogers, 13–43. Ithaca, NY: Cornell University Press, 2001.

Barber, Benjamin. *Strong Democracy: Participatory Politics for a New Age, Twentieth Anniversary Edition.* Berkeley: University of California Press, 2003.

Barnes, Peter. *Capitalism 3.0: A Guide to Reclaiming the Commons.* San Francisco: Berrett-Koehler Publishers, 2006.

Barnes, Peter. *Who Owns the Sky: Our Common Assets and the Future of Capitalism.* Washington, DC: Island Press, 2001.

Bates, Albert, and Timothy Miller. "The Evolution of Hippie Communal Spirituality: The Farm and Other Hippies Who Didn't Give Up." In *America's Alternative Religions,* edited by Timothy Miller, 371–378. Albany: State University Press of New York, 1995.

Bauer, Catherine. *Modern Housing.* Boston and New York: Houghton Mifflin Company, 1934.

Becker, Eric, and Patrick McVeigh. "Social Funds in the United States: Their History, Financial Performance, and Social Impacts." In *Working Capital: The Power of Labor's Pensions,* edited by Archon Fung, Tessa Hebb, and Joel Rogers, 44–66. Ithaca, NY: Cornell University Press, 2001.

Belasco, Warren. *Appetite for Change: How the Counterculture Took on the Food Industry,* 2nd updated ed. Ithaca, NY: Cornell University Press, 2007.

Berry, Wendell. *Bringing It to the Table.* Berkeley: Counterpoint Press, 2009.

Berry, Wendell. *The Unsettling of America.* San Francisco: Sierra Club Books, 1977.

Birch, Eugenie L. "Five Generations of the Garden City: Tracing Howard's Legacy in Twentieth-Century Residential Planning." In *From Garden City to Green City: The Legacy of Ebenezer Howard,* edited by Kermit Parsons and David Schuyler, 171–200. Baltimore, MD: Johns Hopkins University Press, 2002.

Bishop, Bill. *The Big Sort: Why the Clustering of Like-Minded America Is Tearing Us Apart.* New York: Houghton Mifflin Company, 2008.

Blackburn, Robin. *Banking on Death, or, Investing in Life: The History and Future of Pensions.* London: Verso, 2002.

Blasi, Joseph R., Richard B. Freeman, and Douglas L. Kruse. *The Citizen's Share: Putting Ownership Back into Democracy.* New Haven, CT: Yale University Press, 2013.

Bookchin, Murray. *The Third Revolution: Popular Movements in the Revolutionary Era, Volume 1.* New York: Cassell, 1996.

Botsman, Rachel, and Roo Rogers. *What's Mine Is Yours: The Rise of Collaborative Consumption.* New York: Harper Collins, 2010.

Brewer, Priscilla J. "The Shakers of Mother Ann Lee." In *America's Communal Utopias,* edited by Donald Pitzer, 37–56. Chapel Hill: University of North Carolina Press, 1997.

Brewer, Richard. *Conservancy: The Land Trust Movement in America.* Hanover, NH: Dartmouth College Press, 2003.

Brienes, Wini. *Community and Organization in the New Left, 1962–1968: The Great Refusal.* New Brunswick, NJ: Rutgers University Press, 1989.

Bryan, Frank. *Real Democracy: The New England Town Meeting and How It Works.* Chicago: University of Chicago Press, 2004.

Calabrese, Michael. "Building on Success: Labor-Friendly Investment Vehicles and the Power of Private Equity." In *Working Capital: The Power of Labor's Pensions,* edited by Archon Fung, Tessa Hebb, and Joel Rogers, 93–127. Ithaca, NY: Cornell University Press, 2001.

Calthorpe, Peter. "A Short History of Twentieth Century New Towns." In *Sustainable Communities: A New Design Synthesis for Cities, Suburbs, and Towns,* edited by Sim Van der Ryn and Peter Calthorpe, 189–234. San Francisco: Sierra Club Books, 1986.

Calthorpe, Peter. *Urbanism in the Age of Climate Change.* Washington, DC: Island Press, 2011.

Calthorpe, Peter, and William Fulton. *The Regional City: Planning for the End of Sprawl.* Washington, DC: Island Press, 2001.

Carberry, Edward J. "Employee Ownership and Shared Capitalism: Assessing the Experience, Research, and Policy Implications." In *Employee*

Ownership and Shared Capitalism: New Directions for Research, edited by Edward Carberry, 1–26. Champaign, IL: Labor and Employee Relations Association, 2011.

Cassidy, John. *How Markets Fail: The Logic of Economic Calamities.* New York: Farrar, Straus and Giroux, 2009.

Cervero, Robert, Aaron Golub, and Brendan Nee. *San Francisco City CarShare: Longer-Term Travel-Demand and Car Ownership Impacts.* Berkeley: University of California at Berkeley Institute of Urban and Regional Development, May 2006, https://citycarshare.org/wp-content/uploads/2012/09/Cervero-Report-May-06.pdf.

Chandler, Alfred D. Jr. *Scale and Scope: The Dynamics of Industrial Capitalism.* Boston: Harvard University Press, 1990.

Chandler, Alfred D. Jr. *Strategy and Structure: Chapters in the History of the American Industrial Enterprise.* Cambridge, MA: MIT Press, 1962.

Chandler, Alfred D. Jr. *The Visible Hand: The Managerial Revolution in American Business.* Cambridge, MA: Belknap, 1977.

Cheney, George. *Values at Work: Employee Participation Meets Market Pressure at Mondragon.* Ithaca, NY: Cornell University Press, 1999.

Cornell, Andrew. *Oppose and Propose: Lessons from Movement for New Society.* Oakland, CA: AK Press/Institute for Anarchist Studies, 2011.

Crane, Keith, Liisa Ecola, Scott Hassell, and Shanthi Nataraj. "Energy Services Analysis: An Alternative Approach for Identifying Opportunities to Reduce Emissions of Greenhouse Gases." RAND Corporation, 2012, http://www.rand.org/content/dam/rand/pubs/technical_reports/2012/RAND_TR1170.pdf.

Cranz, Galen. *The Politics of Park Design: A History of Urban Parks in America.* Boston: MIT Press, 1989.

Croft, Thomas. "Helping Workers' Capital Work Harder: A Report on Global Economically Targeted Investments." Heartland Capital Strategies, 2009, www.heartlandnetwork.org/images/pdfs/heartland%20cwc%20global%20eti%20report%202009.pdf.

Curl, John. *For All People: Uncovering the Hidden History of Cooperation, Cooperative Movements, and Communalism in America,* 2nd ed. Oakland, CA: PM Press, 2009.

Davies, Stephen. "Laissez-Faire Urban Planning." In *The Voluntary City: Choice, Community and Civil Society,* edited by David Beito, Peter Gordon, and Alexander Tabarrok, 18–46. Ann Arbor: University of Michigan Press, 2002.

Davis, Gerald F., Doug McAdam, W. Richard Scott, and Mayer N. Zald. *Social Movements and Organization Theory.* Cambridge: Cambridge University Press, 2005.

Davis, John. "Origins and Evolution of the Community Land Trust in the United States." In *The Community Land Trust Reader,* edited by John Davis, 3–47. Boston: Lincoln Institute of Land Policy, 2010.

Davis, John, and Rick Jacobus. *The City-CLT Partnership: Municipal Support for Community Land Trusts.* Boston: Lincoln Institute of Land Policy, 2008, www.lincolninst.edu/pubs/1395_The-City-CLT-Partnership.

Davis, John, and Alice Stokes. "Land in Trust, Homes That Last: A Performance Evaluation of the Champlain Housing Trust." Champlain Housing Trust, 2009, www.champlainhousingtrust.org.

De Landa, Manuel. *A Thousand Years of Nonlinear History.* New York: Zone Books, 1997.

Devine, Patrick. *Democracy and Planning: The Political Economy of a Self-Governing Society.* Cambridge: Polity Press, 1988.

Duany, Andres, Elizabeth Plater-Zyberk, and Jeff Speck. *Suburban Nation: The Rise of Sprawl and the Decline of the American Dream.* New York: North Point Press, 2000.

Dubb, Steve, Sarah McKinley, and Ted Howard. "Achieving the Anchor Promise: Improving Outcomes for Low-Income Children, Families and Communities." The Democracy Collaborative, August 2013, http://community-wealth.org/sites/clone.community-wealth.org /files/downloads/Achieving%20the%20Anchor%20Promise_com posite_FINAL.pdf.

Dubb, Steve, Sarah McKinley, and Ted Howard. "The Anchor Dashboard: Aligning Institutional Practice to Meet Low-Income Community Needs." The Democracy Collaborative, August 2013, http:// community-wealth.org/sites/clone.community-wealth.org/files/down loads/AnchorDashboardCompositeFinal.pdf.

Dunham-Jones, Ellen, and June Williamson. *Retrofitting Suburbia: Urban Design Solutions for Retrofitting Suburbs.* Hoboken, NJ: John Wiley and Sons, 2009.

Durham, Sarah. *Brand Raising: How Nonprofits Raise Visibility and Money through Smart Communications.* San Francisco: Jossey-Bass, 2010.

Erickson, David J. *The Housing Policy Revolution: Networks and Neighborhoods.* Washington, DC: Urban Institute Press, 2009.

Fishkin, James S. *When the People Speak: Deliberative Democracy and Public Consultation.* Oxford: Oxford University Press, 2009.

Fishman, Robert. "The American Planning Tradition: An Introduction and Interpretation." In *The American Planning Tradition: Culture and Policy,* edited by Robert Fishman, 1–31. Washington, DC: Woodrow Wilson Center Press, 2000.

Fishman, Robert. *Urban Utopias in the Twentieth Century: Ebenezer Howard, Frank Lloyd Wright, Le Corbusier.* Boston: MIT Press, 1982.

Foldvary, Fred E. "Proprietary Communities and Community Associations." In *The Voluntary City: Choice, Community and Civil Society,* edited by David Beito, Peter Gordon, and Alexander Tabarrok, 258–288. Ann Arbor: University of Michigan Press, 2002.

Frank, Dana. *Purchasing Power: Consumer Organizing, Gender, and the Seattle Labor Movement, 1919–1929.* New York: Cambridge University Press, 1994.

Fraser, Nancy. "Rethinking the Public Sphere: A Contribution to the Critique of Actually Existing Democracy." In *Habermas and the Public Sphere,* edited by Craig Calhoun, 109–142. Cambridge, MA: MIT Press, 1991.

Frug, Gerald. *City Making: Building Communities without Walls.* Princeton, NJ: Princeton University Press, 1999.

Frumkin, Peter. *On Being Nonprofit.* Cambridge, MA: Harvard University Press, 2002.

Fung, Archon, *Empowered Participation: Reinventing Urban Democracy.* Princeton, NJ: Princeton University Press, 2004.

Gansky, Lisa. *The Mesh: Why the Future of Business Is Sharing.* New York: Portfolio Penguin, 2010.

Gansky, Lisa. "Policies for Shareable Cities: A Sharing Economy Policy Primer for Urban Leaders." Shareable and the Sustainable Economies Law Center, www.theselc.org/policies-for-shareable-cities.

Gastil, John, and Katie Knobloch. "Evaluation Report to the Oregon State Legislature on the 2010 Oregon Citizens' Initiative Review." Healthy Democracy Oregon, http://healthydemocracyoregon.org/sites/default/files/Oregon%20Legislative%20Report%20on%20CIR%20v.3-1.pdf.

George, Henry. *Progress and Poverty: An Inquiry into the Cause of Industrial Depressions and of Increase of Want with Increase of Wealth.* Cambridge: Cambridge University Press, 2009 [1879].

Gibson-Graham, J. K. *Postcapitalist Politics.* Minneapolis: University of Minnesota Press, 2006.

Goodwyn, Lawrence. *Democratic Promise: The Populist Moment in America.* Oxford: Oxford University Press, 1976.

Goodwyn, Lawrence. *The Populist Moment: A Short History of the Agrarian Revolt in America.* New York: Oxford University Press, 1978.

Gordon, Linda. *Women, the State, and Welfare.* Madison: University of Wisconsin Press, 1990.

Greenfield, Kent. *The Failure of Corporate Law: Fundamental Flaws and Progressive Possibilities.* Chicago: University of Chicago Press, 2006.

Grossman, Richard L., and Frank T. Adams. "Taking Care of Business: Citizenship and the Charter of Incorporation." In *Defying Corporations, Defining Democracy,* edited by Dean Ritz, 59–71. New York: Apex Press, 2001.

Guarneri, Carl. *The Utopian Alternative: Fourierism in Nineteenth-Century America.* Ithaca, NY: Cornell University Press, 1991.

Guerin, Daniel, ed. *No Gods No Masters: An Anthology of Anarchism, Book One.* San Francisco: AK Press, 1982.

Gutmann, Amy, and Dennis F. Thompson. *Why Deliberative Democracy?* Princeton, NJ: Princeton University Press, 2004.

Hacker, Jacob. "Policy Drift: The Hidden Politics of U.S. Welfare State Retrenchment." In *Beyond Continuity: Institutional Change in Advanced Political Economies,* edited by Wolfgang Streeck and Kathleen Thelen, 40–82. Oxford: Oxford University Press, 2005.

Hall, Peter. *Cities of Tomorrow: An Intellectual History of Urban Planning and Design in the Twentieth Century.* Oxford: Blackwell, 1988.

Hall, Peter, and Colin Ward. *Sociable Cities: The Legacy of Ebenezer Howard.* Chichester, West Sussex: John Wiley and Sons, 1998.

Halpern, Robert. *Rebuilding the Inner City: A History of Neighborhood Initiatives to Address Poverty in the United States.* New York: Columbia University Press, 1995.

Hardin, Garrett. "The Tragedy of the Commons." *Science,* 162 (1968): 1243–1248.

Hardy, Dennis. "Tomorrow and Tomorrow: The TCPA's First Hundred Years, and the Next." Town and Country Planning Association, www.tcpa.org.uk/data/files/18991999.pdf.

Hawken, Paul. "Socially Responsible Investing: How the SRI Industry Has Failed to Respond to People Who Want to Invest with Conscience and What Can Be Done about It." Natural Capital, October 2004, http://www.naturalcapital.org/docs/SRI%20Report%2010-04_word.pdf.

Hayden, Dolores. *Seven American Utopias: The Architecture of Communitarian Socialism, 1790–1975.* Boston: MIT Press, 1976.

Hine, Robert. "California's Socialist Utopias." In *America's Communal Utopias,* edited by Donald Pitzer, 419–431. Chapel Hill: University of North Carolina Press, 1997.

Jackson, Kenneth T. *Crabgrass Frontier: The Suburbanization of the United States.* New York: Oxford University Press, 1985.

Katsiaficas, George. *The Imagination of the New Left: A Global Analysis of 1968.* Boston: South End Press, 1987.

Kazin, Michael. *American Dreamers: How the Left Changed a Nation.* New York: Alfred A. Knopf, 2011.

Kelly, Marjorie. *Owning Our Future: The Emerging Ownership Revolution.* San Francisco: Berrett-Koehler Publishers, 2012.

Kelly, Marjorie, and Violeta Duncan. "A New Anchor Mission for a New Century: Community Foundations Deploying All Resources to Build Community Wealth." The Democracy Collaborative, November 2014,

http://democracycollaborative.org/sites/clone.community-wealth.org
/files/downloads/ANewAnchorMission_FINAL3.pdf.

Klein, Daniel. "The Voluntary Provision of Public Goods? The Turnpike Companies of Early America." In *The Voluntary City: Choice, Community and Civil Society,* edited by David Beito, Peter Gordon, and Alexander Tabarrok, 76–101. Ann Arbor: University of Michigan Press, 2002.

Kostoff, Spiro. *The City Shaped: Urban Patterns and Meanings throughout History.* New York: Bulfinch Press, 1991.

LaFond, Michael. "Cooperative Transport: Berlin's Stattauto (Instead of Cars)." *RAIN Magazine* 14, no. 4 (Summer 1994), http://www.rain magazine.com/archive/1994/cooperative-transport01252014.

Lang, Amy. "But Is It for Real? The British Columbia Citizens' Assembly as a Model of State-Sponsored Citizen Empowerment." *Politics and Society* 35, no. 1 (2007): 35–70.

Lehr, R. L., W. Guild, D. L. Thomas, and B. G. Swezey. "Listening to Customers: How Deliberative Polling Helped Build 1,000 MW of New Renewable Energy Projects in Texas." National Renewable Energy Laboratory (NREL), Golden, CO, June 2003, http://www.osti.gov/sci tech/biblio/15003900.

Lerner, Josh. *Making Democracy Fun: How Game Design Can Empower Citizens and Transform Politics.* Cambridge, MA: MIT Press, 2014.

Levenstein, Harvey. *Revolution at the Table.* Berkeley: University of California Press, 2003.

Libby, James M. Jr., and Darby Bradley. "Vermont Housing and Conservation Board: A Conspiracy of Good Will among Land Trusts and Housing Trusts." In *Property and Values: Alternatives to Private and Public Ownership,* edited by Charles Geisler and Gail Daneker, 259–281. Washington, DC: Island Press, 2000.

Lipset, Seymour Martin, and Gary Marks. *It Didn't Happen Here: Why Socialism Failed in the United States.* New York: W. W. Norton and Company, 2000.

Lynch, Kevin. *Good City Form.* Boston: MIT Press, 1981.

MacLeod, Greg. *From Mondragon to America: Experiments in Community Economic Development.* Sydney, Nova Scotia: University of Cape Breton Press, 1997.

Mandell, Joyce. "CDCs and the Myth of the Organizing-Development Dialectic." COMM-ORG: The On-Line Conference on Community Organizing, 15 (2009), http://comm-org.wisc.edu/papers2009/mandell.htm.

Markusen, Ann. *Profit Cycles, Oligopoly, and Regional Development.* Boston: MIT Press, 1985.

Marx, Karl. "Manifesto of the Communist Party." In *The Marx Engels Reader,* 2nd ed., edited by Robert C. Tucker, 469–500. New York: W. W. Norton and Company, 1978.

Matthei, Chuck. "U.S. Land Reform Movements: The Theory behind the Practice." *Social Policy* (Spring 1992): 36–45.

McDonough, William, and Michael Braungart. *The Upcycle: Beyond Sustainability—Designing for Abundance.* New York: North Point Press, 2013.

McFadden, Steven. "The History of Community Supported Agriculture, Part I." The New Farm, http://newfarm.rodaleinstitute.org/features/0104/csa-history/part1_print.shtml.

McMath, Robert C. Jr. *American Populism: A Social History, 1877–1898.* New York: Hill and Wang, 1993.

McNeill, J. R., and William McNeill. *The Human Web: A Bird's-Eye View of World History.* New York: W. W. Norton and Company, 2003.

Medoff, Peter, and Holly Sklar. *Streets of Hope: The Rise and Fall of an Urban Neighborhood.* Boston: South End Press, 1994.

Moberg, David. "Experimenting with the Future: Alternative Institutions and American Socialism." In *Co-ops, Communes & Collectives: Experiments in Social Change in the 1960s and 1970s,* edited by John Case and Rosemary Taylor, 274–311. New York: Pantheon Books, 1979.

Mollenkopf, John H. *The Contested City.* Princeton, NJ: Princeton University Press, 1983.

Morrison, Roy. *We Build the Road as We Travel.* Philadelphia: New Society Publishers, 1991.

Newman, Peter, and Jeffrey Kenworthy. *Sustainability and Cities: Overcoming Automobile Dependence.* Washington, DC: Island Press, 1999.

Orren, Karen, and Stephen Skowronek. *The Search for American Political Development.* Cambridge: Cambridge University Press, 2004.

Ostrom, Elinor. *Governing the Commons: The Evolution of Institutions for Collective Action.* New York: Cambridge University Press, 1990.

Ostrom, Elinor. *Understanding Institutional Diversity.* Princeton, NJ: Princeton University Press, 2005.

Palmer, R. R. *The Age of Democratic Revolutions: A Political History of Europe and America, 1760–1800: The Challenge.* Princeton, NJ: Princeton University Press, 1959.

Parsons, Kermit. "British and American Community Design: Clarence Stein's Manhattan Transfer, 1924–1974." In *From Garden City to Green City: The Legacy of Ebenezer Howard,* edited by Kermit Parsons and David Schuyler, 131–158. Baltimore, MD: Johns Hopkins University Press, 2002.

Pierce, Neal, and Carol Steinbach. *Corrective Capitalism: The Rise of America's Community Development Corporations.* New York: Ford Foundation, 1987.

Pitzer, Donald. "The New Moral World of Robert Owen and New Harmony." In *America's Communal Utopias,* edited by Donald Pitzer, 88–134. Chapel Hill: University of North Carolina Press, 1997.

Polanyi, Karl. *The Great Transformation: The Political and Economic Origins of Our Time.* Boston: Beacon Press, 1944.

Pollan, Michael. *The Omnivore's Dilemma: A Natural History of Four Meals.* New York: Penguin Press, 2006.

Putnam, Robert. *Bowling Alone: The Collapse and Revival of American Community.* New York: Simon and Schuster, 2000.

Radford, Gail. *Modern Housing for America: Policy Struggles in the New Deal Era.* Chicago: University of Chicago Press, 1996.

Richardson, Harry W., and Peter Gordon. "Market Planning Oxymoron or Common Sense?" *Journal of the American Planning Association* 59, no. 3 (1993): 347–352.

Robinson, Kim Stanley. *2312.* New York: Hachette Group, 2012.

Rodin, Judith. "Innovations in Finance for Social Impact." Rockefeller Foundation, September 5, 2014, http://www.rockefellerfoundation.org /blog/innovations-finance-social-impact.

Roeger, Katie L., Amy S. Blackwood, and Sarah L. Pettijohn, *The Nonprofit Almanac 2012*. Washington, DC: Urban Institute Press, 2012.

Roemer, John. *Equal Shares: Making Market Socialism Work*. London: Verso, 1996.

Rogers, Everett. *Diffusion of Innovation,* 5th ed. New York: Free Press, 2003.

Ross, Tracey. "Eds, Meds and the Feds: How the Federal Government Can Foster the Role of Anchor Institutions in Community Revitalization." Center for American Progress, October 2014, http://www.scribd.com /doc/240183541/Eds-Meds-and-the-Feds-How-the-Federal-Govern ment-Can-Foster-the-Role-of-Anchor-Institutions-in-Community -Revitalization.

Safford, Sean. *Why the Garden Club Couldn't Save Youngstown*. Cambridge, MA: Harvard University Press, 2009.

Sanders, Elizabeth. *Roots of Reform: Farmers, Workers, and the American State, 1877–1917.* Chicago: University of Chicago Press, 1999.

Sassen, Saskia. *Territory, Authority, Rights: From Medieval to Global Assemblages.* Princeton, NJ: Princeton University Press, 2006.

Schor, Juliet. "Debating the Sharing Economy." Great Transition Initiative, http://greattransition.org/publication/debating-the-sharing-economy.

Schweickart, David. *After Capitalism,* 2nd ed. Lanham, MD: Rowman & Littlefield Publishers, 2011.

Shaheen, Susan A., Mark A. Mallery, and Karla J. Kingsley. "Personal Vehicle Sharing Services in North America." *Research in Transportation Business & Management* (2012), doi: 10.1016/j.rtbm.2012.04.005.

Shaw, Randy. *The Activists Handbook: Winning Social Change in the 21st Century,* 2nd ed. Berkeley: University of California Press, 2013.

Shuman, Michael. *Local Dollars, Local Sense*. White River Junction, VT: Chelsea Green, 2012.

Smith, Adam. *Wealth of Nations*. New York: Prometheus Books, 1991 [1776].

Solomon, Dan. *Global City Blues.* Washington, DC: Island Press, 2003.

Souder, Jon A., and Sally K. Fairfax. "In Lands We Trusted: State Trust Lands as an Alternative Theory of Public Ownership." In *Property and Values: Alternatives to Private and Public Ownership,* edited by Charles Geisler and Gail Daneker, 87–119. Washington, DC: Island Press, 2000.

Steffen, Alex, ed. *Worldchanging: A User's Guide for the 21st Century.* New York: Abrams, 2006.

Stein, Clarence. *New Towns for America.* Boston: MIT Press, 1957.

Stocking, George W. Jr. "Franz Boas and the Culture Concept in Historical Perspective." In *Race, Culture, and Evolution: Essays in the History of Anthropology,* 195–233. Chicago: University of Chicago Press, 1982.

Stoecker, Randy. "The CDC Model of Urban Redevelopment: A Critique and an Alternative." *Journal of Urban Affairs* 19 (1997): 1–22.

Streeck, Wolfgang, and Kathleen Thelen. "Introduction: Institutional Change in Advanced Political Economies." In *Beyond Continuity: Institutional Change in Advanced Political Economies,* edited by Wolfgang Streeck and Kathleen Thelen, 1–39. Oxford: Oxford University Press, 2005.

Sviridoff, Mitchell, ed. *The Trials and Errors That Shaped the Modern Community Development Corporation.* New York: New School University, Community Development Research Center, 2004.

Sztompka, Piotr. *Society in Action: The Theory of Social Becoming.* Chicago: University of Chicago Press, 1991.

Sztompka, Piotr. *The Sociology of Social Change.* Oxford: Blackwell, 1993.

Tallen, Emily. *New Urbanism and American Planning: The Conflict of Cultures.* New York: Routledge, 2005.

Teaford, Jon. *The Unheralded Triumph: City Government in America, 1870–1900.* Baltimore, MD: Johns Hopkins University Press, 1984.

Thelen, Kathleen. "How Institutions Evolve: Insights from Comparative Historical Analysis." In *Comparative Historical Analysis in the Social Sciences,* edited by James Mahoney and Dietrich Rueschmeyer, 208–240. New York: Cambridge University Press, 2003.

Tilly, Charles. *Social Movements, 1768–2004*. Boulder, CO: Paradigm Publishers, 2004.

Tocqueville, Alexis de. *Democracy in America, Volume 2*. New York: Vintage Books, 1990.

Voss, Kim. "The Collapse of a Social Movement: The Interplay of Mobilizing Structures, Framing, and Political Opportunities in the Knights of Labor." In *Comparative Perspectives on Social Movements,* edited by Doug McAdam, John D. McCarthy, and Mayer N. Zald, 227–258. Cambridge: Cambridge University Press, 1996.

Ward, Stephen V. "Ebenezer Howard: His Life and Times." In *From Garden City to Green City: The Legacy of Ebenezer Howard,* edited by Kermit Parsons and David Schuyler, 14–37. Baltimore, MD: Johns Hopkins University Press, 2002.

Webb, Beatrice, and Sidney Webb. *The Consumer's Co-operative Movement.* London: Longmans, Green, 1921.

Weir, Margaret. "What Future Social Policy? Urban Poverty and Defensive Localism." *Dissent* 41, no. 3 (July 1994): 337–342.

Whyte, William Foote, and Kathleen King Whyte. *Making Mondragon: The Growth and Dynamics of the Mondragon Cooperative Complex.* Ithaca, NY: Cornell University Press and ILR Press, 1988.

Wiebe, Robert. *The Search for Order, 1877–1920.* New York: Harper Collins, 1977.

Wood, Gordon S. *The Radicalism of the American Revolution.* New York: Random House, 1991.

INDEX

Investing in Frontier Markets

Investing in Frontier Markets

Opportunity, Risk and Role in an
Investment Portfolio

GAVIN GRAHAM AND AL EMID

WILEY

National Library of Canada Cataloguing in Publication Data

Graham, Gavin, author   Investing in frontier markets : opportunity, risk and role in an investment portfolio / Gavin Graham, Al Emid.

Includes index. Issued in print and electronic formats. ISBN 978-1-118-55632-0 (bound); ISBN 978-1-118-55634-4 (ebk); ISBN 978-1-118-55633-7 (ebk)

1. Investments, Foreign–Developing countries. I. Emid, Al, 1946-, author II. Title.

HG5993.G73 2013   332.67'3091724   C2013-904326-8   C2013-904327-6

Production Credits
Cover design: Wiley
Typesetting: LaserWords
Cover image: iStockphoto
Printer: Friesens

Editorial Credits
Executive editor: Karen Milner
Managing editor: Alison Maclean
Production editors: Pamela Vokey and Melissa Lopez

John Wiley & Sons Canada, Limited.
6045 Freemont Blvd.
Mississauga, Ontario

L5R 4J3

Printed in Canada
1 2 3 4 5 FP 16 15 14 13 12

Contents

Acknowledgments

I would like to thank the editors at John Wiley & Sons for their unstinting support of this book and their understanding of how authors go about their tasks. Notwithstanding the obvious fact that authors work in words, defining the relationship between publishers, editors and authors reminds one of trying to answer questions such as "How high is up?" and "What is the meaning of life?"—but in the right set of circumstances, the relationship works well. Fortunately we had those circumstances in crafting this book.

I would also like to thank all of the individuals in the United States, Canada and in emerging and frontier markets for freely giving their time and expert knowledge—and for their patience with what might have seemed like endless back checking.

I would also like to thank those sources who for different reasons I have not specifically named here but whose counsel I valued while shaping the text.

Finally, I would certainly like to extend special thanks to Steve Spector, JD, MLS, for his comprehensive research and appreciation of the intricacies of emerging and frontier markets investing.

Al Emid
September 2013

I would like to thank first of all my wonderful wife, Perianne, without whose help and support my portion of this book would not have been written.

I would also like to thank Don Loney, our original editor at John Wiley, who had the belief that the market was ready for a book on frontier markets, and David Feather, President and Chief Executive Officer at Russell Investments Canada, who had the vision to support the idea. I would also like to thank Xavier Rolet, Chief Executive Officer of the London Stock Exchange Plc, who kindly spent some time to discuss its role in acting as a gateway for frontier markets companies.

Lastly, I would like to thank the various fund managers and experts who provided insight into the frontier markets and their approach to investing in them.

Gavin Graham
September 2013

Foreword

Throughout history, frontiers have represented unexplored opportunities, untapped potential, the promise of riches and the lure of discovery.

For today's investors, frontier markets can offer all that and more. They can offer the chance to invest in some of the fastest-growing economies in the world, most with young, vibrant populations and substantial natural resources. They can open a window to new cultures and new industries. And they can help diversify a portfolio and offer the opportunity for enhanced returns.

In this book, authors Gavin Graham and Al Emid outline the potential that investing in frontier markets can hold for investors. Graham, a noted expert on emerging markets, and Emid, one of Canada's foremost writers on investing, have created a comprehensive study on how investors can benefit from gaining exposure to this new market segment.

They conclude, and Russell Investments agrees, that frontier markets are a logical next step for investors who have already discovered how investments in emerging markets can enhance returns and potentially lower a portfolio's overall risk. They believe that since globalization has had numerous economic benefits for emerging markets, it will likely have the same impact on frontier markets over time.

True, investing in frontier markets also holds risks—many of the countries considered frontier markets are politically unstable, can be influenced by strong governmental control over natural resources and industries, and have economies that are vulnerable to sudden shifts in global trends. Moreover, these markets are often less transparent, less liquid and more volatile even than emerging markets.

But many of the more established emerging markets—Brazil, Russia, India and China—were considered frontier markets not so long ago. They now contain some of the largest companies in the world, have been integrated into the world economy and—importantly—have provided investors with returns that have frequently outpaced those from the developed market economies. Indeed, these countries, known collectively as the BRIC nations, have generally better fiscal accounts, balances of trade and growth prospects than their developed market counterparts.

As Graham and Emid show in this book, the MSCI Emerging Markets (Free) Index delivered a return of 13.4 percent p.a. in the decade ending

October 2012, compared with the MSCI World Index of developed markets, which gained 5.61 percent p.a. in the same period. Russell research found similar results over the longer term: despite greater volatility, since the late 1980s emerging markets produced the best returns among the asset classes analyzed, and since 1988, emerging markets have outperformed Canadian and U.S. equities by a wide margin. Given demographic trends, growing urbanization, rapid industrialization, increased trade flows and other factors, there is potential for continued outperformance from emerging markets.

Russell Investments believes that frontier markets are now essentially where emerging markets were back in the 1980s—relatively unexplored opportunities with great potential. The success that emerging markets have had over the past 30 years is the promise that today's frontier markets now hold.

Moreover, frontier markets show a similarly low correlation with Canadian and U.S. equities as emerging markets did in their infancy. According to Russell research, prior to the global financial crisis in 2008, the rolling correlation was generally below 0.30, and similar to emerging markets, even negative at times. While the crisis caused correlation to briefly spike to over 0.60, it has since trended toward its historical range of 0.20 and lower. However, it would not be surprising for correlations to have episodic spikes due to ongoing macroeconomic uncertainty.

Frontier markets also have very low correlation with other asset classes, making this asset class a great diversifier in traditional portfolios. In fact, the highest correlation exhibited among the asset classes that Russell analyzed with frontier markets is with the international Russell Developed ex-North America Index, at 0.44. In addition, while it would be expected that frontier markets exhibit a strong positive relationship with emerging markets, surprisingly, our analysis shows that has not been the case. The correlation between frontier and emerging markets was 0.41.

Today's frontier markets run the gamut from tiny, agrarian Laos to oil-rich, populous and vibrant Nigeria. They span the globe, including countries in Latin America, the Caribbean, Africa, Asia and Eastern Europe and represent a diverse group of cultures. They are also a growing economic force.

The 40 frontier markets in the MSCI and S&P indices represent 14 percent of global population and 7 percent of global gross domestic product (GDP) on a purchasing power basis (PPB). Expanding that definition to include the exotic frontier markets, such as Myanmar, Iran and Saudi Arabia, frontier markets represent 25 percent of global population and 11 percent of global GDP.

These fledgling emerging markets offer high-growth potential and have attractive valuations compared to the more established emerging markets.

They have attracted risk-embracing investors who want to gain access to the relatively untapped potential offered by these countries. Because of this, a new market segment is being established.

We hope the arguments contained in this book will spark the reader's interest in exploring the potential of emerging and frontier markets.

Russell Investments has been at the forefront of growing investor interest in frontier markets. In the United States, it created the Russell Frontier Index and launched a Frontier Market Pool in 2010. Russell Investments Canada established a frontier market mandate in the Russell Emerging Markets Pool in April 2011.

David Feather
President and Chief Executive Officer
Russell Investments Canada
September 2013

CHAPTER 1

Introducing Emerging and Frontier Markets

O ver the last decade, returns from developed markets have been effectively zero or negative. In the 10 years ending on December 31, 2012, the Morgan Stanley Capital International Developed World Index returned 5.4 percent annually in U.S. dollars in nominal terms. This extremely disappointing record has been accompanied by enormous volatility, giving investors the worst of both worlds—not only have they effectively not made any money in real terms, but they have experienced moves in the markets that have not been seen since the Great Depression of the 1930s.

Over the same period, emerging markets—defined as those countries with a Gross Domestic Product (GDP) per capita of less than US$12,476 (2012) and which are represented by the MSCI Emerging Markets (Free) Index—have delivered 13.7 percent annually in U.S. dollars, more than doubling an investor's initial investment. There are several reasons for this massive outperformance of more-developed markets by less-developed markets, the most important of which were the low and attractive valuations of the developing as opposed to developed markets at the beginning of the decade. Reasons also include their faster rate of GDP growth, younger populations, higher levels of savings and lower levels of government and personal debt. The growth and success of emerging markets will likely be repeated by the next generation of emerging economies—the frontier markets.

This book examines the factors contributing to the performance of emerging and frontier markets and dispenses practical advice for those considering investing in frontier markets. It defines emerging markets and frontier markets and discusses differences between them, explores the diversity of frontier markets and establishes why it is important to differentiate between regions and between individual countries within regions. Furthermore, it considers the risks inherent in investing in such markets, including poor liquidity and regulation, political instability and inadequate financial reporting, and suggests how to manage these risks. It also explains the importance of distinguishing between the popular image of countries and regions and what is actually happening "at ground level."

Investing in Frontier Markets enumerates the key benefits developed market investors can accrue by investing in frontier markets, namely diversification, a low correlation with developed markets and the strong likelihood of frontier markets mirroring the development path followed by longer-established emerging markets, thus delivering strong returns to investors with long-term horizons. The book goes on to examine some of the problems faced by emerging markets during their period of rapid development over the last 15 years. It also looks at the changing role of financial advisors and how they can help position frontier markets in an investor's portfolio and the pitfalls of attempting to "go it alone" when investing in emerging and frontier markets, for example, by using online investing.

Finally, *Investing in Frontier Markets* reviews the various routes available for developed market investors to access frontier markets, beginning with exchange-traded funds (ETFs) and continuing with individual stocks, whether global multinational companies with exposure to emerging and frontier markets or American depository receipts (ADRs) or global depository receipts (GDRs) of emerging and frontier listed companies. The book concludes by looking at mutual and closed-end funds invested in frontier markets, including single-country, regional and global closed-end funds and provides recommendations as to the preferred choice for investors.

EMERGING MARKETS

Antoine van Agtmael, an economist at the International Finance Corporation (IFC), the equity arm of the World Bank, first coined the term "emerging markets" in the early 1980s. The phrase was defined in economic terms: emerging markets were countries with low to middle income per capita. It replaced the earlier description of "less-developed countries," which was seen to have pejorative connotations and has become the accepted description of economies that are moving from developing status to developed status.

Each year on July 1, the World Bank divides countries into four categories, based on annual gross national income (GNI) per capita:

- low income: below US$1,025
- lower-middle income: US$1,026–$4,035
- upper-middle income: US$4,036–$12,475
- high income: US$12,476 or more[1]

---

[1] World Bank, data as of July 1, 2012, http://data.worldbank.org/indicator/NY .GNP.PC.

The World Bank notes that low income and middle income countries are often referred to as "developing economies," but goes on to say that while the term is convenient, it does not imply that all countries in the categories have reached a similar stage of development.[2]

In effect, emerging markets are low and middle income countries. Another way to define emerging markets is to say that they are those countries that do not belong to the Organisation of Economic Co-operation and Development (OECD), which consists of 34 developed countries. This is not the best definition though, since several of the OECD countries, such as Chile, Estonia, Mexico, South Korea and Turkey, are sometimes included in lists of emerging market economies.

The head of the IFC's emerging market database, Farida Khambata, was the first person to use the term "frontier markets," in 1992. Frontier markets are a subset of emerging markets. They are investable but have lower market capitalization and liquidity, or more investment restrictions than the more established emerging markets, or both. These traits make them unsuitable for inclusion in the larger emerging market indices, but nonetheless they display what Marek Ondraschek, Chief Executive Officer of ALNUA Investment Managers, has described as "a relative openness to and accessibility for foreign investors" while not demonstrating "extreme economic and political instability."[3]

The smaller size and lower liquidity of frontier markets means that they are not particularly correlated with other stock markets around the world, including other emerging markets or each other, thus making them attractive to investors looking for potential high returns while lowering the overall volatility of an investor's portfolio.

Despite the fact that emerging markets have been a recognized asset class for the last quarter century, with Franklin Templeton launching the first closed-end emerging market fund in March 1987[4] and Morgan Stanley Capital International (MSCI) launching the first comprehensive emerging markets index in 1988, there are still differences of opinion as to which economies should be classified as emerging. The International Monetary Fund (IMF) and providers of stock market indices such as FTSE, MSCI Barra, Standard & Poor's (S&P) and Dow Jones all produce lists that at

---

[2] World Bank Web site, Data: "How We Classify Countries."
[3] Opalesque TV, interview, September 13, 2010.
[4] Remarkably, Mark Mobius has been the lead manager of the Templeton Emerging Markets Fund (listed on the NYSE with the ticker EMF) since its inception over 25 years ago, a record of longevity with one fund that is almost unparalleled in the fund management industry.

mid-year 2012 had 24, 22, 21, 19 and 22 countries respectively listed as emerging markets.

The countries that are included in all five lists are as follows:

Asia

- China
- India
- Indonesia
- Malaysia
- The Philippines
- Thailand

Europe, the Middle East and Africa

- Hungary
- Poland
- Russia
- South Africa
- Turkey

Latin America

- Brazil
- Chile
- Mexico
- Peru

This makes 15 countries that five major data providers agree should be classified as emerging markets. Twenty-one countries are included in the emerging market indices compiled by S&P and MSCI, the most widely followed indices, which are as follows:

Asia

- China
- India
- Indonesia
- Malaysia
- The Philippines
- South Korea
- Taiwan
- Thailand

Europe, the Middle East and Africa

- Czech Republic
- Egypt
- Hungary
- Morocco
- Poland
- Russia
- South Africa
- Turkey

Latin America

- Brazil
- Chile
- Colombia
- Mexico
- Peru

Interestingly, several markets, such as Israel and South Korea, which would have been classified as "emerging" 15 years ago, are no longer included in many lists as they have now "emerged." By that, we mean that their GNI per capita has surpassed the top end of the middle-income category. FTSE and MSCI upgraded Israel to the list of developed markets in 2008 and 2010, respectively, and FTSE upgraded South Korea in 2009, as did S&P. In the 30 years or so since the IFC first developed an emerging market index, there have been only two other countries that have been upgraded: Greece and Portugal.

A cutoff point of US$25,000 GDP per capita at market exchange rates includes all of the markets classified as developed, with the exception of Israel, which is in the process of being reclassified. The only developed markets with lower GDP per capita are Portugal (which was promoted in 2001) and South Korea (which is in the process of being reclassified).

Using estimated GDP per capita in 1900 from Angus Maddison's historical database, Elroy Dimson, Paul Marsh and Mike Staunton from the London Business School, authors of *Triumph of the Optimists*,[5] ranked developed and emerging markets using the same level of income that corresponds to US$25,000 in 2010. Using this criterion, they note that only

---

[5]Elroy Dimson, Paul Marsh and Mike Staunton, *Triumph of the Optimists: 101 Years of Equity Returns* (Princeton: Princeton University Press, 2002).

seven of the 38 countries with equity markets in 1900 changed status over the following 110 years.

Five markets moved from emerging to developed—Finland, Japan and Hong Kong and, more recently, Portugal and Greece—while Argentina and Chile fell from developed to emerging market status. Adding Singapore, the stock market of which opened in 1911, and the two countries in the process of being reclassified, Israel and South Korea, denotes the eight countries that have "emerged" over 110 years.[6]

The question of whether developing economies will naturally end up achieving developed country status or whether they will require help and guidance from government and international investors is still a hotly debated topic. Some emerging markets have followed the path of Japan, which after the Meiji Restoration in 1868, used government direction of the economy and financial system to create a modern, industrialized state that could hold its own against the Western colonial powers.

Japan took what it considered to be the most successful examples of best practices from the leading powers, so that it modeled its navy and railways on those of Great Britain and its army and educational system on those of Prussia.

Within 40 years it had defeated one of the major powers, Russia, both on land and sea, and within 80, it had inflicted humiliating reversals on the other major colonial nations of Great Britain, France, the Netherlands and the United States. After military defeat in the Second World War, Japan created an industrial powerhouse that within 30 years was the second largest economy in the world, challenging the United States as the largest industrial power.

The Nikkei-Dow Jones Index, the major Japanese stock market index, appreciated by six times during the 1980s, finishing 1989 at 38,900, making Japan's the most valuable stock market in the world. At the time, it comprised just under 30 percent of the MSCI World Index against 25 percent for the United States. Its 75 percent decline since the Nikkei peaked at the end of December 1989 should not detract from its remarkable success between 1949 and 1989.

Some nations, such as South Korea, a Japanese colony from 1910 to 1945, followed the Japanese path of directed economic development very closely. They specialized in similar industries, initially textiles and toys,

---

[6]In the excellent film about Wall Street, *Working Girl*, Cynthia (played by Joan Cusack) attempts to persuade her friend Tess (played by Melanie Griffith) to go out with her. Tess explains she cannot go, as she has to study for a class on emerging markets. "Why can't you let them emerge by themselves?" is Cynthia's response.

then consumer electronics, and most recently steel, telecommunications, automobiles and shipbuilding.

Other countries, including Taiwan, a Japanese colony from 1895 to 1945, chose a different path. With some government direction but also a fair degree of commercial independence, Taiwan specialized in petrochemicals, electronics, telecommunications and computers.

The other members of what were known as the newly industrializing countries (NICs) were existing or former British island colonies: Hong Kong and Singapore. They had no natural resources and larger hostile (or at least ambivalent) neighbors in China, and Indonesia and Malaysia, respectively. Using their positions as major ports and trading hubs, exporting Asian natural resources and low-end manufactured goods in exchange for products from the industrialized nations, they became the wealthiest Asian states ever known, partially due to their inheritance of the rule of law from the British colonial era.

As was constantly stressed by Chris Patten (now Lord Patten of Barnes), the last British governor of Hong Kong (1992–1997), knowing the rules under which commerce would be conducted gives business confidence to invest and grow. Hong Kong offered the closest thing to 19th century laissez-faire capitalism that existed in the 20th century, while Singapore was among the most regulated and organized of countries. However, both succeeded in boosting their GNI per capita more than five times over the last half century.

Interestingly, three of the six countries that have successfully migrated from emerging to developed status over the last 100 years (Japan, Hong Kong and Singapore—four out of eight if we include South Korea and Israel) have been Asian and the remainder European.

None of the NICs were full-fledged democracies during the period of their fastest growth, with South Korea under military rule and Taiwan a one-party state under the Kuomintang Party (KMT), Chiang Kai-shek's nationalist party, until the 1990s. Hong Kong was a British colony until its handover to China in 1997, when it became a Special Administrative Region (SAR) under the "one country, two systems" agreement. Singapore was effectively a one-party state with the Peoples' Action Party (PAP) winning overwhelming majorities with free elections until this decade. Some observers feel that Japan also could have been classified as a one-party state, as the Liberal Democratic Party (LDP) held power for 40 years, starting in 1955.

Whether non-democratic forms of government are a necessary condition for rapid economic growth is a subject that has been fiercely debated.

The argument for an autocratic government, whether a one-party state, a communist regime or a state ruled by the military, is that an autocracy is able to overcome vested interests that benefit from the existing low-growth economic arrangements. In this view, the owners of property and facilities, with little or no interest in encouraging faster growth, can be considered rent takers, whether literally, in the form of land ownership, or by exacting high fees for the use of resources, in the form of trade guilds or monopolies.

On the other hand, the argument against non-democratic regimes stems from their ability to ignore the rule of law and property rights, which makes it unattractive for investors to risk capital that may end up being confiscated in an arbitrary fashion and without due process.

China, with its one-party status and impressive physical infrastructure but constrained human rights, exemplifies the results of belief in autocratic government. India, with its vibrant democracy, highly educated middle class, rule of law and intellectual infrastructure, but with bottlenecks and capacity constraints in power, ports and highways, represents the results of a belief that autocracy is not necessary to achieve rapid economic growth.

Of the 31 countries out of 38 that did not change status in the last 110 years, 17 were classified as developed in 1900 and still are classified as such, and 14 were classified as emerging and remain in that category 110 years later. Thus, while GDP per capita has grown considerably in these countries, their relative rankings have changed far more slowly.

Many reasons explain why emerging markets have not emerged more rapidly, including dictatorship, civil war, corruption, wars, communism without Chinese characteristics (the latter including such features as private ownership of property, companies being allowed to make and retain profits and a relatively high degree of economic, though not political, freedom for individuals), hyperinflation and disastrous economic policies. Dictatorships, which were particularly prevalent in Latin America during the 20th century, but also arose in such European countries as Portugal under Salazar, Spain under Antonio Salazar Francisco Franco and Italy under Benito Mussolini, tended to promote inward-looking policies featuring high-tariff barriers and subsidies to favored domestic industries. These benefited groups that supported the regime at the expense of efficiency and openness to outside influences, but helped maintain the dictatorship's grip on power.

Wars generally have negative effects on economic growth, especially for the losers, but sometimes also, as with the case of the United Kingdom after the Second World War, for the victors as well. Only when a country is geographically isolated, such as the United States, Australia or South Africa, does involvement in a war tend to benefit nations. Civil wars, such as those which occurred in Spain from 1936 to 1939, China from 1928 to 1949 and Russia from 1917 to 1922, are particularly disruptive to economic progress, as they both destroy economic capacity and lead to many of the country's most intelligent and dynamic citizens being killed, imprisoned or driven into exile.

Communism, with its disastrous economic policies of rigid central planning, prohibition of individual enterprise and valuation of party loyalty above competence, ensured that Russia remained economically backward for most of the 20th century, as did Eastern Europe from 1945 to 1989 and China from 1949 to 1979, when Deng Xiaoping introduced a modified form of capitalism ("communism with Chinese characteristics").

■ ■ ■

Finally, governments resorting to the printing press to attempt to solve economic difficulties, whether Weimar Germany from 1922 to 1923, Greece and Hungary from 1944 to 1946 or Argentina, Brazil and Peru from 1989 to 1990 and Zimbabwe from 2007 to 2010, lead to the destruction of savings and a collapse of investor confidence needed to fund investment.

Argentina, which experienced dictatorship under Juan Peron, hyperinflation in the 1970s and 1980s and an unsuccessful foreign war, in 1900 had a GDP per capita equal to France's and higher than Sweden's and Norway's and was one of the five wealthiest countries in the world. Having suffered through this combination of misfortunes particularly since 1950, it has now been relegated to frontier market status by MSCI (in 2009). Several Eastern European markets that were moving toward becoming developed markets in the early 20th century, such as Poland, Hungary, Czechoslovakia and Russia, were hit by the double blow of two world wars and communism.

Unforeseen crises aside, the path to successful economic development is by now widely known and easy to follow if the political elite in a country has an interest in doing so and is willing to overcome the opposition it will face from existing stakeholders. It involves a few major steps such as carrying out a program of land reform to give clear title to small landowners in the agricultural sector and reducing internal and external tariffs and customs duties to encourage the free flow of goods. Other prerequisites include a relatively transparent legal system not dependent upon the whims of the ruler and a focus on raising educational standards so that the workforce required for industrialization is literate and numerate, enabling it to function effectively in an industrial society.

The rule of law, including the recognition of property rights, and the free movement of goods and labor are the necessary underpinnings of economic takeoff. While additional benefits such as provision of a reasonable standard of health care, recognition of workers' rights and a clean environment are desirable in an emerging (or indeed any) economy, they are not vital.

As noted previously, the MSCI Emerging Markets (Free) Index, the best-known index for these markets, has more than doubled over the last decade. Through the 10 years ending October 31, 2012, it returned 85.6 percent in U.S. dollar terms, or a total return of 133.6 percent with dividends included, equivalent to 8.9 percent per annum (p.a.). This is despite the perceived "riskiness" of investing in markets and economies that can be very volatile, where political risks are high, and the quality of information available is low.

The reasons for their outperformance, compared with developed markets, which have returned less than half this amount over the same period, are perfectly straightforward. At the beginning of the last decade, emerging markets were cheap: their valuations were at low levels after the Asian crisis of 1997–98, the Russian default of 1998, the devaluation of the Brazilian real in 1999 and the Argentinean default of 2001. However, their underlying fundamentals, the principal reason for investing, remained attractive. We believe the same situation applies to frontier markets today, where the frontier market index has rebounded only half as much as either the emerging market or, indeed, developed market indices since the financial crisis of 2008–09.

As is the case with frontier markets today, these markets were countries with young populations, low social costs in the form of low or no government expenditures on unemployment payments and pensions, high levels of domestic savings due to the absence of a government safety net in the form of unemployment payments or pensions, rising living standards as they industrialized and improved competitive positions through currency positioning and devaluation.

As a result, they have enjoyed a decade of improving GDP and rising incomes, while also running balance of trade surpluses and keeping government spending under control. Their stock markets have reflected these improvements and delivered excellent returns to shareholders, although fast growth in an economy is not always reflected in stock prices, an economic principle demonstrated by China.

The improvement in the financial situation of the emerging markets is reflected in their credit ratings by the major agencies, where by the end of 2010 57 percent of the JP Morgan Emerging Market Bond Index was investment grade (rated BBB or above), compared to 34 percent in 2002 and only 5 percent in the late 1990s.

By purchasing a fund with broad geographical exposure to these markets, whether actively managed or a passive index fund (the diversification helps to avoid undue exposure to problems in one region or another, such as the Arab Spring of 2010–11), investors will be able to benefit from these trends as they continue for the next few years.

The growth of the middle class in the emerging and frontier markets will also benefit commodity producers in developed countries, such as Australia and Canada, and emerging and frontier commodity producers themselves, particularly those with a major resource sector such as South Africa, Indonesia, Brazil and Colombia.

One additional point to bear in mind is that the improving fundamentals of emerging and frontier markets are reflected in their currencies, which have tended to at least hold their own, if not appreciate gradually, against developed market currencies over the last decade. This reflects their improving fundamentals and superior demographic profile compared to the aging and debt-encumbered Eurozone, Japanese and U.S. economies. Over the past decade, the Chinese Renminbi has appreciated against the American dollar, the Mexican peso and the Brazilian real.

FRONTIER MARKETS

Frontier markets comprise the approximately 60 countries that are not included among the 25 developed stock markets or the 21 emerging markets that we discussed in the previous section. Both MSCI and S&P have frontier market indices, and those 40 countries included in the indices from both index providers are as follows:

Sub-Saharan Africa

- Benin
- Botswana
- Burkina Faso
- Ghana
- Kenya
- Ivory Coast
- Mauritius
- Namibia
- Nigeria
- Senegal
- Zambia

Asia

- Bangladesh
- Kazakhstan
- Pakistan
- Sri Lanka
- Vietnam

Europe

- Bulgaria
- Croatia
- Estonia

- Latvia
- Lithuania
- Romania
- Serbia
- Slovakia
- Slovenia
- Ukraine

Latin America

- Argentina
- Colombia
- Ecuador
- Jamaica
- Panama
- Trinidad and Tobago

Middle East and North Africa (MENA)

- Bahrain
- Jordan
- Kuwait
- Lebanon
- Oman
- Qatar
- Tunisia
- United Arab Emirates (UAE)

This list of countries includes Colombia, which also appears in the emerging market indices. There are another 45 to 50 countries not included in the index providers' frontier indices, which have been described by some investors as exotic frontier markets. They have smaller market capitalizations, lower liquidity and price-to-earnings (P/E) ratios and lower correlation with major developed markets than those countries in the frontier market indices.

These include some quite sizable or resource-rich countries such as Azerbaijan, Belarus and Macedonia in Europe; Angola, Tanzania and Zimbabwe in Africa; and Iran, Iraq and Saudi Arabia in the Middle East. Politics, lack of liquidity or restrictions on foreign ownership exclude them from being included in the indices.

The argument for investing in frontier markets may be stated very simply. Their economies are at a stage of development similar to where the emerging markets were 10 to 15 years ago, and it is highly probable that they will follow the same path of economic development as the emerging markets.

This in turn should be reflected in the performance of their stock markets. In the same way as the emerging markets proved over the last 15 years, from 1998 to 2013, frontier markets will become extremely rewarding investments.

The reason for believing that the frontier markets will likely prove to be rewarding investments is not that high rates of GDP growth will necessarily be reflected in their stock markets, as we discuss in Chapter 4. The reason is that they are attractively valued with a price-to-earnings ratio of 10.3, price-to-book ratio of 1.38 and dividend yield of 4.1 percent (September 2012), which matches where the emerging markets were at the beginning of the last decade.

In addition to being valuable because of their potential income, frontier markets are also a good investment choice because they are not highly correlated with other major stock markets or the other emerging and frontier markets; therefore, although volatile themselves, adding them to a portfolio will reduce its overall volatility.

Frontier markets, moreover, look attractively valued by comparison with emerging and developed markets. This is to be expected, given their lower level of economic development, lack of liquidity and small size. Nonetheless, the MSCI Frontier Markets Index, which lost two-thirds of its value during the global financial crisis of 2008–09, slightly worse than the emerging and developed market indices, has recovered to only about half the level of its 2008 high in the last four years, as opposed to the other global indices, which recovered almost all of their losses. This fact makes them good candidates for investment, as the frontier market economies have continued to grow strongly through this period, in some cases growing more rapidly than the established emerging markets such as Brazil, Russia and India. With more domestically oriented economies, they have been less affected by the slow and patchy GDP growth displayed by the developed economies, especially Europe and Japan, since the financial crisis of 2008–09. Furthermore, as standards of corporate governance improve and access to foreign capital becomes easier, frontier market listed companies are demonstrating strong growth in earnings as they are able to invest newly available capital in attractive opportunities.

Through August 31, 2012, the most recent date for which statistics are available at the time of writing, the MSCI Frontier Markets Index was down −9.83 percent per annum over five years, compared to a barely noticeable −0.07 percent p.a. for the MSCI Emerging Markets (Free) Index. This major underperformance has led to the emerging markets index doing almost twice as well as the frontier index over the last 10 years, up 15.35 percent annualized against 8.33 percent.

The emerging markets index has been more volatile than the frontier market index over the last three years, with an annualized standard deviation of 22.15 against 13.97. That demonstrates the lower level of correlation the illiquid frontier markets exhibit against their much larger and more highly traded emerging market counterparts. Interestingly, this pattern holds true even including the period of extreme volatility that characterized the global financial crisis, with the annualized standard deviation for the two indices since November 30, 2007, which marked the beginning of the crisis, being 29.6 for emerging markets against 24.07 for frontier markets.

This underperformance, despite the lower volatility associated with frontier markets during the crisis, has resulted in a negative Sharpe ratio of −0.05 for the three years ending on August 31, 2012, and of −0.42 for the period since November 30, 2007, against positive numbers of 0.40 and 0.02 for emerging markets over the same periods. This underperformance leaves frontier markets notably cheaper than emerging markets, with a price-to-earnings ratio for the MSCI Frontier Markets Index of 10.27 against 11.72 for the MSCI Emerging Markets, a dividend yield of 4.7 percent against 3.02 percent and a price-to-book value of 1.38 against 1.57.

Thus, quite apart from the long-term attractions of frontier markets and the likelihood of their matching the performance of the more-developed emerging markets, frontier markets have also lagged behind the latter over the last five years and are selling at reasonable valuations in absolute terms. At price-to-earnings and price-to-book-value ratios of 10.3 times and 1.38 times, they are 10 percent cheaper than those of emerging markets, with a 50 percent higher dividend yield.

Naturally, it would be reasonable to expect less-developed and less liquid markets to sell at lower valuations than more-developed markets. However, until frontier markets recently underperformed, they sold at approximately the same valuation as emerging markets, and in some cases, at a premium to the latter. This high valuation reflects the lack of liquidity characteristic of stock markets at an early stage of development, which means that even very small amounts of money entering the market will lead to a rapid rise in valuations, regardless of the attractiveness of the underlying market.

For instance, in 2007 the Vietnam Index (VNI) sold at a P/E ratio of 20.5, even though inflation was accelerating from 12.5 percent to 22.4 percent between 2007 and 2008, and the trade deficit widened from $10.4 billion to $12.9 billion over the same period. Five years later the P/E ratio had contracted to 9.5 in 2011 and a forecast 9 in 2012, even while inflation was down to 6.8 percent and the trade deficit down to a mere $4.2 billion.

In some cases frontier markets may be just as liquid or even more liquid than comparable emerging markets, but there are investment restrictions on foreign ownership that make it difficult or impossible for foreigners to take advantage of the liquidity that is available.

When China began developing its stock markets in the early 1990s, at which stage it would have been classified as a frontier market, it reserved what were known as "A shares," listed on the Shanghai and Shenzhen exchanges, for local residents, while allowing foreign investors to purchase only B shares.

The liquidity in the latter was and remains very low, while the A shares, as one of the only three avenues for Chinese domestic savings (the others being bank deposits and property), were extremely liquid and traded at much higher valuations than the equivalent B shares, which were often quite reasonably valued.

Once the Chinese government began privatizing its state-owned enterprises (SOEs) in the mid-1990s, listing them both as A shares on the Shanghai Stock Exchange and also as H shares on the Hong Kong stock market, foreign investors were in the unusual position of being able to purchase shares in some of the leading blue-chip companies in a major emerging market at substantial discounts compared to the domestically listed shares. With only domestic Chinese investors permitted to own A shares, their valuations soon became much higher than the H shares available to all investors, even though they both provided exposure to the same underlying company. Some frontier markets also maintain restrictions on foreign ownership of locally listed shares or require foreign-owned subsidiaries to list a percentage of the local company on the domestic stock exchange to allow certain domestic investors the opportunity to become owners of leading enterprises, Bangladesh, Kenya and Nigeria among them.

Usually, the situation is reversed: when foreign investors are restricted in the percentage of a domestic company they are permitted to own, foreign shares tend to move at a premium to local shares, as demand from foreigners drives up the price of the shares they are permitted to own. This situation has happened in such markets as Thailand, the Philippines and India, and has led to the creation of mechanisms to permit foreign investors to own a higher percentage of such restricted companies than is permitted by government limits on foreign ownership through participation certificates. These instruments allow foreign investors to enjoy the price performance of the underlying equity without actually becoming shareholders in the company.

The introduction of participation certificates is a characteristic phase that developing markets usually pass through, in which concerns about foreign ownership mean that governments consider it important to cap the percentage in the possession of non-locals. Some frontier markets such as Saudi Arabia specifically ban foreign investment in Saudi-listed companies, although there are persistent rumors at the time of writing (2012–13) that the authorities are considering relaxing these restrictions. We deal with Saudi Arabia in the section on exotic frontier markets, but in the meantime an active market in participation certificates has developed, given the large size of the Saudi market (US$300 billion market capitalization) compared to other frontier markets.

Of course, this sentiment is not confined to developing markets.

One has only to note the U.S. and Canadian restrictions on foreign ownership of defense and media assets, including newspapers, TV and radio stations. These restrictions are designed to protect those companies considered of strategic importance to the economy. This attitude led to Canada banning the foreign takeovers of satellite maker McDonald Detwiler in 2008 and agricultural giant Potash Corp. of Saskatchewan in 2011. It also led to restrictions by the United States on the takeover of oil company Unocal by Chinese National Overseas Oil Corp. in 2005. In 2006, it also led to the argument over Dubai port company DP World taking over the American ports owned by shipping company Peninsular and Oriental (P&O).

Other developed market governments such as the United Kingdom and France have retained what is known as a "golden share" in privatized companies, allowing them the right to control changes in ownership.

While acknowledging that restrictions on foreign ownership are not confined to emerging and frontier markets, it is important to note that this is a stage that almost all developing markets move through, and the removal or loosening of restrictions on foreign investors is a useful sign of changing attitudes by the governments of frontier markets toward foreign investment. Permitting local companies to list on foreign stock exchanges with perceived higher standards of corporate governance and regulatory scrutiny is also an encouraging sign, and certain frontier markets such as Kazakhstan and Nigeria have seen a number of companies list on the London Stock Exchange (LSE) in the last five years.

When considering investing in frontier markets, investors should bear these factors in mind. While selling at attractive valuations at the time of writing, enjoying strong underlying growth in GDP and having attractive fundamentals in terms of young populations and relatively low levels of outstanding debt at time of writing, frontier markets in general have lower standards of corporate governance, less information available and are substantially less liquid than either developed or emerging markets. Any investment in frontier markets should be undertaken on a long-term basis, with investors being prepared to hold their positions for at least five years to benefit from the favorable advantages.

TAKEAWAYS

1. We suggest that the returns from frontier markets will eventually match those of emerging markets.
2. Factors such as diversification, low correlation with developed markets and the strong likelihood of frontier markets mirroring the development path followed by longer-established emerging markets will drive those returns.
3. Frontier markets are much less developed than emerging markets, and exotic frontier markets are the least developed in the frontier category.
4. Generally, a country moves from the exotic frontier category to the more established frontier category, then to the emerging market category and, in some cases, finally moves to the developed nation category.
5. Low levels of liquidity are a major issue in frontier markets, with investors needing to have a long-term time frame for any investment to allow the favorable fundamentals to develop.

CHAPTER 2

Frontier Markets by Region

In this chapter, we include all the usual statistics, such as population, the demographic makeup of the population and gross domestic product (GDP), to show the absolute size of the economy. We also include GDP per capita to illustrate how the wealth of the average inhabitant is the trade balance (whether positive or negative), consumer inflation and the structure of the economy with percentages for agriculture, industry and services.

Moreover, we note the political structure of the frontier countries, whether dictatorship, communist, monarchy, autocracy and limited or open democracy. We also introduce some less traditional measures such as the Transparency International Corruption Perceptions Index and the Gini coefficients for the frontier markets. These are included to give investors some indication of the level of corporate and political governance they may anticipate based on the country's track record and the experience of third party investors, and the level of income disparity between the wealthiest and poorest sectors of the population. These two measures may help to give the investor some sense of the likelihood of political unrest and risk associated with potential investments.

While it has become a cliché to say that "demography is destiny," the structure of a country's population does give some obvious clues as to which sectors or industries are likely to do well or badly. Moreover, when combined with a high level of income disparity between rich and poor and a corporate and government culture that is widely perceived as corrupt and hence unfair, a country with a high percentage of its population under 25 obviously has a higher risk of political unrest, as was witnessed during the Arab Spring of 2010–11.

Young populations that have no stake in the success of the existing regime and are embittered by repressive institutions that they perceive as corrupt have the potential to break out in protests, which can easily turn violent. If the regime has too narrow a base of support, limited to a particular religious or tribal group, for example, as in Libya and Syria, or its foreign sponsor has become less supportive or ambivalent, as in Egypt, and as may be occurring in North Korea, then there is a strong possibility of a regime change. Unrest obviously has implications for successful investment in such markets, and being aware of such social stresses may help give investors advance warning or help determine which countries and regions are more or less attractive as potential investments.

Countries are grouped geographically in this chapter, partially for ease of reference and partially as a result of the fact that they share certain cultural and economic features due to their location. For instance, countries in South and Central America and the Caribbean were part of the Spanish or Portuguese empires with minor exceptions and have their language, religion and legal systems in common. Similarly, countries in South Asia (Pakistan, Bangladesh and Sri Lanka) share a common background of British colonial rule and institutions, and those in central Asia (Kazakhstan, Mongolia, Uzbekistan) have a similar legacy of Russian rule and institutions.

This setup also allows comparisons among countries in the same region, highlighting their respective levels of development and likelihood of proving attractive to investors. Indeed, it would appear more probable that countries that have achieved a higher level of economic development as opposed to their immediate neighbors would be more capable of achieving rapid economic development, if only because of the importance of reaching a "critical mass."

Research by economists and economic historians such as Angus Maddison in *Contours of the World Economy, 1-2030 AD* and Michael Porter have demonstrated that areas with a certain level of income tend to develop much more rapidly than those that have not yet achieved a similar level. While there is no hard and fast income level at which this process begins to occur, Maddison's research indicates that it seems to be associated with the move from low income (below $1,025 GNI p.a. in the World Bank definition) to lower-middle income ($1,026 to $4,035 GNI p.a.). Thus the Netherlands saw its GDP per capita increase almost three times between 1500 and 1700 from $761 to $2,130 in purchasing power parity (PPP) terms, while the United Kingdom's almost doubled between 1600 and 1820 from $974 to $1,706. This fact seems partially to be due to the creation of spare capital resulting from an economic surplus, which in turn is available for investment in capital equipment and other productivity-enhancing developments.

Some of this development of capital equipment and other methods of raising industrial and agricultural output may in turn be due to the ability of wealthier societies to spend some of their economic surplus on education, which leads to further inventions and improvements, creating a virtuous circle.

MEASURES USED IN THIS CHAPTER

This section defines the measures used in this chapter and the reasoning behind their use. These measures allow the reader to compare important economic and social measures between countries in the same region, in an easy-to-read format.

For example, looking at the statistics section shows how large the countries are in absolute terms, such as the size of the population and labor force, gross domestic product (GDP), stock market capitalization, trade and foreign direct investment (FDI). The statistical table also allows readers to see how countries stack up in terms of comparative measures, such as the median age of populations, the composition of GDP, taxes as a percentage of GDP, unemployment, inflation and how well the country scores in terms of income inequality (Gini Index), corruption and human development.

Gross Domestic Product

GDP is the most widely used measure of a country's output and, when divided by the population to produce GDP per capita, gives a measure of the country's poverty or wealth. We have used GDP calculated on a purchasing power parity (PPP) basis in order to get comparable statistics, as many frontier markets, such as Venezuela, have pegged or fixed exchange rates that understate or occasionally overstate their GDP in U.S. dollar terms.

GDP per capita is the simplest method of comparing different economies at the individual level. A country with high GDP per capita, as with most members of the OECD, shows that it has already become relatively wealthy, and its inhabitants enjoy a high standard of living. Therefore it is unlikely to grow exceptionally fast, while its major industries are probably in sectors with a high degree of intellectual capital, such as knowledge-based industries (pharmaceuticals, finance, telecommunications, technology) or those requiring high levels of capital investment (automobiles, aerospace, electronics).

Countries with lower GDP per capita can experience periods of rapid growth driven by industrialization and the move of rural populations into the cities. Their major industries will most likely be ones requiring lower levels of intellectual and physical capital, such as consumer products, textiles, building materials and resources. Investors should be aware of the structure of countries at different levels of GDP per capita when considering their investment strategy.

Gross National Income

As noted, the World Bank, which uses a slightly different measure of economic output in gross national income (GNI), classifies any country for which the GNI per capita is below US$12,475 as a developing economy. There is a major difference between those countries with low- or lower-middle income (below $4,035 GNI p.a.) and those with higher incomes, as the very rapid growth in developing economies tends to occur in the first group. Investors should be aware that it is unreasonable to expect the period of very rapid growth, described by economist Walt Rostow as the "takeoff" phase, to continue for more than 10 to 15 years, as the easy productivity gains from urbanization and industrialization have to be replaced by investment in equipment and infrastructure, requiring large amounts of capital.

Gini Index

The Gini Index is the ratio of the Lorenz curve of family incomes in a country and how far away it is from a 45-degree line where all incomes are perfectly equal. The more equal a country's income distribution, the lower its Gini Index. A Scandinavian country such as Sweden has a Gini Index near 25, while that of a sub-Saharan African country such as Namibia or Angola would be around 50.

Countries with very high Gini Index scores (i.e., those with very unequal income distribution) should be regarded by investors as subject to greater risk of political disturbances, as evidenced by the events of the Arab Spring in 2010–11. In some cases, as with the southern African group that includes South Africa, Namibia and Angola or the Middle East and North Africa (MENA) nations, the countries may be major commodity producers, in these cases minerals and oil and gas respectively. Commodity-dependent economies are vulnerable to the ruling elite appropriating most of the revenues from the resource sector, due to the high capital investment required for exploration and production and the limited number of areas that produce energy or materials.

Corruption Perceptions Index

Transparency International produces the Corruption Perceptions Index, which serves as an effective proxy for the degree of difficulty businesses may encounter when attempting to invest or establish operations in a particular country.

A high score on the Corruption Perceptions Index is a reassurance to investors that business is conducted in a relatively transparent and open fashion with equal treatment for all parties. Improvements in the index are a useful indicator that the climate of corporate governance and political relations has changed in ways that benefit outside investors. A low ranking should not dissuade investors from considering a country for investment, but should alert them to the possibility of decisions affecting them being influenced by non-business factors.

Human Development Index

The United Nations produces the Human Development Index (HDI), which incorporates such measures as literacy, life expectancy and GNI per capita. It was introduced by economist Mahbub ul Haq in 1990 and was based on Nobel laureate Amartya Sen's work on human capabilities and functioning. By incorporating measures of human development, such as life expectancy and education, ul Haq hoped to convince policy makers to evaluate development not only by economic growth but by improvements in human well-being. The calculation was changed in 2010 to incorporate mean and expected years of schooling for the education index rather than literacy rates and GNI per capita rather than GDP per capita.

The Human Development Index enables investors to see whether strong economic growth is being reflected in improvements in living standards as measured by health and education, rather than simply through increasing GDP per capita. If a country's life expectancy is either stagnating or not rising when income is increasing, it suggests that economic benefits are not being widely distributed or achieved at the cost of underinvestment in a country's human capital. Again, a low HDI should not prevent an investor from considering a country; most developing economies will not score highly owing to shorter life expectancies and less time in school for the majority of citizens. However, investors should look for an improving HDI to be combined with strong economic growth.

This format allows readers to understand at a glance whether a specific frontier market is similar to the large emerging markets with relatively low but rapidly growing levels of GDP per capita, such as the BRIC countries (Brazil, Russia, India and China). That is the case with Bangladesh, Pakistan and Vietnam in Asia. This format also highlights smaller but higher income countries, such as Kazakhstan and Sri Lanka, with strengths in particular sectors such as resources or services.

ASIA

Asian frontier markets can be divided into two groups. One consists of the former British colonies of South Asia: Bangladesh, Pakistan and Sri Lanka and the other of former Russian republics or allies that shared a Soviet economic system and a communist ideology: for example Kazakhstan, Mongolia and Vietnam. We also include the second largest emerging market, India, for comparison with these frontier markets, some of which, such as Kazakhstan, are—ironically—substantially wealthier than India on a GDP per capita basis.

Therefore, investors should be aware that frontier markets do not all fall into the same pattern. Some do fit the stereotype of frontier markets in investors' minds; Pakistan, Bangladesh and Vietnam are large countries with low incomes as measured by GDP per capita, where the majority of the population still lives in the countryside. Their growth over the next two decades will, we believe, be derived primarily from the urbanization of their populations as people move from the country to the cities and by the growth of their domestic markets, although they will receive a boost from their export industries. Frontier markets also include, however, smaller and wealthier countries, such as Sri Lanka and Kazakhstan in Asia and the Gulf Co-operation Council (GCC) countries in the Middle East as well as the Baltic states, some of which are major resource exporters and others of which have strong service industries, such as tourism or outsourcing. The major feature that distinguishes them from established emerging markets is the size of their local stock market, which will tend to be small both in absolute terms and in relation to the size of their GDP compared to established emerging markets.

We have followed the same pattern of including emerging markets in other regional sections, with Brazil being included for Latin America, Russia for Eastern Europe, Turkey and Egypt for the Middle East and North Africa (MENA) and South Africa for sub-Saharan Africa. This allows you to make comparisons between emerging economies whose markets have already "emerged" and those economies that share many of the same characteristics but which are still regarded as being less developed, either in their capital markets or in the structure of their economy.

Although frontier markets are less developed, we strongly believe that they will follow the path trodden by the established emerging markets since 2000 and produce equally attractive returns for investors over the next decade.

Large Economies: Bangladesh, Pakistan and Vietnam

The first fact to emphasize is that three of the six Asian frontier markets have populations that rank in the top 15 worldwide (Pakistan 6th, Bangladesh 8th and Vietnam 13th). Let us just repeat that fact: three of the largest 15 populations in the world are Asian frontier markets. If they follow the example of China and India, they will continue to grow the size of their economies over the next 20 years and move up into the top 25 economies in the world in terms of absolute size.

This means that they have large domestic consumer markets, a factor that reduces their vulnerability to downturns in world trade and recessions in the developed world. Secondly, despite relatively low GDP per capita, with Vietnam ranking 166th at US$3,400 in 2011, Pakistan 174th at US$2,800 and Bangladesh 198th at US$1,700, their large populations mean that their economies already rank 28th (Pakistan), 42nd (Vietnam) and 46th (Bangladesh) in total GDP on a purchasing power parity (PPP) basis. India, by comparison, is only slightly wealthier on a GDP per capita basis than Vietnam (US$3,700 to US$3,400) but its enormous population of 1.2 billion means it is the fourth largest economy in the world.

Obviously, a large economy in absolute terms means that it will be a major market for exporters both of commodities and from developed countries. China, for instance, ranks among the top 10 consumers of iron ore, coal, copper, oil and numerous other raw materials, thus affecting prices and supply for important industrial commodities. A large economy such as Pakistan, Bangladesh or Vietnam will also have a large domestic market to offset its vulnerability to downturns in global trade, such as occurred during the global financial crisis of 2008–09, and this growth in demand led by the growth of the domestic middle class may provide some attractive investment opportunities.

Between one-quarter and one-third of the population in these countries is 15 years of age or below, with the median age ranging between 22 in Pakistan and 28 in Vietnam. This means that there is a very young population in countries with low levels of income in terms of GDP per capita, leading to the possibility of unrest if economic growth is not high enough to provide jobs for most of the new entrants to the workforce. While Pakistan and Bangladesh do not score particularly well on the Transparency International Corruption Perceptions Index, income inequality measured

TABLE 2.1 South Asia

Country	Bangladesh	Pakistan	India
Population (m)	163.6	193.2	1220.8
Age (%)			
0–14	33	34	29
15–64	62	62	65
65+	5	4	6
Median age	23.9	22.2	26.7
Population growth (%)	1.6	1.5	1.3
GDP (PPP) (US$bn)			
2012	305.5	514.8	4784
GDP growth (%)			
2012	6.1	3.7	6.5
2011	6.5	3	6.8
GDP per capita			
2012	$2,000	2,900	3,900
2011	$1,900	2,800	3,700
Labor force (%)			
Agriculture	45	45	53
Industry	30	21	19
Services	25	34	28
Unemployment (%)	5	5	10
Urbanization (%)	28	36	30
Taxes as percentage of GDP	11.8	12.8	8.8
Inflation			
2012	8.8	11.3	9.2
2011	10.7	11.9	8.9
Exports (US$bn)			
2012	25.8	24.7	309.1
2011	24.5	26.3	305
Imports (US$bn)			
2012	35.1	40.8	500.3
2011	32.6	38.9	390
Mobile phone (%)	51.6	57.4	73.2
Market capitalization (US$bn)			
2011	23.6	32.8	1015
2010	15.7	38.2	1616

(continues)

TABLE 2.1 *(continued)*

Country	Bangladesh	Pakistan	India
Income inequality (lower=more equal)	98/136 (2005)	113/136 (2008)	78/136 (2004)
Corruption 2011	120/183	134/183	95/183
Human Development Index 2012	146/186	146/186	136/186
Government	Democracy	Democracy	Democracy

Sources: United Nations, World Bank, CIA World Factbook, Transparency International.

by the Gini Index of the disparity between the wealthiest and poorest 10 percent of the population is reasonable given their weak showing as far as corruption and the Human Development Index are concerned.

While the possibility exists of an economic downturn leading to a repeat of the Arab Spring of 2010–11 in the Middle East, both Pakistan and Bangladesh have functioning if imperfect democracies, and the regional suzerain, India, stands ready to intervene if it feels that political developments in its neighbors could lead to problems. Vietnam is a communist one-party state, similar to China, and is willing to use its control of the economy to maintain stability and ensure GDP growth remains strong to avoid political unrest. The two Muslim countries are notably younger, although the population growth rate in all four countries is comparable, at between 1.3 percent to 1.6 percent per annum. Agriculture makes up more than 20 percent of Vietnam's and Pakistan's total GDP and accounts for between 45 percent and 52 percent of all four countries' labor forces, giving all of them plenty of workers to make the move from country to town during the urbanization process.

As the developed markets of Europe, Japan and North America experience low (and in some cases negative) birth rates, the young workers needed to produce goods for older consumers in developed countries must come from frontier and emerging markets. The below-replacement birth rates in such developed economies as Japan and most of Western Europe mean that each country's ratio between its workforce and its rapidly growing population over 65 is deteriorating quickly. However, in some frontier and emerging markets such as Russia, Eastern Europe and China (the latter due to its "one child" policy), populations are not growing but shrinking, making frontier countries such as those in South Asia with young populations and a high birth rate all the more attractive.

At present, each of the four countries, including India, has no more than one-third of its population living in cities. That urban–rural split means that over the next couple of decades, migration to the cities will continue, with the attendant increase in consumption of food, power and consumer products that accompanies the move into urban living.

The increase in urban populations should mean continued growth for providers of fast-moving consumer goods such as packaged food/drinks/tobacco, personal care products, computers, cell phones, utilities, cement and construction materials, auto and motorbike manufacturers and providers of financial services. Consumption of these products rises sharply in line with incomes and living in towns and cities. Obviously, companies in these sectors will become beneficiaries of these trends, as has been the case in emerging markets over the last couple of decades.

Any investor thinking about investing in frontier markets should expect whatever investment vehicle they use to have meaningful exposure in companies in these industries that benefit from increasing urbanization, such as food and drink producers, mobile phone companies, providers of building materials, consumer finance and credit card providers and utilities, as more people move into modern buildings with running water and electricity. These sectors proved to be among the best performing in the emerging markets over the last 15 years, while more export-oriented industries often suffered from overcapacity or being used as a means of absorbing the influx of migrants from the countryside at the expense of profits. Interestingly, the degree of income equality, as measured by the Gini Index of the ratio between the highest and lowest incomes, is lower in the South Asian democracies than in Vietnam (one of the three officially communist countries outside China, along with Cuba and North Korea). This finding may simply reflect the ability of the wealthiest segment of the Indian, Pakistani and Bangladeshi communities to keep some of their assets offshore or disguised, but may also indicate that, as with China, communist state–controlled capitalism can also produce meaningful income inequalities.

While official unemployment ranges around 5 percent in Pakistan, Bangladesh and Vietnam as well as India, underemployment is substantial, reaching nearly 40 percent in the South Asian economies. There is also an extensive population of overseas workers, with remittances from this workforce making up a large percentage of inflows to the current accounts of Bangladesh and Pakistan in particular. All four countries rank in the bottom half of Transparency International's Corruption Perceptions Index, and in the bottom half of the United Nations' Human Development Index, the latter reflecting relatively low levels of literacy and life expectancy.

Taxes as a percentage of GDP are only in the 11–12 percent range in South Asia, meaning all three major economies are among the bottom quartile of tax burden (i.e., the lowest 25 percent) globally, as opposed to

Vietnam's 26.7 percent of GDP going to taxes, which places it in the top half of the global league. Therefore, it is unsurprising that India, Pakistan and Bangladesh run budget deficits in the 4–7 percent of GDP range, compared to Vietnam's much lower 2.4 percent of GDP. This has not prevented Vietnam's debt as percentage of GDP from reaching 57 percent, comparable to Pakistan's and above India's 48 percent and Bangladesh's 35 percent.

All four countries suffer from relatively high inflation, averaging around 10 percent annually but with occasional moves into the high teens. This is symptomatic of economies that still subsidize certain products, particularly fuel, for social reasons and which are forced to increase prices abruptly when subsidies are reduced. It also occurs in countries with underdeveloped banking systems, where credit rationing by the government leads to rapid overheating when liquidity is expanded.

With electricity output in 2011 of 94 and 106 billion kilowatt hours (kWh, a measure of how many kilowatts are produced per hour), respectively, Pakistan and Vietnam are among the top third of countries producing electricity worldwide. India's 880 billion kWh output in 2011 makes it the seventh largest producer of electricity in the world, despite its notorious brownouts due to insufficient power generation and rampant theft of electricity in rural areas.

While there is certainly some correlation between a country's electricity output and the size of its economy, Bangladesh's exports of US$24 billion last year were almost as large as Pakistan's, even though its electric output of 25.6 billion kWh is barely a quarter of the latter's.

Revealing the domestic orientation of India's and Pakistan's economies, India's 2011 exports of US$229 billion were barely double that of Vietnam's (US$95 billion), while, as noted, Pakistan's US$25 billion in exports was only marginally higher than Bangladesh's. Thus Vietnam and Bangladesh, although smaller economies in absolute terms than India and Pakistan, had exports that were much higher in relation to the size of their GDP, implying both that they had been more successful in growing their export industries, and also that they were more vulnerable to a downturn in global trade or a move by developed economies to increase barriers to trade, such as raising tariffs.

While all four countries run trade deficits, India's is of a different magnitude than the others', not merely in absolute size (US$232 billion) but also as a percentage of GDP. It can fund this due to the enormous inflows of foreign direct investment (FDI) that it receives, with $430 billion flowing in during 2010–2011.

Showing that sometimes politics trumps economics, among the other three countries Pakistan, with US$31 billion in 2011, received more than double the amount of foreign direct investment that Bangladesh and Vietnam received put together, a result hard to justify on grounds of economic

performance or outlook and most likely reflecting foreign aid for geopoliti-
cal reasons.

This should not prevent investors from considering Pakistani stocks but
should make them aware that the nature of inward capital flows can make
a country vulnerable to a change in foreign policy on the part of their major
allies, such as the United States.

The largest disparity between the frontier markets and India is that
between the absolute size of the economies and their stock markets. While
Pakistan's GDP on a PPP basis is one-tenth of India's (US$494 billion
vs. US$4,515 billion) and Bangladesh's and Vietnam's are one-fifteenth
(US$285 billion and US$304 billion), their market capitalizations are only
2–3 percent of India's US$1 trillion. If these frontier markets saw their
stock markets reach the same relationship to GDP that India has achieved,
they could easily triple over this period.

In addition, if you were to take a very conservative view of their
likely GDP growth over the next decade and assume that Bangladesh's
and Vietnam's growth rates would only match that of Pakistan recently
(2–3 percent p.a.), then an investor would enjoy this re-rating in an
economy that would be one-third to one-half larger than its present size. If
Bangladesh and Vietnam matched the 6–8 percent p.a. GDP growth they
have enjoyed in the last few years, their economies would almost double in
size, making the re-rating that much larger.

Medium-sized Economies: Kazakhstan and Sri Lanka

Kazakhstan and Sri Lanka are two countries that have similar-sized populations, with Sri Lanka being somewhat larger at 21.5 million against 17.5
million for Kazakhstan, making them medium-sized economies (57th and
60th). Both have populations that are older than those of the larger Asian
frontier markets, with less than a quarter aged below 15 and median ages
around 30.

Kazakhstan is more than twice as wealthy in GDP per capita at
US$13,900 against US$6,100 for Sri Lanka, which became poorer due
to the costs of its 20-year civil war with the Tamil rebels, is more than twice
as wealthy in GDP per capita at US$13,200 against US$5,700. Still, both
are substantially wealthier than the larger countries.

The percentage of their GDP derived from agriculture is far lower at
5 percent in Kazakhstan and 13 percent in Sri Lanka. However, they still
have 26 percent and 45 percent of their labor force respectively employed
in this sector, allowing them to benefit from urbanization, particularly
Sri Lanka, which is exceptionally low (13 percent) and to a lesser extent
Kazakhstan, already quite high at 59 percent.

TABLE 2.2 Asia

Country	Kazakhstan	Sri Lanka	Vietnam
Population (m)	17.7	21.7	92.5
Age (%)			
0–14 years	25	25	25
15–64 years	68	67	69
65+ years	7	8	6
Median age	29.5	31.4	29
Population growth (%)	1.2	0.9	1
GDP (PPP) (US$bn)			
2012	231.3	125.3	320.1
GDP growth (%)			
2012	5	6	5
2011	7.5	8.3	5.9
GDP per capita			
2012	$13,900	$6,100	$3,500
2011	$13,200	$5,800	$3,400
Labor force (%)			
Agriculture	26	32	48
Industry	12	24	21
Services	62	42	31
Unemployment (%)			
2012	5.2	4.5	4.5
Urbanization (%)	59	14	30
Taxes as percentage of GDP	20.4	13.7	30.5
Inflation (%)			
2012	5.2	9.2	6.8
2011	8.3	7	18.1
Exports (US$bn)			
2012	88.6	10.5	114.6
2011	88.3	10.5	91.9
Imports (US$bn)			
2012	42.8	19.1	114.3
2011	40.4	20.3	97.4
Mobile phone (%)	142.5	84.4	137.7

(continues)

TABLE 2.2 (*continued*)

Country	Kazakhstan	Sri Lanka	Vietnam
Market capitalization (US$bn)			
2012	35.6	16.9	38.2
2011	43.3	19.4	26
Income inequality (lower=more equal)	119/136 (2011)	24/136 (2010)	75/136 (2008)
Corruption			
2011	120/174	79/174	123/174
Human Development Index			
2012	69/186	92/186	127/186
Government	Autocracy	Democracy	Communist

Sources: United Nations, World Bank, CIA World Factbook, Transparency International.

Kazakhstan's communist heritage is apparent in its very low Gini Index score. It ranks among the top 10 percent in terms of having the lowest levels of income inequality (in other words, its income disparity between wealthiest and poorest is small) while Sri Lanka is almost at the opposite end of the scale, being among the worst 20 percent in terms of inequality, and has grown worse over the last 15 years. Some of that deterioration may be due to the civil war with the Tamil minority.

However, on other social measures, Sri Lanka looks the best placed among the Asian frontier markets as its Human Development Index (HDI) is 97 against 68 for Kazakhstan. It is also much better than any of the South Asian economies that score between 134 and 146 or Vietnam at 128. Its corruption score is better than India's and much better than Kazakhstan's, which ranks below Vietnam and alongside Bangladesh. Only Pakistan scores worse on this measure.

The investment thesis is somewhat different in these two wealthier countries as opposed to the three large Asian frontier markets. Firstly, their market capitalization to GDP percentage is already almost 20 percent for Sri Lanka and over 20 percent for Kazakhstan, 10 times higher than the big three. Kazakhstan, as a major resource producer, has already performed very well over the last decade on the back of rising resource prices, the development of its Caspian Sea oil and gas fields and the building of a pipeline link to western China.

To make one possible comparison, investors could look at the members of the Gulf Cooperation Council (GCC), other resource-rich Muslim states with authoritarian regimes, relatively high GDPs per capita, large positive balances of trade, budget surpluses and relatively low levels of taxation as a percentage of GDP. This allows their domestic companies to enjoy strong revenue and profit growth on the back of rising levels of consumer income. The primary difference is that Kazakhstan's population and GDP are five to ten times as large as those of the GCC states, making it much easier for a foreign institutional investor to invest reasonable amounts.

Sri Lanka will benefit from the end of its civil war and reduced levels of government spending on security and armaments, falling budget deficits (at 79 percent by far the highest of any of the countries mentioned so far) and a chance to develop its large service sector. This is especially true for tourism with the reduction in violence but also outsourcing for technology and service businesses.

While relatively small, Sri Lanka's market capitalization is close to that of Bangladesh and Pakistan, and half that of Vietnam, meaning that it would be a useful complement to the larger, less-developed economies within a regional portfolio.

The Outlier: Mongolia

Lastly, Mongolia is an outlier in this group, as it is small, with a population of only 3.2 million and GDP on a PPP basis of only US$13.4 billion. However, its massive low-cost mineral resources, primarily copper and coal, and geographic proximity to China mean that its economy will grow rapidly over the next decade. GDP growth in 2010–11 accelerated from 6.3 percent to 17.4 percent, while exports increased 80 percent in the same period.

While its taxes as a percentage of GDP are relatively high, most come from the resource industry. The country's level of income inequality is reasonable, and it still has over half its labor force involved in agriculture, giving it spare capacity to build up employment in the resource sector.

If investing in the markets of Vietnam and South Asian must focus partially on the coming growth in domestic consumption and partially on an increase in valuation, bringing these markets closer to the established Asian emerging markets of India and China, then investing in Mongolia is depending upon the growth in output of its world-class commodities and exports, which would lead to rising levels of income.

The major Asian frontier stock markets of Pakistan, Bangladesh and Vietnam form, in our view, the most attractive and most easily accessible frontier markets available to investors. Although relatively small and illiquid by comparison to the established Asian emerging markets of India and China, they still have market capitalizations of $40–50 billion, a number of well-established companies with competent management and a lengthy track record, including subsidiaries of multinational companies with equivalent standards of corporate governance and reporting and strong underlying fundamentals that make them attractive long-term investments. These include young and rapidly growing populations, two-thirds of whom still live in the countryside and will move to the cities over the next couple of decades, much lower labor costs than the established emerging markets, such as China and Brazil, and relatively low levels of external debt combined with a flexible exchange rate to help exports. The real attraction of these major Asian frontier economies, however, is their large potential domestic market for fast-moving consumer goods (FMCG) and services, such as food and drink, retailing, mobile phones, motorbikes and automobiles, and financial services, such as credit cards, auto loans and consumer finance. Investors should consider a diversified global frontier fund with a reasonable percentage of its assets invested in this region. The smaller Asian frontier markets of Sri Lanka, Kazakhstan and Mongolia represent complementary economies with strengths in specific sectors such as tourism and outsourcing for Sri Lanka and resources and utilities for the latter two countries.

AFRICA

Sub-Saharan Africa is often overlooked when considering investment opportunities, due to its poverty, lack of infrastructure and unsettled politics, and unfamiliarity on the part of investors. South Africa is the only sizable stock market on the continent south of the Mediterranean with a heavy exposure to resource stocks. Investors have therefore tended to classify Africa as difficult to access and lacking in suitable investment opportunities even if one did make the effort.

In fact, in our view Africa is the second most attractive frontier market region after Asia, due to its young and rapidly growing population, extensive natural resources, low levels of GDP per capita and cheap valuations. With the appropriate investment vehicle, investors should certainly consider African investment. *The Economist* has pointed out that over the past decade, six of the ten fastest-growing economies in the world have been African, and that the region has enjoyed GDP growth of more than 5 percent over the past three years (2010–12).[1] Mohamed El-Erian, CEO of Pacific Investment Management Co. LLC, which manages $2 trillion in

---

[1] http://www.economist.com/news/finance-and-economics/21575769-strategies-putting-money-work-fast-growing-continent-hottest.

assets under management (AUM), argued in a recent article in *Foreign Policy* magazine[2] that the region is moving beyond its role as an operations base for multinational commodity producers. It is now seeing economic diversification in the form of homegrown small- and medium-sized enterprises, which the World Bank reckons add 20 percent to Africa's GDP and generate some 50 percent of new jobs in sub-Saharan Africa. "These successful businesses are giving rise to internationally competitive companies, thereby providing access to global markets, new business models and technologies and higher wages and salaries," says El-Erian in the article.

Nigeria is the giant of sub-Saharan Africa, with its estimated population of 190 million making it the seventh largest country by population in the world. The population figure is an estimate as Nigeria has been unable to carry out a full census for many years owing to the religious divisions between the Muslim north and the Christian and animist south of the country. However, it is at least three times bigger than the next largest African country, South Africa, with a population of 48.8 million, the 26th largest in the world. The other African countries that appear in the top quartile of world populations are Kenya (43 million), Ghana (24.6 million) and Cote d'Ivoire (Ivory Coast, 22 million). They rank 31st, 48th and 55th respectively, meaning that although African frontier economies share many of the same attractive features as the large Asian economies such as Pakistan, Bangladesh and Vietnam, with young, rapidly growing populations moving from the countryside to the cities, their domestic markets will be much smaller than their Asian counterparts'. Investors should therefore look for consumer and financial companies that are regional players rather than depending on one market, with the exception of Nigeria and South Africa.

Africa is the poorest frontier market region when considering income per head, using GDP per capita on a PPP basis. The only economies in Africa with GDPs per capita above $10,000 p.a. are South Africa ($11,100) and Botswana ($16,200), both mature resource-based economies, with the latter regarded as probably the best-governed country in Africa, and the finance and tourism center of Mauritius ($15,100). Almost all other African frontier markets are lower-middle income countries as defined by the World Bank, with annual GNI per capita between $1,036 and $4,035, with the exception of diamond and uranium producer Namibia, which has a GDP per capita of $7,500. As a result, they probably come closest, along with the large Asian frontier economies, to the popular conception of what is meant by a frontier market: young, rapidly growing populations, overwhelmingly living in the countryside, very low incomes and a high dependence upon agriculture and

---

[2]http://www.foreignpolicy.com/articles/2013/04/29/into_africa?page=0,1.

TABLE 2.3 Africa

Country	Ghana	Kenya	Nigeria
Population (m)	25.2	44	174.5
Age (%)			
0–14	39	42	44
15–64	57	55	53
65+	4	3	3
Median age	20.7	18.9	17.9
Population growth (%)	2.2	2.3	2.5
GDP (PPP) (US$bn)			
2012	83.2	76.1	450.5
GDP growth (%)			
2012	8.2	5.1	7.1
2011	14.4	4.4	7.4
GDP per capita			
2012	$3,300	$1,800	$2,700
2011	$3,200	$1,800	$2,600
Labor force (%)			
Agriculture	56	75	70
Industry	15	12	10
Services	29	13	20
Unemployment (%)	11	40	23.9
Urbanization (%)	51	22	50
Taxes as percentage of GDP	20.9	17.6	8.6
Inflation (%)			
2012	9.1	10.1	12.1
2011	8.7	14	10.8
Exports (US$bn)			
2012	13.6	5.9	97.5
2011	12.8	5.8	92.5
Imports (US$bn)			
2012	17.5	14.4	70.6
2011	16	13.8	61.6
Mobile phone (%)	84	64	55

(*continues*)

TABLE 2.3 (*continued*)

Country	Ghana	Kenya	Nigeria
Market capitalization (US$bn)			
2011	3.1	10.2	39.3
2010	3.5	14.5	50.9
Income inequality (lower=more equal)	65/136 (2005)	49/136 (2008)	47/136 (2003)
Corruption			
2012	64/174	139/174	139/174
Human Development Index			
2012	135/186	145/186	153/186
Government	Democracy	Democracy	Democracy

Sources: United Nations, World Bank, CIA World Factbook, Transparency International.

other primary industries. This means that, starting from a low base, their GDPs and particularly GDPs per capita should grow rapidly, as populations mature, birth rates fall, and the rural population migrates to the cities, where they enter the cash economy and increase their productivity substantially.

These low GDPs per capita, despite quite large populations in certain countries, mean that frontier African economies do not rank very high in the global GDP table. South Africa's $562 billion ranks it as 26th largest, and Nigeria, with $419 billion, is 31st, but only Ghana and Kenya from the remaining countries make it into the top 100, at 81 and 83 respectively. However if Africa continues to produce high absolute rates of GDP growth, as it has done over the last decade, then its frontier economies should continue to improve their rankings sharply, as has been the case for the more established emerging markets. Investors wishing to benefit from this process should consider a diversified regional fund that can overweight those countries displaying faster growth.

Sub-Saharan Africa has one of the youngest populations in the world. Only the wealthier southern African countries of Botswana, Mauritius, Namibia and South Africa have more than two-thirds of their population over the age of 15, while Ghana, Kenya, Cote d'Ivoire, Senegal and Zambia all have at least 39 percent of their population aged under 15. They also have among the highest birth rates (above 2 percent p.a.) and lowest median ages (below 20) in the world, with the exception of Ghana, which comes close at 1.8 percent p.a. and 21.7 years. As is always the case, higher incomes mean lower birth rates, as families do not feel compelled to secure their future by having lots of children to look after them in old age, as they feel confident they will earn enough during their working life to provide for themselves. Wealthier countries can also afford to provide citizens with some form of pension.

South Africa, however, is the exception among African countries, having both an older population (median age 25.3 years) but also a negative birth rate (−0.4 percent), reflecting the ravages of HIV/AIDS among its population. Its unattractive demographics make South Africa the outlier among African economies and pose a longer-term threat to its finances. The falling percentage of its workforce compared to an aging population and the large number of orphaned children needing child-care and medical treatment place a major drag upon its economic potential and may account for the unimpressive performance of its stock market over the last decade and a half since the end of apartheid.

All sub-Saharan African frontier economies have very low rates of urbanization, in some cases even lower than the one-third level in the major Asian frontier markets. Apart from South Africa and Botswana, which have 61 percent of their population living in cities, every other country has less than half its population living in towns. Ghana and Cote d'Ivoire, two relatively small, long-settled West African states, have 50 percent urbanization rates, Zambia's is 36 percent and Kenya's a remarkably low 22 percent. Agriculture represents more than a quarter of the GDP in the poorer frontier markets, with the exceptions of Kenya, Senegal and Zambia and more than two-thirds of the labor force in all counties where such a breakdown is available.

Investors should be aware that, as in Europe and North America in the 19th century, and in the emerging markets in the last half of the 20th century, the move from the countryside to the towns leads to a sharp rise in consumption as workers enter the cash economy, leading initially to rapid growth in sales of fast-moving consumer goods (FMCG), such as food and drink, alcohol and tobacco and services, and then as incomes rise further, to increases in sales of building materials and cement, utilities and motorcycles and autos, along with financial services, such as credit and debit cards, car loans and consumer finance.

Unemployment rates in frontier African economies when available tend to be persistently high, as subsistence agriculture suffers from seasonal underemployment, with Namibia, Senegal and Kenya having reported unemployment rates of 51 percent, 48 percent and 40 percent, and even Nigeria and South Africa recording unemployment over 20 percent. The United Nations Human Development Index, which takes such factors as literacy and life expectancy into consideration, ranks all of the frontier African markets in the bottom half of the global league table, with the exception of Mauritius (77th). South Africa, Botswana, Ghana and Namibia ranked highest, but even they were only between the 120th and 135th. Investors

TABLE 2.4 Africa

Country	Botswana	Namibia	South Africa
Population (m)	2.1	2.2	48.6
Age (%)			
0–14	33	33	28
15–64	63	63	66
65+	4	4	6
Median age	22.7	22.4	25.5
Population growth (%)	1.3	0.8	−0.5
GDP (PPP) (US$bn)			
2012	32.7	16.9	578.6
GDP growth (%)			
2012	7.7	4.6	2.6
2011	5.1	4.9	3.1
GDP per capita			
2012	$16,800	$7,800	$11,300
2011	$16,400	$7,600	$11,100
Labor force			
Agriculture	NA	16	9
Industry		22	26
Services		61	65
Unemployment (%)			
2012	17.8	51.2	22.7
Urbanization (%)	61	38	62
Taxes as percentage of GDP	36.7	36.9	24.4
Inflation (%)			
2012	7.4	5.8	5.2
2011	8.5	5	5
Exports (US$bn)			
2012	4.5	4.7	101.2
2011	5.5	4.4	102.9
Imports (US$bn)			
2012	6.2	5.8	106.8
2011	6.3	5.3	100.4
Mobile phone (%)	138	102	133

(*continues*)

TABLE 2.4 (*continued*)

Country	Botswana	Namibia	South Africa
Market capitalization (US$bn)			
2012	4.4	1.1	1038
2011	4.1	1.2	855.7
Income inequality (lower=more equal)	3/136 (1993)	6/136 (2010)	2/136 (2005)
Corruption			
2012	30/174	58/174	69/174
Human Devolopment Index			
2012	119/186	128/186	121/186
Government	Democracy	Democracy	Democracy

Sources: United Nations, World Bank, CIA World Factbook, Transparency International.

should note that Africa's legacy of poor government and poverty has left it well behind in terms of realizing its human potential.

South Africa, Botswana and Namibia, the countries in southern Africa with large mining and resource sectors and a history of racial segregation through the apartheid system, rank as the most unequal in the world in terms of income distribution, as ranked by the Gini Index, which ranks how far a country's income distribution diverges from being perfectly equal. The Gini Index showed Namibia to be the most unequal country in the world in its most recent calculation in 2005 and South Africa as the second most unequal (2003). Botswana was ranked as fourth most unequal, although its Gini Index was last calculated in 1993. Recent incidents of labor unrest in the mining sector and the growing pressure within the ruling African National Congress in South Africa to enact legislation to nationalize resource assets are issues that concern many investors and will need to be closely monitored. Other examples of foreign-owned assets being expropriated by African governments include the Democratic Republic of the Congo (DRC) taking over several mines in 2009–10 and Zimbabwe ordering the seizure of farms owned by colonial settlers in 2000–02.

Most African frontier markets are resource exporters, with Nigeria and South Africa both exporting more than $100 billion in 2012, concentrated in oil, gas and gold, and platinum and diamonds respectively, although South Africa is also a major exporter of coal and foodstuffs. Ghana (gold and oil and gas) and Cote d'Ivoire (cocoa) are the only other African countries with exports of more than $10 billion annually. With many countries dependent upon subsistence agriculture, and food forming a large percentage of the consumer price index in African countries, sharp spikes in inflation can sometimes occur, reflecting the prevalence of drought and occasionally famine, but tend to drop out of the index again when conditions improve. The dreadful example of Zimbabwe and its descent into hyperinflation over the last decade may have helped to stiffen the resolve of policy makers elsewhere in the continent to maintain conservative monetary policies, which is reflected in inflation rates in the mid–single digit range for most countries.

Corruption, often seen to be a particular issue for frontier African economies, varies widely among African countries, with the wealthier and better governed southern African group of Mauritius, Botswana, Namibia and South Africa as well as Ghana all ranked between 48 and 69 in Transparency International's Corruption Perceptions Index. That puts them in the top half of the global league table, implying they are regarded as less corrupt. Zambia, at 91, is the only other African country to rank in the top half of the rankings, an unsurprising result given Africa's very low GDP per capita and the absence of a government provided social security or pension system. Most countries show an improvement in the Corruption Perceptions Index as GDP per capita and government benefits rise to provide an adequate safety net, and the tendency of government officials to use their positions to supplement inadequate incomes is reduced. Investors should not be dissuaded from investing in Africa by concerns about corporate governance, as many local listed companies are subsidiaries of global multinationals and have the same reporting and governance standards, while some local incorporated African companies such as Nigeria's Zenith Bank and Diamond Bank have listed on the London Stock Exchange, meeting the standards required to obtain a listing.

■ ■ ■

The principal difficulty for investors wishing to access African frontier markets' strong GDP growth is the small size and limited liquidity of almost all local stock markets. South Africa's stock market capitalization has ranged between $700 billion and $1 trillion over the last three years (2010–12), equivalent to 140 percent to 190 percent of its GDP, a similar ratio to developed markets such as the United States and the UK. It is overwhelmingly the largest stock market in sub-Saharan Africa, with Nigeria's market capitalization only totaling $60 billion at the end of 2012 and Ghana's $18 billion, equivalent to 12 percent and 25 percent of their GDPs. Only Mauritius and Cote d'Ivoire's stock markets were worth more than $5 billion at the end of 2012, and many countries have no stock market or extremely illiquid ones, such as Sierra Leone, where its two listed stocks trade a couple of days a week. Investors should therefore be aware that the small and illiquid nature of their stock markets makes it very difficult to gain access to this growth through the countries themselves. We would recommend, as noted in this section, that investors consider a diversified African regional fund if they wish to obtain exposure to the strong underlying fundamentals of the African frontier markets.

EASTERN EUROPE

Russia is the largest established emerging market in Eastern Europe, being one of the BRIC nations, and we have included it to allow comparisons between an "established" emerging market and frontier markets, which in some cases have higher GDPs per capita than the regional leader. This is the case in Eastern Europe, where (in order of GDP per capita) Slovenia, Slovakia, Estonia, Lithuania and Croatia all enjoyed higher incomes per head than Russia's $17,000 in 2011.

The first point that emerges from an examination of Eastern European frontier markets is their small size, both in terms of population, where only Ukraine, with 44 million inhabitants (30th largest in the world), and Romania, with almost 22 million (56th largest), have more than 7.5 million people. In total, the Eastern European frontier markets' population of 100 million is less than two-thirds of Russia's 143 million, which ranks it as ninth largest globally.

Compared to other frontier and emerging markets, Eastern Europe's demographic structure is much less attractive, with the percentage of populations below age 15 at less than 16 percent in every country and among the highest median ages of any region in the world, averaging 38–42 in all countries including Russia. Every Eastern European frontier market has a negative birth rate (except Slovakia, which has a 0.1 percent positive rate), and they rank at the bottom of all countries worldwide in this regard.

Therefore, the case for investment in Eastern Europe does not depend on young populations with high birth rates and low levels of urbanization, leading to a rapid increase in domestic demand as the population moves from the countryside to the cities, as in Asia or Africa. Urbanization rates are not as high as in South America, ranging from 50 percent in Slovenia to 73 percent in Russia, but they are notably higher than in Asia or Africa. Income levels are already high enough to classify most of these countries as high income using the World Bank definition, where a gross national income (GNI) per capita of over US$12,475 in mid-2012 was enough to classify the country as high income.

Only Ukraine, which had a GDP per capita of US$7,300 in 2011, and Serbia, at US$10,800, were in the high middle-income category, although Romania (US$12,600) and Bulgaria (US$13,800) were close to that level.

TABLE 2.5 Eastern Europe

Country	Bulgaria	Romania	Ukraine
Population (m)	7	21.8	44.5
Age (%)			
0–14	14	15	14
15–64	67	70	70
65+	19	15	16
Median age	42.3	39.4	40.3
Population growth (%)	−0.8	−0.3	−0.6
GDP (PPP) (US$bn)			
2012	103.7	274.1	335.4
GDP growth (%)			
2012	1	0.9	0.2
2011	1.7	2.2	5.2
GDP per capita			
2012	$14,200	$12,800	$7,600
2011	$14,000	$12,700	$7,300
Labor force (%)			
Agriculture	7	32	6
Industry	35	21	26
Services	58	47	68
Unemployment (%)			
2012	9.9	6.5	7.4
Urbanization (%)	71	57	69
Taxes as percentage of GDP	33.8	32.5	30.3
Inflation (%)			
2012	2.4	5	0.6
2011	4.2	3.1	8
Exports (US$bn)			
2012	27.7	67.7	69.8
2011	28.2	58.7	69.4
Imports (US$bn)			
2012	30.3	78.3	90.2
2011	30.9	66	85.7
Mobile phones (%)	150	107	125

(continues)

TABLE 2.5 (*continued*)

Country	Bulgaria	Romania	Ukraine
Market capitalization (US$bn)			
2012	8.3	29.6	25.6
2011	7.3	21.2	39.5
Income inequality (lower=more equal)	39/136 (2007)	97/136 (2011)	120/136 (2009)
Corruption 2012	75/174	66/174	144/174
Human Development Index 2012	57/186	56/186	78/186
Government	Democracy	Democracy	Democracy

Sources: United Nations, World Bank, CIA World Factbook, Transparency International.

Their small populations, despite their reasonably high incomes, mean that Eastern Europe's frontier economies are small, with only Ukraine's $334 billion (39th) and Romania's $271 billion (47th) ranking among the top 50 in terms of GDP. Slovakia and Bulgaria rank 64th and 70th, the former Yugoslav republics of Croatia, Serbia and Slovenia rank 79th, 80th and 89th, and the Baltic republics of Lithuania, Latvia and Estonia are 86th, 106th and 112th. Russia's GDP on a PPP basis, by contrast, is $2.4 trillion, making it the seventh largest economy in the world.

Agriculture accounts for less than 10 percent of all the frontier economies' GDPs, although in Romania and Serbia the sector employs 30 percent and 22 percent of their labor forces, respectively, and Lithuania and Ukraine have around 15 percent employed in that sector. Unemployment is high and persistent, with all the frontier markets experiencing unemployment rates in the mid-teens, with the exception of Romania, Russia and Ukraine, where the relatively high percentage of each workforce employed in agriculture disguises the situation.

With the exception of Russia and Bulgaria, ranked just in the top half globally in terms of income inequality by the Gini Index, all of the remaining frontier markets in Eastern Europe are among the most equal globally in terms of income distribution, doubtless a legacy of their communist heritage.

Perhaps another inheritance from the communist era is that taxes as a percentage of GDP are ranked among the top half globally, with Croatia ranking 25th at 47.2 percent and Slovenia 37th at 42.9 percent, while every other state has taxes between the 30.3 percent of GDP in Ukraine and the 39 percent of GDP in Serbia. Ironically, thanks to its flat tax reforms, Russia's tax as a percentage of GDP, at 20.7 percent, ranks it 157th.

TABLE 2.6 Eastern Europe

Country	Lithuania	Slovenia	Russia
Population (m)	3.5	1.99	142.5
Age (%)			
0–14	14	13	16
15–64	69	69	71
65+	17	18	13
Median age	40.8	43.1	38.8
Population growth (%)	−0.3	−0.2	−0.02
GDP (PPP) (US$bn)			
2012	64.8	58.1	2504
GDP growth (%)			
2012	3.5	−2	3.4
2011	5.9	0.6	4.3
GDP per capita			
2012	$20,100	$28,600	$17,700
2011	$19,400	$28,800	$17,000
Labor force (%)			
Agriculture	8	2	8
Industry	20	35	27
Services	72	63	65
Unemployment (%)			
2012	13.2	11.9	5.7
Urbanization (%)	67	50	73
Taxes as percentage of GDP	22.5	45.1	20.6
Inflation (%)			
2012	3.4	2.6	5.1
2011	4.1	1.8	8.4
Exports (US$bn)			
2012	29	28.4	530.7
2011	28.1	29.6	522
Imports (US$bn)			
2012	31.4	29.8	335.4
2011	30.2	31	323.8
Mobile phone (%)	142	110	166

(*continues*)

TABLE 2.6 (*continued*)

Country	Lithuania	Slovenia	Russia
Market capitalization (US$bn)			
2012	4.1	6.3	845.4
2011	5.7	9.4	796.4
Income inequality (lower=more equal)	86/136 (2009)	135/136 (2008)	52/136 (2011)
Corruption			
2012	48/174	37/174	133/174
Human Development Index			
2012	41/186	22/186	55/186
Government	Democracy	Democracy	Democracy

Sources: United Nations, World Bank, CIA World Factbook, Transparency International.

The region's dependence upon Russia's economy was illustrated by the collapse of the surrounding countries' GDPs in 2009, when Russia's GDP shrank −7.8 percent. Ukraine and the Baltic nations saw their GDPs shrink by between an astonishing −14.3 percent and −17.7 percent, and every other Eastern European economy saw its GDP fall by at least −5 percent, except for Serbia, which fell by −3.5 percent, and Romania, which rose by 6.6 percent. Russia is primarily an exporter of resources, particularly oil and gas, and its exports can change dramatically depending upon the price of energy, increasing 30 percent between 2010 and 2011 from $400 billion to $520 billion as prices rose.

On the other side of the coin, Eastern Europe depends heavily upon Russia as its energy supplier, a fact that Russia has not hesitated to use as a means of gaining political advantage. Russia accounts for one-third of Ukraine's and Lithuania's total imports and over 10 percent of Serbia's, Slovakia's and Bulgaria's imports. Likewise, Russia accounts for between 12 percent and 27 percent of the Baltic nations' and Ukraine's exports, making the region very vulnerable to any slowdown or crisis in Russia, as occurred in 2009 and 1997–98.

On the Corruption Perceptions Index compiled by Transparency International, Ukraine and Russia rank near the bottom, at 153rd and 142nd out of 182. Most of the Eastern European frontier economies rank in the top half of the table, with Estonia, Slovenia and Lithuania ranking in the top quartile, at 29th, 35th and 50th, respectively.

Meanwhile the United Nations Human Development Index also has Slovenia, Slovakia and the Baltic nations scoring very highly in terms of

TABLE 2.7 Eastern Europe

Country	Croatia	Serbia	Slovakia
Population (m)	4.5	7.2	5.5
Age (%)			
0–14	15	15	16
15–64	68	68	71
65+	17	17	13
Median age	40.8	41.7	38.4
Population growth (%)	−0.1	−0.5	0.1
GDP (PPP) (US$bn)	79.1	78.4	132.4
GDP growth (%)			
2012	−1.8	−2	2.6
2011	0	1.6	3.3
GDP per capita			
2012	$18,100	$10,500	$24,300
2011	$18,300	$10,600	$23,700
Labor force (%)			
Agriculture	2	22	4
Industry	29	20	27
Services	69	58	69
Unemployment (%)	20.4	22.4	12.8
Urbanization (%)	58	56	55
Taxes as percentage of GDP	33.6	44.9	34.4
Inflation (%)			
2012	4.7	6.2	3.6
2011	2.1	11.2	3.9
Exports (US$bn)			
2012	12.3	11.4	77.8
2011	13.4	11.8	78.5
Imports (US$bn)			
2012	20.8	19	74.3
2011	22.7	19.5	75.1
Mobile phones (%)	114	142	109

(continues)

TABLE 2.7 (*continued*)

Country	Croatia	Serbia	Slovakia
Market capitalization (US$bn)			
2012	21.3	9.5	4.7
2011	22.4	8.4	4.1
Income inequality (lower=more equal)	105/136 (2010)	121/136 (2008)	129/136 (2005)
Corruption			
2012	62/174	80/174	62/174
Human Development Index			
2012	47/186	64/186	35/186
Government	Democracy	Democracy	Democracy

Sources: United Nations, World Bank, CIA World Factbook, Transparency International.

education levels, wealth and life expectancy, with Slovenia at 21st, ranked above Finland, Spain, Italy, Singapore and the UK, and the others ranked above Malta, Qatar and Portugal.

The other former Yugoslav republics and Romania and Bulgaria also score among those countries with high levels of human development. Investment themes emerging from these statistics include knowledge-based industries, such as information technology, pharmaceuticals and medical devices, autos, capital equipment, mid-level consumer goods and service-based industries, particularly tourism.

Privatizations of many formerly state-owned enterprises (SOEs) have taken place in some countries but others still remain to be concluded, particularly in such countries as Serbia, giving opportunities to foreign investors as efficiencies are introduced and labor forces reduced.

Foreign direct investment (FDI) remains at relatively low levels with the exception of in Russia, where natural resources have attracted major foreign investments, totaling almost $1 trillion in 2010–2011. Slovakia, Bulgaria and Romania attracted over US$50 billion in both 2010 and 2011, and Ukraine attracted US$50 billion in 2010 and US$60 billion in 2011, although these figures represent much smaller percentages of GDP than the others, and the high level of perceived corruption and government interference combined to deter inward investment.

Russia's stock market capitalization has ranged between US$800 billion and US$1 trillion in the last three years, largely reflecting the fluctuations of energy prices. This represents 35–40 percent of Russia's GDP, but the Eastern European frontier stock markets trade at a much lower percentage of

GDP, with every country's stock market capitalization bar one representing less than 10 percent of its GDP.

The exception is Croatia, whose US$22 billion market capitalization at the end of 2011 was approximately 25 percent of its US$81 billion GDP. Croatia's is also the second largest stock market in Eastern Europe after Ukraine (US$26 billion), and it is about the same size as Romania's. No other Eastern European stock market is worth more than US$10 billion.

Overall, Eastern European frontier markets represent a relatively limited investment opportunity among the various frontier regions, owing to their small size, relatively high income levels, vulnerability to their former ruler Russia's political and economic problems and unattractive demographics. This does not mean that there not some interesting opportunities, especially given their high levels of human development, the embracing of flat tax regimes in some cases and strengths in certain industries such as pharmaceuticals and engineering.

LATIN AMERICA

The frontier markets in the Latin American region are located in South America and the Caribbean. Brazil is the "established" emerging market in this region, as one of the BRIC nations, but it is notable, as in Eastern Europe, that some of the frontier markets have higher GDPs per capita than the regional leader.

This is the case in South America, where Argentina and Venezuela's GDPs per capita were US$17,700 and US$12,700 in 2011 against Brazil's $11,900, and Colombia and Peru were close to Brazil with GDPs per capita of US$10,400 and US$10,200.

The major conclusion to be drawn from these numbers is that South America is a continent where countries are upper-middle income (defined by the World Bank as annual gross national income per capita of US$4,035–12,475), as opposed to Asian frontier markets such as Bangladesh, India, Pakistan and Vietnam, which are lower-middle income (annual GNI per capita of US$1,036–4,035). This means the investment case for these countries is different in some respects than that for the larger, poorer Asian frontier and emerging markets, although they share some of the same characteristics. As noted below, their higher incomes and extremely high levels of urbanization mean that, unlike Asian and African frontier markets, the major drivers of economic performance are unlikely to come from rising incomes as the population moves from the countryside to the cities and experiences a major increase in its productivity.

TABLE 2.8 South America

Country	Argentina	Colombia	Brazil
Population (m)	42.6	45.7	201.1
Age (%)			
0–14	25	26	24
15–64	64	67	69
65+	11	7	7
Median age	31	28.6	30.3
Population growth (%)	1	1.1	0.8
GDP (PPP) (US$bn)			
2012	746.9	500	2360
GDP growth (%)			
2012	2.6	4.3	1.3
2011	8.9	5.9	2.7
GDP per capita			
2012	$18,200	$10,700	$12,000
2011	$17,900	$10,400	$12,000
Labor force (%)			
Agriculture	5	18	16
Industry	23	13	13
Services	72	68	71
Unemployment (%)			
2012	7.2	10.3	6.2
Urbanization (%)	92	75	87
Taxes as percentage of GDP	24.7	28.5	37.6
Inflation (%)			
2012	25	3.2	5.5
2011	21	3.4	6.6
Exports (US$bn)			
2012	85.4	60	242
2011	84.3	56.2	256
Imports (US$bn)			
2012	87.3	55.5	238.8
2011	70.7	50.7	226.2
Mobile phone (%)	129	101	121

(*continues*)

TABLE 2.8 *(continued)*

Country	Argentina	Colombia	Brazil
Mobile phone (%)	129	101	121
Market capitalization (US$bn)			
2012	43.6	201.3	1229
2011	63.9	208.5	1546
Income inequality (lower=more equal)	36/136 (2009)	8/136 (2011)	17/136
Corruption	102/174	94/174	69/174
Human Development Index	45/186	91/186	85/186
Government	Democracy	Democracy	Democracy

Sources: United Nations, World Bank, CIA World Factbook, Transparency International.

They have reasonably large domestic markets, but much of the initial growth generated by the increased consumption of rural populations moving to the cities has already occurred. Urbanization rates in Brazil and the other five frontier markets in South America are already extremely high, with Venezuela and Argentina at a remarkable 93 percent and 92 percent respectively, Brazil at 87 percent and Peru and Colombia at 77 percent and 75 percent each. Only Ecuador, at a still-high 67 percent, has less than three-quarters of its population in cities and towns. None of the Asian markets has more than 38 percent of its population in cities, and African markets are even lower.

The three Central American and Caribbean markets of Panama, Jamaica and Trinidad are a contrast in being small, with populations of 3.5 million, 2.9 million and 1.2 million, having higher GDP per capita in the case of Trinidad and Panama (US$20,300 and US$14,300) and having small stock markets (US$15 billion, $11 billion and $7 billion).

They may still offer interesting investment opportunities in specific areas such as ports and infrastructure in Panama, tourism in Jamaica and oil and gas in Trinidad. Brazil, host of the 2014 soccer World Cup and the 2016 Summer Olympics, has the fifth largest population in the world, at just under 200 million, but several other South American frontier markets are in the top 50 in population, with Colombia having 45.2 million (29th largest) and Argentina 42.2 million (32nd largest).

Peru and Venezuela are one level below these markets, with 29.5 million (42nd) and 28.1 million (45th), and Ecuador's 15.2 million gives it the 67th largest population.

Unlike those in Asia and Africa, South American frontier countries have older populations, with the median age ranging from 26 in Ecuador to 30.7 in Argentina. The percentage of their populations below 15 is 29 percent (in Venezuela) or below, with Brazil, interestingly, having the lowest percentage of young people, at 24.7 percent. However, the birth rate is over 1 percent in all of these economies, perhaps reflecting the fact that they are all overwhelmingly Roman Catholic, with all countries except Peru (81 percent) and Brazil (74 percent) having more than 90 percent professed Catholics. Younger populations, as reflected in the percentage of the population aged below 15, and with a younger median age, mean more entrants into the labor force, hence more rapid GDP growth due to the number of workers increasing, and a lower median age indicates a relatively healthy population, with lower medical and pension expenses for a society. Of course, too high a percentage of young people can result in high unemployment as the economy attempts to absorb all of these new entrants. It can lead to civil unrest and violence if the regime is perceived as corrupt or is unable to allow peaceful expression of dissent, as with the Arab Spring in 2010–11.

While Brazil's large population and reasonably high GDP per capita make it the eighth largest economy in the world, with GDP on a purchasing power parity (PPP) basis of $2.3 trillion in 2011, the other four frontier markets were all in the top 45 economies last year. Argentina's higher GDP per capita and rapid growth over the last few years meant it was the 22nd largest economy, with a GDP of $726 billion.

Colombia was relatively close behind Argentina, being 29th largest at $478 billion. Venezuela's higher GDP per capita, despite a small decline over the last couple of years, was enough to give it 35th place with a GDP of $378 billion, ahead of Peru in 41st place with $306 billion in GDP.

Agriculture represents less than 10 percent of the GDP of all these economies, although it still employs 18 percent, 20 percent and 28 percent of the labor force in Colombia, Brazil and Ecuador respectively. The service sector employs more than 56 percent of the workforce in all the economies except Argentina, where industry represents 60 percent of the total, perhaps reflecting its heritage as the third wealthiest country in the world on a per capita basis a century ago.

Most of the South American countries are major resource producers, with some, such as Venezuela, deriving more than 10 percent of their GDP from their principal commodity, in this case oil and gas. Energy also accounts for 95 percent of its exports and more than 40 percent of government revenues. While other economies are less dependent upon one source of income, Brazil (with iron ore and oil and gas), Colombia, Argentina and Ecuador (with food and oil and gas) and Peru (with copper,

TABLE 2.9 South America

Country	Ecuador	Peru	Venezuela
Population (m)	15.4	29.8	28.5
Age (%)			
0–14	29	28	29
15–64	64	65	65
65+	7	7	6
Median age	26.3	26.7	26.6
Population growth (%)	1.4	1	1.4
GDP (PPP) (US$bn)	134.7	325.4	402.1
GDP growth (%)			
2012	4	6	5.7
2011	7.8	6.9	4.2
GDP per capita			
2012	$8,800	$10,700	$13,200
2011	$8,600	$10,400	$12,800
Labor force (%)			
Agriculture	28	1	7
Industry	19	24	22
Services	54	75	71
Unemployment			
2012	4.1	7.7	8
Urbanization	67	77	93
Taxes as percentage of GDP	21.7	29	34.4
Inflation (%)			
2012	5.3	3.6	20.9
2011	4.5	3.4	26.1
Exports (US$bn)			
2012	23.8	47.4	96.9
2011	22.3	46.3	92.6
Imports (US$bn)			
2012	24.7	41.1	56.7
2011	23.2	37	46.4
Mobile phone (%)	99	109	101

(*continues*)

TABLE 2.9 (*continued*)

Country	Ecuador	Peru	Venezuela
Market capitalization (US$bn)			
2012	5.8	153.4	5.1
2011	5.3	160.9	3.99
Income inequality (lower=more equal)	27/136 (2012)	34/136 (2010)	69/136 (2011)
Corruption	118/174	92/174	165/174
Human Development Index	89/186	77/186	71/186
Government	Democracy	Democracy	Democracy

Sources: United Nations, World Bank, CIA World Factbook, Transparency International.

gold, zinc and lead) are vulnerable to sharp moves in the price of their major exports.

While Brazil's exports of US$256 billion in 2011 were more than double Venezuela's and Argentina's at US$93 billion and US$84 billion, they amount to only approximately 10 percent of its GDP, similar to those of Colombia and Peru, while oil exporters and OPEC members Ecuador's and Venezuela's exports are around 20 percent.

Most of these countries run current account deficits with the exception of Argentina and Venezuela, which have difficulty accessing global capital markets. This reflects their recent defaults or rescheduling of their foreign debts (Argentina in 2001 and Venezuela in 2004). Argentina's default was the largest in the world to that date, with US$90 billion of debt affected, although the subsequent compulsory restructuring of Greek sovereign debt in 2012 for private investors has now overtaken that dubious distinction.

South America has some of the higher levels of income inequality in the world. The Gini Index for the five South American frontier markets, plus Brazil, shows Colombia and Brazil among the most unequal countries in the world, and Peru, Ecuador and Argentina in the top quartile. Even the Bolivarian revolution of Hugo Chavez has brought Venezuela to only a mid-table ranking for equality, while taxes as a percentage of GDP are actually substantially higher in Brazil, at 39 percent of GDP, to 29 percent for Venezuela, and the mid- to high 20 percent for the remaining countries.

Social unrest is an ongoing problem for investors in South America, as is nationalization as a response to economic problems, with Venezuela, Argentina and Bolivia expropriating private and foreign investments in recent years. In Venezuela its president, the late Hugo Chavez, stripped major international oil companies of their control of the massive Orinoco oil fields in 2007; nationalized the cement industry in 2008; steel plants in 2008 and 2010, to meet infrastructure and home building goals; the rice processing industry in 2009; and supermarkets and glass plants in 2010 in an attempt to control high inflation. In Bolivia, upon his election President Evo Morales nationalized the gas industry in 2006, the largest telecom company in 2008, the largest hydroelectric plant in 2010 and the electric grid in 2012. The Kirchner government in Argentina renationalized the Buenos Aires water utility in 2006, pension funds in 2008, the national airline in 2009 and its largest oil and gas company in 2012.

While most South American countries have emerged from military rule in the last 30 years, actions such as the Argentine default in 2001–02 and the Brazilian devaluation of 1999 demonstrate that democratic governments in the area are equally likely to take actions that are harmful to investors. Transparency International's Corruption Perceptions Index has only Brazil, Peru and Colombia above median, while Venezuela ranks a remarkably bad 176th, above only such regimes as Myanmar and Afghanistan. Apart from Argentina's 45th place and Brazil's 58th, a legacy of their former status as developed markets, the Human Development Index scores of the rest of the frontier markets are only slightly above the median.

Inflation, formerly a perennial problem in the region, has been effectively addressed in most countries, with the exception of Argentina and Venezuela, where governments have pursued policies that have produced high and accelerating inflation. While Brazil's stock market capitalization is over US$1.2 trillion, equivalent to 50 percent of GDP, only Colombia and Peru have stock markets that are worth more than US$100 billion, which is equivalent to 30–35 percent of their GDP. This state of affairs indicates that the pro-growth policies followed by governments in these two nations in the last decade or so have been reflected in the higher valuations accorded their stock markets.

Argentina's capitalization barely exceeds 5 percent of its GDP, a reflection of the wealth-destroying policies pursued by governments for the last 60 years, as is also the case with Ecuador, while Venezuela's market capitalization is a pitiful 2 percent of GDP.

These disparities demonstrate the effect of good and bad government policy on the fortunes of investors. It would be reasonable for investors looking at this region to concentrate on those countries that have followed sensible economic policies that have led to rising living standards and have been reflected in the stock market.

Sectors that appear attractive to investors in the South American frontier markets include beneficiaries of rising living standards, such as utilities, housing, telecommunications, fast-moving consumer products and automobiles. However, the potential upside from these sectors is more limited than in poorer, less-developed economies, due to their higher incomes and degree of urbanization and the possibility of government price controls or increased taxation.

Export sectors such as resources, agriculture, and manufactured goods, and services such as information technology, tourism and media also appear likely to do well at the correct stage of the cycle, although some governments have introduced export taxes, tariffs on imported capital equipment and requirements for local sourcing of goods and materials that make these sectors more attractive as trades rather than long-term holds.

MIDDLE EAST AND NORTH AFRICA (MENA)

The "established" emerging markets in the region, in this case Egypt and Turkey, are in many cases substantially poorer than some of the frontier markets, such as the small, wealthy members of the Gulf Cooperation Council (GCC).

Some countries, such as several of the GCC states in the Persian Gulf, not only have higher GDPs per capita than the regional leaders but have higher GDPs per capita than most members of the developed world. In fact, three of the Gulf states—Kuwait, Qatar and the United Arab Emirates (UAE)—are among the top 20 countries in the world in terms of individual wealth.

With Turkey and Egypt ranking among the 20 largest countries by population in the world, it is unsurprising that their GDPs per capita at US$14,700 and US$6,600 are below those of the GCC countries.

The Middle East and North Africa (MENA) frontier markets can be divided into two groups. There are the countries near the Mediterranean Sea, consisting of Jordan, Lebanon and Tunisia, which have relatively larger and poorer populations, with GDPs per capita of US$6,000, US$15,700 and US$9,600, respectively, and there are also the small, resource-rich Gulf states with very small populations and high GDPs per capita.

Urbanization has reached very high levels in the Persian Gulf, with Kuwait, Qatar, Bahrain and the UAE having 98 percent, 96 percent, 86 percent and 80 percent of their populations living in cities. Even the Mediterranean economies and Oman have relatively high levels of urbanization, with Lebanon reaching 87 percent, Jordan 79 percent, Oman 73 percent and Tunisia 67 percent, in line with Turkey's 70 percent. Egypt is the country with the lowest proportion of its people living in towns, at 43 percent, but the vast majority of its population lives within a few miles of the Nile River Valley. The move from countryside to cities is therefore not a factor when considering these economies, especially as the Gulf states and Jordan are in a desert zone.

TABLE 2.10 Middle East and North Africa

Country	Tunisia	Lebanon	Egypt
Population (m)	10.8	4.1	85.3
Age %			
0–14	23	22	32
15–64	69	69	63
65+	8	9	5
Median age	31	30.9	24.8
Population growth (%)	0.9	−0.04	1.9
GDP (PPP) (US$bn)			
2012	104.4	63.7	537.9
GDP growth (%)			
2012	2.7	2	2
2011	−1.8	1.5	1.8
GDP per capita			
2012	$9,700	$15,900	$6,600
2011	$9,500	$15,800	$6,600
Labor force (%)			
Agriculture	18	NA	32
Industry	32		17
Services	50		51
Unemployment (%)	18.8	NA	12.5
Urbanization (%)	67	87	43
Taxes as percentage of GDP	23.8	22.3	22.2
Inflation (%)			
2012	5.9	5.5	8.5
2011	3.5	5.1	10.2
Exports (US$bn)			
2012	17.9	5.7	28.4
2011	17.6	5.4	27.9
Imports (US$bn)			
2012	23.5	20.7	58.8
2011	22.9	19.3	57.1
Mobile phone (%)	115	82	98

(*continues*)

TABLE 2.10   (*continued*)

Country	Tunisia	Lebanon	Egypt
Market capitalization (US$bn)			
2011	9.7	10.2	48.7
2010	10.7	12.6	82.5
Income inequality (lower=more equal)	61/136 (2005)	NA	90/136 (2001)
Corruption			
2011	75/174	128/174	118/174
Human Development Index			
2012	94/186	72/186	112/186
Government	Democracy	Democracy	Democracy

Sources: United Nations, World Bank, CIA World Factbook, Transparency International.

From an investor's viewpoint, the MENA region frontier markets are likely to be a relatively small part of a diversified portfolio, given their small size and dependence upon a limited number of resources, primarily oil and gas. Their market-leading positions in some industries and services, such as tourism, airlines and infrastructure (particularly transport-related facilities), offer interesting possibilities.

Despite their small populations, their enormous energy resources mean that the UAE, Qatar and Kuwait have GDPs ranking in the top 60 worldwide, with the UAE at US$262 billion (50th), Qatar at US$185 billion (57th) and Kuwait at US$156 billion (60th). This gives them larger GDPs than Tunisia's US$102 billion (79th), despite the latter's 10.2 million population being double that of the UAE and four to five times that of Kuwait and Qatar. Turkey's GDP was US$1.1 trillion in 2011 for its 80 million population, and Egypt's US$526 billion for 83 million, ranking them 17th and 27th largest in the world on a PPP basis.

The Gulf States' high GDPs are also reflected in their stock market capitalizations, which are US$125 billion for Qatar, US$101 billion for Kuwait and $94 billion for the UAE. Those numbers approach Turkey's US$202 billion and are more than double that of Egypt's US$43 billion, although Egypt's market capitalization halved over 2010–11 due to the Arab Spring.

The Arab Spring began in Tunisia, resulting in the overthrow of a long-established regime, and was followed by similar events in Egypt. There has also been unrest in Bahrain, and any potential investor considering the MENA frontier economies will have to take into account the likelihood of further social and political unrest occurring over the next few years,

TABLE 2.11 Middle East and North Africa

Country	Kuwait	Qatar	UAE
Population (m)	2.7	2	5.5
Age (%)			
0–14	27	13	21
15–64	71	86	78
65+	2	1	1
Median age	28.8	32.4	30.3
Population growth (%)	1.8	4.2	2.9
GDP (PPP) (US$bn)			
2012	165.9	189	271.2
GDP growth (%)			
2012	6.3	6.3	4
2011	8.2	14.1	5.2
GDP per capita			
2012	$43,800	$102,800	$49,000
2011	$42,400	$88,300	$48,500
Labor force (%)			
Agriculture	NA	NA	7
Industry			15
Services			78
Unemployment (%)	2.2	0.5	2.4
Urbanization (%)	98	96	84
Taxes as percentage of GDP	61.2	33.9	36
Inflation (%)			
2012	3.2	1.9	1.1
2011	4.7	1.9	0.9
Exports (US$bn)			
2012	109.4	117.7	300.6
2011	104.3	112.4	281.6
Imports (US$bn)			
2012	24.1	23.5	220.3
2011	22	26.9	202.1
Mobile phone (%)	183	115	213

(continues)

TABLE 2.11 *(continued)*

Country	Kuwait	Qatar	UAE
Market capitalization (US$bn)			
2011	100.9	125.4	93.8
2010	119.6	123.6	104.7
Income inequality (lower=more equal)	NA	NA	NA
Corruption			
2012	66/174	27/174	27/174
Human Development Index			
2012	54/186	36/186	41/186
Government	Monarchy	Monarchy	Monarchy

Sources: United Nations, World Bank, CIA World Factbook, Transparency International.

especially with the civil wars in Libya in 2011 and the civil war still continuing to rage in Syria (2011–13).

The smaller GCC states of Bahrain and Oman have both smaller GDPs at US$32 billion and $83 billion, and substantially lower GDPs per capita at $27,900 and $26,900, reflecting their smaller exposure to energy.

Qatar and the UAE score highly on Transparency International's Corruption Perceptions Index (22nd and 28th) and the United Nations Human Development Index (HDI), which takes into account such factors as education and life expectancy as well as wealth (37th and 30th). Bahrain is also in the top quartile on these measures (46th and 42nd), but the tensions between its Shia minority and the Sunni regime show that there may be dissatisfaction even when the economic scene is apparently benign.

Tunisia and Egypt, the first two countries where long-standing existing regimes were overturned by the Arab Spring in 2010–11, have corruption perception rankings of 73rd and 112th and HDI scores of 94 and 113. However, their Gini Index scores, which measure income inequality, place them around the middle of the global table, which may reflect the ability of their well-connected elite to disguise the extent of their holdings.

The other Mediterranean frontier markets of Jordan and Lebanon have respectable HDI scores of 95 and 73, but Lebanon is regarded as notably corrupt (134). By comparison, Turkey's corruption perception and HDI scores are 61 and 92.

The major states in the MENA region in terms of population and size of GDP are Iran, Iraq and Saudi Arabia, all of which are difficult to access for foreign investors. Iran is under European, U.S. and Canadian sanctions for its suspected nuclear weapons program, despite having a stock market worth more than US$100 billion. Saudi Arabia generally prohibits investment by foreigners, although there is speculation that this may change in the near future, and Iraq's turbulent politics, high level of violence and lack of security make it unattractive for all but the most hardened of frontier market investors.

As with Saudi Arabia's restrictions on outside investment, any fundamental change in these circumstances would put these markets on the radar screen. Until such time as these issues are addressed (and there are persistent rumors that Saudi Arabia will open its stock market to foreign investors at the time of writing, 2013), from an investor's point of view the MENA region frontier markets are likely to be a relatively small part of a diversified portfolio. This is due to the small size of their economies and dependence upon a limited number of resources for most of their GDP, primarily oil and gas (Kuwait, UAE, Qatar) but also including phosphates (Jordan) and aluminum (UAE). However, their market-leading positions in some industries and services, such as tourism, airlines and infrastructure (particularly transport-related facilities), offer interesting possibilities.

Ironically, the GCC markets comprise over 60 percent of the MSCI Frontier Markets 100 Index, launched in late 2012 to give investors access to the 100 largest frontier market companies by market capitalization, with Kuwait representing 30 percent of the index on its own. This reflects the large size of the GCC countries' stock markets compared to other frontier markets, and even the established emerging markets in the region, with Kuwait, Qatar and the UAE's market capitalizations of around $100 billion each being double Egypt's and half the size of Turkey's.[3] Should Saudi Arabia open its market to foreign investors, the overrepresentation would become even greater, as its market capitalization is more than $300 billion.

EXOTIC FRONTIER MARKETS

The exotic frontier markets, as was noted in the first chapter, are those which, while in many cases quite sizable, are not included in either of the S&P or MSCI frontier market indices. The reasons for their absence include restrictions on foreign ownership, sanctions imposed by some major countries on investment, lack of liquidity or public stock markets or perceived exceptionally high levels of political risk. We have included statistics on nine

---

[3]In June 2013, MSCI announced that Qatar and the United Arab Emirates, which comprise almost 30% of the MSCI Frontier Markets Index, will be reclassified as emerging markets effective May 2014, while Morocco will be downgraded from emerging to frontier market status effective November 2013.

of the largest and most interesting potential investment opportunities. Other observers can doubtless make their own lists of exotic frontier markets, and it will be instructive to see which of the countries listed here graduate to inclusion in the indices over the next few years.

Our list of exotic frontier markets includes five countries that rank among the 50 largest countries in the world by number of inhabitants, namely Iran (78.9 million), Myanmar, formerly Burma, (54.6 million), Tanzania (46.9 million), Iraq (31.1 million) and Saudi Arabia (26.5 million), and two, Iran and Saudi Arabia, that rank among the top 25 by gross domestic product (GDP) on a PPP basis. Their GDPs per capita range from the 55th wealthiest (Saudi Arabia again) at $24,500 to the 226th, Zimbabwe, the inhabitants of which have a GDP per capita of $500 p.a. after experiencing hyperinflation in the last decade.

The exotic markets range from countries with extremely young populations and some of the highest birth rates in the world, such as Angola (17th highest), Tanzania (15th), Zimbabwe (2nd) and Iraq (35th), to communist or post-communist countries with very high median ages and negative birth rates. In general, these countries tend to conform to the regional characteristics we have noted elsewhere in this section, with Africa (Angola, Tanzania and Zimbabwe) and Asia (Cambodia, Laos and Myanmar) having younger populations, higher birth rates and lower levels of urbanization. Only Angola among these six countries, with an urbanization rate of 59 percent, has more than 38 percent of its population living in cities, meaning that over the next couple of decades one-third or more of the population will migrate from the country to the towns and cities.

With this move comes an attendant sharp rise in incomes and consumption of consumer goods and services. As one example, mobile phone penetration rates will tend to rise from the 50–70 percent range they have reached at present in all of these markets, except Myanmar with its extraordinarily low 2 percent rate. It could move closer to the 80–100 percent range in such exotic frontier markets as Bolivia, Costa Rica, Iraq and Belarus, let alone the 140–200 percent penetration achieved in wealthier exotic markets like Uruguay and Saudi Arabia.

The economies of these Asian and African countries depend heavily upon agriculture, and over 70 percent of their labor forces work in this sector. As much of this is subsistence agriculture to feed themselves, they are vulnerable to external shocks such as droughts and floods, and GDP is low as not much of these economies is conducted on a cash basis, and there is persistent underemployment (Zimbabwe's is estimated at a remarkable 95 percent). But as the Green Revolution leads to rising output of food and more of the crops they produce become commercial, GDP per capita rises very rapidly.

At present, the GDPs per capita of these countries are very low, between $500 and $2,700 per annum, with the exception of Angola, whose oil- and

TABLE 2.12 Exotic Markets

Country	Angola	Tanzania	Zimbabwe
Population (m)	18.6	48.3	13.2
Age (%)			
0–14	44	45	39
15–64	52	51	57
65+	4	4	4
Median age	17.7	17.3	19.5
Population growth (%)	2.8	2.8	4.4
GDP(PPP) (U$bn)			
2012	126.2	73.5	6.9
GDP growth (%)			
2012	6.8	6.5	5
2011	3.9	6.4	9.4
GDP per capita			
2012	$6,800	$1,700	$500
2011	$6,000	$1,600	$500
Labor force (%)			
Agriculture	85	80	66
Industry	7	10	10
Services	8	10	24
Unemployment (%)			
2012	NA	NA	95
Urbanization (%)	59	26	38
Taxes as a percentage of GDP	48.8	21.7	NA
Inflation (%)			
2012	10.3	15.3	8.3
2011	13.5	12.7	5.4
Exports ($bn)			
2012	71.9	5	3.3
2011	65.8	4.8	2.9
Imports ($bn)			
2012	22.3	9.7	4.7
2011	19.8	9.6	4.4

(*continues*)

TABLE 2.12 (*continued*)

Country	Angola	Tanzania	Zimbabwe
Mobile phone (%)	51	53	70
Market capitalization (US$bn)			
2011	NA	1.5	10.9
2010		1.3	11.5
Income Inequality (lower=more equal)	NA	2007 77/136	2006 23/136
Corruption 2011	168/174	100/174	154/174
Human Development Index 2012	148/186	152/186	NA
Government	Democracy	Democracy	Democracy

Sources: United Nations, World Bank, CIA World Factbook, Transparency International.

diamond-based wealth gives it a GDP per capita of $6,000 per annum, but they should begin to rise quite quickly over the next decade. Of course, this assumes that their governments encourage this process. Zimbabwe, known as the "breadbasket of Southern Africa" as recently as the 1980s, when it had large exports of such commercial agricultural products such as tobacco and maize, has been reduced to importing food from its neighbors amidst widespread malnutrition within its population. This provides an example of what damage can be caused by misguided policies.

This group of exotic markets includes a couple of countries with large populations, namely Myanmar and Tanzania, but all are quite sizable, the smallest country being Laos with almost 7 million inhabitants. This fact makes them interesting to investors in that they will develop sizable domestic markets to offset a dependence on exports of low value-added goods such as textiles, toys and low-end consumer electronics. Those have been the traditional sectors that early-stage emerging markets specialize in due to the competitive advantage that their low labor costs give them in such labor-intensive industries.

These sectors, however, are vulnerable to changes in tariff barriers in the developed markets to which they export, which remove their competitive advantage. Furthermore, recent negotiations for free trade deals and tariff reductions between developed and emerging markets have often seen the removal or reduction of such tariffs being used as bargaining chips in budget negotiations in the developed markets, such as the Central American Free Trade Area ratification in the United States.

TABLE 2.13 Exotic Markets

Country	Cambodia	Laos	Myanmar (Burma)
Population (m)	15.2	6.7	55.2
Age (%)			
0–14	32	36	27
15–64	64	60	68
65+	4	4	5
Median age	23.7	21.6	27.6
Population growth (%)	1.7	1.6	1.1
GDP (PPP) (US$bn)			
2012	36.6	19.2	89.2
GDP growth (%)			
2012	6.6	8.3	6.2
2011	7.1	8	5.5
GDP per capita			
2012	$2,400	$3,000	$1,400
2011	$2,300	$2,800	$1,300
Labor force (%)			
Agriculture	56	75	70
Industry	17	12	7
Services	27	13	23
Unemployment (%)	NA	2.5	5.4
Urbanization (%)	20	33	34
Taxes as percentage of GDP	14.4	22.3	4.1
Inflation (%)			
2012	2.9	4.9	3.1
2011	5.5	7.6	5
Exports (US$bn)			
2012	6.1	2.3	8.5
2011	6.1	2.1	8.2
Imports (US$bn)			
2012	8.8	2.6	7.1
2011	8.2	2.3	5.9
Mobile phone (%)	90	82	2

(continues)

TABLE 2.13 (*continued*)

Country	Cambodia	Laos	Myanmar (Burma)
Market capitalization (US$bn)			
2011	NA	NA	NA
2010			
Income inequality (lower=more equal)	73/136 (2008)	81/136 (2008)	NA
Corruption			
2012	157/174	160/174	172/174
Human Development Index			
2012	138/186	138/186	149/186
Government	Democracy	Communist	Autocracy

Sources: United Nations, World Bank, CIA World Factbook, Transparency International.

The export-led model of economic development followed by Japan and the Asian newly industrializing countries (NICs) from the 1950s to approximately 2000 was dependent upon the wealthy developed markets' willingness to allow relatively low tariff imports of manufactured goods, even in such high value-added sectors as automobiles and electronics.

With a prolonged period of low GDP growth likely over the next decade and their aging demographics putting strains on their government finances, the developed markets may be much less willing to see high-paying manufacturing jobs being outsourced to emerging markets with cheap labor and low environmental and human rights standards.

That economic reality makes the export-led model more risky as a means of achieving rapid GDP growth, although the emerging middle classes in the more-developed emerging markets such as the BRIC nations are already starting to provide alternative export markets for the less-developed frontier economies. Many low-end manufacturing jobs moved from Guangdong Province in southern China to northern Vietnam in the last decade.

A number of the exotic countries do not have Gini rankings, in some cases reflecting their low absolute GDPs per capita. The lack of a Gini ranking can also reflect the nature of the countries' regimes, as with the communist regime in Laos or the military junta in Myanmar, and their unwillingness to allow an accurate analysis of income distribution.

The political policies of the ruling party also account for some of the variation in such matters as taxes as a percentage of GDP. Some resource-based economies with large unofficial and unreported sectors, the so-called black economies of, for example, Iraq, Angola and Saudi Arabia, have very high taxes as a proportion of GDP. Resources are easy to tax for a government that may not have sufficient capacity to easily collect sales or property taxes and usually provide half or more of GDP and more than half of government revenues in resource-based economies.

Iraq actually has the highest percentage of taxes to GDP in the world, at a remarkable 79 percent in 2011, but Saudi Arabia ranks 16th at 51.2 percent and Angola 22nd at 48.8 percent. Most Eastern European economies have taxes that represent more than 35 percent of GDP.

Some of these countries do not have public securities markets, owing to the ideologies of the ruling regime, as in Myanmar, or their extremely small size due to their very low GDPs in both absolute and per capita terms. Laos, for example, has only two companies traded on its stock exchange.

However, among the exotics there were a couple of major exchanges worth more than US$100 billion at the end of 2012. They were Saudi Arabia, the market capitalization of which was US$338 billion with 152 companies listed on it and Iran, at US$107 billion. At present, non-Saudi nationals are not permitted to invest in Saudi-listed shares, but there is evidence that the Saudi authorities are contemplating opening up the Tadawul, as the Saudi exchange is known, to foreign investors, although there is uncertainty over the timing.

One of the reasons given for gradually admitting foreign investors is partially to help counteract the volatility caused by ownership being confined to domestic institutions and individuals. The authorities are also reported to be keen to encourage more listings by family-owned businesses.

Iran's stock market has risen substantially over the last couple of years, reflecting not so much an improving economy as its position as one of the only places to benefit from the sanctions on Iranian trade and finance that have been imposed due to its nuclear development program. The state-owned domestic companies listed on the Tehran Stock Exchange have benefited from their domestic sources of supply to gain market share from importers hit by a depreciating currency and restrictions on imports into Iran.

These restrictions have been imposed due to international sanctions arising from the regime's nuclear development program, but thanks to the strong performance of the state-owned sector, the index hit an all-time record in nominal terms in late 2012. While the authorities loosened restrictions on foreign investors in 2010, and Iran made the list of Goldman Sachs' Next Eleven Emerging Markets, the continued growth of international restrictions on dealing with Iran has deterred would-be investors. A change in policy or in the regime itself would make Iran one of the largest frontier markets open to foreign investors by market capitalization.

The same phenomenon of the stock market acting as a refuge from a deteriorating economy occurred in Zimbabwe during the hyperinflation of

TABLE 2.14 Exotic Markets

Country	Iran	Iraq	Saudi Arabia
Population (m)	79.8	31.9	26.9
Age (%)			
0–14	24	37	28
15–64	71	60	69
65+	5	3	3
Median age	27.8	21.3	26
Population growth (%)	1.5	2.3	1.5
GDP (PPP) (US$bn)			
2012	997.4	155.4	740.5
GDP growth (%)			
2012	−0.9	10.2	6
2011	2	8.9	7.1
GDP per capita			
2012	$13,100	$4,600	$25,700
2011	$13,400	$4,300	$24,800
Labor force (%)			
Agriculture	25	22	7
Industry	31	19	21
Services	45	59	72
Unemployment (%)			
2012	15.5	16	10.7
Urbanization (%)	71	66	82
Taxes as percentage of GDP	13.8	79.9	47.8
Inflation (%)			
2012	25.2	6.4	4.6
2011	21.5	5.6	5
Exports (US$bn)			
2012	66.4	88.3	381.5
2011	128.6	79.7	364.7
Imports (US$bn)			
2012	66.9	56.9	136.8
2011	93.6	47.8	120
Mobile phone (%)	57	85	199

(continues)

TABLE 2.14 (*continued*)

Country	Iran	Iraq	Saudi Arabia
Market capitalization (US$bn)			
2011	107.2	4	338.9
2010	86.6	2.6	353.4
Income inequality (lower=more equal)	45/136	NA	NA
Corruption 2012	133/174	169/174	66/174
Human Development Index 2012	76/186	131/186	57/186
Government	Islamic Republic	Democracy	Monarchy

Sources: United Nations, World Bank, CIA World Factbook, Transparency International.

2005–08, where equities were the only asset that maintained their value in real inflation-adjusted terms. At the end of 2011, Zimbabwe's stock market was worth US$10.9 billion, making it the largest exotic frontier market after Saudi Arabia and Iran, despite Zimbabwe having the lowest GDP per capita among the exotic economies covered in this section. Of the other countries, Iraq's market was worth US$4 billion at the end of 2011.

These are the only ones worth more than US$1.5 billion. At present, the exotic markets are either too small or unavailable to be practicable as a potential investment choice for frontier market investors. This could rapidly change with the opening of Saudi Arabia to foreign investors at some stage in the next couple of years.

It would be reasonable for investors to expect that some of the exotic frontier markets will make the transition to being included in the frontier market indices over the next few years, as they remove restrictions on foreign investment (Saudi Arabia), or a change in the attitude of the ruling regime leads to the development of a domestic stock market (Cambodia and Myanmar). Given that this list, which is by no means complete, includes several sizable countries in terms of population and GDP, there is the potential for some of them to become major components of any frontier market index. At present, however, we recommend that investors focus on those countries that are included in the indices and on those countries that come closest to the popular view of frontier markets, i.e., poorer countries with large populations making the move from the countryside to the cities, primarily in Asia and sub-Saharan Africa, although there are interesting sectors in the other frontier markets.

TAKEAWAYS

1. Understanding factors such as demographics and various indices such as the Gini Index helps investors determine the prospects for a specific country.

2. Frontier markets may be divided into two main groups: one group has Asian and African nations, which match the popular stereotype of frontier markets as large, poor countries with young populations overwhelmingly living in the countryside and with high birth rates; the other group includes Eastern Europe and the Middle East and North Africa (MENA), which exhibit few if any of these characteristics.

3. Latin America falls somewhere between the two blocs, although its remarkably high level of urbanization restricts the potential benefits that accrue to countries experiencing the move of populations from the countryside to the cities.

4. We would suggest investors primarily focus on the Asian and African countries, as their superior demographics and low levels of income and urbanization mean that their economic progress is likely to be rapid over the next decade. The underdeveloped nature of their stock markets also makes their valuations relatively attractive.

5. The Eastern European and MENA countries include some very wealthy states in the GCC, whose stock markets account for over 60 percent of the MSCI Frontier Markets Index capitalization at present. Their small populations, with low or negative birth rates and high median ages, mean that economic growth is more likely to be slower than in the larger, poorer countries and largely dependent on resource prices, although there may be some attractive individual company investments in specific sectors.

6. In Latin America, while there are some countries with large domestic markets and their demographics are a lot more attractive than Eastern Europe's or MENA's, with reasonable birth rates and median ages, we would suggest investors focus on countries that have demonstrated an ability to deliver pro-growth policies without resorting to inflationary measures and negative actions against foreign investors.

CHAPTER 3

Volatility: Not the Same as Risk

Many investors have been deterred from investing in emerging markets due to their perceived high level of volatility. Some believe that such volatility relegates these markets to "risky" status, meaning that due to these markets' sharp rises and falls, potential investors will run a high risk of losing some or all of their capital invested in these countries. To believe this is to confuse volatility with risk, an error that is widely made and entirely understandable but that often prevents people from enjoying the benefits of undervalued investments.

Studies of behavioral psychology by numerous observers, including Daniel Kahneman, winner of the Nobel Prize for Economics, conclude that the inherent mental biases that all of us possess make us bad investors. The human habit of using mental short cuts (sometimes called heuristics) makes us bad judges of the attractiveness of different investments, prone to overconfidence in our decisions once we make them—to the extent of ignoring contrary evidence—and reluctant to incur losses if our decisions are incorrect.

Kahneman and others find that the emotional pain of realizing a loss is between two and three times as great as the pleasure of booking a profit. We therefore have a tendency to sell winners and keep losers, the exact opposite of what is required to become a successful investor.

These traits are reinforced by a natural dislike of sudden changes, which the rational part of the human brain is ill-equipped to handle. Studies find that during times when lots of things are happening, or large amounts of information are received in a short period, the instinctive part of the human brain, sometimes known as the lizard brain, will automatically take over. This results in actions that are devoid of any logical basis but which satisfy the instinctive brain's need to reduce the information overload and simplify the situation.

Thus, high levels of volatility make it difficult for investors to behave rationally when considering investments that tend to be more volatile than more-developed markets, such as those in emerging or frontier markets, as volatility tends to reinforce counterproductive actions, such as selling after markets have fallen sharply. While this may appear to be contrary to the human failing of keeping our losers, in fact it reinforces the losses caused by doing so, as investors tend to finally give up on losing positions at the worst possible time—after they have fallen sharply.

This unconscious behavior is reinforced by unfamiliarity, as investors often have very little or no personal knowledge of the emerging markets in question and can be panicked into dumping stocks by unfavorable headlines. In many cases, the country in the headlines is hundreds of miles distant, with a different political, religious or economic history, and the unrest or violence is being driven by completely different factors, but this does not prevent foreign investors from withdrawing their money.

LESSENING VOLATILITY IN EMERGING AND FRONTIER MARKETS

Despite the widely held perception among most investors that emerging markets (including frontier markets) are much more volatile than developed markets, the evidence shows that the difference between them has been narrowing over the last decade. Compared to the volatility (as measured by the standard deviation of returns) of developed markets in the MSCI All Country World Index, the standard deviation of emerging markets in the MSCI Emerging Markets (Free) Index over the decade ending in 2009 was about 30 percent higher (25 percent annual standard deviation vs. 17 percent).

Over the last third of a century, the standard deviation of developed markets has risen by almost two-thirds, from 11 percent a year to 17 percent, while that of emerging markets has also risen, but by a much smaller percentage, from 19 percent to 25 percent. While individual emerging markets remain much more volatile than individual developed markets (32.5 percent vs. 23.5 percent over the decade ending in 2009), the difference has fallen from 43 percent in the 1980s, while that of individual developed markets has risen from 20 percent per annum.

As Elroy Dimson, Paul Marsh and Mike Staunton at the London Business School point out, "For global investors, the high volatility of individual markets does not matter, as long as they hold a diversified portfolio of emerging markets."[1] They go on to note that investors need not

---

[1]Credit Suisse, Global Investment Returns Yearbook 2010, Section 1: Emerging Markets, 5.

even be concerned by the higher volatility of the emerging market index, stating, "What matters is how much an incremental holding in emerging markets contributes to the risk of their overall portfolio."[2] This is measured by the beta (sensitivity) of the emerging market index to global markets, which was 1.3 for the decade ending in 2009.

Dimson, Marsh and Staunton state that a higher beta implies a higher expected return to compensate investors for the higher risk (volatility). They calculate that the long-term expected return from developed markets is 3–3.5 percent p.a. above the return from cash, and that with a beta of 1.3, investors should expect a modestly-higher extra return of 1–1.5 percent p.a. from emerging markets. This extra return is not due to the higher GDP growth of emerging economies but exists to compensate investors for the higher volatility they have to accept when investing in these markets. In other words, investors require higher returns for being willing to accept higher risks.

CORRELATIONS TO OTHER MARKETS (AND LACK THEREOF)

Frontier markets, precisely because of their limited liquidity and the difficulty of executing trades due to high transaction costs, which can amount to as much as 400 basis points (bps) in certain markets, have low correlations with developed markets as represented by the MSCI World Index, much lower than those of emerging markets (0.6 vs. 0.9). As emerging markets have become larger and more liquid, they have seen their correlations with developed markets rise very sharply over the last decade, from 0.75 in 2000 to 0.91 at the end of 2009, suggesting that they are now effectively higher beta versions of the developed markets.

All correlations have risen sharply over the last few years, partially due to the increased globalization of world markets and also to the financial crisis of 2008–09 and its aftermath, as correlations tend to rise sharply during financial turmoil. Correlations between the MSCI Emerging Markets Index and the MSCI All Country World Index rose from 0.8 in 2005 to 0.91 at the end of 2009, reflecting the tendency of correlations to increase greatly during financial turbulence such as that which followed the financial crisis of 2008–09. Nonetheless, even a statistically significant correlation such as 0.91 still allows investors to achieve meaningful risk reduction from diversification between emerging and developed markets.

---

[2]Ibid.

A small position in emerging markets will disproportionately reduce portfolio volatility. A 1 percent allocation to emerging markets by a portfolio entirely invested in developed markets will reduce portfolio volatility by more than 1 percent. Therefore, even if the return from emerging markets is the same as that from developed markets in the future, it is still worth reallocating some of a portfolio to emerging markets.

On the other hand, correlations between emerging markets are still quite low at 0.55, even after rising from almost zero at the beginning of the last decade. Therefore, investors having a diversified emerging-market portfolio, rather than selecting just one or two countries, still benefit greatly from reduced volatility.

Despite their own high volatility, frontier markets are even more useful in reducing overall volatility for a diversified portfolio, as they have low correlations with emerging markets as well as developed markets (0.59). The least developed frontier markets, such as Africa, as represented by the MSCI Frontier Markets Africa Index, have even lower correlations with developed and emerging markets (0.39 and 0.36). This attribute makes investing in frontier markets a very attractive way to reduce the overall volatility of either a global (developed and emerging markets) or emerging-market portfolio.

Furthermore, frontier markets not only have low correlation with developed and emerging markets but very low correlations with each other. As Mark Mobius, the lead manager of the Templeton Frontier Markets Fund notes, "If you take Estonia and compare it to Lebanon ... you find there is zero correlation. They don't move together at all."[3] In fact, according to Morningstar numbers from June 2012, Estonia has 0.07 correlation with Lebanon, and all of the seven markets included in the table have correlations of 0.53 or below, with every market except Kazakhstan and Mauritius having correlations below 0.42—in other words, not statistically significant.

STRUCTURAL REASONS FOR HIGHER VOLATILITY

The structure of capital markets in emerging or frontier economies also serves to reinforce their inherent volatility. In developed markets, by far the largest investors in equity or bond markets are institutions with a very long time horizon, such as life insurers or pension funds. They receive regular inflows every two weeks or every month from their policyholders or members, and the same pattern is observed for individuals using tax sheltered

---

[3] "Franklin Templeton Fund Pushes Frontiers," July 21, 2011, advisor.ca.

savings and pension plans, such as 401(K)s and individual retirement accounts (IRAs) in the United States, registered retirement savings plans (RRSPs) and tax-free savings accounts (TFSAs) in Canada, the mandatory provident fund (MPF) in Hong Kong and the central provident fund (CPF) in Singapore, superannuation in Australia and individual savings accounts (ISAs) in the UK. The inflows are invested into the markets on a regular basis, regardless of the level of the markets, providing a natural hedge against selling by individual and foreign investors.

In emerging and frontier markets there are no, or very few, such institutional investors to offset capital flows generated by individuals and foreign investors. For this reason, one of the major elements used when assessing the attractiveness (or lack of attractiveness) of emerging markets is foreign investor inflows and outflows, including the premiums at which shares available to foreigners are trading. Therefore, bull and bear markets in emerging and frontier markets tend to be more violent than those in the more mature developed markets, as they each become self-reinforcing, with domestic individuals piggybacking on foreign inflows on the way up and attempting to exit before the foreigners on the way down.

Restrictions on domestic institution's investments in many emerging markets either prohibit investment in equities or restrict the percentage to a limited amount (usually below 15 percent of assets) to ensure there is a ready market for government bonds. Institutions are required to invest the vast majority of their assets in government bonds to fund budget deficits and reduce the interest that government pays, a policy that is known as financial suppression.

Market Capitalization

These factors reinforce volatility in already relatively small and illiquid markets. For the six Asian frontier markets that we discussed in the last chapter (Bangladesh, Pakistan, Sri Lanka, Vietnam, Kazakhstan and Mongolia), only one of them (Kazakhstan) has a market capitalization greater than $40 billion, and the valuation of all their stock markets put together only totaled $146.7 billion at the end of 2011, less than 15 percent of India's market capitalization.

Of course, that is the total market capitalization; given the large shareholdings retained by the founding families and state-owned enterprises in quoted companies in frontier and emerging markets, the actual investable universe is usually substantially smaller. This is why certain index providers, such as MSCI, produce two versions of their indices, one of which will be designated "(Free)" to indicate that it reflects the free float of available shares for foreign investors. Most exchange-traded funds (ETFs) investing in emerging or frontier markets state that they attempt to cover a high percentage of the investable universe of stocks—the vital word here being "investable."

The iShares MSCI Frontier Markets 100 Index ETF launched by Blackrock in September 2012 was specifically limited to the 100 most liquid stocks in frontier markets, including measures specifically chosen to ensure adequate trading volumes as well as market capitalization. This focus on liquidity has resulted in a portfolio that at the end of September 2012 had 56.8 percent in financials and 62 percent in four Middle Eastern markets, of which approximately half (30.2 percent) was in Kuwait, and 15.4 percent and 12.6 percent were in Qatar and the UAE.

This lack of meaningful exposure to many frontier markets, including some of the largest in terms of population and GDP, both reinforces the argument that ETFs are not necessarily the best way to play small and illiquid markets such as those of frontier economies and also shows that the composition of emerging stock market indices will likely change radically over time, as new companies go public, multinationals list their local subsidiaries and states decide to raise capital by privatizing SOEs.

Not many experienced international investors would suggest that having almost two-thirds of a frontier market portfolio in Middle East banks and utilities is the best way to gain exposure to less-developed economies and share in their growth, especially as the GDPs per capita of Qatar, the UAE and Kuwait are $105,000, $48,800 and $42,200, making them the second, 12th and 19th wealthiest countries in the world, respectively.

Focusing on market capitalization also leads to weightings that fail to reflect the underlying realities of these markets in terms of fundamentals such as population and absolute size of GDP.

The Middle Eastern stock markets have a 45 percent weight in the frontier market indices, yet account for only 3 percent of the total population, while the Asian markets, with 47 percent of the population, have only a 15 percent weight. Likewise Africa's 29 percent of the total frontier markets' population also has only a 15 percent weight in the indices. The "recognized" frontier markets in Central and South America, Eastern Europe and the Middle East account for 70 percent of the indices' market capitalization while only having 24 percent of their inhabitants.

While the wealthy countries such as the UAE and Saudi Arabia have market capitalizations that are 28 percent and 50 percent of their GDPs, poorer and more populous countries such as Nigeria, Vietnam, Pakistan and Kenya have stock markets that are between only 9 percent and 14 percent of their GDPs. One of the major arguments for investing in such economies is that their market capitalization-to-GDP ratio will rise substantially in line with higher incomes, as has occurred in other emerging markets. India's market capitalization is 60 percent of its GDP at the official exchange rate and has been as high as 100 percent in the last couple of years, and Brazil's and Russia's are 50 percent of GDP.

It is reasonable to believe that if economic growth continues at the same rate as the last decade for some of the frontier markets, then their market capitalization-to-GDP ratios will start to approach the level attained by the BRICs.

As it is, the frontier markets included in the indices represent 14 percent of total global population and 7 percent of global GDP on a PPP basis. This statistic compares to India's 18 percent of global population and 5 percent of global GDP. If one expands the definition of frontier markets to include the exotic frontier markets covered in the previous chapter and other countries that have begun the process of liberalizing their financial markets, such as the Democratic Republic of the Congo, Sudan and Uganda in Africa and the central Asian republics, this expanded frontier market universe has been calculated to represent 25 percent of the global population and 11 percent of global GDP on a PPP basis.[4]

TAKEAWAYS

1. Investors should understand that higher volatility does not always mean higher risk—in fact, due to the frontier markets' low correlation with developed and emerging markets, including a small percentage of frontier markets in an equity portfolio actually reduces its overall volatility. Understanding frontier markets means understanding the radical differences between and among them. Gaining that understanding of a country means looking at everything from its resources to its GDP and all other economic factors.
2. Volatility in emerging and frontier markets has been falling gradually over the last decade, while that of developed markets has been rising, although emerging and frontier markets are still more volatile.
3. Frontier markets are not only not correlated with developed and emerging markets, they are also not highly correlated with each other.
4. Due to the small size of the stock markets in many frontier economies, using market capitalization–weighted vehicles, such as ETFs, is not the most effective way to gain exposure to the larger frontier economies.

---

[4]Zin Bekkali, Daniel Broby and Waseem Khan, "The Frontier Markets' Ship Is Sailing," Silkinvest White Paper, June 2012.

CHAPTER 4

Solid Investment Information
vs. Media Images

Effective decision making in any crucial undertaking, including investing, requires a hard look at the right way and wrong way to make decisions and the right way and wrong way to gather information to underpin those decisions. Understanding the distinction between relevant information and irrelevant noise can make a huge difference in the decision-making process.

When investors look at frontier markets, their opinions are most likely heavily influenced by the news coverage they see or read. The 24-hour news cycle, countless Internet news portals, satellite radio, mobile news screens, conventional radio, television channels, newspapers and magazines combine to keep us instantly and perhaps unrelentingly informed of developments in every news event. The "all news, all the time" format satisfies news junkies, shift workers who may not be able to watch conventionally scheduled newscasts and others who want constant updating on the minutiae of a news story as well as the core details.

The phenomenon started with the launch of CNN in 1980 and accelerated following the launch of CNN2 in 1982, later renamed CNN Headline News and then renamed again to HLN. The success of those networks led to other 24-hour operations in television and radio in the United States and Canada. It also led to the all-news format at the United Kingdom's British Broadcasting Corporation and Sky News as well as operations such as Euronews in Europe and Al Jazeera in the Middle East.

Today, seemingly endless news footage of explosions and flames rivets the attention more than a chart showing investment opportunities. A shouting correspondent ducking gunfire probably commands more interest than a thoughtful analysis of a foreign economy. Airplane crashes and blackened wreckage attract more attention than thoughtful analysis of airline stocks. *Reductio ad absurdum* appears more entertaining than honest discourse.

Investors, like most human beings, tend to overreact to bad news. Dramatic or tragic events—whether natural or man-made—make gripping news stories and provide front-page headlines and lead stories on television and radio news. Wars, riots, rebellions, demonstrations, strikes, earthquakes, hurricanes, fires and medical emergencies provide great pictures and dramatic stories and the 24-hour news cycle means that we cannot help but stay constantly informed of bad news.

However "constantly informed" does not necessarily mean "fully informed." What some professionals call "hit-and-run journalism"—while honest, accurate and professionally intended—does not always deal well with the economic aftermath of today's news.

News media and their audiences tend to focus on these front-page stories and perhaps we shape our worldviews and decisions accordingly, an understandable move, but a very faulty one when it influences investment decision making, for at least two reasons.

First, by the time the traumatic events have made headlines, the financial markets have often already anticipated them, fulfilling their role as predictors of future events. Studies have demonstrated that equity and bond markets will usually lead changes in the economy by six to nine months, meaning that by the time bad economic news hits the airwaves, the markets have priced it into equity values. Markets are famously described as a discounting mechanism, although, as the old joke has it, the stock market has predicted nine of the last five recessions! In other words, sell-offs and increases in market indices do not infallibly predict the direction of the underlying economy, but they do react well in advance of such changes.

Second, dramatic events may anticipate a change in circumstances, meaning that what seems to be bad news may actually anticipate better times ahead. During the European crises of 2011–13, crowds of protesters taking to the streets often led to changes of governments, which in turn made changes in economic policy. Similarly, the Arab Spring of 2010–11 eventually led to changes in the regimes that did not permit rapid growth in the economy due to corruption and the weight of established interests.

Taken together, these factors mean that the tendency to react to dramatic short-term events does not necessarily make for good investing decisions, and when frontier markets appear in the news, the focus on uprisings, wars, revolutions and bombings may well conceal underlying good news on economic progress.

Indeed, when news media focus on explosions and fires, we hear less about some of the more peaceful areas of a region such as the Middle East, and the discrepancy between what we see and the bigger picture may result in missed opportunities in frontier market investing.

In this chapter, we have chosen select examples of countries from different regions and at different stages of development to demonstrate that the popular view of a region such as the Middle East may well be too one-dimensional, and that the tendency of the news media to define a country by one characteristic, such as "war torn" or economically backward, often conceals more than it explains. Investors will hopefully come away with a clearer picture of the opportunities in a couple of the largest Asian frontier markets, appreciate that the Middle East is a "two-tier" market with a number of wealthy and stable regimes that at the time of writing (2013) form the largest percentage of the MSCI Frontier Markets Index, understand the difficulties that ex-Soviet countries face in their move to becoming more capitalist economies and discover that Africa contains well-developed and successful economies, such as Kenya, as well as "exotic" frontier markets, such as Sierra Leone. The pervading theme throughout is that lack of familiarity with frontier markets makes the media and investors, who take most of their information from the regular news outlets, all too willing to put a country or region into a particular category and then assume that nothing has changed, despite many years or even decades having passed.

THE MIDDLE EAST: NOT ALL IN CONFLICT

Throughout much of 2012 and 2013, the electronic, print and online news media regularly featured bombings and shootings in Libya, Syria, Lebanon and other Middle East locales. A casual observer might conclude that the entire Middle East had disintegrated into chaos and mentally dismiss the possibility of investment.

This example illustrates part of the problem in studying any region on any basis. The Middle East does not represent one homogenous region any more than all of Europe or Asia consists of one homogenous region. In fact, making across-the-board statements about "the Middle East" seems as questionable as making across-the-board statements encompassing all of Europe or all of South America.

However, understanding the area means viewing it as a two-tier region, according to Mark Townsend, a Dubai-based journalist who has covered the Middle East for 15 years, reporting for *Al Jazeera, Emerging Markets, Euromoney*, the *Financial Times, Institutional Investor*, Thomson Reuters and the *Washington Times*. During an interview with one of the authors of this book, he explained how the two-tier concept works in the region.[1]

---

[1]Personal interview with Al Emid during the research and writing of this book in 2012.

The two-tier concept describes the contrast between the oil-rich Gulf states of the Gulf Cooperation Council and the Middle Eastern countries such as Tunisia, Libya, Egypt and Syria that have undergone change because of the Arab Spring. The Gulf Cooperation Council consists of Bahrain, Kuwait, Oman, Qatar, Saudi Arabia and the United Arab Emirates, which is a collection of emirates or principalities: Abu Dhabi (also the UAE capital), Ajman, Dubai, Fujairah, Ras al-Khaimah, Sharjah and Umm al-Quwain.

In Townsend's appraisal, Egypt, Libya and Tunisia continue to suffer significant upheaval and uncertainty and have to resolve deeply rooted issues such as unemployment levels and corruption. Moreover, Libya also faces an impending battle for control of its natural resources, while in Egypt the government faces continuing pressure for reform, and the civil unrest in Syria has escalated into a full-blown civil war.

However an investment judgment on the Middle East would suffer if based solely on events in Egypt, Libya and Tunisia, since by comparison the GCC countries, except for Bahrain and Kuwait, remain peaceful and stable at time of writing. "They have a lot of commonalities in the sense that they are benefiting from high oil prices," Townsend explains, adding that those commonalities generally explain the absence of Arab Spring–type revolts. Bahrain and Kuwait, the exceptions, continue to grapple with Sunni-Shia tensions, which is unnerving other Gulf states. Kuwait has the most advanced electoral system, but the ruling monarchy has refused calls for a constitutional monarchy and its refusal has prompted significant riots.

Oil revenues have become the glue holding the region together and to some extent the oil-financed government programs have held off dissent, a state of affairs that will continue for as long as oil revenues continue flowing. Kuwait and Bahrain have certainly experienced dissent to a lesser extent than other areas but are peaceful at time of writing.

Dubai has certainly had economic problems due to a property bust followed by the financial crisis of 2008–09, which led to massive debt problems that required restructuring, but it has continued climbing out of the economic crisis and has created an extraordinary infrastructure. "Their motto was 'build it and they will come,' for years," Townsend says. That strategy led to massive overbuilding and then a huge letdown.

Currently, Dubai's real estate sector has started reviving with rents, prices and transaction volumes rising, according to the National Bank of Kuwait.[2] The bank says that "revival in the real estate market would improve the outlook for banks, which still face asset quality pressures from their real estate loans."[3] The bank also points out that transaction volumes

---

[2] National Bank of Kuwait, GCC Economic Outlook, January 2013, 1.
[3] Ibid.

and prices remain 45 percent below the "build it and they will come" period of 2002–08.

Townsend describes Saudi Arabia as the proverbial economic "elephant in the room" suggesting that its impact on equity markets in the Middle East will eventually be enormous. Saudi Arabia and Qatar currently appear to be the most attractive to foreign direct investment (FDI).

Saudi Arabia has been liberalizing its economy while spending large sums of money on welfare-sponsored programs. In 2012, it started gradually allowing overseas fund managers to deal in Saudi securities but only through complicated swap arrangements.

Meanwhile, Saudi Arabia has announced another record budget for 2013. The *Middle East Economic Survey* characterizes the budget as "prompted by bumper earnings realized last year."[4] The MEES outlook says that this budget "is again expansionary, underlying the government's intention to continue with its large spending program in the aftermath of the Arab spring."[5]

The report underlines the country's health by pointing out that the budget projects an 18 percent increase in total revenue to about US$221.1 billion in 2013 over 2012, a 19 percent rise in total expenditure to US$218.7 billion and a resulting surplus of US$2.4 billion compared to the budgeted surplus of US$3.2 billion in 2012.[6]

Observers suggest that Saudi Arabia has set a course for further liberalization of share trading, and that it will eventually allow direct access by foreigners to the Saudi Stock Exchange in Riyadh, which has representation in most sectors including petrochemicals, financials, retail and manufacturing. At time of writing (2013), the total market capitalization varies between US$350 and $400 billion, which would make it by far the largest frontier market by size if it was readily investable by foreign investors.

Future investment opportunities will include infrastructure projects to replace the current infrastructure shortfalls, Townsend says. "There is great scope for project finance and huge demands for infrastructure spending. It has the largest population in the Gulf," he explains. He also points to Saudi Arabia's plan to boost welfare spending to approximately US$10,000 for every citizen and to build 500,000 homes and create jobs. While Saudi Arabia has experienced some discontent among the Shia population of its eastern provinces, where its major oil fields are located, the revenues

---

[4]Basim Itayim and Melanie Lovatt, *Middle East Economic Survey* 56, no. 1 (January 4, 2013), 17.
[5]Ibid.
[6]Ibid.

generated by its massive natural resources have enabled the government to assuage dissent by such generous welfare programs.

Elsewhere in the region, the National Bank of Kuwait projects real GDP growth for Qatar at 5.0 percent and 4.9 percent in 2013 and 2014 respectively.[7] The figures represent a slowing but still healthy outlook. Pointing to a determination to diversify for the future into non-oil GDP, the NBK projects growth by 8 percent and 7.6 percent respectively in the same years.

Qatar has also had what the report terms "a remarkable decade of investment and expansion in the country's gas sector which has delivered double-digit average annual growth and seen Qatar assume the mantle of the world's largest liquid natural gas (LNG) exporter and highest per capita income country."[8] With the rapid expansion of U.S. shale gas production, the large price disparity between the Asian markets of Japan, South Korea and China, to which Qatar is exporting its LNG at high prices (over US\$15 per million cubic feet), and the much lower prices (below US\$5 per million cubic feet) that prevail in North America is likely to close, but the enormous revenues that Qatar derives from its long-life, low-cost gas reserves will continue to allow the country to remain prosperous and stable.

Looking to the future, Townsend sees a pent-up demand for initial public offerings in the GCC states as the owners of large family businesses monetize parts of their ownership in these companies. A report by Delhi, India–based KuicK Research underlines the GCC's future potential leadership in solar energy. The report says that the region's climate and near-constant sunlight provide continuous solar radiation for most of the year. It points out that Saudi Arabia, the UAE, Kuwait and Oman have each declared their plans to produce at least 10 percent of electricity from renewable sources of energy by 2020 and are leaving no stone unturned to secure their future with renewable sources of energy.[9]

More broadly, the entire region has initiatives underway against the day when oil revenues no longer finance all public needs. Middle Eastern and North African regional-electricity generators announced numerous major projects as they moved to meet rising power demand:

> While the region holds some of the world's largest oil and gas producers and reserves, countries with large and small hydrocarbon resources alike sought to develop projects using a variety of fuels

---

[7]National Bank of Kuwait, GCC Brief, February 19, 2013.
[8]Ibid.
[9]"GCC Renewable Energy Sector Analysis," KuicK Research, August 1, 2012.

and technologies. With oil producers seeking to maintain their export revenues and oil importers seeking to control spending, last year saw notable progress in nuclear and renewable projects as well as in more conventional oil and gas-fired capacity.[10]

The UAE could see "real non-oil GDP" grow to 4 percent over the next two years, though well below its 2001–08 annual average of 9 percent, according to the National Bank of Kuwait's forecasts. "Parts of the economy—notably trade, tourism and business services—now seem to be doing well, helped by the country's strong trade links with emerging markets, high-quality infrastructure and possibly a boost to competitiveness from a sustained spell of low inflation," the bank says.[11]

With their high GDPs and liquid stock markets that are open to foreign investors, the GCC states form the largest portion of the MSCI Frontier Markets Index and the Frontier Markets 100 Index, comprising over 60 percent of the former, with Kuwait on its own making up more than 30 percent of the index. This high weighting is more a reflection of the high market capitalization of the GCC stock markets and their openness to foreign investors than a genuine representation of their importance among the frontier economies. The GCC region has other active stock exchanges compared to the official stock exchanges of Kuwait, Dubai, Abu Dhabi, Qatar and Bahrain, including the NASDAQ Dubai exchange, the Dubai Financial Market and the Abu Dhabi Securities Exchange, but they lack the critical mass, liquidity and regulations to qualify as major exchanges, Townsend explains.

The GCC economies have some successful companies, primarily in the finance, telecommunications and infrastructure sectors, reflecting their strategic geographic position, their exceptionally strong capital reserves and a pro-business attitude on the part of their governments.

However, the picture does have some limitations and cautions for the unwary. The GCC economies are generally very wealthy and enjoy enormous energy resources, but they are small, with none of them having a population over 3 million except the UAE, with 5.3 million, and much of their populations are comprised of foreign contract workers. Their location in a desert zone means they are dependent upon imports for their food supplies, and their proximity to Iran's radical regime creates political tensions with their Shia minorities. In a practice that would make

---

[10]David Knott, "MENA Power Generators Pushed Diversity in 2012," *Middle East Economic Survey* 56, no. 1 (January 4, 2013). www.archives.mees.com/issues.
[11]Ibid.

many Westerners uncomfortable, government ministers often chair large companies, ignoring the obvious questions about conflicts of interest. The GCC Board Directors Initiative, a voluntary organization, however, works to improve governance and oversight in GCC boardrooms. It defines itself as the leader of regional debate on best practices in governance.

Moreover, Moody's Investors Service has a negative outlook on the UAE banking system, citing problem loans, many of them related to real estate, at Dubai-based banks.[12] Meanwhile, the GCC markets' high weight in the MSCI Frontier Markets Index is partially responsible for its relative underperformance since the financial crisis of 2008–09, as the legacy of financial companies' exposure to problem loans in Dubai has detracted from performance.

Should Saudi Arabia reduce the effect of this issue in future and permit foreign investment in its stock market, its large size by comparison with the other countries in the GCC markets should change the equation. As noted, the wild card for investors in the region is the progress of opening up Saudi Arabia's Tadawul stock market to foreign investors. At the time of writing in early 2013, there is speculation that this opening will occur before the end of the year, but the same thing was confidently expected by many observers to happen in 2012, a forecast that proved to be incorrect. One of the principal factors apparently causing delay is a difference of opinion over the length of the settlement period for share transactions.

Should Saudi Arabia open its stock markets to direct foreign investments, its US$350 billion size would immediately make it the largest frontier market not just in the region but globally, and would likely see flows of capital into Saudi Arabia. At present, foreign investors are using participation certificates (known as P-notes or P-certs) sponsored by investment banks to give them exposure to the price performance, but not ownership, of individual Saudi stocks.

Investors contemplating a position in the Middle East need to realize that there is a major difference between the larger, poorer countries around the Mediterranean that have experienced civil unrest and changes in governments over the last three years, such as Tunisia, Libya and Egypt, and the much smaller and richer GCC countries around the Persian Gulf. The latter comprise over 60 percent of the MSCI Frontier Markets Index, so any passive market capitalization–weighted investment, such as an ETF, means the investor will effectively be taking a positive view on these countries. While they have successfully largely recovered from the aftermath of the

---

[12] Moody's Investor Services Banking System Outlook, United Arab Emirates, November 2012, 1.

financial crisis of 2008–09 and the property crash in Dubai, and appear politically stable at present, they remain small and very exposed to the price of natural resources. However they are benefiting from their safe-haven status given the present uncertainties in the region and are continuing to develop their non-resource assets to provide diversification.

VIETNAM: A LONG-TERM BET

The path to the Vietnam War that dominated television coverage 40 years ago began in 1858 when France started its conquest of the country and in 1887 made it part of French Indochina. Notwithstanding its declaration of independence from France after the Second World War, it remained under French rule until 1954 when the communist forces of Ho Chi Minh defeated the French. The Geneva Accords of 1954 provided for the division of the country into the communist North and the anti-communist South.

That division played a major part in the outbreak of the Vietnam War, which actually began on November 1, 1955. The United States provided increasingly large quantities of economic and military aid to South Vietnam throughout the 1960s in order to sustain the South Vietnamese government as the war between the two halves became ever more bitter and costly. American armed forces departed in 1973 following the ceasefire between the two halves, and two years later North Vietnamese forces took over South Vietnam. The war officially ended on April 30, 1975.

Over the following decade, the united Vietnam had little economic growth due to a range of factors including conservative communist leadership, the persecution and exodus of some crucial groups, including successful merchants and supporters of the former South Vietnamese regime, leading to the exodus of the "boat people" in 1978–80. Its growing isolation from other nations culminated in border wars with two other communist neighbors, Cambodia in 1978 and China in 1979.

As a turning point, and the beginning of its path to becoming a South Asian power, Vietnam embarked on its Doi Moi or "renovation" policy in 1986. The program, which might remind one of Russia's Glasnost, called for increased economic liberalization, structural reforms and private ownership.

Now the World Bank calls Vietnam "a development success story." In its Vietnam Overview, the World Bank suggests that the Doi Moi transformed Vietnam from one of the poorest countries in the world, with per capita income below $100, to a lower-middle income country within a quarter of a century with per capita income of $1,130 by the end of 2010.[13]

---

[13]World Bank, Vietnam Overview.

The same report says that the "ratio of population in poverty has fallen from 58 percent in 1993 to 14.5 percent in 2008, and most indicators of welfare have improved."[14]

More recently, Vietnam has increasingly moved onto the world stage. It chaired the 2009 annual meetings of the Boards of Governors of the World Bank Group and the International Monetary Fund and carried out the Chairmanship of the Association of Southeast Asian Nations (ASEAN) in 2010.

Viewed from a Western perspective, Vietnam has several economic ironies, including a nominally communist regime embracing a controlled form of capitalism and becoming an outsourcing base for its former enemy, China. Chinese and other companies outsource some of their back office, manufacturing and software program writing, according to Michael Shari, an award-winning financial journalist who has covered emerging markets and frontier markets and has written for publications such as *Barron's*, *Time* magazine, *Business Week*, *Institutional Investor* and *Bloomberg*.[15]

The relationship between Vietnam and China appears logical; although the two countries do not share a colonial past or colonial tradition, they do share a Confucian tradition, Shari explains. That similarity means that the two countries share some common views on areas such as self-cultivation, the family, social civility, moral education, individual well-being and the role of the state.

Several factors besides the China trade drive Vietnam's move to frontier status, including inexpensive labor and its status as the world's second largest rice exporter and second largest coffee exporter, Shari says. This would amount to history repeating itself as Vietnam has started down the same road as China and Thailand, both of which are now considered strong emerging markets. "There is a lot of evidence that this is how countries evolve," Shari explains. Looking again to history, Vietnam has the potential to become the next South Korea within the next 10 to 20 years. Shari notes that it's "hardly a coincidence" that Korean electronics giant Samsung Electronics moved 40 percent of its cellular telephone manufacturing to Vietnam from South Korea in 2012.

Vietnam's economy and capital markets are growing rapidly on a strong natural resource base, low wages and the expansion of ports, including the former military bases of Da Nang and Hue on one of the world's longest coastlines.

---

[14]Ibid.

[15]Personal interview with Al Emid during the research and writing of this book in 2012.

The stock market has benefited from historically high oil prices because some of the largest companies listed on the local exchange are subsidiaries of Petro Vietnam, the national oil company, which recently appeared in portfolios run by Acadian Asset Management in Boston and Singapore.

Such experienced frontier market players have demonstrated that it is possible to overcome the headaches that many foreign investors face, such as regulations that limit the percentage of any local company's equity that a foreign investor can own.

Foreign portfolio managers see their investments in Vietnam as long-term bets and believe that they are picking high-quality companies that they expect to deliver strong returns over the long term, despite the volatile price swings of frontier markets.

Meanwhile the Vietnam investment picture has several complications including unclear limits on foreign ownership of Vietnam companies. "There are local [stock]brokers who do know the limit from word of mouth and to them it's very clear, but to outsiders it's not transparent," Shari says, adding that Vietnam, like other frontier markets, has some issues such as limited liquidity in its stock trading. "Every frontier market has some really serious issues in how you sell a stock."

Moreover, government-owned enterprises hesitate to become publicly listed companies because this means surrendering control to shareholders they have never met, Shari explains. Nevertheless, the government has continued to move forward with a gradual privatization program, partially to address budget problems arising from overenthusiastic lending by some of the state-owned banking sector in 2009–10.

In fact, the policy of partial privatization has created limited liquidity, which means greater control over share prices by the companies, Shari says. That helps stabilize the value of the corporation since the issue of shares worth 10 percent or 20 percent actually establishes a new outside valuation for the company. American and British portfolio managers say they depend on word of mouth to find out from Vietnamese brokers about the opportunity to buy into a domestic company.

However, Vietnam's adoption of Doi Moi has not led to enormous returns for investors in the Vietnamese stock exchange. As one of the earliest frontier markets to allow in foreign capital, several Vietnam country funds were launched in the early to mid-1990s, of which the Vietnam Enterprise Investment Fund Ltd. (VEIL) is the largest still extant, with US$460 million in assets under administration in early 2013. Its compound annual return after fees since inception in 1995 is 6 percent p.a., and that of its sister fund, the Vietnam Growth Fund (VGF), which was launched almost a decade later, in 2004, is 8.3 percent p.a. While these mid–to high–single digit returns compare favorably with the returns from many developed markets over the same period, many investors might understandably feel they should receive a higher return from investing in a frontier market, given the higher volatility and lack of liquidity involved.

One benefit of these restrained returns is that the valuations for Vietnamese equities are now reasonable, with the VNF Index selling at less than 11 times 2014's forecast earnings and yielding 3.5 percent. Investors in frontier markets should not expect strong GDP growth to automatically translate into strong stock market returns, as the example of China in the last decade illustrates. They should instead concentrate on the quality of individual companies and their management.

KENYA: A SLOW REDUCTION IN RISK

For some individuals, Masai warriors and spectacular nature photography define their views of Kenya. That seems understandable, given the number of documentaries and even feature magazine spreads that portray those aspects of the country. For others, the Kenya picture involves fights over food in areas bordering Somalia and Ethiopia. For still others, the image of packed Nairobi rush hours comes to mind. And others remember most clearly the news reports of ethnic violence following a disputed election in December 2007.

All of those representations are correct. However, looking to the present and future, Kenya's Vision 2030 plan calls for an average gross domestic product growth rate of 10 percent annually, according to a British Broadcasting Corporation analysis.[16]

The same BBC report explains that a new constitutional order sets limits on "the arbitrary and discretionary powers used by politicians and civil servants to steal public money."[17] This very direct description of a process that occurs in virtually every emerging and frontier market, and which is a major concern for investors, should remind us that corporate governance at both the company and government levels is something that must be considered when investing in lower income countries. We have included Transparency International's Corruption Perceptions Index score for most of the countries discussed in the book as a guide to their relative ranking.

The obvious reason for widespread corruption by public officials in low income countries is that their wages are very low. The absence of

---

[16]"Viewpoint: Will Corruption Kill off Kenya's Vision 2030 Plans?" BBC News Africa, October 10, 2012.
[17]Ibid.

a social "safety net" in the form of pensions or welfare payments in most emerging markets means that officials regard their time in office as a means of amassing sufficient wealth to provide for their families in the event of sickness or old age. This is usually a transitional stage for emerging and frontier markets as rising GDP per capita allows governments to pay employees enough to remove the temptation to take advantage of their positions.

The BBC report also says that "the key elements of Kenya's economy include wholesale and retail, transport and communication, manufacturing, financial services and agriculture and forestry."[18]

Certainly, Kenya's problems provide fodder for naysayers commenting on the country's future. However, Kenya may become another example of history repeating itself, suggests financial journalist Michael Shari. "My general feeling about frontier markets is that the things that people say about them now are pretty much the same things that people used to say about China or Russia or India or Brazil 10 or 20 years ago."

Trading stocks (outside of global funds) comes with several unfamiliar risks, Shari explains. Settlement periods can range up to 30 days, a difference from North American or European trading practice that many would have trouble understanding. Political risk is greater, corporate governance within a corporation is not as well defined as within North America and the legal system has not become established enough for individuals to know what to expect.

These criticisms would include whether a specific country has bought into the idea of equity as well as debt, Shari says. Critics will suggest that these countries are like Europe of several decades ago. "They'll say these countries are like Europe used to be—quite debt focused and not yet equity focused," he continues. "They say all sorts of things that sound familiar—the same stuff people used to say about China or Russia or Brazil."

"Then people will say that in this country income is less than $1,000 annually [and that] there's no way to take the country seriously," Shari explains, adding that changes in income level are also part of the evolutionary process, along with upgraded educational and political systems.

"There is really no reason to believe that Kenya or Morocco, Vietnam or Cambodia are not going to follow this evolutionary development," he says.

Kenya now has to overcome some of the challenges also faced by South Korea. Kenya is next door to a politically volatile neighbor—Somalia—while South Korea is next to North Korea. (Somalia, however, is

---

[18]Ibid.

not hostile to Kenya in the same way that North Korea is hostile toward South Korea.)

Both countries have a liability in terms of appearing to be in "a bad neighborhood." However, as with South Korea, which has become a member of the Organisation for Economic Co-operation and Development (OECD) and is in the process of graduating to developed market status, Kenya has every chance to follow the same path that other markets which we now call frontier markets have taken to become emerging markets, including Indonesia and Colombia.

Kenya has a strong cohort of English-speaking administrative people, viable manufacturing and retail sectors and even provides outsourced expertise for companies based in India. "There's another sign at how it's moving up the evolutionary chain to becoming a more investible market," Shari says. "In the same way that when American companies want to cut costs and move some of their back office operations to a cheaper country . . . when Indian companies start out and they want to outsource to a cheaper country for their back office [functions], they pick Kenya."

Growth in gross domestic product could exceed 5 percent in 2013, according to the International Monetary Fund, although the IMF adds the now-standard caveat that the euro crisis poses threats to the country's performance.[19]

Not surprisingly, at time of writing, the top 10 Kenyan stocks based on five-year growth records mirror the country's top industries. Growth figures exclude dividends:[20]

1. British American Tobacco–Kenya: +185.3 percent US$, 265.9 percent Kenyan shilling[21]
2. City Trust: +163.2 percent US$, 237.6 percent Kenyan shilling
3. Scangroup: +124.2 percent US$, 187.6 percent Kenyan shilling
4. Athi River Mining: +115.7 percent US$, 176.7 percent Kenyan shilling
5. Kakuzi Ltd.: +79.8 percent US$, 130.7 percent Kenyan shilling
6. East African Breweries: +45.9 percent US$, 87.1 percent Kenyan shilling
7. Equity Bank: +45.8 percent US$, 87.0 percent Kenyan shilling

---

[19] "IMF Concludes Fourth ECF Review Mission to Kenya," International Monetary Fund Release, September 12, 2012.

[20] "The 10 Best Kenyan Stocks Over the Past Five Years," compiled by Ryan Hoover, editor of InvestinginAfrica.net, based on data from Bloomberg News and Xe.com, effective January 13, 2013.

[21] The conversions between U.S. dollars and Kenyan shillings vary because the shilling depreciated against the U.S. dollar during the five-year period ending January 13, 2013.

8. Williamson Tea Kenya: +44.4 percent US$, 85.2 percent Kenyan shilling
9. Diamond Trust Bank: +41.0 percent US$, 80.9 percent Kenyan shilling
10. Nation Media Group: +30.1 percent US$, 66.9 percent Kenyan shilling

One fact that the list above makes clear is that foreign investors in frontier markets need to factor currency movements into their return calculations. As this list of Kenyan returns illustrates, U.S. dollar–based investors have seen their returns reduced by almost half over the five-year period, as the Kenyan shilling has weakened against the U.S. dollar and other developed market currencies. Often a weakening currency is a deliberate policy on the part of the frontier market's government, to encourage the development of export industries earning foreign exchange and to restrict the import of expensive consumer goods. In some cases, frontier markets such as Argentina and Venezuela have maintained more highly valued official exchange rates that permit well-connected companies and individuals to benefit from purchasing foreign goods at an artificially high exchange rate.

The authors believe that the strong absolute returns to be expected from frontier markets over the next decade will more than compensate investors for some currency depreciation. Over time, currencies of successful and fast-growing economies should appreciate to reflect their improving performance, as has happened with Singapore and China over the last decade.

KAZAKHSTAN: BORAT PAINTED THE WRONG PICTURE

Understanding the genuine investment potential of individual frontier market countries means setting aside inaccurate impressions resulting from media closer to home than the investment locale. The impression that many Westerners have of Kazakhstan would range from drawing a blank, to a vague recollection that it had formed part of the former Union of Soviet Socialist Republics (USSR), to the fairly ridiculous, owing to a 2006 movie release entitled *Borat: Cultural Learnings of America for Make Benefit Glorious Nation of Kazakhstan*.

The film revolves around the adventures of Borat Sagdiyev, played by British actor and TV prankster Sacha Baron Cohen. He delivers a bizarre characterization of a television reporter from Kazakhstan who goes to the United States to produce a documentary about American society. He decides to go to California in search of Pamela Anderson and encounters some hilarious aspects of American culture along the way.

The dismally unflattering view of Kazakhstan in the opening scenes (actually filmed in Romania) sets the tone for a film for which the phrase "lowbrow" seems unjustifiably high praise. Not surprisingly, Kazakhstanis took offense to the image of their country in the film, although several years later they credited the film with increasing tourism to the country.

However, Western audiences have few other points of reference for Kazakhstan, the largest of the republics that constituted the USSR except for Russia.

In fact, Kazakhstan started along the path to a market economy in 1991, according to Damir Seisebayev, an Almaty, Kazakhstan–based independent equity analyst.[22] It still has a long way to go, he concedes. Kazakhstan has a transitional economy, meaning that it continues to evolve from tight government controls to a market economy. Actually, in some ways government control is increasing, given examples such as the merger of some pension funds.

To expedite the transition—or at least the Western view of the transition—Kazakhstan hired former British prime minister Tony Blair to provide economic advice and "to present a better face to the West," according to the *Financial Times*.[23] His cachet in the West can reasonably be expected to raise Kazakhstan's credibility, or at least visibility, on the world financial stage.

Kazakhstan's future depends on its ability to monetize its oil reserves and mineral resources. The country's future also depends on its ability to diversify into non-oil areas, Seisebayev suggests. It has focused on increasing the diversity of its economy after the plummet in its GDP during the financial crisis of 2008–09 owing to its high dependence on energy and mineral exports, which had powered strong growth in GDP through the previous decade.

That dependency became a double-edged sword during the financial crisis of 2008–09 as the drop in oil and commodity prices worsened the country's fragile economy. Government devaluation of the currency and injection of about US$10 billion in economic stimulus helped recovery, and rising commodity prices since that time have helped revive the economy.

Still, like some Middle Eastern governments, Kazakhstan's government knows that it must diversify the economy to prepare for the day when oil reserves and mineral resources become depleted or when the world

---

[22]Personal interview with Al Emid during the research and writing of this book in 2012.

[23]Robert Budden, "Blair Venture Revenues Up 33 percent to £16M," *Financial Times*, January 6, 2013.

customers stop buying. In response, Kazakhstan has embarked on an ambitious diversification program, aimed at developing targeted sectors such as transport, pharmaceuticals, telecommunications, petrochemicals and food processing.

Approximately 130 equities trade on the Kazakhstan Stock Exchange, but they break down into two main categories: those that form part of the KASE Index (which are liquid), and those with limited liquidity. The Kazakhstan Stock Exchange Index or KASE contains equities that Seisebayev considers more liquid than the remainder.

At time of writing (first quarter of 2013), the KASE Index consists of:

- Bank CenterCredit JSC, a financial institution with a capitalization of US$241 million
- Eurasian Natural Resources Corporation PLC, cross-listed on the LSE, a diversified mining stock with exposure to ferroalloys, iron ore, aluminum and energy, producing 17 percent of Kazakhstan's electricity with a capitalization of US$6.756 billion
- Kazakhmys PLC, one of the leading global copper miners, cross-listed on the London Stock Exchange (LSE) with a capitalization of US$6.776 billion
- Halyk Savings Bank of Kazakhstan JSC, with a capitalization of US$2.537 billion
- Kazkommertsbank JSC, with a capitalization of $975 million
- Kaztelekom JSC, the leading telecoms operator with a market capitalization of $1.2 billion
- KazMunaiGas EP JSC, one of the three largest Kazakh energy companies with GDRs listed on the LSE, which raised US$2 billion in its IPO in 2006 and has a market capitalization of $8,112 billion
- KazTransOil (ticker KZTO), the largest oil pipeline network, under the People's IPO program
- K'Cell (KCELL), a subsidiary of Nordic telecommunications operator TeliaSonera, with over 11 million subscribers, which raised $525 million in an IPO in December 2012

These nine stocks have more of a free float and therefore more liquidity than the other listed companies, according to Seisebayev. In many cases the government maintains control of a state-owned organization by allowing the sale of shares representing only 10–15 percent of its value, "meaning that these are not true privatizations."

Notwithstanding its economic possibilities, Kazakhstan has a daunting range of socioeconomic problems to resolve, including wealth inequality, with its consequences for education; chemical sites due to former defense industries (including some of the bases used to launch Soviet-era space flights); industrial pollution; poisonous dust storms and infrastructure problems.

Nonetheless, with its extensive energy resources and large mineral reserves, Kazakhstan has large foreign exchange reserves and enjoys a very positive trade balance, allowing it to address many of the same social and infrastructure problems of other members of the former Soviet Union.

Listing its major resource companies on the London Stock Exchange has allowed it to raise capital from international investors without forcing them to negotiate issues of the low liquidity and unfamiliarity that deter many international investors from investing in frontier markets. While the economy suffered a sharp slowdown during the global recession in 2008–09, the recovery in energy and mineral prices has seen a sharp rebound in GDP growth, aided by the completion of major infrastructure projects such as the gas export pipeline to China. While at present investment opportunities in Kazakhstan are almost totally confined to the resource sectors, as the economy grows and the liquidity on the Kazakh stock exchange improves, it would be reasonable to expect the government to list more of its domestically oriented businesses, such as utilities and transport, as evidenced by the recent listing of KazTransOil.

Investors should note that the strategy followed by Kazakhstan of listing several of its largest and most profitable companies on the London Stock Exchange since 2006 is now being followed by other frontier markets such as Nigeria; several banks in Nigeria have followed suit since 2011. This tactic has not been without its own problems as issues of corporate governance and limited public float have dogged certain Kazakh issuers, notably diversified resource stock ENRC. However, with the LSE pursuing a policy of attracting issuers from frontier economies due to the limited liquidity and lack of awareness among foreign investors that characterize most frontier markets' domestic stock exchanges, it would be reasonable to expect further new issues on established exchanges by other frontier market companies to make the expense and public scrutiny worthwhile. This does not mean they will prove to be successful investments; as with all IPOs, investors should consider the reasons for the company raising capital and how the proceeds of the issue will be used.

BANGLADESH: NOT A BASKET CASE

Sometimes in history, an unthinking utterance by a powerful individual resonates well beyond its moment and becomes enshrined in conversation well beyond its original meaning. General Douglas MacArthur's "I shall return," uttered when he was forced to leave the Philippines due to the Japanese invasion in 1942, an otherwise simple phrase, became forever connected to him, even for individuals who may not know the context or much about the man. In the trench warfare of some corporate situations, "live to fight another day" describes an attitude toward political survival in an environment of corporate infighting.

In an epithet often attributed to Henry Kissinger, Bangladesh was derided as an "international basket case" during the aftermath of the separation of the then-East Pakistan from Pakistan.

At the time, the economy was shattered as a result of the conflict. The war had left East Pakistan in ruins.

The Economist recalls:

> *In the last days of 1971 the country then called East Pakistan was engulfed by torture, rape, mass-killing and other acts of genocide. The main perpetrators were Pakistani troops bent on preventing secession from "West Pakistan." But the army had the support of many of East Pakistan's fundamentalist groups, including Jamaat-e-Islami, which remains Bangladesh's largest Islamic party. Estimates of the death toll vary from around 300,000 to the current government's reckoning of 3m[illion]—one in 20 of the population at that time.*[24]

Notwithstanding whether the "basket case" epithet had any merit at the time, Kissinger never supported the separation or liberation, preferring a strong Pakistan as a counterweight to India, a proudly non-aligned nation. He reportedly believed that an independent Bangladesh would align itself with either the then-threatening Union of Soviet Socialist Republics or China. Kissinger's view appears to have sprung from his belief in "realpolitik," a political philosophy best described as a non-ideological and totally pragmatic approach to a country's interests in politics, including foreign relations.

He later demonstrated the ultimate application of this philosophy by working toward then-President Richard Nixon's first trip to China. In fact, as a figure of speech, the phrase "Nixon going to China" became a political shorthand to describe an expected move by a politician. Kissinger sidestepped questions about the basket case remark in later years, but it rankled with Bangladeshis for several decades.

---

[24] "Trying War Crimes in Bangladesh: The Trial of the Birth of a Nation," *The Economist*, December 15, 2012.

Currently Bangladesh suffers from the usual image of South Asian countries as poor and overpopulated but, in absolute terms, appears arguably less politically risky than Pakistan.

Understanding the country's investment potential means looking more deeply into present accomplishments and future potential, explains Manirul Ahsan, a Dhaka, Bangladesh–based senior investment specialist and 23-year veteran of investment analysis.[25]

Bangladesh's socioeconomic indicators excel compared to those of some neighboring countries, he argues, advocating for a deeper look at the country, its potential, what it has achieved and stands to achieve. These positive indicators include: rising entrepreneurship; increasing workforce participation by women; a huge number of young and available workers (increasing by about 3 million annually), many of them foreign-educated; poverty reduction programs and the participation of non-governmental agencies.

The Bangladesh economy has grown 5–6 percent per year since 1996 despite the war in 1971, infrastructure problems, insufficient power supplies and slow implementation of economic reforms, according to *The World Factbook*.[26]

Although Bangladesh generates more than half of its gross domestic product through the service sector, 45 percent of Bangladeshis work in the agriculture sector, with rice as the single most important product. Garment exports totaled $12.3 billion in 2009, and remittances from overseas Bangladeshis totaled $11 billion in 2010, accounting for almost 12 percent of the country's gross domestic product.[27]

Bangladesh's growth in GDP should range around 7 percent annually until 2050, according to the PricewaterhouseCoopers LLP study entitled The World in 2050: Beyond the BRICs—a broader look at emerging market growth prospects.[28]

---

[25] Personal interview with Al Emid during the research and writing of this book in 2012.

[26] *The World Factbook*, Central Intelligence Agency, Bangladesh segment updated December 12, 2012, https://www.cia.gov/library/publications/the-world-factbook/geos/bg.html. segment updated December 12, 2012.

[27] Ibid.

[28] John Hawksworth and Gordon Clarkson, "The World in 2050: Beyond the BRICs—a broader look at emerging market growth prospects," Pricewaterhouse-Coopers, LLP, March 2008, 3.

Bangladesh has improved in other ways, according to a recent video by *The Economist*:

Without anybody noticing it very much, the country has quietly achieved some of the most impressive gains in basic living standards ever seen. The simplest measure of this is how long people live. A Bangladeshi born in 1990 would expect to live until 56—not much. Now life expectancy is 68 and four years longer than the average Indian lifespan even though Indians are so much richer.[29]

Not surprisingly, the PricewaterhouseCoopers report explains the benefits of the long-range view:

The general message is that investors with long-time horizons should look beyond the BRICs (Brazil, Russia, India and China); there are many other alternatives worth considering depending on the nature of the investment and the risk tolerance of the investor.[30]

This positive picture of Bangladesh omits some of the country's drawbacks, including annual flooding due to monsoon rains that cover about one-third of the total territory, hamper development and cause water pollution and soil degradation in areas of extremely dense population.

The PricewaterhouseCoopers report warns that economic projections for Bangladesh "are contingent on avoiding major natural disasters, notably those associated with long-term rising sea levels due to global warming."[31]

The World Bank also sees some near-term risks connected to the European crisis and suggests that a worsening of the crisis would hurt Bangladesh's exports but points to the stability provided by the International Monetary Fund's Extended Credit Facility as a stabilizing factor.[32]

Ahsan ranks energy, infrastructure, telecommunications, electronic transactions, media and entertainment as the most promising investment sectors. Bangladesh has made huge strides in shaking off the "basket case" image.

---

[29] "Bangladesh: A Remarkable Improvement: Making Great Strides," video datelined November 16, 2012, http://www.economist.com/blogs/feastandfamine/2012/11/bangladesh-remarkable-improvement.
[30] Hawksworth and Clarkson, "The World in 2050."
[31] Ibid.
[32] Bangladesh Economic Update, October 2012, 2.

The use of countries such as Bangladesh with large, low-paid workforces as outsourcing production hubs for developed market companies, particularly in industries such as textiles, garments, toys and low-end electronics, where labor costs form a major percentage of the total cost of the products, means that investors in these companies need to be aware of potential reputational damage when accidents occur. Such dramatic incidents as the collapse of a garment factory complex in the capital of Dhaka in early 2013, with the loss of more than 1,000 lives, made the supply chains that supply retailers in North America and Europe very visible. Pressure from foreign customers to avoid a repetition of such incidents may well lead to more stringent enforcement of existing safety standards and the introduction of higher standards and increased production costs in addition to rising wages. All of these factors would pose a problem for countries such as Bangladesh that rely on low-cost labor as one of their major attractions for customers.

SERBIA: A PROMISING CANDIDATE

During the Yugoslav Wars, Serbia appeared in the news regularly as we watched the former Socialist Federal Republic of Yugoslavia dissolve into its parts. Until 1991, Yugoslavia—an artificial construct of a nation at the best of times—consisted of eight jurisdictions. These included six republics: Bosnia and Herzegovina, Croatia, Macedonia, Montenegro, Serbia and Slovenia along with the two semi-autonomous provinces of Kosovo and Vojvodina (at the time part of Serbia).

The dissolution actually began in 1989 as political and ethnic divisions led to massive protests in Serbia and elsewhere. Following referenda, Croatia and Slovenia declared independence in June 1991. After its own referendum, Macedonia declared independence in September of the same year.

Bosnia and Herzegovina made the same move in March 1992. Not surprisingly, tensions escalated and what we generally call the Bosnian conflict began in the same month, when Serbian paramilitary forces attacked Bosnian villages.

The killing of a Bosnian protester in Sarajevo in April triggered the start of full warfare. In April, Serbia and Montenegro formed the Federal Republic of Yugoslavia.

Hostilities in the western regions ended in 1995 when talks in Dayton, Ohio, led to the Dayton Agreement. The Kosovo War between Serbia and Montenegro against Bosnia began in 1996 and ended with the North American Treaty Organization (NATO) bombing of Serbia in 1999.

By some estimates the hostilities reduced the GDP of the Yugoslav economy by half, when compared to before the beginning of the wars in 1991.

Since then, the region has had less attention from Western broadcast media. In the Hollywood category, a gritty film entitled *Behind Enemy Lines* released in 2001 stars Gene Hackman as an unlikely hero going behind the lines to rescue a navy navigator during Bosnian hostilities. The plot is reminiscent of countless earlier cavalry-to-the rescue films. In some television fiction dramas the filmmakers traced a villain's murderous insanity in America back to his experiences in the war zone.

The former Yugoslavia's fissiparous tendencies had not been exhausted however, and in February 2003, the Federal Republic of Yugoslavia became the State Union of Serbia and Montenegro. That union broke up when Montenegro declared independence in June 2006 after a referendum.

Finally, Kosovo declared independence from Serbia in February 2008, a move upheld in July 2010 by the International Court of Justice in the Hague. Serbia based its appeal on United Nations Resolution 1244, which Serbia claimed was a guarantee of its borders. The court decided that the resolution did not prevent a unilateral declaration such as that made by Kosovo.

Since the end of hostilities, Serbia has worked at staking its place on the world economic and political stage. Investors should be aware that although the dissolution of the former Yugoslavia has been unusually lengthy and bloody, several other frontier markets have seen conflicts arising after the end of the Cold War and the fall of the Soviet regime in 1989, now that such conflict is no longer regarded as a move in the international chess match of U.S.–Soviet rivalry. In such African countries as Somalia and Ethiopia, the early 1990s saw a descent into warlordism, with chaos in the former and the independence of the former Italian colony of Eritrea in the latter. This was then followed by a war over boundaries between Ethiopia and its former allies in Eritrea between 1998 and 2000. Similarly, in the Caucasus, conflicts between the former Soviet republics of Armenia and Azerbaijan over the disputed Armenian enclave of Nagorno Karabakh led to fighting between 1991 and 1994, and as recently as 2008, Georgia and Russia were involved in a brief war over Russia's support for separatist rebels in South Ossetia.

For Serbia, the transition has not occurred without pain, according to Dr. Milan R. Kovačević, a Serbian economist who specializes in foreign investment financing.[33] He has acted as a consultant for international corporations such as PepsiCo Inc., General Motors Company and the IKEA Group.

---

[33]Personal interview with Al Emid during the research and writing of this book in 2012.

Kovačević suggests that Serbia's move from closed communist system to market economy could never have happened easily, a judgment borne out as other countries made the same shift. Similarly, states in Eastern Europe, such as Romania, Bulgaria and Ukraine, with large agricultural sectors, a reliance on inefficient Soviet-era industries such as heavy manufacturing and petrochemicals supplied by cheap Russian gas, also found it especially difficult to adapt to the post-communist era. In this case it involved a near-total overhaul of Serbian society. "We were a very closed country—no exports, no imports, only smuggling money, smuggling goods and so on," Kovačević recalls.

Serbia currently has relatively low restrictions on foreign investment in the country. "We have a direct foreign investment law which enables foreigners to have 100 percent share in almost all areas," Kovačević says.

For the future, in March 2012 Serbia achieved the status of "candidate" for entry into the European Union. Admission would mean better trade relations with other European nations and would provide a "seal of approval" on the world stage for Eastern and Southern European states emerging from communism. It affirms a country's economic viability and provides access to various forms of aid, including farm support payments.

Croatia expects to reap numerous economic benefits from its admission to the European Union, scheduled for 2013, and Serbia could eventually reap similar benefits, according to a knowledgeable Belgrade-based Serbian journalist, who asked not to be identified.

The promising picture does have some question marks overhanging it. Despite a major joint venture between the government and the U.S.–Italian carmaker Fiat announced in 2011 to build Fiat cars in Serbia, the Serbian government has delayed some of the payments due to Fiat under the terms of the joint venture until some time in 2013, according to reports in Bloomberg News.

Meanwhile, although Serbia has few restrictions on foreign investment, the stock exchange in Belgrade provides very limited opportunities. In a typical privatization scenario, a majority shareholder, often an American company, buys up between 65 percent and 80 percent of an organization privatized by the Serbian government while the remainder of shares goes to employees and other individuals who often sell their shares to the same majority shareholder.

Moreover, the exchange has a very limited trade in bonds.

Serbia would not be classified among the more attractive frontier markets even within Eastern Europe, owing to the legacy of the Bosnia conflict and the uncertainty over its willingness to recognize Kosovo's independence. When added to the high cost and uncompetitive structure of the Serbian economy, there are limited investment opportunities for foreign investors.

Nonetheless, its strategic geographic position, relatively large size compared to other European frontier markets (only Romania and Ukraine have larger populations, and only Croatia, Romania and Ukraine have larger stock markets), and its well-educated population as well as its relatively cheap valuation mean that there may be several individual companies that will prove to be successful investments over the next five years. Possible approval of EU entry would provide a major boost to Serbia's international reputation and credibility.

SIERRA LEONE: NO LONGER WAR TORN

A decade ago, Sierra Leone definitely qualified as a "war-torn" African nation, embroiled in a costly and bloody civil war. For some, the 2006 film *Blood Diamond*, starring Leonardo DiCaprio as the tormented Danny Archer, surrounded by the war, may be the most enduring image, even seven years later.

The civil war partially revolved around the desire to control the diamond business and the sale of the notorious "blood diamonds"—that is, diamonds produced in conflict zones such as Sierra Leone, under appalling conditions by exploited workforces. This led to the establishment of a certification system that benefited established producers such as Namibia, South Africa, Australia and Canada at the expense of poorer African countries like Angola and Sierra Leone.

The "war torn" label still turns up periodically—and inaccurately, according to Kimberly S. Johnson, a veteran financial journalist covering Sierra Leone for media organizations such as the *Financial Times* and *Africa Magazine*, and previously with CNN, the Associated Press and the *Boston Globe*.[34] "There are a few international journalists that insist on putting that in every single one of their stories," she explains.

More accurately, the civil war ended in 2002 after many thousands of deaths and the forced relocation of roughly a third of the population. With the departure of United Nations peacekeepers in 2005, the country's military forces assumed responsibility for security and have worked for its stability. The military forces remained neutral during the presidential contests of 2007 and 2012.

Understanding the evolution of investment markets may increase a financial professional's grasp of the divisions between market categories.

---

[34]Personal interview with Al Emid during the research and writing of this book in 2012.

Sierra Leone typifies two important concepts in the study of frontier markets. Its low level of development gives it the rank of exotic frontier market, meaning that the MSCI and FTSE indices do not currently include it as a full frontier market. Moreover, it provides an example of a country that could move from exotic status to full frontier status, and possibly in a decade or more, move to emerging market status.

In fact, development of Sierra Leone's other major natural resource, its extensive and high-quality iron ore deposits, is already in full swing with London Alternative Investment Market (AIM)–listed African Minerals (AMI-L) having invested over $2 billion over the last five years to develop the Tonkolili iron ore mine, with forecast production of 20 million tonnes per annum by mid-2013. Furthermore, Sierra Leone has state-controlled China Railway Minerals as a 12.5 percent shareholder in African Minerals, as China's appetite for iron ore to make steel continues to grow.

Other neighboring West African countries, such as Guinea and Mauritania, also possess extensive high-grade iron ore deposits, which major mining companies are looking at developing.

Ironically, the low level of market development provided a sort of cushion from the global financial crisis in 2008–09. In comparison, Nigeria and Ghana felt the impact of the crisis more directly since they have better developed equity, bond and exchange markets. Sierra Leone has a limited bond market, which deals almost exclusively in short-term local bonds, Johnson explains.

Now fragile economically—but not war torn—the country grapples with rebuilding. Its economic future rests on its ability to develop bountiful natural resources including diamonds, oil, iron ore, bauxite and rutile. President Ernest Bai Koroma's priorities appear to include development, job creation and eradication of corruption.

The country's resources have attracted a list of international companies from the United Kingdom, including iron mining companies African Minerals Ltd. and London Mining PLC, American oil companies Chevron and Anadarko Petroleum, as well as Australian exploration and development company Cape Lambert Resources Ltd. and Russia's Lukoil Oil Company.

Sierra Leone has two indigenous banks, the Sierra Leone Commercial Bank and the Rokel Commercial Bank (Sierra Leone) Ltd. The government owns 51 percent of Rokel with the remainder trading on the Sierra Leone Interim Trading Facility in Freetown, which operates for only two days per week and has very few stocks available for trading.

For the future, the outcomes of several scenarios would go a long way in deciding Sierra Leone's economic viability. Currently foreign companies extract the country's resources and typically ship them offshore. "There's no processing. There's no refining here or anything like that," Johnson says. A shift to domestic processing would create jobs and incomes.

The ability of the Koroma government to succeed in its goals of development, job creation and eradication of corruption would provide the kind of reassurance that foreign companies require in order to undertake lengthy periods of research and to commit large amounts of money. Moreover, the Koroma government must also work to reduce the country's illiteracy rate, which currently stands in the 60 percent range, according to Johnson.

On the financial side, if the Koroma government finds a balance between increasing royalties from multinational mining companies and driving up their costs so much that they exceed the benefits of investing in the country, the country's cash-starved administration would have much-needed revenues to provide national infrastructure. The Koroma government must also achieve national stability and then demonstrate that stability to outside companies and investors.

The population has a determination to raise themselves and their country. "They want to go to school. They want to send their kids to school. They want to go to college," Johnson says. In some ways, they have bought into the globalization phenomenon, she continues. "Everyone's on Yahoo. Everyone's on Facebook."

More broadly, if Sierra Leone does make the shift from the exotic to the indexed frontier market category, it would serve as an example for promising but underdeveloped African frontier markets that have low gross domestic product per capita, very young populations, low levels of urbanization, low taxes as a percentage of GDP and small or nonexistent stock markets. This role becomes even more important if, as some analysts have suggested, Africa becomes "the new China"—a reference to its economic and market potential.

CONCLUSION

By definition, exotic frontier markets such as Sierra Leone have the potential to see their GDPs per capita double or triple from a very low base, with the attendant rise in consumption, infrastructure, development of domestic industries and development of stock and bond markets.

Investors might consider investing in these countries when thinking about frontier markets, as the potential return is likely to be much higher than the small, wealthy Gulf Cooperation Council countries or the relatively well-off Eastern European states with shrinking, aging populations, notwithstanding promising individual companies. The difficulty for investors is accessing these markets, as they are usually at a lower stage of development than those countries included in the index. Using companies listed in developed markets, which have projects or exposure to exotic frontier markets, can be one route to follow.

Looking at the range of frontier markets in this chapter and the strategies they have adopted to develop their capital markets and grow their economies, investors should come away with some feeling for the enormous range of countries at different stages of development that comprise the universe of frontier markets. They encompass every type of developing economy from the large, relatively poor, but fast-growing Asian behemoths such as Bangladesh and Vietnam, through ex-Soviet and communist command economies such as Kazakhstan and Serbia, to African economies including both middle income countries such as Kenya and exotic markets such as Sierra Leone.

Making generalizations about individual countries on the basis of their geographical location or their closeness to more troubled nations is not a sensible approach and is as fallacious as much of the Western media coverage that lumps all countries in a region into one stereotype. It is important for investors to be aware of the differences between frontier markets at different stages of development and with different economic backgrounds.

TAKEAWAYS

1. When considering investment in frontier markets we need to set aside media images and focus on the more accurate data, analyses and projections.
2. We need to avoid generalizations about regions, such as the Middle East, and identify areas, such as the United Arab Emirates, that are relative safe havens and promising investments.
3. Some frontier market investments require a much longer-term horizon than others, particularly those with a high percentage of their population still living in rural areas and with high birth rates and a young population.
4. Investment generalizations based on an entire region can be costly, whether in actual dollars or in opportunity costs.

CHAPTER 5

Economic Strengths of Emerging and Frontier Markets

A number of reasons explain the attractiveness for investors of emerging markets and frontier markets, which we describe as developing markets. These reasons include their lack of correlation with developed markets, which means adding developing markets to a traditional portfolio can reduce its overall volatility. Another reason often cited is their faster rate of economic growth compared to developed markets. The question investors must ask, however, is whether their accelerated growth has translated into superior returns compared to developed markets.

RETURNS FROM EMERGING MARKETS

As we noted in Chapter 1, over the last decade, emerging markets, as represented by the MSCI Emerging Markets (Free) Index, have delivered substantially higher returns than developed markets, as represented by the MSCI World Index. This does not necessarily prove, however, that higher economic growth results in higher stock market returns. For the decade ending October 31, 2012, the MSCI Emerging Markets Index delivered annual price-only returns of 13.4 percent p.a. and total returns of 16.1 percent p.a. against returns from the MSCI All Country World Index of 5.6 percent p.a. and 8.3 percent p.a. respectively. This return is more than double that of developed markets. It is largely due to the low valuations of emerging markets at the beginning of the last decade, when they had recently been through the Asian crisis of 1997–98, the Russian default and devaluation of 1998 and the Brazilian devaluation of 1999.

Over the last decade, GDP growth in emerging markets has grown much more rapidly than in developed markets, with the BRIC countries and other countries in the emerging market indices experiencing GDP growth of 5–10 percent p.a., apart from the two recession years of 2002 and 2009.

By contrast, the G7 developed economies have experienced lower levels of GDP growth, averaging 2–3 percent p.a. before the financial crisis of 2008–09 and 0–2 percent p.a. subsequently.

This difference in GDP growth reflects not only their higher starting levels of income but also their less attractive demographics and higher levels of debt.

As a result, while 20 years ago (1992) developing markets accounted for only 19 percent of global GDP, today they account for 36 percent at market exchange rates. Using purchasing power parity (PPP), developing markets today account for more than 50 percent of global GDP.

They also account for 70 percent of world population (over five times that of developed markets) and 46 percent of its land mass (twice that of developed markets). Given their rapid GDP growth compared to developed markets, this percentage will continue to increase over the next decade.

Using projections for future GDP growth to 2050 by Pricewaterhouse-Coopers (PwC), Elroy Dimson, Paul Marsh and Mike Staunton of the London Business School suggest that emerging markets will continue to grow rapidly, with the BRIC nations comprising four of the five largest economies ranked by GDP by 2050, China displacing the United States as the world's largest economy by 2020, and India overtaking the United States by 2050.[1]

The growth in GDP has lifted the developing markets' percentage of global stock market capitalization from 2 percent in 1980 and 6 percent in 2004 to 13 percent in 2012. In a 2009 ranking of the top 100 global companies ranked by market capitalization by *Forbes* magazine, three of the top five companies were from emerging markets and 11 of the top 100 were from China—the most from any country except the United States.

However, the market capitalization of developing markets is well below their share of world GDP, largely due to the restrictions on which stocks foreigners can hold. Chinese A shares remain inaccessible to foreign investors who do not meet the qualifications to become qualified foreign institutional investors (QFIIs). Some frontier markets, such as Saudi Arabia, do not permit foreigners to own shares listed in the country, while others, such as Iran, are under sanctions by major developed economies such as the United States and Canada. Similarly, many emerging and frontier market stocks have only a small proportion of their shares in public hands.

Even if emerging markets' capitalization grew only in line with the GDP projections from PwC, Dimson, Marsh and Staunton note it would

---

[1] Credit Suisse, Global Investment Returns Yearbook 2010, Section 2, 13.

account for 30 percent of the world total by 2050, more than double its present weight, and with markets tending to become more open to foreign investment as economies mature and the free float available rises, they speculate that its share could reach 40–50 percent of total world capitalization by that date.[2]

There is not always a direct correlation between GDP growth and stock market performance, as witnessed in China over the last decade. Nonetheless, strong absolute growth in GDP usually results in strong revenue growth for companies, which in turn makes possible high growth in their earnings.

THE LACK OF CORRELATION BETWEEN GDP GROWTH AND EQUITY RETURNS

While it is likely that the market capitalization of developing markets will grow, both in absolute terms and relative to the developed world, this does not mean that stronger GDP growth automatically translates into stronger stock market returns. For the 34 years from 1976 to 2009, the annualized return from emerging markets was 9.5 percent per annum compared to returns from developed markets of 10.6 percent p.a.

Although emerging markets have outperformed developed markets strongly over the last decade, it is likely that the degree of outperformance will be lower going forward, as the valuations for both emerging markets and developed markets are now similar.

Meanwhile, it is worth reiterating that emerging markets underperformed developed markets in both the 1980s and 1990s before their substantial outperformance over the last decade, and that over the period starting in 1976 for which emerging market returns have been measured, there has been little difference between their returns and those of developed markets.

If, as conventional wisdom suggests, corporate earnings will constitute a roughly constant share of national income, then dividends should grow in line with the growth of the real economy. Thus, fast-growing economies should experience higher stock returns due to higher growth in dividends; Dimson, Marsh and Staunton show that there is a high correlation (0.87) between real dividend growth and real equity returns for the 19 countries for which there are records for the period between 1900 and 2009.

However, the evidence suggests that real dividend growth has lagged behind real GDP per capita growth in 18 of the 19 countries over this

---

[2]Ibid.

110-year period, and the correlation is negative (−0.30). Even more importantly, the association between real growth in GDP per capita and real
equity returns is also negative (−0.23)!

Dimson, Marsh and Staunton find a very low (0.12) correlation between
growth in real GDP per capita and real equity returns—one so low as to
be statistically insignificant. Therefore, it is correct to state that there is no
evidence of economic growth being a predictor of stock market performance.

Reasons for the Lack of Correlation

There are several possible explanations for the lack of correlation. As Robert
D. Arnott and Peter L. Bernstein (who co-authored an award-winning article
on the sources of equity market returns[3]) point out, private enterprises in
entrepreneurial countries contribute to GDP growth but not to quoted
company dividends. It is also notable that even public companies in certain
sectors such as technology and health care may retain a higher proportion of
their earnings for research, thus reducing the correlation between earnings
growth and dividend growth.

There is therefore a gap between GDP growth and dividend and earnings
growth, which also explains why the relationship between GDP growth and
returns from the stock market is so "noisy." Many successful countries
attract immigrants, which also impacts the growth of their GDP per capita.

Professor Jeremy Siegel, author of *Stocks for the Long Run*, points out
that the largest firms quoted on most developed markets are multinationals
whose profits depend on global, rather than domestic, GDP growth, thus
reducing the correlation between GDP growth and stock market returns.
This finding does not suggest that economic growth is not relevant to stock
market returns, but rather that both depend upon the state of the global
economy and the domestic economy in which stocks are listed.

Economic growth reflects growth in the real economy, which is not
always the same as stock market capitalization. Even growth in stock
market capitalization does not necessarily mean that investors' portfolios
will appreciate, due to privatization, equity issuance, demutualization and
other instances of new stock being issued by companies for such purposes
as acquisitions or spin-offs.

As we have discussed elsewhere, often foreign investors are unable to
share in increases in values in emerging and frontier markets, due to limited
free floats and government restrictions, while companies listed in developing

---

[3]Robert D. Arnott and Peter L. Bernstein, "What Risk Premium Is Normal?" *Financial Analysts Journal*, March/April 2002.

markets may be dependent upon growth in the developed world. Indeed, sometimes multinationals listed in developed markets may provide better exposure to growth in developing markets, a phenomenon that we discuss later when considering the best ways for foreign investors to gain access to emerging and frontier markets.

The strong growth in the GDP of emerging and frontier markets has been common knowledge for the last decade or so at least, and this is reflected in the valuations in which these markets trade. There is little difference between the price-to-earnings ratio of the developed markets and the established emerging markets at present, but in previous periods, such as the early to mid-1990s, emerging markets traded at substantially higher valuations than developed markets and produced disappointing returns by comparison.

Frontier markets, however, are somewhat cheaper than emerging markets on a valuation basis, partially due to having underperformed, notably since the end of the financial crisis. They also have younger populations than developed markets and many emerging markets, lower incomes per capita and are at an earlier stage of economic development where gains in GDP per capita are more easily achieved as productivity rises in the agricultural sector and workers migrate from the countryside to the cities.

This strong GDP growth has translated into rising levels of consumer income, creating an emerging market middle class, defined as those citizens whose GDP per capita in PPP terms is over US$5,000 per annum. Developing markets represent 70 percent of the global population, and their population is growing faster than that of the developed markets. Individuals in developing markets have become wealthier, with wealth among the developing markets having increased five times over the last decade.

Developing market consumers hold a high percentage of their wealth in the form of cash savings, leaving significant room for discretionary spending. Sales of fast-moving consumer goods (FMCG) and other products such as financial services have experienced rapid growth over the last decade, and sales of consumer durables such as autos have also risen sharply in the last five years. Consumers in the developing markets now purchase more automobiles than those in the developed markets, and China passed the United States in 2009 as the largest auto market in the world.

We believe that investors are likely to enjoy strong absolute returns from investing in a diversified portfolio of frontier market companies, given their relatively attractive valuation and the strong growth in consumer incomes and spending. While there is no direct correlation between GDP growth and stock market returns, the strong GDP growth experienced by frontier markets over the last decade has improved their governments' revenues and ability to invest in infrastructure and raise living standards. Investors should therefore consider not only companies that benefit from the rise of the developing markets' middle class, but also those companies that provide materials, equipment and resources to help support the improvement in countries' physical and human capital.

The sectors that would benefit from rising consumer incomes would include the obvious makers of consumer products, especially FMCG (breweries, food and beverage makers, personal care products and consumer electronics) and those that provide services to the same group, such as fast food restaurants, mobile phone companies, Internet service providers and banks and other financial services groups. Sectors that would benefit from the latter process would include building materials (cement and steel), utilities, capital equipment makers and providers of infrastructure such as toll roads and ports.

The developing economies have made remarkable progress in improving their financial condition in the last decade, with the percentage of developing countries ranked investment grade by the ratings agencies rising from 5 percent in 1992 to 47 percent in 2012. Meanwhile, developed countries have been experiencing downgrades, and while developing countries' debt-to-GDP ratio is 40 percent, for developed countries it was more than 100 percent in 2012.

At the corporate level, companies in developing markets are becoming more creditworthy and corporate balance sheets and profitability have been improving, with growth in equity substantially outpacing growth in net debt over the last decade. As a result, developing market companies are better equipped to compete with multinationals and companies in developed markets. Several companies headquartered in emerging markets are among the global leaders in their industries, such as Brazilian resource giant Vale; energy companies PetroChina, Gazprom in Russia and Petrobras in Brazil; mobile telecom providers China Mobile and VimpelCom (in Russia and elsewhere) and Brazilian brewer InBev.

Many developing market companies, such as those listed in the last paragraph, have American depositary receipts (ADRs) and global depositary receipts (GDRs) listed in New York and London, requiring them to produce reports that comply with Generally Accepted Accounting Principles (GAAP) or International Financial Reporting Standards (IFRS) standards, improving their disclosure. According to MSCI, over 40 percent of developing market issuers now report their financials in such fashion, up from 5 percent a decade ago. As discussed in Chapter 4 when looking at frontier markets that have followed this route, Kazakhstan has listed several of its largest and most profitable companies on the London Stock Exchange (LSE), including energy company KazMunaiGas, mining companies Kazakhmys and Eurasian Natural Resources Corp., and a couple of banks, Halyk Savings Bank and Kazkommertsbank. These have not all proved to be successful investments, but other frontier economies are now following this path. Five Nigerian companies are listed on the LSE, including two Nigerian banks, Guaranty Trust Bank and Diamond Bank, which were already listed on the LSE in 2012, and a third, Zenith National Bank, which listed GDRs in March 2013, meaning that the two largest Nigerian banks are now listed on the LSE.

According to the LSE, it has 58 emerging market banks listed with a market capitalization of US$75 billion. Ninety-seven sub-Saharan African–focused companies are listed on or admitted to LSE markets, including 23 companies and two GDRs on the main exchange and 70 admissions and two GDRS on the Alternative Investment Market (AIM), while US$6.75 billion has been raised by Africa-focused issuers since 2008.[4]

As with any other company, investors considering investment in such frontier market issuers should conduct suitable due diligence, and while having GAAP- or IFRS-compliant accounts offers some comfort, there is no guarantee that the companies willing to pay international accountants to produce them will prove to be successful investments. However, the willingness to produce such accounts does demonstrate that management is prepared to spend some money to make its financials comprehensible to international investors. Having locally audited accounts should not disqualify companies from being considered as possible investments. If the business is in a relatively straightforward industry, such as manufacturing, retailing or construction, then there is less room for accounting subterfuge, and if the company is relatively small, the expense of hiring an expensive international auditor may not be felt to be justified.

Frontier market valuations appear attractive at the time of writing, as the faster growth earnings by companies in developing markets have offset the rise in their prices over the last three years since the end of the financial crisis. Frontier markets also look attractively valued compared to the emerging markets whose valuations are at present (2013) approximately equal to those of the developed markets, at around 12 to 14 times earnings; by comparison, the MSCI Frontier Markets Index sells at 10.5 times this year's forecast earnings.

The attractiveness of some of the developing markets is heightened by their appreciating currencies. As noted elsewhere in the book, as the financial situations of the emerging markets have improved over the last decade, so have their currencies appreciated against those of the developed markets, especially since the financial crisis erupted in 2008, and the central banks in the United States, Europe and Japan responded by starting quantitative easing programs, which involved effectively creating extra liquidity by printing money.

China, which runs a controlled float against its major trading partners for its currency, the yuan (also known as the Renminbi), has allowed it

---

[4]Press release, London Stock Exchange, March 21, 2013.

to appreciate from Y8.21=US$1 to Y6.22=US$1 over the past half-dozen years to 2013, a rise of almost 25 percent. The Brazilian real rose from US$1=BRL2.55 in late 2008 to BRL 2. At one stage in 2011, the real appreciated to R1.6, and the Brazilian government introduced negative interest rates to dissuade inflows from foreign investors into the currency. Among frontier markets, the Colombian peso has appreciated from US$1=P2550 in late 2008 to P1750 in 2013, the Peruvian new sol from US$1=NS3.15 to NS2.63, and the Philippine peso from US$1=P50 to P41.50.

Not all developing markets' currencies appreciate, of course; in some cases their governments will deliberately run a weak currency policy to encourage exports and generate foreign currency reserves, with the Kenyan shilling and Ghanaian cedi both depreciating by almost 50 percent over the last five years, while stifling the demand for expensive imported consumer luxuries. Nonetheless, given the strong underlying fundamentals of most frontier market economies and the quantitative easing programs of the developed countries, it would be reasonable to assume that at least frontier market currencies should not depreciate too rapidly over the next few years.

TAKEAWAYS

1. The lack of correlation between frontier markets on the one hand and emerging and developed markets on the other explains a large part of their potential. The strong returns from emerging markets and frontier markets over the last decade as opposed to those from developed markets is in large part due to their low valuations at the beginning of the decade. Frontier markets still appear attractive, as they have not rebounded as much as emerging markets since the financial crisis ended in early 2009 and are now selling at lower valuations than either emerging or developed markets.

2. It is also important to note that frontier markets do not correlate with each other. Despite the strong GDP growth of emerging and frontier markets compared to developed markets, investors should be aware that there is little correlation between GDP growth and stock market returns.

3. Much of the explanation lies in the low valuations. Investors should look for sectors that will benefit from the factors that make frontier markets attractive, namely companies supplying goods and services to the rising middle-class consumers in these countries.

Past Emerging Market Upheavals and What They Can Teach Frontier Market Investors

In life, love and career, earlier traumas can impact on present decisions and thinking—perhaps without any direct-line connection between the past and the decision in question. The status of frontier markets as a subset of emerging markets may mean that past upheavals color present investment decisions. If our thesis is correct—that frontier market investments, given time, will yield solid returns—then the tendency to fear the repetition of history could prove costly. In order to avoid the outcome of opportunity costs, we must look at each frontier market investment possibility with an open mind.

This is important because behavioral finance experts include memory on the list of factors that influence decision making in investing as well as in other areas of life. However, allowing memories of bygone traumas to influence decision making in the present can become costly in investing as well as in other areas of life.

Five well-known emerging and frontier market crises may cloud some investors' views of emerging markets and frontier markets, both in general and with respect to the five regions involved: Argentina, Mexico, the Asian economies (including Japan), Russia and Brazil.

Clarifying one's perspective in the investing process means—in a sense—overruling the old memory in favor of more relevant facts in the present. That strategy certainly applies to emerging and frontier markets. "Emerging markets are going to have a majority of the world's middle classes," argues James Awad, a 43-year veteran of capital management and managing director of New York–based Zephyr Management LP, which has US$2 billion in assets under management[1].

---

[1] Personal interview with Al Emid during the research and writing of this book in 2012.

The scale of these markets and their potential is inescapable. "They already have a majority of the world's population. They are going to have a majority of worldwide gross domestic product," Awad says. Moreover, many of these countries now have a bigger and wealthier middle class than previously.

Emerging market stock prices are currently below the valuations they reached before the financial crisis in 2008–09 and below those of more established frontier markets such as those of the BRIC countries (Brazil, Russia, India and China), meaning that they do not fully reflect their true value—one of the factors underpinning our argument about the potential for future returns.

As with many emerging and frontier market concepts, the positive news does not apply across the board; several examples of what happened with emerging markets when they seemed sure winners in the early 1990s provide a warning to investors that there may be bumps in the road ahead.

ARGENTINEAN DEFAULT OF 2001

Argentina was a developed market that slid back to emerging market status and then to frontier market status. As noted in Chapter 1, at the beginning of the 20th century, Argentina's GDP per capita was equal to that of France and higher than that of Sweden and Norway.[2] Fifty years of political instability, military coups, hyperinflation and regressive economic policies that began with the rule of dictator Juan Peron and his wife Eva ("Evita") in 1941 culminated in the largest-ever sovereign debt default in 200 years (in 2001). Despite enjoying bountiful natural resources, a temperate climate, a well-educated elite and large inflows of foreign investment from British, American, German and Italian investors, Argentina failed to deliver on its early promise and already had a history of defaulting on its foreign debt, including the episode in 1890 that almost led to the bankruptcy of Barings, at the time one of the leading global investment banks.

It was late in pegging its peso at 1:1 to the American dollar in an attempt to conquer hyperinflation, a strategy chosen by the government in 1989 after the overthrow of the military junta following the Falklands invasion in 1982. This worked in reducing inflation but made Argentina very expensive during the 1990s, hurting its export competitiveness, an especially severe consequence given its dependence on resources.

---

[2]Dimson, Marsh and Staunton, Credit Suisse Global Investment Returns Yearbook 2010, Section 1, 5.

Eventually, after the successors to the flamboyant regime of Carlos Menem, Argentine President from 1989 to 1999, had seen the current account deficit blow out during the economic crisis of 2001–02, the government defaulted on about $90 billion worth of foreign debt (much of which had been sold to foreign investors as higher-yielding U.S. dollar–denominated debt) in 2001 and devalued the peso by 75 percent in early 2002, after imposing capital controls. The economic crisis that followed led to shortened careers for several presidents and continued unrest.

In the same year, the Argentinean economy bottomed out and left an estimated 60 percent or more of Argentineans in poverty. The same factors that were so disastrous in 2002—the restructured debt picture and the huge labor supply—helped generate 7–8 percent annual increases in GDP for about six years, but eventually President Nestor Kirchner imposed price controls, export taxes and other measures and—reportedly—understated inflation numbers.

In 2007, Cristina Fernandez de Kirchner succeeded her husband as president after he passed away in office and growth slowed, first due to export taxes and other anti-business domestic policies such as freezing utility tariffs, then due to the fall in demand caused by the global financial crisis. The situation was exacerbated by drought in 2009–10, and despite being re-elected as president in 2011, President Kirchner continues to face challenges caused by weaker Chinese demand for commodities, rising inflation (officially running at 12–13 percent p.a. but reportedly twice as high) and American judicial rulings forcing it to pay the outstanding interest on the unsettled portion of its unpaid foreign debt.

The Buenos Aires Merval Index is no higher in U.S. dollar terms than it was a decade ago, and while individual Argentinean companies, some of which have American Depository Receipts (ADRs) listed in New York, can provide good returns to foreign investors on a short-term (one to two years) basis, most analysts and managers do not recommend holding a major position in the country. Currently, analysts believe that government policies risk worsening the country's high inflation rate. The government has imposed foreign exchange controls. And although the Merval Index had risen by 37 percent in peso terms to an all-time high in local currency terms by the end of April 2013, Argentina does not rank highly as a favored investment among frontier market funds.

Investors should be aware that a country's history of dealing with foreign investors (especially when there is a long track record, which is the case for most Latin American countries) can be a valuable guide to its attitude toward property rights and how minority shareholders and bondholders are treated. Thus Argentina has defaulted or rescheduled its debt five times since 1950 and three times in the last 30 years, most recently in 2001. Peru has defaulted or rescheduled five times since 1969, most recently in 1984, and Venezuela four times since 1983, most recently in 2004. Of course, Brazil (an established BRIC emerging market) defaulted or rescheduled three times between 1961 and 1983, but while it has devalued since then, as we note elsewhere in this chapter, it now has a 30-year history of repaying its foreign creditors.[3]

MEXICAN DEVALUATION OF 1995

The Mexican devaluation provides another emerging market example of the potentially bumpy road ahead and illustrates a lesson about volatility and uncertainty. As part of a series of economic reforms, the government of Mexico had pegged the peso at a rate of 2.21 pesos to the American dollar in January 1988. The peg and the reforms apparently reassured several Wall Street firms, who began selling Mexican Treasury bonds, called "tesobonos," which carried higher yields than U.S. debt. The tesobonos, denominated in pesos, had coupons and principal indexed to the American dollar. At the time, it appeared that the move resolved several problems including an increasing current account deficit, partially triggered by the appreciating peso.

When then-Federal Reserve chairman Alan Greenspan began raising American interest rates from 3 percent at the beginning of February 1994, money flowed out of Mexico, and the Mexican government used up most of its foreign exchange reserves to protect the currency peg.

It could not sustain this strategy and devalued the peso effective December 20, 1994. By March 1995 the rate had fallen to 7.75 pesos to the American dollar for what was a peak-to-trough drop of 70.3 percent.

This devaluation led to a major sell-off of the tesobonos and the administration of then-president Bill Clinton had to use the Federal Reserve's special reserves to help bail out Mexico. Holders of tesobonos lost around 30 percent of their capital due to the devaluation. It also led to soaring inflation and a serious recession in Mexico.

The government had not foreseen other fallout from the peg, including imported inflation. "When you peg a currency to the dollar what you are really doing is [...] importing the lower inflation [of the United States]," explains Fernando X. Donayre, founder and chief investment officer of Miami-based Inca Investments LLC and a professional investor in Latin

---

[3]Carmen M. Reinhart and Kenneth S. Rogoff, *This Time Is Different: Eight Centuries of Financial Folly* (Princeton: Princeton University Press, 2009).

America since 1990.[4] At the time, Mexico had the higher inflation rate, so the peg forced Mexican industry to forego price increases in excess of American increases. Mexican producers could not pass on increases because that would have made their goods uncompetitive against relatively cheaper American goods. "You can think of the government passing off the burden of fighting inflation from government to private industry," Donayre says. "A peg only works when both countries have approximately the same inflation rate over a sustained period of time," he continues.

This approximates much of the problem with the euro in Europe in 2010–13, since the one currency amounts to a peg for all participating countries. Underlying fundamentals of countries subscribing to a peg need to remain relatively similiar for the peg to work. In Mexico's case, the current account deficit became so serious the government had no choice but to cancel the peg and let the peso float.

In the absence of a country's ability to control its inflation, the peg becomes what Donayre calls a "gimmick": "It's only going to work on a short-term basis; that's why they had to remove the peg to the dollar in Mexico," he says.

The devaluation proved once again an unhappy rule of currency fluctuations: a devalued currency does not gradually drop to the most appropriate level and rest there. It can overshoot the correct threshold and gyrate before finding the appropriate exchange rate—as occurred again with the Mexican peso. This devaluation also proved another unhappy rule—the relationship between currency fluctuation and economic outlook.

Due to its major devaluation in 1995, Mexico and its economy still do not inspire as much confidence as the economies of the United States and Canada; therefore, the Mexican currency has had a more volatile exchange rate than the two other North American currencies.

Times change, currencies change and economies change. Since the devaluation crisis, Mexico, the United States and Europe have all changed, and in some ways Mexico now enjoys a more favorable comparison with the United States and has more room to maneuver, according to James Awad. "The U.S. and Europe have more debt in proportion to GDP than the emerging markets and are growing slowly and are basically broke," he says. That means that their currencies do not have as much of a "safe-haven appeal" on the margin as they had in the 1990s. "The Mexican peso has somewhat more leeway versus the dollar and the euro than it did back then, so the Mexicans can afford to make a few more mistakes, [all other things] being equal," Awad suggests.

---

[4]Personal interview with Al Emid during the research and writing of this book in 2012.

For that and other reasons, a currency flight from Mexico within the near future could occur only if the country faced a worse crisis than in 1994, an unlikely turn of events. Even more reassuring, at time of writing, Mexico has a lower debt-to-gross-domestic-product ratio than the United States.

Mexico now officially has a free-floating exchange rate, meaning that it moves with market forces unhampered by government interference. Perhaps more accurately, the government influences rates at a much-reduced level through rate setting by the Banco de Mexico, the country's central bank.

Now with the 11th largest population in the world, about 115 million people, Mexico has a unique set of advantages (including its proximity to the United States) and disadvantages (including seemingly endless drug wars).

Mexico's largest advantage—its next-door neighbor—means it will continue benefiting from the American recovery in terms of exports to the United States and outsourced contracts from there. It also has a wealthier middle class now than during the crisis, which means it conforms to the view that the emerging and frontier markets will have a majority of the world's middle classes and the largest proportion of worldwide gross domestic product within a couple of decades.

Frontier markets that have experienced a major devaluation like Mexico did in 1995, such as Argentina in 2001–02 and Vietnam in 2010–11, experience strong GDP growth, as they stand to benefit from increased competitiveness because their costs drop compared to their major export partners, and they see their trade balances improve sharply. Countries can help the process by signing free trade agreements with their counterparts. Mexico has a lengthy list of trade agreements because it saw joining the global economy as the way to grow, Donayre says. In fact, Mexico has more trade agreements with more countries than any other country in the world, he continues.

In Donayre's appraisal, Mexico understands the need to stick to its best competencies—which include manufacturing and exporting to the United States, a strategy that allows it to capitalize on its proximity to American markets, a good rail network and lower transportation costs when compared with other emerging markets.

Mexican shipments to the United States typically take about two days, while Chinese shipments can take from 20 days to two months. These factors have converged profitably. During the first half of 2011, Mexican manufacturing exports increased by 17 percent and growth in exports will result in capital inflows and a rise in the Mexican stock market, according to an Inca forecast.

As with any country, the positive picture has some huge drawbacks. In Mexico, these include drug wars that drain resources from both countries and have cost more than 57,000 lives since December 2000. The illegal immigration issue further complicates Mexico–U. S. relations and has no easy solution. In fact, the problem could worsen if the American economy recovers sufficiently to start attracting large numbers of undocumented Mexicans again. Mexico also has low real wages, underemployment and low mobility for Amerindians in its poor southern states.

Taken as a whole, these factors lead to a two-part conclusion. "Mexico still has a lot of problems that we think about with underdeveloped countries, not very business friendly, too bureaucratic sometimes," Donayre says. "But Mexico has done one thing spectacularly well. They have managed their fiscal and money side very well. They lived within their means." Put differently, it has come a long way from the crisis of 1994.

As with other emerging markets, it makes sense for investors to concentrate on sectors where Mexico enjoys a competitive advantage and which benefit from the growth of the middle class. Mexico's telecommunications and media companies have used their quasi-monopoly position in the local market to expand into other Latin American countries. For example, telephone company Telmex controls 90 percent of the landline market and 80 percent of the mobile phone market in Mexico, while America Movil is the largest mobile phone operator in Latin America. They are both controlled by billionaire Carlos Slim. This makes America Movil (NYSE: AMX) an interesting investment in emerging markets such as Chile and Brazil, and frontier markets in Latin America, such as Argentina, Colombia, Ecuador, Paraguay, Peru and Uruguay, as well as most of the countries in Central America.

Media group Televisa (NYSE: TV) is the largest mass media entertainment company in Latin America and the Spanish-speaking world and has an exclusive contract with Univision, the largest Spanish-language TV channel in the United States. It earned $248 million from royalties in 2012 for its Univision programs from other Spanish-speaking markets and an additional $198 million in export sales, making it a good play on rising consumer incomes in Latin American frontier markets.

Meanwhile, Mexico's stock market includes such consumer stocks as Wal-Mart de Mexico (OTC: WMMVY) and Coca-Cola FEMSA (NYSE: KOF), the largest beverage company in Latin America and the biggest independent Coca-Cola bottler in the world. The latter also owns OXXO, the biggest convenience store chain in Latin America, and a 20 percent stake in Heineken, which it received in exchange for its brewing operations. Since it makes and sells its soft drinks in the frontier markets of Colombia, Venezuela, the Philippines and Argentina as well as Mexico, Brazil and four Central American countries, it is an obvious beneficiary of rising consumer incomes, although its good performance over the last five years has made it quite expensive in valuation terms at 33 times 2012 earnings.

Mexican banks that survived the peso crisis in the mid-1990s, such as Grupo Financiero Banorte S.A.B de C.V. (TC: GBOOY) and Banco Azteca, are also attractive investments that profit from consumers acquiring their first credit card, car loan and mortgage.

Frontier market banks benefit from the same underlying drivers of growth as banks in emerging markets, such as Banorte and Azteca. They are able to make excellent profits from the margin between borrowing at low or controlled rates from savers who are earning enough money to begin saving for the first time and are not aggressively seeking higher interest rates on their deposits, and lending to businesses and individuals at rates that are high enough to make a decent margin.

What Mexico's experiment with pegged exchange rates demonstrates, as do the Asian and Russian crises of 1997–98, is the danger of borrowing too much in a seemingly cheap foreign currency and then being exposed to very large foreign exchange losses when the domestic currency is devalued. Foreign banks such as Canada's Scotiabank (Bank of Nova Scotia) and Spain's Banco Santander ended up purchasing Mexican banks that had sound franchises but were temporarily insolvent due to mismatches between their borrowing and lending currencies. Investors looking at frontier market banks such as those from Nigeria, Pakistan or Argentina should be aware of the currency breakdown of their funding structures and how much of their borrowing is in short-term interbank deposits, insofar as this is possible.

The present health of Mexico overshadows its past economic problems and demonstrates that a period of volatility and uncertainty does not necessarily mean disaster. This kind of roller coaster ride may well be in store for frontier market investors, but just as foreign investors suffered large losses in U.S. and developed currency terms during the devaluation crisis of 1994–95, so they have benefited from the strong growth of the Mexican economy over the last decade after it regained its competitiveness. Similarly, the Argentine stock market did well in both local and U.S. dollar terms after the 2001 devaluation and default, and Vietnam has produced strong returns over the last two years since its devaluation.

ASIAN MELTDOWN OF 1997–98

In a strategy generally resembling the pegging of Mexico's peso to the American greenback, several Asian economies ran similar U.S.-dollar linked currency floats throughout the 1990s. They based their strategy on the success of the Hong Kong dollar peg to the greenback, which started in 1983.

However, they missed some important details. The Hong Kong dollar was a currency board, and the Hong Kong authorities simply mirrored the actions of the United States Federal Reserve and created or reduced liquidity and raised or lowered interest rates exactly in line with the Reserve.

Meanwhile, Thailand, South Korea, Indonesia and other nations had what is known as a "dirty float," more delicately called a "managed float" against the American dollar.

Arguably, the word "float" can be viewed as misleading, since a genuine floating rate precludes direct intervention. These governments shadowed the American greenback without explicitly admitting the strategy while paying higher interest rates.

This strategy enabled faster growth in spite of trade deficits due to import imbalances, as they had huge sums of foreign cash flowing in to get what appeared to be American dollar investments providing higher yields than available in the United States.

In a calamity somewhat resembling events in Mexico, as American interest rates started rising in 1996–97, and their current accounts became heavily negative due to foreign money flowing back out, these countries had to devalue their currencies, beginning with Thailand in July 1997. Within one year, Malaysia, Indonesia, the Philippines and South Korea had all been forced to devalue—their stock markets crashed. Foreign investors lost between 50 percent in U.S. dollar terms in markets that were not forced to devalue, such as Singapore and Hong Kong (which maintained its currency board), and up to 90 percent in U.S. dollar terms in South Korean and Indonesian investments, when currency devaluation was combined with falls in their stock markets.

At the time, emerging markets were regarded as a disaster and foreign investors repatriated their capital to take advantage of the technology boom in the United States and other developed markets. Times have changed, Awad argues, outlining several economic realities. Emerging markets have higher secular growth and more of their growth is among themselves. "That's not to say that they are unaffected by what's going on in the West, but they've got a higher secular growth rate than they did in the 1990s," he explains. "They are a generator of world growth. They have tremendous accumulated savings, and they can withstand worldwide economic turmoil better than they could then," he adds.

In fact, in an ironic twist, Japan and South Korea competed for access to the Myanmar stock market in 2012, according to the *New Straits Times*. In an article entitled "Asian Bourses Vie for Foothold in Myanmar," the *Times* reported that:

> *Two of Asia's biggest stock exchanges are fighting for dominance in the world's hottest new frontier market as investors beat a path to Myanmar following the end of decades of military rule. The*

operator of the Tokyo Stock Exchange announced last month a deal with Myanmar's central bank to open a stock market in the country formerly known as Burma along with Japan's Daiwa Securities, after years of discussions. . . . But they face competition from South Korea, whose exchange also aims to open a stock market in the state, according to a spokesman for Korea Exchange in Seoul.[5]

Some of the original "Asian Tiger" markets such as South Korea and Hong Kong have rebounded and reached their old highs in recent years. However, some of the ASEAN (Association of Southeast Asian Nations, counting among its members the emerging nations of Thailand, Malaysia, the Philippines, Indonesia and Singapore) markets are still below the levels they reached 20 years ago, despite the fact that their economies are much larger and wealthier in real terms than was the case in the 1990s.

This underperformance has led to attractive investment opportunities for knowledgeable investors who are prepared to recognize that the countries have changed their policies to prevent a recurrence of the Asian crisis.

As in Mexico's case, these countries no longer follow a dirty float policy for their exchange rates, instead allowing a free float, which has both constrained imports and encouraged exports, helping them rebuild their current account balances and foreign exchange reserves. Furthermore, the harrowing effect of the crisis has made company managements "get religion" as far as controlling foreign currency debt and maintaining strong balance sheets.

Therefore, there are numerous beneficiaries of rising incomes, such as mobile phone companies, including PLDT in the Philippines and Telkom Indonesia; consumer product companies, often subsidiaries of multinationals, such as Guinness Malaysia, Nestlé Malaysia, Unilever Indonesia and Multi Bintang (the Heineken brewer in Indonesia); and banks such as Bangkok Bank and Siam Commercial Bank in Thailand, and Maybank, CIMB and Public Bank in Malaysia. These are now attractively valued compared to their developed-market counterparts and exposed to economies with much better demographics and growth prospects.

Given that many of the larger Asian exotic frontier markets, such as Myanmar, do not have a stock market or, as in the case of Laos, have only a few listed stocks that trade infrequently, often companies such as these that are listed in their established emerging market neighbors, such as Thailand and Malaysia, are the only practical way to invest in these countries. While

---

[5] "Asian Bourses Vie for Foothold in Myanmar," *New Straits Times*, May 13, 2012.

the three largest Asian frontier markets (Pakistan, Bangladesh and Vietnam) were somewhat insulated from the 1997–98 Asian crisis, partially due to not following the managed currency float policy as aggressively as the more established Asian emerging markets but principally due to the difficulty of foreign investors being able to invest large amounts of money into their illiquid stock markets, the traumatic experience suffered by many Asian countries 15 years ago still exerts a strong influence on their policies.

Investors should note that some of the ASEAN stock markets are still selling well below their 1997 highs in U.S. dollar terms, even though the underlying economies have easily surpassed the level reached at that time. While it is tempting to invest in developing markets when conditions look good and growth has been strong, paying too high a valuation for even the most attractive growth story can result in long-term underperformance. We believe the reasonable valuations in most frontier markets remove much of the risk of overpaying for their strong fundamentals, but caution is necessary when they become more widely accepted as a suitable asset class for developed market investors.

RUSSIAN DEBT DEFAULT OF 1998

The International Monetary Fund and the World Bank intervened during the Asian crisis of 1997–98, but the ripple effect meant that markets in the United States, Europe and Russia declined as a result and triggered, among other consequences, the Russian devaluation and default in August 1998.

Russia, which had been one of the fastest-growing and most popular of the emerging markets due to the boom released by Boris Yeltsin's crony capitalism, saw its interest costs shoot up as a result of the crisis. It burned through its foreign exchange reserves, devalued the ruble and defaulted on its foreign currency debt, costing some investors up to 90 percent of their capital. The Asian crisis and Russian default together led to the notorious collapse of the big hedge fund Long-Term Capital Management (LTCM), which had enormously leveraged bets that yields on all sorts of emerging market government debt would converge, just as had happened with European countries during the mid-1990s in the run-up to the introduction of the euro.

LTCM had maintained that emerging markets were not correlated with each other, leading to the conclusion that what happened in Asia would not affect countries such as Russia and that the fund could invest with enormous amounts of leverage without risk. They were proven wrong, despite employing Nobel Prize–winning economists Myron Scholes and

Robert Merton, coinventors of the well-known and widely used Black-Scholes option pricing model, and their collapse almost brought down several Wall Street banks, which had big loans outstanding to LTCM, an event that became an ironic sort of dry run for the collapse of Lehman Brothers 10 years later.

The United States Federal Reserve then bailed out the investment banks that were at risk due to LTCM's collapse, as detailed in Roger Lowenstein's excellent history of LTCM, *When Genius Failed.*[6]

Fifteen years later, Russia has become one of the BRIC nations, the rise in commodity prices has resulted in a rapid rebuilding of its foreign exchange reserves and trade balance, and Yeltsin's willingness to dismantle the pervasive Russian state, largely through a flawed system of privatizations via vouchers distributed to the entire population, has been replaced by former KGB operative Vladimir Putin's desire to use Russia's resources as a tool of foreign policy.

Russia provides a study in two extremes—corruption and economic possibility. There is a pervasive belief that Russia remains corrupt, although its rank in the Transparency International Corruption Perceptions Index is better than that of a number of former Soviet states and some other autocratic regimes. There is a strong belief by many observers that it has not gotten over its past history of crony capitalism and that those who could make money in Russia have moved their money outside the country. The recent expropriation of a portion of all bank deposits over €100,000 in Cyprus in March 2013 was justified by the assertion that much of this money represented offshore deposits of Russian criminal syndicates and the ill-gotten gains of well-connected Russian oligarchs, without much being produced in the way of evidence to support these statements.

Russia remains very dependent on oil revenues. That reliance on oil could bring weakening pressures in 2013 and 2014, according to an executive briefing on Russia published by Scotiabank Economic Research. The report describes the pressures as "underpinned by the nation's heavy reliance on oil exports and stagnation in economic reforms."[7]

However, the same report forecasts growth in gross domestic product at 3.5 percent for 2013 and 4 percent in 2014 but points out that:

> *Over the longer-term, Russia will struggle to attract the investment needed to maintain current oil production levels, address infrastructure deficiencies and diversify the economy away from natural*

---

[6]Roger Lowenstein, *When Genius Failed: The Rise and Fall of Long-Term Capital Management* (New York: Random House, 2000).
[7]Executive briefing, "Russia Global Economic Research," Scotiabank, January 2013.

resources; oil and gas shipments account for roughly two-thirds of exports.[8]

At time of writing, the administration of Vladimir Putin is "embroiled in the ongoing conflict in Syria," the report points out, adding that it expects only minimal impact in the near term from Russia's entry into the World Trade Organization.[9]

The same report says that the current account surplus, amounting to 4.5 percent of GDP in 2012, will narrow as strong import growth outpaces exports while the income deficit widens, risking ruble devaluation and, possibly, a twin deficit situation in the years to come.

Despite this, several Russian companies have attracted substantial foreign interest, not merely the obvious oil and gas and natural resource plays but other companies dependent upon consumer demand. A recent study by Sberbank CIB, the investment banking arm of Russia's top bank, Sberbank, noted that the middle class (defined as those earning between US$6,000 and $15,000 p.a.) in Russia comprised 55 percent of the population (compared to 30 percent in Brazil, 21 percent in China and 11 percent in India), and consumer-oriented sectors accounted for two-thirds of its GDP in 2012.[10]

Among Russian stocks with exposure to the consumer are mobile phone groups such as MegaFon, MTS and VimpelCom, the sixth largest mobile phone company in the world, which owns a majority of Orascom Telecom, with frontier market operations in Algeria, Pakistan and Bangladesh. As with Mexican multinationals such as America Movil and FEMSA, established emerging market companies such as VimpelCom and Orascom are able to operate successfully in other, less-developed emerging markets as they are familiar with many of the obstacles faced by businesses operating in lower income countries, including the problems of dealing with sometimes arbitrary and changing government regulations. Food retailers Magnit and Dixy, real estate owners and developers LSR and Etalon and Internet stock Yandex are stocks that should also benefit from the growth of the consumer market and that generally sell at a discount to their emerging market peers.

Given Russia's strong influence over many of its former satellites in Eastern Europe, Russian companies may often be the best way to gain access to these frontier markets, especially given the small size and low liquidity of many of the stock markets in these countries. They may also end up being the principal beneficiaries of growth in certain countries; Russian

---

[8] Ibid.
[9] Ibid.
[10] "Consumers to Power Russian Economy," Reuters, February 5, 2013.

influence was felt by many observers to be a major factor in the result of the most recent Ukrainian presidential election, and Belarus's economic policies often appear to be heavily influenced by Russia's strategic interests.

The Russian default provides another example of the volatility and risk that investors can expect in even the largest and most well-established emerging markets and should prepare them for the high volatility that accompanies frontier market investing. That said, the strong performance of the Russian stock market in both local and foreign currency terms over the last decade illustrates the fact that large natural resources such as those possessed by many frontier economies can often trump even relatively poor corporate governance and political uncertainty. Investors should note, however, that these factors result in such countries' stocks trading at a discount to those in other countries that are believed to have higher standards.

BRAZILIAN DEVALUATION OF 1999

Brazil was running a dirty float against the American dollar and had to devalue its own currency, the real, by 30 percent in January 1999. Due to the financial crisis of 1997-98 and the subsequent sharp fall in commodity prices, Brazil's oil revenues collapsed.

Indeed, emerging markets such as Mexico, Thailand and Brazil ran dirty floats to help reduce their high inflation and the cost of borrowing but had not realized that a government might control interest rates or exchange rates but cannot control both financial levers.

The implicit lesson is that keeping a country's currency pegged at a certain exchange rate requires a willingness to increase interest rates when foreign money begins flowing out, which then can cause a slowdown or even a recession.

Unwillingness to raise interest rates means that the government has to let the currency slide, making imports more expensive and raising the cost of servicing debt denominated in a foreign currency.

Mexico, Brazil (and the Asian countries) were unwilling to do either and thus used up all their currency reserves trying to defend a fixed exchange rate; they then were forced to devalue, regardless of their intentions. By this stage, emerging markets had lost all their gains from the late 1980s to the early 1990s and had done much worse than major developed markets like the United States. That may have left a legacy of resistance to the concept of emerging market investing, bringing with it at least some resistance to frontier markets.

By the end of the 1990s, investors had more than tripled their money in the S&P500, quadrupled it in the NASDAQ and more than doubled it in Europe, leaving emerging markets seemingly relegated to "yesterday's story."

However, above-average economic growth, driven by several factors including the world's appetite for commodities, meant that Brazilian equities performed well during the last decade, explains Fernando Donayre at Inca Investments LLC. "Brazilian equities went through a period of high performance beginning in 2003 that basically lasted through 2009," he says. After that, they took hits from the global financial crisis but have since bounced back.

At time of writing in 2013, Brazil has a strong economy, driven by internal consumption as well as high commodity prices. In Brazil, "you have a strong economy [and] relatively high interest rates," Donayre says. "What happens [is] a lot of investment goes into the domestic currency and you get a lot of people basically doing a carry trade where you borrow currency in a low-cost currency like the dollar or the yen (and invest in the higher-yielding currency)."

Certainly, Brazil faces several risks including the possibility of another recession in the developed world and the continuation of the decline in the appetites of several countries, including China, for its commodities.

As a result GDP growth slowed sharply from 7.5 percent in 2010 to 1 percent in 2012, and the central bank responded by cutting interest rates by 5.25 percent to a record low of 7.25 percent. With its equity index dominated by resource stocks such as government-controlled Petrobras S.A. and iron ore giant Vale S.A., which bought Canadian nickel producer Inco Ltd. in 2007, Brazil's stock market performance has depended on resource prices and investors' perception of their direction. However, proving again that recovery can follow volatility and even disaster, analysts are expecting 3–4 percent GDP growth in 2013, helped by infrastructure spending by the government ahead of the soccer World Cup in 2014 and the summer Olympics in 2016.

With its rapidly growing middle class, Brazil is also a major consumer market with many well-managed companies servicing this sector. Among them are Brazil's largest retailer, Grupo Pao de Acucar S.A., in which major French food retailer Casino Guichard-Perrachon (PA: CO) took a controlling stake in 2012. Casino demonstrates another method for investors to gain exposure to emerging and frontier markets, as it also controls Colombia and Thailand's largest food retailers, Exito and Big C as well as Big C's Vietnamese operation, and derives over 56 percent of its revenues and 67 percent of its profits from fast-growing emerging and frontier markets. Another Brazilian consumer stock is the largest domestic tobacco company, Souza Cruz S.A., controlled by multinational British American Tobacco (LSE: BAT; NYSE: BTI) which derives 75 percent of its revenue from emerging and frontier markets and has growing operations in frontier markets such as Colombia, Pakistan, Bangladesh, Cambodia and Ukraine as well as the emerging markets of Brazil, Turkey, Egypt, Russia, Indonesia and Mexico. Investors should examine the possibility of purchasing global companies such as Casino and BAT, and we examine several other multinational companies that derive the majority of their revenues and profits from emerging and frontier markets elsewhere in the book.

Brazilian consumer stocks include cosmetics producer Natura Cosmeticos S.A., food producers BRF Brasil Foods S.A. and Cosan S.A., residential home builders Gafisa S.A. and Rossi Residencial S.A. and banks Banco Bradesco and Banco Santander Brazil. As with the other major Latin American established emerging market, Mexico, many of Brazil's companies have exposure to their neighboring frontier markets, such as Argentina, Uruguay, Colombia and Peru.

Investors in frontier markets should take into consideration the problems faced by the more established emerging markets such as Mexico, Russia, Brazil and the Asian Tiger economies between 1994 and 2000. They should also consider that, regardless of the frontier markets' excellent underlying fundamentals, including young and rapidly growing populations, the process of urbanization and much lower levels of external and internal debt than many developed markets, stock markets and economies do not progress in a straight line. Setbacks such as those experienced in the mid-to late 1990s are inevitable with rapidly growing economies, usually due to over-rapid growth or attempts to maintain fixed or managed exchange rates and an overreliance on debt to maintain growth. A less volatile way to gain exposure to the emerging and frontier markets is to invest in the sovereign and corporate debt issued by these countries, which has the advantage of providing investors with a substantially higher yield than is at present available from investment-grade debt in developed markets. Investors are also likely, if our thesis is correct, to benefit from appreciating currencies, as the favorable fundamentals of the emerging and frontier markets will most probably lead to their currencies gaining against those of developed markets. In the next section, we examine the case for emerging and frontier market debt.

THE PLACE OF FIXED INCOME IN THE EMERGING AND FRONTIER EQUATION

The fixed-income picture in these (and other) emerging and frontier markets appears to be as complex as the investment picture and equally unsuited to across-the-board generalizations.

Understanding the fixed-income picture means understanding the different components of risk, explains Mohamed A. El-Erian.[11] He is the chief executive officer and co-chief investment officer of Newport, California–based Pacific Investment Management Company, LLC (PIMCO), which has US$1.8 trillion in assets under management; the chairman of U.S. President Barack Obama's Global Development Council;[12] and the author of *When Markets Collide: Investment Strategies for the Age of Global Economic Change.*

El-Erian lists the major types of these investments as foreign currency bonds and domestic fixed income for countries such as Mexico and Brazil, which issue domestic bonds in local currency. These are sometimes available to foreign investors through private equity vehicles or externally managed fixed-income funds, which can also hold foreign currency–denominated bonds such as sovereign debt bonds issued in a foreign currency and corporate bonds issued by multinational or domestic companies to finance their activities.

Corporate bonds are denominated in American dollars and sometimes in the domestic currency and issued in countries such as Brazil, Mexico, Peru and Russia. "Once the market accepts the sovereign bonds the appetite for the corporate bonds goes up," El-Erian says. "You get paid a risk premium above the sovereign [bond] because [. . .] that's the next step in the process," he continues. "Here it is not enough to have a view on the sovereign side; you also have to have a view on the company. That means understanding the sector, understanding the competition it faces domestically and abroad and understanding how the company is run." In many of these cases, the bonds are issued by major multinationals based in developed countries to finance projects in the emerging or frontier markets.

In any venue, if one invests in fixed income, it amounts to underwriting a risk, although the nature and breadth of the risks involved have changed. "In 'the old days' the major risk was creditor default," El-Erian recalls. Now investors have more choices in the risks they underwrite—including currency risk, liquidity risk and volatility risk. "There's a whole list of risk factors that now an investor—depending on which developing countries he or she goes to—can get exposed to," El-Erian says.

Some risks are unique to the category of investments, such as private equity vehicles that contain internal fixed-income investments. "The biggest

---

[11] Personal interview with Al Emid during the research and writing of this book in 2012.

[12] Created in 2012 to promote global economic development; the appointment was announced in a statement on December 21, 2012. Alexis Leonida, "Obama Picks El-Erian to Lead Global Development Council," *Bloomberg News*, December 24, 2012.

problem when you go internal is [. . .] liquidity risk," El-Erian says, noting that PIMCO has no connection with these vehicles. The capital remains locked up for between five and seven years and is used to service the mortgage market within the country. In exchange for taking the risk on individuals in emerging markets who might not otherwise qualify for a mortgage, unit holders get a risk premium.

Risks to the fixed-income picture in emerging markets and frontier markets include whether an individual country can maintain its credit improvement programs and whether it can become "contaminated" by the fiscal problems of the Western world. "If—God forbid!—the U.S. were to go into recession, that would impact negatively on the price of those bonds," El-Erian says. Indeed, these countries generate trade surpluses and add to their reserves by selling to the United States.

Some risks can be reduced where the government has the necessary political will and authority. In Brazil's case the government overcame the liquidity risk by measures such as restoring the dollar float and by pointing out its commitment to stability to the population. It then made fiscal adjustments which reduced credit risk and default risk and then embarked on serious structural reform.

Generally Brazilian fixed-income investments do not currently offer the potential for the gains at the levels of past years but can provide an income flow. Russia also presents some unique risks. "When you go to countries like Russia you are underwriting the rule of law as well," El-Erian says, referring to Western complaints about how business is done in Russia. "That's why you want to be paid a risk premium as an investor—because you are underwriting legal risk."

Not all of the types of fixed-income investments are sold all the time in all emerging and frontier markets. For example, with respect to China, Westerners have had access only to foreign currency sovereign bonds, as the Chinese government has ample supplies of cash. Understanding fixed income in these markets also means examining these investment assets on a case-by-case basis. "Don't believe that this is a generalized story—it's a very specific story; each name has to be looked at," El-Erian says.

While the debt ratings agencies, such as Standard & Poor's (S&P), Moody's and Fitch have suffered damage to their reputations and are facing lawsuits for their role in the sub-prime mortgage debacle in the United States, their country ratings for sovereign debt and company ratings for corporate issues are still regarded as good indicators of the relative attractiveness and risks of investing in different regions and countries. Investors can look at the credit ratings for the emerging and frontier markets to get some idea of how different economies rank the direction of their upgrades and downgrades to see how the circumstances are changing, although the latter are not always especially timely. However, it is much simpler and more practical to allow a professional bond manager to undertake this analysis and run the portfolio, especially as it is almost impossible for an individual investor to purchase a sufficient variety of bonds to have a well-diversified portfolio. Investing in developing countries is an area where paying a manager a reasonable fee to carry out the necessary due diligence to take into account the various risks enumerated by El-Erian is an expense that is well justified in the authors' view.

Generalizations also can be dangerous. A rise in GDP in a country—seemingly a positive indicator—may not necessarily provide reassurance. "It's a continuous element so [the fact that] the GDP went up by 'X' last year is not a good one. The GDP can go down by 'Y' this year. Even a trade surplus does not provide ironclad assurance," El-Erian says. "We have known countries that have gone from trade surplus to trade deficit. If you look at Argentina, that sounds a cautionary note, because Argentina used to be among the top seven richest economies of the world and is no longer."

Emerging market debt has become an increasingly popular asset class for investors looking for higher yields than have been available in the G7 countries since the financial crisis of 2008–09. Whether issued by governments (sovereign debt) or corporates, either in foreign currencies such as U.S. dollars, euros, yen or other developed market currencies, or in local currencies, yields on emerging and frontier market debt issues were generally above 10 percent as recently as four years ago in 2009, but have come down substantially as the risk premiums over developed market debt have contracted. Yields on U.S. Treasuries, German bunds and UK sterling gilts have fallen to 60-year lows.

There are numerous emerging and frontier market debt funds available to investors in Europe and North America. While an attractive diversifier and provider of yield to fixed-income investors, for investors looking to benefit from the longer-term growth and low correlations of frontier and emerging markets, we would not recommend them as a suitable route to gain access to these markets. In the end, fixed-income funds are driven by interest rate movements and will tend to be highly correlated at the time when this is least wanted.

Still, apart from these risks, positive signs can provide reassurance of satisfactory returns. These signs include what El-Erian refers to as durable elements "hardwired" into the system, such as building useful institutions and having the buy-in of the population.

Those emerging markets that have enjoyed the most success tend to possess certain characteristics that investors should look for when considering frontier markets. Briefly, these may be summarized as respect for property rights and the rule of law when applied to business and commerce, even if the political system of the country is not a traditional democracy. A willingness to challenge existing vested interests, usually expressed through a reform of the traditional landowning system but also through reforming restrictive practices such as trade guilds or long-established labor unions is also an indicator that enough members of the ruling elite recognize the importance of removing barriers to higher GDP growth, thereby fostering sustainable improvement in living standards.

The Asian Tiger economies, which almost all observers would classify as the most successful among the emerging markets over the last quarter century, used an export-led model to build up sufficient reserves of capital to develop their physical infrastructure, while stressing the importance of education in raising the productivity of their work force. While there were some groups within these economies that did not share fully in the benefits derived from these successful policies, a sufficient majority did perceive themselves as becoming better off, and particularly, that their children had the possibility of enjoying a much more prosperous and successful future.

When South Korea and Taiwan made the transition to full-fledged democracy in the early 1990s, the repercussions for the former rulers, whether the the former military dictators in Korea, or the Kuomintang National Party in Taiwan, were limited. In fact, the Nationalist Party has returned to power in Taiwan and is pursuing a "One China" policy of cooperation with its former communist rivals on the mainland. Other countries such as Malaysia and Thailand carried out effective land reforms and have developed vibrant if sometimes fractious democracies, while Indonesia has been able to successfully adapt to the ending of a one-party autocratic system. In Latin America, Mexico, Brazil, Colombia and Chile have successfully emerged from periods of military or effective one-party rule and have become well-regarded developing economies, combining high rates of GDP growth with functioning democracies.

It is when one looks at countries that were formerly much wealthier, both on an absolute and relative basis, than their neighbors in the same region, such as the Philippines, Myanmar and Sri Lanka in Asia or Argentina, Cuba and Venezuela in Latin America, that the absence of these factors becomes apparent. Where the main aim of the ruling elite is to maintain power and suppress any opposition, control is more important than growth, and living standards stagnate (when they do not actually decline, as is the case in Cuba and Myanmar).

Similarly, when the ruling elite is partisan and intent on maintaining its privileges and rewarding its supporters rather than growing the overall economy, as in Argentina, the Philippines and Venezuela, there may be a period of prosperity and growth, but the process can not be self-sustaining under such circumstances. Almost inevitably it will be terminated by an economic crisis, unless natural resources allow the population to be effectively bribed with the country's own wealth.

Other unique positive factors to look for in developing markets include proximity to trading partners, such as Mexico's proximity to the American border, which allows it relative ease of selling and shipping into the United States—a factor that El-Erian terms "an external anchor." Similarly, China, South Korea and Taiwan benefit from their proximity to Japan.

Historical relationships between former colonies and their imperial rulers can sometimes allow easy access to the former ruler's markets. The low tariffs that many African and Caribbean frontier markets enjoy when shipping goods to the European Union reflect British and French ownership of most of these regions in the 19th and 20th centuries. India acts in a role similar to that of a previous imperial ruler toward Bangladesh and Sri Lanka, and Thailand does the same toward Laos and Cambodia.

In the end, improvements in emerging markets and the apparent global shift in wealth point to a need to shift investment strategies along the same lines. "The emerging markets are going to have a majority of the world's middle classes," to repeat the words of James Awad at Zephyr Management. "They already have a majority of the world's population." Frontier markets alone had 25 percent of the world's population and 11 percent of its GDP on a PPP basis at the end of 2012, according to the United Nations, and look set to increase their share of GDP to at least match their share of population over the next two decades.

TAKEAWAYS

1. Checking the history of a market is a valid means of investment research, but checking the present and future outlook is more important.
2. Pegging emerging and frontier markets' currencies to a developed market currency, usually the U.S. dollar, via a so-called "managed float" or "dirty float" caused a number of problems in the past, including the Mexican peso crisis of 1994–95, the Asian and Russian crises of 1997–98, the Brazilian devaluation of 1999 and the Argentinean devaluation and default in 2001–02. Those problems may still color the attitudes of some investors.
3. Look for factors that are "hardwired" in a country, such as attitudes toward foreign investment, cultural aspects (the status of landownership as opposed to commerce) and the country's track record on inflation and default.
4. In examining a country's potential, look to its natural resources prospects as well as its past.
5. Define the exact nature of risk in any emerging market or frontier market investment. Is it political or demographic? Is the issue one of illiquidity or of settlement, or are there more serious underlying concerns? Risk in Russia differs from risk elsewhere.
6. Are investors being compensated for the risks they are taking, either by higher yields on fixed-income investments or by low valuations on equities?

The Global Investment Landscape: Why Developed Markets Appear Unattractive at Present

Dealing effectively with the global investment landscape means viewing the investment dynamics of different areas and connecting the global dots between them. Truly understanding any complex investment premise—or for that matter any complex premise in any discipline—means looking at factors in the proverbial "big picture" in order to better grasp the fundamentals of the premise. The concepts involved in understanding emerging markets, while complex, have become at least somewhat familiar to many investors while the concepts involved in frontier markets remain truly puzzling to many financial professionals and to most investors. Achieving some understanding means starting with a global perspective.

One central thesis of this book is that frontier markets are at a stage of development that is equivalent to that of the "established" emerging markets of Southeast Asia, Russia and Latin America 15 to 20 years ago, with GDPs per capita that are at the same level as those of the emerging markets at that time and with the potential to follow the same path of development and growth that the emerging markets did over the last 15 years. While there is no guarantee that their stock markets will perform as well as the emerging markets have done over the last 15 years since the Asian and Russian crises of 1998, their relatively low valuations should give investors confidence that the absolute returns from a diversified portfolio of frontier markets will prove to be attractive, especially compared with the low returns likely from the major developed economies.

In this chapter we examine the outlook for the major developed economies over the next few years and conclude that they are facing major structural challenges that will make it difficult for investors to realize strong absolute returns. In fact, despite the fact that the stock market indices are hitting new all-time highs in the United States and Germany at the time of writing, and the United Kingdom and Japan have risen back to levels last achieved in 2007–08, investors have essentially made no money in nominal terms over the last dozen years. In the opinion of many commentators and analysts, some of them in this chapter, the long-term challenges these markets face from their unattractive demographics and the enormous debt overhang resulting from the financial crisis of 2008–09 and the measures taken to overcome it mean that it is highly unlikely that their returns will substantially improve over the next decade. Therefore, we believe that investors should have meaningful exposure to the faster-growing emerging and frontier markets in their portfolios, with the proviso that they should have a specific allocation for frontier markets as a means of reducing a portfolio's overall volatility, given their low correlation with both developed and emerging markets.

Investors in developed markets, of course, may already have substantial exposure to emerging markets through their existing developed market holdings, either directly or through the mutual funds that they hold and perhaps employer pension plans. This is due to the growth of globalization over the last 25 years, which has seen many multinational companies substantially increase their exposure to emerging markets. Elsewhere in this book are examples of a number of sizable U.S.- and UK-listed companies that derive at least 40 percent of their revenues from emerging and frontier markets.

The International Monetary Fund traces the roots and evolution of the term "globalization":

> *The term "globalization" began to be used more commonly in the 1980s, reflecting technological advances that made it easier and quicker to complete international transactions—both trade and financial flows. It refers to an extension beyond national borders of the same market forces that have operated for centuries at all levels of human economic activity—village markets, urban industries, or financial centers.*[1]

Viewed from that perspective, globalization matters in all areas of our lives and yields economic and political benefits to countries and individuals

---

[1] *Globalization: A Brief Overview*, International Monetary Fund, May 2008.

embracing it. Its current form amounts to an electronic version of a centuries-old concept.

The IMF also describes the impact of globalization:

> *There is substantial evidence, from countries of different sizes and different regions, that as countries "globalize" their citizens benefit in the form of access to a wider variety of goods and services, lower prices, more and better-paying jobs, improved health, and higher overall living standards. It is probably no mere coincidence that over the past 20 years, as a number of countries have become more open to global economic forces, the percentage of the developing world living in extreme poverty—defined as living on less than $1 per day—has fallen by half.*[2]

More simply, globalization defines the process and benefits of international integration that result from flows of communications and telecommunications, large-scale capital flows, culture, resources, literature and even terrorism. Already underway before the advent and widespread use of the Internet, globalization increased in pace and breadth with the explosion of web technology and the rapid acceptance of the Internet for communication, including accessing stock and bond market data and company information.

Extending the principles of globalization to investment means including an emerging market weighting and frontier market weighting in an individual's or institution's holdings along with investments in developed markets, which in most cases will constitute the majority of an investor's holdings.

It also means recognizing two distinct realities about equities in developed markets (and therefore mutual funds holding them). Many of these developed market equities are exposed to growth in emerging and frontier markets, a proposition easily demonstrated by the Canadian stock market index, the S&P/TSX Composite, which has a weighting approaching 40 percent in energy and materials companies, giving it a heavy exposure to foreign commodity purchases. At the same time domestically focused equities in developed markets have limited growth potential, especially when compared with the potential that we suggest lies ahead with emerging and frontier markets. In such situations, the line between the potential of emerging and frontier markets cannot be drawn firmly given the status of frontier markets as a subset of emerging markets.

---

[2]Ibid.

CANADA

Canada has a relatively small number of publicly traded investment categories, a factor that makes diversification difficult but analysis easier than in other markets. Natural resources stocks, including oil and gas, forestry and mining, account for 36 percent of total market capitalization on the Toronto Stock Exchange effective November 30, 2012, and financials account for 24 percent of market capitalization on the TSX on the same date. Investors have regarded commodity-based developed markets such as Canada and Australia as being a lower-risk way to gain exposure to the growth of the middle class in emerging and frontier markets, as rising consumer incomes lead to higher consumption of raw materials, including base metals such as iron ore, coal, copper, aluminum, nickel, and zinc as well as energy, including oil and gas, particularly liquefied natural gas (LNG), which is capable of being transported long distances, and uranium for nuclear power plants.

The outlook for the natural resources sector depends on the outcome of two main issues, according to Gordon Pape, a Toronto-based newsletter publisher and author.[3] "An environment of rising commodity prices is going to have a very positive effect on the Toronto Stock Exchange," he suggests. China's influence on world commodity prices means that its success in engineering a soft landing and reversing the decline in the growth rate of its gross domestic product would sustain world commodity prices with a positive effect on the Canadian resource sector.

A soft landing would restore confidence in China's ability to keep its growth GDP in the 7–8 percent range. Slower growth in Chinese GDP would mean lower demand for commodities, Pape suggests. At the same time, a successful re-acceleration in Chinese growth would go a long way to reinforcing faith in frontier markets, since some who feel uncertain about frontier markets point to uncertainties surrounding China.

Outside of the China trade, the other main factor affecting the Canadian resources category is the demand for oil—which is a macroeconomic factor not specific to Canada—and the current deep discounts to the benchmark world oil prices such as West Texas Intermediate (WTI) and North Sea Brent for oil and gas that have seriously affected Canadian oil revenues. This latter factor has been at least partially due to the rapid growth of shale gas production in the United States—which has substantially reduced the demand for Canadian gas, always the largest energy export to the United States—and also due to the shortage of pipeline capacity to permit Canadian

---

[3]Personal interview with Al Emid during the research and writing of this book in 2012.

exports to reach other potential customers. Moreover, the increasing trend toward railway transport for oil as opposed to pipelines, due to many of the shale gas discoveries not being tied into the pipeline networks, adds to the cost of producing and distributing oil and exerts downward pressure on oil company profitability and therefore on share prices.

The American economy has had an enormous but uneven impact on Canada for over 150 years, and that connection will continue indefinitely, given that over 60 percent of Canada's exports still go to the United States. The American government's degree of effectiveness in dealing with its fiscal problems, avoiding recession and cutting its deficit will inevitably affect the Canadian economy, Pape suggests. "The deficit obviously can't go on at the current rate forever," he says. This fact alone calls into question the potential for serious long-term growth in the American equity market, notwithstanding the rally underway at time of writing.

The negative effect of the lack of sufficient pipeline capacity and the discount attributable to Canada's heavier oil has been increased by the shale gas boom in the United States. The rapid rise in U.S. natural gas production in the last three years due to successful extraction of formerly tight gas reserves through "fracking" (hydraulic fracturing of the sandstone containing the gas) has driven the price of gas to 15-year lows and curtailed Canadian gas exports to the United States.

On the other hand, approval of the Keystone XL Pipeline extension, postponed in November 2011, would have a positive effect on Canadian oil revenues and therefore share prices. During the run-up to the American 2012 federal election, American federal officials postponed their decision on the proposed Keystone XL Pipeline route and issued plans to consider a new route.

As proposed by Calgary-based TransCanada Corporation, the pipeline would link the Alberta oil patch to Texas refineries. The postponement essentially guaranteed that authorities would not make a decision until at least late 2013 and perhaps 2014. Lack of sufficient pipeline capacity has driven down the price of oil sands crude, meaning lowered revenue for industry and federal and provincial governments. Rejection or continued postponement of the Keystone extension would telegraph lowered interest in Canadian oil and therefore exert downward pressure on oil revenues.

Even with approval of the extension, any improvement in the commodity's outlook would be four to five years away. "We're still looking at 2017–18 before it actually becomes comes into play," Pape suggests, adding that energy stock prices would likely increase ahead of that time in anticipation of profit increases.

Investors should not, therefore, assume that purchasing commodity-producing companies in developed economies such as Canada will give them direct access to the growth of emerging and frontier markets through rising commodity prices. Whether or not the commodity boom of the past decade has come to an end, the performance of the S&P/TSX energy and materials sectors over the last five years has been extremely disappointing, given that commodity prices have recovered sharply from the lows that they reached during the financial crisis. The S&P/TSX Capped Energy Index returned −6.3 percent p.a. in the five years ending in April 2013 and the S&P/TSX Capped Materials Index −5.9 percent p.a. The controversies over constructing the necessary infrastructure to permit commodity producers such as Canada and Australia to fully benefit from the continued growth in demand for resources from the emerging and frontier markets are a reminder that using developed markets as a proxy for investing directly in frontier markets can lead to disappointing performance as factors that are specific to those countries can override what are apparently strong fundamentals.

While the Canadian stock market does offer stability, its long-term growth prospects do not match those of either the emerging markets or frontier markets. The financial sector of the Canadian market does not appear poised for major growth at time of writing. Dividends paid by Canadian financial institutions do not appear threatened and the Canadian banking sector began to raise its dividends again after a two-year hiatus in 2011, but major share price appreciation seems unlikely as long as interest rates remain low.

The low rates would make a significant increase in life-insurer share prices unlikely within the near future. "It's really difficult to see how there is going to be any strong move to the upside [under these circumstances]," Pape says. Meanwhile insurers have to deleverage the liabilities flowing from their long-term contracts, another factor working against share price appreciation within the near future. The sale by Sun Life of Canada of its American annuity business in early 2013 relieved it of costly long-term obligations.

While Canadian bank dividends appear likely to continue to be unthreatened indefinitely, low interest rates and an uncertain economy work against significant upside of shares in these institutions. The dividends will provide a reasonably stable return, but share price growth exceeding 5–6 percent within the near future appears unlikely, with one possible exception.

That exception is the Canadian financial institution most heavily exposed to emerging and frontier markets. Long a major player in the Caribbean through a series of acquisitions over the last two decades, the Bank of Nova Scotia (TSX; NYSE: BNS) is now the fourth largest bank in Mexico, the sixth largest in Chile and the second largest in Peru. It recently bought a top 10 bank in Colombia and has minority stakes in several banks in China and Thailand. However, despite deriving more than one-third of its profits from its Latin American and Asian operations, its stock price has only marginally outperformed the S&P/TSX Composite Index return of 9.3 percent p.a. over the last decade (ending April 2013). Investors should be aware that even the most internationally exposed developed market companies will be more affected by their domestic market's performance than by their international operations, unless the overwhelming majority of their revenues and profits are perceived by investors to be generated from emerging or frontier market operations.

THE UNITED STATES

With its broad segments and limited diversification, the Canadian economy and stock market present a relatively straightforward picture, but the American market has far greater diversity in equity categories, weightings, investment products and capitalization levels, giving it a huge advantage for investors but presenting a much more difficult task for analysts. When examining the challenges faced by the U.S. economy over the next few years, most observers have focused on the explosive growth in government debt taken on to overcome the effects of the financial crisis of 2008–09; that debt has tripled in the last five years. Demographics in both Canada and the United States do not present as much of a challenge as they do in Europe and Japan, as population growth through birth and migration has remained reasonably robust. However, with the federal deficit close to US$1 trillion a year for the last five years and public debt to GDP rising sharply to 100 percent (excluding debt held by the Federal Reserve), the U.S. government faces the challenge of reducing the burden of the high level of debt to GDP, especially as any rise in government bond yields will lead to a rapid rise in interest payments.

Investors attempting to gain access to emerging and frontier markets by investing in U.S. companies face the same difficulty already noted in the Canadian section. The importance of the performance of the domestic economy and company- and country-specific factors will carry much greater weight in most investors' minds than even a substantial exposure to the more rapidly growing and attractively valued emerging and frontier markets, unless that exposure accounts for a very high percentage of a company's revenues.

Pape enumerates three priorities for the American stock market, starting with the urgent need for Washington to clarify policies in areas such as corporate taxation so that corporations will know their upcoming tax liabilities.

That leads to the second priority. American corporations have huge amounts of cash on their balance sheets earning negligible returns due to record low interest rates. Typically, these corporations hesitate to make large-scale capital acquisitions or hiring decisions in the absence of clarity, Pape suggests, adding that a clearer outlook might induce spending and new business enterprises. "All this cash is not being deployed in an era when interest rates are near zero. It's not earning them much money, obviously, so it's going to be in their interest to put the money to work in productive ways," he says. "We know the money is there." Some productive uses for the cash pile might be investment in new capacity in the U.S., as the rise in labor costs in traditionally low-wage emerging economies and the increasing cost of transporting goods back to the U.S. have started making manufacturing in the U.S. more attractive. When combined with reductions in real wages and health care and pension costs by the corporate sector over the last few years, there are even some examples of companies "onshoring" i.e., moving production back from emerging markets, as discussed later in this section.

One factor specific to the United States is that profits earned overseas are subject to a 35 percent withholding tax if repatriated into the United States. This leads to some anomalous situations, such as Apple's decision in early 2013 to borrow $100 billion to pay higher dividends and repurchase stock, rather than use the cash on its balance sheet, a large proportion of which had been earned outside the United States. Therefore, even those U.S. companies with a very high foreign exposure may not be given full credit for achieving success, as the cash thus generated is not always available to their shareholders in a tax-effective form.

At time of writing the S&P 500 trades in the middle of its historic price-to-earnings ratio at approximately 14 times 2013's forecast earnings, making it fair value. Meanwhile an improvement encouraged by clarity in Washington policies and the resulting release of cash could create significant upside in the share prices of companies benefiting from increased investment, such as suppliers of capital equipment, technology and infrastructure plays. These uncertainties do not generally have parallels in emerging and frontier markets and therefore do not threaten growth in those markets.

The third priority is the extent to which major American corporations can continue to grow their overseas sales revenues, which means that emerging and frontier markets hold the key to continued growth in some equities in developed nations. In some cases, these corporations earn 40–50 percent of revenues overseas, leaving them less dependent on the domestic market and more dependent on the troubled European and uncertain Chinese markets. A resolution of the European crisis and economic stability in China would augur well for the American multinationals with operations in these countries, such as highly rated KFC- and Pizza Hut–operator Yum! Brands Inc., which derives more than 75 percent of its revenues internationally and over 40 percent of its revenues from China. We look at Yum! Brands and several other U.S. multinational companies with high emerging and frontier market exposure in more detail in Chapter 10.

A fourth priority—job creation—generally flows from the outcomes of government clarity, business confidence and overseas sales. Economists and analysts generally believe that 250,000 new jobs every month for several successive months would indicate real progress. Those numbers would increase tax revenues, consumer spending and, perhaps equally importantly, see a restoration of consumer confidence, which in turn would be reflected in a greater willingness to spend and to invest in growth-oriented assets such as equities. This scale of job creation—and with it the economic health that creation on this scale would result in—appears unlikely in the United States in this decade, another factor that will restrict growth. Furthermore, the constrained-income growth in the United States over the last decade has led to a reduction in export growth among the more export-dependent emerging markets, such as South Korea and Taiwan, and even in the United States's largest trade partner, China. This reinforces the importance for investors of focusing on those emerging markets that have a higher dependence upon their domestic market, which includes most frontier markets, as their export industries are less developed. We find the most attractive markets are in Asia and Africa, in countries with larger populations and thus more capacity to develop a large domestic market.

Traditional job creation engines seem unlikely to provide 250,000 new jobs.

The housing market, afflicted with falling prices, huge numbers of foreclosures, negative equity and formerly large inventories has recovered somewhat in 2012–13, and the auto industry will make a limited contribution.

The factors limiting American job growth—and therefore the benefits for consumers of that growth—comprise a daunting list. Real income growth in the United States over the 2000–10 decade was the lowest since the 1930s, and the degree of income inequality in the United States is approaching that of such notably economically stratified countries as Argentina, the Philippines and Nigeria. The ratio of chief executive officer earnings to those of the average employee has increased from 42:1 in 1982 to 354:1 in 2012, according to the AFL-CIO. Any analysis of the American economy needs to recognize that, broadly, the mood of the American consumer appears—understandably—more focused on hedging against job uncertainties and deleveraging debt than on new homes and possessions.

Retail sales have remained lackluster more than 5 years into a recovery and with stock market indices hitting new all-time highs. That huge shortfall points to the uncertain mood of individuals and business owners, includes the continued hoarding of cash by both groups and could lead to a drop in

GDP. Weak retail sales over the second half of 2012 and the first half of 2013 mark the lowest growth in retail sales since the 2008 recession.

As well as the huge amounts of cash on corporate balance sheets, the American economy has several strong points, according to James Awad, managing director of New York–based Zephyr Management. Chief among these, according to Awad, is the reversal of some of the forces that drove jobs out of the United States. The American dollar has depreciated while wages have fallen in America and risen in emerging markets. Jobs are now being "onshored"—moved back from some of the traditional emerging market destinations such as China—to the United States, or in some cases Mexico, partially due to the rising cost of transport, with the price of a barrel of oil having risen five times over the decade of 2000 to 2010. Investors should be aware that as wages rise in traditional low-cost manufacturing centers such as China, Brazil, the Caribbean, Thailand and Indonesia, the attractions of moving production to lower-cost centers in the frontier economies becomes stronger. Vietnam has been gaining textile manufacturing and electronics assembly business from southern China, and Bangladesh, in turn, has been gaining business from Thailand and India.

Sectors where the United States and other developed markets retain an advantage, such as technology, software, telecoms and media, are also attractive to investors as they retain high barriers to entry, requiring large, well-educated workforces and ready access to large amounts of risk capital, factors which few emerging markets are able to supply. Observers such as Awad also stress the American tradition of innovation, especially among large technology corporations, including Google, Facebook and Apple, many of which did not even exist 20 years ago.

These factors suggest the viability of undervalued large-capitalization stocks in companies paying stable dividends, getting the majority of their revenues from within the American market but also deriving a large portion from emerging and frontier markets. As noted, however, investors have to be prepared to receive the majority of their potential outperformance after the market has finally come to recognize the importance of the revenues from non-developed markets to these companies. Technology companies, infrastructure companies with operations in emerging markets and energy companies with strong revenues from outside the United States seem attractive sectors that fit this description as long as investors pay reasonable valuations, as do consumer-oriented sectors such as consumer staples and consumer discretionary companies (food, beverage and personal products makers, for example), although their defensive nature and high dividend yields have seen their valuations increase.

EUROPE

Our belief in the investment potential of frontier markets lies partially in the potential for growth in these markets and partially in the limited potential of other markets, including Europe. Understanding the European crisis and the continued negative impact it will have on European investments means understanding that several crises actually converged together and that they need different solutions.

Examining the European crisis leads to the inevitable conclusion that it will take at least until the end of the decade and likely longer before those countries offer the potential for reasonable returns to investors. This is not to deny that there are attractive individual companies headquartered in the United Kingdom and the Eurozone that derive a high percentage of their revenues and profits from emerging and frontier markets, some of which are described elsewhere in the book, but the unattractive outlook for the domestic European economies will likely limit returns for the broad indices and may hold back returns even for those companies that do not have a high dependence upon their local markets.

The series of crises affecting the members of the Eurozone (those countries that joined the European Monetary Union and adopted the euro as their currency) has unfolded gradually over the period from 2010 onward. Although the finances of the five countries sometimes called the PIIGS—Portugal, Ireland, Italy, Greece and Spain—seemed to unravel at approximately the same time, a look at the root causes of their problems sets Ireland apart from the other countries.

Ireland got into trouble because banks had been caught in a real estate crisis somewhat like that in the United States; it led to bailouts that the government could not afford and was then followed by a debt crisis. However, the problems in Greece, Portugal, Italy and Spain resulted from years of overspending and failure to carry out necessary economic reforms that would have made their economies more flexible and competitive. Spain's crisis was similar to Ireland's in that it suffered from a banking crisis because of a real estate bubble.

Like Ireland, Spain had a low debt-to-GDP ratio before the crisis, and its budget was pretty much balanced. However, it remains to be seen whether Spain can improve its economy's competitiveness and productivity. Portugal is somewhere in between Greece and Spain. In this context, because these countries could no longer devalue their currencies, their economies became increasingly less competitive vis-à-vis their Asian counterparts because they had traditionally relied on manufacturing to power their economies. As a result, the competitiveness of their industrial base gradually eroded and jobs were lost, according to Patrick Leblond, associate professor of Public and International Affairs at the University of Ottawa in Ottawa, Ontario.[4]

Greece and Italy were overdue for reforms for years even before entering the European Union and had not undertaken sufficient reforms since that time, Leblond explains. To gain admission to the EU, Greece had manipulated its finances in a way that would have gotten an entrepreneur seeking a small business loan rejected by every bank in the Western world.

Moreover, before entering the Eurozone, Greece and Italy had maintained their competitiveness by devaluing their currencies, a strategy that boosted exports. Their problems worsened when they entered the Eurozone since this strategy was no longer available due to the common currency.

That increased the obligation to take steps to become more competitive. For example, Greece has monopolies in areas such as the trucking industry. Many of Spain's problems flowed from a real estate bubble, and when the bubble burst, many construction workers formerly absorbed into the construction industry became unemployed. The problems were exacerbated as the collapse of the real estate bubble also left many *caixas* (state-owned regional banks) in a precarious position.

Still weak, but apparently clear of the crisis-a-day period, European economies can improve only very slowly, according to observers such as Leblond. While the crisis arguably could continue for several years, he expresses the conventional wisdom that the European Union will not dissolve nor will the euro disintegrate, and he underpins that analysis by pointing to several historical factors.

History has proven the strength of the EU. Generally, it has been an economic success to date and a review of the political postures of the member nations shows no apparent willingness to sacrifice the entire Union in order to avoid helping some members experiencing difficulties. Since its inception, the EU's political and economic success has flowed from greater integration of European economies, not disintegration, in Leblond's estimation.

The blessing-in-disguise aspect of the crisis may not seem readily obvious, but the crisis may very well turn out to be a blessing if it gives the EU, especially its fiscally disciplined members such as Germany, France and the Netherlands, the means to force undisciplined member countries such as the PIIGS to undertake long-delayed fiscal and structural reforms. In that event, the troubled nations will emerge with stronger and more competitive economies that, in later years, could actually contribute to the EU's prosperity, making the whole EU economically stronger.

---

[4]Personal interview with Al Emid during the research and writing of this book in 2012.

Even when viewed through the prism of a worst-case scenario, the situation should not become as apocalyptic as some analysts have suggested. In the event that a weaker member such as Greece were to leave the EU—a development that observers, including Leblond, view as extremely unlikely—its departure, or that of Cyprus, where a banking crisis resulted in uninsured depositors losing substantial percentages of their savings, would not mean the end of the Union or the euro

Stronger EU members such as Germany, France and the Benelux countries (Belgium, Netherlands and Luxembourg) currently show no risk of default and would be unlikely to revert to having their own national currencies, according to observers such as Leblond. Moreover, German banks are exposed to Greek and Portuguese debt, and disintegration of the euro would be costly at best and disastrous at worst. Pragmatism seems to have triumphed over short-term bandage solutions. Abandoning the troubled nations and forcing them out of the EU would likely do more harm than good overall and would not solve the fiscal problems. If forced outside the EU, the countries would still have their fiscal problems, which would worsen and continue to affect other European economies. Keeping them within the EU allows other members to exert pressure on them to make the necessary reforms. Moreover, if Greece left the European Union the move would create instability in the continent, something none of the member nations would find appetizing.

In 2013, the move to create a single financial supervisor for major banks sends a positive signal of plans for greater financial integration in the EU to financial markets. "I sense that this is about more integration, not less," Leblond says. Europe may have passed through its darkest days. Greece, perhaps the worst hit of the European nations, remains inside the EU though it has had to agree to a series of concessions in order to qualify for bailout financing. Generally, citizens and governments have recognized the need for reforms including reduced spending, albeit in gradual increments, Leblond explains.

He also notes that Europeans have grasped the need for austerity. "The population is becoming, in a way, tired of [it]. At the same there is a general recognition that there is no choice, that it's impossible to keep borrowing and spending more than one earns as a country," Leblond says. The revival in financial markets since the worst of the Eurozone crisis in mid-2012, when the president of the European Central Bank, Mario Draghi, promised to do "whatever it takes" to preserve the euro, has seen bond yields in the peripheral Eurozone countries retreat sharply from the levels of over 7 percent that they reached in Spain, Portugal and Italy. At those levels, it became impossible for these countries to keep financing their government debt.

Ireland, which did not suffer from many of the structural problems afflicting the uncompetitive so-called Club Med economies, has already begun to sell off some of the bad debts it inherited when it nationalized the banks, and is seeing its debt-to-GDP ratio falling rapidly. It could complete a large portion of its bailout program within a couple of years. That would enable it to return to obtaining financing from international capital markets without the need for a European Central Bank guarantee.

In Italy, much will depend on the ability of the government of the day to sustain reforms aimed at stimulating a stagnant economy that has experienced little growth and no improvement in productivity in 10 years. It will take years to turn the situation around and increase productivity and competitiveness.

The era of low interest rates partially explains Greece's predicament, since it enabled the government to spend prodigiously. "The country went on a spending spree in 2000," Leblond recalls, adding that the government essentially lost control of spending. Greece also has to rein in at least part of its underground economy, estimated to account for 30 percent of its GDP. "You have classic overspending by government combined with what I call a moribund economy that is not competitive," Leblond explains.

Meanwhile, private investors in Greek sovereign debt lost over 70 percent of their principal in a forced redenomination early in 2012, and such losses are likely to be experienced by the multinational lenders such as the International Monetary Fund in the near future.

In Greece, the government's ability to convince the population of the need to rein in spending and continue implementing austerity programs will determine its ability to continue getting the bailout financing that stabilizes the country. Harsh realities such as these will discourage investments in Greece and elsewhere in Europe for the foreseeable future. In relative terms, frontier markets provide a safer haven.

In Spain, the national banks are stronger than regional banks that encountered problems because of large property loans, some of them politically motivated, Leblond suggests. "They were not very well managed and as a result the government had to basically bail out the banks," he says. With unemployment at 26 percent and youth unemployment at over 50 percent, the effects of the austerity program being imposed by the Eurozone and Spain's political elite rapidly eroded support for the European project and even threatened the unity of the country itself, as Catalonia, the wealthiest region, in 2012 elected a regional government that openly discussed separation from Spain.

As with other crisis-hit peripheral economies, Italy, Spain and Portugal may end up having to accept a Eurozone bailout of their banks with the attendant stringent conditions, meaning that the outlook for anything other than a protracted recession is unlikely for several years for much of Europe. Both Spain and Greece, as well as Portugal, are all heavily dependent upon tourism, but their membership in the EU makes them expensive by comparison with other destinations outside, such as Turkey.

Overall, the economic situation in Europe will remain subdued for several years while governments and banks work out the massive restructuring necessary to return the PIIGS to prosperity. For that reason, investment prospects in Europe have to be viewed as long-term buying opportunities at best.

For those reasons, the attractiveness of investments in European multinationals has less to do with the economies in which they have their headquarters and more to with their exposure to the fast-growing emerging and frontier markets. Europe possesses many world-class competitors that sell at a discount to their American rivals, due to the lackluster outlook for their domestic markets, but have major exposure to emerging market and frontier market consumers.

Major energy producers such as London-based BP PLC; the Hague–based Royal Dutch Shell PLC; Paris-based Total S.A. and pharmaceutical companies Novartis AG, based in Basel; GlaxoKlineSmith, based in London; and Sanofi (formerly Sanofi-Aventis), based in Paris fall into this category.

Also worth considering are consumer product companies such as Unilever PLC (based in London), Nestlé S.A. (based in Vevey, Switzerland) and Reckitt Benckiser PLC (based in Slough, UK). Drinks companies benefiting from the emerging markets' middle-class demand include London-based Diageo PLC, SABMiller PLC (also London based) and Heineken N.V. (based in Amsterdam).

Some of these companies, such as Diageo PLC and SABMiller PLC, have huge exposures to emerging and frontier markets, adding to their strengths and attractiveness. Many investors prefer to gain exposure to what they regard as riskier, faster-growing economies through blue-chip multinationals of this type, and there are several other examples later in the book. However, what the descriptions of Canada, the United States and Europe contained in this chapter should have conveyed to investors is that risk is not confined to less-developed countries, but, in fact, risk in certain asset classes in the developed markets is just as high. For example, investors contemplating buying conventional sovereign government debt issued by developed countries, such as the United States, Japan and most members of the Eurozone, at nominal yields below 2 percent in the United States and Europe and below 1 percent in Japan, face the strong possibility of losing money in inflation-adjusted terms over the next decade. In some cases, such as Greece, private sector investors have already lost more than 60 percent of their original nominal investment.

Even investing in developed equity markets has not proven to be a successful investment strategy for the period since 2000. Returns from equities from 2000 to 2010 were the lowest since the 1930s, and taken as a whole, these factors lead to the inescapable conclusion that investing in most U.S. and European companies at this time would not be likely to produce attractive real returns for some years to come. That again underpins the argument for investors having a meaningful exposure to emerging and frontier markets and to confine investments in developed equity markets to those companies and sectors that have a significant exposure to these areas.

TAKEAWAYS

1. Notwithstanding the importance of emerging and frontier market investing, advisors and clients can constructively "locate" them within the broader global investment landscape. Our faith in frontier markets lies partially in their own fundamentals and partially in the conservative or even muted outlook for other regions.
2. The health of emerging and frontier markets contributes to the health of the Canadian economy and other commodity-producing nations, such as Australia, Brazil and South Africa.
3. The American and European parts of the economic landscape continue changing, but the outlook for the United States appears much more attractive than for Europe over the next few years.
4. Much of the investment potential of European multinationals flows from their emerging and frontier market strategies.

CHAPTER 8

Online Trading in Emerging and Frontier Markets and Why It's a Bad Idea

The most appropriate and least appropriate venues for taking advantage of any investment should form an integral part of any detailed discussion of that investment. Online trading by novice or sophomore investors in emerging market or frontier market investments easily falls into the inappropriate category.

THE DANGEROUS APPEAL OF GOING IT ALONE

Online trading has several appealing aspects, many of them similar to the advantages of online shopping, whether for preliminary research when buying a home, as a means of cost-saving, booking travel, or buying books, clothes or furniture. It also has emotional appeal in terms of independence and self-determination.

"Going it alone" has a certain cachet for some individuals, whether in life, business or investing. Some television commercials show well-known television actors evoking investors' rugged individualism, independence of spirit and self-determination.

Other commercials appeal to the simplicity of online trading, belying its actual complexity. A familiar television commercial shows a very young child sitting at a computer keyboard and executing a trade through an online trading site. The child recounts how "a lot of people," presumably nervous adults, question whether he should trade stocks. He then presses a few keys on the keyboard and exclaims, "I bought a stock. You just saw me buy a stock."

He goes on to the main message in this series of commercials: anyone can do online trading and make serious money. "If I can do it, you can do it," he says. This veneer of simplicity reduces online trading to child's play, but to treat online trading this way can become expensive.

These and other appealing aspects may seduce the unwary into trying online trading without understanding the work and risks involved—a risky enough undertaking when dealing with familiar equities, and an even riskier one when dealing with emerging market or frontier market equities.

The advantages of online trading seem especially attractive to those who felt disappointed in the fallout of the financial crisis that began in 2008. The crisis apparently divided investors into three broad groups.

Some individuals have become so concerned about their investments and financial health that they place greater value on expert advice than ever and have become more open to working with professional advisors than ever before.

Another group believes that financial experts let them down during the market crisis and aftermath, citing faulty investment choices, failure to adapt investment portfolios to the realities of the period and even lack of communications during the most traumatic parts of the crisis. As a form of retaliation, members of this group have become determined to take greater charge of their affairs, and many of them see online trading as the solution and point to the mentioned advantages.

They see the television commercials for online trading sites that point to the fact that control is in the hands of the investor, the investor tools are available as part of the package and getting started is easy. Just stare at the graphs, think it over, press a few buttons and bingo! You too can become a hot market trader!

Perhaps that does happen for a small minority of online traders, but this scenario does not take into account the risks that come with the emotional appeal.

The third group consists of those for whom keeping their money "under the mattress" seems like the best investment. As a group, they have countless trillions of dollars in low-interest bank accounts and larger-than-necessary holdings of bank certificates. This behavior is occurring while interest rates in developed markets are at generational lows and show no sign of increasing for the foreseeable future. While short-term interest rates have been 0.25 percent or less in Japan for the last 15 years, their arrival in the United States, Europe and Australia has been a novel development in the five years since the financial crisis of 2008–09. This amounts to a policy of "financial suppression" by central banks and governments and has resulted in investors being forced into riskier investments in search of a reasonable yield. While it may seem tempting to go it alone by using online trading to gain access to higher-yielding investments, such as emerging and frontier markets, we would not recommend this as a strategy.

THE RISKS OF ONLINE TRADING

Risks are the flip side of independence, since the online trader may not have access to a knowledgeable financial advisor acting as a buffer in the decision-making process, and the trader might even have an emotional inability to deal with daily or hourly swings in share price movements.

The novice may not have the self-discipline to deal well with the commitment involved in online trading. While trading sites trumpet their quality research and investor tools, these assets do not help an investor who finds reading reports a bore, dislikes navigating through the tools or simply does not have enough time to approach trading with the rigor required by any complicated task.

The emotional risks of online trading also include the stress involved in watching stocks rise, fall and rise again—or just keep falling—during a trading day, compounding the stress of a market environment in which volatility has become the new normal and appears likely to remain volatile for at least another two years. An otherwise intelligent choice can become a severely eroded holding with a sudden development that even the most careful online trader could never have foreseen.

Self-understanding in any context, especially when appraising one's own abilities, can be painfully difficult. Deciding if online trading is truly for you requires self-understanding as well as an understanding of the dynamics of frontier markets.

Prospective traders must ask themselves if they have the ability to resist the urge to buy or sell a stock as a reaction to short-term market developments, such as a negative report in the morning's news. The impulse to trade in the short term can result in severe losses in opportunity cost or in hard dollars.

Online trading also requires insights into one's own decision-making processes. Some online traders tend to make choices to buy or sell a stock based on intuition or gut feelings rather than objective analysis. Hearing of the latest disturbance in Nigeria could lead one to doubt investments in frontier exchange-traded funds with holdings there. Still, Nigeria ranks as one of the leading frontier markets and is a thriving market for developed market multinationals.

Others have a more disciplined style and make decisions based on careful analysis and mathematical calculations. Some traders, of course, combine both approaches.

It requires a huge commitment of time and self-discipline to be an online trader. First, there are large amounts of research required to become fully informed about a company, its recent past and its outlook, before making a decision. Second, one must become familiar and comfortable with the tools offered by the online trading site in order to reach a strong comfort level with them. Online trading for the non-professional is at best a part-time avocation even when trading in developed markets. Adding to that the dynamics and complexities of frontier markets means an additional level of research needs to be undertaken by the serious online trader.

It also requires the trader to separate reality from glamor. It is exciting to trade on a stock exchange in a distant city—in this case halfway around the world—but the reality is that the only practical approach to access many frontier-market stocks via online trading is to buy and sell American depository receipts (ADRs) and global depository receipts (GDRs) on North American and European exchanges. This both limits the opportunity to those stocks that are large and liquid enough to have listed their shares on major foreign exchanges yet still requires the time to become familiar with a much broader range of stocks and opportunities than otherwise.

It may sound impressive to chat in casual conversation about the frontier exchange-traded funds (ETFs) in one's portfolio, but the online trader, working without the buffering effect of a financial advisor, may not have checked the volatility of such an ETF against his or her risk tolerance. Worse still, where the advisor administers most of the individual's assets, he or she may not be aware of risks that the client is taking in the online account and conceivably may have included some higher-risk investments in the portfolio.

Online trading is far closer to gambling than many would like to admit. There is nothing fundamentally wrong with gambling provided the individual knows how to handle it. The individual has to accept that some choices will become quite profitable and some will become losers—and to react appropriately.

For the professional advisor, this equation has added fallout since many advisors believe that when a stock in an individual's online trading portfolio drops dramatically in value, the disappointment extends to decision making in his or her other holdings, including those handled by an advisor. An individual who takes some losses in the online trading portfolio tends to want to reduce their involvement with both the online portfolio and the assets handled by the advisor. That increases the need to understand the effect of the individual's emotional makeup.

Given the higher volatility of developing markets, as mentioned in Chapter 3, individuals' emotional reactions to sharp moves in these markets may both affect their overall portfolio, including that portion handled by an advisor, and color their approach to investing in promising, fast-growing markets in the future. With the MSCI Frontier Markets Index falling over 50 percent between late 2007 and the beginning of 2009, many investors would have sold their positions with large losses and been reluctant to re-enter. A couple of the individual frontier market companies with ADRs and GDRs that are discussed in Chapter 10 provide good examples of the volatility that can affect even the best-positioned, best-managed frontier-market stocks.

Panama-based regional airline Copa Holdings (NYSE: CPA) dropped 73 percent in the 15 months between the beginning of July 2007 and late November 2008, while South Asian and North African mobile phone operator Orascom Telecom (LSE: OTLD) fell 78 percent between the beginning of 2008 and March 2009. Meanwhile their underlying businesses continued to grow and produce positive cash flow. It is reasonable to assume that many investors would have sold their shares at some point during this period and been reluctant to return to them even after the global economy recovered.

Understanding Your Financial Behavior

Understanding one's own financial behavior starts with determining one's financial decision temperament, according to Victor Ricciardi, an assistant professor of finance at Goucher College in Baltimore, Maryland, whose credits include more than 10 years of research into behavioral finance.[1] He defines behavioral finance as the study of investor behavior across all types of individuals. Behavioral finance attempts to understand the processes by which an individual determines the important factors in financial decision making.

Ricciardi identifies two main categories of financial decision makers. The analytical type makes decisions based on a large quantity of information. In an example outside of investing, an analytical decision maker considering a car purchase checks factors such as safety, maintenance records and price and then determines a broad selection of, let's say, five cars.

When considering an investment, this type of individual assesses the risk of a stock by checking its financial information, its industry, its beta or market-related risk and its standard deviation variance, a formula that measures its risk against a historical track record.

In comparison, an intuitive thinker works more from personal psychology and emotional processes. "They go with their gut feeling," Ricciardi says. This kind of individual can be optimistic and may tend to

---

[1]Personal interview with Al Emid during the research and writing of this book in 2012.

overconfidence. An intuitive thinker might look for a flashy sports car and make a decision based on which one just seems "right."

In investment decision making this kind of individual might be prone to making decisions without the kind of information required by the analytical individual. During the Internet bubble, some intuitive thinkers bought unproven stocks with no valuations and few financial analyses and regretted it afterward. Throughout this book we suggest that not all areas of emerging and frontier markets are the same, and an intuitive thinker might not make that distinction.

Not surprisingly, many individuals combine attributes of both types in their decision making. After identifying the broad category of five most suitable cars (taking an analytical approach), the person with a blend of attributes might go for the sportiest car within that group (taking a more intuitive approach). In investment decision making, this kind of person might perceive a company with a familiar and trusted product or service, such as a cellular telephone company, as a good stock choice, Ricciardi says.

Another way of looking at the two types of financial behavior centers on risk. An analytical person, for instance, tends not to like debt and generally restricts it to the house mortgage, which he or she tends to pay off as rapidly as possible. Ricciardi defines these issues in their simplest terms as decisions that allow an individual to sleep at night. "Thinking about decisions that you made in your lifetime, are you able to sleep based on your current financial decisions that you have made during your lifetime?" he asks. A heavily indebted analytical person might have more trouble sleeping at night than a heavily indebted intuitive person; generally, the extent to which a person can sleep at night is the same as the extent to which he or she can deal with risk.

This kind of self-analysis helps an individual sort through his or her risk tolerance. A popular theory teaches that during the buoyant stock market before the financial crisis of 2008–09, many individuals felt they had a high risk tolerance, only to find that they were not as risk tolerant when the market crashed. In contrast, Ricciardi argues that for many individuals, the crash led to a reappraisal of perceptions more than an actual shifting of category. "It's our perceived versus our true risk or our perception of risk," he says.

In his estimation, these individuals did not really change their risk tolerance because of the financial crisis but had not clearly understood their tolerance in the first place.

"I don't even think, necessarily, they are shifting from categories. I think people don't have a clear sense of what their propensity is to assess true risk," he suggests. Generally, someone with a high level of risk tolerance can face a 20–30 percent drop in their portfolio and take a long-term view, while someone with a lower tolerance would find that kind of drop much less acceptable.

Ricciardi questions whether some investors clearly make the connection between risk and return—meaning that they may or may not understand the risk-to-return ratio, a concept that teaches that the higher the risk, the greater the potential reward.

Attitudes toward risk also involve factors such as age (younger individuals might be more comfortable with risk than older individuals) and marital status (a married individual with the customary family responsibilities might be less prone to risk-taking than a single individual). Entrepreneurial individuals might be more accepting of risk than individuals in conventional salaried occupations. Those closer to retirement are often less accepting of risk than those with a longer income-earning horizon.

These and other concepts converge in the asset allocation strategy, which reconciles a large list of factors into a coherent investing plan. However, many investors do not adjust their allocation in retirement plans and other investments regularly to stay within the allocation and unknowingly end up with an allocation with an unsuitable level of risk.

As a result of a bull market, an investor originally in a 60 percent stock and 40 percent fixed-income allocation may find himself or herself with a higher weighting of stocks, possibly going to 80 percent stock and 20 percent income. "Depending on the market cycle, [such as] a bull market, they wind up having a lot more money than they would have [otherwise], but also they are exposed to a lot more downside risk," Ricciardi says.

The 80 percent/20 percent weighting means that the individual, possibly without realizing it, has moved into a higher-risk category. "They're up a lot of money, but they're also ensuring that they are in a higher risk category because they never adjusted their asset allocation strategy on a yearly basis," Ricciardi says. Resolving that means checking the portfolio at least once yearly to check for unintended changes in portfolio weightings.

For some individuals, relating their values to Abraham Maslow's motivational theory will help them understand their overall needs and place themselves into one of the categories. In a paper released in 1943, Maslow first outlined his hierarchy of needs, represented by the familiar pyramid showing human needs as layers, with physiological needs at its base and self-actualization at its apex. Maslow postulated that the most basic needs (that is, the physiological needs) had to be satisfied before an individual would reach for higher needs (that is, self-actualization).

Ricciardi believes that this kind of self-understanding and introspection will assist each individual to assess propensity for risk and to become a better decision maker. "I would say it's fair to say they're going to look inside themselves," he says.

This kind of self-understanding and introspection actually becomes more important in online trading than in other areas of a person's financial affairs, since the individual trading online generally does not have the advice and buffering effect of a knowledgeable financial advisor.

(Certainly that may be present in other areas of the individual's investing and financial planning.)

Arguably, the complexities of online trading increase exponentially for the novice or sophomore trader who trades on emerging market or frontier market stock exchanges. Indeed, Ricciardi questions whether the online trader can knowledgeably sift through the information overload, much of it from foreign sources.

The overload makes assessing the correct price point for a purchase more difficult than ever, he says. Knowing when to gamble and when to fold becomes exponentially more difficult with increased distances and cultures. When a stock in a distant frontier market takes a sudden drop, calculating its chances for recovery becomes more difficult than when a familiar North American name suddenly drops.

The overload may lead to what Ricciardi calls "representativeness," the act of coping with overload by latching on to one piece of information and using it to represent the larger situation. "You have a small amount of information and draw a major conclusion from it," he explains. The absence of reliable information can also lead to what Ricciardi calls "anchoring," a decision-making process in which someone may have a successful investment in one distant country and assume that he or she can easily duplicate that success in another distant country.

Another danger is that an individual who is culturally connected to a frontier market may believe he or she understands the investments in that market. "If you felt more connected because you emigrated [from a frontier market country] to North America, would you have a cultural bias?" Ricciardi asks. "Maybe you can feel more confident because you think you know it and are more likely to invest in that."

In effect, the first screen the individual uses in this case is a cultural screen. "I think I know a lot about Croatia because I have roots there," Ricciardi says. In fact, an investor must learn to recognize thinking that stems from cultural biases, and approach his or her thinking with the normal due diligence, checking all the usual categories of financial information and resisting the urge to decide based solely on the cultural screen.

PROFESSIONAL ADVISORS AND ONLINE TRADING

A professional advisor who discourages a client from getting involved in online trading or suggests limitations on a client's online trading may worry that the client will misread the advisor's motives and figure that the advisor wants more assets under his or her control. The advisor may also worry that the client will read the suggestion as implying a lack of faith in the client's judgment. When any professional works in the business of giving advice, he or she can suffer from fear of misinterpretation. A financial professional may already have more than his or her fair share of relationship fears in dealing with a client. Still, an advisor who has sufficient rapport with the client can convey the realities online trading without offending the client's belief in his or her own talents.

However, an advisor may identify a client who should simply not handle money, and dissuading him or her from online activity offers a polite way of expressing concern. Alternatively the advisor may suggest that the client restrict online trading to familiar names and participate in emerging markets and frontier markets through a carefully selected global fund.

TAKEAWAYS

1. At this time, online trading has limited usefulness for emerging market investing and even less relevance for frontier market investing.
2. An investor who decides to try online trading in these categories requires greater investment savvy than when trading in developed markets.
3. An investor who undertakes online trading in these categories has to make a deliberate attempt to set aside any cultural biases.
4. Online trading decisions made by an investor, whether novice, moderately knowledgeable or extremely sophisticated, lack the "buffer" effect of a professional advisor acting in the client's best interests.

CHAPTER 9

The Changing Role of Financial Advisors

The professional financial advisor looking to interest clients in a larger exposure to emerging market investments, or to initiate exposure to frontier market investments, faces one or more professional tasks before that conversation. Every advisor–client relationship is unique, but as a financial professional you may have to tackle these tasks before broaching the topic of emerging or frontier market investments.

These tasks fall into four major categories: responding to increased challenges after the financial crisis, accepting volatility, coping with increased reliance on financial advisors and convincing hesitant clients.

RESPONDING TO INCREASED CHALLENGES AFTER THE FINANCIAL CRISIS OF 2008–09

A financial advisor has to help investors overcome their post–financial crisis hesitation to invest in any asset category. As with corporations following a crisis, investors keep larger-than-necessary amounts in cash and in investments with low-paying interest because of continued volatility and a wariness about the future.

Some advisors believe that memories of the crisis and stock market crash of 2008 continue to linger. For this reason some investors still hesitate to increase their exposure to equities, while other investors have become determined to "catch up" and recoup losses as quickly as possible.

An advisor also has to reinforce investors' belief in the quality of professional financial advice. Indeed, the crisis that shook much of the financial system starting in 2008 also caused many investors to rethink their core values and perspectives. For many investors who were clients of advisors, the crisis also damaged their confidence in the abilities of the sources of financial counsel they had entrusted to look after their fiscal health. Some advisors still have to work at regaining the trust of clients and perhaps shoring up client rosters.

The crisis eroded the visions of many individuals as well as their faith in their own destinies, as otherwise seemingly secure employees received pink slips, and established entrepreneurs found their companies faltering or failing completely. For many individuals over the age of 50, the crisis spoiled their lifestyle outlook and led to a rethinking of retirement plans and an increase in their level of apprehensiveness as they approached retirement age. Some have had to advance their retirement plans due to abrupt terminations by their employers and others have had to delay their plans due to erosion of their finances. A number of individuals in this age bracket have had to rethink estate and inheritance issues, ultimately reducing assets intended for familial and philanthropic beneficiaries. Many of these individuals need more income accumulation and may also need to reconcile their future plans with the reality of the resources they have available.

At the time of writing, as we find ourselves in the midst of a slow and uncertain recovery, advisors and clients need to take measures aimed at rebuilding new wealth. At the same time, they also need to protect assets from the next downturn—whenever it comes. They have to ensure that it does not wreak as much havoc with their finances as did the cataclysmic tumult of 2008–09. We believe this means being willing to include non-correlated asset classes such as frontier markets even though superficially their volatility may seem to make them unattractive. That means considering some new rules, such as recognizing that volatile assets may have a place even in conservatively positioned portfolios, and revisiting some old ones that remain relevant.

The new rules would differ from client to client but they would include one or more of the following:

- Careful calculation of the weighting of frontier investments, in most cases not to exceed 5 percent of the individual's international equity weighting; that is not an absolute rule but a good general threshold.
- Generally the dollars deposited in frontier investments should be funds that the client will not reasonably need for at least five years or more.
- This category could include some allocation of frontier market bond funds as well as equity funds.
- Outside of frontier market considerations, the new rules would include continued participation in equity funds even after retirement, compared with the earlier rule that a client's involvement in equities would decrease or cease altogether with the onset of retirement.
- For clients who have more apprehensions than others, advisors may consider increased frequency of portfolio rebalancing.

ACCEPTING VOLATILITY

Many financial experts say that "volatility has become the new normal." While some would dismiss the phrase as a cliché, the reason that any phrase becomes a cliché is that it resonates with truth for a sufficient number of people who use it to describe a common view. Recognizing that and planning accordingly head the list of rules for the present investment climate.

Some advisors and clients recognize that volatility has become and will continue to define the new normal, and accept it as a reality and work within it. The proof of this new maxim surrounds us every day: U.S. morning newscasts focus on the latest job numbers, which are often discouraging, and American consumer-sensitive stocks decline within hours. Thousands of miles from major stock exchanges, militants engage in hostilities and the news reverberates into the price of oil for everyone. In North America and Europe, formerly stable blue-chip equities—such as bank stocks—no longer guarantee stable capital preservation and predictable growth, a lesson learned in several countries.

Accepting volatility does not mean avoiding it; investors should not shun assets perceived to be risky, such as equities, by moving their funds into developed market government bonds, as has occurred en masse since 2009. Most advisors recommend using investment-grade and high-yield corporate bonds and emerging market debt to diversify investors' bond holdings and purchasing dividend-paying equities in developed markets. The use of other asset classes that are not correlated with major stock markets, such as market neutral– and absolute return–focused hedge funds is also commonly recommended to reduce volatility of portfolios. Noting that frontier markets have very low correlations with developed and emerging markets as well as with each other is another tactic that advisors may consider recommending to their clients.

One important strategy for helping clients cope with volatility is revisiting the client's risk tolerance, the subjective measure of how much risk an investor can absorb emotionally with his or her investment. Each advisor and client needs to frankly appraise exactly how much risk the client can tolerate—emotionally and financially—in his or her investments. Right up until the crash of 2008–09, many individuals did not recognize the old maxim "a rising tide lifts all boats," referring in this case to the buoyant days before the crash.

Not all financial crises are the same, however, and it can be difficult for advisors and clients to spot the signs and understand the true nature of the risk of a particular investment or strategy. In fact, using the word "crash" for what happened is arguable; some say that the events did not resemble earlier market crashes, such as those in 1929 and 1987. Those crashes happened over short periods while the crisis of 2008–09 happened in waves. Moreover, while the actual meltdown involved mainly the financial sector, the panic selling occurred across almost all asset classes.

Those individuals who sold their assets in a panic overestimated their risk tolerance when the markets provided good returns before the crisis, and found to their dismay that their real tolerance was much lower than they had thought.

In order to avoid a mismatch between risk tolerance and the nature of the investments they suggest to their clients, advisors should walk investors through a self-examination that focuses on several questions:

- Do sharp portfolio swings trouble you?
- If your portfolio declined tomorrow by 15 percent would you lose sleep?
- Would that decrease have a major effect on your financial health?
- If the portfolio declined tomorrow by 15 percent and you considered the decline temporary, would you still feel a strong temptation to sell the depreciating assets?
- If the decline appeared permanent, would you have lost too much maneuvering room in your finances and have to make major sacrifices?
- Would the decline have an irreparable effect on your plans for your beneficiaries?
- If you lost your job or business tomorrow, would you have to liquidate investments to pay ongoing expenses?

If a client answers "yes" to all or most of these questions, he or she has a low threshold for risk and volatility and needs to redefine his or her risk tolerance and the structure of his or her finances.

Some advisors and investors look for a perfect investment combination or tool, when in fact a mixture will most often produce the best results. Unfortunately, advisors and clients may find it easier to narrow their views than to build an understanding of all options and determine a suitable combination of them.

Several more promising strategies for coping with volatility can include increasing liquidity, opting for more conservative investments, avoiding sector funds with narrow mandates, reducing exposure to troubled equity markets and increasing exposure to blue-chip stocks.

Ultimately, however, both investors who have become accustomed to volatility and those who have become emotionally insulated from it can become receptive to increased investment in emerging markets and starting or increasing their investments in frontier markets. One method of establishing an exposure to inherently volatile asset classes such as emerging and frontier markets for investors is using dividend-paying stocks with income that reduces volatility as well as addressing some investors' income needs. An advisor who truly believes in his or her rapport with clients can work to educate clients on emerging and frontier market investing issues such as non-correlation and long-term horizons.

COPING WITH INCREASED RELIANCE ON FINANCIAL ADVISORS

For individuals or institutions interested in emerging or frontier markets, coping with the new reality will mean turning more than ever to a professional advisor or advisors, according to Jim Ruta, a consultant to advisors, and professional speaker.[1] Ruta proposes that making the most of the lessons of the recovery means an altered advisor–client relationship.

For some that will mean a new or renewed trust in professional advisors. Broadly speaking, individuals fall into one of two categories in their attitudes toward professional financial advisors. Some feel that they want and need professional advice more than ever and appreciate the value of professional financial advice, while others feel that "the professionals" let them down during the financial crisis.

Many of the individuals in the latter group understand that the forces that led to the crisis exploded outside their grasp and beyond what any advisor could have anticipated. However, they believe that their advisors should have communicated more frequently during the darkest days of the crisis.

Several cartoonists at the time captured this predicament with cartoons that portrayed advisors hiding under their desks, refusing to answer their telephones, a comic image that Ruta sees as rooted in reality. "That isn't so far-fetched—I know people who were figuratively hiding under their desks and would not take calls from clients," he recalls.

Now, advisors and clients work—or should work—with new rules in what Ruta describes as a "reset" of the relationship. Arguably, this could become more important within the context of emerging and frontier market investing, as successful investing in an unfamiliar area helps disillusioned investors regain faith in an advisor's value. An advisor's role goes beyond increasing wealth and includes wealth protection. "My job is not so much to help you get rich. My job is to help you not be poor," Ruta says, paraphrasing what some advisors now tell clients at the outset of a working

---

[1]Personal interview with Al Emid during the research and writing of this book in 2012.

relationship. The advisor who defines that part of the mandate at the outset has taken the first step in a strong and genuine engagement, Ruta continues.

"People think the first step in the financial planning process is to set goals and objectives or to find facts [...] or to think about the future," Ruta says. Instead, he notes, the real first step is engagement.

Clearly defining the client's risk tolerance, as we explained in the previous section, is another step. "One of the things that the crash proved is that people are very bad self-assessors of their risk tolerance," Ruta says, explaining that the crisis left many individuals who had overestimated their risk tolerance "whimpering in corners" at their investment losses or looking for someone to blame.

Since individuals can misjudge their own risk tolerance and ability to accept risk, a wise advisor needs to work with them to balance wealth creation with wealth preservation. Today, this is called "behavioral finance."

"It turns out that return *of* your money is every bit as important as return *on* your money," Ruta says. Engagement flows from understanding what the advisor will do, how he or she will do it and what the expected benefits are.

Most advisors explain the risk/reward paradigm, meaning the higher the risk, the greater the potential reward. Now, in this fragile recovery, a client also needs grounding in the risk/loss paradigm.

That means taking measures to avoid losses in the event of another crisis during the portfolio-construction process. As one example, social media stocks may become the next costly bubble and those accepting this belief should reduce or eliminate exposure to this investment category. In the context of emerging market and frontier market investments, it means restricting those investments to funds that the client can leave untouched for at least five years or more.

Making the most of the recovery also means dispensing with some of the old rules that have become obsolete. For example, in earlier years, an advisor would have recommended that a client approaching retirement get out of equities and go into a stable investment such as bonds. Now, the continued low-interest environment of the recovery means that individuals need continued involvement in equities at all ages as otherwise they will not keep up with the drain caused by taxes and inflation.

The very nature of the relationship has changed and a power shift has taken place, in Ruta's estimation. Before financial information became so freely available on the Internet, radio, television and in the print media a financial advisor had broad knowledge of all financial matters and issues to a degree not available to the client. Now, clients have access to financial planning software and unlimited financial information on the Internet and from other sources. Moreover, as well as increased access, investors' panic at dropping portfolio values and disappointment with "professional" advice likely drives their interest in obtaining more financial information.

In the context of emerging market and frontier market investing, the increased access to information means that the client may have formed impressions of these countries and markets before the advisor has had an opportunity to explain them. This fact, in turn, has led to a demystification of financial planning processes and issues; the individual can understand and therefore exert more control over his or her finances, creating a power shift in the financial planning process. "Consumers can now know what to expect and what to ask for. [...] That's the power shift," Ruta says.

The power shift represents a quantum leap from what Ruta calls "the dump and pray" approach, referring to clients who dump all of their financial records, assets and issues on an advisor and then just pray that everything will work out.

The sense of burden felt by most people today just from their own work and family responsibilities leaves little time for sufficient knowledge of the increasingly complex financial markets in general and certainly of the increasingly intricate emerging markets and frontier markets. That, in turn, increases reliance on a well-versed financial advisor.

In this newly reset relationship, clients expect more direct and personal communications from their advisors, so that the cartoonists no longer have lack of communication as a comic foil. Before the onset of electronic communication, many advisors would call clients regularly; they may now sidestep telephone calls in favor of text messages and emails. Advisors should anticipate that clients will expect a communication plan, spelling out how often that can expect to hear from the advisor and how the communication will take place, whether by telephone, email or other means, and design such a plan accordingly.

That leaves the advisor looking for the imaginary line between respecting the power shift and what Ruta calls "optioneering" or detailing a long list of options from which clients are expected to make their own decisions. "Optioneering is a mistake today and a problem for clients," Ruta says. "Clients deserve to have advisors knowledgeable enough about them, the markets and the investments to be able to recommend the best course of action. Clients deserve leadership from their advisors."

Still, the reset—where it has occurred—does not reduce the judgment and expertise retail and institutional clients so greatly need from their advisors.

The equation is not complicated. Simply put, when an advisor proposes investments to a client, his or her ability to frame the proposed investment—whether a traditional asset or global fund with a large frontier market component—within the context of the role it will play in the client's overall investment picture will likely reassure an otherwise hesitant client.

For the advisor looking to introduce clients to frontier market investing, this strategy imposes a layer of discipline on portfolio recommendations and may act as a restraint against having more specialty holdings than necessary. Building a purpose-driven portfolio requires that each component play a role in getting the client closer to where they need to go, and the importance of carefully demonstrating the role becomes an integral part of the recommendation procedure.

At the same time, while clients have become more knowledgeable, many still want their advisors to indicate their own convictions, to drive the proverbial stake into the ground and declare their beliefs. It's a matter of being an actual "advisor." In spite of the apparent obligation to provide a client with all available options, a strong advisor will still indicate that he or she considers one option better than the others so that a client does not leave the office wondering, "What the heck was he saying?"

The possibility of that head-shaking can increase with the complexities of faraway markets. Suggesting to a client that having (for example) a 5 percent exposure to frontier markets will round out the portfolio by giving exposure to faster-growing and cheaper global markets and allow the client to take advantage of their lack of correlation with developed markets clearly indicates the benefits likely to result from following this advice.

Where it exists, a client's sophistication and grasp of emerging markets can provide a platform for the move to frontier markets. This may mean stating the premise of this book to a client: frontier markets are now what emerging markets were previously—underdeveloped and experiencing rapid economic growth, spurred on by globalization.

It may also mean reviewing and explaining the low correlation between frontier markets, emerging markets and developed markets, meaning that events in one category do not necessarily affect investment returns in another category and also meaning that the categories are somewhat fluid. The changing status of some countries can further confuse the issue. In one of the most notable changes, Argentina slid from being a developed nation in the first half of the 20th century to an emerging market and now is classified as a frontier market by the compilers of indices such as MSCI and S&P.

"The relationship between the three has changed as emerging economies have become more developed, and new countries and companies have been added to the list of frontier markets," explains Daniel Morillo, PhD, writing on the iShares Blog.[2]

Emerging markets have become correlated with each other and more correlated with developed economies. In the last 10 years, the MSCI

---

[2]Daniel Morillo, "Rethinking Risk in Frontier Markets," iShares Blog, October 16, 2012. http://isharesblog.com/blog/2012/10/16/rethinking-risk-in-frontier-markets.

Emerging Markets Index has had a correlation of around 90 percent with the MSCI Developed Markets Index, compared with around 70 percent in the 10 years previous to that.[3]

By comparison, "frontier markets have remained reasonably different from one another. Their economies are not as integrated into global markets, and they are subject to a wide range of idiosyncratic local economic and political dynamics."[4]

Moreover, the overall correlation between frontier markets and developed markets is lower than the correlation of emerging markets to developed markets, averaging less than 50 percent apart from the period of the financial crisis of 2008–09, Morillo points out on the same blog. Indeed, "since January 2008, the correlation between the MSCI Emerging Markets Index and the MSCI Developed Markets Index was 92 percent compared with 78 percent for the [MSCI] Frontier Markets Index."[5]

The new relationship between advisors and clients may also mean having more candid conversations with clients about costs. Some advisors believe that their clients would prefer to get emerging or frontier market exposure through shares in Coca-Cola and other multinational equities rather than more varied exposure through a global fund, believing that they save on management costs.

However, in such a case, the client may not see the risks of taking this approach, including the fact that these equities do not derive (in most cases) as much as even 50 percent of revenues from the frontier market, leaving the remainder to come from low-growth and saturated development markets. That, in effect, creates a mix of risks. Furthermore, the majority of these multinationals' performance will be due to their domestic market rather than the faster-growing emerging and frontier markets.

That leads us back to the reason investors need exposure to frontier and emerging markets in the first place. One possible objection from clients may be the perceived high cost of using a specialized frontier market fund, where the management expense ratio (MER) may be 2.5 per cent or more, which leads clients to prefer exposure through familiar and lower-cost vehicles such as global multinationals.

However, as noted above, these seemingly "cheaper" alternatives are largely correlated with their domestic markets, removing the benefit of volatility reduction, and as will be apparent when we examine their track records in Chapter 10, actively managed funds have managed to beat the

---

[3] Ibid.
[4] Ibid.
[5] Ibid.

relevant index even with the disadvantage of their high fees, demonstrating that frontier markets are an asset class where active managers do add value.

Clients may also not realize that where the advisor works on a fee-based basis, this approach may not make any difference in total costs.

Perhaps in this case a narrow view actually means more costs in the end.

All this does not mean becoming a financial planning Pollyanna. Globalization has a downside: changes in distant markets can affect a country's own. If growth slows or becomes negative in developed markets, frontier market countries will sell fewer exports into them, possibly slowing job growth and the rise of the middle-class consumer in these countries. If nervous Western bankers pull back on lending to frontier markets, or if American jobs are repatriated to the United States in substantially larger numbers than currently, frontier markets' actual growth may fall below analysts' more optimistic projections.

In the same way that emerging markets did not necessarily suit risk-averse investors several years back, frontier markets may not appeal to risk-averse investors or those who do not have a long-term outlook—and advisors must ensure that their clients are suitable for frontier market investing.

CONVINCING HESITANT CLIENTS

Retail Clients

Although some clients may be initially mistrustful of investing in developing nations, emerging market investments have an unshakeable place in all portfolios, according to Charles Stanley, a 23-year veteran of financial services and wealth manager at the La Jolla, California, office of Trovina LLC, a wealth management firm.[6] Trovina has a strong belief in emerging markets, fully integrates them into client portfolios and plans to eventually participate in frontier markets.

Stanley convinces his clients of his views by defining a comprehensive portfolio as a highly diversified construct of domestic, international, developed and emerging markets and stating that each should be included in every client's holdings. "Our position, basically, is you take risk where you get paid for risk, and if you're not going to get paid for it you don't take it," he says. Trovina uses the fixed-income portion of the portfolio to reduce its

---

[6]Personal interview with Al Emid during the research and writing of this book in 2012.

volatility and believes that there is a risk of negative return with durations longer than five years.

Most of Stanley's clients are retired or approaching retirement, and so he does reduce the exposure to equities over time. "That way we still have the advantage of the more risky asset classes like emerging markets," he says.

For its major fund supplier to include a country in its offerings, the sub-advisor will investigate key factors such as the liquidity, both in terms of the equity and at the exchange level. The checklist of a fund management company looking at investing in a particular market will also include market capitalization and regulation listing requirements, settlement practices, political risks, the existence of repatriation restrictions and the impact of taxes on yields.

An advisor analyzing how to persuade his or her client to consider investing in frontier markets might follow one of the strategies used by Trovina, which when it eventually includes frontier market investments, would likely accomplish that through a global or emerging market fund, Stanley suggests. It sees that strategy as providing more diversification than a fund investing solely in frontier markets. That move would ensure liquidity of the fund holdings, he continues. Trovina's fund supplier would begin by adding the frontier market or markets into its emerging markets funds. This strategy would reduce the perceived risk of investing in frontier markets, owing to the lack of correlation between emerging and frontier markets, and allow investors to accept more controlled risk, and is followed by such fund management groups as Tradewinds of Los Angeles, CA and Russell Investments, who include a percentage of frontier markets in their emerging market funds.

Advisors should ensure that they, like Trovina, explain their philosophy to the client and have a firm set of investment principles—instead of acting on unconscious drivers of investor behavior, such as fear and greed, at the beginning of the relationship.

Institutional Clients

Effective strategies for advisors to use to recruit investors to frontier markets can operate differently with institutional clients, as opposed to retail clients, according to Timothy Morris, a nine-year veteran of financial services, vice-president of J.P. Morgan Asset Management and a client portfolio manager to institutions and foundations.[7] Morris's role involves working

---

[7]Personal interview with Al Emid during the research and writing of this book in 2012.

with the company's emerging market equity team and representing J.P. Morgan to institutional clients, including public pensions, endowments and foundations across North America. Morris sees countries that are not classified as "developed" as offering a potential investment in the emerging market or frontier market categories. Like many analysts and experts, he views frontier markets as a subset of emerging markets. In practice, this means advising these institutions and their pension fund clients on whether and how they should increase or initiate investments in emerging markets or frontier markets.

For example, the Ontario Municipal Employees Retirement System (OMERS), a provincial Canadian pension plan with a global view of investments, had a 5 percent weight in emerging markets in its public equity portfolio at the end of 2011, equivalent to C$538 million (US$531.1 million) or approximately 1 percent of its total assets. The Ontario Teachers' Pension Plan had a 3.7 percent weight in the MSCI Emerging Markets ETF, worth C$1,918 million (US$1,894 million) or just over 1.5 percent of its total assets at the end of 2011. The Canada Pension Plan had 9.6 percent in emerging markets in its public equity portfolio at the end of 2011, or 5.1 percent of its total assets.

Major public sector pension plans such as these can work with longer time horizons than other institutional investors such as mutual funds or hedge funds with shorter-term objectives. While at present their exposure to developing markets is confined to established emerging markets, for reasons of liquidity among other considerations, it is reasonable to assume they will gradually initiate positions in frontier markets as the latter grow large enough for the pension plans to obtain positions that would make a difference to their overall performance.

Working with institutional clients requires convincing multiple levels of decision makers. In a typical scenario, there may be one or more levels of decision makers and decision making.

Morris and his colleagues will work with the person or persons within an organization designated to supervise existing investment opportunities and to investigate new ones. At a later stage in the investment process, perhaps when approaching an investment decision or manager selection, the group will hold what they may call a "semi-finals" or "finals" meeting with two or more potential managers. The involvement of these groups reflects the degree of discretion placed by clients in the investment team and— where appropriate—outside "gatekeepers" such as pension consultants. It is estimated that more than 80 percent of institutions in North America use outside consultants to advise them on asset allocation and the choice of third-party managers.[8]

---

[8] Guardian Capital Inc., Annual Report, 2012.

Typically, these investments are placed in pooled funds, the institutional version of the retail mutual fund. The advisor may suggest pooled funds to clients for several reasons, among them the reduced costs of investment management fees, custodian and dealing costs due to economies of scale.

That preference increases in emerging market and frontier market investing, given the variety of local laws and oversight, restrictions and requirements for registration, Morris explains.

"The requirements for registration in the individual markets in order to own securities are quite onerous [...] in overseas markets," Morris says. The alternative that an advisor may propose to a client is a separate account, which it would own directly and which J.P. Morgan or another company would manage on its behalf. That becomes expensive in terms of custody costs and time consumed, and an advisor should make institutional investors aware of the difference to costs between using pooled funds and the alternative, showing clients the value that they bring to the relationship.

Generally, a pension plan with more than US$200 million in investable assets may become a candidate for a standalone investment fund, according to Morris. An advisor might encounter assets of this magnitude with a client that is a medium-sized corporation or not-for-profit institution. Nonetheless, the higher transaction and administration costs involved in the less efficient and liquid emerging and particularly frontier markets, including bid-offer spreads that can often exceed 200 basis points and in some cases 300 basis points, mean that advisors should recommend that all but the largest institutions should use pooled funds to gain access.

The exposure to emerging market investments varies by size and type of plan and by the sophistication of its managers. Endowments and foundations are somewhat more aggressive, often qualifying as "earlier movers" in this category, due at least in part to their longer investment horizon and fewer variables in financial commitments.

Pension funds might have less flexibility in this area than endowments and foundations since pension funds have an obligation for existing pension payments to members. The scale of projected payments may act as a restriction on aggressive investing, and is something of which a successful institutional advisor should be well aware and make recommendations accordingly.

Among other hurdles in the proposal process, Morris and others encounter the perception that emerging markets involve greater risk than other equity asset classes, including periods of general risk aversion that are not what he terms "emerging-markets specific."

Generally, institutional investors tend to be less likely to react to jumps in political or financial risk than retail investors and overreaction by small investors can provide buying opportunities.

Another hurdle in the proposal process involves an institution's low level of familiarity with emerging market equity investing. "We sometimes need to educate trustees or boards (about) how we address concerns such as corporate governance [...] financial disclosure and issues like that which are all things that any equity investor should be focused on," Morris says. Advisors should make investors aware that the quality of information and company management in emerging markets has improved over the past decade.

American depository receipts and global depository receipts of emerging and frontier market companies, whether held directly or through a fund, provide another reassurance for hesitant institutional clients. "In either case, when they list those depository receipts they also comply with all of the same disclosure requirements (and) accounting rules as any other company that lists on that exchange. So they're meeting all of the same requirements that any developed market company is meeting," Morris explains. Indeed, as well as applying to the companies listed in the United States or on European markets, that requirement indirectly pressures companies with which these frontier- and emerging-market companies compete for capital to meet similar standards, Morris says. An advisor's explanation of this proviso tends to ease investors' concerns and satisfy external auditors.

Institutional plans that have five years or more of successful history of emerging market investing and have continued to increase their exposure over time tend to become receptive to frontier markets. "Typically what you find in those settings is that they will begin to use what we would characterize as a core and satellite approach where the satellites may be, for instance, a manager that specifically focuses on frontier markets or small cap names within the asset class," Morris explains.

An advisor looking to provide context, color and comfort with frontier market equities to investors can also cite the scale of frontier markets. "Few people realize how big the so-called frontier markets are. If you take them as a group, they represent about 15 percent of the world GDP today," says Marko Dimitrijevic, founder and chief investment officer of Miami, Florida–based Everest Capital LLC, which currently has an optimistic view of Nigeria, Saudi Arabia, Colombia and Bangladesh.[9]

The "scale" reassurance seems powerful: "And 15 percent, to put it in context, it's larger than the Chinese economy. So, when people focus on 'China, China, China—what's China doing and how's China growing?' China is about 13 percent of the world economy. The frontier markets that

---

[9]Interview with FundFire, a *Financial Times* service, December 20, 2012.

we're talking about, the smaller emerging markets, represent 15 percent of the world economy," Dimitrijevic says.[10]

Certainly, the advisor looking to increase client interest in frontier investing has a wealth of precedents with which to give clients reassurance. A report issued in 2012 by Pyramis Global Advisors, a Fidelity Investments company, states: "Globally, 24 percent of investors surveyed said they will increase allocations to emerging market debt over the next few years."[11]

Referring to the report, Charles Morrison, the company's president of fixed income, says that the future looks positive for emerging and frontier market investment. "With historically low yields in many safe-haven bond markets and increased credit risk in a number of European countries, it is not surprising that many institutional investors are beginning to look beyond their borders," he says in a statement.[12]

TAKEAWAYS

1. The advisor's post-crisis role has become more difficult and varied, even without considering emerging and frontier market investing. Adding the complexities of those investments to the mix clearly adds to an advisor's challenges.
2. The advisor's role—important in any investment, at any time— becomes even more important in emerging and frontier markets.
3. Whether working with retail or institutional clients, advisors may have to spend more time and effort in educating clients on the investment potential of emerging and frontier markets than with more traditional investments.
4. Less experienced or sophisticated clients may accept frontier market investing more readily after success with emerging markets.
5. Emerging and frontier market investing increases the advisor's obligation to explain basic terminology such as American depository receipts and global depository receipts and the assurances built into them.

---

[10] Ibid.
[11] Pyramis Global Advisors, survey announcement, December 6, 2012.
[12] Ibid.

Different Ways to Invest in Frontier Markets: ETFs, ADRs, Local Stocks and Closed-end Mutual Funds

Every financial investment has at least four major aspects requiring careful consideration: its place in a portfolio, its design features, its profitability and its accessibility. We have set out the investment case for frontier markets as an asset class and described the markets—and market opportunities—in detail in earlier chapters.

We believe that frontier markets, the "emerging" emerging markets, should form part of a well-rounded portfolio. Frontier markets will likely repeat the excellent performance of the developing economies that have doubled investors' money over the last decade.

However, even if frontier markets do not fully replicate that performance, their low correlation with both developed and emerging markets and low valuations mean that they should form part of any equity portfolio, as they will reduce its overall volatility and produce good absolute levels of return.

Given that concept, as a professional advisor working with institutional or retail clients you may ask, "What is the best way to invest in frontier markets?" In this chapter, we answer this question with definite opinions on the most and least advisable approaches.

Let us start in reverse order and save our preferred method of gaining exposure until the end of the chapter. Looking first at the methods available in a developed economy such as North America, Western Europe or Australasia, and in reverse order of popularity, they would be as follows:

1. Exchange-traded funds (ETFs)
2. Regional funds investing in specific regions, such as the Middle East and North Africa (often referred to as MENA funds), Africa, or Latin America

3. Sector funds, investing in specific sectors, such as telecommunications, health care or technology
4. Single-country funds investing in a single nation such as South Africa or Vietnam
5. Individual equities in multinational companies with large exposures to emerging and frontier markets listed on major exchanges, such as KFC-operator Yum! Brands, spirits company Diageo PLC, consumer product group Unilever or emerging market bank Standard Chartered PLC
6. American depository receipts (ADRs) and global depository receipts (GDRs), which are United States–listed and Europe-listed instruments giving exposure to individual companies in frontier markets, such as Egypt-based mobile phone operator Orascom Telecom Holding S.A.E.; Viña Concha y Toro S.A., a Chilean wine company; or the Philippine Long Distance Telephone Company
7. Global frontier market funds—both traditional mutual funds and closed-end funds

Each of these approaches has advantages and disadvantages.

EXCHANGE-TRADED FUNDS

Exchange-traded funds (ETFs) have become one of the most popular methods of gaining access to market and asset classes over the last decade. Their popularity stems from their low cost, transparency and liquidity—all desirable characteristics in any investment. They also deliver few surprises and that certainly provides another desirable characteristic. As an investment professional, you know that you will receive the return of the underlying index less the moderate expenses of running the fund.

Supporters of using ETFs also point out that studies demonstrate that between two-thirds and three-quarters of actively managed mutual funds fail to beat the index. They argue that investors should instead buy a low-cost index product such as an ETF and put the investment away to provide their exposure to market and asset classes.

This approach requires several caveats. First, it assumes that stock market indices will deliver positive returns over the long term, which has historically been the case during the secular bull markets of 1921–1929, 1949–1966 and 1982–1999. However, as we have seen during the last decade, developed markets have long periods when indices and the index-linked products based on them do not provide positive returns. In that scenario, owning an ETF provides you with a low-cost, liquid and transparent way to make zero or negative returns in nominal terms, even before factoring in inflation.

Secondly, with index or index-based investments such as ETFs, the vast majority consist of various stocks weighted by market capitalization. This means that the largest positions have far more influence on the performance of the index than the smaller positions, and that the more the stock price of the largest companies rises, the greater their weight in the index-based investment. That can lead to anomalous situations such as the S&P/TSX Composite Index in 2000 having Canadian telecom stock Nortel Networks as its largest component, comprising almost 35 percent of the index at the time. Subsequently Nortel fell over 95 percent in value in the next two years and eventually ended up filing for bankruptcy.

This anomaly defeats the purpose of indexing, which is to achieve diversification in a low-cost and simple fashion. It also runs counter to what both intuition and numerous studies have demonstrated: selling stocks with rising valuations and buying stocks with falling or constant valuations is the simplest and most successful way to generate outperformance. Buying market capitalization–weighted index products such as ETFs requires investors to do the exact opposite. The ETF is required to buy stocks with rising valuations and sell stocks with falling valuations. As a result, market capitalization–weighted ETFs have tended to underperform index-linked products that used a different methodology such as equal-weight or fundamentally based ETFs.

Since we believe that frontier markets will appreciate substantially over time, this objection matters less than with other types of ETFs. Even if market capitalization–weighted ETFs are an inefficient way to gain exposure to a market, they can still deliver excellent returns as happened with the MSCI Emerging Markets ETF (NYSE: EEM) over the last decade. Anyone who bought EEM at the end of 2001, after the traumatic events of 9/11, and continued holding it through the financial crisis of 2008–09 would have received a return of 89.4 percent a decade later.

However, the other negative point about market capitalization–weighted instruments such as ETFs applies here. These instruments concentrate on a few large stocks. That characteristic both defeats the objective of diversification and makes these funds vulnerable to underperformance when new companies become listed on the stock exchange and available for trading. The ETF will eventually be able to buy enough shares in the new listing to represent that company's weight in the index, but only over time. It will also need to sell down its existing holdings to reduce their weightings, which could depress the index and the fund's performance.

This structural disadvantage becomes massively compounded when considering frontier market ETFs. Given the undeveloped, concentrated and illiquid nature of stock markets in developing economies, the issues of overconcentration in a few countries and stocks are so great as to almost defeat the actual purpose of using an ETF. The plain vanilla MSCI Frontier Markets Index is comprised of the 141 largest companies adjusted for their free float in the 25 countries that comprise the index, which have an average market capitalization of $3 billion.

However, owing to the more developed and liquid stock markets in the Middle East region, the five Gulf Cooperation Council (GCC) countries make up 57 percent of the total index, with Kuwait on its own comprising more than 30 percent. The other 20 countries, which include such populous and economically important countries as Argentina, Bangladesh, Kazakhstan, Kenya, Nigeria, Pakistan, Ukraine and Vietnam, account for only 43 percent of the index.

The MSCI Frontier Markets 100 Index ETF (FM) was launched in 2012 to provide a representative and more easily replicable alternative to the broader index and includes 100 of the largest and most liquid constituents of the parent index. Back-tested data demonstrate that the MSCI Frontier Markets 100 Index does indeed closely follow the broader index, with returns of 15.2 percent vs. 16.8 percent over 1 year, 7.2 percent per annum vs. 6.8 percent p.a. over 3 years and −9.7 percent p.a. vs. −9.2 percent p.a. over 5 years.

The small difference in performance between the two indices over the different time periods indicates that they closely track each other and that buying the Frontier Markets 100 ETF should provide investors with virtually the same performance as the wider index.

The problem of overconcentration is almost as great, however, with the top 10 holdings comprising 40.9 percent of the fund, and Kuwait, Qatar and the UAE respectively making up 28.3 percent, 16.7 percent and 10.9 percent of the Frontier Markets 100 ETF. The only other countries to have weights above 4 percent are Nigeria (13.3 percent) and Pakistan (4.4 percent). Thus, almost 75 percent of the ETF consists of only five countries, three of which are wealthy GCC states with very small populations, not what investors think of when considering investing in frontier economies.

The problem worsens with single-country ETFs. For example, two new Deutsche Bank ETFs, based on the MSCI indices for Bangladesh and Pakistan and launched in mid-2012, had 60 percent and 24 percent respectively in their top five holdings. The db (Deutsche Bank) x-trackers MSCI Pakistan IM Index ETF has 22 percent in one holding—Oil and Gas Development (OGD). Regardless of OGD's investment merits, having almost a quarter of a supposedly diversified fund in one stock is the "Nortel in 2000" situation repeated, with the attendant vulnerability to company-specific problems.

Therefore, while ETFs appear to be the easiest and lowest-cost way to access frontier markets, we would caution advisors and investors against merely going out and buying market capitalization–weighted frontier market ETFs. While frontier markets are likely to continue to appreciate, giving investors attractive absolute returns, we believe there are better and more effective ways of gaining exposure. The same caveat applies even more strongly to regional or single-country ETFs, where the concentration issue is much more of a problem.

Furthermore, as with emerging market ETFs, the cost is not especially low. Management expense ratios for these funds run between 0.7 percent and 0.85 percent, as compared with the 0.15 percent or even below 0.1 percent charges for ETFs in the liquid and efficient developed markets of North America.

If there were to be an equal-weight emerging market ETF, with each position starting at the same weight and automatically being rebalanced every six months, as is the case for a few developed market ETFs, then both the overconcentration issue and the obligation to buy more expensive companies while selling cheaper ones would be addressed. However, the liquidity issues for many frontier markets make this a difficult proposition. There is the Rydex MSCI Emerging Markets Equal Weight ETF, but none for the frontier markets.

Another potential indexing method involves looking at the companies' underlying performance in terms of revenues and profits. That is known as "fundamental" indexing, and both back tests and the record of accomplishment of funds using this approach indicate that it addresses the valuation concern. The PowerShares FTSE RAFI Emerging Markets Portfolio (PXH) uses this approach, but unfortunately not in frontier markets.

Apart from the iShares MSCI Frontier Markets 100 ETF, the Guggenheim Frontier Markets ETF (FRN) invests in New York– and London-listed ADRs and GDRs. That leaves it heavily weighted toward South America, with over 70 percent of the fund consisting of companies from Chile (37.2 percent), Colombia (15.2 percent), Argentina (10.1 percent) and Peru (8.3 percent). Only Argentina is included in the MSCI Frontier Markets Index, the other three countries being classified as emerging markets. Therefore, what is described as a frontier markets ETF actually has over one-third of its assets in one of the wealthier emerging markets (Chile) and another 24 percent in two emerging markets (Colombia and Peru) that are included only in some versions of the MSCI Frontier Markets Index.

There are also regional frontier market ETFs with a narrower focus, such as the Market Vectors Africa Index ETF (AFK), the Market Vectors Gulf States Index ETF (MES), the iShares MSCI Emerging Markets Latin America (EEML) and the PowerShares MENA Frontier Countries ETF (PMNA), which cover specific geographical areas. There are also the S&P SPDR Emerging Asia Pacific (GMF), Emerging Middle East and Africa

(GAF) and Emerging Europe (GUR). Finally, there are a few single-country emerging and frontier market ETFs.

The only indisputably frontier market ETF at time of writing is the Market Vectors Vietnam ETF (VNM), but five of the smaller emerging markets, known as "crossover markets" are included in the MSCI Frontier Emerging Markets Index (uncapped). These are Colombia, Egypt, Morocco, Peru and the Philippines, which comprise 53 percent of the index owing to their much larger stock market capitalizations. There are single-country ETFs for four of them. Colombia has two, Global X FTSE Colombia 20 ETF (GXG) and Market Vectors Colombia ETF (COLX), while the others have one each: Egypt has Market Vectors Egypt ETF (EGPT), Peru has iShares MSCI All Peru Capped Index Fund (EPU) and the Philippines has iShares MSCI the Philippines Investable Market Index Fund (EPHE).

Therefore, buying an ETF such as the iShares MSCI Frontier Markets to gain exposure to global frontier markets, while apparently a logical decision, in fact leaves the investor with a concentrated exposure to a few small, wealthy Middle Eastern markets, not what most people would anticipate when purchasing this investment vehicle. Even those regional ETFs such as the Market Vectors Africa and Middle East and single-country ETFs such as the Market Vectors Colombia, Egypt and Vietnam funds and the iShares Peru and Philippines funds will find that the top 10 holdings form at least 55 percent of the portfolio, meaning a heavy concentration in a few large stocks, many of which are in the same industry. Investors should take care to do their research into what is in the supposedly diversified ETF they are considering, and whether it truly reflects those aspects of frontier markets to which they wish to gain exposure.

REGIONAL FUNDS

Funds investing in specific geographical areas are often the first pooled vehicles for investors who become interested in a specific area. They are usually described as "story funds": the promoters identify an area that has gained public attention or is perceived as the "next big thing" and launch products to take advantage of demand.

We do not mean that there is no truth in the story. In Hong Kong in the early 1990s, residents who had been there for a while got used to meeting enthusiastic foreign investors, usually from the United States, who came back from a few days in China boundlessly enthusiastic about the potential of the Chinese market. "After all," these converts to the China story declaimed, "There are 1.3 billion Chinese. If we could just sell them all a soda, or a pair of running shoes, think how much money we could make!"

The listener's sober response to this enthusiasm would have been to point out that there were only about 250 million middle-class Chinese living in the coastal provinces and cities, and they were the only people in China who could afford such luxuries. Secondly, they would have noted that the cost and difficulties of transportation within China made it very difficult to reach many potential consumers. And lastly, the listener would have enquired why the Chinese government would have been willing to allow its citizens to spend so much of their disposable income on foreign companies' products unless it received some benefits from the process, whether as taxes, employment for its people or joint ownership. As it turned out, the anticipated profits very often did not materialize and profitability of foreign companies in China has not been especially impressive. Indeed, investors should be aware that rapid GDP growth does not automatically translate into superior stock market returns.

In fact, countries such as China illustrate that the interests of minority shareholders are often secondary to other social and political aims, such as absorbing the 12–15 million migrants from rural provinces who arrive in China's coastal cities every year and have to be found employment, or building up foreign exchange reserves. At the time of writing, China's Shanghai A Share Index was still well below its all-time high, which was achieved in 2007, and has been a notable underperformer among major global indices over the last couple of years. Similarly, in such frontier markets as Pakistan, Nigeria and Vietnam, the move of several million rural laborers every year into the teeming cities of Karachi, Lagos and Ho Chi Minh City present the governments of these countries with many problems of absorption, overstraining their existing infrastructure and providing the breeding ground for possible civil unrest. Investors should not become too excited about the size of the possible market opportunities in such developing economies, remembering that products still have to be able to reach their eventual consumers, regardless of how fast their incomes are growing.

More importantly from an investor's point of view, however, was the issue of how to gain investment access to these rapidly growing middle classes. When Morgan Stanley's chief investment strategist, Barton Biggs, returned from China in late 1993 and famously declared himself "maximum bullish"[1] on China, his suggested list of companies to invest in consisted largely of Hong Kong conglomerates, trading houses and property companies. There simply were not many available ways to access the Chinese economy, as foreigners were restricted to owning what were known as B shares in Chinese-listed companies.

---

[1] Recapped in obituary of Barton Biggs, *Financial Times*, July 16, 2012.

Meanwhile local Chinese investors drove A shares, restricted to Chinese domestic investors, to new heights. It was only when the Chinese government started listing minority stakes in its blue-chip, state-owned enterprises such as the state oil companies, toll roads and telecom stocks in the mid-1990s that foreign investors began to have some choice of domestically oriented stocks. Even if the case for investment is valid, such as accelerating GDP-growth driven by rapidly growing youthful populations moving from the countryside to the cities, finding ways to allow investors to share in this growth can be more difficult than many people might imagine. This is due both to the underdeveloped state of local stock markets resulting in few investable companies being available for investors and the absence of physical infrastructure to allow goods and services to be delivered to potential consumers. Those companies that are perceived to be participating in the strong growth thus are bid up to expensive valuations owing to a supply/demand imbalance.

Thus, regional or industry funds are usually launched after stock markets have already risen sharply, meaning most of the good news is already reflected in the share prices. In some cases, the story may not develop as anticipated, as many Japanese investors discovered when they bought European funds after the fall of the Berlin Wall in 1989.

Instead of the expected European boom, Germany's reunification led to punishingly high interest rates to counteract the inflationary effect of converting East German Ostmarks at too high a valuation, and Europe went into a deep recession. That led to the collapse of the Exchange Rate Mechanism, the predecessor to the euro. Likewise, funds launched after South Africa emerged from apartheid in the mid-1990s did not prove to be great investments.

Therefore, as happened with Latin American and Asian funds in the late 1980s and early 1990s and Eastern European funds in the mid-2000s, regional frontier funds such as Middle East and North Africa (MENA) funds and sub-Saharan Africa funds launched in the last few years have not delivered tremendous returns for their owners. The Market Vectors Africa and Middle East Funds, launched in 2008, have returned −4.2 and −8.7 percent per annum through mid-2013. Focusing on only one region or industry also risks substantial erosion in value due to the contagion effect. In a crisis, investors will tend to lump all markets in a region together and condemn them all to the rubbish bin, regardless of the fact that the problems of Libya have very little to do with Turkey or that Nigeria is driven by very different factors than the Congo.

In another example, one only needs to think of the crisis in the Euro-zone, where the economic situation of Spain or Italy was much superior to that of Greece, yet all were put into the same category by frightened investors and saw their bond markets and ability to raise funds devastated. These were investment-grade European democracies familiar to most investors from personal experience. How much greater is the contagion effect in obscure countries that may be difficult to find on a map, where few, if any, foreign investors have visited or have any direct knowledge of the country?

Therefore, due to the shortage of suitable investments in the majority of developing markets and the tendency of these to become unduly expensive due to inflows of foreign capital in a short period, we would suggest that financial professionals and their clients treat regional funds with caution.

Moreover, early-stage emerging markets and frontier markets are extremely volatile and subject to a high degree of perceived political risk, although this can have an upside. The Arab Spring of 2010–11, which saw the replacement of long-standing regimes in North Africa and continues to have repercussions in the Persian Gulf and the Middle East, may eventually lead to the development of much more attractive investment opportunities in the region. However, when gun battles in capital cities appear on the nightly news, investors are understandably reluctant to risk their money there.

If investors are optimistic on the outlook for a particular region, as many well-informed professionals are about sub-Saharan Africa at the time of writing, then it is perfectly reasonable to maintain a long-term position in a regional fund, despite the caveats we have referred to in this and earlier sections. This should be undertaken with at least a five-year time horizon, and with a determination not to be worried by highly visible bad news, such as (in Africa) civil wars, the menace of HIV/AIDS, the threat of Islamic fundamentalism, hyperinflation or the break-up of certain countries. In the Middle East and North Africa, investors would be prepared to regard the overthrow of long-established regimes and the attendant bloodshed as the precursor of more investor-friendly regimes pursuing capitalist and free-market economic policies, and that Western interventions in the region would be confined to short, successful actions such as occurred in Libya in 2011.

As with global frontier funds and ETFs, investors in highly volatile developing markets must be prepared for a major sell-off, such as happened in 2008–09, at some stage in the next five years, caused either by accelerating economic growth and rising interest rates in developed markets or by the developing markets becoming overvalued due to an inflow of foreign capital driving up valuations in these countries' stock markets.

SECTOR FUNDS

Sector funds are another method of investing in emerging markets that has not yet spread to frontier markets because of the small number of sectors in many of these markets. At the time of writing there are several emerging market sector ETFs, including the EG Shares Emerging Market Consumer ETF (ECON) and Metals/Mining ETF (EMT) as well as the EG Shares Energy GEMS ETF (OGEM). Lastly, there is the PowerShares Global Emerging Markets Infrastructure ETF (PXR). All of these are almost entirely invested in emerging markets rather than frontier markets. However, all have the same issues of concentration and valuation that underpin our recommendation that advisors and investors not use regional or industry funds as a means of accessing frontier markets.

Those choosing this strategy must have sufficient confidence to stand the shock of a major sell-off in the frontier markets, which will undoubtedly occur in the next five years. Given the illiquid and volatile nature of these markets, their lack of correlation with both developed and emerging markets vanishes during financial crises, as was illustrated by the jump in correlations to over 0.6 during the global financial crisis in 2008–09. While diversified global frontier market funds will at least have the ability to change their weightings to increase their exposure to more defensive sectors and countries, single-industry and single-country funds have no such defense.

When the authorities in developed markets are sufficiently assured about deflation no longer being a concern and begin to raise interest rates, then the evidence of the last 20 years is that, as happened in 1994, 1997 and 2007, more volatile and economically leveraged markets such as the emerging and frontier markets will sell off, and sell off more than the developed markets, regardless of their superior fundamentals.

SINGLE-COUNTRY FUNDS

The arguments against regional funds apply even more strongly to single-country funds. While less likely to be driven by "story" investing, they do not even have the limited diversification benefit of different countries at different stages of development that provides modest protection from sell-offs in regional funds. In regional funds, good active managers may add value by underweighting countries at the wrong stage of the economic cycle or when culture and government are unfavorable and by overweighting those that look attractive.

Obviously, this is not the case in single-country funds, and while one could argue that active managers can under- and overweight different sectors within the country, frontier stock markets are normally not well diversified. There may be few, or no, defensive companies such as utilities and consumer products available in a specific frontier market.

In general, too, when frontier and emerging markets sell off, everything goes down at the same time. Most investors are either local individuals or foreign institutions, with no domestic long-term buyers such as pension funds and insurance companies to offset their selling of shares, as is the case in developed markets. That means that when emerging markets start falling, there is little to stop them.

There is also the unpleasant fact that sometimes we make mistakes. The country that we were convinced was destined to be successful and lead the region into the developed world may, for whatever reason, fail to achieve success.

Indeed, in the 1950s, the three Asian capitals that were the most prosperous and which had economies that appeared to be best positioned were Manila in the Philippines, Rangoon (now Yangon) in Burma (now Myanmar) and Colombo in Sri Lanka. At that time, no one would have given much chance at survival to Hong Kong (a British colonial possession next to a communist regime), South Korea (devastated by a fierce civil war and with an aggressive communist neighbor), Taiwan (under threat of invasion by China) or Singapore (a Chinese enclave between two resurgent states). They have survived and prospered in the meantime, and Hong Kong and Singapore have become the wealthiest Chinese societies in history.

That resulted from a two-part combination: the entrepreneurial culture of the overseas Chinese and the common-law system inherited from their former colonial ruler, Great Britain, which guarantees the property rights of entrepreneurs and gives them confidence to invest.

As noted in the section on regional funds, Vietnam is the only frontier market with several large investment funds and an ETF available to give investors access. Apart from the four crossover markets—ETFs for Colombia, Egypt, Peru and the Philippines, the recently launched Bangladesh and Pakistan ETFs and the Ukrainian and Iraqi country funds which we will briefly look at later in this section—investors have limited choices for frontier market exposure to individual countries.

While one could make the case that certain countries, such as Indonesia and Colombia, are large and diversified enough to justify a view that they will survive and prosper, investors should confine such bets to a small part of their frontier and emerging market portfolio.

MULTINATIONAL COMPANIES WITH LARGE EMERGING MARKET EXPOSURE

When you tell some investors about the reasons to invest in emerging and frontier markets, they will respond, "Oh, I agree with your thesis about

investing in emerging and frontier markets, for all the reasons you state."
They then go on to assert that they already have a lot of exposure to these
markets because they own [insert name of multinational here]. Their point,
which is a valid one, is that the multinational company gets 25 percent
to 55 percent of its revenues from these markets, and they can trust the
accounting. Obviously the management were smart enough to get into these
fast-growing economies 10 years ago. So why would they want to take a
risk on people they don't know running local companies, with accounting
that isn't transparent and whose liquidity is very low?

Those are good points. KFC (part of Yum! Brands), Johnson & Johnson,
Philip Morris International and Procter & Gamble in the United States or
Diageo PLC, Unilever PLC, BAT PLC, Anheuser-Busch InBev S.A., Siemens
AG and Nestlé S.A. in Europe have undoubtedly done an excellent job of
servicing the rising middle class in the emerging markets. Yet even those
successes rarely derive more than 50 percent of total revenues from emerging
and frontier markets. This means at least half or two-thirds of their revenues
come from low-growth, fiercely competitive developed markets. That leads
us back to the reason investors need exposure to frontier and emerging
markets in the first place.

The superior demographics, rising incomes, rapid GDP growth and
aspirational buying of brand-name goods make the emerging middle class
in developing markets very attractive to consumer product companies and
sellers of consumer durables such as autos and electronics.

Furthermore, being large multinationals listed on developed market
exchanges means that such stocks trade primarily due to North American,
European or Japanese factors, rather than the longer-term growth of emerging and frontier markets. Certainly, while such stocks have outperformed
the developed market indices over the last decade (which have lost investors
money) they have, in general, not done as well as emerging and frontier
markets, partially due to the drag from their developed market exposure.

For those reasons, we would not advise using multinational stocks as the
only means of accessing frontier markets, although many companies with
large emerging and frontier market exposure have proved to be excellent
investments. We discuss some of those companies in this chapter, as we
wanted to show how some well-managed and experienced businesses headquartered in mature markets, as well as a couple of regional frontier market
companies with ADRs/GDRs, have successfully positioned themselves to
take advantage of the excellent long-term growth prospects in emerging and
frontier markets and have selected representative samples drawn from many
different industry sectors.

These examples of successful multinational and regional companies
with serious frontier market exposure demonstrate these concepts and
their potential for investors. While we do not necessarily recommend them

for individual portfolios, as each investor's circumstances are unique, if an investor wanting to gain exposure to developing markets purchased a basket of these or similar stocks, we feel their performance over the next few years should provide attractive returns.[2]

DIAGEO PLC (NYSE: DEO, LSE: DGE)

Status: the largest global spirits company—45 percent of revenues from emerging and frontier markets

Diageo, a name adopted when brewer and Scotch-whisky producer Guinness & Co. merged with conglomerate Grand Metropolitan PLC in 1997, is the world's largest spirits company. As well, it produces Guinness stout and Harp Lager and such well-known wine brands as Blossom Hills and Beaulieu Vineyard. It also owns a 34 percent stake in French wine and spirits group Moët-Hennessy Louis Vuitton S.A. (PA: LVMH).

Diageo's leading brands include Johnnie Walker, Crown Royal, Seagram's VO, J&B, Bushmills and Buchanan's whiskies; Smirnoff, Ketel One and Ciroc vodkas; Captain Morgan's Rum; Gordon's and Tanqueray gin and Bailey's Irish Cream. An agreement to distribute Jose Cuervo Tequila ends in 2013, but Diageo is examining alternative sources of the spirit. Scotch makes up the largest percentage of its sales at 29 percent, with beer second at 21 percent and vodka next at 12 percent.

Exposure to Emerging and Frontier Markets

In 2012, Diageo had 15 percent of the global premium spirits market by volume compared to 9 percent for Pernod Ricard S.A. and 5 percent each for Bacardi Ltd. and Indian group United Spirits Ltd. More importantly, owing to its higher-value brands, it had 24 percent of global spirits sales by value against 15 percent, 8 percent and 3 percent respectively for its nearest rivals. In the six months to December 31, 2012, almost 40 percent of its revenues came from the faster-growing frontier and emerging markets.

In November 2012, it announced an agreement to purchase a 53.4 percent stake in United Spirits, India's leading domestic spirits producer, from its controlling shareholder. Subject to Indian government approval, this deal will further strengthen its leading position with the combined group, accounting for 20 percent of global spirits by volume and 27 percent by value.

---

[2]Both of the authors own Diageo personally, and one of them also owns SABMiller, Standard Chartered, Mead Johnson, Unilever and Sherritt.

This acquisition will also reinforce Diageo's growth in emerging and frontier markets, which has grown by one-third between 2010 and 2012 from 32 percent to 39 percent of its £10.76 billion (US$17.2 billion) in revenues.

Recent Track Record

Organic sales, after taking out currency fluctuations, grew between 4 percent and 9 percent in each fiscal year ending on June 30 between 2001 and 2008. After flat sales during the global financial crisis in 2008–09, organic sales growth accelerated again to average 6 percent per annum between June 30, 2010, and June 30, 2012. Operating profits before exceptional items grew at least 7 percent per annum between 2001 and 2008, and still grew by 2 percent in 2008–09 and 4 percent in 2009–10 before accelerating to 9 percent between 2010 and 2012. Free-cash-flow generation has been strong, enabling the company to reduce its net debt even though it has made five takeovers in emerging markets in the last two years, ignoring the United Spirits transaction.

Diageo provides a relatively low-risk way for investors to benefit from the growth of the middle class in emerging and frontier markets and the move toward higher-priced premium alcoholic beverages in developed markets. The company has a solid balance sheet (it is rated A- by Standard & Poor) and experienced management. Its wide geographical reach, enormous variety of brands and different price points are all major pluses.

Middle-class consumption of alcoholic beverages in emerging and frontier markets was estimated to total US$7 trillion in 2010 by consultancy IHS Global Insight Inc. They and Diageo believe it has grown 20 percent since then, reaching US$8.5 trillion by the end of 2012, and will have almost tripled by 2022 to US$20.5 trillion. Of that, 33 percent will be in China, another 25 percent in the other BRIC countries of Russia, India and Brazil and a further 13 percent in Mexico, Turkey and Indonesia.

Given this strong growth, Diageo has expanded its emerging and frontier market presence recently, buying leading Turkish spirits-maker Mey Icki Sanayi ve Ticaret A.S. for US$2.1 billion in 2011. This deal enables it to distribute its premium international brands through Mey Icki's local network of 57,000 outlets, or 80 percent of the total outlets in Turkey. Mey Icki's portfolio includes not merely being the largest maker of the fiery Turkish spirit raki, with 85 percent of total sales accounting for 25 percent of the alcohol market in Turkey. It also has strong positions in beer (57 percent of the total market) and vodka (5 percent). Sales of Scotch by value for Diageo in Turkey have increased from 20 percent to 50 percent of the market in the last two years, showing the benefit to global companies of owning or having access to a strong local-distribution network.

Continuing its expansion in emerging markets' spirits, Diageo in July 2011 increased its stake from 48 percent to 53 percent in Chinese company Sichuan Chengdu Quanxing Group, which owns 39.7 percent, the largest share, of listed Chinese super-premium white-spirits maker Sichuan Shui Jing Fang.

In June 2012, it bought a further 10.6 percent stake for £14 million in Hanoi Liquor Joint Stock Company, maker of Vietnam's best-selling vodka, Vodka Hanoi, to add to its 34.9 percent stake purchased in several tranches for approximately £40 million between January and June 2011.

Diageo also bought the second largest Ethiopian beer maker, Meta Abo Brewer S.C., for US$225 million in January 2012. Consultancy Access Capital estimates that Meta Abo has a 15 percent share by volume of the Ethiopian beer market, which is expected to grow by 10 percent p.a. until 2015. Commenting on the deal, United Kingdom Trade Minister Lord Green noted, "Sub-Saharan Africa is not only a trillion-dollar market, but the IMF forecasts it will have seven of the world's 10 fastest-growing economies over the next five years."[3]

Further growing its African beer operations, where Nigeria has now become the largest market for Guinness in the world, Diageo's subsidiary East African Breweries Ltd. bought out SABMiller's 20 percent stake in Kenya Breweries Ltd. in June 2011 for US$225 million, and its 51 percent subsidiary Serengeti Breweries Ltd. opened a new US$55 million brewery in Tanzania in November 2011.

Outlook for Emerging and Frontier Market Growth

Its most recent deal before the United Spirits transaction was the £300 million acquisition of Ypioca Group, one of the leading cachaca brands in Brazil, in May 2012. Cachaca is the largest spirits category in Brazil, and Ypioca is the leading premium brand, ranking number two by value and number three by volume in the total cachaca market, with sales of approximately £60 million (US$96 million) in 2011. Ypioca has an extensive sales and distribution network in the northeast of Brazil and the second largest retail penetration nationwide.

As Diageo CEO Paul Walsh notes, "Brazil is an attractive fast growing market for Diageo with favorable demographics and an increasing disposable spirits category and will also provide [us] with an enhanced platform

---

[3]Diageo release, January 10, 2012.

[for] the long term growth of our premium international spirits brands in Brazil."[4]

The United Spirits transaction is another example of the same strategy at work, with the total 53.4 percent stake in the Indian business costing Diageo £1.28 billion (US$2.05 billion) and expected to be earnings accretive in the second year after the deal closes. As an additional benefit, Diageo is buying 50 percent of United National Breweries traditional sorghum beer business in South Africa from United Spirits for US$36 million.

Valuation

At a price of £18.85 in February 2013, Diageo had a market capitalization of £47.5 billion and was selling at a price-to-earnings ratio of 17.4 times, a price-to-earnings-growth ratio of 1.3 and yielding 2.3 percent. Over the previous five years, it had appreciated over 83 percent against a 10 percent increase in the FTSE100 Index over the same period.

■ ■ ■

SHERRITT CORPORATION (TSX: S)

Status: leading global nickel company; produces 10 percent of Cuba's electricity and 20,000 barrels of oil a day

Sherritt Corporation is one of the world's largest producers of lateritic nickel ore and cobalt from its 50 percent–owned Moa joint venture in Cuba and its recently developed Ambatovy refinery and mine in Madagascar, forecast to become the largest nickel mine in the world.

Exposure to Emerging and Frontier Markets

Sherritt has operated in Cuba for over 50 years and produced approximately 34,500 tonnes of nickel and 3,400 tonnes of cobalt in 2011. It also has oil and gas operations in the ocean off Cuba's shores that produced 20,888 barrels of oil equivalent daily in 2011, making it the largest independent oil producer there. It also owns a one-third interest in the Energas S.A. joint venture with Cuban state oil and power companies, which operates three

---

[4]Diageo release, May 28, 2012.

electric power plants. These plants have a capacity of 356 megawatts (mW) and produce approximately 10 percent of Cuba's electricity output, making Energas the largest independent electric producer in the country. Sherritt's Cuban exposure has meant that the company's senior management is banned from visiting the United States, and it is not allowed to list its securities on U.S. exchanges. However, U.S. investors can purchase shares in Sherritt on the Toronto Stock Exchange in Canada, as can all other global investors.

In addition, its 40 percent–owned operation in Madagascar started producing nickel and cobalt in the second half of 2012 and has a capacity of 60,000 tonnes of nickel and 5,600 tonnes of cobalt a year when in full operation. Built at a cost of US$5.5 billion, the Ambatovy mining endeavor is the largest foreign investment in Madagascar. It includes a 220-kilometer pipeline to transport the ore-bearing slurry from the mine to the refinery and port at Toamasina and has an estimated 27-year life.

As well as its emerging and frontier market exposure, with 21 percent of its assets located in Cuba and 31 percent in Madagascar, Sherritt also produces 95 percent of the thermal coal (used by power stations) sold in Canada, with seven domestic mines for Canadian electricity output and two export mines that ship coal to Asian markets. It also produces phosphate fertilizer as a by-product from the Fort Saskatchewan refinery, where it refines and processes the nickel from its Moa joint venture in Canada.

Recent Track Record

Sherritt's operating performance over the last five years has been robust, despite the sharp falls in the commodity sectors in which it operates during the financial crisis of 2008–09. Even during that period, while prices of nickel and cobalt fell by 75 percent, Sherritt maintained its operating earnings.

The price of thermal coal was much more resilient, with domestic prices actually rising from $15 per tonne to $17.55 between 2008 and 2012. Meanwhile, the price of Sherritt's oil fell, but only from US$56 per barrel in 2008 to US$45.05 in 2009, as Sherritt receives 71–76 percent of the market price of oil, with the Cuban government receiving the remainder. Its electricity prices remained in a range of $41–$46.79 per megawatt hour.

The escalating cost and delays of its major growth project, the Ambatovy nickel mine in Madagascar, due to changes in the project design and the need to replace some of the contractors, combined with a coup in Madagascar, however, saw investors abandon the stock, which at C$5.75 is down almost 75 percent from its highs in 2007.

Despite this disappointing performance, its earnings before interest, taxation, depreciation and amortization (EBITDA) have ranged between

$495 million and $643 million in the last four years and its operating cash flow between $354 million and $495 million. Nickel, oil and coal each have generated over $200 million EBITDA over this period, although the nickel and cobalt division has seen its EBITDA fall to below $150 million in the last 12 months. The power division's EBITDA has fallen much lower, to $25 million p.a. for the last three years, following a change in its pricing in 2008. However, a 130 mW expansion is due to come on line in 2013, providing an increase of one-third in capacity.

Outlook for Emerging and Frontier Market Growth

With the Ambatovy mine reaching full capacity by 2014, Sherritt's nickel and cobalt production will almost double, as its 40 percent share will be 24,000 tonnes of nickel and 2,240 tonnes of cobalt per year. Taxation of profits on the project is 10 percent for the mine and 25 percent for the refinery, and while expenses will start to be fully accounted for by Sherritt once it reaches 70 percent of its capacity, the increase in production combined with more stable, or even rising, metal prices should see a substantial increase in earnings.

    With higher oil and electricity production in Cuba, combined with continued Asian demand for thermal coal as growth accelerates again, the outlook for growth in Sherritt's revenues and profits from emerging and frontier markets appears promising.

Valuation

With a debt-to-equity ratio of 28 percent (US$1.78 billion excluding its non-recourse share of the Ambatovy debt against equity of US$3.79 billion), the company's balance sheet is strong, and it has been able to issue US$500 million of 7.5 percent BB+ rated bonds maturing in 2020 to extend its debt maturities. Due to the sharp fall in its share price, down 61 percent over the last five years to February 2013, Sherritt has dramatically underperformed on both the S&P 500 Index, up 12 percent over the same period, and the S&P/TSX Metals and Mining Index, up 32 percent. Selling at less than half its book value and less than one times sales, Sherritt is on a forecast price-to-earnings ratio of 10 times 2013's earnings and yields of 2.6 percent. These valuations are reasonable and if the company delivers its expected growth in revenues and earnings over the next few years, they are cheap.

■ ■ ■

MEAD JOHNSON NUTRITION (NYSE: MJN)

Status: leading infant-nutrition company—over two-thirds of its revenues from Asia and Latin America

Mead Johnson Nutrition, as one of the largest manufacturers globally of infant formula under such well-known brands as Enfamil, Sustagen and Enfagrow, was spun off from its parent, drug-manufacturer Bristol-Myers Squibb, in 2009. Since then it has delivered strong and consistent growth in revenues and earnings, with occasional hiccups such as overstocking in its China operations in 2012, a misstep that led to slower revenue growth than anticipated.

Exposure to Emerging and Frontier Markets

Among the companies that will be beneficiaries of the continued strong growth in the emerging and frontier markets' middle classes, to invest in Mead Johnson Nutrition is to take advantage of one of the strongest and most predictable factors in economic life, namely demographics.

Birth rates in some developed countries, including Japan and most of continental Europe, have fallen well below the population replacement rate of 2.1 children per couple. Most of these nations currently average birth rates of 1.2 to 1.5, but this is emphatically not the case in most emerging and frontier markets.

The long-term growth in consumption of infant nutrition products is based upon more births in the fledgling middle class in emerging and frontier markets, more women entering the workforce, thus reducing the period of time spent breast-feeding, current low levels of consumption of infant formula and a desire to purchase the best possible product for one's children.

A study by the Nielson Company shows that the percentage of the global infant-formula market comprised of premium products, the area where Mead Johnson competes, had increased from two-thirds to almost three-quarters of total consumption between 2008 and 2011, despite the global recession.

While consumption of infant formula was 47 kilograms (kg) per annum, per live birth in North America and 35 kg in Europe, it was only 20 kg in Asia (including Japan) and 12 kg in Latin America. In other emerging and frontier regions, the amount consumed is a still-lower 7 kg p.a. per birth.

China is the largest infant nutrition market in the world, worth US$8 billion and has been progressively moving toward premium infant formula, where Mead Johnson competes strongly. A company-commissioned third-party survey estimated that middle-class consumers will represent 45 percent of the country's 1.3 billion population by 2015.

The infant formula market is fragmented and competitive, with more than 30 entrants. Mead Johnson is the number-one infant nutrition company in China, with 18 percent market share, having regained the share it lost in 2012 due to its new product introduction at a higher price. It is also number one in Thailand, number two in the Philippines and Malaysia and number three in Vietnam.

Forecasts for Latin America call for growth in its share of the global infant-nutrition market from 6 percent in 2006 to 14 percent in 2017, and Mead Johnson believes its sales in the region will quadruple to US$1 billion by 2015. This is due both to its strong position in existing markets—where it is number one in Mexico, its third largest market globally, as well as in Peru, Ecuador and Colombia—and through acquisitions such as Sancor Bebe in Argentina, which made it number one in that market.

In Brazil, which is already one of its top 10 markets, the premium segment is underdeveloped, and Mead Johnson is targeting growth here in infant formula to build on the success of its nutritional complement business, where it is number one.

Recent Track Record

Mead Johnson is one of the most global companies listed in North America, selling more than 70 products in 50 countries around the world. Its Enfa range of infant formulas exceeded US$3 billion in sales for the first time in 2012. More than two-thirds (US$2.72 billion, up 11 percent from 2011) of its US$3.9 billion in revenues last year was from its Asia/Latin America division, as opposed to the US$1.18 billion (down 4 percent) from its North America/Europe division, while its earnings before interest and tax (EBIT) were up 11 percent to US$911 million in the former against a 20 percent decline to US$246 million in the latter.

For the company as a whole, revenues in constant currency terms grew 7 percent to US$3.9 billion, with constant currency revenues up 12 percent in Asia/Latin America against a 3 percent decline in the more mature markets. While some of the latter can be attributed to the long-term decline in the birth rate in these more-developed countries, CEO Stephen Golsby mentioned higher dairy and other commodity costs, exacerbated by lower production volumes, partially due to unfounded rumors of contamination at the beginning of the year which the company took time to recover from.[5]

---

[5]Mead Johnson Nutrition annual report (2012) announcement, January 31, 2013.

Operating net earnings per share were up 10 percent in 2012 and are forecast by the company to grow by 4.7–7.2 percent in 2013.

Interestingly, Mead Johnson is experiencing sales growth even in China, where the one-child policy has seen the country's birth rate plummet to well below replacement rate. After a fall in sales in the first half of 2012 due to overstocking by wholesalers there and the introduction of a new product with a double-digit price increase, the company regained market share in the second half and grew sales by more than 5 percent in constant currency terms for the year for China/Hong Kong.

Excluding China, the other Asian/Latin America markets had organic revenue growth in the mid-teens in the fourth quarter of 2012, and including an Argentine acquisition made in March 2012, the segment experienced over 20 percent revenue growth, of which 6 percent was from price increases. Even North America/Europe saw sales growth of 4 percent in the fourth quarter, although this comprised a 5 percent price increase and 1 percent volume decline.

Outlook for Emerging and Frontier Market Growth

With the relatively high birth rates in most emerging and frontier markets, Mead Johnson is well positioned to benefit from rising living standards allowing new parents to purchase infant-nutrition products to help their children grow and advance. While the growth of their sales is somewhat dependent upon access to safe drinking water to mix with the infant formula, the adulteration scandals for locally sourced products in such markets as China have reinforced the strong position of such international nutrition companies as Mead Johnson, Abbott Laboratories Inc. and Nestlé S.A., as their high-quality standards and rigorous safety regime have insulated them somewhat from consumer concerns.

Valuation

The combination of strong revenue growth and price-insensitive products has made Mead Johnson an attractive investment over the period since its spin-off. With revenue growth over the period from 2006–2010 averaging 8 percent p.a. compound and 11.3 percent for the three years ending December 31, 2012, and net profits and earnings per share growing by more than 14 percent, the stock price has more than doubled since its spin-off in October 2009 and is up 75 percent over the last three years. Due to its stumble in China, however, Mead Johnson sold off sharply in 2012, making it reasonably priced for a growth stock at a price-to-earnings ratio of 25 times 2012's earnings and 21 times 2013's forecast earnings.

Generating more than $200 million of free cash flow each year, Mead Johnson has paid down $0.5 billion of the $2 billion in debt it inherited from Bristol-Myers four years ago and pays a modest dividend of $1.20 per share, equivalent to a 1.6 percent yield, an increase of 70 percent since 2009. As of February 2013, Mead Johnson is selling at a relatively expensive valuation, but if it is able to deliver continued growth in revenues in line with the last few years, the company should continue to produce earnings growth in the mid-teens.

■ ■ ■

UNILEVER PLC (NYSE: UL/UN, LSE: ULVR/UN)

Status: third largest global consumer product company—55 percent of revenues from emerging and frontier markets

Unilever is the third largest global food and consumer product company, making ice cream, packaged food, and personal care and cleaning products. Most investors will have used a Unilever product in the last month; the company calculates that it sells 190 billion packs of its products annually and that their products are used more than 2 billion times a day.

With operations in 100 countries and sales in 190, Unilever employs more than 171,000 people and had sales of €51.3 billion (US$66.7 billion) in 2012, a 10.5 percent increase on the previous year (6.9 percent on an organic basis after accounting for foreign exchange and acquisitions).

With its wide range of products and operations, Unilever is extremely well placed to benefit from rising levels of consumer expenditure by the growing middle class in emerging and frontier markets, especially as many of its products are the type of small, affordable pleasures that consumers tend to purchase with incremental amounts of additional income.

Exposure to Emerging and Frontier Markets

Unilever has several listed local subsidiaries in emerging and frontier markets, such as Hindustan Unilever in India and Unilever Indonesia, which provide more concentrated exposure to these markets. However, as shown by the increase in royalties that Unilever charges subsidiaries as announced in 2012, there are geographic and operational risks involved in buying the local company rather than the parent. Unilever Indonesia's share price fell 25 percent in December 2012 when the change in the royalties it pays to its parent company from 3.5 percent to 5 percent by 2014 was announced.

Unilever has focused its attention in recent years on development and global promotion of its major power brands, such as Dove Soap, Hellmann's Mayonnaise, Knorr Soup, Lipton's Tea, Vaseline body lotion and Persil laundry detergent, aiming to grow the brands to over €1billion (US$1.3 billion) in sales each. Magnum Ice Cream and Sunsilk Shampoo achieved this target in 2012, giving the group 14 products in this category. This also enables Unilever to benefit from economies of scale in the global marketing of its fast-moving consumer goods (FMCG) portfolio.

Advertising and marketing costs were equivalent to approximately 13 percent of Unilever's revenues in 2012. Sales growth has been largely derived from the emerging and frontier markets, which now account for 55 percent of its revenues, and which had organic growth of 11.4 percent in 2012, offsetting volume declines in the mature and recession-hit European markets from which it derives one-third of its revenues.

The other source of growth in recent years has been acquisitions, particularly in the faster-growing personal care division, where former–Nestlé S.A. and Procter & Gamble Inc. veteran-CEO Paul Polman has been focused, while selling off smaller, lower-growth brands in the food area. Thus Unilever bought Sara Lee Corporation's Radox division for US$1.3 billion in 2010 and the Alberto Culver Company (VO5 and TRESemmé shampoos) for US$3.7 billion, also in 2010. While Unilever had to sell the VO5 shampoo business in the United States and the Sanex division in Europe when it bought Radox, it used some of the US$890 million sale proceeds to buy the Colgate-Palmolive Company's Colombian laundry detergent business for US$215 million, swapping low-growth assets for a faster-growing emerging market business.

Similarly, it sold its Findus Frozen Foods business in Italy for €805 million (US$1.05 billion) in 2010 to Birds Eye Ltd., its mature Bertolli's and P.F. Chang's frozen meals business in North America to Conagra Foods Inc. for US$287 million in 2012 and its Skippy Peanut Butter operation to Spam maker Hormel Foods Corp. in early 2013 for US$700 million. These sales reduced its exposure to low-growth developed food markets.

Outlook for Emerging and Frontier Market Growth

In emerging and frontier markets, the company continues to roll out existing products such as Magnum ice cream in the Philippines, TRESemmé shampoo in Brazil, Indonesia and India, Lipton tea in Turkey and Lifebuoy hand wash in Russia.

Meanwhile the Lux brand has done well across all emerging markets thanks to a successful re-launch with new fragrances and advertising. Brooke

Bond Tea did well in 2012 in both value and premium segments in India and Cif cleaner was helped by product innovations in Argentina.

Apart from the ubiquitous nature of its products, Unilever's ability to introduce existing global brands to new emerging and frontier markets and to modify package sizes and delivery mechanisms means that it has an extremely robust business model that is resilient in the face of economic uncertainty.

Unilever intends to double its revenues from €40 billion (US$64 billion) in 2010 to €80 billion (US$128 billion) over the next few years, which will be dependent upon continued growth in its emerging and frontier market revenue. By comparison, its mature European and North American businesses, especially in the food segment, its second largest, are unlikely to see more than low–single digit growth, due to recessionary conditions and tough competition. It would be reasonable to assume that Unilever will make other emerging market acquisitions such as that of Russian beauty and skincare company LLC Concern Kalina, with sales of €300 million (US$420 million), of which it bought 82 percent for €550 million (US$715 million) in 2011.

Valuation

The success of Unilever's focus on emerging and frontier markets has driven its share price to increase almost 60 percent in the five years to early 2013 against a 10 percent increase in the FTSE100 Index over the same period. It sells at a price-to-earnings ratio of 17 times 2012 earnings, a price-to-earnings growth ratio of 1.7 times and has a yield of 3.5 percent. While no longer cheap, its ability to produce high–single digit revenue growth in its faster-growing emerging and frontier markets and body and personal care divisions would suggest its valuation is reasonable.

■ ■ ■

YUM! BRANDS (NYSE: YUM)

Status: leading fast food restaurant chain with 44 percent of revenues from China

Yum! Brands, owner of the KFC (formerly Kentucky Fried Chicken), Pizza Hut and Taco Bell chains, is one of the largest global fast food restaurant operators, with more than 37,000 outlets in 2011.

Exposure to Emerging and Frontier Markets

Yum! derived over three-quarters of its US$12 billion in revenues from outside of the United States and 44 percent from China alone in 2012. Yum! was the first quick-service restaurant chain to enter China, in 1987, and today KFC is the leading quick-service brand there, opening a new restaurant every day and with more than 4,000 restaurants in more than 800 cities at the end of last year.

Pizza Hut was the first pizza restaurant chain to open in China, in 1990. It introduced pizza delivery in 2001 and had more than 700 outlets in 120 cities at the end of 2012 and 140 Pizza Hut Home Service units. In 2012 alone Yum! opened 889 new outlets in China, but saw its same-store sales growth turn negative in the fourth quarter on reports of excessive levels of antibiotics in chickens supplied to KFC; it anticipates continued negative sales for the first half of 2013. It also created Yum! Brands India as a separate division in 2011, which had 220 KFC, 170 Pizza Hut and more than 100 Pizza Hut Home Service outlets in 2012.

Recent Track Record

In 2012, Yum! Brands opened 1,976 new outlets internationally and grew its earnings per share (EPS) by 13 percent to US$3.25 per share (excluding special items). This was the 11th consecutive year that Yum! has managed to grow its EPS by at least 13 percent. Its system sales worldwide in 2012 grew 5 percent before adjusting for foreign currency and 8 percent excluding the impact of the disposal of the Long John Silver's and A&W restaurants in the United States in 2011; these results were due in part to the fact that 2011 contained an extra (53rd) week owing to the timing of the company's year end and to the acquisition of the 425-outlet Little Sheep dine-in Chinese restaurant chain in China. Its sales grew 17 percent in China, 7 percent in Yum! Restaurants International (YRI), which excludes China and India, and 5 percent in the United States.

Its same-store sales growth, which compares sales at restaurants open at least one year, grew 4 percent in China, 3 percent in YRI markets and 5 percent in the United States; its worldwide margin increased 0.6 percent to 16.6 percent and its operating profit grew 12 percent before currency translation. Of the 1,976 new restaurants opened, 889 were in China, 949 in YRI markets and 138 in India, with 83 percent of its new units in emerging markets.

Yum! has gradually reduced its company ownership in mature markets, such as the United States and United Kingdom, selling 468 restaurants to franchisees in the United States last year and 376 in YRI, meaning that it owns only 11 percent of its restaurants in the United States and 8 percent of its YRI restaurants. However, it owns 79 percent of its Chinese outlets. Among YRI markets, Latin America accounts for 11 percent of sales and grew 9 percent after currency translation last year, and the Middle East accounts for 8 percent of sales and grew 11 percent.

Smaller YRI emerging markets include Africa at 7 percent (up 17 percent) and Russia, Thailand and South Korea, all at 2 percent of sales and up 46 percent, 14 percent and 11 percent respectively in 2012.

Outlook for Emerging and Frontier Market Growth

The chicken-supply health scare in the fourth quarter of 2012 saw Chinese same-store sales fall 6 percent for the quarter with KFC sales up only 3 percent for the year and down 8 percent for the quarter. Yum! reported that same-store sales were down 37 percent in January 2013, off 41 percent at KFC and 15 percent at Pizza Hut. Part of this decline is due to the timing of Chinese New Year, which fell in February in 2013, and therefore some of the decline will be reversed in February, but Yum! has forecast a 25 percent decline in Chinese sales over January and February combined. However, Yum! was not found to be at fault, and no fine was assessed by the Chinese authorities in regard to the chicken-supply scare.

The company is also forecasting that earnings per share (EPS) will drop in 2013. Furthermore, it says that Chinese same-store sales will be flat for the year, with a decline in the first half being followed by a recovery in the second half. Yum! still aims to open 700 new units in China in 2013, has tightened up its supply-chain practices and is confident that growth will be restored once consumer confidence is regained.

Valuation

In the meantime, the fallout from the health scare has led to a sharp decline in the Yum! stock price, which had risen by almost 450 percent over the last decade, far outperforming the S&P 500 or the MSCI Emerging Markets Index. Over the last 12 months to February 2013, however, the stock was flat, against a 15 percent increase in the S&P 500, leaving the stock selling at a price-to-earnings ratio of 19.6 times 2012's EPS after special items and a dividend yield of 2.12 percent after a 21 percent increase in its quarterly dividend to $0.34.

Assuming that Yum! has successfully addressed consumer concerns over the safety of its supply chain, its focus on growing its emerging and frontier market business with high levels of company ownership, while reducing its company exposure in mature markets, such as the United States and Europe, should mean that earnings growth will re-accelerate over the next few years, making Yum!'s valuation sustainable.

■ ■ ■

ORASCOM TELECOM HOLDING (LSE: OTLD, Egypt EY: ORAT)

Status: leading mobile phone operator in Algeria, Pakistan and Bangladesh

Orascom Telecom, formerly owned by Egyptian mobile phone entrepreneur Naguib Sawiris, is majority owned (51.9 percent) by Russian mobile phone operator VimpelCom (NYSE: VIP), which merged its operations with Wind Telecom in 2011 to become the sixth largest mobile phone company in the world.

Exposure to Emerging and Frontier Markets

Orascom Telecom Holding is a major mobile phone operator with 85 million subscribers in emerging and frontier markets. It is the largest operator in Algeria (Orascom Telecom Algerie, or OTA) and Pakistan (Mobilink) and the second largest in Bangladesh (Banglalink). It also has indirect equity ownership of Globalive Wireless Canada (Wind Mobile) and of Telecel Zimbabwe and its subsidiary Telecel Globe, which operates in Burundi and the Central African Republic. The population of the countries in which Orascom operates was 450 million in 2012, with an average wireless penetration of 56 percent.

Orascom Telecom formerly operated a leading mobile network in Tunisia but sold it in 2011 for a more-than $700 million profit, which it used to reduce debt. It is at present in negotiations to sell one part of its Algerian operations, which operates under the brand name Djezzy, to the Algerian government, which has been restricting Orascom's ability to launch promotions to attract subscribers in a dispute over taxes.

In December 2012, the chair of Orascom Telecom Algérie announced that VimpelCom Ltd. and the government of Algeria had agreed to a joint venture to operate Djezzy, in which the Algerian government would own 51 percent. It also announced in late 2012 that it was undertaking a strategic review of its operations in Africa, which might lead to the sale of all or part of its indirect equity holdings in these businesses.

In 2011, Algeria accounted for 51 percent of its revenues, Pakistan 32 percent and Bangladesh 14 percent, while Telecel Global and Wind Mobile Canada accounted for 2 percent of the total.

Recent Track Record

Subscribers grew 14 percent between the third quarter of 2011 and the third quarter of 2012, from 75 million to 85 million, while organic revenues and earnings before interest, taxation, depreciation and amortization (EBITDA) grew 6 percent. Due to the decline of the Algerian, Pakistani and Bangladeshi currencies against the U.S. greenback, which is the Orascom reporting currency, revenues in U.S. dollars were down 4 percent from $925 million to $885 million in the third quarter 2012 and EBITDA was down 5 percent from $448 million to $425 million, while its EBITDA margin was down from 48.4 percent to 48.1 percent.

Subscriber numbers were up 9 percent in Algeria, 8 percent in Pakistan and 21 percent in Bangladesh year-on-year while Telecel Global subscribers were up almost 50 percent year-on-year, driven by strong growth in Zimbabwe. Revenues in local currency terms were up 2 percent in Algeria, 4 percent in Pakistan and 23 percent in Bangladesh while EBITDA was up 1 percent, 10 percent and 9 percent, respectively. With 17.7 million subscribers and a 56 percent market share, OTA in Algeria generated DZD63.4 billion in EBITDA and DZD61.3 billion in free cash flow (EBITDA less capital expenditures) in the first nine months of 2012.

Mobilink in Pakistan has 36 million subscribers and a 30 percent market share and generated PKR33.9 billion and PKR26.2 billion in EBITDA and free cash flow, respectively, in the first nine months of 2012. Banglalink in Bangladesh is the fastest-growing mobile operator with 25.7 million subscribers and a 27 percent market share at the end of the third quarter of 2012. Starting after the other two Orascom operators, it has only recently become cash-flow positive, with BTK11.5 billion and BTK4.1 billion in EBITDA and free cash flow in the first three quarters of 2012.

Outlook for Emerging and Frontier Market Growth

While the potential sale of its Algerian operations to the government will reduce Orascom's revenues and EBITDA, as happened following the sale of its Tunisian business in 2011, it is likely that Orascom will receive a substantial price for its share, which it can use to reduce its net debt, which was US$2.98 billion at the end of September 2012.

With the renewal of its mobile license in Bangladesh for 15 years and the potential introduction of 3G services in both Pakistan and Bangladesh in 2013, where mobile penetration rates are still relatively low at 63 percent and 60 percent, continued growth of both revenues and EBITDA appears likely over the next few years.

Valuation

At its price of $3.25 in February 2013, Orascom Telecom sells at an estimated 12.8 times the price-to-earnings ratio of 2012's earnings and does not pay a dividend. While the likely sale of its Algerian operations will reduce its earnings, the proceeds should also reduce its debt, and the growth in its Pakistan and Bangladesh operations with the introduction of 3G in 2013 should lead to higher average revenues per user, making the valuation appear reasonable.

■ ■ ■

COPA HOLDINGS S.A. (NYSE: CPA)

Status: leading Latin American airline with regional hub in Panama

Copa Holdings S.A. (NYSE: CPA) is a leading regional airline based in Panama that provides passenger and freight services to 65 destinations in South, Central and North America and the Caribbean. It operates a fleet of 83 modern aircraft, with an average age of 4.3 years, consisting of 57 Boeing 737-700s and 737-800s and 26 Embraer 190 jets.

Exposure to Emerging and Frontier Markets

Copa is a member of the global airline network, and from its hub at Tocumen International Airport, Panama City, it offers the most destinations and international flights of any hub in Latin America, including eight destinations in the United States, as well as Toronto, Canada. Tocumen's convenient location, excellent weather and sea level altitude contribute to Copa's excellent on-time record and ability to act as the center of a major hub-and-spoke operation, allowing travelers to reach any destination within Central and South America with only one stop.

Copa has expanded rapidly over the last decade, going public in 2005 and using the access to public markets to grow and modernize its fleet. Its low costs are due to its modern fleet, efficiencies of operating one major hub in the center of its major markets and the competitive cost of labor in Panama.

Copa carried 10.1 million passengers in 2012, a 17 percent increase on the previous year, and experienced a 24 percent increase in capacity as it added 10 new Boeing 737 aircraft. In 2005, it purchased the second largest Colombian airline and now operates an extensive schedule of internal and international flights in Colombia.

Recent Track Record

Copa Holdings sold a 49 percent stake to Continental Airlines in 1998 and entered an extensive alliance, which provided for code sharing, joint marketing and technical exchanges. At the time, Copa had a fleet of 13 Boeing 737-200s flying to 24 destinations in 18 countries. Copa introduced its first 737-700s in 1999, its first 737-800s in 2003 and its first Embraer 190s in 2005, becoming the launch customer for the Brazilian manufacturer. It went public on the New York Stock Exchange in 2005, as Continental reduced its stake to 27.3 percent.

In two subsequent sales, Continental reduced its holding to 10 percent in mid-2006 and sold out completely in 2008. Since going public, Copa shares have risen four times, and over the last five years they have risen 170 percent against a 12 percent increase for the S&P 500.

In the year to December 2012, Copa had operating income of $402.5 million, up 4.6 percent, on revenues up 22.9 percent to $2.25 billion, as it increased capacity 22 percent. Adjusted net earnings of $336.5 million ($7.57 per share) were up 7 percent and 7.2 percent respectively, although its operating margin was down from 21 percent to 17.9 percent on higher fuel costs and slightly lower revenue per available seat mile.

As a result, the shares dropped sharply when earnings for the fourth quarter fell below expectations, leaving Copa selling at a price-to-earnings ratio of 13.5 times 2012's earnings and a dividend yield of 2.1 percent.

Outlook for Emerging and Frontier Market Growth

With its new membership in the Star Alliance as of mid-2012, Copa should benefit from increased traffic from members of other airline loyalty schemes, especially that of the merged United Continental, as Copa added Las Vegas to its route network in 2012 and is adding Boston in 2013.

With the widening of the Panama Canal by 2016 expected to add substantially to trade and visitors to Panama, and with the boost to Copa's capacity through adding 7 new Boeing 737-800s scheduled for 2013, it is reasonable to expect Copa's traffic to rise over the next few years.

Assuming that the airline keeps its costs competitive and maintains its conservative policy of fuel hedging to offset the risk of higher fuel prices,

Copa should be able to maintain its margins at around present levels and remain a profitable and successful airline benefiting from the rising demand for travel from the growing Latin American middle class.

Valuation

With a price-to-earnings ratio of 9.8 times its forecast 2013 earnings and a dividend yield of 2.2 percent, Copa is attractively valued for a cyclical business like an airline, assuming that the forecast growth in capacity for 2013 can be filled.

■ ■ ■

SABMiller PLC (LSE: SAB, OTC: SABMRY)

Status: second largest global brewer with 76 percent of revenues from emerging and frontier markets

SABMiller PLC is the second largest global brewer, with more than 200 beer brands and 70,000 employees in more than 75 countries. The group's portfolio includes global brands, such as Pilsner Urquell from the Czech Republic, Peroni Nastro Azzurro from Italy, Miller Genuine Draft (U.S.) and Grolsch (the Netherlands). It also includes leading local brands, such as Aguila (Colombia), Castle (South Africa), Miller Lite (U.S.), Snow (China), Victoria Bitter (Australia) and Tyskie (Poland). SABMiller also has a growing soft drinks business and is one of the world's largest Coca-Cola bottlers.

Exposure to Emerging and Frontier Markets

Formed by the merger of South African Breweries and Miller in the United States in 2003, SABMiller is the largest brewer in China, with its Snow brand being the best-selling beer in the world. SABMiller derived 76 percent of its revenues from emerging and frontier markets in the year to March 2012.

It has purchased leading European brewers such as Peroni, Tyskie and Grolsch in the last decade and in 2011 bought Foster's Group, the largest Australian brewer, to gain access to the Australian market and control of the Foster's brand, which it already distributed in the U.S.

In 2006, SABMiller bought majority control of Bavaria Brewery (Colombia), the second largest brewer in South America and the number one brewer in Colombia, Peru, Ecuador, Honduras, El Salvador and

Panama and number three in Argentina. SABMiller has a joint venture with Andolu Efes, which covers 16 European countries including Russia, Turkey and Ukraine, and formed a joint venture (MillerCoors) in 2008 with Molson Coors, which is the number two brewer in the United States, with 29 percent market share.

Recent Track Record

Over the five years ending in March 2012, SABMiller's revenues, including its share of associates and joint ventures, have grown 31.7 percent to $31.4 billion earnings before interest, taxation and amortization (EBITA), 36 percent to $5.6 billion and adjusted earnings per share (EPS) 50 percent to $2.14 per share. Volumes of beer have grown by a lower 10.9 percent to 229.3 million hectoliters and soft drinks 14.2 percent to 49.5 million hectoliters, illustrating SABMiller's ability to raise prices and increase EBITA margins to 17.9 percent from 16.4 percent by migrating consumers to higher-priced premium beers and raising prices above commodity-cost inflation while still growing volumes.

Its recent acquisition of Foster's in December 2011 for $10.2 billion shows its willingness to purchase attractive brands in low growth developed markets at a reasonable price. It also shows confidence in its ability to manage the assets more efficiently and market the acquisition's brands through its international network, as it has done with Birra Peroni S.r.l. in Italy and Royal Grolsch NV in the Netherlands.

Similarly its joint venture with Molson Coors Brewing Co. in the U.S. has continued to extract efficiencies even though beer volumes are declining in the U.S., with underlying net income for the year to December 2012 for the joint venture up 9.5 percent to $1.22 billion even though sales were down 1.3 percent for the year due to increasing sales of premium craft beers and gaining market share for Coors Light.

Meanwhile its emerging and frontier market operations continue to expand, with Latin America, its largest contributor to EBITA at 32 percent, growing 14 percent to March 2012; Asia Pacific (6 percent of EBITA) up 30 percent; Africa, excluding South Africa (13 percent of EBITA) up 16 percent; and South Africa (22 percent of EBITA) up 14 percent. On the other hand, Europe (14 percent of EBITA) saw its EBITA fall 9 percent, hit by recession, increases in duties and a move to lower-margin home consumption.

Outlook for Emerging and Frontier Market Growth

With the recent acquisition in February 2013 of Kingsway Breweries in China for $864 million, SABMiller acquired seven breweries with sales of

9.3 million hectoliters in 2012 and a capacity of 14.5 million hectoliters, including four in one of the wealthiest and fastest-growing provinces, Guangdong, with three other breweries in Tianjin, Sichuan and Shaanxi. The operations are highly complementary to SABMiller's CR Snow's existing operations and may help raise the very low margins that breweries receive in China, as the top five breweries now have 65 percent of the total market.

With beer volumes up 2 percent in the last quarter of 2012 and soft drink volumes up 3 percent, group revenue was up 8 percent, and including the Foster's acquisition, group volumes were up 6 percent and revenues up 17 percent. Including the 27 percent of group revenues that come from the shrinking markets of the United States and Europe, SABMiller appears able to continue growing its volumes at low– to mid–single digits for the next few years and its revenues by mid– to high–single digits as it continues to sell more premium beer and raise its prices ahead of cost inflation. Markets such as India, where it is the number two brewer, and Vietnam, where it has bought out its joint venture partner and is exporting to other countries in Indochina, still represent a very small percentage of its revenues, leaving more room for growth.

Valuation

Analysts are expecting further progress from SABMiller, which has risen over 600 percent in the last decade, well ahead of the FTSE100 Index, which is up 70 percent. It has also substantially outperformed the FTSE100 Index over the last 5 years, up 190 percent to February 2013 against a 10 percent increase and is reasonably valued given its high–single digit revenue growth at a price-to-earnings ratio of 18 times 2012's earnings and a 1.8 percent dividend yield.

■ ■ ■

STANDARD CHARTERED BANK (LSE: STAN, HK: 2888)

Status: long-established global bank with more than 90 percent of its profits from Africa, Asia and the Middle East

Standard Chartered Bank PLC is a London-headquartered commercial and investment bank rated A+ by S&P and A2 by Moody's Investors Service Inc., with 1,700 branches in Africa, Asia and the Middle East. It employs more than 85,000 people in 71 countries.

Exposure to Emerging and Frontier Markets

Formed by the merger in 1969 of Chartered Bank (founded in 1858 in Shanghai, Mumbai and Kolkata) and Standard Bank (founded in 1862 in South Africa), Standard Chartered is one of the three note-issuing banks in Hong Kong and has the government of Singapore's investment company, Temasek, as its largest shareholder with 11.5 percent. A consortium of Asian investors took a large position in the bank in the late 1990s to prevent a potential takeover by Lloyds Bank of the UK, which had made an unsuccessful takeover attempt in 1986. Since then, Standard Chartered has focused on building up its emerging and frontier market business and selling off its European and U.S. operations.

In 2000, it purchased Grindlays Bank in India from the Australia and New Zealand Banking Group (commonly called ANZ), making it the largest foreign bank in India. In 2004, it acquired control of Permata Bank in Indonesia in cooperation with Astra International, and in 2005 it outbid HSBC for Korea First Bank while integrating its Thai operations with recently purchased Nakornthorn Bank.

In 2006, Standard Chartered bought 81 percent of Pakistan's sixth largest bank, Union Bank of Pakistan, for US$511 million and took control of Taiwan's seventh largest private bank, Hsinchu International Bank. In 2007 and 2008, the bank bought majority control of both Indian broker UTI and Cazenove Asia, a leading investment bank and, also in 2008, bought American Express Bank for US$823 million. In 2010, it bought the African custody business of Barclays and strengthened its strategic relationship with the largest Chinese bank, Agricultural Bank of China.

Recent Track Record

Operating income grew by more than 50 percent over the five years between 2007 and 2011, from $11 billion to $17.6 billion, of which consumer banking accounted for 38 percent. Hong Kong, the largest single market, contributed 17 percent, Singapore 12 percent and Korea 10 percent, with other Asia-Pacific countries (primarily Indonesia, Taiwan, Thailand and Malaysia) contributing 20 percent. India contributed 10 percent, the Middle East and other South Asian markets 13 percent and Africa 8 percent, while the developed markets of the Americas, United Kingdom and Europe made up the remaining 10 percent.

As well, 24 different markets delivered more than US$100 million in operating profit in 2011, making the bank exceptionally well diversified. The consumer side of the bank saw profits before tax rise 26 percent in 2011 to US$1.65 billion, and the wholesale side of the bank's pretax profits rose 9 percent to US$5.2 billion. Pretax profits for the bank as a whole rose 11 percent to US$6.8 billion on assets up 16 percent to $599 billion. Its core Tier 1 ratio has been at 11.8 percent for 2010 and 2011, above the Basel III requirements, which have set increased levels of core shareholder capital in order to prevent a recurrence of the financial crisis of 2008–09.

In 2012, the New York State Department of Financial Affairs fined Standard Chartered US$340 million, and other regulators, including the New York Federal Reserve and the Department of Justice, levied fines of US$327 million for money laundering. The bank was alleged to have misreported US$250 billion in transactions for Iranian clients, of which US$24 million for Iran and US$109 million for other countries (Burma, Sudan and Libya) breached U.S. sanctions.

Despite these setbacks, the bank indicated that it expected 2012 earnings to be up by high–single digits and up low–double digits after removing the effect of weakening Asian currencies against the U.S. dollar and before considering the fines. Africa, China, Indonesia and Malaysia as well as the Americas, the UK and Europe are expected to grow their income by double digits, while its largest market, Hong Kong, will grow at a high–single digit rate.

Outlook for Emerging and Frontier Market Growth

The revival in Chinese economic growth in late 2012 and 2013 and the revival in U.S. domestic demand should lead to stronger GDP growth in export-oriented economies such as South Korea and Taiwan, as well as the commodity-oriented ASEAN economies. While the South Asia markets of India and Pakistan are experiencing slower growth and higher inflation, Standard Chartered has the ability to gain market share due to the strength of its balance sheet. This enables it to offer more competitive terms to its clients, and its ready access to global funding puts it in a strong position. Its African operations are expected to enjoy renewed strength on the back of stronger commodity prices.

Valuation

With Standard Chartered's well-diversified geographical exposure and 60/40 wholesale/consumer banking business mix, it is well positioned to benefit from both rising consumer incomes and strong corporate activity in its emerging and frontier markets. At £17 (US$25.50) a share in early 2013, it outperformed the FTSE100 Index over 10 years, rising 170 percent against 70 percent, but over five years is up only 20 percent, in line with the index, and sells at a price-to-earnings ratio of 13.8 times 2011's earnings and a dividend yield of 2.8 percent.

As noted at the beginning of the section, there are a number of other multinational companies that have extensive exposure to emerging and frontier markets. Investors can find out the size of this exposure by seeing what percentage of revenues and profits is derived from developing economies. Anything above 35 percent of revenues should mean that the company has sufficient exposure to be meaningful, and that investors should give the management credit for building up this business. Investors should, however, examine the correlation of the company's share performance with its domestic stock market, and be aware that domestic factors may have a greater influence on the stock performance than its emerging and frontier market exposure, at least in the short term.

■ ■ ■

FRONTIER MARKET AMERICAN DEPOSITORY RECEIPTS

Frontier market American depository receipts (ADRs) represent shares in companies listed locally in a frontier nation and subsequently listed as ADRs in New York. Global depository receipts (GDRs) are listed in London or Luxembourg. In a few cases, the company may list in London or New York directly, without a local listing. However, as the recent spate of accounting issues for U.S.- and Canada-listed Chinese companies, such as Sino-Forest, in Canada has shown, there can be issues of corporate governance involved when the company is listed in one jurisdiction, headquartered in another and operating in a third. Sino-Forest, which claimed to have harvesting rights to forests in China, was suspended in 2011 when it was accused of operating a fraudulent business, an accusation that was subsequently proven to be correct, with the company filing for bankruptcy in March 2012. Its auditor, Ernst & Young, agreed in March 2013 to pay a C$117 million settlement to investors to settle class action claims.[6] This proviso should not be taken as a blanket condemnation of companies from frontier and emerging markets being listed on developed stock markets but merely as an indication that investors should examine companies with a primary listing in a foreign jurisdiction with more caution.

Over 20 percent of the London Stock Exchange's listings are foreign (non-UK) companies, including such major world-class companies as

---

[6]Peter Koven, "Judge Approves Ernst & Young Settlement for Sino Forest Shareholders," *National Post*, March 20, 2013.

SABMiller PLC, the world's second largest brewer, insurance company Old Mutual PLC, leading commodities producer Glencore Xstrata PLC and several Russian companies, such as Evraz Group SA and Polymetal International PLC.

Looking just at ADRs and GDRs restricts the investor to companies that are listed and regulated in one jurisdiction but that have U.S. dollar– or pound sterling–denominated securities in a developed market linked to the underlying security. Companies issuing ADRs and GDRs have to meet minimum accounting and reporting standards in the country in which they are listed.

Therefore investors are able to compare "apples to apples" when looking at the financial accounts of such issuers and have the comfort of knowing the reports have been audited by a recognized developed market accountancy firm, although even this may not prevent cases of fraud or misrepresentation.

Thus, each ADR of Nestlé S.A. represents five Swiss franc–denominated underlying shares. Investors can buy them through their usual U.S. broker and have them held by a U.S. depository institution and receive dividends in U.S. dollars.

While this may be a comfortable situation for investors in major global companies with established track records, the same cannot be said for frontier market issuers. There will be problems concerning lack of familiarity and liquidity as well as concerns that some of the issuers may prove to be in similar situations to those of the Chinese companies that listed on North American exchanges in 2009–2011. These companies may be suspected of being shells designed to extract funds from foreign investors unfamiliar with the underlying business.

The disadvantage for investors is that they are investing in a single frontier market company, with all the issues that brings. That includes management quality, competition, currency and political risk. While there are a number of blue-chip ADRs from emerging markets—notably telecom, energy, infrastructure and utility stocks—their performance has depended very much on individual factors.

Some of the London-listed frontier market stocks included among frontier market funds' top 10 holdings are Diamond Bank (Nigeria), Kazakhmys and KazMunaiGas Exploration Production (Kazakhstan), Bank of Georgia (Georgia), Zenith Bank and First Bank of Nigeria (Nigeria) and Dragon Oil (Turkmenistan).

It is entirely possible that an investor could be correct in choosing a specific frontier market that provides a good opportunity, and an industry within that country that does well, yet find that the individual ADR he or she has chosen does not reflect these positive developments owing to poor management, a change in regulations, or political developments.

Notwithstanding the wired world, those factors are still difficult to research from thousands of miles away.

As with regional and country funds, we would recommend against investing in individual frontier market ADRs or GDRs unless the investor or advisor has a high comfort level with his or her stock-picking skills in addition to familiarity with the country or region and a robust tolerance for risk. Among ways of developing familiarity with a country or region would be attending school or college there, working there for a few years, having family connections or, of course, being a citizen of the country who has emigrated to the developed world. All of these would remove the likelihood of making decisions based on lack of knowledge or dependence on media reports. Developing a high comfort level with stock picking, as noted in the section on behavioral finance in Chapter 8, is becoming aware of one's own inherent biases and hardwired investment behavior.

GLOBAL FRONTIER FUNDS

Finally, we *do* recommend investing in frontier markets through global funds, especially those where the mandate allows the portfolio manager a large amount of flexibility. By now, readers will probably have gathered that we do not feel that passive index investing is the best way to invest in illiquid markets that are heavily concentrated in a few stocks, especially as economic development and privatization likely mean that the composition of the index will change rapidly over the next few years. We also argue that attempting to pick regions or countries that will do well is a strategy that will not be successful, except in a few cases where investors have good local knowledge and strong nerves.

While multinational companies with a high percentage of their revenues from emerging and frontier economies may be attractive investments in their own right, their exposure to low-growth developed markets and the influence that developed market factors exercise on their stock price can make them unsuitable as a part of a portfolio's frontier market weighting.

Likewise, ADRs and GDRs for frontier market companies involve investors in the selection of single companies in developing markets, with the attendant risk factors.

Therefore, we would recommend that investors choose an actively managed global frontier market fund with a reasonable expense ratio, taking into account the fact that active investment in frontier markets is a relatively expensive business, involving a fair amount of travel for local research and, in some cases, the maintenance of offices in several regions. At present, the longer-established global frontier market funds have management (or total) expense ratios (MERs or TERs) of between 2.1 percent per annum to 2.3 percent p.a. Frontier and emerging markets are two of the areas where competent active managers have consistently been able to add value above the indices.

In an actively managed portfolio, the fund managers, through the exercise of their skill and judgment, attempt to outperform the relevant benchmark index. That justifies the additional management fee over and above the fee of a passive index-tracking vehicle such as an ETF. In this section, we will be comparing each fund with its most relevant index, which includes not merely the MSCI Frontier Markets Index but also the MSCI Emerging Frontier Markets Index, which includes five of the smaller and less liquid emerging markets, specifically Colombia, Egypt, Morocco, Peru and the Philippines.

Templeton Emerging Markets Fund

By comparing the performance of a long-established emerging market fund such as the Templeton Emerging Markets Fund, the longest-established retail fund investing in emerging markets, against the MSCI Emerging Markets Index ETF (EEM), you will see that even after paying an MER of 1.9 percent p.a. against one of 0.4 percent for the ETF, the actively managed fund has outperformed the MSCI Emerging Markets (Free) Index by between 1 percent and 2 percent p.a. over any period of longer than three years.

We believe that an actively managed global frontier fund will demonstrate the same outperformance over the next five to ten years. Although there are only a few global frontier funds and none have a longer track record than five years, the evidence so far supports our belief.

Several straightforward reasons explain this outperformance. First, active managers can identify mispriced shares in inefficient and illiquid markets. Second, and perhaps more importantly, active managers can over- and underweight various geographical regions at different stages of the economic cycle or where political considerations are overriding economic fundamentals.

Global frontier market funds have existed for about five years and there are still only a limited number available. The oldest and largest is the Templeton Frontier Markets Fund, managed, like the Templeton Emerging Markets Fund, by Mark Mobius and his team. Templeton launched the U.S. version in October 2008 and had $764 million in assets under management (AUM) at the end of 2012. The company launched the European version at the same time and had $1.25 billion in AUM at the end of December 2012. The U.S. version returned 13.45 percent p.a. from inception to the end of 2012 and the European version 12.53 percent, both in American dollars, after deducting a management expense ratio of 2.15 percent against a negative return from the MSCI Frontier Markets Index over the same 4.25-year period of −4.98 percent p.a.

These numbers indicate the growing interest of developed market investors in frontier markets that led to large inflows into both versions of the fund. There were assets of $1.2 billion for the U.S. version and US$1.8 billion for the European version by the end of April 2013. Templeton announced at the end of May 2013 that they would be closing the U.S. fund (and its Canadian-sibling fund) and the European fund to new investors, effective the end of June 2013.

Part of the difference in performance between the two funds reflects their different currency denominations and part reflects the slightly different holdings between the funds; the U.S. version has 90 positions and the European version has 97 positions. The weightings in individual stocks also differ between the two funds.

The 97 holdings in the European version of the Templeton Frontier Markets Fund at the end of December 2012 had a combined price-to-earnings ratio of 7.5 times, a price-to-cash-flow ratio of 4.78 times and a price-to-book ratio of 1.24 times, meaning that the companies in its portfolio were cheap on a number of measures, a situation which in the past has produced superior returns over time.

The 90 positions in the U.S. version had slightly higher combined price-to-earnings and price-to-book ratios at 8.66 times and 1.65 times, but the two portfolios are very similar in characteristics, as would be expected. The price-to-earnings ratio, price-to-cash-flow ratio and price-to-book ratio of a portfolio, combined with its volatility (as measured by its standard deviation) and how it tracks its benchmark index (as measured by its beta) give a convenient description of whether the portfolio is value- or growth-oriented, how much it is likely to move around and whether it goes up and down more or less rapidly than the index.

The European portfolio had moderate volatility, as evidenced by its standard deviation of returns of 15.53 over the previous three years. Both versions of the fund owned a number of the same companies, with KazMunaiGas Exploration Production, Qatar Telecom, Dragon Oil PLC, Zenith Bank PLC and First Gulf Bank featuring among both versions' top 10 holdings. In mid-2011 Templeton launched a Canadian version of the U.S. fund, which has tracked the U.S. fund after taking currency movements into account.

While this is a short comparison period, the size of the outperformance by the actively managed funds against the passive index is notable.

The MSCI Frontier Markets Index is very heavily weighted in Gulf Cooperation Council (GCC) countries, with the five GCC countries of Kuwait, Qatar, the UAE, Bahrain and Oman comprising 57 percent of the index and Kuwait on its own comprising more than 30 percent.

The other 20 non-GCC frontier states make up only 43 percent of the index, even though such countries as Argentina, Bangladesh, Kazakhstan, Kenya, Nigeria, Pakistan, Romania, Ukraine and Vietnam have much larger populations and economies than the GCC states.

The MSCI Frontier Markets Index is free float–adjusted market capitalization, which means that the positions in the index are weighted according to the size of the freely available shares rather than the total market capitalization. Those countries with the largest stock markets and most freely investable shares dominate it. That means that the Gulf states are overrepresented in the index.

Part of the explanation for the outperformance by the actively managed fund is due to its managers' ability to take positions that are not included in the index. In the European version, the fund has a 7.6 percent weight in Saudi Arabia and a 4.1 percent weight in Egypt, neither of which are included in the MSCI Frontier Markets Index. The fund also has major overweight positions in Kazakhstan (9.6 percent vs. 4 percent in the index), Vietnam (7.2 percent vs. 2.1 percent), Romania (4.7 percent vs. 1.2 percent) and Ukraine (4.2 percent vs. 0.2 percent), while being underweight in some GCC counties, such as Kuwait, Qatar and the UAE.

On a sector basis, the fund is underweight in financials (40 percent vs. 51.2 percent) and telecoms (11.7 percent vs. 14.9 percent) while being overweight in energy (16.1 percent vs. 8.3 percent) and materials (10.8 percent vs. 3.1 percent), allowing it to be overweight in those sectors more geared to economic growth. This gives it a higher exposure to the larger frontier markets where resources have higher weights in the indices. The MSCI Frontier and Frontier 100 indices have very large exposures to GCC countries and financials, neither of which might be regarded as characterizing the elements of frontier markets that foreign investors wish to access.

Harding Loevner Frontier Emerging Markets Fund

Other global frontier market funds available to investors in the developed markets include one from Harding Loevner LP, which launched its U.S. institutional Frontier Emerging Markets Fund in May 2008, with a U.S. retail version launched in December 2010. The funds are managed by the team of co–portfolio managers Rusty Johnson and Pradipa Chakrabortty. The two mandates had $88 million in assets under management at the end of December 2012. Over the 4.5-year period since inception, the institutional fund had produced a negative return of −5.89 percent p.a. after a gross expense ratio of 1.87 percent, against a negative return of −6.64 percent p.a. from the MSCI Frontier Emerging Markets Index. The retail version had produced a negative return of −2.98 percent p.a. after a capped net expense ratio of 2.25 percent against a negative return of −0.17 percent p.a. from the MSCI Frontier Emerging Markets Index over a two-year period.

The MSCI Frontier Emerging Markets Index is a free float–adjusted, market capitalization–weighted index comprised of 25 frontier markets and five of the smaller emerging markets (Colombia, Egypt, Morocco, Peru and the Philippines). While an improvement over the MSCI Frontier Markets Index, the MSCI Frontier Emerging Markets Index is dominated by the five crossover emerging markets, which comprise 53 percent of the index owing to their large size by comparison with the frontier markets. The GCC countries now make up 27 percent of the index and the 20 non-GCC countries only 20 percent.

The portfolio of the Harding Loevner LP Frontier Emerging Markets Fund resembles the Templeton Frontier Markets Fund, with its 78 holdings having a combined price-to-earnings ratio of 11.9 times vs. 13.5 for the index, a price-to-cash-flow ratio of 5.2 times vs. 7.4 times and a price-to-book ratio of 1.8 times, comparable to that of the index. The higher price-to-earnings and price-to-book ratios most likely reflect the inclusion of more established emerging markets, while the standard deviation at 14.03 against the index's 14.16 is lower than Templeton's, perhaps reflecting the non-correlation between frontier and emerging markets.

The presence of such companies as Cementos Argos and Ecopetrol S.A. from Colombia, Credicorp and Alicorp from Peru and Universal Robina and Bank of the Philippine Islands from the Philippines among the Harding Loevner LP Frontier Emerging Markets Fund's top 10 holdings indicates that its managers have a greater focus on the smaller emerging markets than those funds, such as Templeton, that are exclusively focused on the frontier markets.

HSBC GIF Frontier Markets Fund

HSBC GIF Frontier Markets Fund is a retail product that was launched as HSBC SIF Frontier Markets Fund in February 2008, making it the oldest of these global funds. It was re-launched as GIF (Global Investment Funds) Frontier Markets Fund in December 2011, and a U.S. retail mutual fund was launched in September 2011. Along with an institutional mandate, these funds had US$158 million in assets under management at the end of September 2012. Managed by Andrew Brudenell and Chris Turner, the funds had produced a negative return of −5.31 percent p.a. in the 4.7 years ending November 2012, after capped net management expenses of 1.87 percent, against a negative return of −11.94 percent for the MSCI

Frontier Markets Index and −8.81 percent p.a. for the MSCI Frontier Emerging Markets Capped Index over the same period.

This latter index is a proprietary customized index developed and maintained for HSBC by MSCI, which solves the high concentration issue inherent in both the MSCI Frontier and Frontier Emerging Markets indices by capping individual countries' weights in the index. Thus, the five crossover emerging markets' combined weight is capped at 25 percent, which is reset back to 25 percent when their combined weight breaches 30 percent of the index. All other countries, including the five GCC countries, have a maximum initial weight of 10 percent each, which gets reset back to 10 percent when it breaches 12 percent.

Therefore, the MSCI Frontier Emerging Markets Capped Index has 25 percent in the five crossover emerging markets of Colombia, Egypt, Morocco, Peru and the Philippines, 31 percent in the five GCC countries and 44 percent in the 20 non-GCC frontier markets.

The 70–90 holdings in the portfolio have a combined price-to-earnings ratio of 9.91 times against the index's 9.19 times, but have a higher dividend yield of 4.38 percent against 3.67 percent. While holding many of the same names as the other frontier funds among its top 10 holdings, such as KazMunaiGas, Colombia's Bancolombia and Ecopetrol, and Qatar Telecom and First Gulf Bank, it also holds less recognizable names such as Hub Power Company Ltd. and Pakistan Petroleum from Pakistan, and Etihad Etisalat from Saudi Arabia. Additionally, it has significant overweights in Saudi Arabia, Pakistan, Nigeria, Qatar and the UAE, the latter two against the capped index weights.

The most important point about all three of these actively managed global frontier market funds is that they have all beaten their respective indices, whether the straightforward MSCI Frontier Markets Index or some variant of the broader MSCI Frontier Emerging Markets Index over any period longer than two years. This after taking into account the drag of the 1.87–2.25 percent management expense ratios carried by these funds; the indices, of course, do not suffer from the deduction of fees.

The management fees on the frontier market ETFs such as the iShares MSCI Frontier Markets 100 Index and the Guggenheim Frontier Markets Index are 0.79 percent p.a. and 0.65 percent p.a. plus dealing and administrative expenses. Given the extremely concentrated and illiquid nature of the frontier market equities that passive investments such as ETFs have to invest in, it is unsurprising that active managers have beaten the indices. They are inefficient markets where active managers find it much easier to add alpha by virtue of research and taking positions away from the index weightings.

Other Global Frontier Funds

The longest-established retail frontier market fund is actually run by a Danish company, BankInvest; its New Emerging Market Equities Fund was launched in December 2007. Managed by Hans-Henrik Skov and James Bannan, after five years ending January 2013 it had €46 million (US$60 million) in AUM and returned 0.5 percent p.a. after a management expense ratio of 2.75 percent since inception against a negative return of −1.3 percent p.a. from its benchmark. This is a 50/50 blend of the MSCI Frontier Markets Index and the MSCI Frontier Markets Index excluding the GCC, both with dividends reinvested. While its portfolio has slightly higher price-to-earnings (11.36 times) and price-to-book (2.05 times) ratios than some of its competitors, its volatility as measured by standard deviation is lower, at 12.85.

The portfolio has some less familiar names among its top holdings, such as Bank of Georgia, Nestlé Nigeria PLC and Vietnam Dairy Products JSC. It also has a large exposure to sub-Saharan Africa, with Nigeria as its largest country weight at 22.2 percent, Kenya at 8 percent and Senegal at 5 percent. Again, despite having a higher expense ratio for its retail class than other funds, BankInvest has still managed to outperform the index over the last five years.

Other global frontier funds that have started within the last two years up to early 2013 include the US$57 million in AUM Schroder Frontier Markets Equity Fund, started in December 2010, and the US$110 million Lloyd George (LG) Frontier Markets Fund, launched in December 2011. The US$54 million Morgan Stanley Investment Management's Frontier Emerging Markets Portfolio was converted from a closed-end NYSE-listed investment company in August 2012, although it is actually one of the longer-established frontier market funds, having been listed in August 2008.

The point worth reiterating about all of these actively managed funds is that they have all beaten the MSCI Frontier Markets Index over the last year and over all periods other than two years for the Harding Loevner fund. This sole example of underperformance is only marginal, so it is reasonable to say that all actively managed frontier market funds with a two-year track record or longer have beaten their indices, after accounting for expense ratios, by well over 2 percent in almost all cases and with widely differing investment approaches in terms of geographical weightings, sector allocations and valuation measures.

In inefficient markets such as the frontier markets, with low volumes and limited distribution of information, active managers can consistently add value against the index, especially when the indices in question are very heavily weighted in a small number of countries or industries, as is the case at present with those for frontier markets.

Closed-end Country Funds

One of the more interesting ways to access developing markets is through closed-end country funds. These are investment funds listed on the stock market with a limited number of issued shares, unlike open-ended investment vehicles such as mutual funds in the United States and Canada and open-ended investment companies (OEICs) in Europe, which can create new shares when investor demand is high.

As a result, closed-end funds, known as investment trusts in the UK, trade at a premium or discount to the value of their underlying assets, reflecting investor enthusiasm or pessimism about the prospects for a country or region.

Among the open-ended mutual funds and OEICs, there are several Latin American regional funds, sub-Saharan African funds and especially Middle East and North Africa (MENA) regional funds available to investors, most of which have been launched in the last five years as awareness of frontier market investing has grown among investors. We discussed the merits of the regional and single-country approach while discussing ETFs, and the same arguments apply to mutual funds and OEICs. A list of those available can be found in the appendix.

In the United States, there are over two dozen closed-end country or regional funds, including a number that invest in emerging markets. Among them at the time of writing (first quarter of 2013), the only country fund trading at a premium to its underlying net asset value (NAV) was the Chile Fund (CH). There are three Chinese funds, two Indian funds, two Thai funds, two Mexican funds, two Taiwanese funds, two Korean funds and an Asian regional fund (Templeton Dragon Fund).

There are individual funds for Indonesia, Malaysia, Singapore and Turkey. All of these sell at discounts to their NAVs, which range from 5 percent to 15 percent, reflecting how investor enthusiasm for new investments waxes and wanes. The only closed-end U.S.-listed fund that has some frontier market exposure is the Templeton Russia and Eastern Europe Fund (TRF), which has around 8 percent in two Ukrainian agricultural companies and 1 percent in a Kazakh energy stock, with the remaining 90 percent in Russian companies.

London-listed closed-end funds do include some frontier market single-country funds, including the Ukraine Opportunities Trust and the Iraq Euphrates Fund. Vietnam has the VinaCapital Vietnam Opportunities Fund as well as two Dublin-listed funds, Vietnam Enterprise Investments Ltd. (VEIL) and Vietnam Growth Fund. VEIL was launched as long ago as 1995 and Vietnam Opportunities and Vietnam Growth were launched in 2003 and 2004 respectively, and between the three of them they have US$1.4

billion in AUM, showing that the appetite of investors for frontier markets is by no means a recent phenomenon.

The closed-end structure also allows the funds to invest in private equity and real assets such as property, which are illiquid but offer a great exposure to the long-term growth of the country for patient investors.

The Ukraine Opportunities Trust, at $20 million, is more characteristic of the size of frontier market funds, where the small size of local stock markets and illiquidity combine to make it impracticable to invest large sums of money. Over 85 percent of its assets are in private equity holdings and its listed shareholdings are extremely illiquid. Interestingly, the $44 million Euphrates Iraq Fund is more liquid and recently participated in the $1.3 billion IPO of mobile phone operator Asiacell, the largest IPO in the Middle East for four years.

Another closed-end frontier market fund, and one of the largest by AUM (£83 million [US$133 million] at the end of December 2012) is the BlackRock Frontiers Investment Trust PLC, which was listed on the LSE in December 2010. It returned a negative −3.4 percent p.a. since inception against a negative −10 percent p.a. for the MSCI Frontier Markets Index (both in U.S. dollar terms).

BlackRock manager Sam Vecht has allotted, among the larger positions, more than 4 percent to Bangladesh and Panama and more than 5 percent to Ukraine and Vietnam, while Kazakhstan represents 9 percent of the portfolio. Its top 10 holdings include Air Arabia (UAE), Halyk Savings Bank in Kazakhstan and Hrvatski Telekom in Croatia, as well as the more expected KazMunaiGas, First Gulf Bank, and Zenith Bank in Nigeria. It sold at a 6 percent discount to its net asset value as at the end of December 2012, enabling investors to buy US$1 of assets at 94 cents.

Another closed-end fund investing in frontier markets is the LSE-listed Advance Frontier Markets Fund, which is actually one of the longest-established funds investing in these countries, having been started in June 2007. With approximately U$150 million in AUM, the fund primarily invests in other closed- and open-end frontier market funds, either European registered, such as the Africa Opportunity Fund, Ashmore Emerging Markets Middle East Fund, the Qatar Investment Fund and the Vietnam Opportunity Fund, or those established in local markets. These include its largest position, the EFG Hermes-Saudi Arabia Fund. Its asset mix has a high African exposure (41 percent, with Nigeria at 15 percent), while its 23 percent in the Middle East has a high Saudi weight and almost no positions in Kuwait. Asia is at 15 percent, Eastern Europe at 6 percent and Latin America at 4 percent. Managed by Dr. Slim Feriani and selling at a 10 percent discount to its NAV, the fund offers a discounted means of accessing frontier markets as many of its closed-end fund holdings also sell at discounts to their own NAVs.

The conclusion for investors is plain: for those investors wanting to invest in frontier markets—the next generation of emerging markets—buying an actively managed global frontier market fund will almost certainly produce attractive returns in absolute terms and will outperform a passive investment approach. In the final section, we summarize the arguments for frontier market investing, discuss the pros and cons of various approaches, and recap some recommendations for gaining exposure to this attractive asset class.

TAKEAWAYS

1. Rely on actively managed vehicles rather than passively managed ones.
2. Reasonably priced, actively managed global frontier funds should achieve attractive absolute returns over the next few years and most likely outperform a passive index frontier fund as well.
3. Be wary of individual stock purchases for which you do not have access to comprehensive financial information.
4. While investing in North American companies with revenues from emerging markets and frontier markets is a valid approach, consider their exposure to slow-growth developed markets and their correlation with their home country's indices.

Conclusion

In this book, we have described the emerging world of frontier markets and examined the differences between the various regions. We have explained why adding investments from these markets can reduce a portfolio's overall risk despite their high volatility, made investors aware of the importance of understanding their own inherent biases when considering investing in these economies and finished by examining the different methods of gaining access to them.

We have demonstrated our belief that frontier markets are in the same position as the original emerging markets were 15 years ago. Then, after an initial period of strong performance in the early 1990s, emerging markets became overvalued and most experienced severe economic difficulties from 1995 to 1999, when their policy of operating a fixed– or managed–float exchange rate led to banking and foreign exchange crises. Similarly, after strong performance from frontier markets in the five years until the financial crisis of 2008–09, there was a dramatic sell-off, which saw the MSCI Frontier Markets Index fall more than 65 percent.

After the Asian and Russian crises of 1997–98 and the Brazilian real devaluation of 1999, emerging markets sold at cheap valuations with floating exchange rates that had fallen sharply. Over the following decade from December 31, 2000, to December 31, 2010, the MSCI Emerging Markets (Free) Index produced a return of 182 percent in U.S. dollars, equivalent to more than 15 percent per annum. Even taking into account the period from September 30, 2002, the bottom of the 2000–02 bear market, the MSCI Emerging Markets (Free) Index produced a return of 13.4 percent p.a. against 5.6 percent for the MSCI All World Index.

Since the financial crisis of 2008–09, however, the MSCI Frontier Markets Index has rebounded only moderately, with a negative return of 0.3 percent p.a. for the three years ending December 30, 2011, against a strongly positive return of 17.4 percent p.a. for the MSCI Emerging Markets (Free) Index over the same period. Since then, frontier markets have begun to outperform emerging markets, with the MSCI Frontier Markets Index up 12.5 percent in the 12 months to April 30, 2013, against 1.3 percent for the MSCI Emerging Markets (Free) Index. Combined with their previous underperformance, this means that over the five years ending April 30, 2013, the MSCI Frontier Markets Index returned −12.7 percent p.a. against the

MSCI Emerging Markets (Free) Index return of −2.7 percent p.a. This has left the frontier markets selling at lower price-to-earnings (11 times 2012 earnings) and price-to-book value (1.2 times) than the emerging markets and with a higher dividend yield (4.5 percent).

We believe that the strong underlying fundamentals of the frontier market economies, with young populations (over 60 percent under the age of 30), high GDP growth (seven of the ten fastest-growing economies in the last decade) and populations moving from the countryside to the cities will lead to them delivering strong absolute performance over the next decade when combined with their attractive valuations.

To that analysis we need to add a caveat for the unwary. Investors need to be prepared to take at least a five-year time horizon when considering frontier markets, as their higher volatility and lower liquidity will mean that they will experience sharp price movements in both directions during that period. Therefore we would not recommend frontier markets as an investment for those who have a low tolerance for volatility, despite the excellent returns we anticipate from this asset class over the next few years.

An additional advantage of investing in frontier markets for developed market investors is that, due to their low liquidity and smaller market capitalization, frontier markets are not correlated with either emerging or developed markets or with each other. That means that adding a small percentage of frontier market exposure to a global equity portfolio will reduce the overall volatility of the portfolio even though the volatility of frontier markets is higher than that of developed markets. While their correlation with emerging and developed markets has increased over the last decade from 0.2, the highest correlation is a still an insignificant 0.44 with developed markets outside of North America and 0.41 with emerging markets.

When considering which vehicle to use to gain access to frontier markets, our research has pointed us in the direction of actively managed global frontier market funds as the preferred solution. While there are several regional exchange-traded funds (ETFs) that have operated for more than three years, they suffer the disadvantage of providing exposure only to regions such as Latin America or the Middle East. Those regions may not display the attractive characteristics that caused investors to choose frontier markets. Investors who wish to buy frontier markets to gain exposure to their young populations and fast-growing economies should ensure that the vehicle they choose has a large exposure to the markets of South Asia and sub-Saharan Africa, which are the areas that have the most countries that match these requirements.

Even the recently launched global iShares MSCI Frontier Markets ETF has almost 60 percent of its holdings in small Middle Eastern countries, demonstrating that in rapidly developing markets the index reflects which countries have the largest market capitalizations rather than the largest economies. Even the MSCI Frontier Emerging Markets Index, used as a benchmark by several fund managers, has the disadvantage that the five smaller emerging markets included in it account for more than 50 percent of the index, leading to similar issues of overconcentration. Moreover, the composition of an index at an early stage of development, such as with frontier markets, can be very concentrated in a few stocks or industries, defeating the benefits of diversification usually associated with ETFs. We would caution investors against making ETFs their automatic choice for investment in less-developed markets such as those of frontier economies.

While investing in global multinational companies with large emerging and frontier market exposure listed on major stock exchanges or regional frontier market companies with listed American depository receipts (ADRs) or global depository receipts (GDRs) has proven to be a rewarding tactic over the last decade, there are several disadvantages. The first is that many of the companies still have a high exposure to slow-growth mature developed markets, which reduces their growth, while the second is that their stock prices are more highly correlated with their local index, removing much of the benefit of non-correlation that investors receive by buying pure frontier market investments. While a carefully selected portfolio of such global companies deriving a high percentage of their revenues and profits from emerging and frontier markets will doubtless continue to provide positive absolute returns, we feel investors will likely do better by choosing a diversified global frontier market fund that represents a purer connection with these economies.

Our research indicates that buying an actively managed global frontier market fund, even after paying a relatively high expense ratio of 2.1–2.5 percent, leads to investors outperforming the relevant frontier markets index. In the period since the first frontier funds were launched in 2007–08, almost all managers have managed to outperform the index after deduction of fees. While this reflects the geographically concentrated nature of the indices, it also reflects the inefficiency of immature markets with imperfect information, dominated largely by domestic retail investors and with low liquidity and high dealing costs. These are ideal conditions for active management to demonstrate that it can add value and, to their credit, virtually all the fund management companies have done so.

While at present (early 2013) the experience of investors who have bought frontier market funds and ETFs has not been very profitable, with the exception of recently launched funds that have benefited from the strong upturn in frontier markets in 2012–13, we believe that over the next decade the frontier markets will deliver strong positive absolute returns to investors, hopefully similar to those received by investors in emerging markets over the last decade. Even if the returns are not as high in absolute terms, we believe the strong underlying fundamentals of frontier markets will provide positive returns, while their low correlation with both emerging and developed markets means that every investor should have at least a small percentage (3–5 percent) of the international portion of their equity portfolio invested in a diversified frontier market fund.

Frontier Market Open-end Funds as of May 2013

GLOBAL FRONTIER FUNDS

European Registered

Barings Frontier Markets Fund

Charlemagne Magna New Frontiers Fund

HSBC GIF Frontier Markets

Lloyd George (LG) Frontier Markets Fund

Renaissance Frontier Markets Fund

Sarasin EmergingSar–New Frontiers

Schroder ISF Frontier Markets Equity

Templeton Frontier Markets (Closed to new investors from June 30, 2013.)

U.S. Registered

Harding Loevner Frontier Emerging Markets (HLEMX)

HSBC Frontier Markets Fund (HSFAX)

Morgan Stanley Investment Management's Frontier Emerging Markets (MFMIX)

Templeton Frontier Markets (TFMAX) (Closed to new investors from June 30, 2013.)

Canadian Registered

Templeton Frontier Markets (Closed to new investors from June 30, 2013.)

EMERGING EUROPEAN EX-RUSSIA FUNDS

European Registered

Aviva Investors European Convergence Fund
Parvest Equity Europe Converging
SEB Eastern Europe ex-Russia Fund
U.S. Global Eastern Europe Fund (EUROX)

U.S. Registered

U.S. Global Investors Eastern Europe Fund

AFRICAN FUNDS

European Registered

Alquity Africa
Bellevue Funds African Opportunities
Charlemagne Africa Fund
Coronation Universal Fund–African Frontiers Fund
DWS Africa
Invest AD Emerging Africa Fund
Investec Global Strategy Fund–Africa Opportunities
JP Morgan Funds–Africa Equity
Julius Baer Multistock–Africa Opportunities
Julius Baer Multistock–Northern Africa
Neptune Africa
Nordea–1 African Equity Fund
Renaissance Pan-African Fund
Renaissance Sub-Saharan Fund
Sanlam African Frontier Markets Fund
Silk African Lions
Standard Africa Equity
Templeton Africa Fund
WIOF African Performance Fund

U.S. Registered

Commonwealth Africa Fund (CAFRX)
Nile Pan African Fund (NAFAX)

MIDDLE EAST AND NORTH AFRICA (MENA) FUNDS

European Registered

Amundi Funds Equity MENA Fund
Ashmore Emerging Markets Middle East Fund
Barings MENA Fund
Charlemagne Magna MENA Fund
Concord Egypt Fund
Emirates MENA Top Companies Fund
Franklin MENA Fund
JP Morgan Funds–Emerging Middle East Equity Fund
Mashreq Arab Tigers Fund
Schroders ISF–Middle East Fund
Silk Arab Falcons Fund
Silk Road Frontiers Fund
T. Rowe Price Mid-East & African Fund
WIOF Middle East Performance Fund

U.S. Registered

T. Rowe Price Africa & Middle East Fund (TRAMX)

Index